T0280768

Lecture Notes in Mechanical Engineering

Lecture Notes in Mechanical Engineering (LNME) publishes the latest developments in Mechanical Engineering - quickly, informally and with high quality. Original research reported in proceedings and post-proceedings represents the core of LNME. Volumes published in LNME embrace all aspects, subfields and new challenges of mechanical engineering. Topics in the series include:

- Engineering Design
- Machinery and Machine Elements
- Mechanical Structures and Stress Analysis
- Automotive Engineering
- Engine Technology
- Aerospace Technology and Astronautics
- Nanotechnology and Microengineering
- Control, Robotics, Mechatronics
- MEMS
- Theoretical and Applied Mechanics
- Dynamical Systems, Control
- Fluid Mechanics
- Engineering Thermodynamics, Heat and Mass Transfer
- Manufacturing
- Precision Engineering, Instrumentation, Measurement
- Materials Engineering
- Tribology and Surface Technology

More information about this series at http://www.springer.com/series/11236

D N Badodkar · T A Dwarakanath
Editors

Machines, Mechanism and Robotics

Proceedings of iNaCoMM 2017

 Springer

Editors
D N Badodkar
Division of Remote Handling
  and Robotics
Bhabha Atomic Research
  Centre (BARC)
Mumbai, India

T A Dwarakanath
Division of Remote Handling
  and Robotics
Bhabha Atomic Research
  Centre (BARC)
Mumbai, India

ISSN 2195-4356   ISSN 2195-4364   (electronic)
Lecture Notes in Mechanical Engineering
ISBN 978-981-13-4195-3   ISBN 978-981-10-8597-0   (eBook)
https://doi.org/10.1007/978-981-10-8597-0

This Springer imprint is published by the registered company Springer Nature Singapore Pte Ltd.
The registered company address is: 152 Beach Road, #21-01/04 Gateway East, Singapore 189721, Singapore

Preface

This volume contains the papers presented at the **3rd International and 18th National Conference on Machines and Mechanisms (iNaCoMM)**. iNaCoMM 2017 under the aegis of AMM and IFToMM was successfully organized by the Division of Remote Handling and Robotics (DRHR), Bhabha Atomic Research Centre (BARC), Mumbai, from 13 to 15 December 2017. The conference was held at the DAE Convention Centre, Anushakti Nagar, Mumbai. The conference brought together researchers and students, working on various aspects of design, analysis of machines, mechanisms and robotics to deliberate through oral, poster and design contest presentations on recent advances. Dr. D N Badodkar, Distinguished Scientist, BARC, served as the Chairman and Convener, and Dr. T A Dwarakanath, Scientific Officer-H, DRHR, BARC, served as the Co-Convener of iNaCoMM 2017.

iNaCoMM 2017 featured eminent researchers as plenary speakers. On 13 December 2017, Dr. R. K. Sinha, Ex-Chairman, Atomic Energy Commission, inaugurated the conference and gave an inaugural address. Prof. C Amarnath, President, AMM, and Dr. Rama Rao, former Director, Reactor Design and Development Group of BARC, were the honourable guests for the inaugural session. Dr. Rama Rao delivered a talk on assessment of vibration in structures, and Prof. C Amarnath reminisced about the formation of the Association for Machines and Mechanisms, India, and the first iNaCoMM during his talk in the inaugural session. In keeping with the tradition of iNaCoMM, the two prestigious memorial lectures were hosted. On 14 December 2017, Prof. B. M. Belgaumkar Memorial Lecture was delivered by Prof. Paulo Flores, University of Minho, Portugal, on the challenges and future developments towards the modelling of frictional contacts in dynamics of mechanisms. On 15 December 2017, Prof. K. Lakshminarayana Memorial Lecture was delivered by Prof. Ashitava Ghosal, IISc, Bangalore, on the analysis and design of robots and multi-body computer-controlled mechanical systems. The inaugural and memorial lectures were followed by interesting morning and afternoon presentations and poster sessions on various topics of the conference.

A total of 211 research papers were submitted out of which 72 papers were accepted for oral presentation during the conference after a rigorous two-stage peer review process. The research papers were presented in two parallel sessions having six papers per session. Twenty shortlisted papers were displayed during the poster presentation session in the conference. The best papers in the student category as well as in the general category were awarded. Also, the two best poster presentations were awarded.

One of the key objectives of the Association for Machines and Mechanisms (AMM) is to promote innovation among the students. Towards this end, iNaCoMM 2017 hosted Student Mechanism Design Contest (SMDC) for students. A total of 22 teams had submitted their projects out of which eight teams were shortlisted after a two-stage review process. The shortlisted teams exhibited their working design out of which the best three working models were given awards.

The iNaCoMM 2017 details and the conference photographs are available in the website: www.inacomm2017.org.

I would like to acknowledge AMM and IFToMM for supporting the event, BRNS for funding the conference, the reviewers of the papers, the organizing committee members of iNaCoMM and the participants of iNaCoMM 2017 for making it a monumental success. We would like to thank Springer Nature Singapore Pte Ltd., Singapore, for publishing the digital proceedings of the iNaCoMM 2017 in a book series: *Lecture Notes in Mechanical Engineering (LNME)*.

Mumbai, India   Dr. D N Badodkar
December 2017

Review Committee of iNaCoMM 2017

Abhishek Jaju
Amaren Prasanna Das
Amarnath Chitta
Anirban Guha
Anupam Saraswat
Arun Misra
Arun Samantaray
Ashish Dutta
Ashitava Ghosal
Asim Kar
Asokan Thondiyath
B Sony
Balamurugan G
Balasubramaniam R
Bhagyesh Deshmukh
Bhaiya Ram
Bhaskar Dasgupta
Chandrahas Handa
Cheruvu Siva Kumar
D C Kar
Debanik Roy
Dewangan T K
Dibakar Sen
Dinesh Sarode
Dr. D N Badodkar
Dr. Vijayananda
G K Ananthasuresh
G. Aravamuthan
Gaurav Bhutani
Girdhar Sharma
Gurunathan Saravana

Sandipan
Sangamesh R Deepak
Sanjay Panwar
Sanjeev Sharma
Santiranjan Pramanik
Sashindra Kumar Kakoty
Satish Reddy
Saurabh Pandharikar
Saurin Sheth
Shubhangi Shrikhande
Shubhashis Sanyal
Soumen Sen
Sourav Rakshit
Srinivasa Prakash Regalla
Sudipto Mukherjee
Sumit Sinha
Suril Vijaykumar Shah
Surojit Bose
T A Dwarakanath
Ushnish Sarkar
V K Mishra
Vaibhav Dave
Vamshi Krishna
Venkata P P K
Vinay Kumar Shrivastava
Vineet Vashista
Vitthal Arajpure
Vivek Mahadev

Technical Committee of iNaCoMM 2017

Dr. D N Badodkar, Chairman & Convener iNaCoMM 2017, DRHR, BARC
Dr. T A Dwarakanath, Co-Convener iNaCoMM 2017, DRHR, BARC
Prof. Anirban Guha, IIT Mumbai
Prof. Prasanna S. Gandhi, IIT Mumbai
Dr. D. C. Kar, DRHR, BARC
Shri. P. V. Sarngadharan, DRHR, BARC
Shri. Sanjeev Sharma, DRHR, BARC
Shri. R. V. Sakrikar, DRHR, BARC
Shri. V. K. Shrivastava, DRHR, BARC
Shri. Abhishek Jaju, DRHR, BARC
Smt. Bimmi Bharadvaj, DRHR, BARC
Shri. D. C. Biswas, DRHR, BARC
Dr. Gaurav Bhutani, DRHR, BARC
Shri. Hemanta Swain, DRHR, BARC
Shri. Jagdish Kota, DRHR, BARC
Shri. Kamal Sharma, DRHR, BARC
Smt. Meher Tabassum, DRHR, BARC
Smt. Namita Singh, DRHR, BARC
Shri. S. K. Sinha, DRHR, BARC
Shri. S. S. Saini, DRHR, BARC
Shri. Shishir K. Singh, DRHR, BARC
Shri. Sreejith P., DRHR, BARC
Shri. Teja Swaroop, DRHR, BARC
Shri. Ushnish Sarkar, DRHR, BARC
Shri. Vaibhav Dave, DRHR, BARC
Shri. Venkata P. P. K., Computer Division, BARC

Contents

About the Editors

Dr. D N Badodkar is a postgraduate in Electrical Engineering and joined BARC Training School in the year 1980. After successful completion of the one-year orientation training in Nuclear Science and Technology, he joined the Reactor Control Division, BARC, Mumbai, in 1981 as Scientific Officer-C. Subsequently, he obtained his Ph.D. degree from Mumbai University. Presently, he is Distinguished Scientist, Director, Reactor Design and Development Group and Head, Division of Remote Handling and Robotics. He is also a senior professor in engineering sciences at Homi Bhabha National Institute (HBNI) and is the chairperson of various doctoral committees at HBNI and Raja Ramanna Centre for Advanced Technology. His expertise includes special-purpose electrical drives, electromagnetic actuators, reactor control mechanisms and application-specific automation systems. He is the recipient of DAE's Technical Excellence Award-2000 and Group Achievement Award-2008, 2014, 2015 and 2016.

T A Dwarakanath graduated in Mechanical Engineering from the University of Mysore. He pursued master's degree and continued to obtain his Ph.D. degree from the Indian Institute of Science, Bangalore, in 1994. He joined BARC in 1993 as Scientific Officer-D. He was awarded the BOYSCAST Young Scientist Fellowship Award by the Department of Science and Technology (DST) in the year 1997. He was Visiting Research Scholar at the University of Florida, USA, from 1998 to 1999. He was associated with Prof. Joseph Duffy and Prof. Carl Crane on the design of compliant platforms. Presently, he is Scientific Officer-H in BARC and holds a faculty position in the Homi Bhabha National Institute. His interest and expertise are in the design and development of applications for parallel mechanism-based systems.

Elastic Stability of Lift Support Structure of RPC Trolley

Sandip Patel, S. P. Prabhakar, N. S. Dalal and Saurabh Pathak

Abstract Iron-based calorimeter is used for the study of Neutrino consisting of huge electromagnet and a large number of RPC detectors in India-based Neutrino Observatory (INO) project. RPC detectors are handled by a customized rail-mounted-movable RPC-handling trolleys. In this paper, the problem of static stability of trolley support structure has been discussed. Lift support structure of RPC handling trolley is modeled and analyzed considering trolley self-weight and weight of platform including payload. Using FEM solver, the critical buckling load is estimated and found within a safe limit. Results obtained from FEM analysis are also practically validated on a scaled down fabricated model of lift support structure of RPC trolley subjected to an equivalent load. This study is beneficial for optimum material use for working forces and for the safety of working staff.

Keywords INO · RPC detector · Design · Electromagnet · Trolley · FEM analysis · ANSYS workbench · Buckling · Elastic stability · Accuracy and alignment

1 Introduction

India-based Neutrino Observatory (INO) is an underground laboratory in which atmospheric neutrinos will be studied by an iron-based magnetized detector-iron

S. Patel (✉) · S. P. Prabhakar · N. S. Dalal · S. Pathak (✉)
Division of Remote Handling & Robotics, Bhabha Atomic Research Centre,
Trombay, Mumbai, Maharashtra, India
e-mail: patel.sandip932@gmail.com

S. Pathak
e-mail: Saurabhp@barc.gov.in

S. P. Prabhakar
e-mail: satya@barc.gov.in

N. S. Dalal
e-mail: Nilesh.dalal@gmail.com

© Springer Nature Singapore Pte Ltd. 2019
D N Badodkar and T A Dwarakanath (eds.), *Machines, Mechanism and Robotics*, Lecture Notes in Mechanical Engineering,
https://doi.org/10.1007/978-981-10-8597-0_1

calorimeter (ICAL) [1]. To facilitate preliminary studies about the neutrinos and to establish an engineering model, a scaled-down prototype ICAL detector is being built at Madurai (IICHEP, Madurai) of size is $8 \times 8 \times 7.25 \, \mathrm{m}^3$.

In ICAL, a muon path generated through the interaction of neutrino and iron, will be tracked using resistive plate chamber detector (RPC) [2]. These RPCs will be kept at different gap layers at different elevations in ICAL magnet.

RPC detector is a glass-based gas-filled detector of size 2 m × 2 m and is highly fragile [2]. For handling and placing the detectors at different positions and elevations, a RPC handling trolley is developed. The RPC handling trolley is a tall lift structure with the accurate movement of its platform for proper alignment with gap layer. Trolley consists of three major subassemblies.

a. Bottom cart assembly
b. Lift support structure
c. Lift platform

Long slender columns sometimes fail well before the yield stress of the material in compression due to load causing buckling. Hence buckling study becomes important for the stability of tall structures [3–5]. Criticality of buckling is also dependent on the geometry of column [6].

RPC handling trolley has been designed to handle a payload of 1.5 tons. The shelf structure weighs 4.5 tons including payload. Maximum vertical movement is 9 m whereas trolley can travel horizontally on a pair of rails with movement accuracy of horizontal 5 mm, vertical 2 mm. Size of the trolley is 6.5 m × 2.6 m × 12 m (ht.) with gross weight of 30 tons. Elastic stability study of lift support structure has been done using FEM analysis in this paper. Results obtained from FEM analysis has been validated on a scaled down fabricated model with equivalent loading pattern.

2   Theory of Stability Analysis

In the mechanical parlance, "stability implies resistance to changes, deterioration or displacement of functions of a system and to remain in a position of equilibrium". The stability of operation of heavy machines is one of the main factors determining their working ability and safety. The question of the stability of various forms of equilibrium of a compressed bar can be investigated by using the same theory as used in investigating the stability of equilibrium configurations of rigid-body systems (Fig. 1, [7]). Hence structural stability is governed by buckling behavior of the structure. Different geometries show a different kind of post-buckling behavior. In the design against buckling study carried by Robert M. Jones shows relative nature of buckling event on the basis of geometries like plates, bars shells, etc. (Fig. 2, [6]). Observation shows that bar failure in buckling is a relatively catastrophic event. So the factor of safety against bar buckling must be quite high as a comparison to plate buckling.

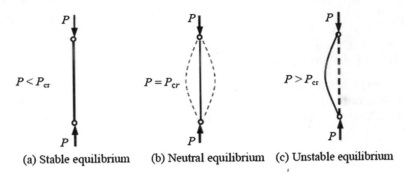

(a) Stable equilibrium   (b) Neutral equilibrium   (c) Unstable equilibrium

Fig. 1 State of equilibrium for column [7]

Fig. 2 Relative nature of buckling event [6]

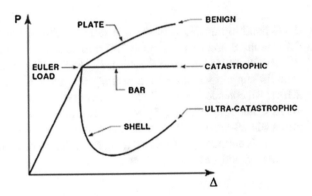

Nature of buckling of the geometries decides minimum safety margin, a design should keep avoiding failure due to buckling. Buckling analysis is a technique used to determine the critical buckling load and buckling mode when structure starts being unstable. There are two techniques to carry the buckling analysis: eigenvalue buckling analysis (linear buckling) and nonlinear buckling analysis. Linear buckling can be evaluated as classical Euler's buckling formula

$$P_{cr} = \frac{\pi^2 EI}{K^2 L^2} \tag{1}$$

where

E   Young's modulus of the material,
I   minimum area moment of inertia,
L   length of the column

Eigenvalue buckling is solved in FEM analysis to get the load multiplier λi and buckling mode $\{\psi i\}$ using following linear equation:

$$([K] + \lambda i[S])\{\psi i\} = 0 \tag{2}$$

where

[K]   is the stiffness matrix
[S]   is stress stiffness matrix

Buckling analysis is carried out using small deflection theory assuming the linear elastic behavior of material. Study of buckling becomes important in case of a tall structure. Various studies related to buckling of columns, tanks have been carried out [8, 9].

3 Modeling

RPC handling trolley (Fig. 3) is a tall movable lift structure made using various MS standard sections (columns 200 mm × 200 m^2 section, stiffener ISA100, cart ISMB300, and top frame ISMB200). The RPC trolley is made of three subassemblies. The lift support structure subassembly is individually modeled and analyzed using FEM [10] considering the effects of other assemblies as well as payload. The meshing of RPC handling trolley (Fig. 4) has been done using such element which is higher order 3D 20-node solid element that exhibits quadratic displacement behavior. The element is defined by 20 nodes having three degrees of freedom per node: translations in the x, y, and z directions.

3.1   Material of Construction

Section Material: Mild steel.

Young's modulus = 2.1E5 N/mm^2
Density = 7850 kg/m^3
Poisson's ratio = 0.3.

4   FEM Analysis

4.1   Assumptions

Lift support structure is welded over the cart structure. Assuming the cart structure as rigid, end of four columns of the lift support structure is made fixed in the analysis. Pulleys mounted on the top frame beams have not been modeled in the analysis but applied loads have been considered on the top frame.

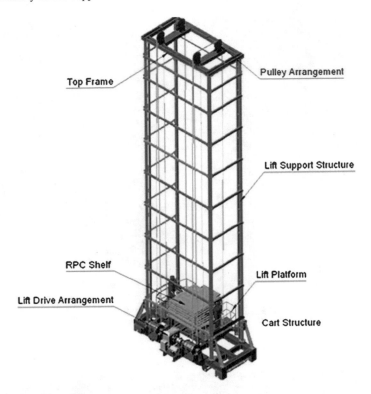

Fig. 3 RPC handling trolley

4.2 Load Conditions

Self-weight of the structure + Load of the lift on the four pulley locations.

Total weight of the lift platform including payload (4.5 T) will be lifted using four wire ropes which will be wounded over drums at cart passing through four pulleys; mounted on the top frame of lift support structure. The tension in each wire rope will be equal to one-fourth of the weight of the lift platform and load on the top frame will be equal to reaction at pulley locations which will equivalent to twice of rope tension. Earth gravity is considered as an input parameter. Assembly is studied for the static condition.

Total load on the top frame $= 2 \times 4.5$ T $= 88,290$ N
This load is working in eight rope segment on four pulley locations.
Load on each location $=$ Total load on the top frame/8 $= 11,036$ N $= 11,050$ N (approx.)

Initial boundary condition of lift support structure is shown in Fig. 5.

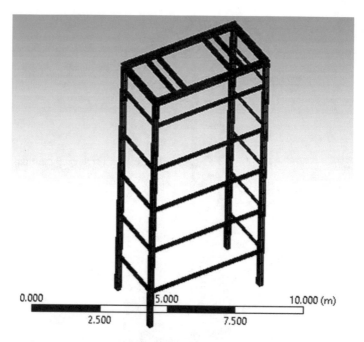

Fig. 4 Meshing of lift support structure

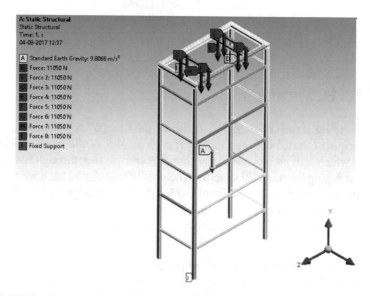

Fig. 5 Initial boundary condition of lift support structure

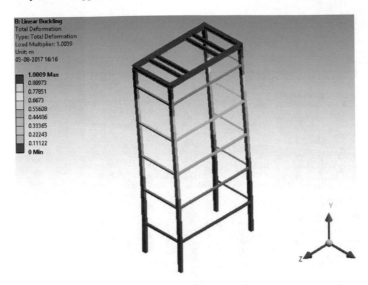

Fig. 6 First mode of buckling

4.3 Analysis

Another form of structure linear buckling analysis theory, expresses the linear buckling eigen value as below

$$([\mathbf{K_E}] + \lambda[\mathbf{K_G}])\{\delta\} = 0 \tag{3}$$

$[\mathbf{K_E}]$ is stiffness matrix of linear buckling analysis structure, $[\mathbf{K_G}]$ is geometric stiffness matrix, λ denotes the loading parameter. When the structure has not any initial defect, it represents the upper limit of buckling loading. δ is the buckling modal vector of the structure [3].

In the analysis, first three modes of buckling have been evaluated and analyzed. It is found that critical buckling load for the first mode is found to be 104 T with load multiplier value 1.003. It is also found that critical buckling load for third mode is 9% higher than the second mode and critical buckling load for second mode is 253% higher than first buckling mode. All three modes of buckling are shown in Figs. 6, 7, and 8.

In all the cases of buckling, critical buckling load is more than 11 times of operating load. Results are shown in Table 1.

B: Linear Buckling
Total Deformation 2
Type: Total Deformation
Load Multiplier: 1.0171
Unit: m
03-08-2017 16:42

1.0001 Max
0.88902
0.77789
0.66676
0.55564
0.44451
0.33338
0.22225
0.11113
0 Min

Fig. 7 Second mode of buckling

Table 1 Summary of result of buckling analysis

Mode	Critical buckling load	Difference w.r.t critical buckling load of first mode
1	104 T	
2	367 T	253%
3	400 T	284%

5 Validation

5.1 Fabrication of Scaled Down Model

A geometrically similar experimental set up was made to validate above results obtained from simulations. A 1/8 scaled down model of lift support structure, size 587.5 mm × 290 mm × 1390 mm (ht.) has been fabricated. Lift support structure columns and I section of top frame has been changed to hollow square section based on equivalent section modulus and area moment of inertia about relevant axes. Sketch of the scale down model is shown in the Fig. 9.

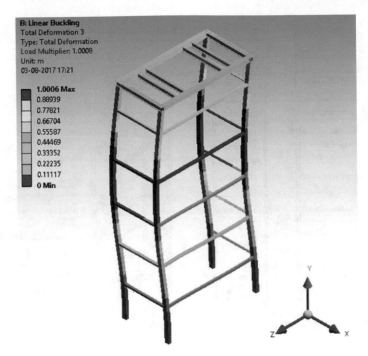

Fig. 8 Third mode of buckling

Model columns are of size 20 mm × 20 mm × 1 mm (thk) and top frame beams are of hollow square section of dimension 20 mm × 20 mm × 1 mm (thk). Stiffener is changed to angle 15 mm × 15 mm × 1.5 mm (thickness). Above sizes of the sections are selected on the basis of section of closest dimensions available in market. The construction material of lift support structure and model is same.

5.2 Boundary Conditions

The equivalent loading pattern on scaled-down-fabricated model has been derived using nondimensional analysis.

Length scale factor (S_L) used for making the model of lift support structure is 1/8.

$$\text{Density} = \text{Weight/volume}$$
$$\rho_p/\rho_m = S_L/S_f \tag{4}$$
$$\text{If } \rho_p = \rho_m, \text{ then } S_f = S_L$$

If we keep the density of material for model (ρ_m) and prototype (ρ_p) same then stress scale factor (S_f) must be equal to the length scale factor (S_L).

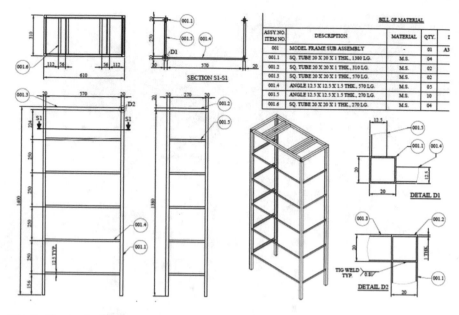

Fig. 9 Sketch of scale down model

Hence $S_f = 1/8$, corresponding stresses will reduce by a factor of 8. Force applied on the top frame will also accordingly reduce. Force applied on the top frame for getting reduced stresses is calculated using Eq. 5.

$$Force = stress \times area$$
$$Hence, P_p/P_m = 1/(S_f S_L^2) \tag{5}$$

where P_p is load on the prototype and P_m is load on the model.
If, $P_p = 22100$ N, $S_f = S_L = 1/8$

$$22,100/P_m = (8 \times 8^2)$$
$$P_m = 43.164\,N$$

5.3 FEM Analysis of Scaled Down Model

This analysis has been necessitated to accept adopted change in the structural section in scaled-down model.

Analysis is carried out for above boundary conditions (Fig. 10) and critical buckling load for the first mode has been evaluated and found to be 3.2 T with load multiplier 1.0008 (Fig. 11).

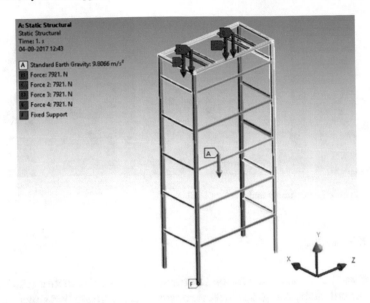

Fig. 10 Boundary condition of model

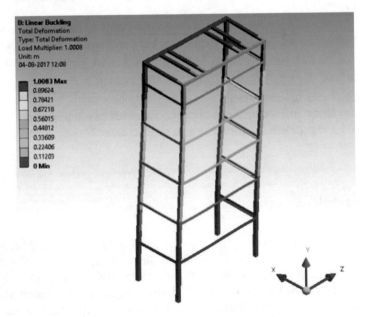

Fig. 11 First buckling mode of model

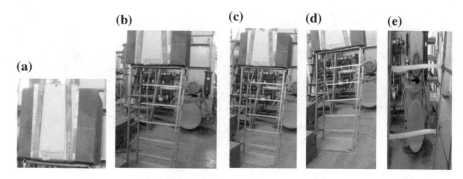

Fig. 12 Behavior of the model under 3 T of load

5.4 Lab Testing

Buckling test has been conducted on the model using the destructive technique to validate the critical buckling load for scale down model of lift support structure. Load of 3 T is applied on the top frame of the model and the model behavior was observed during (Fig. 12).

Figure 12 shows different stages of application of 3 T load on scaled-down-fabricated model. Buckling of the model has been initiated at 3 T load which is 6.25% lower than the simulation result value of 3.2 T. This mismatch in result may be due to following reasons:

1. Variation in the loading pattern
2. Variation in the fixing conditions of the bottom ends of the columns
3. Material and geometric imperfections in the sections of columns and top frame of beams

6 Observations

Buckling design of the bars requires a sufficient high factor of safety because of catastrophic failure. Considering this in the trolley design, the factor of safety in buckling of lift support structure has been kept more than 10. This entails that the trolley does not experience any unwanted failure during unassuming circumstances.

In the validation part of the thesis, it is seen that buckling in a structure is dependent on many parameters (material, geometry, section, etc.). During the manufacturing of the structure, a small deviation in parameters will result in multiplying stress several folds. This was seen in the lab during validation test that if the end support of the columns is not properly fixed then structure may lead to prior failure.

7 Conclusions

It is found that the lift support structure of RPC handling trolley can bear 104 T load on its top frame without buckling. The FEM analysis results are validated using 1/8 scale model of lift support structure with similar geometry. The 1/8 scale model is analyzed using FEM with the same solver and estimated critical buckling load is 3.2 T. The experimental critical buckling load of one-eighth model is found 3 T. Hence, the accuracy of FEM analysis is found within 7%. Since one-eighth model is representing similar lift support structure of RPC handling trolley the FEM analysis result may be considered within 7% actual and less than the estimated.

The critical buckling load of the lift support structure of RPC trolley considering 104 T, factor of safety found to be 11.5, which is widely acceptable range and in safe limit.

References

1. http://www.ino.tifr.res.in/ino/
2. S. Bheesette, *Design and Characterisation Studies of Resistive plate Chambers*, Ph.D. Thesis, IIT Bombay, 2009
3. J. Bi, Stability analysis on large-span steel tubular truss based on finite element simulation, in *International Conference on Smart Grid and Electrical Automation* (2016)
4. Kraav, T., Lellep, J.: Elastic stability of uniform and hollow columns. Procedia Eng. **172**, 570–577 (2017)
5. R.H. Wood, Effective length of columns in multi-storey building. Struct. Eng. **52**(7–9) (1974)
6. R.M. Jones, *Buckling of Bars, Plates and Shells* (Bull Ridge Publishing, 2006), p. 702
7. S.P. Timoshenko, J.M. Gere, *Theory of Elastic Stability*, 2nd edn. (McGraw-Hill Book Company, 1963)
8. G. Shi et al., Experimental study on column buckling of 420 MPa high strength steel circular tubes. J. Constr. Steel Res. **100**, 71–81 (2014)
9. Anna Halicka, Jerzy Podgorski, Designing of cylindrical concrete tanks with regard to buckling and second order effects. Procedia Eng. **193**, 50–57 (2017)
10. R.D. Cook, D.S. Malkus, M.E. Plesha, *Concepts and Applications of Finite Element Analysis*, 3rd edn. (Wiley, 1989)

Recovering Free Space from a Single Two-Point Perspective Image for Mobile Robot Navigation for Indoor Applications

V. Bhanu Chander, Thondiyath Asokan and Balaraman Ravindran

Abstract The problem of identifying free space in an environment from a given single image is a subject matter of interest in the field of computer vision and robotics. The aim of this paper is to construct a scaled 2D floor map from a single two-point perspective (2PP) image for visualizing the relative dimensions and poses of the objects, by taking minimal information. This is done by proposing a new simple method which utilizes the perspective property of the given image, viz., vanishing points. This paper introduces necessary geometrical constructions by introducing the notion of the side view of an image, using which few simple geometrical relations will be derived, that will help in constructing a 2D floor map. To the best of our knowledge, this is the first work of its kind, which introduces architectural concepts for map construction and for measurements from it, thus proving novelty of the introduced method.

Keywords Single-view metrology · Mathematical imagining
Single-image analysis · Computational geometry · Robotic mapping

1 Introduction

In the field of mobile robotics, the ability of the robot to navigate is a very basic requirement to perform any task. For the robot to plan a path, it either needs a pre-fed map of the environment or needs to build the map on-the-go. In either case, a knowl-

V. Bhanu Chander (✉) · T. Asokan
Department of Engineering Design, Indian Institute of Technology Madras, Chennai, India
e-mail: bhanu.lntecc@gmail.com

T. Asokan
e-mail: asok@iitm.ac.in

B. Ravindran
Department of Computer Science & Engineering, Robert Bosch Centre for Data Science & AI,
Indian Institute of Technology Madras, Chennai, India
e-mail: ravi@cse.iitm.ac.in

© Springer Nature Singapore Pte Ltd. 2019
D N Badodkar and T A Dwarakanath (eds.), *Machines, Mechanism and Robotics*, Lecture Notes in Mechanical Engineering,
https://doi.org/10.1007/978-981-10-8597-0_2

edge of the environment in the form a map is essential. Robotic mapping addresses the problem of acquiring spatial models of physical environments through mobile robots. The mapping problem is generally regarded as one of the most important problems in the pursuit of building truly autonomous mobile robots [1]. Robotic mapping is usually tedious and existing methods for finding free space using resources like sensors (LIDARs, range sensors, and/or using multiple vision system) turn out be costly, laborious and time-consuming.

Since vision-based sensors are inexpensive, research focus is turning toward usage of vision sensors (especially cameras) for robotic mapping. If cameras are considered, then the process of camera calibration is needed which is human involvement. Robust methods are yet to be developed for constructing 3D maps from single images taken from monocular cameras. Finding a way to deduce required free-space information from a single image and without the need of camera calibration is a huge requirement and will turn out to be a demanding platform for several applications (robotics, autonomous navigations, Virtual Reality (VR), Augmented Reality (AR), etc.), once proper benchmarking methods are established. Unfortunately, there are very few attempts on single-image floor mapping and thus there is no notion of standardizing an algorithm or a method yet. These attempts were shown to be incomplete and demanded a huge set of training data. These learning algorithms are also computationally complex.

1.1 Related Works

Few works are observed which had dealt with spatial layout estimation of indoor scenes. Some of the works are on finding salient directions in structured scenes [2] and modeling captured worlds in terms of simple bounding blocks [3]. Noticeable methods for recovering spatial layout from cluttered scenes are observed [4–6], which was applied to indoor scenes. Researchers have tried using single images for spatial layout estimations [7, 8]. Their focus was not on finding free space which helps in constructing a map of the given scene, but, their intention was rather on constructing a 3D model, mostly for visualization purpose. The earliest work on single-view metrology [9] dealt with 3D affine measurements from single perspective images. Their work was able to reconstruct 3D models of the scenes, but, just like the other works, they were not able to give the notion of obtaining a free space map from the 3D models, and the work structure needed manual labeling, which, according to [10] is laborious. Techniques for obtaining depth maps are available [11], but, as noted from [4], depth maps are not applicable for path planning tasks.

Out of the available research works on spatial layout estimation, so far, very few of them have actually worked on the notion of free space maps [12, 13]. Unfortunately, existing works (on floor map buildings) modeled objects which need to be aligned along the axis of the identified walls and the floor. Objects boundaries in the constructed floor maps are made parallel to the walls even if they are not parallel in the real world. Apart from that, the methods employ learning-based techniques which need a large set of training images, which again is human involvement. Owing to the gap observed in the existing works and the benefits of obtaining maps from single images, this paper aims at introducing an easy method that will help in eliminating the costly as well as laborious calibration and training process involved. The proposed work might thus fuel the research in a different perspective which has not been tried yet. This paper makes an assumption that objects in the image will be assumed as fitted with bounding boxes.

2 Background

This section introduces the basics and the background needed for understanding the proposed method. Most of the captured images will be either in two-point (2PP) or three-point (3PP) perspective. Type of perspective is defined by the number of vanishing points in the given scene. More about vanishing points are available in [14, 15]. Many works exist for finding vanishing points in a given perspective image [16, 17]. Given an object in 2PP, there is a standard way [14] in architecture for constructing its top view to some scale, with respect to the camera position in the world. Although the step-by-step explanation of the construction process is out of scope for this paper, Fig. 4 has been introduced for better understanding to the readers about the procedure involved, showing the inputs and outputs related to this construction process.

Figure 1 shows the common camera configuration and the terminology used in this paper. More introductions to this subject on camera models are available in [18]. The common terminologies used in this paper are listed below:

1. Camera center is considered as the origin of the camera frame, and this is usually referred as "View point" denoted by "V". Height of V from the ground plane denotes the "eye level" of the camera, which is usually represented as a line called "Horizon line". Camera frame is represented in terms of X_C, Y_C, and Z_C.
2. Viewing direction is along the positive Y_C direction.
3. World coordinate system is represented in terms of X_W, Y_W and Z_W.
4. "Image Plane" represents the plane on which the scene will be captured and is available to us in the form of an image. Point of intersection of the image plane with Y_C is termed as "Image Center".
5. Camera pose is represented by 6 degrees of freedom (DoF). Its coordinate position (x, y, z) represents 3 DoF while its three orientations (pitch, roll and yaw) represent another 3 DoF.

The concept of top and side views has been marked in Fig. 1. While the top view is obvious, the notion of the side view and measurements from the image are bit confusing and so we discuss them here introducing our geometry. In Fig. 2, a simple line drawing of a captured image is shown to the right with two objects, enclosed in green borders, denoting the image. Let the vanishing points of the objects lie along the line connecting VP_1 and VP_2, which in the side view will be at V, as shown

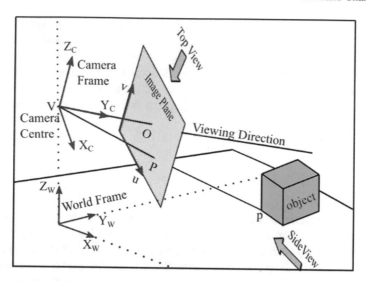

Fig. 1 Standard camera model considered in this work, depicting camera, world, and image frames. Camera center is denoted as "V", while image center is denoted as "O". Notion of top and side views used in this works are shown with arrows. Top and side views are considered such that image plane is perpendicular to the viewing planes from both the directions. Projection of object's base corner (say p) onto the image plane is denoted as P

in Fig. 2 (left side). This line indicates the eye level or height of the camera from the ground. This straight horizontal line through V is also termed as "Horizon line". Note that ground level is not known to us in the side view and so it will be taken at some arbitrary level. Image plane in the side view is shown by a green vertical line at a distance d (equal to the focal length of the camera) from the viewpoint.

Let P_1 and Q_1 be the bottom and top nearest corners of the first object, near to the camera as shown in the image. Its position in the side view is shown, marked as P_1 and Q_1. Similarly, let P_2 and Q_2 be the bottom and top nearest corners for the second object, the same will be captured in the image plane as shown in the side view. We can now make measurements from the image, like say if we want the height of the camera from the ground, according to the first objects scale as in the image, we can measure it by h_1 as shown in Fig. 2 in both the image and the side view. We will be utilizing a similar kind of image-based measurements for finding parameters required for building the map, like for example object height, relative distances, etc.

Given an image with multiple objects in it, trying to get a 2D map by following the construction procedure given in [14] will give top views of all the objects in different scales. Apart from that, all the objects will be positioned along the same horizon line, which is not the correct representation. This situation is shown in Fig. 3a considering three objects B1, B2, and B3. If we follow the standard procedure of construing top view for all the three objects individually, we will get a new top view as shown in Fig. 3b. But, their actual relative positions are shown in Fig. 3c.

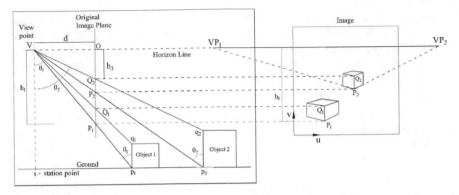

Fig. 2 An example image with two objects line drawing is shown to the right and its side view is shown on the left. In the side view, we can see the camera center V as well as objects placed on the ground, while the vertical green line represents the image plane. The height of V from the ground is not known yet, but based on our assumption that the surface is flat, we can show the objects on the same horizontal at some depth from V. Station point "s" represents the vertical projection of the viewpoint V onto the ground

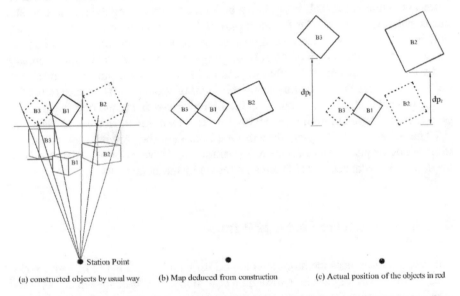

(a) constructed objects by usual way   (b) Map deduced from construction   (c) Actual position of the objects in red

Fig. 3 a An example scenario with three objects (B1, B2, and B3) shown in magenta color. Constructed top view of the objects will assume rectangular shapes lying above the horizon line. **b** A 2D Map that can be deduced from the construction. Objects B2 and B3 are not positioned exactly relative to object B1 and the station point, as they are aligned in the real world. **c** Actual positions of the three objects, relative to one another, shown in red color. Note that the map is scaled and the object dimensions and positional distances are all scaled by a common scale factor

All the objects' nearest corners will have the same y distance from the station point in the general procedure. But, we need a transformation by which they are placed more or less at the same relative position with respect to a reference object. We are interested in finding this new transformation. Denoting the distance to be shifted by d_p (call it "offset distance"), we need to find d_p for all the objects, for which we introduce a novel geometrical method which has not been viewed by researchers in this geometrical perspective way yet. This paper thus happens to be the first work of its kind which employed geometrical approach for map-building application using single images.

3   Overview of Methodology

Figure 4 shows the structure of the procedure that will be followed in the proposed generalized algorithm for getting floor maps. Inputs for the system will be a single-captured image from which the details of vanishing points and objects corners will be extracted and fed to it. This paper is not concerned with getting the required inputs but is rather concerned with the later part of building floor maps. So, the inputs will be fed manually to the algorithm that we designed. Our program builds the top views for all the identified objects, employs the concept of side view geometry and the mathematics related to that for evaluating the offset distance d_p for all the objects, evaluates scale factor by using the input of ground truths, scales down the actual ground truth of objects and then finally it overlays the found object top views onto the scaled ground truth view, taking into consideration the measured distances d_p. The outputs from the program will be a floor map showing the objects' scaled dimensions (say with scale factor S_k) positioned relative to one another to some accuracy, the distances of which are also scaled by the same factor S_k.

4   Floor Map from Single 2PP Image

This section introduces the proposed method for building a 2D view of a given 2PP image with several objects in it, through a case study. The basic idea that we follow here is very simple. Considering an example image with two objects, base corners of which are denoted as P_1 and P_2 as shown in Fig. 5a, depth of first objects base corner P_1 from the horizon is say h_1, while the depth of second object base corner P_2 from the same horizon line is h_2, which is lesser than h_1 as shown in Fig. 5b. We know that in the real world both the objects will be lying on the same flat surface. So, if we can project second object such that its depth also measures h_1, then, we can get the required offset distance, for which our proposed concept of side view, as shown in Fig. 5, will come handy.

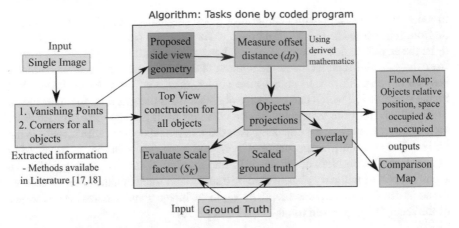

Fig. 4 A flowchart depicting the general methodology proposed in this paper with all the modules (inputs and outputs) involved for map building. Blocks in yellow color are the inputs taken, while the rest blocks are part of this paper's contribution

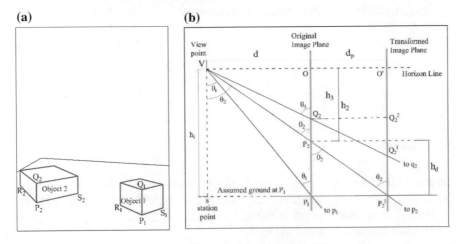

Fig. 5 **a** Line drawing of an example image in 2PP, considering with two objects on the ground, nearest base corners of which are marked as P_1 and P_2. **b** Constructed side view for the scenario with two objects. Camera viewpoint is denoted by V and the original image plane is represented by the vertical line at O in green colour. Object 1 and object 2 makes θ_1 and θ_2 angles with V. Their base corner projection onto the image plane is denoted as P_1 and P_2. Projection of P_2 and Q_2 onto the new image plane through O' is represented as P_2^1 and Q_2^1, respectively

4.1 Side View Geometry

Figure 5b shows the side view of the arrangement, with all the notations considered for this case study with two objects, base corners of them being at P_1 and P_2, marked in the original image plane. Trying to project P_2 to the same depth as P_1 will result in a new image plane, positioned parallel to the original image plane at a distance d_p from it as shown in Fig. 5b, denoted as *"Transformed Image Plane"*. Let θ_1 and θ_2 be the angles made by the two objects' base corners with viewpoint V, as viewed from the side view and let the perpendicular distance between the reference objects base corner and the second object base corner, measured by P_1P_2 in the original image plane be h_d, which can be easily obtained from the given image. Distance d of the object from the viewpoint can be obtained from the top view construction. Apart from that, we can get objects' base corners vertical depths (with respect to the horizon line) from the image, denoted by h_1 and h_2 as shown in Fig. 5, considering two objects. Our problem of interest is to find the shift distance d_p, using which the second object's imaginary plane would be transformed, such that the object measures the same depth as the reference depth h_1. Q_2 in the image plane denotes the top corner of the second object. From triangle VOP_2 in Fig. 5.

$$\tan \theta_2 = \frac{OV}{OP_2} = \frac{d}{h_2} \tag{1}$$

Now, from triangle $P_2P_1P_2^1$ and using (1), we get

$$\tan \theta_2 = \frac{d_p}{h_d} \tag{2}$$

$$d_p = h_d \cdot \tan \theta_2 = \frac{h_d \cdot d}{h_2} \tag{3}$$

5 Case Study

We now take the example image with two objects, line drawing of which is shown in Fig. 5a (magenta colour denotes objects). Considering the scenario, we now list out the steps to be followed for constructing the map, given that we have two objects in the example image considered in Fig. 6:

1. Construct the top view for the first object and find the dimensions. Measure the depth h_1 and make it as reference depth.
2. Construct the top view for the second object (with the base corner at P_2), and find the ground depth h_2 with respect to the horizon line.
3. Determine the distance d_p using Eq. (3) for the second object.
4. Marking the station point at O', position the top views of both the objects along the same horizon line. After that, draw construction lines for the second object.
5. Offset top view of the second object such that its base corner, denoted by P_h is now at P_p^1. This transformation is done such that the vertical distance between P_h and P_p^1 is d_p as shown in Fig. 6. All other corners must lie on their corresponding projection lines and must make the same angle with the horizontal, as found in the actual top view.

Fig. 6 Construction of a 2D map from an image with two objects. Second object's base corner P_h in top view has to be projected to P_p^1 such that the vertical distance between the measures d_p. With this new projection, both the objects are scaled to some scale factor say $1/S_k$ to their actual dimensions and their relative positions are in proper proportion to the actual positions in the real world

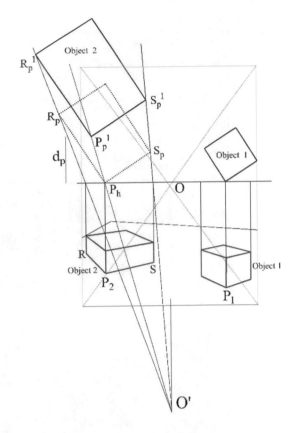

If there are multiple objects (more than two) in the image, repeat the process by keeping the nearest object's depth as the reference.

6 Experimental Results

We coded the proposed algorithm in Mathematica™, captured several real-world images in 2PP, measured ground truths of the objects along with their relative distances and used them for our experiments. Our program evaluated a scaled factor for each input image data and compared the obtained result of the floor map with the scaled ground truth maps. A 2D floor map obtained from Mathematica result is shown in Fig. 8a, for the example scenario, considered in Fig. 7a (line diagram of which is shown in Fig. 3a). Objects constructed using the proposed methods are shown as filled polygons in yellow color, while, corresponding ground truths of the same objects are shown as rectangles in magenta color overlaid on top, relative to the station point (position of the camera in top view) which is shown as a cyan color blob.

(a)

(b)

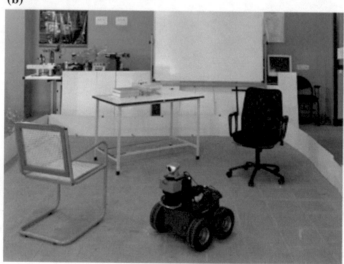

Fig. 7 **a** An example image with three objects, taken from a monocular camera. **b** Another scene with a robot, two chairs, and a table. Some of the edges and corners are partly occluded

In another example shown in Fig. 7b, nonrectangular and partly occluded objects have been considered with some of their edges and corners not clearly visible, thus validating the competency of the proposed method. The comparison map in Fig. 8b shows that there is a good match with the obtained map and the scaled ground truth. We tested the same code for several more case studies. In all the cases, it showed

(a)   **(b)**

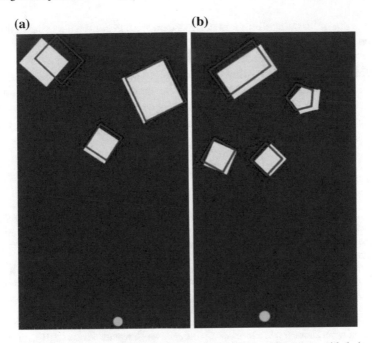

Fig. 8 Resulting images depicting the comparison between obtained floor maps with their measured ground truths. Circles in cyan color represents the camera position in top view. Objects constructed are shown as filled polygons in yellow color, while the corresponding ground truths are shown in magenta colour, overlaid on top. **a** For the example image shown in Fig. 7a. **b** For the example image shown in Fig. 7b

very good performance in terms of the match. We found that errors in dimensions mismatch were within ±7% which is a pretty good approximation of the actual dimensions.

7 Conclusions and Future Works

In this paper, a new geometrical method for building floor maps that capture the relative poses of objects and the approximate floor space occupied by them from a given single two-point perspective (2PP) image has been introduced. This method is very simple, involving very few mathematical relations obtained from the geometry of the side view that we proposed here for the first time, proving the novelty of the algorithm. This work differs from the existing methods in that it does not depend on the requirement of huge training dataset for letting the algorithm learn; as well as this is the first work which accurately captured the exact bounding space occupied by the objects unlike the few existing works which made improper approximation that turn out to be not applicable for applications such as robotic navigation tasks.

Results are quite compelling and comparison with ground truths shows the better performance of the method. It has to be noted that all the distances (and dimensions) that have been obtained here are scaled by a common scaling factor S_k. If at least one actual dimension (say a robot dimension or length or depth of an object like a table) is known, then, we can straight away get all the estimates as in real environment (to some accuracy level). Extending the method for constructing a 3D free space map as well as solving three-point perspective methods by modifying the existing method will be considered as future works.

References

1. S. Thrun, *Robotic Mapping: A Survey: Exploring Artificial Intelligence in the New Millennium* (Morgan Kaufmann Publishers Inc., San Francisco, CA, USA, 2002). ISBN 1-55860-811-7
2. J. Kosecka, W. Zhang, Extraction, matching, and pose recovery based on dominant rectangular structures. J. Comp. Vis. Underst. **100**(3), 274–293 (2005)
3. L. Pero, J. Guan, E. Brau, J. Schlecht, K. Barnard, Sampling bedrooms, in *Proceedings of the IEEE Conference on Computer Vision and Pattern Recognition* (2011), pp. 2009–2016
4. V. Hedau, D. Hoiem, D. Forsyth, Recovering the spatial layout of cluttered rooms, in *Proceedings of the International Conference on Computer Vision* (2009), pp. 1849–1856
5. V. Hedau, D. Hoiem, D. Forsyth, Thinking inside the box: using appearance models and context based on room geometry, in *European Conference on Computer Vision* (2010), pp. 224–237
6. D. Lee, A. Gupta, M. Hebert, T. Kanade, Estimating spatial layout of rooms using volumetric reasoning about objects and surfaces, in *Proceedings of Advances in Neural Information Processing Systems (NIPS)*, vol. 23 (2010), pp. 1288–1296
7. F. Han, S.C. Zhu, Bayesian reconstruction of 3D shapes and scenes from a single image, *in Proceedings of the International Workshop on Higher-Level Knowledge in 3D Modeling and Motion Analysis* (2003). ISBN:0-7695-2049-9
8. S. Yu, H. Zhang, J. Malik, Inferring spatial layout from a single image via depth-ordered grouping, in *Proceedings of the IEEE Conference on Computer Vision and Pattern Recognition* (2008), pp. 1–7. https://doi.org/10.1109/cvprw.2008.456297
9. A. Criminisi, I.D. Reid, A. Zisserman, Single view metrology. Int. J. Comp. Vis. **40**(2), 23–148 (2000)
10. D. Hoiem, A. Efros, M. Hebert, Recovering surface layout from an image. Int. J. Comp. Vis. **75**(1), 151–172 (2007)
11. A. Saxena, S.H. Chung, A.Y. Ng, 3-D depth reconstruction from a single still image. Int. J. Comp. Vis. **76**(1), 53–69 (2008)
12. V. Hedau, D. Hoiem, D. Forsyth, Recovering free space of indoor scenes from a single image, in *IEEE Conference Computer Vision and Pattern Recognition* (2012), pp. 2807–2814. https://doi.org/10.1109/cvpr.2012.6248005
13. M. Hebert, J. Lin, S. Satkin, Data-driven scene understanding from 3D models. Br. Mach. Vis. Conf. (2012). https://doi.org/10.5244/C.26.128
14. F.D.K. Ching, S.P. Juroszek, *Design Drawing*, 2nd edn. (Wiley Publications, Washington, 2010). ISBN 978-0-470-53369-7
15. J. Jang, J.R. Rossignac, *Determination of the Correct Eye Position for Viewing Perspective Images of 3D Scenes* (Georgia Institute of Technology, 2001)
16. J. KoSecki, W. Zhang, Efficient computation of vanishing points, in *Proceedings of the IEEE International Conference on Robotics & Automation* (2002). https://doi.org/10.1109/robot.2002.1013365
17. C. Rother, A new approach for vanishing point detection in architectural environments. J. Image Vis. Comput. **20**(9–10), 647–655 (2002)
18. K. Byres, J. Henle, Where the camera was. This Mag. **77**(4), 251–259 (2004)

Image-Based Data Preparation for Robot-Based Neurosurgery

Abhishek Kaushik, T A Dwarakanath, Gaurav Bhutani, P. P. K. Venkata and Aliasgar Moiyadi

Abstract The purpose of the paper is to formulate the optimum robotic surgical framework to perform a high-precision neurosurgery. The DICOM data tags are meticulously identified and used to build the optimum robotic surgical framework to develop accurate neuro-registration and neuronavigation. Algorithm along with GUI is developed for neuro-registration and neuronavigation. The different Unique Identifiers (UIDs) of DICOM are studied and all the slices of the various views are classified and stored as a data series file. From a single DICOM series, the three orthographic views, an oblique view of choice and a 3D model of the patient's brain are reconstructed and displayed. The DICOM data information of patient posture is extended to develop optimum robotic surgical framework to perform a high-precision neurosurgery. Surgical Coordinate Measuring Mechanism (SCMM)-based neuro-registration and neuronavigation are demonstrated on the various phantoms and a real human skull to validate the data preparation for neuronavigation. The test procedures are found to be in accordance with the neurosurgical standards. A neuro-surgical procedure is demonstrated by utilizing workspace of the surgical robot. The SCMM-based neuro-registration procedure eliminates the 'line of sight' constraint

A. Kaushik (✉)
Homi Bhabha National Institute, Anushakti Nagar, Mumbai, India
e-mail: abhishekk@barc.gov.in

T A Dwarakanath (✉) · G. Bhutani (✉)
Division of Remote Handling & Robotics, Bhabha Atomic Research Centre, Trombay, Mumbai 400085, India
e-mail: tad@barc.gov.in

G. Bhutani
e-mail: bhutani@barc.gov.in

P. P. K. Venkata
Computer Division, Bhabha Atomic Research Centre, Trombay, Mumbai 400085, India
e-mail: panikv@barc.gov.in

A. Moiyadi
Advanced Centre for Treatment Research & Education in Cancer, Navi Mumbai, India
e-mail: aliasgar.moiyadi@gmail.com

© Springer Nature Singapore Pte Ltd. 2019
D N Badodkar and T A Dwarakanath (eds.), *Machines, Mechanism and Robotics*, Lecture Notes in Mechanical Engineering,
https://doi.org/10.1007/978-981-10-8597-0_3

as in camera-based neuro-registration procedures. The utility of optimum workspace strategy of the robot helps in bringing highest manipulability at the required region.

Keywords Neuro-registration · Neuronavigation · Neurosurgery · DICOM Medical imaging · Image-guided surgery · Robot-based neurosurgery

1 Introduction

Robotic neurosurgery and neuronavigation involves various technologies to guide the neurosurgeon to locate and operate on the problem area within the confines of the brain. During neuronavigation, the tip of the surgical tool is projected as crosshairs in the different projections of the reconstructed CT/MRI image data. In the text of the paper, MR implies CT/MRI, unless explicitly specified. During the surgery, the surgeon can view in real time, the position of the surgical tool along with the reconstructed MR image of the patient on the computer workstation. The prerequisite of the neuronavigation is the determination of the relationship of the tumor with the surgical tool, which is obtained in the neuro-registration process. Before neuro-registration, an estimate of the relationship between the tumor point and the platform of the robot (end effector) is obtained. The surgical tool position has to be tracked with respect to the patient's image throughout the neurosurgery.

The medical images generated by the medical imaging modalities are in DICOM format. DICOM is a set of standards formulated to maintain the standardization among the various stack of images, data types, and the communication between various modalities, workstations, and other devices. It records image-related parameters such as patient 3D position, sizes, and orientations slice thickness, modality used, information related to the patient, the doctor and the hospital [1, 2]. These DICOM images need to be processed for obtaining useful information related to the anatomy of the brain and the tumor. The reconstructed images are interfaced with the various neuronavigation devices and can be used to guide the surgical tool during surgical procedures.

2 Data Preparation for Robot-Based Neurosurgery

DICOM image data always have a DICOM entity called DICOMDIR. This DICOMDIR is read first as it contains all information. DICOM images are arbitrarily arranged and need to be segregated. The images are segregated based on the DICOM Unique Identifiers (UIDs). A patient can have multiple scans like MR scan of the neck or MR of the brain. All scans of the patient come under one unique patient ID (UID) and patient can have different studies and allotted different study instance UIDs (0020, 000D), which is unique for each study. A further study can have multiple series based on directions like axial, coronal, and sagittal either based on a scan with contrast medium or without a contrast medium. In DICOM, each series is assigned with series instance UIDs (0020, 000E) which is unique for each series. Each series may have multiple images and each image has a unique Service-Object Pair (SOP) instance UID (0008, 0018). A software module based on the given methodology is developed to read the UIDs of the images and arrange them in their pre-designated locations in the series and study. Generally, images belonging to a particular series have the same orientation. Basically, two coordinate systems are used in the acquisition of medical images namely patient coordinate system and image coordinate system. The anatomical or patient coordinate system [P] is fixed and fully defined by the lying posture of the patient on imaging couch. The image coordinate system, is a 2D coordinate system, is attached to each image. The MR Scanner generates a regular rectangular array of images. From these images, the axial, coronal, and sagittal images can be generated [2, 3]. Images acquired by the MR scanner are in 2D and it is required to map the position and orientation of these 2D images with reference to the 3D patient coordinate system. For this, the procedure given in the DICOM standard 3.0 [2] is adopted. The image plane and the pixel spacing attributes mentioned below are used to map the position and orientation of the 2D images with respect to patient coordinate system [P].

- Image Position with respect to the patient coordinate system, (S_x, S_y, S_z): DICOM Tag (0020, 0032), (S_x, S_y, S_z) are the Image position coordinates of the center of the first voxel at the top left corner of the image from the patient coordinate system.
- Image Orientation with respect to the patient coordinate system, (X_x, X_y, X_z), (Y_x, Y_y, Y_z): DICOM Tag (0020, 0037), (X_x, X_y, X_z) are the values of the row (X) direction cosines of image orientation and (Y_x, Y_y, Y_z) are the values of the column (Y) direction cosines of image orientation.
- Pixel Spacing $(\Delta i, \Delta j)$: DICOM Tag (0028, 0030), Pixel spacing $(\Delta i, \Delta j)$ is the column and row pixel resolution of the pixel spacing in mm.

The coordinates of the voxel (i, j) in the image plane with respect to the patient coordinate system [P] (in mm) is given as:

$$P_x(i, j) = X_x \cdot \Delta i \cdot i + Y_x \cdot \Delta j \cdot j + S_x \tag{1}$$

$$P_y(i, j) = X_y \cdot \Delta i \cdot i + Y_y \cdot \Delta j \cdot j + S_y \tag{2}$$

$$P_z(i, j) = X_z \cdot \Delta i \cdot i + Y_z \cdot \Delta j \cdot j + S_z \tag{3}$$

where i, j are the column and row index to the image plane [2]. The stated procedure has been incorporated to develop the software module for neuronavigation. The above methodology will also be used to obtain the homogenous transformation between the patient coordinate system [P] and fiducial coordinate system [F], ${}_P^F T$.

3 Optimization of the Robot Posture with Respect to the Patient

Neuro-registration is the process of determining the relationship of the patient frame with respect to the surgical tool frame (attached to the robot). Before conducting neuro-registration, the setup of the surgical robot in relation with the patient has to be estimated. The setup should be such that it leads to an optimum performance of the robot. The estimation of the setup can be obtained on the basis of the patient-specific information provided in the DICOM tags of the particular patient. It helps in simulating the complete robotic surgery environment like relative positions of the robot, the surgical couch, the mobility of the surgical team, the patient and the related instruments. More importantly, the robot posture estimation and the placement ensure that the Region of Interest (ROI) for surgery and the entry point is within the workspace of the robot and is reachable with an optimum operating efficiency. The concept of the robot posture estimation is illustrated in Fig. 1. The task comprises of the various components from which the data is drawn to set up the robot posture with respect to the patient. Six reference frames are established (1) Image coordinate system [I], (2) Patient coordinate system [P], (3) Fiducial coordinate system [F] (4) Surgical couch coordinate system [SC], (5) Robot platform coordinate system [RP] and (6) Robot base coordinate system [RB]. During robotic neurosurgery, the aim is to fix the posture of the robot in a way that the ROI/tumor is in the centre of the workspace of the robot. Considering the Region of Interest as a point representing

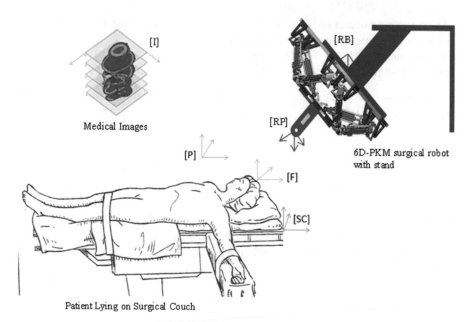

Fig. 1 Principle of the robot posture estimation based on patient

a tumor in the image coordinate system [I], Eqs. (4) and (5) are used to find the relationship between the tumor point and the robot platform and to estimate the robot posture based on the patient coordinate frame (before actual neuro-registration).

$$
{}_T^{RP}P = {}_{RB}^{RP}T \cdot {}_{SC}^{RB}T \cdot {}_F^{SC}T \cdot {}_P^{F}T \cdot {}_I^{P}T \cdot {}_T^{I}P \tag{4}
$$

$$
{}_P^{RP}T = {}_{RB}^{RP}T \cdot {}_{SC}^{RB}T \cdot {}_F^{SC}T \cdot {}_P^{F}T \tag{5}
$$

where ${}_T^{I}P$ are the coordinates of the tumor point with respect to image coordinate system, ${}_I^{P}T$ is the transformation of [I] with respect to [P], ${}_P^{F}T$ is the transformation of [P] with respect to [F], ${}_F^{SC}T$ is the transformation of [F] with respect to [SC], ${}_{SC}^{RB}T$ is the transformation of [SC] with respect to [RB], ${}_{RB}^{RP}T$ is the transformation of [RB] with respect to [RP], ${}_T^{RP}P$ are the coordinates of the tumor point with respect to the robot platform coordinate system [RP], ${}_I^{RP}T$ is the transformation of [I] with respect to [RP]. In DICOM, Image position (0020, 0032), Image orientation (0020, 0037) and pixel spacing (0028, 0030) DICOM tags can fully define a stack of images (series) with respect to the patient coordinate system [P] (as discussed in Sect. 2). The orientation of patient coordinate system [P] depends on how the patient is lying on the surgical couch. A fiducial coordinate system [F], with similar orientation as that of the patient coordinate system [P], is fixed at the center of the any of the fiducial marker (whose position is known with respect to [P]) on the surface of the head. This defines [P] with respect to [F]. Usually, in DICOM standards, the patient position tag (0018, 5100) specifies the patient position relative to the imaging equipment space. The methodology of relating the patient position with respect to the imaging equipment has been extended to establish the relationship between the patient coordinate system [P] and the surgical couch coordinate system [SC] using fiducial coordinate system [F]. The proper positioning of the patient is required to maintain blood circulation, to prevent nerve damage, to provide sufficient exposure to the operating area and to prevent the sensitive parts of the body from the pressure caused due to self-weight of the body [4].

By and large the postures of patient are well classified and given as: Head First-Prone (HFP), Head First-Supine (HFS), Head First-Decubitus Right (HFDR), Head First-Decubitus Left (HFDL), Feet First-Decubitus Right (FFDR), Feet First-Decubitus Left (FFDL), Feet First-Prone (FFP) and Feet First-Supine (FFS) [2, 5].

In DICOM standards, these positions are defined with respect to the imaging equipment and in this paper, a similar analogy is suggested for relating the patient position with respect to the surgical couch during neurosurgery. The surgical couch coordinate system [SC] has been attached at a suitable place on the surgical couch such that the relationship between [SC] and [F] is easily determined. The robot base coordinate system [RB] is a predefined coordinate system (attached at the base of the robot) with respect to [SC]. A near optimum posturing of robot with respect to the patient based on the visual clues is obtained, ${}_P^{RP}T$ is approximately determined for home position of [RP] with respect to [RB]. The robot platform coordinate system [RP] is attached to the platform (surgical tool). The inverse kinematics approach is developed to obtain the relationship between [RB] and [RP] of a 6 DOF Parallel

Kinematic Mechanism (6D-PKM) robot developed in the author's laboratory (shown in Fig. 6). The positioning of the robot should ensure that the tumor or region of interest should be within the workspace of the robot. The workspace represents the scope of the robot's motion and provides an important constraint for the robot motion planning and control. The complete workspace of a 6D-PKM robot is in a six-dimensional (6D) space. The achievable workspace is determined from the constraint of leg ranges, l_{min} and l_{max} (minimum and maximum leg lengths of 6D PKM). The workspace points satisfy the constraints given by the Eq. (6) [6, 7].

$$l_{min} \leq \left\| \overrightarrow{l_i} \right\| \leq l_{max} \quad \text{where}, i = 1, \ldots, 6 \tag{6}$$

l_i is the leg length connecting the base connection point to the corresponding platform connection point of the 6D PKM. For a given translation and rotation of the platform, the inequality Eq. (6) is solved to obtain the equations of 12 (6 pairs) spheres, six with minimum leg lengths and six with maximum leg lengths. The workspace is given by the intersection set of all the 12 spheres. This approach is used to develop a C++ software module which employs an analytical method to generate the workspace. The desired workspace is the 3D intersection of these 12 spheres as shown in Fig. 2 (shown in light blue color). Figure 2 also illustrates the 3D translation workspaces and maximum pivot region (shown in blue color) for rotations of the platform about the X-axis. Similarly, the maximum pivot regions for rotation about the Y and Z axes can also be determined. The optimum robot placement should ensure that the Region of Interest (ROI) for surgery is close to the maximum pivot region for rotation about X, Y, and Z axis of platform.

4   Patient Preparation and Neuro-registration

Neuro-registration is a process of determining the relationship of the anatomical frame with respect to a surgical tool frame. The task lies in identifying the point in the image and accessing it for measurement in real space. To map the MR image of the body part with the corresponding anatomical portion of the real body, specific points on the image are registered with the corresponding real-life anatomical points. Mathematical requirements should be taken care such that, no three fiducials should be collinear or near collinear to avoid singularity or ill-conditioning. In case of four fiducials being used for neuro-registration, care should be taken that all of the four should not lie in a plane. To start with the neuro-registration, the DICOM directory (DICOMDIR) is imported and read so that the axial, coronal and sagittal views are reconstructed and displayed in a window of the GUI as shown in Fig. 4. Now for neuro-registration, four predefined points at the center of the cylindrical hole of a fiducial are marked in different views of the real-time visualization.

A high-precision, lightweight, portable Surgical Coordinate Measuring Mechanism (SCMM) is developed in the author's laboratory at DRHR, BARC, Mumbai for

Fig. 2 3D model workspace of 6D-PKM

neuro-registration and neuronavigation. It is a passive four degree of freedom serial mechanism with encoders mounted at each joint and with a base fixture. Neuro-registration experiments are carried out using SCMM [6]. After selecting points in the images, the corresponding points are measured by using the SCMM in its reference frame. By using a 3D model, it is possible to register very complex shapes. Two acrylic blocks of different sizes, spherical glass jar phantom and a human skull are affixed with fiducial markers. All are successfully registered using the 3D model and the SCMM. Figure 3 shows the prototype of the SCMM used for registration of the human skull. The complete procedure and detail of neuro-registration using SCMM can be found in one of the author's previous paper [6, 7]. The SCMM is used to determine the exact value of $^{RP}_{P}T$ after optimum placement of the robot. Figure 4 shows the real-time visualization of the registration, a window showing the DICOM coordinates and the corresponding SCMM coordinates of the selected points is displayed. After the point selection, the registration between the anatomical frame and the surgical tool frame is carried out.

5   Neuronavigation and Robot-Based Neurosurgery

A real-time visualization has been developed, based on procedure discussed above, using wxWidgets, VTK and PyDICOM in python language. The 3D surface model is generated using the Marching cube algorithm [8]. Along with the axial, coronal,

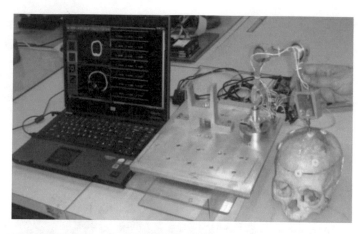

Fig. 3 Registration of a human skull by SCMM

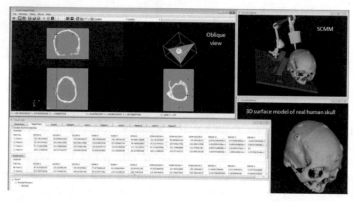

Fig. 4 GUI shows all run-time views and the relationship of SCMM with respect to a 3D human skull model after neuro-registration

and sagittal views, an oblique view is also generated. This oblique view is a real-time image of the brain normal to the axis of the moving tool. As seen in Fig. 4, the top right window shows the generated 3D model of the skull along with the actual position and orientation of the SCMM during neuronavigation. After neuro-registration, the neuronavigation framework is tested for its accuracy. Table 1 shows the DICOM and SCMM coordinates of two anatomical points in the DICOM and SCMM frame of reference and their registration errors (bold). The neuro-registration errors are less than 1 mm. The experiments are performed with the CT scan data of two acrylic blocks, a spherical jar phantom and an actual human skull. The implementation of the SCMM-based neuronavigation is illustrated in Fig. 4. It shows the SCMM and its simulated model when the user is traversing the surface of the skull. Neuronavigation procedure is found to be satisfactory in all the cases. In Fig. 5, the patient's head

Table 1 Zoomed view of table shown in Fig. 4 showing DICOM points, SCMM points and the neuro-registration error

Points	DICOM X	DICOM Y	DICOM Z	SCMM X	SCMM Y	SCMM Z	SCMM DICOM X	SCMM DICOM Y	SCMM DICOM Z	Error X	Error Y	Error Z
5	47.41	133.42	−178.40	77.87	65.39	93.85	47.83	134.39	−178.16	**0.42**	**0.97**	**0.237**
6	114.36	137.44	−155.56	76.53	132.93	108.75	114.31	137.74	−155.02	**0.05**	**0.29**	**0.54**

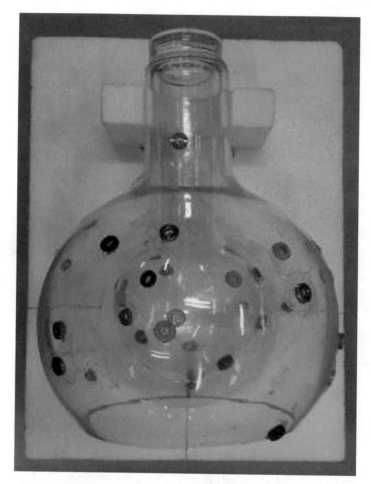

Fig. 5 A spherical glass jar phantom

is simulated using a spherical glass phantom whereas tumor is simulated by inner glass jar. Neuro-registration and neuronavigation procedure is carried out using glass jar phantom and the coordinates of the tumor point and entry point are determined (using Eq. (4)) and passed to 6D-PKM robot (developed at author's laboratory at DRHR, BARC, Mumbai) for neurosurgical procedures (Fig. 6). Figure 6 shows the surgical needle attached to the 6D-PKM robot postured optimally with respect to the glass jar phantom and accessing the ROI after neuro-registration.

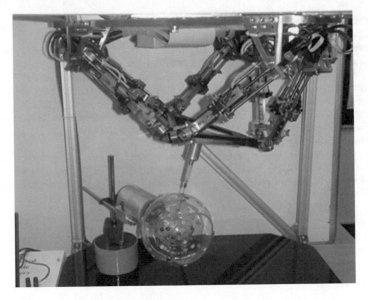

Fig. 6 Surgical needle attached to the 6D-PKM

6   Conclusions

A methodology has been developed for optimizing robot posture estimation prior to neuro-registration with respect to the patient. A neuro-registration and neuronavigation system have been developed using SCMM and the software interface conforming to the DICOM standards. The ease of neuro-registration is enhanced by generating a 3D model from the DICOM images. The experiments have been established to validate the SCMM-based successful neuro-registration and neuronavigation procedure. The visualization of run-time navigation of SCMM relative to the 3D model of the phantom enhances surgical perception. The SCMM-based neuro-registration procedure eliminates the camera mounts and 'line of sight' constraint as in camera-based neuro-registration procedures. The optimum robotic surgical framework to perform a high precision neurosurgery is formulated and a successful neuro-registration, neuronavigation, and neurosurgical procedures have been demonstrated using SCMM and 6D-PKM. The procedure to point to the infinitesimal region repetitively is developed to minimize the error in measurement.

References

1. T.M. Deserno, *Biomedical Image Processing* (Springer, 2011)
2. *Digital Imaging and Communications in Medicine (DICOM), Part 3: Information Object Definitions. PS 3.3* (2011)

3. Coordinate System, http://www.slicer.org/slicerWiki/index.php/Coordinate_systems. Accessed 24 Aug 2017
4. I. Rozet, M.S. Vavilala, Risks and benefits of patient positioning during neurosurgical care. Anesthesiol. Clin. Neurosurg. Anesth. Crit. Care **25**(3), 631–653 (2007)
5. R.M. Schmitz, O. Telfer, R.W. Townson, S. Zavgorodni, *Generalized Coordinate Transformations for Monte Carlo (DOSXYZnrc and VMC++) Verifications of DICOM Compatible Radiotherapy Treatment Plans* (2014)
6. G. Bhutani, T.A. Dwarakanath, Neuro-registration and navigation unit for surgical manipulation, in *Proceedings of the 1st International and 16th National Conference on Machines and Mechanisms*, 18–20 Dec 2013 (IIT Roorkee, India, 2013)
7. G. Bhutani, Modeling, *Design and Development of Frameless Stereotaxy in Robot Assisted Neurosurgery*, Ph.D. Thesis, Homi Bhabha National Institute, Mumbai India, November 2014
8. T.S. Newman, H. Yi, A survey of the marching cubes algorithm. Comput. Gr. (Elsevier) **30**, 854–879 (2006)

Gearbox Fault Detection Using Exponentially Weighted Moving Average Control Charts

Heera Lal and Prasad V. Kane

Abstract Gearbox is commonly used in many manufacturing and engineering applications. An accurate condition monitoring and health assessment is necessary and important to detect faults in gearbox to monitor machinery performance and avoid machine breakdown. This paper aims to demonstrate an approach for the condition monitoring of gearbox to recognize the fault at an initial stage by applying control chart as a tool by analyzing the acceleration-time domain signals. In this paper, time series model is used to extract the features characterizing faults and the exponentially weighted moving average control (EWMA) charts are obtained to monitor the deviations in the feature values. The variation of these features is monitored using EWMA control charts. The gear fault can be simulated in gearbox by different techniques. The most commonly observed fault in the gearbox is gear tooth failure due to scoring, wear, pitting and tooth fracture and it can be simulated by partial tooth removal during the experiment. In this study experiment, the fault with increasing severity is simulated on the spur gear tooth by filing operation. Experimental data for healthy gear and gear with three stages gear tooth removal, i.e. 37.5, 75 and 100% is acquired. EWMA charts were plotted using the data collected for the above severity of faults and it is observed that the control chart is an effective tool in identifying the deviation from the normal condition.

Keywords Gearbox · Gear tooth faults · EWMA charts · Vibration
acceleration-time data

H. Lal · P. V. Kane (✉)
Department of Mechanical Engineering, VNIT, Nagpur, India
e-mail: prasadkane20@gmail.com

H. Lal
e-mail: heera19jiet@gmail.com

© Springer Nature Singapore Pte Ltd. 2019
D N Badodkar and T A Dwarakanath (eds.), *Machines, Mechanism
and Robotics*, Lecture Notes in Mechanical Engineering,
https://doi.org/10.1007/978-981-10-8597-0_4

39

1 Introduction

The gearbox is a vital part on most types of machinery for changing the shaft speed, the torque, and the power. It is important to detect any faults at an early stage to prevent breakdown. There are several techniques available for the early detection of failure, and one of the most useful is vibration analysis.

Monitoring the condition or the status of the machine to avoid impending failure is a challenging task. It helps to avoid breakdown by corrective action and also helps to plan for preventive maintenance schedules. Same is valid for the structural components. Statistical control charts provide an effective way to monitor the status of the machine by extracting the performance features and its graphical display [1]. The upper and lower control limits and the center line can be obtained from the features extracted from the healthy status of the machine or the structure under observation. The deviation from the healthy status due to the presence of faults can be ascertained from the outliers of the control charts. The severity of the fault can also be detected based on the number of the points lying outside the control limits. Application of control charts like X-bar control chart, EWMA control charts, multivariate control chart T^2, and Q have been effectively demonstrated by researchers [2–10]. P. Srinivasa Rao and Ch. Ratnam implemented time series models and exponentially weighted moving average control charts for damage identification of welded structures [2]. S. S. Lampreia analyzed gas turbine condition by Q and multivariate Q control chart by plotting vibration level [3]. S. S. Lampreia et al. also demonstrated the application of T^2 modified multivariate control charts applied to vibration level to control the condition of electro-pump [4]. Amor Messaoud et al. discussed the application of time series analysis and control charts for an industrial application demonstrating the selection of different parameters for analysis [5]. N. Baydar et al. demonstrated application of principal component analysis, squared prediction error and T^2 statistics for fault detection in rotating machinery [6]. Jyrki Kullaa implemented Shewhart T, Hotelling T, MCUSUM, MEWMA, Shewhart, x chart, CUSUM and EWMA control charts to identify the ability of different charts to identify damage in Z24 bridge of Switzerland using the vibration based approach. The author used the modal parameters like natural frequencies, mode shapes, and damping ratios to plot the control charts and techniques like PCA is implemented for important feature selection. The authors concluded that Hotelling T control charts for individual variables are a good choice if false alarms are to be avoided, because it is insensitive to small shifts. The author proposed that CUSUM and EWMA charts are sensitive to small shifts [7].

Zhang, Sheng et al. proposed new statistical process control tool, the Weighted Loss function CUSUM (WLC) chart, for the detection of condition variation of the machine. The authors obtained the control limits using baseline condition data with an autoregressive model and the residuals. The changes of mean and variance of the statistic's distribution against baseline condition are used to indicate the variation from the baseline data and it can be detected by a single Weighted Loss function CUSUM (WLC) chart. The approach is presented with the case study, which shows that the chart can detect faulty conditions as well as their severity [8]. Hoon Sohn et al. demonstrated the application of X-bar control chart for the vibration-based damage diagnosis of concrete bridge column [9]. Haitao Wang has demonstrated the application of EMWA control charts for the applications like Variable-Air-Volume-Air Handling unit [10]. EMWA charts are used in this work due to its ability to respond to small shifts in the vibration characteristics which is discussed in the following section.

1.1 EWMA Control Chart

EWMA control chart due to its ability to respond to small shifts in the process provides an edge over the conventional Shewhart control charts. The EWMA control limits, i.e., upper control limit (UCL), center line (CL), and lower control limit (LCL) are defined as follows:

$$\text{UCL} = \bar{x} + \text{L}\sigma\sqrt{\frac{\lambda}{2-\lambda}[1-(1-\lambda)^{2i}]} \tag{1}$$

$$\text{CL} = \bar{x} \tag{2}$$

$$\text{LCL} = \bar{x} - \text{L}\sigma\sqrt{\frac{\lambda}{2-\lambda}[1-(1-\lambda)^{2i}]} \tag{3}$$

where L and λ are the design parameters of EWMA control chart.

2 Experimental Set up

The experimental setup shown in Fig. 1, consists of the gearbox with spur gear-box connected to D.C. motor. The speed of gearbox was controlled by D.C. motor speed controller. The data acquisition system consists of a piezoelectric accelerom-eter (vibration sensor with a sensitivity of 98 mV/g), a data acquisition card, and computer with data acquisition software. Vibration signals were acquired by mount-ing the accelerometer on bearing housing. The sampling frequency selected for data acquisition was 20 kHz. The acceleration signals were acquired for different fault conditions shown in Figs. 2, 3, 4 and 5 for healthy gear tooth (0 mm broken tooth), Fault level 1 (1.5 mm broken tooth), Fault level 2 (3 mm broken tooth), Fault level 3 (4 mm broken tooth), respectively, as shown in Table 1. It was observed that the amplitude level of vibration signals increases with increasing fault levels of gear tooth.

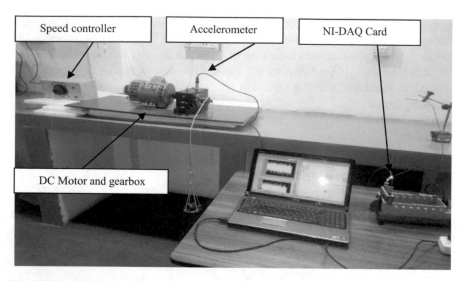

Fig. 1 Experimental setup

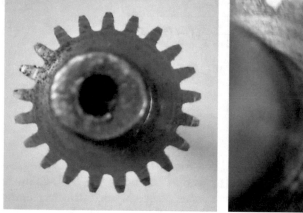
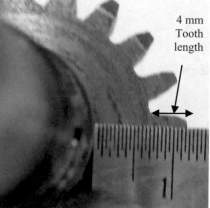

Fig. 2 Good gear tooth

The control limits were first constructed based on the measurements obtained from the initial healthy gearbox. Then, data for the faulty condition with the increasing severity was monitored against the control limits of EWMA control charts to assess the ability of control chart to identify gearbox faults.

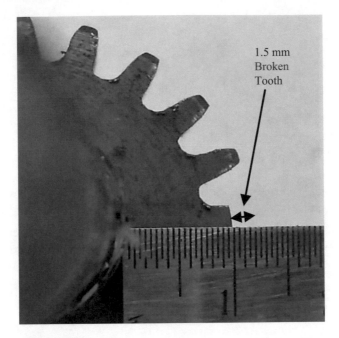

Fig. 3 Gear tooth fault level-1

Fig. 4 Gear tooth fault level-2

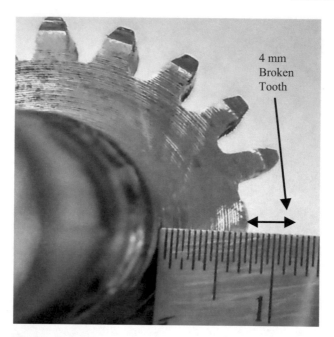

Fig. 5 Gear tooth Fault level 3

Table 1 Different gear tooth fault levels with increasing fault severity

S. no.	Gear tooth fault levels	Fault condition
1	Good gear (4 mm tooth length)	0 mm broken tooth
2	Gear tooth Fault level 1	1.5 mm broken tooth
3	Gear tooth Fault level 2	3 mm broken tooth
4	Gear tooth Fault level 3	4 mm broken tooth

3   Result and Discussion

In this study, based on time series modeling and EMWA control charts, fault monitoring is proposed. In this work, three fault levels are investigated as mentioned in Table 1. By simulating these three faults in the test setup, acceleration-time data is acquired to plot EWMA control charts as shown in Figs. 6, 7, 8, and 9. EWMA control charts are plotted for individual observation using 1000 data features. The values of L and λ, are selected as 3 and 0.2, respectively, to plot EWMA control chart in this work.

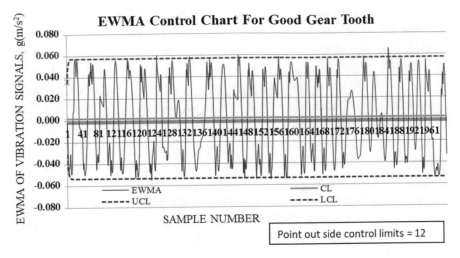

Fig. 6 EWMA control chart for good gear

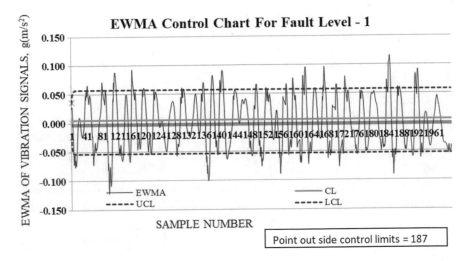

Fig. 7 EWMA control chart for gear tooth Fault level 1

H. Lal and P. V. Kane

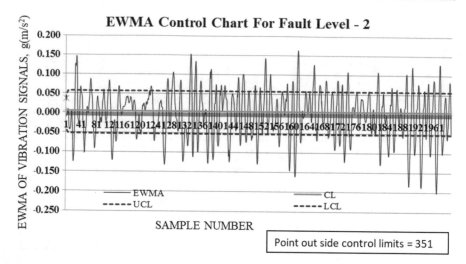

Fig. 8 EWMA control chart for gear tooth Fault level 2

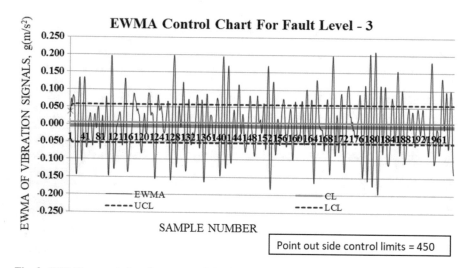

Fig. 9 EWMA control chart for gear tooth Fault level 3

Table 2 Points outside control limits for different fault conditions

S. no.	Fault severity	Points outside control limits
1	Good gear tooth	12
2	Gear tooth Fault level 1	187
3	Gear tooth Fault level 2	351
4	Gear tooth Fault level 3	450

The limits of the control chart EWMA for healthy gear tooth is shown in Fig. 6 and it is found that only 12 points out of 1000 data points are lying out of the control limits (UCL and LCL). Further, the data features obtained faulty gear conditions are plotted against the same control limits and the number of data points lying out of the control limit are evaluated which is summarized in Table 2. With the increasing severity of faults, i.e., Level 1, 2, and 3, the EWMA control charts are plotted and are shown in Figs. 7, 8, and 9. It is observed that outliers, i.e., data points outside control limits are significant in number for these faults. It is observed that 187, 351, and 450 points are lying outside the control limits with the increasing severity of Fault level 1, 2, and 3, respectively. Thus, it can be concluded that the EMWA control charts are responsive and sensitive to the severity of faults and can be applied as condition monitoring tool for the similar applications.

References

1. D. Jennings, P.R. Draket, Machine tool condition monitoring using statistical quality control charts. Int. J. Mach. Tools Manuf. **37**(9), 1243–1249 (1997)
2. P. Srinivasa Rao, Ch. Ratnama, Damage identification of welded structures using time series models and exponentially weighted moving average control charts. Jordan J. Mech. Ind. Eng. **4**(6), 701–710 (2010)
3. S.S. Lampreia, J.G. Requeijo, Analysis of an equipment condition by Q & multivariate Q control charts. Analysis **150**, 200–205 (2012)
4. S.S. Lampreia, J.G. Requeijo, J.M. Dias, V. Vairinhos, T² charts applied to mechanical equipment condition control, in *Proceedings IEEE 16th International Conference on Intelligent Engineering Systems* (2012), pp. 441–446
5. A. Messaoud, C. Weihs, F. Hering, *Time Series Analysis, Control Charts: An Industrial Application* (Fachbereich Statistik, University at Dortmund, Germany, 2005), pp. 1329–1337
6. N. Baydar, A. Ball, U. Kruger, Detection of incipient tooth defect in helical gears using multivariate statistics. Mech. Syst. Signal Process. **15**(2), 303–321 (2001)
7. J. Kullaa, Damage detection of the Z24 bridge using control chart. Mech. Syst. Signal Process. **17**(1), 163–170 (2003)
8. S. Zhang, J. Mathew, L. Ma, Y. Sun, A.D. Mathew, Statistical condition monitoring based on vibration signals, in *Proceedings VETOMAC-3 & ACSIM-2004* (2004), pp. 1238–1243
9. H. Sohn, J.A. Czarnecki, C.R. Farrar, Structural health monitoring using statistical process control. J. Struct. Eng. **126**(11), 1356–1363 (2000)
10. H. Wang, Application of residual-based EWMA control charts for detecting faults in variable-air-volume air handling unit system. J. Control Sci. Eng. **2016**, 8 (2016)

Generalized Point Correspondence Algorithm for Neuro-Registration

Surya Dwarakanath, Gaurav Bhutani, P. P. K. Venkata
and Abhishek Kaushik

Abstract The objective of this paper is to generate a unique and robust correspondence between two sets of points, one from the image frame of reference and the other from a set of points in the surgical tool frame of reference; irrespective of the alterations in the number of points or in the sequence of measurement of the points in the image or the tool frame. The radio-opaque markers (affixed to the scalp of the patient before MRI/CT Scan) serve as a reference in neuro-images. The coordinates of the markers on the patient's scalp with respect to the robot (surgical tool) frame are measured during neurosurgery. From the data, the relationship between the anatomical frame and the tool frame is established. Distance and uniqueness criteria between the markers are used to determine the correspondence. Validation is obtained by conducting correspondence on the phantoms with various configurations of marker points.

Keywords Neuro-registration · Neuronavigation · Image-guided surgery
Image-to-patient data correspondence

S. Dwarakanath (✉)
Indian Institute of Technology Madras, Chennai, Tamil Nadu, India
e-mail: me14b098@smail.iitm.ac.in; suryadwar@gmail.com

G. Bhutani (✉)
Division of Remote Handling & Robotics, Bhabha Atomic Research Centre, Trombay, Mumbai
400085, India
e-mail: bhutani@barc.gov.in

P. P. K. Venkata
Computer Division, Bhabha Atomic Research Centre, Trombay, Mumbai 400085, India
e-mail: panikv@barc.gov.in

A. Kaushik
Homi Bhabha National Institute, Anushakti Nagar, Mumbai, India
e-mail: abhishekk@barc.gov.in

© Springer Nature Singapore Pte Ltd. 2019
D N Badodkar and T A Dwarakanath (eds.), *Machines, Mechanism
and Robotics*, Lecture Notes in Mechanical Engineering,
https://doi.org/10.1007/978-981-10-8597-0_5

49

1 Introduction

Neuro-registration is conventionally based on the classic frame-based stereotaxy [1–4]. Even though the accuracy of the frame-based model is high, owing to the disadvantages of patient discomfort and the sophistication of image-guided surgery, frameless stereotaxy is slowly gaining acceptance [5–8]. Radio-opaque markers called fiducials serve as a reference in neuro-images [9]. The fiducials are affixed on the scalp with a well-spaced distribution based on certain geometric constraints. The coordinate measurements in the image are primarily for establishing a relationship between these reference points (markers) and the rest of the brain region, especially the tumour region. Neuro-registration is mandatory to facilitate neuronavigation on image-guided surgical procedures [9, 10]. Neuro-registration is the standard procedure which localizes the brain region with respect to the surgical tool frame as well as the image frame. Once registered, navigation of the physical surgical tool tip inside the brain can be visualized in the sections of the CT volume and the surgical tool in the reconstructed 3D model.

The outlook of this paper is to free the surgeon of the measurement of points in the image as a standard operating procedure under patient preparation in the operation theatre. The task of scanning, image reconstruction, reconstruction of the 3D model and the image measurement can take place in a distributed manner at an entirely different geographic location and at a different instance of time. Registration errors may occur if the number of points of measurement is inconsistent in either frame or if the sequence of measurement of the points varies in the two frames of reference.

Section 2 presents the data preparation pre-requisite for neuro-registration. Section 3 presents the algorithm for establishing point correspondence. Section 4 gives the geometrical constraints required for point correspondence. Section 5 gives the results and Sect. 6 concludes the paper.

2 Data Preparation for Establishing Correspondence

MRI scans of the patient give three series of DICOM images of the patient and each image in a series can be treated as a cross section of the patient's head [11]. The location of any point in the brain in the 3D space can be determined with respect to the image frame of reference, I^r. The coordinates of the reference point of all the markers are determined in I^r. Similarly, the location of the reference point and the approximate centroid of the tumour region is also determined with respect to I^r. This leads to the positions of the tumour and all the markers to be fully defined in I^r. For point correspondence between I^r and the robot reference frame, R^r, the spatial coordinates of the radio-opaque markers on the scalp are to be measured accurately by some means with respect to R^r. An accurate and unique correspondence leads to an accurate neuro-registration. A successful neuro-registration localizes every point in the brain with respect to R^r (Fig. 1).

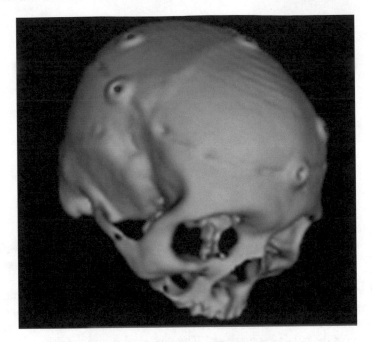

Fig. 1 3D model of a real human skull with markers affixed on the scalp

In the current procedure, measurement of the phantom representing the patient is done using the Surgical Coordinate Measuring Machine (SCMM). Figure 2 shows the SCMM during neuro-registration. It is highly precise, lightweight, portable and made of high-strength aluminium. It is a passive four degrees of freedom serial mechanism with a base fixture and encoders fixed at all joints [9, 12, 13]. The SCMM is equipped with an end probe. The geometry of the end probe is designed to nest with the central cylindrical hollow indent of the markers [12, 13]. For measurement, the surgeon must nest the end probe in the cylindrical indentation of the marker. Proper nesting triggers the electrode switch to record the coordinates of the point with respect to $\mathbf{R^r}$. Such a geometrical constraint results in a highly accurate coordinate measurement.

3   Algorithm for Establishing Correspondence

After obtaining coordinates of the markers in the DICOM images with respect to $\mathbf{I^r}$ and coordinates of the markers on the scalp of the patient with respect to $\mathbf{R^r}$, the correspondence of the points between the two reference frames must be established. Information needed by the algorithm for obtaining the correspondence of points between the two different reference frames are (i) the number of markers affixed on the scalp, (ii) coordinates of the markers in both $\mathbf{I^r}$ and $\mathbf{R^r}$ and (iii) distance error

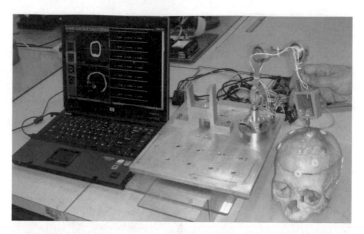

Fig. 2 Prototype of a surgical coordinate measuring mechanism (SCMM) during neuro-registration

limit. The distance error limit is the admissible tolerance in distance, within which the probability of wrong correspondence is negligible. Value of the distance error limit depends on the sparseness between the markers and the accuracy with which coordinates of the points are measured. The empirical rule is to set its value to one-tenth of the smallest distance between any two markers. In the present work, it is assumed to be 3 mm considering that the least distance between any of the markers is 30 mm. It should be noted that this parameter does not influence the correctness of the correspondence. If absolute differences between the distances are within 3 mm, they are considered to be equal. The tolerance value can be set according to the least distance between any of the markers. Markers in the image frame of reference, I^r, are labeled as points P_1, P_2, ..., P_n and the markers in the robot frame, $\mathbf{R^r}$, are labeled as points R_1, R_2, ..., R_n. The distance set of a point is defined as the set of all the distances associated with that point. For example, the distance set of P_1 are the distances between P_1P_1, P_1P_2, P_1P_3, ..., P_1P_n. In the subsequent subsections, the correspondence algorithm is explained by taking various cases.

3.1 Unique Correspondence

Distance set of all the points for both the frames of reference are calculated separately. A numerical case study showing the spatial coordinates and distance sets of all the points in I^r and $\mathbf{R^r}$ are given in Tables 1 and 2, respectively. Distances within the distance set of a point are then sorted in the ascending order of magnitude for further usage. All the distances are in mm.

The next step is a comparison of the distance sets across the two frames. For comparing distance sets of the points across the two frames, the distance sets of both the points are checked element by element. The comparison is illustrated in Table 3

Table 1 Distance sets of points in the image frame I^r

No. of markers = 4				Dist. set of P_1		Dist. set of P_2		Dist. set of P_3		Dist. set of P_4	
Pts.	P_X	P_Y	P_Z								
P_1	100	0.0	0.0	P_1P_1	0.0	P_2P_1	223.6	P_3P_1	316.2	P_4P_1	100.0
P_2	0.0	200	0.0	P_1P_2	223.6	P_2P_2	0.0	P_3P_2	360.5	P_4P_2	200.0
P_3	0.0	0.0	300	P_1P_3	316.2	P_2P_3	360.5	P_3P_3	0.0	P_4P_3	300.0
P_4	0.0	0.0	0.0	P_1P_4	100.0	P_2P_4	200.0	P_3P_4	300.0	P_4P_4	0.0

Table 2 Distance sets of points in the robot frame $\mathbf{R^r}$

Pts.	R_X	R_Y	R_Z	Dist. set of R_1		Dist. set of R_2		Dist. set of R_3		Dist. set of R_4	
R_1	200	100	0.0	R_1R_1	0.0	R_2R_1	316.2	R_3R_1	223.6	R_4R_1	300.0
R_2	200	0.0	300	R_1R_2	316.2	R_2R_2	0.0	R_3R_2	360.5	R_4R_2	200.0
R_3	0.0	0.0	0.0	R_1R_3	223.6	R_2R_3	360.5	R_3R_3	0.0	R_4R_3	100.0
R_4	200	0.0	0.0	R_1R_4	100.0	R_2R_4	300.0	R_3R_4	200.0	R_4R_4	0.0

No. of markers = 4

Table 3 Element-by-element comparison of distance sets of points across two frames

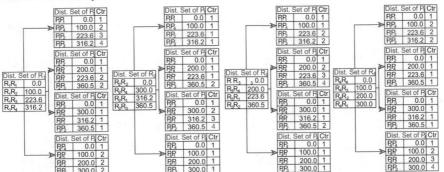

Table 4 Matching and uniqueness value (U_V)

Pts.	P_1	P_2	P_3	P_4	U_V
R_1	1	0	0	0	1
R_2	0	0	1	0	1
R_3	0	1	0	0	1
R_4	0	0	0	1	1

for all the distance sets of points. The distance set of each point in R^r is compared with the distance sets of all the points in I^r. If the absolute difference between the elements is inside the error limit, a counter is incremented starting from 0 (see the counter column in Table 3). This is done for all the elements. If the counter is equal to the total number of markers (highlighted in colour in Table 3) the comparison is deemed as successful and the points are said to be matched. A point in R^r when compared with all the points of I^r may match with any number of points ranging from 0 to the total number of markers.

Further, the uniqueness test is conducted to check the unique correspondence. Uniqueness value, U_V, is the extent of match of the data set points in R^r to the number of data set points in I^r. A U_V of 0 means that it matches with nothing whereas a U_V of 1 means that it matches exactly with one point in I^r and a U_V of more than 1 represents that it matches with multiple points in I^r. It can be seen in Table 3 that each point in R^r is matched to only one point in I^r (that is when the counter gets incremented to the total number of markers, 4). Hence, we can conclude that the U_V of each point in R^r is 1 and hence the points in both the frames uniquely correspond. The uniqueness value (U_V) of points for the given example is shown in Table 4. A match in a point of R^r with a point in I^r is marked as 1 and the sum of the row leads to U_V of the point in R^r.

Table 5 Element by element comparison of distance sets of points across two frames, a non-unique case

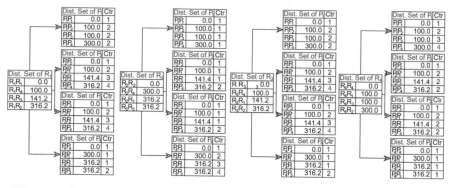

Table 6 Matching and uniqueness value (U_v)

Pts.	P_1	P_2	P_3	P_4	U_v
R_1	0	1	1	0	2
R_2	0	0	0	1	1
R_3	0	1	1	0	2
R_4	1	0	0	0	1

3.2 Non-unique Correspondence

A situation to demonstrate the failure of unique correspondence is considered, the ordered distance set in both the frames is given in Table 5. Since the distance set of R_1 is equal to both P_2 and P_3, R_1 matches with both P_2 and P_3. Similarly, even R_3 matches with both P_2 and P_3, thus clearly indicating the non-possibility of unique correspondence. Uniqueness value (U_v) of the points given in Table 6 indicates non-uniqueness of points R_1 and R_3. Such distance sets can be easily avoided by following simple empirical rules. The rules and the detailed geometrical conditions are discussed in the next section.

3.3 Correspondence with Difference in the Number of Markers

There may arise cases when the number of points in $\mathbf{R^r}$ is less than those in $\mathbf{I^r}$ during neuro-registration. The algorithm can accommodate this situation. Let us assume there are n points in $\mathbf{R^r}$ and m points in $\mathbf{I^r}$ and there is no element of symmetry in the arrangement of fiducials. The distance set of a point in $\mathbf{I^r}$ is divided into all possible subsets with n elements in each of the subset. The distance set of each point in $\mathbf{R^r}$ is compared to all subsets of all the points in $\mathbf{I^r}$. The comparison is done element by

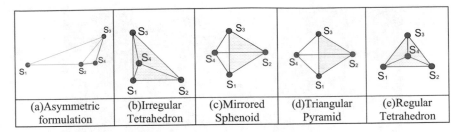

Fig. 3 Edge equivalence diagram of different arrangements in 3D space

Table 7 Description of different types of arrangement of markers

Arrangement	Remarks
Irregular tetrahedron	All points have $U_v = 1$
Mirrored sphenoid	2 points have $U_v = 2$ and the other 2 points have $U_v = 1$
Triangular pyramid	3 points have $U_v = 3$ and the other point has $U_v = 1$
Regular tetrahedron	All points have $U_v = 4$

element and a flag is incremented if the compared elements lie within an error limit. If the flag becomes equal to the number of points in $\mathbf{R^r}$, the point in $\mathbf{I^r}$ to which the compared subset belongs and the point in consideration in $\mathbf{R^r}$ are said to match. Further, uniqueness value (U_v) calculation is done and correspondence is established if possible.

4 Geometrical Considerations for Successful Correspondence

Even though three non-collinear markers on the patient's scalp will lead to a successful neuro-registration, redundant markers are generally used. This practice is to improve the spacing of reference points. The average accuracy of neuro-registration and hence neuronavigation is enhanced by using redundant markers. The present algorithm is generalized and poses no limit on the number of markers and works for any number of points. In this section, for simplicity of discussion, n = 4 has been considered. However, the idea can be easily extrapolated to any number of points. An edge equivalence diagram of all the types of the tetrahedron formed by four points is shown in Fig. 3. Table 7 discusses the consequences in U_v due to different types of arrangements of markers on the patient's scalp.

Out of the four markers arranged on a patient's scalp, the probability of three of them being collinear is extremely low. If only three fiducials are being used, the empirical rule for successful correspondence is to arrange the three points in the form

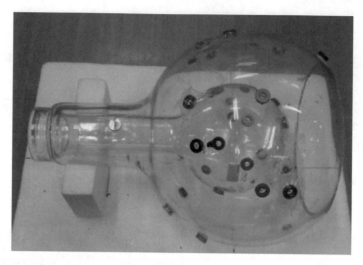

Fig. 4 Phantom with markers on the spherical surface

of a scalene triangle as shown by points S_1, S_2, S_3 in Fig. 3a. An arrangement in the form of an irregular tetrahedron always leads to a successful correspondence. One option out of many is to use the fourth point S_4 as shown in Fig. 3a, to formulate a scalene triangle again with the shortest length of the earlier triangle as the largest side of the new scalene triangle.

5 Validation and Results

The algorithm has been tested on various geometrical formations of markers. The experiments were repeated after changing the sequence of the measurement. The distance error limit value has been rigorously assessed in each case and an empirical rule to set its value to one-tenth of the smallest distance between any two markers has been found.

It was found that asymmetry in marker formation satisfying other requirements lead to successful correspondence all the time. The algorithm is validated by testing against known cases of correspondence (Figs. 4 and 5). For all the cases, the correspondence code based on the algorithm generated correct results of correspondence. It generated corresponding points across the two frames in case of a unique correspondence. It generated non-uniqueness alerts and put out the reason(s) for the unsuccessful correspondence. Time taken for the correspondence in all the cases has been observed to be within 1 s. The maximum number of markers taken is 8. The module has been successfully incorporated in a medical initiative being developed at the author's laboratory.

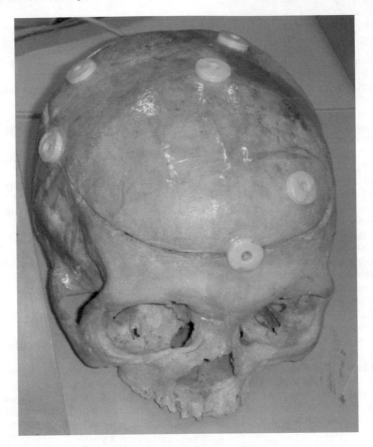

Fig. 5 Markers on the scalp with a subset of symmetrical markers

6   Conclusions

Development of the point correspondence algorithm has removed the requirement of the surgeon having to view the image data for the correct correspondence of markers. The probability of occurrence of a human error is minimized as the sequence of selection of points does not in any way influence successful correspondence; also, it is not required to be consistent with the number of markers on either of the frames. Any number of markers can be used in either the image or on the patient based on the minimum requirement criteria. A subset of four markers arranged in the formation of an irregular tetrahedron results in successful correspondence. The algorithm asserts that fiducials placed with good spatial distribution and geometrical asymmetry assure successful correspondence.

References

1. L. Leksell, Stereotactic apparatus for intercerebral surgery. Acta Chir. Scand. **99**, 229–223 (1949)
2. L. Leksell, The stereotaxic method and radiosurgery of the brain. Acta Chir. Scand. **102**, 316–319 (1951)
3. Elekta Systems, https://www.elekta.com/neurosurgery/. Accessed 1 Jan 2017
4. Leksell Stereotactic System, Elekta Instrument AB, Manual (Document number 1007063 Rev. 02 (2008/10))
5. N.L. Doward, Frameless stereotactic biopsy with the EasyGuide. Medicamundi **42**(1), 33–37 (1998)
6. O. Ganslandt, S. Behari, J. Gralla, R. Fahlbusch, C. Nimsky, Neuronavigation: concept, techniques and applications. Neurol. India **50**(3), 244–255 (2002)
7. S. Frey, R. Comeau, B. Hynes, S. Mackey, M. Petrides, Frameless stereotaxy in the nonhuman primate. NeuroImage **23**(3), 1226–1234 (2004)
8. G. Eggers, J. Muhling, R. Marmulla, Image-to-patient registration techniques in head surgery. Int. J. Oral Maxillofac. Surg. **35**, 1081–1095 (2006)
9. G. Bhutani, T.A. Dwarakanath, K.D. Lagoo, A. Moiyadi, P.P.K. Venkata, Neuroregistration and navigation unit for surgical manipulation, in *Proceedings of the 1st International and 16th National Conference on Machines and Mechanisms (iNaCoMM2013)*, 18–20 Dec 2013 (IIT Roorkee, India, 2013)
10. Digital Imaging and Communications in Medicine (DICOM). Part 3: Information Object Definitions, PS 3.3-2011
11. M.S. Alp, M. Dujovny, M. Misra, F.T. Charbel, J.I. Ausman, Head registration techniques for image-guided surgery. Neurol. Res. **20**, 31–37 (1998)
12. G. Bhutani, *Modeling, Design and Development of Frameless Stereotaxy in Robot Assisted Neurosurgery*, Dissertation, Homi Bhabha National Institute, Mumbai, India
13. A. Kaushik, G. Bhutani, P.P.K. Venkata, T.A. Dwarakanath, A. Moiyadi, Image based data preparation for neuronavigation, in *Presented in 2nd International and 17th National Conference on Machines and Mechanisms (iNaCoMM2015)*, IIT Kanpur, 16–19 Dec 2015

Stability Analysis of a Rigid Rotor Supported on Gas Foil Bearings Under Different Loading Conditions

Kamal Kumar Basumatary, Sashindra K. Kakoty and Karuna Kalita

Abstract Gas foil bearings (GFBs) has been considered as an alternative to traditional bearings in turbopumps, turbocompressors, and turbochargers. The popularity of this bearing has motivated the researchers and people from industries to explore its capabilities. In this context, a nonlinear transient analysis of a rigid rotor supported on airfoil bearing under unidirectional constant load and unidirectional periodic load is carried out. The nondimensional form of the Reynolds equation is discretized using Finite Difference Method while the Crank–Nicolson method and Newton–Raphson method are used to obtain the pressure at every time step. Mass parameter, which is a function of the speed of the rotor, has been considered as the parameter of stability. It has been observed that a rotor stable under unidirectional constant load can be unstable under unidirectional periodic load.

Keywords Gas foil bearing · Crank–Nicholson method · Unidirectional constant load · Unidirectional periodic load

1 Introduction

The applications of Gas Foil bearing (GFB) in oil-free turbomachinery have undergone an extensive investigation in the recent years. The implementation of this technology provides significant advantages like weight reduction with lower maintenance requirements and high operating speed [1]. However, they are constructed to have very low radial clearance for the generation of dynamic pressure and a source of

K. K. Basumatary (✉) · S. K. Kakoty · K. Kalita
Department of Mechanical Engineering, Indian Institute of Technology Guwahati, Guwahati 781039, Assam, India
e-mail: kamalbasumatary3@gmail.com; k.basumatary@iitg.ac.in

S. K. Kakoty
e-mail: sashin@iitg.ac.in

K. Kalita
e-mail: karuna.kalita@iitg.ac.in

© Springer Nature Singapore Pte Ltd. 2019
D N Badodkar and T A Dwarakanath (eds.), *Machines, Mechanism and Robotics*, Lecture Notes in Mechanical Engineering,
https://doi.org/10.1007/978-981-10-8597-0_6

61

nonlinear effects in the system. Despite its several advantages, the stability of the rotors supported on GFBs is a major concern for engineers and researchers as they have low damping characteristics. Hence, it is needless to say that stability analysis of rotors supported on GFB is important from an engineering perspective. Therefore, the rigorous effort has been made both experimentally and numerically to predict the accurate dynamics of GFB. A numerical investigation of rotors supported on GFBs requires the coupled solution of rotor equation and Reynolds equation along with the compliance of top and bump foil.

In this regard, Bou-Said et al. [2] used both linear and nonlinear approach to predict the threshold stability of GFB. The investigation showed the limitations of using linear approach beyond a certain operating range. Recently, Bonello and Pham [3] suggested an algorithm with an alternative dependent variable, which allowed the solution of time domain explicitly at each time step. A comparison was made between frequency domain and time domain simulation to demonstrate the efficiency of the algorithm. Further, Larsen et al. [4] pointed the inaccuracy of frequency domain method for stability analysis for the GFBs. Therefore, it is evident that a nonlinear transient analysis although time consuming but provide information than the frequency domain method. Hence the stability analysis is carried out using a nonlinear transient analysis. Further, in applications like a crankshaft or connecting rod of automotive engines, the bearings are subjected to periodic loads where the directions of applied load changes with time. In this context, Majumdar and Brewe [5] investigated the stability of rigid rotor supported on oil film journal bearings under dynamic loading. Their analysis suggested that under the similar operating condition, the stability of bearing is greatly affected by different loading conditions. Similar results were obtained in case submerged oil journal bearings [6, 7]. Recently, Zarbane et al. [8] presented a numerical study on the behavior of lubricant film under periodic loading. The investigation showed that when the fluid film is periodically squeezed, the load-carrying capacity is proportional to the frequency of oscillations while inversely proportional to the average film thickness.

In this work, a theoretical analysis on stability characteristics of rigid rotors supported on airfoil bearing under unidirectional constant load and the unidirectional periodic load is carried out. Finite Difference Method has been used to discretize the nondimensional form of the Reynolds Equation. The Crank–Nicolson method and the Newton–Raphson method are used to obtain the pressure at every time step. The time transient solution has been carried out and thereby the trajectories of the journal center are obtained for various compliance coefficients and eccentricity ratios. The critical mass parameter, a function of speed, has been found out for different operating conditions and identify the stability threshold speed of the GFB under different loading conditions.

2 Mathematical Model

Figure 1 shows the coordinate system of GFB. The governing equation for GFBs is described by the Reynolds equation for isothermal perfect gas written in nondimensional form as

$$\frac{\partial}{\partial \theta}\left(\bar{P}\bar{H}^3\frac{\partial \bar{P}}{\partial \theta}\right) + \frac{\partial}{\partial \bar{Z}}\left(\bar{P}\bar{H}^3\frac{\partial \bar{P}}{\partial \bar{Z}}\right) = \Lambda\frac{\partial \bar{P}\bar{H}}{\partial \theta} + 2\Lambda\frac{\partial(\bar{P}\bar{H})}{\partial \tau} \tag{1}$$

In Eq. (1), $\bar{P}$ is the normalized pressure, $\bar{H}$ is the film thickness, $\bar{Z}$ is nondimensional axial bearing length, Λ is the bearing number, τ is the nondimensional time, c is the clearance, and r is the radius of the bearing.
Where

$$\Lambda = (6\mu\omega/P_a)(R/c)^2 \quad \bar{Z} = z/r$$
$$\bar{P} = p/P_a \qquad\qquad \tau = \omega t$$
$$\bar{H} = h/c \qquad\qquad x = r\theta$$

The discretized form of Eq. (1) in (i, j)th node or qth node can be written in a quadratic form as

$$\left(\bar{P}_q^e\right)^T \mathbf{A}_q^e \, \bar{P}_q^e + \mathbf{b}_q^e \, \bar{P}_q^e = \frac{\partial \bar{P}\bar{H}}{\partial \tau} \tag{2}$$

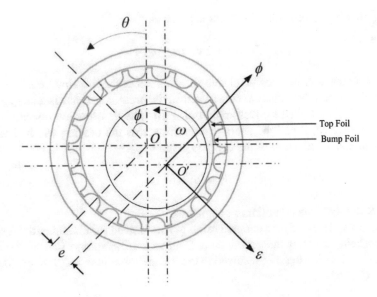

Fig. 1 Detailed view of bump-type GFB

where $P_q^e = \left\{ P_{(i,j-1)} \ P_{(i-1,j)} \ P_{(i,j)} \ P_{(i+1,j)} \ P_{(i,j+1)} \right\}^T$ and its size is 5×1

$$\mathbf{A}_q^e = \begin{bmatrix} \dfrac{\bar{H}_{(i,j-1)}^3}{4(\Delta\bar{Z})^2} & 0 & 0 & 0 & -\dfrac{\bar{H}_{(i,j-1)}^3}{4(\Delta\bar{Z})^2} \\[2ex] 0 & \dfrac{\bar{H}_{(i-1,j)}^3}{4(\Delta\theta)^2} & 0 & -\dfrac{H_{(i-1,j)}^3}{4(\Delta\theta)^2} & 0 \\[2ex] \dfrac{\bar{H}_{(i,j)}^3}{(\Delta\bar{Z})^2} & \dfrac{\bar{H}_{(i,j)}^3}{(\Delta\theta)^2} & -\dfrac{2\bar{H}_{(i,j)}^3}{(\Delta\theta)^2} - \dfrac{2\bar{H}_{(i,j)}^3}{(\Delta\bar{Z})^2} & \dfrac{\bar{H}_{(i,j)}^3}{(\Delta\theta)^2} & \dfrac{\bar{H}_{(i,j)}^3}{(\Delta\bar{Z})^2} \\[2ex] 0 & -\dfrac{\bar{H}_{(i+1,j)}^3}{4(\Delta\theta)^2} & 0 & \dfrac{\bar{H}_{(i+1,j)}^3}{4(\Delta\theta)^2} & 0 \\[2ex] -\dfrac{\bar{H}_{(i,j+1)}^3}{4(\Delta\bar{Z})^2} & 0 & 0 & 0 & \dfrac{\bar{H}_{(i,j+1)}^3}{4(\Delta\bar{Z})^2} \end{bmatrix}$$

$\mathbf{A}_q^e$ is a 5×5 nonsymmetric matrix;

$\mathbf{b}_q^e = \begin{bmatrix} 0 & \dfrac{\Delta\bar{H}_{(i-1,j)}}{2(\Delta\theta)} & 0 & -\dfrac{\Delta\bar{H}_{(i+1,j)}}{2(\Delta\theta)} & 0 \end{bmatrix}$ is a row vector of size 1×5.

The quadratic form of equation can be easily solved using Newton–Raphson Method as described by Jamir et al. [9]. Using the boundary conditions (3), Eq. (2) is solved using Crank–Nicholson Method to obtain the normalized pressure at every time step.

$$\bar{P} = 1 \text{ at } (\bar{Z} = \pm L/2, \theta)$$
$$\bar{P} = 1 \text{ at } (\bar{Z}, \theta = \pi) \tag{3}$$
$$\bar{P} = \bar{P} \text{ at } (\bar{Z}, \theta = 0) \text{ and } (\bar{Z}, \theta = 2\pi)$$

The nondimensional film thickness is given as

$$\bar{H} = 1 + \varepsilon \cos(\theta - \phi) + \bar{w}_t \tag{4}$$

where $\bar{w}_t$ is the nondimensional elastic deformation of the foil structure.

The elastic support structure considered in the present analysis is a simple foundation model, described by Heshmat et al. [10]. The deformation depends on the bump compliance, α and the average pressure across the bearing width. Thus, the nondimensional deflection of the bump is given by

$$\bar{w}_t = S(\bar{P} - 1) \tag{5}$$

where $S = \dfrac{\alpha P a}{c}$ is the compliance coefficient.

Equations (2) and (5) are coupled using (4) and solved for obtaining the resulting pressure field, which is integrated using Simpsons 1/3rd rule to find the fluid film forces, $\bar{F}_\varepsilon$, $\bar{F}_\phi$ of the bearing resolved in the ε and ϕ direction, respectively, is given by Eqs. (6) and (7).

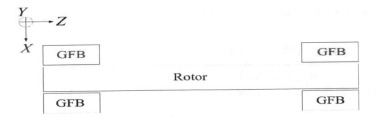

Fig. 2 Rotor bearing configuration

$$\bar{F}_\varepsilon = - \int_0^{2\pi} \int_0^{L/R} \bar{P}(\theta, \bar{Z}) \cos(\theta - \phi) d\theta d\bar{Z} \tag{6}$$

$$\bar{F}_\phi = - \int_0^{2\pi} \int_0^{L/R} \bar{P}(\theta, \bar{Z}) \sin(\theta - \phi) d\theta d\bar{Z} \tag{7}$$

The rotor is mounted on two identical gas foil journal bearings as shown in Fig. 2. Under the assumption that the rotor is rigid with mass M per bearing, the trajectory of the journal center is computed using the following nondimensional equations of motion [5].

$$\bar{M} \bar{W}_0 \left[\ddot{\varepsilon} - \varepsilon (\dot{\phi})^2 \right] = \bar{F}_\varepsilon + \bar{W}_c \cos \phi \tag{8}$$

$$\bar{M} \bar{W}_0 \left[\varepsilon \ddot{\phi} + 2 \dot{\varepsilon} \dot{\phi} \right] = \bar{F}_\phi - \bar{W}_c \sin \phi \tag{9}$$

where $\bar{W}_0$ is the nondimensional load.

The nondimensional terms are defined as

$$\bar{W}_0 = \frac{W_0}{P_a R^2} \quad \bar{F}_{\varepsilon,\phi} = \frac{F_{\varepsilon,\phi}}{P_a R^2} \quad \bar{M} = \frac{M c \omega^2}{W_0}$$

The equations of motion and the solution of dynamic Reynolds equation are then solved under unidirectional constant load and unidirectional periodic load at every time step to simulate the journal center trajectory and thereby estimate the mass parameter which is a function of speed. The trajectories are obtained by plotting the attitude angle and eccentricity ratio at every time step showing the position of journal orbit at various time steps. By observing these trajectories it can be ascertained whether the rotor system is stable, unstable, or in critical condition. A bearing is considered unstable if this trajectory grows continuously, tending to reach the clearance circle. However, if the trajectory curls in and regains the static equilibrium position, then the bearing is said to be stable. If the journal center trajectory traverses over a loop, the bearing is said to be in a critically stable condition. The corresponding value of the mass parameter at which the trajectory is critically stable is known as a critical mass parameter, $\bar{M}$. This process is repeated for a number of times for different values of mass parameter until critically stable trajectories are obtained.

The two loading conditions investigated in this work are described in the following sections.

Case 1: Unidirectional Constant Load:

In this case, the applied load is assumed to be constant and acting in a constant direction. The applied load is taken as the nondimensional steady-state load, i.e.,

$$\bar{W}_c = \bar{W}_0 \tag{10}$$

Case 2: Unidirectional Period Load:

In this case the applied load is assumed to be periodic, however, acting in a constant direction [5]. Therefore,

$$\bar{W}_c = \bar{W}_0\left(1 + \sin\frac{\tau}{2}\right) \tag{11}$$

3   Results and Discussion

To validate our current formulation, the trajectory of rotor under unidirectional constant load is compared with the trajectory simulated in Ref. [3]. Figure 3 shows the trajectory simulated using the current method. The bearing geometry used for validation is a familiar configuration taken from literature which is shown in Table 1. There is a slight change in the trajectory in comparison with the trajectory presented by Bonello and Pham et al. [3]. This might have happened due to the difference in solution method and calculation of bump foil deflection. However, both of the trajectories converge to the same equilibrium point which confirms that simulation method is correct. This probably indicates the validity of our current formulation. While for validation fixed coordinate is used, other investigation in this work are done in polar coordinates as it gives better understanding of the clearance limit of the bearing. After satisfying ourselves that our formulation for constant load is correct, the program was modified to incorporate the unidirectional periodic load.

The results of the current investigation are limited to the length to diameter ratio of 1. Many trajectories of the rotor center have been drawn for different mass parameters until the transition from stable to unstable is observed. However, only few of these trajectories are presented here.

Table 1 Geometry and material properties of GFB [3]

Gas foil bearing (GFB)	
Bearing length	38.10 mm
Bearing radius	19.05 mm
Bearing clearance	32 μm
Rotor weight	3.061 kg

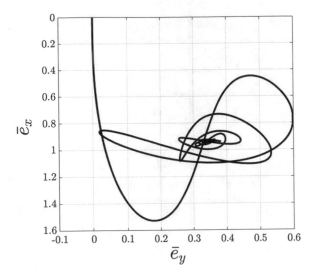

Fig. 3 Rotor response when dropped from centre while rotating at 10,000 rpm

In Fig. 4, the trajectory of journal center for different mass parameters under unidirectional constant load is shown. Figure 4a shows a stable case for mass parameter 5. At mass parameter 6.1 the rotor becomes critically stable in which the rotor neither curls back to an equilibrium position nor increases its size of radius. The radius of rotor trajectory increases with the further increase of mass parameter making the system unstable as seen in Fig. 4b. In Fig. 4c, the journal trajectory for mass parameter 6.5 is shown. Therefore, for the bearing configuration of $\varepsilon = 0.5$, $\Lambda = 1$, $S = 1$, the critical mass parameter is found to be 6.1 in which the rotor traverses a closed loop.

It has been established that under similar operating conditions a system can be stable under unidirectional constant load while unstable under a unidirectional periodic load [8–10]. In Fig. 5, trajectory of rotor supported on GFB under unidirectional periodic load is shown. Interesting trajectory can be observed. The trajectory neither seems to curls towards equilibrium nor traverses outwards. It tends to move in a closed loop. The only difference in the trajectory is that with the increase of mass parameter the radius of the loop increases. Therefore, at a certain mass parameter the trajectory reaches the clearance limit and can lead to bearing failures. This mass parameter at which the trajectory reaches the clearance zone is identified as the critical mass parameter. In Fig. 5a, the rotor trajectory for mass parameter 1 is shown. The rotor traverses a closed loop within the stable limit. As the mass parameter is increased to 1.2 the trajectory reaches the bearing clearance limit as observed in Fig. 5b. Further increment in mass parameter to 1.5 increases the radius of the orbit, exceeding the clearance limit as seen in Fig. 5c. Similar trajectories have been obtained for determining the different values of critical mass parameter for different eccentricity ratio, compliance and bearing number to investigate its effects on stability of GFB.

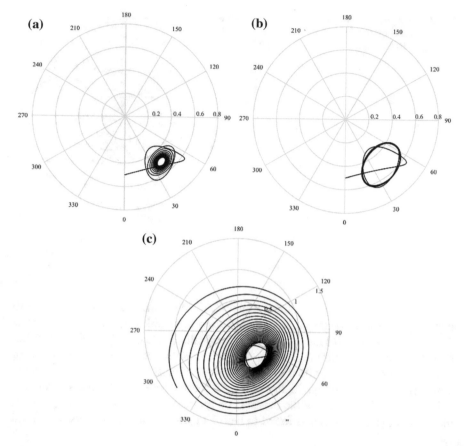

Fig. 4 Trajectory of journal centre under unidirectional constant load for $\varepsilon = 0.5$, $\Lambda = 1$, $S = 1$. **a** $\bar{M} = 5$, **b** $\bar{M} = 6.1$, **c** $\bar{M} = 6.5$

3.1 Effect of Eccentricity Ratio

In Fig. 6, the effect of eccentricity on the loading conditions are shown. It is seen that with the increase of eccentricity ratio the value of mass parameter also increases in the case of unidirectional constant load. This implies that in GFBs, the load carrying capacity increases as the speed increased. On the other hand, in case of unidirectional periodic load, the mass parameter decreases with the increase of eccentricity ratio. Therefore, it can be implied GFBs cannot support heavy periodic load.

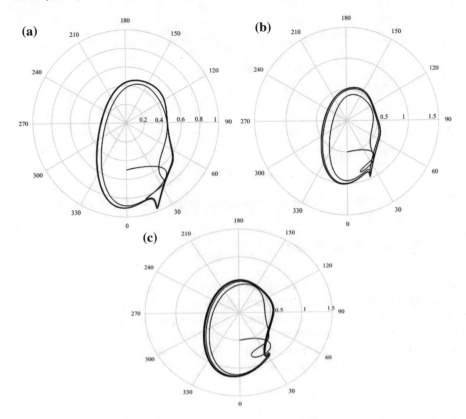

Fig. 5 Trajectory of journal centre under unidirectional periodic load for $\varepsilon = 0.5$, $\Lambda = 1$, $S = 1$. **a** $\bar{M} = 1$, **b** $\bar{M} = 1.2$, **c** $\bar{M} = 1.5$

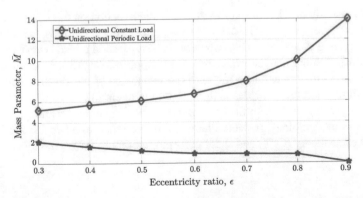

Fig. 6 Effect of eccentricity ratio on mass parameter for unidirectional constant and periodic load

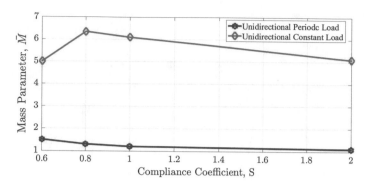

Fig. 7 Effect of Compliance on mass parameter for unidirectional constant and periodic load

3.2 Effect of Compliance

In Fig. 7, the effect of various compliance coefficient on mass parameter is shown. It has been observed that for unidirectional constant load the mass parameter first increases with the increase in compliance coefficient, but decreases after a certain point. While in case of unidirectional periodic load, the mass parameter decreases with the increase of compliance coefficient. This indicates that with higher compliance coefficient the stability of GFB decreases.

4 Conclusions

The present study provides a stability map for stable operation of GFB under unidirectional constant and periodic loads. In similar operating conditions, the rotor under periodic loading showed unstable behavior. A heavy periodic load is very much susceptible to instability than constant load rotor supported on GFB. Moreover, higher compliance coefficient can also increase the instability of the system. The present study, although simple, provides insight about the operating range of GFB and can be used to generate results for different values of bearing numbers and aspect ratios. Further, the methodology presented here can be extended to other foil models like classical plate theory (CPT) and shear deformation theory (SDT) models.

References

1. G.L. Agrawal, Foil air/gas bearing technology—an overview, in *Proceedings of the ASME Turbo Expo*, Orlando, Florida, USA, Paper no. 97-GT-347 (1997)
2. B. Bou-Said, G. Grau, I. Iordanoff, On nonlinear rotor dynamic effects of aerodynamic bearings with simple flexible rotors. J. Eng. Gas Turbines Power **130**, 012503-1-9 (2008)

3. P. Bonello, H.M. Pham, The efficient computation of the nonlinear dynamic response of a foil-air bearing rotor system. J. Sound Vib. **333**, 3459–3478 (2014)
4. J.S. Larsen, I.F. Santos, S.V. Osmanski, Stability of rigid rotors supported by air foil bearings: comparison of two fundamental approaches. J. Sound Vib. **381**, 179–191 (2016)
5. B.C. Majumder, D.E. Brewe, Stability of a rigid rotor supported on oil-film journal bearings under dynamic load, NASA Technical Memorandum 102309 (1987)
6. R. Pai, B.C. Majumdar, Stability of submerged four-lobe oil journal bearings under dynamic load. Wear **154**, 95–108 (1992)
7. J. Ramesh, B.C. Majumder, N.S. Rao, Non-linear transient analysis of submerged oil journal bearings considering surface roughness and thermal effects. Proc. Inst. Mech. Eng. Part J: J. Eng. Tribol. **201**(1), 53–61 (1995)
8. K. Zarbane, T. Zeghloul, M. Hajjam, A numerical study of lubricant film behaviour subject to periodic loading. Tribol. Int. **44**, 1659–1667 (2011)
9. T.M. Jamir, S.K. Kakoty, K. Kalita, Gas foil bearing analysis and the effect of bump foil thickness on its performance characteristics using a non-linear matrix equation solver. Int. J. Recent Adv. Mech. Eng. **3**(3), 15–31 (2014)
10. H. Heshmat, J.A. Walowit, O. Pinkus, Analysis of gas lubricated foil journal bearings. ASME J. Lubr. Technol. **105**, 647–655 (1983)

Optimization of Rendering Data, Generation, and Isolation of ROI for Focused Neuronavigation

R. S. Nikhil Krishna, Surya Dwarakanath, Abhishek Kaushik, Gaurav Bhutani, P. P. K. Venkata, T A Dwarakanath and Rahul Jain

Abstract Identifying and generating the Regions Of Interest (ROIs) in a set of images is an important step towards planning treatment in neurosurgery. Existing Neuronavigation software require manual marking of a specific ROI in consecutive slices of the DICOM images to generate the solid model of a ROI. The volumetric shape and position of the ROI serves as a reference to the surgical tool during neuronavigation. The paper presents an algorithm for the semiautonomous generation of ROI from the slices of images using a single click. This paper is aimed at isolating the ROI in a CT/MRI scan, along with eliminating all non-ROI regions. This reconstruction in 3D along with the real-time 3D superposition of the surgical

R. S. Nikhil Krishna (✉) · S. Dwarakanath (✉)
Department of Mechanical Engineering, Indian Institute of Technology Madras,
Chennai, India
e-mail: rsnk96@gmail.com; me14b088@smail.iitm.ac.in

S. Dwarakanath
e-mail: suryadwar@gmail.com; me14b098@smail.iitm.ac.in

A. Kaushik
Homi Bhabha National Institute, Anushakti Nagar, Mumbai, India
e-mail: abhishekk@barc.gov.in

G. Bhutani (✉) · T A Dwarakanath · R. Jain (✉)
Division of Remote Handling and Robotics, Bhabha Atomic Research Centre,
Trombay, Mumbai 400085, India
e-mail: bhutani@barc.gov.in

T A Dwarakanath
e-mail: tad@barc.gov.in

R. Jain
e-mail: rahulj@barc.gov.in

P. P. K. Venkata
Computer Division, Bhabha Atomic Research Centre, Trombay, Mumbai 400085, India
e-mail: panikv@barc.gov.in

© Springer Nature Singapore Pte Ltd. 2019
D N Badodkar and T A Dwarakanath (eds.), *Machines, Mechanism and Robotics*, Lecture Notes in Mechanical Engineering,
https://doi.org/10.1007/978-981-10-8597-0_7

tool provides for a highly focused visualization of the surgical problem, along with significantly improved rendering performance.

Keywords Region of interest in brain · Autonomous generation of ROI · Isolation of ROI · Focused visualization · Flood fill · 3D Flood fill · 3D contour generation Point cloud optimization · DICOM optimization · Neuro-registration Neuronavigation

1 Introduction

In robot assisted surgery, neuronavigation guides the neurosurgeon to locate the tumor/region of interest within the confines of the brain and then to carry out the required surgical procedures for its treatment. A CT/MRI scan of the patients head provides multiple images of the brain in the DICOM format. In this paper, MR implies CT/MRI, unless explicitly mentioned. The reconstructed MR images superimposed with the moving surgical tool are available to the neurosurgeon real time on his/her computer workstation [1]. Presently, selection of ROI from the set of DICOM images requires the surgeon to manually go through all the DICOM images and draw the contours of the desired region in each image. This process, though very accurate, is very time consuming and cumbersome [2–5].

This paper aims at isolating ROIs (tumour/safe regions) in a 3D model recon-structed from a set of MR images semiautonomously and significantly reducing the computational complexity of the rendering process. The algorithm has been vali-dated by successful tests on the DICOM images from the MR scans of the patients as well as the skull phantoms with different objects inside them representing ROIs. This reconstruction in 3D shown along with the surgical tool in real time allows for a highly focused visualization of the surgical program. The development pre-sented in the paper is a module of a Neuronavigation Suite being developed by the authors in the Robotics Lab, Bhabha Atomic Research Centre. The details of the Neuronavigation Suite are well presented in [6].

2 Optimization of Data to be Rendered

A major factor in the total memory demand for rendering is the cardinality of the point cloud. The cardinality of the point cloud influences the computational complexity in two ways, the first being a larger amount of data to be rendered and the second being an increase in the complexity of the Delaunay triangulation. It is well known that the complexity of the Delaunay triangulation of N points in 3D space, i.e., the number of its faces, can be $\Omega(N^2)$, and under a mild uniform sampling condition, the complexity reduces to $O(N \log^2 N)$ [7]. However, this is additional computation nonetheless, and it is shown later in this paper that the entire need to perform Delaunay triangulation can be avoided in the context of neuronavigation, and this helps further reduce the overhead.

A simple way of reducing the cardinality would be to simply threshold the DICOM data. However, the resulting point cloud is not useful, as points still sparsely populate the interiors of the brain, which significantly complicates mesh generation. Two approaches to optimization are presented in the paper. The first is the optimization of the content to be rendered from the data obtained through the MR scan. The second is the filtering of the extracted outer skull point cloud resulting in lesser noise, and a more realistic convex shape. Both approaches are described in more detail in the subsequent sections.

3 Outer Contour Extraction

Although low-level algorithms like Canny edge detector [8] are widely used to detect and link the adjacent high-contrast pixels, the extraction of a structured line information is still an active research topic, especially in areas like medical imaging. Given the fact that MRs are captured in the form of slices, one approach would be to generate the 2D contour from the axial view, and then to connect the generated contours in 3D [8–10]. However, in doing so, we provide no orientation-invariant neighborhood structure. Analyzing the structure for contours by constructive geometry (CAD or CSG) would require a prior semantic structure to perform efficiently [11–13].

In the context of neuronavigation, we can assume that the entirety of the DICOM data need not be rendered and that the outer skull along with the selected ROIs will suffice. We also consider the outer skull to be the outermost excited region in the MR scan of the patient undergoing neurosurgery. The proposed algorithm utilizes both of these assumptions reducing the content to be rendered volumetrically by over 40-fold and resulting in an effective reduction in the memory requirement for rendering by over one-third for surface mesh generation and one-fourth for volumetric renders (Table 3).

3.1 Our Methodology

With the MR scan data converted into a suitable form for analysis, a linear scan is performed through all voxels along the X and Y axes, which are normal to the sagittal and coronal plane. For each of the axes, a scan is performed starting from every point on a plane perpendicular to the axis under consideration along the axis itself, which ends when a voxel with an intensity beyond a certain set threshold is encountered. The same scan is then performed in the opposite direction, covering the opposite half of the DICOM data. This is followed by a scan in the Z axis. However, the scan in z-axis is performed along only one direction, as computing and rendering the lower part of the head leading to the spinal cord is unnecessary in the context of

Neuronavigation. For maintaining an orientation invariant point cloud density, this scan must not only be done along the three axes, but in every possible direction. To account for this, the point cloud obtained after scanning in the three axes is filtered by convolving it through specific kernels, as discussed below (Fig. 1).

3.2 Refining the Outer Contour

Even after using the aforementioned approach, a few points remain in the point cloud which are not representative of the outer skull of the patient, and significantly increase the complexity of the triangulation. Noise removal can be achieved by performing median filtering in 3D. This will be followed by another filtering process to perform functions like blurring, hole closing, and enforcement of convexity. This can be followed by a thresholding applied on the convolved DICOM data. The availability of fast multidimensional convolution algorithms allows these operations to be performed with minimal overhead. Three kernels that were tested.

The box kernel is one of the most basic kernels, and represents a constant weight averaging. Consequently, it can be used for closing purposes by performing a subsequent thresholding operation. The Gaussian Kernel can act as a much more effective small cavity closer due to its resemblance to a point spread function, preferentially closing smaller radii holes. The convolution can in fact be performed fairly quickly since the equation for the 3-D isotropic Gaussian is separable into x, y and z components. The third kernel suggested in the context of reducing the time complexity of the Delaunay Triangulation is the Convexity Filter (CF) Kernel, which is a dynamically updating Gaussian-derived kernel. The kernel updates its values based on its relative position with respect to the center of the DICOM data such that it enforces sparsity in that direction and density orthogonally. Future work could involve Gaussian kernel where the weights are decayed angularly rather than truncating the kernel angu-

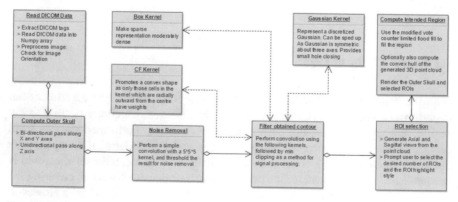

Fig. 1 The flow of control of the program using the techniques mentioned in the paper

Table 1 Axis parallel view of the kernels

	The box kernel	3D Gaussian kernel (σ = 2.5 along all axes)	The CF kernel
Point projection			
Parallel projection			

Table 2 Isometric view of the different kernels

	The box kernel	3D Gaussian kernel (σ = 2.5 along all axes)	The CF kernel
Point projection			
Parallel projection			

larly. The CF kernel provides for an interesting study, due to its ability to potentially simplify the mesh generation process by enforcing a more convex surface.

The visualizations of these types of kernels for a $5 \times 5 \times 5$ kernel have been provided below in Tables 1 and 2 using Mayavi [14]. The size of the sphere represents the voxel intensity.

It is observable in the axis parallel view of the CF kernel that the center voxel, in red, is visible and that it is not visible in the case of a simple 3D Gaussian Kernel. The isometric view gives a better view of the direct visibility of the centre voxel without any partial occlusions, like in the 3D Gaussian kernel, due to the sparsity enforced by the CF. In both views, the CF kernel has been visualized at an instant when the center of the DICOM data is along the positive x-direction of the kernel (Axis orientation at bottom left of each image).

It is also noticed that for the purpose of Neuronavigation, there is no need for mesh generation, as the position of the surgical tool relative to the chosen regions of interest, usually a tumor, is what is of interest. Hence, the rendering of the DICOM data can be done volumetrically, as seen in Fig. 2c, d. To quantify the improvement in performance, we took an MR scan and measured the RAM consumption that the original methods and the proposed methods took for the rendering. The results have been recorded in Table 3.

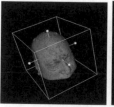   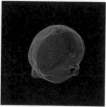

(a) Isosurface Mesh generated out of the thresholded DICOM data   (b) Simplified Mesh of outer contour extracted using proposed methods   (c) A volumetric render of the point clouds of points extracted using the proposed method   (d) Alternate View of (c)

Fig. 2 Simplified mesh and volumetric rendering of point cloud

Table 3 Computational requirements, averaged over 3 runs, on a computer with 1.7 GHz Intel Core i5-4210U with 8 GB of RAM

RAM used (MB)	Rendering process
1350	Isosurface mesh generation of entire DICOM data
315–385	Isosurface mesh of thresholded DICOM data
205–240	Simplified mesh of outer skull computed by proposed methods
205–255	Volumetric render of entire DICOM data
200–210 (extends by about 35 MB on addition of a region of interest)	Volumetric render of outer skull computed by proposed methods
165	Volumetric render of a completely empty 3D array

4 Semiautonomous Region Growth

Other methods in recent literature like using superpixels rely purely on clustering, and are not yet completely implementable on a large scale, in terms of both computational requirements and accuracy [15]. The method proposed for Region of Interest (ROI) selection is a vote counter limited modification of the flood fill algorithm. The user can navigate through the slices and choose a point of interest as the seed point for the region growth. Traditionally, a flood fill would initiate from this seed point and spread in all directions up to a point depending on the intensity of the flood. However, the proposed method offers an alternative which is more beneficial as it allows us to generate a heuristic for the probabilities of each voxel belonging to the intended region.

In the proposed method, a counter is used to count paths to a particular voxel, by incrementing a counter every time the flood fill encounters that voxel along its path. One essential modification to the base flood fill algorithm to permit this type of counters to function properly is to not stop the flood fill every time a visited voxel is reached in the 3D array generated by DICOM. Formulating the vote counter this way, the number of votes represent the total number of paths from the seed point, selected using the aforementioned method, to the given point. Hence, if normalized, it represents the probability of a given voxel belonging to the intended region, as is well known in Ensemble Theory in Statistics.

The next step in the proposed region selection method is by choosing which voxels are to be highlighted based on the vote counter. Applying a low cut off limit on the counter after the flood fill will give us a larger region, but at the cost of a greater possibility of overgrowing the region. The effects of such an overgrowth, however, can be minimized by reducing the intensity of the flood fill. Applying a larger threshold ensures that only regions very likely to be part of the intended region will be selected.

The above algorithm was seen to perform well in the case of flood fill with a fixed range (that is, the region grows from a given point depending on the intensity difference with the seed point, not the point itself). However, in cases where regions that have an internal gradient, it is known to not completely occupy the intended region. In such cases, generally, a variable range flood fill is used. The drawback of using this method for all cases is that it is known to overgrow in most cases. This problem, if the variable range flood fill is to be used, can be tackled by penalizing the growth depending on its distance from the seed point, along with using the aforementioned vote counter procedure.

For the purpose of this application, a larger threshold is chosen. This gives us a sparse point cloud of the possible voxels that are affected by the tumor. This is important as in the automated surgery, it should not remove any unnecessary tissues from the brain. If a little bit of approximation can be permitted, then the convex hull

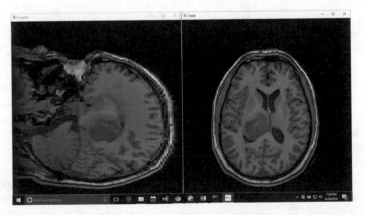

Fig. 3 The seed point selection interface for generation of ROI

(a)

(b)

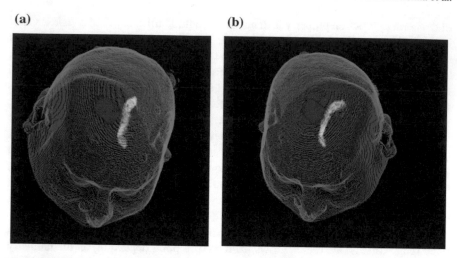

Fig. 4 ROI generated using modified vote counter flood fill algorithm

can be taken as the selected region. If minimal approximation is to be taken, then a hole filling algorithm can be implemented. In our laboratory tests, it was seen that taking the convex hull gives relatively better results for tumor selection.

Figure 4 shows ROIs that have been generated using the proposed modified vote counter flood fill algorithm, without convex hull, displayed with one-pixel wide outer contour extracted using methods proposed in Sect. 4. The red region in Fig. 4 represents a tumor as seen in the axial slices of Fig. 3 and the yellow region a safe region. Both regions lie inside the brain.

5 Conclusions

The proposed method provides a computationally very efficient method for focused Neuronavigation in Neurosurgery that is scalable in its implementation. The presented methodology reduces the size of the data to be rendered by over 40-fold and reduces the memory complexity of the rendering phase over one-fourth by rendering only the outer skull along with the various ROIs and eliminating the inner contents. The reliability of the development is validated using the skull phantom in which different objects of different sizes and materials are filled to represent the different ROIs. The algorithm and the software module are also successfully demonstrated on the MR image data of the phantoms and the patients to validate the semiautonomous generation of the ROIs for neuronavigation. The region selection method is a much more reliable method than existing algorithms due to its self-reinforcement in the form of an incremental vote counter.

References

1. P.P.K. Venkata, T.A. Dwarakanath, A. Moiyadi, A. Kaushik, G. Bhutani, Image-based data preparation for neuro-navigation, in *2nd International and 17th National Conference on Machines and Mechanisms* (2015)
2. T.M. Deserno, *Biomedical Image Processing* (Springer, 2011)
3. O.S. Planykh, *Digital Imaging and Communications in Medicine (DICOM). Part 3: Information Object Definitions. PS 3.3* (Springer, 2011)
4. *Introduction to CT Physics* (2004)
5. G. Dougherty, *Digital Image Processing for Medical Applications* (Cambridge University Press, 2009)
6. G. Bhutani, *Modeling, Design and Development of Frameless Stereotaxy in Robot Assist.* Ph.D. thesis, Homi Bhabha National Institute, Mumbai, India, 2016
7. A. Lieutier, D. Attali, J.D. Boissonnat, Complexity of the Delaunay triangulation of points on surfaces the smooth case, in *Proceedings of the 19th Symposium on Computational Geometry* (2003), p. 201210. https://doi.org/10.1145/777792.777823
8. K.A. Schaper, D.A. Rottenberg, R.M. Leahy, D.W. Shattuck, S.R. Sandor-Leahy, Magnetic resonance image tissue classification using a partial volume model. Neuroimage 856–876 (2001)
9. H. Bischof, M. Hofer, M. Maurer, Line3d: efficient 3d scene abstraction for the built environment, in *German Conference on Pattern Recognition* (2015), pp. 237–248
10. C. Heipke, F. Rottensteiner, U. Soergel, V. Toprak, A.O. Ok, J.D. Wegner, Matching of straight line segments from aerial stereo images of urban areas. ISPRS J. Photogramm. Remote Sens. **74**, 133–152 (2012)
11. A. Zisserman, C. Schmid, Automatic line matching across views, in *1997 IEEE Computer Society Conference Computer Vision and Pattern Recognition, 1997, Proceedings* (1997). https://doi.org/10.1109/CVPR.1997.609397
12. Y. Chrysanthou, A. Sharf, D. Cohen-Or, N.J. Mitra, Y. Li, X. Wu, Globfit: consistently fitting primitives by discovering global relations, in *ACM SIGGRAPH* (2011)
13. Y. Furukawa, J. Xiao, Reconstructing the world's museums. Int. J. Comput. Vis. **110**, 243–258 (2014)
14. R. Klein, R. Schnabel, R. Wahl, Efficient ransac for point-cloud shape detection. Comput. Gr. Forum **26**, 214–226 (2007)
15. T. Lambrou, N. Allinson, T.L. Jones, T.R. Barrick, F.A. Howe, X. Ye, M. Soltaninejad, G. Yang, Automated brain tumour detection and segmentation using superpixel-based extremely randomized trees in flair MRI. Int. J. Comput. Assist. Radiol. Surg. **12**, 183–203 (2017)

Comparison of Hybrid and Parallel Architectures for Two-Degrees-of-Freedom Planar Robot Legs

Aditya Varma Sagi and Sandipan Bandyopadhyay

Abstract A comparative analysis between a hybrid and a parallel manipulator, to study the influence of their architecture on performance, is presented in this paper. The two manipulators are modifications of a serial 2-R manipulator and a five-bar manipulator, respectively. They are altered in a way that they both share the same arrangement of the links, while having a distinction only in the actuator arrangement. Indices of performance, such as the measure of manipulability, local conditioning index, and global conditioning index are used to compare their performance.

Keywords Legged robot · Hybrid manipulator · Parallel manipulator
Velocity Jacobian · Measure of manipulability · Condition number

1 Introduction

The locomotory devices in organisms, such as fins in fishes, wings in birds, or legs in terrestrial animals, are appendages that exert forces on the environment, helping the animals move. These appendages are called *manipulators* in engineering terminology. The basic requirement of such manipulators is to be able to generate motion and to produce forces over a desired region in the space around the body. To provide two-degrees-of-freedom (DoF) motion in the sagittal plane, a serial-chain linkage, such as a serial 2-R manipulator, or a closed-loop linkage, such as a five-bar manipulator can be used as a robot leg.

A. V. Sagi · S. Bandyopadhyay (✉)
Department of Engineering Design, Indian Institute of Technology Madras,
Chennai 600036, Tamil Nadu, India
e-mail: aditya.sagi13@gmail.com

S. Bandyopadhyay
e-mail: sandipan@iitm.ac.in

© Springer Nature Singapore Pte Ltd. 2019
D N Badodkar and T A Dwarakanath (eds.), *Machines, Mechanism
and Robotics*, Lecture Notes in Mechanical Engineering,
https://doi.org/10.1007/978-981-10-8597-0_8

Both the serial as well as parallel actuation schemes are incorporated in the legs of terrestrial animals. The bones are primarily arranged in a serial fashion, but the muscles are arranged in both the serial as well as parallel architectures. There are muscle groups that connect adjacent bones providing force and reaction on them. These resemble the actuators in a serial-chain linkage that provide action–reaction pairs on adjacent links. Other muscle groups span multiple joints to connect two bones, e.g., *rectus femoris* muscle in the human thigh connects the hip to the shank of the leg, while spanning the hip joint and the knee. From an actuation perspective, the arrangement of these muscles resembles the actuation in a parallel manipulator, where a distal link is actuated from the base through a linkage. Serial manipulators have an inherent disadvantage that the inertia of the links are high due to the placement of the actuators, to drive the subsequent link, at the distal end. With the actuators contributing a significant amount to the mass of the robot, a considerable amount of torque is demanded to move these actuators along with the links, which also leads to a significant wastage of energy. This drawback is addressed by placing the actuators at the proximal end of the links, and using a transmission element to transfer the motion from the actuator to the subsequent links. Such an arrangement forms a hybrid architecture due to the presence of closed loops in the mechanism. Walking robots have been built using leg manipulators with the serial [1], hybrid [2] as well as parallel [3, 4] architectures. The aim of this work is to present a comparative analysis of the performance of a planar two-DoF manipulator when arranged in the hybrid and parallel architectures. In this work, the performance of the manipulators is evaluated based on kinematic indices such as the measure of manipulability, local conditioning index, and global conditioning index. Since the legs are usually designed to have low mass and inertia, the contribution of external loads outweighs the contribution of dynamic loads (due to the movement of the leg) to the motor torques for low-speed applications. Hence, the scope of this work was restricted to kinematics and statics alone.

The rest of the paper is organized as follows: details on the architecture of the two manipulators are presented in Sect. 2. The performance indices that will be used for comparison are introduced in Sect. 3. The numerical results and inferences are presented in Sect. 4, followed by the conclusions in Sect. 5.

2   Mechanical Design

Commonly used robotic leg architectures, to generate two-DoF planar motion, are the serial 2-R manipulator [1] (see Fig. 1a) and the five-bar manipulator [3, 4] (see Fig. 1b). A modification of these manipulators is shown in Fig. 1c. The serial 2-R manipulator can be modified by re-locating the second motor closer to the base and adding a linkage (l_4-l_3-l_{2e}) to drive the distal link as shown in Fig. 1c. This modification addresses a major drawback in the serial architecture, namely, the inertia due to the placement of the second motor at the distal end of the first link. This manipulator will be referred to as a *hybrid manipulator* in the rest of the paper.

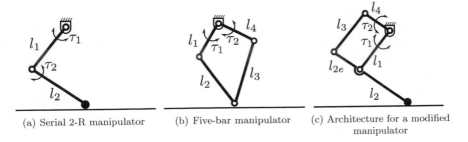

(a) Serial 2-R manipulator   (b) Five-bar manipulator   (c) Architecture for a modified
                                                                          manipulator

Fig. 1 Planar two-DoF manipulator architectures generally used in the design of walking robot legs

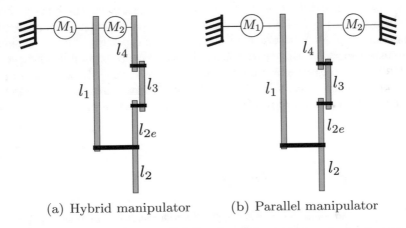

(a) Hybrid manipulator   (b) Parallel manipulator

Fig. 2 Actuator connection diagram of hybrid and parallel manipulators showing the connection of motors M_1 and M_2. The stator of motor M_1 is attached to the ground, while its rotor is attached to link l_1 in both the manipulators. The motor M_2 has its rotor attached to link l_4, while its stator is attached to the ground in the parallel manipulator, and it is connected to the link l_1 in the hybrid manipulator

A five-bar manipulator can also be modified to have an architecture similar to Fig. 1c by extending one of its links (l_2 in this case). Since this manipulator has a parallel architecture, it will thus be referred to as a *parallel manipulator* in the rest of the paper.

Though the two manipulators have similar kinematic sketches (see Fig. 1c), they differ in the way the second motor is connected. As shown in Fig. 2a, the modified serial 2-R manipulator (i.e., the hybrid manipulator) has the second motor, M_2, situated on the first link (i.e., the stator is attached to the first link), with its rotor being co-axial with that of motor M_1, and driving the four-bar mechanism (l_1-l_4-l_3-l_{2e}). In contrast, the modified five-bar manipulator (i.e., the parallel manipulator) has the second motor fixed to the base (i.e., the stator is attached to the ground) with the rotor being co-axial with that of motor M_1 as shown in Fig. 2b.

The two manipulators are similar in multiple respects; they have the same workspace and also the same singularities within the workspace (when the links l_3 and l_{2e} line-up)[1]. This is desirable as the difference in performance of the manipulators can then be attributed to the one point of difference, i.e., the actuation scheme of the manipulators.

3 Performance Indices

The kinematic design of a robotic manipulator can be evaluated based on the size of the workspace and the *quality* of the available workspace. The quality of the workspace region may be determined based on its *distance* from singular configurations of the manipulator and also the force production capability of the manipulator within that workspace. Many performance indices have been used to evaluate the quality of the workspace of a manipulator (for example, see [6]) based on the *singular values* of the velocity Jacobian matrix of the manipulator. Some common measures are: the measure of manipulability [7], and the reciprocal of the condition number [8].

3.1 *Measure of Manipulability*

The *measure of manipulability* (MoM), μ, of a manipulator is defined in [7] as:

$$\mu(J) \triangleq \sqrt{\det(JJ^{\top})},$$

where J is the (forward) velocity Jacobian matrix of the manipulator. For nonredundant manipulators, such as the ones under consideration, the measure is equal to $\mu(J) = Abs\,(\det(J))$. The MoM of an n-DoF nonredundant manipulator can thus be expressed in terms of the singular values, σ_i, of its Jacobian matrix as:

$$\mu = \prod_{i=1}^{n} \sigma_i. \tag{1}$$

It has been observed that the MoM remains the same for both the manipulators (when they have identical link lengths) at any configuration over the entire workspace. This

---

[1] This is the gain-singular configuration (refer to [5] for details) of the manipulator when $\phi_2 - \phi_3 = 0, \pi$ (see Fig. 6). In this configuration, the forward velocity Jacobian matrices of the manipulators are undefined due to the presence of the term $\sin(\phi_2 - \phi_3)$ in the denominator (refer to Appendix).

can be attributed to the structure of the velocity Jacobian matrices[2] of both the manipulators which are of the form:

$$J_p = \begin{bmatrix} a & b \\ c & d \end{bmatrix}, \qquad\qquad J_h = \begin{bmatrix} a+b & b \\ c+d & d \end{bmatrix}, \qquad (2)$$

where J_p and J_h are the velocity Jacobian matrices of the parallel and hybrid manipulators respectively, and a, b, c, and d are substitutes for the elements of the Jacobian matrices. The relation between the determinants of the two matrices may be obtained easily as follows:

$$\det(J_h) = \begin{vmatrix} a+b & b \\ c+d & d \end{vmatrix} = \begin{vmatrix} a & b \\ c & d \end{vmatrix} + \begin{vmatrix} b & b \\ d & d \end{vmatrix} = \begin{vmatrix} a & b \\ c & d \end{vmatrix} = \det(J_p).$$

This shows that the measure of manipulability of the two manipulators (with the same corresponding link lengths) at a given configuration will be identical. Since the MoM of both the manipulators is the same, it does not prove useful as a measure for comparing the performance of the two designs by itself. However, the index will be useful when used in conjunction with other indices, as will be discussed in Sect. 4.

3.2 Local Conditioning Index and Global Conditioning Index

The condition number, $\kappa_F(A)$, of a matrix, A, based on the Frobenius norm of the matrix, $\|A\|_F$, is defined as:

$$\kappa_F(A) \triangleq \|A\|_F \|A^{-1}\|_F,$$

$$\text{where,} \quad \|A\|_F \triangleq \sqrt{\text{Tr}(AA^{\top})}.$$

The condition number of a matrix, of dimension 2×2, can be expressed in terms of its singular values σ_1 and σ_2 as:

$$\kappa_F = \frac{\sigma_1^2 + \sigma_2^2}{\sigma_1 \sigma_2}. \qquad (3)$$

This condition number, κ_F, for the 2×2 matrix, ranges between $[2, \infty)$. It is beneficial to have a performance index that is bounded, for use in the design/analysis of manipulators. One such index can be the reciprocal of the condition number as shown in [8]. This index provides a *local* measure of the performance of the manipulator at a given configuration, and hence shall be referred to as the *local conditioning index*

---

[2]Refer to Appendix.

(LCI). The LCI, γ, of a manipulator, based on the condition number of its Jacobian, is defined as:

$$\gamma = \frac{n}{\kappa_F},$$ (4)

where n is the DoF of the manipulator, and κ_F is the condition number of its Jacobian matrix. The LCI, γ, has a range space of $[0, 1]$, with 0 indicating a singular configuration and 1 indicating an isotropic configuration [9]. To obtain a measure of performance over the entire workspace, W, a *global conditioning index* (GCI), η, was defined in [8] as follows:

$$\eta = \frac{\int_W \gamma \, dw}{\int_W dw}.$$ (5)

The GCI can be considered to be a measure of the closeness of the manipulator to isotropy over the entire workspace.

3.3   Performance of the Manipulators

The analysis of the performance of the manipulators, in terms of velocities and forces, does not take into cognisance any specific use that the manipulators would be put into. It is, therefore, desirable to have a guarantee on the lower bound of the performance of the manipulators. Considering the concept of the velocity and force ellipsoids (for example, see [5], pp. 146–158), the minimum singular value of the velocity Jacobian matrix, σ_{min}, provides a measure of the lower bound in the velocity domain, while the reciprocal of the maximum singular value, i.e., $1/\sigma_{max}$, provides a measure of the lower bound in the force domain. To obtain better performance in terms of velocity it is thus essential to have a high value of σ_{min}, and to get a better performance in terms of force a lower value of σ_{max} is required. In other words, a kinematically isotropic configuration is preferred.

The relation between the singular values, the MoM, and LCI for two-DoF manipulators can be derived from Eqs. (1) and (3) to be:

$$\sigma_{min} = \sqrt{\frac{\mu(1+\gamma)}{2\gamma}}\left(1 - \sqrt{\frac{1-\gamma}{1+\gamma}}\right),$$ (6)

$$\sigma_{max} = \sqrt{\frac{\mu(1+\gamma)}{2\gamma}}\left(1 + \sqrt{\frac{1-\gamma}{1+\gamma}}\right).$$ (7)

If the MoM, μ, is held constant, the value of σ_{min} can be increased while simultaneously bringing down the value of σ_{max} by increasing the value of the LCI, γ. We know that the MoM of both the architectures is same for identical link lengths. The two manipulators can, therefore, be compared purely based on the value of the LCI for any given configuration. A higher value of LCI is desirable. It assures better performance in terms of the velocity output as well and the force transmission capability of a manipulator in comparison to the other.

4 Results and Discussions

The expressions to determine the GCI of the two manipulators can be obtained in closed form (following the procedure outlined in [8]) by using kinematically equivalent but simplified models[3] of the manipulators (see Fig. 3). To indicate the underlying actuation setup, the angle θ_4 is described in a relative sense in the hybrid manipulator (see Fig. 3a), whereas, in the parallel manipulator it is described in an absolute sense (see Fig. 3b).

The expressions for the LCI and GCI of the hybrid and parallel designs are:

$$\gamma_h = \frac{2\sin\theta_4}{\left(\frac{1}{\rho} + 2\rho + 2\cos\theta_4\right)}, \qquad\qquad \gamma_p = \frac{2\sin\beta}{\left(\frac{1}{\rho} + \rho\right)}, \qquad (8)$$

$$\eta_h = \int_0^\pi \frac{\sin^2\theta_4}{\left(\frac{1}{\rho} + 2\rho + 2\cos\theta_4\right)}\,\mathrm{d}\theta_4\,, \qquad \eta_p = \int_0^\pi \frac{\sin^2\beta}{\left(\frac{1}{\rho} + \rho\right)}\,\mathrm{d}\beta\,, \qquad (9)$$

where γ_h and γ_p are the LCI for the hybrid and parallel manipulators respectively, η_h and η_p are the GCI for the hybrid and parallel manipulators respectively, β represents the relative angle between the two links in the parallel manipulator, i.e., $\theta_4 - \theta_1$, and $\rho = \frac{l_2}{l_1}$ is the nondimensional ratio of the link lengths. It can be observed that the GCI is purely a function of the ratio of the link lengths, ρ, and is independent of any individual link dimension. It will, therefore, remain constant even under scaling.

As discussed in Sect. 3.3, it is desirable to have a manipulator be as close to an isotropic configuration as possible. Hence, the design with the maximum value of GCI is preferred. The maxima of the GCI can be determined by checking the necessary condition for optima: $\frac{\mathrm{d}\eta}{\mathrm{d}\rho} = 0$, which leads to the following results:

$$\frac{\mathrm{d}\eta_h}{\mathrm{d}\rho} = (2 - 1/\rho^2)\int_0^\pi \frac{\sin^2\theta_4}{\left(\frac{1}{\rho} + 2\rho + 2\cos\theta_4\right)^2}\,\mathrm{d}\theta_4 = 0\,, \qquad (10)$$

$$\frac{\mathrm{d}\eta_p}{\mathrm{d}\rho} = (1 - 1/\rho^2)\int_0^\pi \frac{\sin^2\beta}{\left(\frac{1}{\rho} + \rho\right)^2}\,\mathrm{d}\beta = 0\,. \qquad (11)$$

---

[3]It should be noted that the linkage (shown in dashed line in Fig. 3) used to drive the distal link, l_2, has been chosen to be a parallelogram linkage to simplify the analysis.

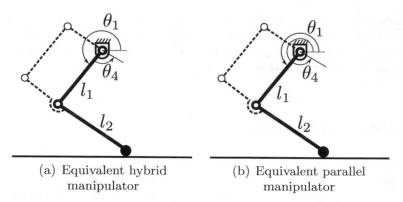

(a) Equivalent hybrid   (b) Equivalent parallel
manipulator   manipulator

Fig. 3 Kinematically equivalent two-link manipulators (indicated with solid lines) for the hybrid and parallel designs with the corresponding references for the measurement of joint angles

Fig. 4 Variation of the GCI of the hybrid and parallel manipulators (η_h and η_p respectively) for different designs with change in the ratio, ρ

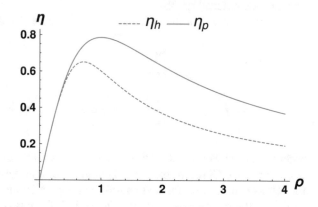

Solving Eq. (10) gives $\rho = \frac{1}{\sqrt{2}}$ for the hybrid manipulator and solving Eq. (11) gives $\rho = 1$ for the parallel manipulator. Correspondingly, $\eta_h = 0.6506$ (which is in accordance with [8]) at $\rho = \frac{1}{\sqrt{2}}$, and $\eta_p = 0.7854$ at $\rho = 1$. For a given maximum reach of the manipulator, i.e., $l_1 + l_2$, the optimal links lengths, in terms of GCI, for a given architecture can be obtained by using the respective value of ρ at which the maxima of the GCI occurs.

The variation of the GCI with the ratio of link lengths is shown in Fig. 4. The peaks for hybrid and parallel designs occur at $\rho = \frac{1}{\sqrt{2}}$ and $\rho = 1$, respectively. It can be observed from Fig. 4 that the parallel manipulator outperforms the hybrid manipulator in terms of the GCI. This indicates that the parallel manipulator is closer to the isotropic configuration over its workspace as compared to the hybrid manipulator for different leg designs (i.e., varying values of ρ).

Figure 5 shows plots of the LCI for the best designs, in terms of GCI, of the hybrid and parallel manipulators, with $\rho = \frac{1}{\sqrt{2}}$ and $\rho = 1$ respectively. It can be observed that, in both the cases, the parallel manipulator has higher LCI for smaller values of the angle β, i.e., when the leg is more outstretched, while the hybrid manipulator

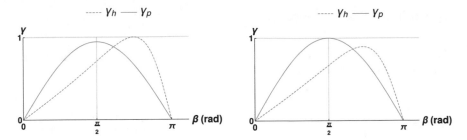

Fig. 5 Variation of the LCI of the hybrid and parallel manipulators (γ_h and γ_p respectively), for $\rho = \frac{1}{\sqrt{2}}$ and $\rho = 1$, with change in the relative angle β. In the hybrid manipulator $\beta = \theta_4$, and in the parallel manipulator $\beta = \theta_4 - \theta_1$

performs better for higher values of β, i.e., when the leg is folded. These plots indicate the regions of best performance of the manipulators in terms of their capability to generate velocity and forces in all directions.

5 Conclusions

A comparison between two manipulators, a hybrid manipulator and a parallel manipulator, that are similar in kinematic design except for the placement of the motors, has been presented in this paper. The performance of these manipulators was evaluated based on three performance indices: measure of manipulability, local conditioning index, and global conditioning index. The evaluation in terms of the GCI indicates that the parallel manipulator performs better than the hybrid manipulator over a large range of the design space, ρ. The evaluation in terms of the MoM and LCI indicates that the hybrid manipulator is closer to isotropic configuration when it is in a folded configuration while the parallel manipulator is closer to an isotropic configuration when it is a little outstretched. Although the analysis indicates that a parallel manipulator provides better performance (in terms of the GCI), no conclusive inferences can be drawn based on just these three indices as to which manipulator is better suited for the application. Other performance indices, such as the Mechanical Cost of Transport (MCoT), which are trajectory specific (unlike the analysis presented in this paper where no specific trajectory is considered), must also be used to gauge the performance of these manipulators for any specific application. The evaluation of the performance of these manipulators has been performed only based on kinematic indices. The performance in terms of dynamics has not been reported as it is out of the scope of this work. This can be considered for future work.

Appendix: Velocity Jacobian

The analytical expressions for the velocity Jacobian matrices of the hybrid and parallel manipulators are given by:

$$
J_p = \frac{1}{l_{2e}s_{23}} \begin{bmatrix} -l_1(l_2 + l_{2e})s_1s_2c_3 + l_1(l_2c_1s_2 + l_{2e}s_1c_2)s_3 & l_2l_4s_2(c_4s_3 - c_3s_4) \\ -l_1(l_2 + l_{2e})c_1c_2s_3 + l_1(l_2s_1c_2 + l_{2e}c_1s_2)c_3 & l_2l_4c_2(c_3s_4 - c_4s_3) \end{bmatrix},
$$

$$
J_h = \frac{1}{l_{2e}s_{23}} \begin{bmatrix} \begin{aligned} -(l_1(l_2 + l_{2e})s_1 + l_2l_4s_{14})s_2c_3 + l_1l_{2e}s_1c_2s_3 \\ + l_2(l_1c_1 + l_4c_{14})s_2s_3 \end{aligned} & l_2l_4s_2(c_{14}s_3 - c_3s_{14}) \\ \begin{aligned} -(l_1(l_2 + l_{2e})c_1 + l_2l_4c_{14})c_2s_3 + l_1l_{2e}c_1s_2c_3 \\ + l_2(l_1s_1 + l_4s_{14})c_2c_3 \end{aligned} & l_2l_4c_2(s_{14}c_3 - s_3c_{14}) \end{bmatrix},
$$

where J_p and J_h are the velocity Jacobian matrices of the parallel and hybrid manipulators, respectively, and l_i's are the lengths of the links as indicated in Fig. 6, c_i and s_i represent the cosine and sine of the angles θ_i, ϕ_i respectively, s_{23} indicates the sine of the compound angle $\phi_2 - \phi_3$, and c_{14} and s_{14} indicate the cosine and sine of the compound angle $\theta_1 + \theta_4$, respectively. It should be noted that the orientation of link l_4 is measured in an absolute sense in the parallel manipulator, whereas it is measured in a relative sense in the hybrid manipulator. Thus, θ_4 in the parallel manipulator is equal to $\theta_1 + \theta_4$ of the hybrid manipulator for a given configuration. The two Jacobian matrices possess the following structure:

$$
J_p = \begin{bmatrix} a & b \\ c & d \end{bmatrix}, \qquad J_h = \begin{bmatrix} a+b & b \\ c+d & d \end{bmatrix},
$$

where $a, b, c,$ and d are substitutes for the elements of the matrices. This structure of the Jacobian matrices arises due to the use of the compound angle $\theta_1 + \theta_4$ to describe

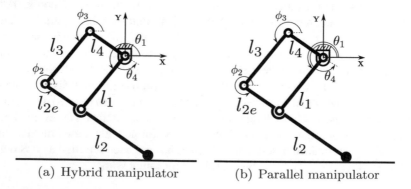

(a) Hybrid manipulator   (b) Parallel manipulator

Fig. 6 Geometric parameters and references to measure link angles in the hybrid and parallel manipulators

the angle made by the link l_4 with the X-axis of the base co-ordinate frame in the hybrid manipulator as opposed to just θ_4 in the parallel manipulator.

The velocity Jacobian matrices for the simplified models of the manipulators (shown in Fig. 3) are:

$$
\boldsymbol{J}_p = \begin{bmatrix} -l_1 \sin \theta_1 & -l_2 \sin \theta_4 \\ l_1 \cos \theta_1 & l_2 \cos \theta_4 \end{bmatrix},
$$

$$
\boldsymbol{J}_h = \begin{bmatrix} -l_1 \sin \theta_1 - l_2 \sin(\theta_1 + \theta_4) & -l_2 \sin(\theta_1 + \theta_4) \\ l_1 \cos \theta_1 + l_2 \cos(\theta_1 + \theta_4) & l_2 \cos(\theta_1 + \theta_4) \end{bmatrix}.
$$

References

1. M. Hutter, C. Gehring, D. Jud, A. Lauber, C.D. Bellicoso, V. Tsounis, J. Hwangbo, K. Bodie, P. Fankhauser, M. Bloesch et al., Anymal-a highly mobile and dynamic quadrupedal robot, in *Proceedings of the IEEE/RSJ International Conference on Intelligent Robots and Systems (IROS)*, Daejeon, Korea, 9–14 Oct 2016, pp. 38–44
2. M. Hutter, C.D. Remy, M.A. Hoepflinger, R. Siegwart, ScarlETH: design and control of a planar running robot, in *Proceedings of the IEEE/RSJ International Conference on Intelligent Robots and Systems (IROS)*, San Francisco, California, USA, 25–30 Sept 2011, pp. 562–567
3. G. Kenneally, D.E. Koditschek, Leg design for energy management in an electromechanical robot, in *Proceedings of the IEEE/RSJ International Conference on Intelligent Robots and Systems (IROS)*, Hamburg, Germany, 28 Sept–02 Oct 2015, pp. 5712–5718
4. W. Bosworth, S. Kim, N. Hogan, The MIT super mini cheetah: a small, low-cost quadrupedal robot for dynamic locomotion, in *IEEE International Symposium on Safety, Security, and Rescue Robotics (SSRR)*, Oct 2015, pp. 1–8
5. A. Ghosal, *Robotics: Fundamental Concepts and Analysis*, 1 edn. (Oxford University Press, New Delhi, India, 2006)
6. G. Kenneally, A. De, D.E. Koditschek, Design principles for a family of direct-drive legged robots. IEEE Robot. Autom. Lett. **1**(2), 900–907 (2016)
7. T. Yoshikawa, Manipulability of robotic mechanisms. Int. J. Robot. Res. **4**(2), 3–9 (1985)
8. J. Angeles, C. Gosselin, A global performance index for the kinematic optimization of robotic manipulators. J. Mech. Des. **113**(3), 220–226 (1991)
9. J.K. Salisbury, J.J. Craig, Articulated hands: force control and kinematic issues. Int. J. Robot. Res. **1**(1), 4–17 (1982)

A Comparative Study of the Configuration-Space and Actuator-Space Forward Dynamics of Closed-Loop Mechanisms Using the Lagrangian Formalism

Anirban Nag and Sandipan Bandyopadhyay

Abstract This paper presents a comparative study between two related methods of formulating the equations of motion, within the Lagrangian framework, for closed-loop mechanisms. Such mechanisms encounter singularities not only at the boundaries of their workspaces, but also inside the workspaces. The latter kind of singularities are detrimental to the operation of the mechanisms and may lead to their mechanical failure. The primary objective of the paper is to investigate the ways in which these singularities impact the two formulations, and to establish a relation between them. A planar five-bar mechanism is used to illustrate that the singularities appearing in one formulation is a subset of those appearing in the other formulation. The second objective is to provide a qualitative analysis of the time-complexities of the respective formulations. A planar five-bar and the Stewart platform manipulator are used to study and compare the computational costs incurred in either of the formulations.

Keywords Configuration-space · Actuator-space · Gain-type singularities
Time-complexity · Stewart platform manipulator (SPM)

A. Nag · S. Bandyopadhyay (✉)
Department of Engineering Design, Indian Institute of Technology Madras,
Chennai 600036, Tamil Nadu, India
e-mail: sandipan@iitm.ac.in

A. Nag
e-mail: nag.anirban16@gmail.com

© Springer Nature Singapore Pte Ltd. 2019
D N Badodkar and T A Dwarakanath (eds.), *Machines, Mechanism and Robotics*, Lecture Notes in Mechanical Engineering,
https://doi.org/10.1007/978-981-10-8597-0_9

95

1 Introduction

Closed-loop mechanisms are known to have a greater number of joints than their degrees-of-freedom (DoF), as a result of which, they have inherent kinematic constraints. Hence, they are also known as *constrained mechanical systems*. Dynamic modeling of such systems using the Lagrangian formulation has been documented well in the literature. A summary of the different variations within the Lagrangian framework has been presented in [1]. The two main approaches involve incorporating the constraint forces in the equation of motion in one formulation, and eliminating the same using the principle of virtual work, in the second. The former one is termed as the *augmented* formulation and the latter is referred to as the *embedded* formulation (see, e.g., [1], pp. 196–200). The two formulations are also referred to as *configuration-space dynamics* and *actuator-space dynamics*, respectively [2]. Dynamics of closed-loop mechanisms have already been studied using both the formulations. For instance, configuration-space dynamic model of the Stewart platform manipulator (SPM) has been presented by Anwar and Bandyopadhyay in [3]. Actuator-space formulation of dynamics of the 3-R̲RR parallel manipulator has been reported by Agarwal et al. in [4]. Abdellatif et al. have presented a similar study on the dynamics of the SPM in [2].

It is well known that any closed-loop mechanism/manipulator suffers from the *gain-type* singularities appearing inside their workspaces, in addition to the *loss-type* or boundary singularities [5]. At these singularities the mechanism gets *locked*, and extremely large (i.e., infinite in theory) efforts are demanded of the actuators, which may lead to the breakdown of the mechanism. It is, therefore, of interest to study the impact of such singularities on the different formulations of dynamics. However, to the best of the knowledge of the authors, a comparative study of such effects have not been reported extensively in literature. The main focus of this paper is to address this gap.

The second aspect which the authors would like to address in this paper is the comparison of the time-complexities of both the formulations. Time-complexity forms an important performance index, while choosing a particular formulation for dynamic modeling. It would be illustrated that the two formulations provide a great contrast, in terms of the number of operations involved. The difference becomes significant for larger mechanisms/manipulators. The five-bar and the SPM have been used as examples to illustrate this point.

The rest of the paper is arranged thus: Sect. 2 deals with the equation of motion in both the configuration-space and the actuator-space formulation, and the singularities involved. An example of the five-bar mechanism is used to look into the matrices involved, and to draw certain inferences. Section 3 presents the complexities involved in both the formulations, as well as a qualitative analysis of the time taken to simulate the dynamics in a computer algebra system. The conclusions of the work are presented in Sect. 4.

2 Singularity Analysis in the Context of the Two Dynamic Formulations

The *active* (i.e., actuated) and *passive* (i.e., unactuated) joint variables present in the mechanism can be defined by the vectors $\boldsymbol{\theta} \in \mathbb{R}^n$, and $\boldsymbol{\phi} \in \mathbb{R}^m$. The configuration-space variable, $\boldsymbol{q}$, is defined as $\boldsymbol{q} = [\boldsymbol{\theta}^\top, \boldsymbol{\phi}^\top]^\top \in \mathbb{R}^p$, $p = n + m$. The number of *independent* constraints defining the system is equal to m, and can be expressed in the vector form as, $\boldsymbol{\eta}(\boldsymbol{q}) = \boldsymbol{0}$. The equation of motion in the configuration-space can thus be written as

$$M(\boldsymbol{q})\ddot{\boldsymbol{q}} + C(\boldsymbol{q}, \dot{\boldsymbol{q}})\dot{\boldsymbol{q}} + G(\boldsymbol{q}) = \boldsymbol{Q}^{nc} + \boldsymbol{J}_{\eta q}^\top \boldsymbol{\lambda}, \tag{1}$$

where $M(\boldsymbol{q})$, $C(\boldsymbol{q}, \dot{\boldsymbol{q}}) \in \mathbb{R}^{p \times p}$ are the *mass* and the *Coriolis* matrices, respectively, and $G(\boldsymbol{q})$ is the gravitational force vector. The vector of externally applied forces is denoted by $\boldsymbol{Q}^{nc}$. The *constraint Jacobian matrix* is given by $\boldsymbol{J}_{\eta q} = \frac{\partial \eta}{\partial q} \in \mathbb{R}^{m \times p}$, and $\boldsymbol{\lambda} \in \mathbb{R}^m$ is the vector of *Lagrange multipliers*, given by:

$$\boldsymbol{\lambda} = -A^{-1}\left(\dot{\boldsymbol{J}}_{\eta q}\dot{\boldsymbol{q}} + \boldsymbol{J}_{\eta q}M^{-1}f\right), \text{ where, } A = \boldsymbol{J}_{\eta q}M^{-1}\boldsymbol{J}_{\eta q}^\top, f = \boldsymbol{Q}^{nc} - C\dot{\boldsymbol{q}} - G.$$

From the expression of $\boldsymbol{\lambda}$ presented above, it is evident that the dynamic model presented in Eq. (1), breaks down, when A^{-1} does not exist, i.e., when $\det(A) = 0$.

The actuator-space formulation involves deriving the equation of motion after elimination of the constraint forces using the principle of virtual work. Since, the mechanism under consideration is an ensemble of rigid bodies, the constraints are *scleronomic*, i.e., they do not change with time, such that

$$\frac{d\eta}{dt} = \boldsymbol{0} \Rightarrow \boldsymbol{J}_{\eta q}\dot{\boldsymbol{q}} = \boldsymbol{0} \Rightarrow \dot{\boldsymbol{q}}^\top \boldsymbol{J}_{\eta q}^\top = \boldsymbol{0}. \tag{2}$$

Pre-multiplying Eq. (1) throughout by $\dot{\boldsymbol{q}}^\top$, and using Eq. (2), the resulting equation devoid of constraint forces is obtained as:

$$\dot{\boldsymbol{q}}^\top M(\boldsymbol{q})\ddot{\boldsymbol{q}} + \dot{\boldsymbol{q}}^\top C(\boldsymbol{q}, \dot{\boldsymbol{q}})\dot{\boldsymbol{q}} + \dot{\boldsymbol{q}}^\top G(\boldsymbol{q}) = \dot{\boldsymbol{q}}^\top \boldsymbol{Q}^{nc}. \tag{3}$$

Again, writing $\boldsymbol{\eta}(\boldsymbol{q}) = \boldsymbol{0}$ as $\boldsymbol{\eta}(\boldsymbol{\theta}, \boldsymbol{\phi}) = \boldsymbol{0}$, differentiation with respect to time leads to the following relation between the *rates* of the active and passive joint variables

$$\frac{d\eta}{dt} = \boldsymbol{J}_{\eta\theta}\dot{\boldsymbol{\theta}} + \boldsymbol{J}_{\eta\phi}\dot{\boldsymbol{\phi}} = \boldsymbol{0} \Rightarrow \dot{\boldsymbol{\phi}} = -\boldsymbol{J}_{\eta\phi}^{-1}\boldsymbol{J}_{\eta\theta}\dot{\boldsymbol{\theta}} = \boldsymbol{J}_{\phi\theta}\dot{\boldsymbol{\theta}}, \tag{4}$$

where $\boldsymbol{J}_{\eta\phi} = \frac{\partial \eta}{\partial \phi} \in \mathbb{R}^{m \times m}$ and $\boldsymbol{J}_{\eta\theta} = \frac{\partial \eta}{\partial \theta} \in \mathbb{R}^{m \times n}$. The underlying assumption for Eq. (4) to hold, is the existence of $\boldsymbol{J}_{\eta\phi}^{-1}$. Using Eq. (4) the configuration-space and actuator-space velocity and acceleration vectors can be related as

$$\dot{q} = J_{q\theta}\dot{\theta}, \quad \ddot{q} = J_{q\theta}\ddot{\theta} + \dot{J}_{q\theta}\dot{\theta}, \tag{5}$$

where $J_{q\theta} = \begin{pmatrix} I \\ J_{\phi\theta} \end{pmatrix} \in \mathbb{R}^{p\times n}$ and $I \in \mathbb{R}^{n\times n}$ is the identity matrix. Using Eq. (5) in Eq. (3), the equation of motion in the actuator-space is given by

$$\dot{\theta}^\top \left[\left(J_{q\theta}^\top M J_{q\theta} \right) \ddot{\theta} + J_{q\theta}^\top \left(M \dot{J}_{q\theta} + C J_{q\theta} \right) \dot{\theta} + J_{q\theta}^\top G\left(q\right) - J_{q\theta}^\top Q^{nc} \right] = 0.$$

Since $\dot{\theta}^\top \neq 0$, in general, the expression in the square bracket in above equation has to vanish, leading to the following equation:

$$M_\theta \ddot{\theta} + C_\theta \dot{\theta} + G_\theta = \tau_\theta, \tag{6}$$

where $M_\theta, C_\theta \in \mathbb{R}^{n\times n}$ are the new *mass* and *Coriolis* matrices, G_θ is the gravitational force vector and τ_θ is the vector of externally applied forces/torques. From the derivation of the equation of motion in the actuator-space, in particular, from Eq. (4), it is evident that the formulation would breakdown when $\det\left(J_{\eta\phi}\right) = 0$. This condition leads directly to the gain-type singularity [5]. Regarding the singularities in the two formulations, which is a direct manifestation of the respective matrices $J_{\eta q}$ and $J_{\eta\phi}$ losing rank, the following conjecture is proposed:

Proposition 1 *Rank deficiency of $J_{\eta\phi}$ does not necessarily lead to the rank deficiency of $J_{\eta q}$; however, the converse is true for any closed-loop mechanism.*

In other words, the set of poses at which $J_{\eta q}$ is singular is a proper subset of the poses at which $J_{\eta\phi}$ is singular. The proof of this proposition follows the structural relationship between the matrices $J_{\eta q}$ and $J_{\eta\phi}$ as shown in Eq. (7)

$$J_{\eta q} = \left[\begin{array}{c|c} J_{\eta\theta} & J_{\eta\phi} \\ (m \times n) & (m \times m) \end{array} \right] \tag{7}$$

Proof The matrices $J_{\eta q} \in \mathbb{R}^{m\times p}$ and $J_{\eta\theta} \in \mathbb{R}^{m\times n}$ are rectangular, while the matrix $J_{\eta\phi} \in \mathbb{R}^{m\times m}$ is always square. Let $J_{\eta\phi}$ be rank deficient due to linear dependence of any two rows. However, this will not affect the rank of $J_{\eta q}$ since, it is also dependent on the rows of $J_{\eta\theta}$ by construction. Hence, the rank deficiency of $J_{\eta\phi}$ does not necessarily result in the rank deficiency of $J_{\eta q}$.

The converse occurs when $J_{\eta q}$ becomes singular due to linear dependence of any two rows. Since, each row of $J_{\eta q}$ is a composition of a row of $J_{\eta\theta}$ and $J_{\eta\phi}$ by construction, this necessarily means, that the corresponding rows in the respective matrices also become dependent. Hence, the rank deficiency of $J_{\eta q}$ always implies rank deficiency of $J_{\eta\phi}$. ∎

2.1 Illustrative Example: Planar Five-Bar Mechanism

To illustrate the above proposition, a planar five-bar mechanism has been used as an example (see Fig. 1). For this mechanism, $\boldsymbol{\theta} = [\theta_1, \theta_2]^\top$, $\boldsymbol{\phi} = [\phi_1, \phi_2]^\top$, $\boldsymbol{q} = [\theta_1, \theta_2, \phi_1, \phi_2]^\top$. Hence, $m = n = 2$ in this case. The constraint equations can be written as:

$$\eta_1 = l\cos\theta_1 + r\cos\phi_1 - l_0 - l\cos\theta_2 - r\cos\phi_2 = 0, \tag{8}$$

$$\eta_2 = l\sin\theta_1 + r\sin\phi_1 - l\sin\theta_2 - r\sin\phi_2 = 0. \tag{9}$$

The matrices $\boldsymbol{J}_{\eta\phi}$ and $\boldsymbol{J}_{\eta q}$ are computed as

$$\boldsymbol{J}_{\eta\phi} = r\begin{pmatrix} -\sin\phi_1 & \sin\phi_2 \\ \cos\phi_1 & -\cos\phi_2 \end{pmatrix}, \quad \boldsymbol{J}_{\eta q} = r\begin{pmatrix} -\rho\sin\theta_1 & \rho\sin\theta_2 & -\sin\phi_1 & \sin\phi_2 \\ \rho\cos\theta_1 & -\rho\cos\theta_2 & \cos\phi_1 & -\cos\phi_2 \end{pmatrix},$$

where $\rho = \frac{l}{r}$, is a nondimensional constant defining the ratio of the active to the passive link length. The rank of both the matrices is m in a nonsingular pose. The condition for the rank deficiency of $\boldsymbol{J}_{\eta\phi}$ is given by $\det(\boldsymbol{J}_{\eta\phi}) = 0$, which, when expanded, leads to: $r^2\sin(\phi_1 - \phi_2) = 0 \Rightarrow \phi_1 - \phi_2 = \alpha\pi, \alpha \in \mathbb{Z}$. It is evident, that one of the gain-type singular poses is given by, $\phi_1 = \phi_2 + \pi$. At this pose, the above matrices reduce to the following forms:

$$\boldsymbol{J}_{\eta\phi} = r\begin{pmatrix} \sin\phi_2 & \sin\phi_2 \\ -\cos\phi_2 & -\cos\phi_2 \end{pmatrix}, \quad \boldsymbol{J}_{\eta q} = r\begin{pmatrix} -\rho\sin\theta_1 & \rho\sin\theta_2 & \sin\phi_2 & \sin\phi_2 \\ \rho\cos\theta_1 & -\rho\cos\theta_2 & -\cos\phi_2 & -\cos\phi_2 \end{pmatrix}.$$

Clearly, $\boldsymbol{J}_{\eta\phi}$ is singular, while the rank of $\boldsymbol{J}_{\eta q}$ is equal to m, same as before.

For the converse, let the rows of $\boldsymbol{J}_{\eta q}$ be some linear combinations of each other, such that there exists $k \in \mathbb{R}, k \neq 0$ such that

$$[-l\sin\theta_1, l\sin\theta_2, -r\sin\phi_1, r\sin\phi_2] + k\,[l\cos\theta_1, -l\cos\theta_2, r\cos\phi_1, -r\cos\phi_2] = \boldsymbol{0}.$$

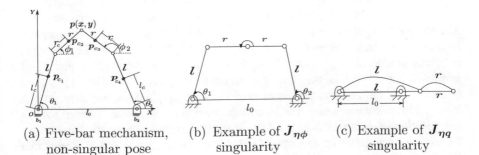

(a) Five-bar mechanism, non-singular pose   (b) Example of $\boldsymbol{J}_{\eta\phi}$ singularity   (c) Example of $\boldsymbol{J}_{\eta q}$ singularity

Fig. 1 Schematics of the five-bar mechanism in different conditions

From the individual components, one finds

$$\tan \theta_1 = \tan \theta_2 = \tan \phi_1 = \tan \phi_2 = k, \text{ provided } \cos \phi_i, \cos \theta_j \neq 0, i, j = 1, 2. \quad (10)$$

Multiplying the second row of $\boldsymbol{J}_{\eta q}$ by k, and using the relation in Eq. (10) the resulting matrix is obtained as

$$\boldsymbol{J}_{\eta q} = \frac{r}{k} \begin{pmatrix} -\rho \sin \theta_1 & \rho \sin \theta_2 & -\sin \phi_1 & \sin \phi_2 \\ \rho \sin \theta_1 & -\rho \sin \theta_2 & \sin \phi_1 & -\sin \phi_2 \end{pmatrix}. \quad (11)$$

A simple row operation on Eq. (11) shows that $\boldsymbol{J}_{\eta q}$ is rank deficient. Another observation shows, that the third and fourth columns of $\boldsymbol{J}_{\eta q}$ forms $\boldsymbol{J}_{\eta \phi}$, which by itself is singular. Hence rank deficiency of the $\boldsymbol{J}_{\eta q}$, necessarily leads to the rank deficiency of $\boldsymbol{J}_{\eta \phi}$, which was the statement of Proposition 1. In summary, one can say that the actuator-space formulation would *always* breakdown if $\boldsymbol{J}_{\eta \phi}$ is rank deficient whereas, the configuration-space formulation would not necessarily breakdown, unless $\boldsymbol{J}_{\eta q}$ is singular.

3 Time Complexities

One consideration while choosing a particular formulation for dynamic modeling is the computation complexity involved. This section presents a comparative study of the computational costs associated with both the formulations. Since the derivation of $\boldsymbol{M}$, $\boldsymbol{C}$ and $\boldsymbol{G}$ matrices in the configuration-space (presented in Eq. (1)) is common in both the formulations, the scope of complexity analysis in this work would be confined to only the additional numerical computations specific to the individual formulations. The time-complexity of the configuration-space formulation is dictated by the time taken to evaluate the vector of constraint forces. For example, both the formulations involve several matrix inversions, which have been performed using the LU decomposition. Hence, the number of basic operations involved in each such inversion is $\frac{2}{3}h^3$, h being the dimension of the matrix [6]. Both the formulations also involve a number of matrix multiplications, whose costs need to be accounted for. The complexity analysis of matrix multiplications is done in the following manner: each entry of a matrix $\boldsymbol{W} = \boldsymbol{U}\boldsymbol{V}$, where, $\boldsymbol{U} \in \mathbb{R}^{m \times p}$, $\boldsymbol{V} \in \mathbb{R}^{p \times n}$, can be viewed as the scalar product of two vectors of length p, requiring p multiplications and $p - 1$ additions. For mn entries, the computational cost[1] is given by $mn(2p - 1)$. It must be noted, that the analysis presented here is mainly qualitative, and complexities involved in conventional numerical methods have been considered. Though a rigorous quantitative treatment was aimed for, in terms of establishing a ratio between the theoretical computation cost involved in each sub-operation to their actual computer run times, an accurate correlation could not be established for reasons explained

---

[1]The addition and multiplication operations have been treated equally, following [6].

in Sect. 3.1. Nonetheless, the distinctive features of both the formulations clearly emerge from the reported results and seem to be in agreement in terms of both the theoretical cost and the actual run times.

Another aspect of the actuator-space dynamics is the computation of the passive joint variables and their corresponding velocities at each integration time-step, for the forward dynamics simulation. This involves the solution of the forward kinematics of the manipulator. This is an expensive step, as the forward kinematics of a parallel manipulator is typically nontrivial and leads to multiple solutions, as it involves the solution of a nonlinear system of equations. This also requires implementation of a root-tracking algorithm, to ensure that *all* the solutions remain on their respective branches as the system evolves with time. Solution of the forward kinematic problem involves bringing the system of multivariate nonlinear equations to a univariate polynomial equation, referred to as the *forward kinematic univariate* (FKU), which itself is solved via the eigenproblem of its *companion matrix*. One of the conventional numerical approaches for solving an eigenproblem is through the application of the QR algorithm, which has a complexity of $\frac{4}{3}\delta^3$ [6], where δ is the degree of the FKU. For example, the forward kinematics of the SPM requires the solution of a 20 degree univariate polynomial [7]. Furthermore, it is essential that one particular forward kinematic solution branch is followed for the entire simulation period. Hence, an effective root-tracking algorithm needs to be implemented. In the present work, the *nearest neighbor* approach is followed, wherein the root closest to the chosen solution in the previous time-step is selected in the present one as the successor of the former. The present analysis assumes that the FKU is obtained in the *closed form*. If the FKU is not present in the closed form, then the complexities involved in the intermediate steps leading to the FKU have to be accounted for. Further, a finite amount of time has to be accounted for the evaluation of the remaining joint and task-space variables, tracing back from the FKU solutions. The passive joint velocities can be evaluated using the relation presented in Eq. (4).

The overall computational cost manifests as the time taken by the ODE solver to solve the final ODE arrived at, by either of the formulations. The fourth-order Runge–Kutta (RK) method is used in both the cases. This would involve, transforming the second-order ODE given in Eqs. (1) and (6) into their respective state-space forms. Let, the state-space vector X be defined by $[x_1^\top, \ x_2^\top]^\top$, such that $x_1 = q$, $x_2 = \dot{q}$. Equation (1), can thus be written as:

$$\dot{x}_1 = x_2, \ \dot{x}_2 = M^{-1}(x_1)F, \text{ where } F = \left(Q^{nc} + J_{\eta q}^\top \lambda - C\left(x_1, x_2\right)x_2 - G(x_1)\right).$$

The above equation is of the standard *state-space* form, $\dot{X} = f(X)$. Since, the RK method involves evaluating the state-derivative $f(X)$, at four different states, typically the time taken by the solver is proportional to the time taken for a single function evaluation. The same procedure is followed for the actuator-space dynamics. Since the composite force vector F is calculated before-hand, the additional costs involved in evaluating $f(X)$, are that of the inversion of the mass matrix M,

Table 1 Expressions/steps and their computational costs in each of the two formulations

Configuration-space	Cost	Actuator-space	Cost
A	$m(m+p)(2p-1)$	M_θ	$n(n+p)(2p-1)$
$J_{\eta q}M^{-1}f$	$(m+p)(2p-1)$	C_θ	$n(n+2p)(2p-1)$
$J_{\eta q}\dot{q}$	$m(2p-1)$	G_θ	$n(2p-1)$
A^{-1}	$\frac{2}{3}m^3$		
λ	$2m^2$	FK solution (via FKU and eigenproblem approach)	$\frac{4}{3}\delta^3$
$J_{\eta q}^\top \lambda$	$(2m-1)p$	Evaluation of passive velocities	$m(2n-1)$
$f(X)$	$\frac{2}{3}p^3+p^2$	$f(X)$	$\frac{2}{3}n^3+n^2$

and multiplying the inverse by F. The theoretical computational costs incurred in the two formulations have been enumerated in Table 1.

3.1 Illustrative Examples

Two examples, one that of the planar five-bar mechanism and the other of the SPM, have been provided to illustrate the time-complexities involved in the two formulations.[2] It is difficult to appreciate the difference in complexities involved in the two formulations from the five-bar example, since the size of the matrices involved is small, owing to the dimension of the configuration-space, which is 4. The main attributes of the respective formulations can nonetheless be understood. The second example, that of the SPM, involves a much larger system and provides a more clearer distinction between the said formulations. To investigate this further, actual numerical simulation is used. The dynamics of both the manipulators have been simulated for a free fall scenario, inside the computer algebra system (CAS), Mathematica 11. Both the simulations were run using the formulations for 100 instances each, on a computer with CPU clock speed of 3.6 GHz, and the mean results are documented.

3.1.1 Computational Cost and Simulation Run Times for the Planar Five-Bar Mechanism

For the five-bar mechanism as presented in Sect. 2.1, $m=2$, $n=2$, $p=4$. The computational cost involved can be obtained by substituting these values in Table 1.

---

[2]Rational values of the computational cost obtained by using Table 1 have been rounded off to their closest integer values.

Table 2 Expressions and their computational costs for the five-bar mechanism

Configuration-space	Cost	Actuator-space	Cost
A	84	M_θ	84
$J_{\eta q} M^{-1} f$	42	C_θ	140
$\dot{J}_{\eta q} \dot{q}$	14	G_θ	14
A^{-1}	5		
λ	8	FK solution (via FKU and eigenproblem approach)	11
$J_{\eta q}^{\top} \lambda$	12	Evaluation of passive velocities	6
$f(X)$	59	$f(X)$	9
$\sum$	224	$\sum$	264

Table 3 CPU time taken in computing the major steps in the two formulations for the five-bar

Configuration-space	Time (ms)	Actuator-space	Time (ms)
A	0.057	M_θ	0.075
$J_{\eta q} M^{-1} f$	0.025	C_θ	0.137
$\dot{J}_{\eta q} \dot{q}$	0.002	G_θ	0.002
A^{-1}	0.005	FK solution (via FKU and eigenproblem approach)	0.002
λ	0.002	Evaluation of passive velocities	0.001
$J_{\eta q}^{\top} \lambda$	0.001		
$f(X)$	0.043	$f(X)$	0.002
$\sum$	0.135	$\sum$	0.219

A symmetric five-bar was considered for this example. The lengths of the base, proximal, and distal links were assumed to be 1.0 m, 0.5 m, and 0.6 m, respectively. The corresponding link masses were 0.425 kg and, 0.509 kg, respectively. The mass moments of inertia about the centroidal axes were 0.008 $kg\,m^2$ and 0.015 $kg\,m^2$, respectively. The dynamics was simulated for 0.5 s in case of both the formulations. The numerical integrator used steps of 0.01 s in time.

From the data presented in Tables 2 and 3, it may be inferred that the ratio of the theoretical cost and the actual run times, correlate in some cases, and differ in others. However, a qualitative analysis shows that the computation of the A matrix is the most expensive step in the configuration-space formulation, whereas the same holds true for the computation of the Coriolis matrix C_θ in case of the actuator-space formulation. A notable mismatch is noticed in the cost and run time data for the inversion of the A matrix. In general, it is difficult to establish the cause of the mismatch, when the number of operations involved is known to be small. Since all the operations were performed inside a CAS, it may as well happen, that a certain overhead was involved in calling the in-built function used for matrix inversion, and hence, the rise in the observed run time. It may be noted that, most of the sub-expressions for this example can be obtained in closed form. The FKU is quadratic in this case and the solutions can be obtained in closed form. However, the problem is solved numerically, to develop an algorithmic structure, which may be used for solving any closed-loop mechanism. Furthermore, root-tracking algorithms are not needed for this particular example as any one of the two forward kinematic solutions may be used throughout, without the possibility of branch switching.

3.1.2   Computational Cost and Simulation Run Times for the SPM

For the SPM dynamics as presented by Anwar and Bandyopadhyay [3], $m = 12$, $n = 6$, $p = 18$. When used in Table 1, these numbers lead to the cost figures presented in Table 4.

The mass and inertia parameters of the platform were adopted from [3]. The dynamics was simulated for 0.3 s. The numerical integrator used steps of 0.01 s in time.

The overall numerical data indicates that the actuator-space formulation is more computation intensive in this case. Similar to the previous example of the five-bar mechanism, the theoretical cost computations are not in exact proportion with their corresponding computer run times, as listed in Table 4 and Table 5, respectively. The reasons for these are many, including the fact that a computer algebra system was used for the implementation, which has a number of features such as operator overloading, internal function call and memory management overheads, etc. An implementation in a numerical language, such as C should yield a clearer picture, and it is planned next. However, the tables do identify, without any ambiguity, the most expensive step in

Table 4 Expressions and their computational costs for SPM

Configuration-space	Cost	Actuator-space	Cost
A	12,600	M_θ	5040
$J_{\eta q} M^{-1} f$	1050	C_θ	8820
$J_{\eta q} \dot{q}$	420	G_θ	210
A^{-1}	1152		
λ	288	FK solution (via FKU and eigenproblem approach)	10,667
$J_{\eta q}^{\top} \lambda$	414	Evaluation of passive velocities	132
$f(X)$	4212	$f(X)$	180
Σ	20,136	Σ	25,049

Table 5 CPU time taken in computing the major steps in the two formulations for the SPM

Configuration-space	Time (s)	Actuator-space	Time (s)
A	0.128	M_θ	0.040
$J_{\eta q} M^{-1} f$	0.016	C_θ	0.178
$\dot{J}_{\eta q} \dot{q}$	0.005	G_θ	0.004
A^{-1}	0.047	FK solution (via FKU and eigenproblem approach)	0.181
λ	0.003	Root-tracking	0.120
$J_{\eta q}^\top \lambda$	0.003	Evaluation of passive velocities	0.003
$f(X)$	0.052	$f(X)$	0.007
$\sum$	0.244	$\sum$	0.530

either formulation. In the case of the configuration-space formulation, for the SPM, the computation of the matrix A is clearly the most expensive step, while in the other formulation, it is the combination of the forward kinematics and the root-tracking procedure which must follow it. Thus, it is clear that to improve the computational performance of either formulation, one has to focus on these steps, more than the others. In the present setup, the configuration-space formulation seems to outperform the other, in spite of its apparent bulk in terms of the sizes of the matrices involved.

4 Conclusion

A comparative study between two formulations of Lagrangian dynamics, from the perspectives of the singularities encountered and the time-complexities involved, have been presented in this paper. It has been illustrated, that, both approaches have respective breakdown points, namely, at singularities. Further, it has been shown that a singularity in the actuator-space formulation need not lead to a singularity in the configuration-space formulation, though the converse is necessarily true. It was shown, using a five-bar mechanism as an example, that the configuration-space singularity is actually a subset of the actuator-space singularity. The latter part of the paper compares the time-complexities of the two methods, using the examples of the five-bar and the SPM. The most expensive steps in either formulation are identified through a theoretical estimate, and confirmed via actual numerical computations.

References

1. A.A. Shabana, *Computational Dynamics* (Wiley, New York, 2009)
2. H. Abdellatif, B. Heimann, Computational efficient inverse dynamics of 6-DoF fully parallel manipulators by using the Lagrangian formalism. Mech. Mach. Theory **44**(1), 192–207 (2009)
3. S.M. Anwar, S. Bandyopadhyay, Trajectory-tracking control of semi-regular Stewart platform manipulator, in *Proceedings of the 15th National Conference on Machines and Mechanisms, (NaCoMM 2011)* ed. by S. Bandyopadhyay, G. Saravana Kumar, P. Ramu (Narosa Publishing House, India, 2011), pp. 446–454
4. A. Agarwal, C. Nasa, S. Bandyopadhyay, Dynamic singularity avoidance for parallel manipulators using a task-priority based control scheme. Mech. Mach. Theory **96**(Part 1), 107–126 (2016)
5. S. Bandyopadhyay, A. Ghosal, Analysis of configuration space singularities of closed-loop mechanisms and parallel manipulators. Mech. Mach. Theory **39**, 519–544 (2004)
6. G.H. Golub, C.F. Van Loan, *Matrix Computations*, 3rd edn. (Johns Hopkins University Press, Baltimore, MD, USA, 2012)
7. T.-Y. Lee, J.-K. Shim, Algebraic elimination-based real-time forward kinematics of the 6–6 Stewart platform with planar base and platform. Proc. IEEE Int. Conf. Robot. Autom. **2**, 1301–1306 (2001)

Synthesis of Stationary-Active Axes Parallel Mechanisms and Applications

K. D. Lagoo, T A Dwarakanath and D N Badodkar

Abstract The paper presents the synthesis of Stationary-Active (St-Ac) axes mechanisms starting from two DOF to six DOF parallel manipulators. The St-Ac type of parallel mechanisms show certain advantages over the moving axes or pivoted axes type of actuators. Due to the Stationary Actuator feature, certain design features are possible, which are not feasible in case of the pivoted axis or moving active axes type of parallel mechanisms. The paper shows the overriding characteristics of St-Ac axes configuration that will influence its choice in certain applications. The mechanical master–slave manipulator design, common shaft control of St-Ac Parallel Manipulators and the prototype of St-Ac has been demonstrated.

Keywords Stationary-active axes parallel manipulator · Manipulator applications · Master–slave arrangement · Single actuator manipulator

1 Introduction

The design synthesis of parallel mechanisms has been continuously evolving; the structural synthesis is evolving in various joint combinations and permutations. A few of the parallel mechanism architectures have been well adopted by the industry. By far, the most popular parallel mechanism based architectures are the 6-Universal-Prismatic-Spherical (6-UPS) and the 6-Spherical-Prismatic-Spherical (6-SPS)-jointed kinematic chains [1]. The mechanism originated with the prototype development for an application rather than translating theoretical designs into

K. D. Lagoo · T A Dwarakanath (✉) · D N Badodkar (✉)
Division of Remote Handling & Robotics, Bhabha
Atomic Research Centre, Trombay, Mumbai 400085, India
e-mail: tad@barc.gov.in

D N Badodkar
e-mail: badodkar@barc.gov.in

K. D. Lagoo
e-mail: klagoo@barc.gov.in

© Springer Nature Singapore Pte Ltd. 2019
D N Badodkar and T A Dwarakanath (eds.), *Machines, Mechanism
and Robotics*, Lecture Notes in Mechanical Engineering,
https://doi.org/10.1007/978-981-10-8597-0_10

107

practice [2]. The former is popular for its larger workspace and the latter because of its simplicity in construction. In most of the parallel mechanisms, the active axes undergo pivot mobility. The actuators undergo rotational motion about the passive pivot axes at the base. Though the actuators are located close to the base, the rotational motion of the actuators increases the rotational inertia of the leg. The design syntheses of parallel mechanisms, in which the active axes are stationary, have also been reported [3]. The limited three degree of freedom parallel mechanism-based system, known as the delta robot has been well adopted and has been highly successful in high-speed pick and place applications. This paper discusses and presents many designs and case studies of the stationary axis type of parallel mechanisms. The invariance of the axis of actuation has a large influence on basing parallel mechanisms for many applications. This single attribute can give rise to many useful design concepts to devise many applications. This is a critical requirement for high-speed and remote actuation motion mechanisms. The elimination of the actuator mass inertia and the high mean time before fatigue failures are the other main features of the stationary-active axes configuration.

The stationary axis feature of the manipulators can be utilized in several ways. For example, all the active axes can be coupled by a drive train and driven by a single actuator. Since the axes are stationary, the corresponding axes of two parallel manipulators of the same design can be coupled in a one-to-one correspondence, resulting in a master–slave mechanism. This master–slave idea has been implemented for two DOF, three DOF and six DOF Stationary Actuator Mechanisms. The disadvantage of these stationary axis manipulators is its limited workspace.

2 Master–Slave Arrangement

The master–slave arrangement is the oldest form of manipulation still in use largely because of its man-in-loop control. Offline or autonomous robot regulation is impracticable even in common routine manipulations. There has been an extensive development based on the serial mechanism–based Master–Slave arrangement [4, 5]. The large number of passive joints and floating active axes, however, were the impediments for the development of a practicable parallel mechanism based Master–Slave arrangement. This section shows how the St-Ac axes-based parallel manipulator overrides these impediments in providing a practicable solution.

Two St-Ac parallel manipulators identical in kinematics serve as a Master and a Slave. The master receives the trajectory input through its end effector and the slave reflects the trajectory as the output at the end effector. The transmission of force and motion from the master to the slave takes place through the common stationary axis of each kinematic chain. The one-to-one correspondence of the master and the slave connectors along a common stationary axis results in the identical motion response at the slave for the given motion input at the master. The advantage of the St-Ac axes-type master–slave is in its uncoupled and direct transmission compared to the master–slave

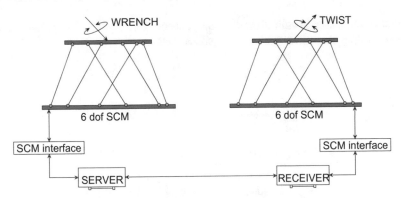

Fig. 1 Bilateral wrench communication scheme

mechanisms of the serial manipulator type, which involve multiple axis (arm) motion transmission. However, the limitation of this type is the limited workspace.

2.1 Wrench Communication System

A bilateral wrench communication scheme has been developed to connect the two manipulators, which are separated. The scheme is intended to establish a wrench reflection between the master and slave manipulators. The master, which takes the operator's input at its end effector while the other termed as the slave reflects the output at its end effector. A two-way data communication is considered for an effective wrench reflection and control. Therefore, the role of the master and the slave are interchangeable. Figure 1 shows the main components and connectivity of the wrench reflection scheme. The inherent Jacobian balancing between the master and the slave has been established. The input at the master end effector would result in supporting the wrench provided that the environment (or contact media) is present. In the absence of contact media the manipulator tends to twist in the direction of the applied wrench [6]. The external wrench at the slave side is reflected back to the master. The St-Ac axes mechanical master–slave arrangement gives very high fidelity because of the inherent nature of Jacobian balance.

The Jacobian matrix comprising the line vectors of the slave J_s are matched with those of the master J_m. This increases the stiffness of the configuration state and the configuration state remains the same even in the absence of the contact media. The external wrench which is sensed at the slave side is reflected back to the master. The input on the master side will experience a proportional resistance to twist in the direction of the reflected wrench. In other words the master twists the hand of the operator with the same wrench with which the slave twists the environment. The desired task space values are transformed to the joint space (connector space) and the control algorithm is built in the connector space. The control law applied on each of the six connectors on either side is given as follows:

$$Fm_i = K_{dpm}\big(\bar{L}_{dm}(i) - \bar{L}_m(i)\big) + K_{dvm}\Big(\bar{\dot{L}}_{dm}(i) - \bar{\dot{L}}_m(i)\Big)$$

$$+ \sum_{j=1}^{6} K_{pm}\big(Jm_{ij} - Js_{ij}\big) + K_{vm}\Big(\bar{\dot{L}}_m(i) - \bar{\dot{L}}_s(i)\Big) \qquad (1)$$

$$Fs_i = K_{dps}\big(\bar{L}_{ds}(i) - \bar{L}_s(i)\big) + K_{dvs}\Big(\bar{\dot{L}}_{ds}(i) - \bar{\dot{L}}_s(i)\Big)$$

$$+ \sum_{j=1}^{6} K_{ps}\big(Js_{ij} - Jm_{ij}\big) + K_{vs}\Big(\bar{\dot{L}}_s(i) - \bar{\dot{L}}_m(i)\Big) \qquad (2)$$

where L_{dm}, L_m are the desired and the actual connector lengths of the master and $\dot{L}_{dm}$, $\dot{L}_m$, are the desired and actual linear velocities of the master, respectively. Similarly L_{ds}, L_s are the desired and the actual connector lengths of the slave and $\dot{L}_{ds}$, $\dot{L}_s$ are the desired and actual linear velocities of the slave, respectively. The Ks in the above equations are gains set in the software and values. All the safety and corrective actions are assumed to be taken by the respective local controllers. If the safety threshold is surpassed, an action to suspend all the actions of the slave is issued. The control action of Eqs. 1 and 2 are inherently built in St-Ax axes mechanical master–slave mechanisms.

2.2 2-PRR Master–Slave Mechanism

2-PRR Parallel Mechanism is the simplest type of St-Ac axes-type parallel manipulator. The basic design is shown in Fig. 2. It consists of 2 legs; each leg is a PRR chain.

Fig. 2 2 PRR manipulator-based master slave

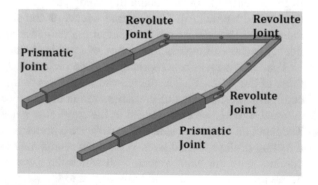

Fig. 3 2 PRR master–slave

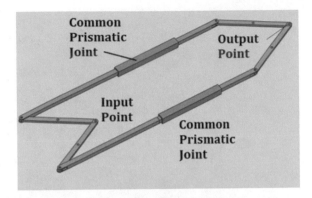

Fig. 4 Profile machining

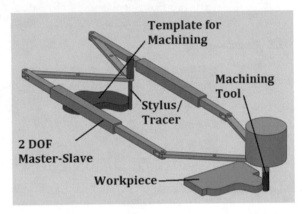

Now, if the prismatic joint of the two PRR manipulators is correspondingly united, the resulting mechanism can be operated in a master–slave configuration as shown in Fig. 3. Due to the common prismatic joints, the motion of the input point is copied at the output point. The typical 2-PRR Master–Slave applications are 2D Profile machining (see Fig. 4), in which a profile is to be machined on a workpiece as per the template. The stylus centered on the revolute joint of the master side follows the template; the corresponding revolute joint of the slave side can be the machining cutter which duplicates the profile and other trajectory characteristics. In pattern matching, where the holes are to be drilled in a workpiece as per the pattern are marked on the template. The locating pin is centered on the master side common revolute joint. The drilling head is centered on the slave side common revolute joint as shown in Fig. 5. The locating pin will be inserted into the reference hole in the template and the drilling head will be lowered on the workpiece to carry out the drilling operation to reproduce the pattern accurately. A screen shot of the simulation of a 2-PRR master–slave wiping the surface is shown in Fig. 6.

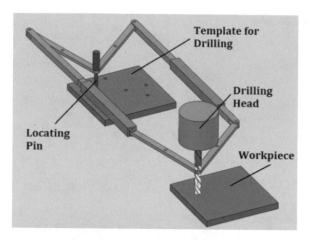

Fig. 5 Pattern matching

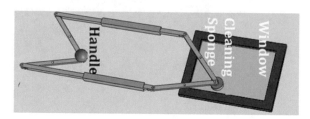

Fig. 6 Remote surface cleaning

2.3 Delta Master–Slave-Based Manipulator

Delta is one of the most popular 3 DOFs in-parallel mechanism configurations, which consists of three stationary actuators, either linear or rotary. Each of the three actuators is connected through a spatial parallelogram mechanism to the end effector platform.

The parallelogram mechanism in the chain constrains the platform orientation and allows only translational degree of freedom. Rotary and prismatic actuator based delta robots are shown in the Figs. 7 and 8 respectively. Two delta mechanisms are connected back to back in the stationary-active axis in the Master–Slave configuration. This synthesis is shown for both the revolute joint and prismatic joint based delta mechanisms (Figs. 9 and 10).

In the revolute delta-based master–slave, the drive transmission is enabled through gears. The corresponding active revolute joints are coupled with a 1:1 gear ratio. Therefore, the corresponding revolute joints of the master and the slave move through identical angles, but in opposite directions. Hence, mirrored motion of the slave platform is obtained. In the prismatic delta-based master–slave, the prismatic joint is common for both the master and the slave. Due to this, both the master and

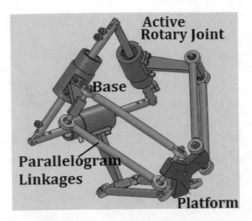

Fig. 7 Rotary actuator-based delta

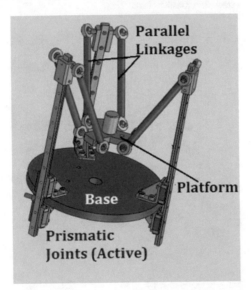

Fig. 8 Prismatic actuator-based delta

slave platforms undergo the same movement in three dimensions. The applications discussed earlier for a 2-PRR are simulated for the delta master–slave configuration and shown in Figs. 10, 11 and 12, respectively, to show its feasibility in spatial dimensions.

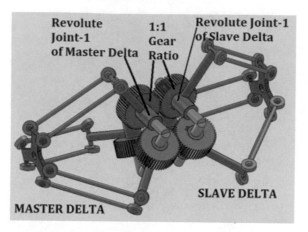

Fig. 9 Revolute joint delta-based master–slave

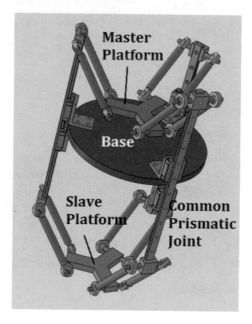

Fig. 10 Prismatic delta-based master–slave

2.4 Six PSS-Based Master–Slave

A 6-PSS-based Master Slave consists of 6 PSS chains between the base and the platform, where the prismatic joint is the active axis. A schematic of a 6 PSS parallel manipulator is shown in Fig. 13 and the corresponding master–slave arrangement is shown in Fig. 14.

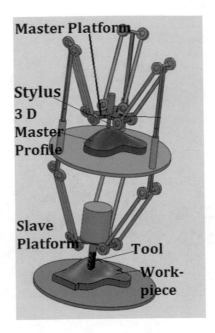

Fig. 11 3D profile machining

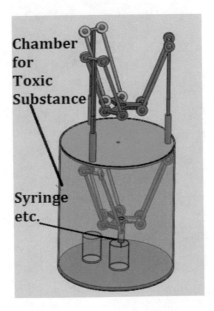

Fig. 12 Handling of toxic liquids

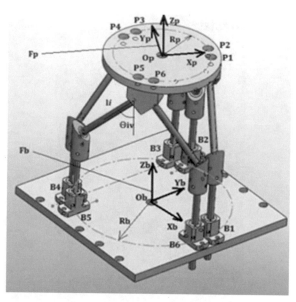

Fig. 13 6 PSS manipulator

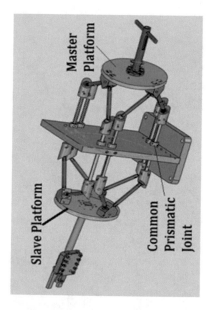

Fig. 14 Six PSS-based master–slave

This 6 PSS-based Master–Slave will give the 6 DOF Motion of the Slave Mechanism, as is obtained in the conventional Master–Slave mechanisms. The kinetic arrangement, design parameters, and the variables are shown in Fig. 13. Two coordinate frames, $F_B = [x_b, y_b, z_b]^T$ and $F_P = [x_p, y_p, z_p]^T$ are defined at the circumcenter of the base and the platform disc respectively. The six legs connecting the platform and the intermediary base is of constant length l. The leg connection points $B_i(B_{ix}, B_{iy}, B_{iz})$ and $P_i(P_{ix}, P_{iy}, P_{iz})$, $i = 1, \ldots, 6$, both at the base and the platform form the vertices of a semi-regular hexagon.

The points are represented with respect to F_B. R_b and R_p are the circum-radius of the connection points at the base and the platform, respectively. They are in cyclic symmetry about Z_b and Z_p axis, respectively. The origin of the frame F_P with respect to F_B is given as $O_P = [O_x, O_y, O_z]^T$ and $^B_P R$ is the rotation of frame F_P with respect to F_B. p_i is the coordinate of the leg connection point at the platform with respect to F_P. P_i, the coordinate of the leg connection point at the platform with respect to F_B is

$$P_i = O_P + {}^B_P R p_i \tag{3}$$

The projection of the leg i on the X_b-Y_b plane is given as

$$\bar{l}_{ixy} = (P_{ix} - B_{ix})\hat{i} + (P_{iy} - B_{iy})\hat{j}; \quad l_{ixy} = \|l_{ixy}\|;$$

$$\theta_{iv} = \sin^{-1}\left(\frac{l}{l_{ixy}}\right); \quad \bar{l}_i = \bar{l}_{ixy} + (P_{iz} - S_i)\hat{k} \tag{4}$$

Then the prismatic actuating distance, S_i along $\hat{k}$ for the given position and the orientation of the platform is given as:

$$S_i = P_{iz} - l \cos \theta_{iv}$$

Limited joint-based inverse kinematics of active stationary axis manipulators can be obtained in a similar manner and is not discussed in this paper.

3 Common Shaft Control

In St-Ac axes type of manipulators, since the active axes are stationary, they can be driven by means of a single motor, through transmission arrangement. For example, in a delta robot with prismatic active axes, each prismatic axis can be operated by means of a cam arrangement and the camshafts can be connected together by means of mechanical transmission arrangement and driven by a single motor (Fig. 15). In this concept, each prismatic joint is driven by a separate cam (an eccentric cam in this design). The cam profile for each prismatic joint can be different. Since the cam profiles are fixed, the platform follows a specific trajectory for one rotation of the shaft. This type of arrangement is useful where a cyclic motion of the platform is desired, for example, in shakers used in labs, etc. Depending upon the motion profile of the platform, the individual displacements of the prismatic joint can be calculated

Fig. 15 Cam-controlled
delta

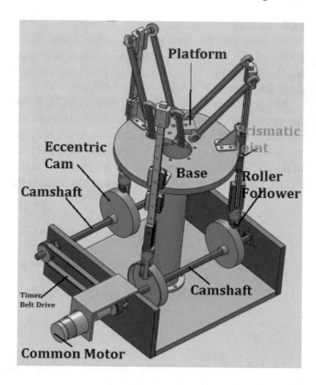

for one complete cycle and the cam profiles can be designed accordingly for each prismatic joint [6]. The advantage of this arrangement is that a simple motor (plain or geared motor) can operate the mechanism and the components like ball screws, multiple number of stepper or servo motors, drives, controllers, software, etc., are not needed, resulting in a simple and a low-cost solution. However, if there are frequent changes, changing the motion profile would mean changing the cam design, and fabricating the newly designed cams, which will be expensive.

3.1 6-PSS Manipulator Controlled by a Single Motor

In this type of manipulator, the prismatic axes, which are active axes, are stationary. Similar to the earlier concept shown in Fig. 15, each prismatic joint is driven by a separate cam, and the cam profile can be different for each prismatic joint. All these cam shafts are connected together by a linkage mechanism and hence they can be driven by a single actuator [7]. The schematic of the single actuator driven manipulator [8, 9] is shown in Fig. 16 and the actual prototype is shown in Fig. 17.

Fig. 16 Single-shaft control for six PSS manipulator

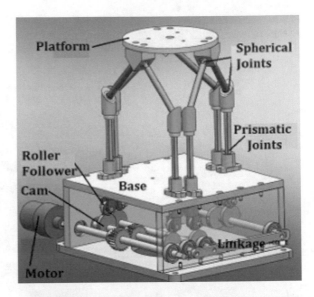

Fig. 17 Prototype of single-shaft control for six PSS manipulator

Fig. 18 Sun tracking for a
solar panel

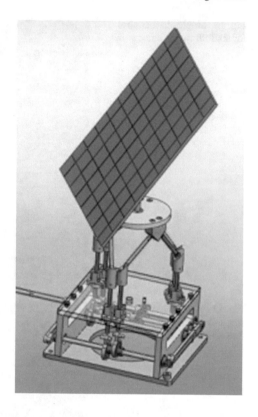

Some suggested applications of Single Actuator—6 PSS Manipulator are shown
in the Figs. 18, 19 and 20.

4   Conclusions

The synthesis of St-Ac axes-type-based parallel mechanism show advantages in
kinematic construction of mechanical master–slave manipulators. The manipulator
syntheses of the practically useful master–slave arrangement are shown. A multi-
component repeatable cyclic trajectory at the platform is generated using the simple
cam and the leg follower or mechanism drive system. The design of a single actuator
shaker to operate in six-dimensional space based on 6-PSS joint configuration has
been described. The idea of using a single actuator driven manipulator to perform
repeatable trajectories and serving stationary points is presented. The advantage of
stationary-active axes in 6-PSS mechanisms in serving various applications has been
demonstrated.

Fig. 19 Motion cycle
having fixed station points

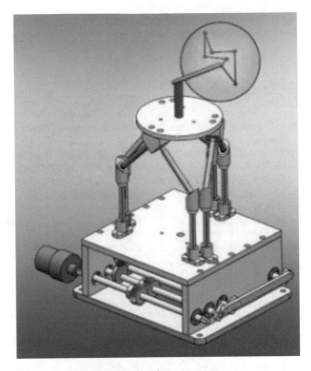

Fig. 20 Shaker for
biological labs

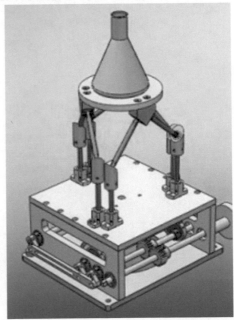

Acknowledgements The co-authors condole the sad demise of the first author K. D. Lagoo and greatly acknowledge his contribution in nurturing the present work to the application stage.

References

1. V.E. Gough, Contribution to discussion to papers on research in automobile stability and control and in tyre performance. Proc. Auto. Div. Inst. Mech. Eng. 392–394 (1956–1957)
2. D. Stewart, A platform with six degrees of freedom. Proc. Inst. Mech. Eng. **180**, 371–378 (1965)
3. Z. Du, R. Shi, W. Dong, Kinematics modeling of a 6-PSS parallel mechanism with wide-range flexure hinges. J. Cent. South Univ. **19**(9), 2482–2487 (2012)
4. K. Jayarajan, Remote handling technology in nuclear industry. Mod. Manuf. India **1**(3), 22–25 (2013)
5. Advanced Master Slave Manipulators, http://barc.gov.in/technologies/msm/msm.html. Accessed 10 Nov 2017
6. T.A. Dwarakanath, G. Bhutani, Beam type hexapod structure based six component force-torque sensor. Mechatronics **21**(8), 1279–1287 (2011)
7. H.A. Rothbart, *Cam Design Handbook: Dynamics and Accuracy* (McGraw-Hill Professional, 2003)
8. K.D. Lagoo, T.A. Dwarakanath, D.N. Badodkar, Single actuator shaker design to generate infinite spatial signatures, in *2nd International and 17th National Conference on Machines and Mechanisms iNaCoMM2015* (2015)
9. T.A. Dwarakanath, K.D. Lagoo, D.N. Badodkar, 6-PSS based parallel manipulators, in *New Advances in Mechanisms, Mechanical Transmissions and Robotics. Mechanisms and Machine Science*, vol. 46, ed. by B. Corves, E.C. Lovasz, M. Hüsing, I. Maniu, C. Gruescu (Springer, 2017)

Direct Dynamics of a Space Robot Actuated by Control Moment Gyros

Yinghong Jia and Arun K. Misra

Abstract This paper presents a direct formulation of dynamical equations for a space robot actuated by control moment gyros (CMGs). The space robot consists of a service satellite and a robotic manipulator comprising an arbitrary number of rigid links connected by spherical joints. A cluster of CMGs is mounted on the base and on each link. The static and dynamic imbalances of the gimbals and the rotors are both considered. Dynamical equations for the robotic system level are derived using Kane's equations. The nominal output torques of the CMGs and the disturbance torques caused by the imbalances are separated, with each having explicit expressions. A feedback controller based on the nominal model is also proposed for system trajectory tracking control. Simulation comparisons based on different imbalance parameters show that the controller works, but the imbalances may cause both high-frequency and low-frequency disturbance torques, which may distinctly decrease system-control accuracy.

Keywords Dynamics · Space robot · Control moment gyros · Dynamic imbalance · Static imbalance

1 Introduction

In recent years, a new concept has been proposed to actuate manipulator links; that is to employ control moment gyros (CMGs) as reactionless actuators for space robots [1]. The CMG actuation has several advantages over traditional joint motor actuation; for example, reduction of peak attitude control torque [2], improvement of system-level pointing performance [2, 3], and power saving for high-agility maneuvers [1, 4].

Y. Jia
School of Astronautics, Beihang University, Beijing 100191, China
e-mail: jia_yingh@163.com

A. K. Misra (✉)
Mechanical Engineering Department, McGill University, Montreal, QC H3A 0C3, Canada
e-mail: arun.misra@mcgill.ca

© Springer Nature Singapore Pte Ltd. 2019
D N Badodkar and T A Dwarakanath (eds.), *Machines, Mechanism and Robotics*, Lecture Notes in Mechanical Engineering,
https://doi.org/10.1007/978-981-10-8597-0_11

Another advantage is that spherical joints can be employed to replace the traditional revolute joints since the joints are free, which means more degrees of freedom (DOFs) of the manipulator end effector can be obtained by using fewer joints [5, 6].

To promote the technological development of CMG actuation, several studies have been conducted on the dynamics of the CMG-actuated space robotic systems. Carpenter and Peck [7, 8] investigated the dynamics of a multibody system comprising an arbitrary number of bodies with each actuated by a scissored pair of CMGs. Jia et al. [5, 6] developed the dynamical equations for a CMG-actuated space robotic system allowing generic CMG configurations and a movable base. Hu et al. [9] proposed a recursive formulation of dynamical equations for flexible multibody systems with variable speed control moment gyroscopes (VSCMGs). The CMG rotor usually spins at high speed to generate large angular momentum, and the imbalances of such a high-speed rotating rotor can produce notable disturbances [10]. Therefore, it is necessary to consider CMG imbalances when deriving the dynamical equations. However, none of the aforementioned studies concerning system dynamical modeling have taken CMG imbalances into account.

There are two primary motivations for this research work. One is to develop accurate dynamical equations for a CMG-actuated space robotic system with full consideration of the static and dynamic imbalances of the CMGs. The other motivation is to provide a model for system controller design. For this purpose, the dynamical model is separated into two parts: the nominal part without CMG imbalances and the uncertain part stemming from CMG imbalances, with each part having explicit expressions. The system controller can be designed based on the nominal model with/without consideration of the uncertainty, and the uncertainty expressions can be used to analyze the characteristics of the uncertainty, such as upper bound and frequency, so as to facilitate controller design.

2 System Description and Reference Frames

Consider a space robotic system consisting of a rigid base (B_0) and a manipulator arm comprising N rigid links ($B_1, B_2, ..., B_N$), as shown in Fig. 1. The $N+1$ composite bodies are connected by N spherical joints denoted by $o_1, o_2, ..., o_N$, respectively. A cluster of CMGs is mounted on each composite body to actuate the system. The total number of the CMGs mounted on B_i is denoted by n_i ($i = 0, 1, ..., N$). Each CMG is viewed as a multibody system consists of a gimbal and a rotor. $B_{i.gj}$, $B_{i.rj}$ and $B_{i.cj}$ are used to denote the jth gimbal, the jth rotor and the whole jth CMG mounted on B_i, respectively ($i = 0, 1, ..., N, j = 1, 2, ..., n_i$). For each CMG, it is reasonably assumed that the gimbal axis is perpendicular to the rotor spin axis, and the two axis lines intersect at one point. For $B_{i.cj}$, the intersection point is denoted by $o_{i.cj}$.

To describe the motion of the system, some reference frames are introduced as follows: $\mathcal{F}_I(o_I - \bar{x}_I \bar{y}_I \bar{z}_I)$ is the inertial reference frame located at an arbitrary point o_I in the inertial space, and whose constituent unit vectors are $\bar{x}_I$, $\bar{y}_I$ and $\bar{z}_I$. $\mathcal{F}_i(o_i - \bar{x}_i \bar{y}_i \bar{z}_i)$ is the body-fixed reference frame of B_i ($i = 0, 1, ..., N$). $\mathcal{F}_0$ is located at

Fig. 1 Space robot with
CMGs

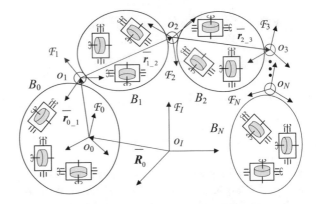

Fig. 2 Illustration of B_i with
the jth CMG

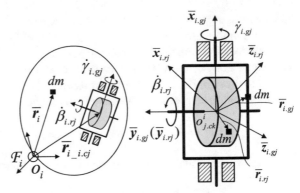

an arbitrary point o_0 on B_0, while $\mathcal{F}_i$ is located at point o_i ($i = 1, 2, ..., N$). For
each CMG, both the gimbal-fixed reference frame $\mathcal{F}_{i.gj}(o_{i.cj} - \bar{x}_{i.gj}\bar{y}_{i.gj}\bar{z}_{i.gj})$ and
the rotor-fixed reference frame $\mathcal{F}_{i.rj}(o_{i.cj} - \bar{x}_{i.rj}\bar{y}_{i.rj}\bar{z}_{i.rj})$ are located at $o_{i.cj}$. $\bar{x}_{i.gj}$ and
$\bar{y}_{i.rj}$ are along the directions of the gimbal rate and the rotor angular momentum,
respectively. Moreover, $\bar{y}_{i.gj}$ is in the same direction with $\bar{y}_{i.rj}$ (Fig. 2).

3   Dynamical Equations in General Form

We use $f_* = [\bar{x}_*, \bar{y}_*, \bar{z}_*]^T$ to denote the vectrix of an arbitrary reference frame $\mathcal{F}_*$.
With the definition of f_*, an arbitrary three-dimensional vector $\bar{u}$ can be expressed
as $\bar{u} = f_*^T u$, where $u = [u_x, u_y, u_z]^T$ is the column component matrix of $\bar{u}$ in
$\mathcal{F}_*$. With the definition of the vectrix, the velocities of the element masses dm on B_i,
$B_{i.gj}$, and $B_{i.rj}$ ($i = 1, 2, ..., N$) can be given by

$$\bar{V}_i^{dm} = f_I^T \dot{R}_0 - \sum_{l=0}^{i-1} f_l^T \tilde{r}_{l\_l+1} \omega_l - f_i^T \tilde{r}_i \omega_i$$

$$\bar{V}_{i.gj}^{dm} = f_I^T \dot{R}_0 - \sum_{l=0}^{i-1} f_l^T \tilde{r}_{l\_l+1} \omega_l - f_i^T (\tilde{r}_{i\_i.cj} + A_{\mathcal{F}_{i.gj}}^{\mathcal{F}_i} \tilde{r}_{i.gj} A_{\mathcal{F}_i}^{\mathcal{F}_{i.gj}}) \omega_i - f_{i.gj}^T \tilde{r}_{i.gj} \Gamma_g \dot{\gamma}_{i.gj}$$

$$\bar{V}_{i.rj}^{dm} = f_I^T \dot{R}_0 - \sum_{l=0}^{i-1} f_l^T \tilde{r}_{l\_l+1} \omega_l - f_i^T (\tilde{r}_{i\_i.cj} + A_{\mathcal{F}_{i.rj}}^{\mathcal{F}_i} \tilde{r}_{i.rj} A_{\mathcal{F}_i}^{\mathcal{F}_{i.rj}}) \omega_i$$

$$- f_{i.gj}^T A_{\mathcal{F}_{i.rj}}^{\mathcal{F}_{i.gj}} \tilde{r}_{i.rj} A_{\mathcal{F}_{i.gj}}^{\mathcal{F}_{i.rj}} \Gamma_g \dot{\gamma}_{i.gj} - f_{i.rj}^T \tilde{r}_{i.rj} \Gamma_r \dot{\beta}_{i.rj} \qquad (1)$$

where R_0 is the position of o_0 in $\mathcal{F}_I$; r_{i_i+1} and $r_{i\_i.cj}$ are the positions of o_{i+1} and $o_{i.cj}$ in $\mathcal{F}_i$, respectively; $r_\star$ is the position of the element mass dm on $B_\star$ in $\mathcal{F}_\star$ ($\star$ is i, $i.gj$ or $i.rj$); ω_i is the angular velocity of $\mathcal{F}_i$; $\gamma_{i.gj}$ and $\beta_{i.rj}$ are the gimbal angle and the rotor angle of the jth CMG on B_i, respectively; $A_{\mathcal{F}_\#}^{\mathcal{F}_*}$ represents the rotational transformation matrix from $\mathcal{F}_\#$ to $\mathcal{F}_*$; the symbol "~" signifies the cross-product matrix associated with the 3×1 column matrix; $\Gamma_g = [1, 0, 0]^T$; $\Gamma_r = [0, 1, 0]^T$. The expressions of the velocities of the element masses on B_0, $B_{0.gj}$, and $B_{0.rj}$ are similar to those in Eq. (1) and are not presented here.

The generalized speeds of the system are defined as follows:

$$u_1 = \dot{R}_0, \quad u_2 = \omega_0, \quad u_3 = \omega_1, \quad \dots, \quad u_{N+2} = \omega_N \qquad (2)$$

Kane's dynamical equations for the system can be written as

$$F_{I,l} + F_{A,l} = 0, \quad (l = 1, 2, \dots, N+2) \qquad (3)$$

where $F_{I,l}$ and $F_{A,l}$ are the lth generalized inertia force and the lth generalized active force, respectively. The lth generalized inertia force $F_{I,l}$ can be evaluated as

$$F_{I,l} = \sum_{i=0}^{N} \int_{B_i} \frac{\partial \bar{V}_i^{dm}}{\partial u_l} \cdot \frac{d\bar{V}_i^{dm}}{dt} dm + \sum_{i=0}^{N} \sum_{j=1}^{n_i} \int_{B_{i.gj}} \frac{\partial \bar{V}_{i.gj}^{dm}}{\partial u_l} \cdot \frac{d\bar{V}_{i.gj}^{dm}}{dt} dm$$

$$+ \sum_{i=0}^{N} \sum_{j=1}^{n_i} \int_{B_{i.rj}} \frac{\partial \bar{V}_{i.rj}^{dm}}{\partial u_l} \cdot \frac{d\bar{V}_{i.rj}^{dm}}{dt} dm, \quad (l = 1, 2, \dots, N+2) \qquad (4)$$

Substituting the velocity expressions into Eq. (4) and collecting terms, the dynamical equations of the robotic system can be obtained through Eq. (3):

$$M\dot{u} + Q_{nl} = F_{cmg} + F_A \qquad (5)$$

where $u = [\dot{R}_0^T, \omega_0^T, \omega_1^T, \dots, \omega_N^T]^T$ is the generalized speed vector; M is the symmetric mass matrix; Q_{nl} is the inertia force nonlinear in the generalized speeds; F_{cmg} is the force generated by the CMGs; F_A is the generalized active force.

4 Output Force of the CMGs

For each body $B_\star$ ($\star$ is i, $i.gj$ or $i.rj$) in the system, the basic inertia parameters are defined as follows: $m_\star$ is the mass of $B_\star$; $S_\star = \int_{B_\star} r_\star dm$ and $I_\star = \int_{B_\star} \tilde{r}_\star^T \tilde{r}_\star dm$ are the first inertia moment and the inertia matrix of $B_\star$, respectively. In the nominal case, the centroids of the gimbal and the rotor are both located at the intersection point $o_{i.cj}$; moreover, the body-fixed frames, $\mathcal{F}_{i.gj}$ and $\mathcal{F}_{i.rj}$, are the inertial principal axis frames of the gimbal and the rotor, respectively. As a result, the nominal first inertia moments of the gimbal, the rotor and the whole CMG are all zero, and the corresponding nominal inertia matrices have diagonal matrix form, i.e.,

$$\hat{S}_{i.*j} = \mathbf{0}, \quad \hat{I}_{i.*j} = diag(\hat{I}_{i.*jx}, \hat{I}_{i.*jy}, \hat{I}_{i.*jz}), \quad (* = g, r, c) \tag{6}$$

Due to installation and machining errors, Eq. (6) may not hold in the actual case. We denote $\mathcal{F}'_{i.gj}(o'_{i.gj} - \bar{x}'_{i.gj}\bar{y}'_{i.gj}\bar{z}'_{i.gj})$ and $\mathcal{F}'_{i.rj}(o'_{i.rj} - \bar{x}'_{i.rj}\bar{y}'_{i.rj}\bar{z}'_{i.rj})$ as the inertial principal axis frames of the gimbal $B_{i.gj}$ and the rotor $B_{i.rj}$, respectively. In the actual case, the centroids, $o'_{i.gj}$ and $o'_{i.rj}$, may have small deviations from $o_{i.cj}$; moreover, the unit vectors of $\mathcal{F}'_{i.gj}/\mathcal{F}_{i.rj}$ may not be coincident with those of $\mathcal{F}'_{i.gj}/\mathcal{F}'_{i.rj}$. The centroid deviations, denoted by $\rho_{i.gj}$ and $\rho_{i.rj}$, are referred to as the static imbalances of the gimbal $B_{i.gj}$ and the rotor $B_{i.rj}$, respectively; the rotational transformation matrices, $A_{\mathcal{F}_{i.gj}}^{\mathcal{F}'_{i.gj}}$ and $A_{\mathcal{F}_{i.rj}}^{\mathcal{F}'_{i.rj}}$, are defined as the dynamic imbalances of the gimbal $B_{i.gj}$ and the rotor $B_{i.rj}$, respectively. We denote $\Delta S_{i.*j} = S_{i.*j} - \hat{S}_{i.*j}$, and $\Delta I_{i.*j} = I_{i.*j} - \hat{I}_{i.*j}$ ($* = g, r, c$). It is clear that $\Delta S_{i.*j}$ and $\Delta I_{i.*j}$ represent the uncertain deviations of the first inertia moments and the inertia matrices stemming from the imbalances. A simple analysis shows that $\Delta I_{i.gj}$ can be characterized by three small Euler angles between $\mathcal{F}'_{i.gj}$ and $\mathcal{F}_{i.gj}$, denoted by $\varphi_{i.gj}$, $\theta_{i.gj}$ and $\psi_{i.gj}$; while $\Delta I_{i.rj}$ can be characterized by only two small Euler angles between $\mathcal{F}'_{i.rj}$ and $\mathcal{F}'_{i.rj}$, denoted by $\varphi_{i.rj}$ and $\psi_{i.rj}$.

With the definition of the imbalances, the output force of the CMGs in Eq. (5) can be written as

$$F_{cmg} = [(\Delta F_{cmg0}^{sta})^T, T_{cmg0}^T, T_{cmg1}^T, \ldots, T_{cmgN}^T]^T \tag{7}$$

where ΔF_{cmg0}^{sta} is the disturbance force of the CMGs acting on the base caused by the static imbalances; T_{cmgi} is the torque of the CMGs acting on B_i, which can be divided into several parts as

$$T_{cmgi} = T_{cmgi}^{nom} + \Delta T_{cmgi}^{sta.s} + \Delta T_{cmgi}^{sta.out} + \Delta T_{cmgi}^{dyn}, (i = 0, 1, \ldots, N) \tag{8}$$

where T_{cmgi}^{nom} is the nominal output torque of the CMGs acting on B_i; ΔT_{cmgi}^{dyn}, $\Delta T_{cmgi}^{sta.s}$ and $\Delta T_{cmgi}^{sta.out}$ are the disturbance torques acting on B_i stemming from the dynamic imbalances of the CMGs, the static imbalances of the CMGs on B_i, and the static imbalances of the CMGs on the outboard bodies of B_i, respectively. The expressions of T_{cmgi}^{nom}, ΔF_{cmg0}^{sta}, ΔT_{cmgi}^{dyn}, $\Delta T_{cmgi}^{sta.s}$, and $\Delta T_{cmgi}^{sta.out}$ are given by

$$T_{cmgi}^{nom} = -A_{gi}\hat{I}_{i.cx}\ddot{\gamma}_i - \left(\hat{C}_{gli}(\omega_i) + A_{ti}\hat{I}_{i.ry}d[\dot{\beta}_i]\right)\dot{\gamma}_i - \tilde{\omega}_i A_{ri}\hat{I}_{i.ry}\dot{\beta}_i$$

$$\Delta F_{cmg0}^{sta} = A_{\mathcal{F}_0}^{\mathcal{F}_I}\sum_{i=0}^{N}\left[\Delta P_{gi}\ddot{\gamma}_i + \Delta D_{gi}\dot{\gamma}_i^2 + \Delta D_{ri}\dot{\beta}_i^2 + \left(\Delta G_{gi}(\omega_i) + \Delta D_{gri}d[\dot{\beta}_i]\right)\dot{\gamma}_i + \Delta G_{ri}(\omega_i)\dot{\beta}_i\right]$$

$$\Delta T_{cmgi}^{dyn} = -\Delta B_{gli}\ddot{\gamma}_i - \Delta R_{gli}\dot{\gamma}_i^2 - \Delta R_{rli}\dot{\beta}_i^2 - \left(\Delta C_{gli}(\omega_i) + \Delta R_{grli}d[\dot{\beta}_i]\right)\dot{\gamma}_i - \Delta C_{rli}(\omega_i)\dot{\beta}_i$$

$$\Delta T_{cmgi}^{sta.s} = -\Delta B_{gsi}\ddot{\gamma}_i - \Delta R_{gsi}\dot{\gamma}_i^2 - \Delta R_{rsi}\dot{\beta}_i^2 - \left(\Delta C_{gsi}(\omega_i) + \Delta R_{grsi}d[\dot{\beta}_i]\right)\dot{\gamma}_i - \Delta C_{rsi}(\omega_i)\dot{\beta}_i$$

$$T_{cmgi}^{sta.out}\begin{cases} \tilde{r}_{i\_i+1}A_{F_0}^{F_i}\sum_{l=i+1}^{N}[\Delta P_{gl}\ddot{\gamma}_l + \Delta D_{gl}\dot{\gamma}_l^2 + \Delta D_{rl}\dot{\beta}_l^2 + (\Delta G_{gl}(\omega_l) + \Delta D_{grl}d[\dot{\beta}_l])\dot{\gamma}_l \\ +\Delta G_{rl}(\omega_l)\dot{\beta}_l], & i = 0, 1, \ldots, N-1 \\ \mathbf{0}, & i = N \end{cases} \tag{9}$$

therein, $\hat{I}_{i.ry} = diag\,\hat{I}_{i.r1y}$, $\hat{I}_{i.r2y}$, $\ldots \hat{I}_{i.rn_iy}$, $\hat{I}_{i.cx} = diag(\hat{I}_{i.c1x}, \hat{I}_{i.c2x}, \ldots, \hat{I}_{i.cn_ix})$; $\gamma_i = [\gamma_{i.g1}, \gamma_{i.g2}, \ldots, \gamma_{i.gn_i}]^T$, $\dot{\gamma}_i^2 = [\dot{\gamma}_{i.g1}^2, \dot{\gamma}_{i.g2}^2, \ldots, \dot{\gamma}_{i.gn_i}^2]^T$; $\beta_i = [\beta_{i.r1}, \beta_{i.r2}, \ldots, \beta_{i.rn_i}]^T$, $\dot{\beta}_i^2 = [\dot{\beta}_{i.r1}^2, \dot{\beta}_{i.r2}^2, \ldots, \dot{\beta}_{i.rn_i}^2]^T$; $d[x]$ is an operator which returns the square matrix with the elements of the column matrix x on the main diagonal; A_{gi}, A_{ri}, and A_{ti} are $3 \times n_i$ matrices, whose columns are the unit column vectors along the directions of the gimbal axis, rotor momentum, and transverse axes of the jth CMG on B_i, respectively; $\hat{C}_{gli}(\omega_i)$ is a coefficient matrix associated with ω_i; ΔP_*, ΔD_*, ΔG_*, ΔC_*, ΔR_* and ΔB_* are coefficient matrices associated with the CMG imbalances.

5 Controller Design Example

System controller design is based on the following model derived from the system dynamical equation:

$$\hat{M}\ddot{u} + \hat{Q}_{nl} + \hat{Q}_{inr} = F_c + \Delta F \tag{10}$$

where $\hat{M}$ and $\hat{Q}_{nl}$ are the nominal parts of M and Q_{nl}, respectively; $\hat{Q}_{inr} = [\mathbf{0}^T, (\tilde{\omega}_0 A_{r0}\hat{I}_{0.ry}\dot{\beta}_0)^T, (\tilde{\omega}_1 A_{r1}\hat{I}_{1.ry}\dot{\beta}_1)^T, \ldots, (\tilde{\omega}_N A_{rN}\hat{I}_{N.ry}\dot{\beta}_N)^T]^T$ is the nominal interaction force; ΔF is the "lumped" system uncertainty containing the disturbance force stemming from the imbalances and the active disturbance forces; $F_c = [F_{o_0}^T, (T_{cmg0}^c)^T, (T_{cmg1}^c)^T, \ldots, (T_{cmgN}^c)^T]^T$ is the control force, where F_{o_0} is the translational control force acting on B_0 whose line of action passes through o_0, and

$$T_{cmgi}^c = -A_{gi}\hat{I}_{i.cx}\ddot{\gamma}_i - \left(\hat{C}_{gIi}(\omega_i) + A_{ti}\hat{I}_{i.ry}d[\dot{\beta}_i]\right)\dot{\gamma}_i, (i = 0, 1, \ldots, N) \quad (11)$$

is the nominal control torque of the CMGs on B_i.

The control objective is to make the manipulation variable $\Psi = [R_0^T, \sigma_0^T, R_E^T, \sigma_E^T]^T$ to track the desired trajectory Ψ_d, where R_E is the position of the reference point on the end effector (the tip link) in $\mathcal{F}_I$; σ_0 and σ_E represent the attitudes of B_0 and the end effector, respectively, both defined as the Rodrigues parameters (MRPs) with respect to $\mathcal{F}_I$. Since development of robust control algorithms is not the focus of this study, a feedback controller is proposed based on Eq. (10) by neglecting the lumped system uncertainty ΔF:

$$F_c = \hat{M}[-K_u(u - u_d) + \dot{u}_d] + \hat{Q}_{nl} + \hat{Q}_{inr} \quad (12)$$

where K_u is a positive-definite matrix; $u_d = J^+[\dot{\Psi}_d - \Lambda(\Psi - \Psi_d)]$ is the desired trajectory of the generalized speed u, in which Λ is a positive definite matrix, J is the Jacobian matrix satisfying $\dot{\Psi} = Ju$, and $J^+ = J^T(JJ^T)^{-1}$. It can be verified that $\Psi \to \Psi_d$ and $\dot{\Psi} \to \dot{\Psi}_d$ under the control law (12) if the lumped system uncertainty ΔF is neglected.

Once F_c is determined by Eq. (12), the control torque $T_{cmgi}^c (i = 0, 1, \ldots, N)$ can be obtained. To provide the desired control torque T_{cmgi}^c, and avoid CMG configuration singularities simultaneously, the following steering law with gimbal null motion is adopted assuming that $n_i \geq 4 (i = 0, 1, \ldots, N)$:

$$\dot{\gamma}_i = -\frac{1}{h_i}A_{ti}^T(A_{ti}A_{ti}^T)^{-1}T_{cmgi}^c + \varepsilon_i[E_{n_i} - A_{ti}^T(A_{ti}A_{ti}^T)^{-1}A_{ti}]\frac{\partial \xi_i}{\partial \gamma_i}, (i = 0, 1, \ldots, N)$$
$$(13)$$

where ε_i is a positive scalar parameter; $\xi_i = det(A_{ti}A_{ti}^T)$ is the measurement of CMG configuration singularity for the CMGs on B_i; h_i is the nominal rotor angular momentum of the CMGs on B_i, i.e., $\hat{I}_{i.r1y}\dot{\beta}_{i.r1} = \hat{I}_{i.r2y}\dot{\beta}_{i.r2} = \cdots = \hat{I}_{i.rn_iy}\dot{\beta}_{i.rn_i} = h_i$.

6 Simulation and Analysis

In most cases, two simulation comparisons are of particular interest. One is the comparison between the nominal output torque and the real output torque considering the imbalances of the CMGs, while the other is that between the control accuracies with and without consideration of the imbalances. In this section, simulation results are presented for the above two comparisons.

The robotic system and the CMG configuration used in the simulation are shown by Figs. 3 and 4, respectively. The space robotic system containing a cube-shaped base and a three-link arm. The reference point of the end effector is selected as the

Fig. 3 Illustration of the
robotic system

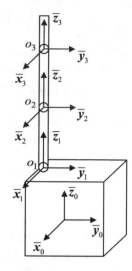

Fig. 4 CMGs in pyramid
configuration

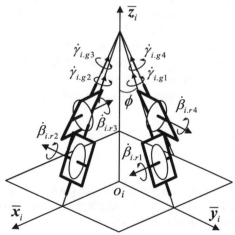

tip of B_3. A cluster of CMGs arranged in the pyramid configuration with the skew
angle of $\phi = 53.1°$ is installed on the base and each link to actuate the system.

6.1 CMG Torque Comparison

In this section, we assume that the CMG cluster is mounted on a stationary platform. The four CMGs have the identical rotor angular momentum of $h_i = 18.85$
N.m.s. The CMGs also have the identical static imbalance parameters of $\rho_{i.gj} =$
$[5, 5, 5]^T \times 10^{-6}$ m, and $\rho_{i.rj} = [3, 3, 3]^T \times 10^{-6}$ m, as well as the identical

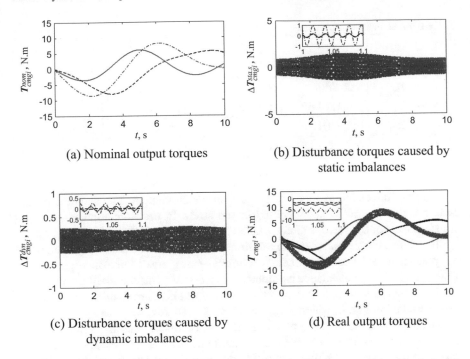

(a) Nominal output torques

(b) Disturbance torques caused by static imbalances

(c) Disturbance torques caused by dynamic imbalances

(d) Real output torques

Fig. 5 Output torques of the CMGs (solid line: torque about $\bar{x}_i$; dash line: torque about $\bar{y}_i$; dash–dot line: torque about $\bar{z}_i$)

dynamic imbalance parameters of $[\varphi_{i.gj}, \theta_{i.gj}, \psi_{i.gj}]^T = [3, 3, 3]^T \times 10^{-5}$ rad and $[\varphi_{i.rj}, \psi_{i.rj}]^T = [2, 2]^T \times 10^{-5}$ rad. The gimbal angular velocities are chosen as $\dot{\gamma}_{i.gj} = a_{i.gj} \sin(b_{i.gj}t)$, where $a_{i.g1} = 30$ °/s, $a_{i.g2} = 25$ °/s, $a_{i.g3} = 15$ °/s, and $a_{i.g4} = 10$ °/s; $b_{i.g1} = b_{i.g3} = 0.1\pi$ rad/s, and $b_{i.g2} = b_{i.g4} = 0.15\pi$ rad/s.

Figure 5 presents the output torques of the CMGs. The disturbance torques, including those caused by the static imbalances and the dynamic imbalances, have hybrid frequency characteristics. Further investigation shows that the high-frequency characteristics stem from the high spin rates of the rotors, while the low-frequency characteristics are mainly caused by the gimbal angular velocities.

6.2 Control Accuracy Comparison

In this section, simulations are carried out for the closed-loop system constructed by the control law and the steering law proposed in Sect. 5. The control objective is identical to that in 6. The control parameters are chosen as $\Lambda = 0.5E_{12}$, $K_u = 0.5E_{15}$, and $\varepsilon_i = 0.5$ ($i = 0, 1, 2, 3$). Since the main objective of this simulation is to investigate the effect of the imbalances on the control accuracy, the active

Table 1 Small imbalance parameters of the CMGs

	$\rho_{i.gj}$, 10^{-5} m	$\rho_{i.rj}$, 10^{-5} m	$[\varphi_{i.gj},\ \theta_{i.gj},\ \psi_{i.gj}]^T$, 10^{-4} rad	$[\varphi_{i.rj},\ \psi_{i.rj}]^T$, 10^{-4} rad
CMGs on B_0	$[2, 2, 2]^T$	$[1.5, 1.5, 1.5]^T$	$[1.5, 1.5, 1.5]^T$	$[1.2, 1.2]^T$
CMGs on B_1	$[1.6, 1.6, 1.6]^T$	$[1.2, 1.2, 1.2]^T$	$[1.2, 1.2, 1.2]^T$	$[1, 1]^T$
CMGs on B_2	$[1.2, 1.2, 1.2]^T$	$[1, 1, 1]^T$	$[0.8, 0.8, 0.8]^T$	$[0.6, 0.6]^T$
CMGs on B_3	$[1.2, 1.2, 1.2]^T$	$[1, 1, 1]^T$	$[0.8, 0.8, 0.8]^T$	$[0.6, 0.6]^T$

disturbance forces are assumed to be zero in the simulation. The actuator for the base position control is not specified in the study. In the simulation, the desired translational control force is directly taken as the actual translational control force.

To achieve clear comparison conclusions, three sets of imbalance parameters are adopted: zero imbalance parameters (nominal case), small imbalance parameters (Table 1), and large imbalance parameters (twice as large as the small parameters).

The position tracking errors and the velocity tracking errors of the end effector are presented in Fig. 6, where $\Delta R_E = \|\Delta R_E\|_2$ and $\Delta\sigma_E = \|\Delta\sigma_E\|_2$. The CMG imbalances decrease both the position tracking accuracies and the velocity tracking accuracies, while the effects on the velocity tracking accuracies are greater than those on the position tracking accuracies due to the high-frequency characteristics of the disturbance torques. The larger the imbalances, the greater the effects. The adverse impacts are embodied in high-frequency chattering around the nominal control responses. It should be noticed that the chattering cannot be suppressed by system controller due to the bandwidth limit, and therefore the feasible method for reducing the chattering is to reduce the imbalance parameters by improving installation and machining accuracies, or employ vibration isolation platforms for the CMG clusters as proposed in [11].

7 Conclusions

A direct formulation of dynamical equations for a space robot actuated by CMGs is proposed using Kane's equations with full consideration of the static and dynamic imbalances of the CMGs. The formulation allows an arbitrary number of manipulator links and generic CMG configurations. To facilitate system analysis and controller design, the dynamical model is also separated into two parts: the nominal part and the uncertain part. A feedback control law based on the nominal dynamical model is proposed to accomplish trajectory tracking control. Simulation results show that the disturbance torques stemming from the imbalances have both high-frequency and low-frequency characteristics, and that the disturbance torques may decrease system tracking control accuracies, especially the velocity tracking accuracies.

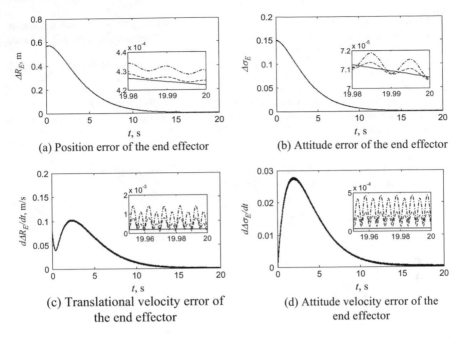

(a) Position error of the end effector

(b) Attitude error of the end effector

(c) Translational velocity error of the end effector

(d) Attitude velocity error of the end effector

Fig. 6 Control errors of the end effector (solid line: result with zero imbalance parameters; dash line: result with small imbalance parameters; dash–dot line: result with large imbalance parameters)

Acknowledgements This work was supported by the National Natural Science Foundation of China (11272027).

References

1. M.A. Peck, M.A. Paluszek, S.J. Thomas, J.B. Mueller, Control-moment gyroscopes for joint actuation: a new paradigm in space robotics, in *Proceedings of the 1st Space Exploration Conference: Continuing the Voyage of Discovery*, Orlando, FL, USA, 30 Jan–1 Feb 2005 (AIAA 2005-2522)
2. D. Brown, Control moment gyros as space-robotics actuators, in *AIAA Guidance, Navigation and Control Conference and Exhibit*, Honolulu, HI, USA, 18 Aug–21 Aug 2008 (AIAA 2008-7271)
3. D. Brown, M.A. Peck, Energetics of control moment gyroscopes as joint actuators. J. Guid. Control Dyn. **32**(6), 1871–1883 (2009)
4. M.A. Peck, Low-power, high-agility space robotics, in *AIAA Guidance, Navigation and Control Conference and Exhibit*, San Francisco, CA, USA, 15 Aug–18 Aug 2005 (AIAA 2005-6243)
5. Y. Jia, S. Xu, Decentralized adaptive sliding mode control of a space robot actuated by control moment gyroscopes. Chin. J. Aeronaut. **29**(3), 688–703 (2016)
6. Y. Jia, A.K. Misra, Robust trajectory tracking control of a dual-arm space robot actuated by control moment gyroscopes. Acta Astronaut. **137**, 287–301 (2017)

7. M.D. Carpenter, M.A. Peck, Minimum-power robotic maneuvering using control-moment gyroscopes, in *AIAA Guidance, Navigation and Control Conference and Exhibit*, Hilton Head, SC, USA, 20 Aug–23 Aug 2007 (AIAA 2007-6324)
8. M.D. Carpenter, M.A. Peck, Dynamics of a high-agility, low-power imaging payload. IEEE Trans. Rob. **24**(3), 666–675 (2008)
9. Q. Hu, Y. Jia, S. Xu, Recursive dynamics algorithm for multibody systems with variable-speed control moment gyroscopes. J. Guid. Control Dyn. **36**(5), 1388–1398 (2013)
10. R.A. Masterson, D.W. Miller, R.L. Grogan, Development of empirical and analytical reaction wheel disturbance models, in *40th AIAA/ASCE/AHS/ASC Structures, Structural Dynamics and Materials Conference and Exhibit*, St. Louis, Missouri, USA, 12 April–15 April 1999 (AIAA 99-1204)
11. Y. Zhang, J. Zhang, S. Xu, Parameters design of vibration isolation platform for control moment gyroscopes. Acta Astronaut. **81**, 645–659 (2012)

A Two-Degree-of-Freedom RSSR-SSR Manipulator for Sun-Tracking

Vimalesh Muralidharan and Sandipan Bandyopadhyay

Abstract A two-degree-of-freedom RSSR-SSR manipulator is proposed for the sun-tracking application. A detailed study of its forward and inverse kinematic problems is presented. It is illustrated through an example that the requisite range of motion can be achieved for exact tracking at the chosen location without encountering singularities or violating the limits of commercially available spherical joints. Static analysis is also performed to show that the load is significantly distributed among the two limbs, thereby reducing the strength requirement on the foundations at base pivots.

Keywords Sun-tracking mechanism · Tip-tilt platform · Parallel manipulator

1 Introduction

Solar trackers are classified into three types based on the number of actuators used, namely, static (i.e., stationary panels), one-axis, and dual-axis trackers [1]. It is shown in [2], that the additional cost incurred in tracking with two actuators as opposed to a static panel can be recovered in 450 days, thereby justifying the use of trackers over static ones.

The existing dual-axis trackers are typically serial in their architecture, with tip-tilt or pan-tilt motions [3], mounted on a *heavy* central pole to withstand the wind load and self-weight of the panel [4]. Additionally, the tracking error is more pronounced in the platforms of serial architecture since the error in each of the actuators is cumulatively reflected on the end-effector. These limitations are overcome through the use of parallel manipulators, where the load is distributed among the limbs connecting the

V. Muralidharan · S. Bandyopadhyay (✉)
Department of Engineering Design, Indian Institute of Technology Madras,
Chennai 600036, Tamil Nadu, India
e-mail: sandipan@iitm.ac.in

V. Muralidharan
e-mail: m.vimalesh94@gmail.com

© Springer Nature Singapore Pte Ltd. 2019
D N Badodkar and T A Dwarakanath (eds.), *Machines, Mechanism and Robotics*, Lecture Notes in Mechanical Engineering,
https://doi.org/10.1007/978-981-10-8597-0_12

moving platform to the ground and the tracking error is bounded above by the largest error in any of the limbs.

Recently, parallel manipulators have been considered for sun-tracking in [4–9]. Shyam and Ghosal [4] have shown that the 3-RPS architecture has a lighter support structure and better deflection characteristics compared to the serial pan-tilt platform under the same loading conditions. Pramanik and Ghosal [5] have proposed the 3-UPU wrist architecture as a low-energy sun-tracking solution, since the centre of mass remains stationary while tracking. However, both these solutions include an additional degree-of-freedom (DoF) which is redundant in this application. Parallel versions of two-DoF pan-tilt and tip-tilt mechanisms have been proposed in [6, pp. 15–17]. The pan-tilt arrangement suggested is not completely parallel in that the second actuator is not fixed on the ground, but carried around by the first. Hence, the drawbacks of serial architectures listed above apply to this design as well. The tip-tilt spherical manipulator presented in that work requires *eight* rotary joints, with all axes meeting at the centre of a sphere. Such design specifications make manufacturing accuracy and assembly critical to its functionality, thereby increasing the fabrication complexity and cost.

Cammarata [7] has proposed a two-DoF U-PUS manipulator for sun-tracking. A complete analysis on the requisite range of motion, intermediate joint forces, and vibration modes has been performed in this work. A similar architecture, U-PUS-PRS, was derived through Grassman geometry by Wu et al. [8] and its dynamics was discussed and compared with a serial counterpart. Both these topologies incorporate a heavy vertical pole supporting all the loads, like in the platforms of serial architecture. Quaglia and Maurino [9] have designed an interesting arrangement with two planar four-bars one on top of the other, that decouples the diurnal and seasonal motions completely. However, the design is quite complicated with additional support trusses and beams for the load carried by the mechanism. In view of the reported solutions to the sun-tracking problem and the respective issues pointed out, this work proposes a two-DoF parallel manipulator for the stated application that alleviates the aforementioned issues.

The rest of the paper is organized as follows: the architecture and kinematics of the proposed manipulator are presented in Sect. 2, followed by the sun-tracking application requirements in Sect. 3. Static analysis and their results are discussed in Sect. 4, followed by some practical considerations in Sect. 5. Finally, the paper is concluded in Sect. 6.

2   The RSSR-SSR Manipulator

The CAD model of the proposed RSSR-SSR manipulator is shown in Fig. 1. It consists of two R-S-S-R (R and S denote rotary and spherical joints, respectively) kinematic loops which are identified as b_1-p_1-p_2-b_2-b_1 and b_3-p_4-p_3-b_{12}-b_3, forming a planar and a spatial four-bar loop, respectively. The DoF of this manipulator, as per the Grüebler's formula (see, e.g., [10, pp. 69–71]) is *three*, distributed as one

Fig. 1 Schematic of the
R͟SS͟R-SS͟R manipulator with
the solar panel. The panel is
attached to the manipulator
at the vertices p_1, p_2 and p_3

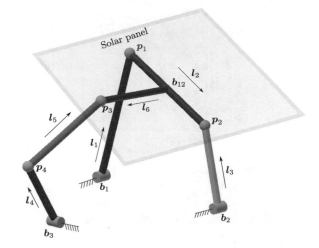

per loop, in addition to the unconstrained rotation of link l_5 (see Fig. 1) about its
own axis. This axial rotation does not contribute to relative motion between the links
and hence, for all practical purposes, the manipulator is considered to possess only
two DoF. The ternary link, in the form of a triangular platform $p_1 p_2 p_3$, acts as the
end-effector of this manipulator, whose roll and pitch motions are controlled by the
actuated rotary joints at the locations b_1 and b_3.

2.1 Loop-Closure Equations

The kinematics of the R͟SS͟R-SS͟R manipulator is depicted schematically in Fig. 2. The
actuated joint variables are given by $\boldsymbol{\theta} = [\theta_1, \theta_2]^\top$, while the passive joint variables,
which also form the *task-space* of this manipulator, are given by $\boldsymbol{\phi} = [\psi_1, \phi_2]^\top$.
The global frame of reference {0}, designated as o_0-$X_0 Y_0 Z_0$, is positioned at the
pivot point b_1, without any loss of generality. The base pivots and link vectors of
the planar four-bar loop, confined to $X_0 Z_0$ plane (see Fig. 2), are defined as[1]: $b_1 =$
$[0, 0, 0]^\top$, $b_2 = [b_{2x}, 0, b_{2z}]^\top$; and $l_1 = [l_1 \cos\theta_1, 0, l_1 \sin\theta_1]^\top$, $l_2 = [l_2 \cos\psi_1, 0,$
$l_2 \sin\psi_1]^\top$, respectively. The pivot locations and link vectors of the spatial four-bar
loop are given by: $b_3 = [b_{3x}, b_{3y}, b_{3z}]^\top$, $b_{12} = b_1 + l_1 + \rho l_2$; and $l_4 = {}_1^0 R [l_4 \cos\theta_2,$
$l_4 \sin\theta_2, 0]^\top$, $l_6 = {}_2^0 R [l_6 \cos\phi_2, l_6 \sin\phi_2, 0]^\top$, where ${}_1^0 R = R_Y(\pi/2) R_Z(\pi/2)$ and
${}_2^0 R = R_Y(\pi/2 - \psi_1) R_Z(-\pi/2)$ are rotation matrices[2] describing the orientation of
frames {1} and {2} w.r.t. frame {0}. The loop-closure equations of the planar and
spatial four-bar loops are formulated as, $\boldsymbol{\eta} = [\eta_1, \eta_2]^\top = [0, 0]^\top$, where

---

[1]For brevity, all vectors expressed in global frame of reference are typed without any leading
superscripts.
[2]The symbol $R_k(\beta)$ represents the rotation matrix corresponding to rotation about k-axis by an
angle β in the counterclockwise sense (see, e.g., [10, pp. 22–25]).

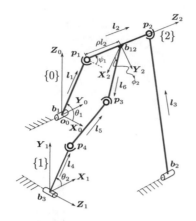

{0} - Global stationary frame
{1} - Local stationary frame
{2} - Local moving frame
$\rho \in [0, 1]$

Fig. 2 Kinematic diagram of the R̲S̲SR-SS̲R̲ manipulator

$$\eta_1(\theta_1, \psi_1) \overset{\Delta}{=} \|b_1 + l_1 + l_2 - b_2\|^2 - l_3^2 = 0, \tag{1}$$

$$\eta_2(\theta_1, \psi_1, \theta_2, \phi_2) \overset{\Delta}{=} \|b_3 + l_4 - (b_{12} + l_6)\|^2 - l_5^2 = 0, \tag{2}$$

physically signifying the rigidity of the links l_3 and l_5, respectively. It is observed that η_1 is a function of θ_1 and ψ_1 only, implying that the planar four-bar is not influenced by the motion of the spatial loop. On the other hand, η_2 contains θ_1 and ψ_1, in addition to θ_2 and ϕ_2, indicating that the configuration of the spatial loop keeps changing as the planar four-bar moves. This *one-way coupling* permits a sequential kinematic analysis, in which the planar four-bar is solved first, followed by the spatial loop, as illustrated in the Sects. 2.2 and 2.3.

2.2   Forward Kinematics

The forward kinematic problem involves finding the output variables, ϕ, for given inputs, θ, from the loop-closure constraint equations. The variable ψ_1 is the only unknown in Eq. (1), which is of the following form:

$$A_1 \cos \psi_1 + B_1 \sin \psi_1 + C_1 = 0, \tag{3}$$

where $A_1 = -2l_3(-b_{2x} + l_1 \cos \theta_1)$, $B_1 = -2l_3(-b_{2z} + l_1 \sin \theta_1)$ and $C_1 = b_{2x}^2 + b_{2z}^2 + l_1^2 - l_3^2 + l_3^2 - 2l_1 b_{2x} \cos \theta_1 - 2l_1 b_{2z} \sin \theta_1$. The closed-form solution to Eq. (3) is given by

$$\psi_1 = \text{atan2}(B_1, A_1) \pm \arccos\left(-C_1 / \sqrt{A_1^2 + B_1^2}\right). \tag{4}$$

For each value of ψ_1, Eq. (2) reduces to a form that is analogous to Eq. (3):

$$A_2 \cos \phi_2 + B_2 \sin \phi_2 + C_2 = 0, \tag{5}$$

where

$A_2 = 2l_6(b_{3y} + l_4 \cos \theta_2),$

$B_2 = 2l_6(\cos \psi_1(b_{3z} - l_1 \sin \theta_1 + l_4 \sin \theta_2) + (-b_{3x} + l_1 \cos \theta_1) \sin \psi_1),$

$C_2 = b_{3x}^2 + b_{3y}^2 + b_{3z}^2 + l_1^2 + l_4^2 - l_5^2 + l_6^2 + l_2^2\rho^2 + 2b_{3y}l_4 \cos \theta_2 + 2(-b_{3x}l_1 \cos \theta_1$

$\quad + l_1 l_2 \rho \cos \theta_1 - \psi_1 - b_{3z}l_1 \sin \theta_1 + l_4(b_{3z} - l_1 \sin \theta_1) \sin \theta_2 - l_2\rho(b_{3x} \cos \psi_1$

$\quad + (b_{3z} + l_4 \sin \theta_2) \sin \psi_1)).$

The solutions to Eq. (5) are obtained by a formula similar to Eq. (4). Totally, there are *four* solutions to the forward kinematic problem.

2.3 Inverse Kinematics

The inverse kinematic problem involves finding the input variables, θ, for the desired output coordinates, ϕ, using the same loop-closure equations, Eqs. (1) and (2). The Eq. (1) is of the following form:

$$A_3 \cos \theta_1 + B_3 \sin \theta_1 + C_3 = 0, \tag{6}$$

where $A_3 = 2l_1(-b_{2x} + l_2 \cos \psi_1)$, $B_3 = 2l_1(-b_{2z} + l_2 \sin \psi_1)$ and $C_3 = b_{2x}^2 + b_{2z}^2 + l_1^2 + l_2^2 - l_3^2 - 2b_{2x}l_2 \cos \psi_1 - 2b_{2z}l_2 \sin \psi_1$. The solutions to Eq. (6) are given by expressions similar to those in Eq. (4). For each value of θ_1, Eq. (2) reduces to a form that is identical to Eq. (5), whose solutions are also obtained similarly. Thus, the inverse kinematics problem also has *four* solution branches.

3 Sun-Tracking Application

The analytical procedure for finding the position of the sun, as observed from any geographical location on earth, is well-established and available in standard textbooks, such as [1]. In this study, Chennai (13.0827° N, 80.2707° E) is chosen as the place of interest. The paths traced by the sun on three special days, summer solstice (June 21), equinox (September 21) and winter solstice (December 21), between 7 a.m. and 5 p.m., are plotted in Fig. 3. The sun moves approximately in parallel planes on each day of the year, the extreme planes being marked by the solstices.

Fig. 3 Sun paths on
solstices and equinox at
Chennai

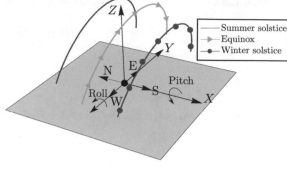

Fig. 4 Feasible design of
the manipulator for exact
tracking at Chennai

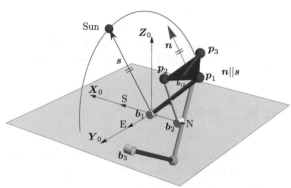

A solar tracker is said to track the sun in an exact manner if it manages to maintain
the normal to the panel parallel to the position vector of the sun throughout the desired
duration of tracking, as seen from the place of interest (see Fig. 4). For exact tracking,
throughout the year, it is necessary that the tracker possesses two rotational DoF,
azimuth-elevation, or equivalently, roll-pitch motions. Let the roll and pitch motions
be defined as rotations about body-fixed Y-and X-axis, respectively, as shown in
Fig. 3. It may be noted that the chosen order of rotations is roll, followed by pitch.
The variations of these angles are plotted for the said three days in Fig. 5. It is
inferred that the ranges of angular motions required are: roll $\in [-80°, 55°]$ and pitch
$\in [-85°, 80°]$, for exact tracking at this location. It is observed that the roll motion
is nearly constant for the most part of the day, while the pitch covers around $180°$
every day.

Figure 4 depicts a feasible design of the manipulator that is capable of generating the requisite range of roll and pitch motions without encountering any singularities. The geometric parameters of this design are[3,4]: $b_2 = [-0.162, 0, 0]^\top$;
$b_3 = [-0.146, 0.369, 0]^\top$; $\{l_1, l_2, l_3, l_4, l_5, l_6, \rho\} = \{0.369, 0.200, 0.221, 0.402, 0.538,$

---

[3]These numbers were obtained from an optimal design process, whose details are not included here
for want of space.

[4]All length dimensions are in metres, angles in degrees, and forces in Newtons.

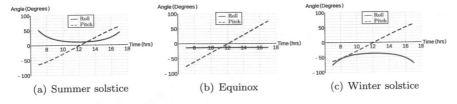

Fig. 5 Variation of the roll and pitch angles at Chennai

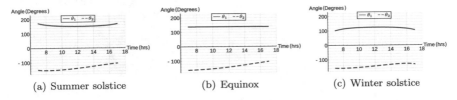

Fig. 6 Variation of actuated angles on solstices and equinox at Chennai

0.200, 0.500}. The range of motion of the actuators for the specified roll and pitch motions are obtained as $\theta_1 \in [99°, 173°]$ and $\theta_2 \in [-164°, -101°]$, whose variations on the solstices and equinox are plotted in Fig. 6. It is noted that the variation of θ_1 is less than 20°, while that of θ_2 is about 60° on a given day.

Self-weight of the support frame of the panel, and the wind thrust experienced by the panel, constitute the major loads in the system. Since the angular motion of the sun is very slow, i.e., about 180° in 12 hours, all inertial forces are negligible in comparison, and hence, not considered in this work. The symmetric geometry of the panel causes the net force to act at the centroid of the frame. The panel is mounted on the manipulator such that its centroid is coincident with the point b_{12} on the coupler of the planar four-bar as shown in Fig. 1. This arrangement ensures that the centre of mass does not move significantly during the diurnal motions, thereby reducing the energy spent in tracking.

4 Static Analysis

The self-weight (f_g) and the wind load (f_w) forces are determined following the data presented in [4]. The details are as follows[5]:

- A 15 kg frame imposes a constant vertical load given by, $f_g = [0, 0, -147]^\top$.
- The magnitude of drag force due to *uniform wind* (in the horizontal plane) on the panel is equal to $f_w = (1/2)C_d \rho_{air} v^2 A$, where $C_d = 1.18$, is the coefficient of drag; $\rho_{air} = 1.25 \text{ kg/m}^3$, is the density of air; $v = 22$ m/s, is the assumed wind velocity and $A = 4 \sin \alpha \text{ m}^2$ (see Fig. 7), is the projected area in the direction of

---

[5] All the link masses are neglected in this study, since their contribution is outweighed by payloads significantly.

Fig. 7 Wind load on the
panel

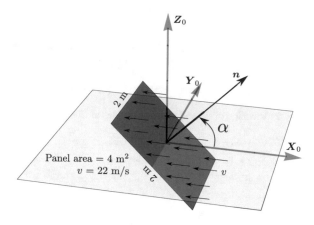

wind. The maximum impact of wind load is experienced by the actuator at b_1,
when the pitch angle (ϕ_2) is *zero*, i.e., $f_w = f_w[-1, 0, 0]^\top$.

The static torques at the actuated joints, $\tau = [\tau_1, \tau_2]^\top$, are computed as:

$$\tau = J_v^\top (f_g + f_w), \tag{7}$$

where J_v is the velocity Jacobian matrix corresponding to the point b_{12}, which is
derived in the following equations. The position vector b_{12}, defined in Sect. 2.1, when
differentiated with respect to time, yields:

$$v_{12} = \frac{\partial b_{12}}{\partial \theta}\dot{\theta} + \frac{\partial b_{12}}{\partial \phi}\dot{\phi} = J_{p\theta}\dot{\theta} + J_{p\phi}\dot{\phi}. \tag{8}$$

Differentiating the constraint equations Eqs. (1) and (2) with respect to time yields:

$$\frac{\partial \eta}{\partial \theta}\dot{\theta} + \frac{\partial \eta}{\partial \phi}\dot{\phi} = J_{\eta\theta}\dot{\theta} + J_{\eta\phi}\dot{\phi} = 0. \tag{9}$$

Eliminating $\dot{\phi}$ between Eqs. (8) and (9), the velocity of b_{12} is obtained as:

$$v_{12} = J_v\dot{\theta} = (J_{p\theta} - J_{p\phi}J_{\eta\phi}^{-1}J_{\eta\theta})\dot{\theta}. \tag{10}$$

It is noted that $J_v^\top$ is a (2×3) matrix whose second row is null. Consequently, τ_2 is
identically zero, and the static analysis of this manipulator reduces to the analysis of
the planar loop only, as depicted in Fig. 8. The holding torque values are plotted in
Fig. 9 and the magnitude of the ground reaction forces are plotted in Fig. 10.

It is observed that the load is almost equally distributed among the two pivots,
unlike in the case of serial counterparts where a single pole transmits all the forces
to ground. This feature provides an advantage from the construction point of view,
where a single deep foundation could be replaced by two shallow ones.

Fig. 8 Forces on the system

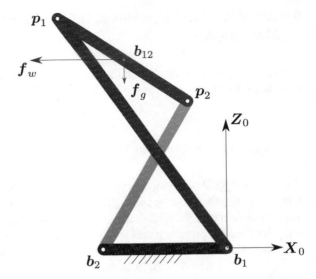

Fig. 9 Holding torque of the actuator at b_1 for the applied loads

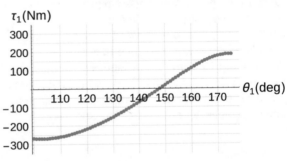

Fig. 10 Magnitude of ground reaction forces

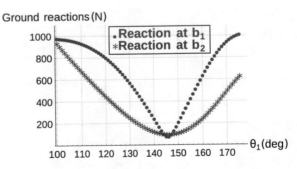

5 Practical Considerations in the Design of the R̲SSR-SS̲R̲ Manipulator

The relevant practical issues with the proposed design are pointed out and suitable remedies are suggested in this section.

5.1 Equivalent Kinematic Design

The proposed R̲SSR-SS̲R̲ topology of the tracker leads to some practical issues, with four spherical joints arranged in a successive manner. Limitations in the realizable range of motion (see Sect. 5.2) and misalignment due to clearances within the spherical pairs form the primary issues in this design. In order to cope with these issues, an equivalent kinematic design is presented in Fig. 11. The following modifications are incorporated in the R̲SSR-SS̲R̲ architecture to arrive at this design. The two spherical joints in the planar four-bar are replaced by rotary joints, whose axes are perpendicular to the X_0Z_0 plane. In order to enable rotation about the coupler link p_1p_2, another rotary joint is introduced at the b_{12} location. Finally, the spherical joint at p_3 is replaced by a *universal* joint to eliminate the unconstrained rotation of the S-S link, namely, l_5. These modifications leave behind only one spherical joint at the p_4 location in the manipulator. It may be noted that both these designs differ only under practical considerations, while they are equivalent from the perspective of the overall kinematic behaviour of the manipulator.

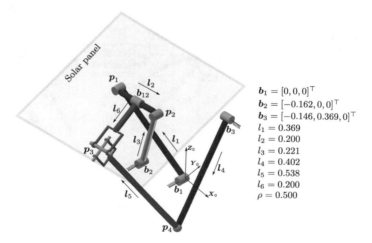

$$b_1 = [0, 0, 0]^\top$$
$$b_2 = [-0.162, 0, 0]^\top$$
$$b_3 = [-0.146, 0.369, 0]^\top$$
$$l_1 = 0.369$$
$$l_2 = 0.200$$
$$l_3 = 0.221$$
$$l_4 = 0.402$$
$$l_5 = 0.538$$
$$l_6 = 0.200$$
$$\rho = 0.500$$

Fig. 11 CAD model of the manipulator designed for sun-tracking at Chennai

Fig. 12 Angle between the two links l_4 and l_5 attached by a spherical joint

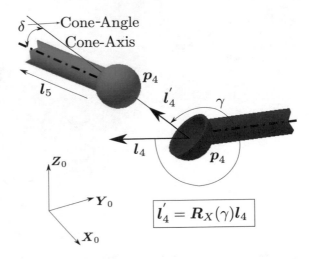

$$l'_4 = R_X(\gamma)l_4$$

5.2 Range of Motion of the Spherical Joint

The motion capabilities of the spherical joints are characterised by their cone-axes and maximum permissible cone-angle denoted by l'_4 and γ, respectively, in Fig. 12. Commercially available spherical joints are known to have an allowable range of motion between $-30°$ and $+30°$ in general, see, e.g., [11]. The only spherical joint in the manipulator is located at p_4, and it is instructive to verify if the range of motion required for exact tracking can be catered to. The spherical joint is affixed to link l_4 such that, its cone-axis is along the vector l'_4 (see Fig. 12) which is defined as: $l'_4 = R_X(\gamma)l_4$. The angle γ is an architecture parameter and an appropriate value for it is found to be $-100°$ in this problem.[6] The spherical joint angle or the cone-angle, δ is computed as follows:

$$\delta = \arccos\left(\frac{l'_4 \cdot l_5}{l_4 l_5}\right). \tag{11}$$

The variation of δ while tracking the sun across all days in a year between 7 a.m. and 5 p.m. is plotted in Fig. 13. From the figure, it is inferred that the required range of motion at the spherical joint is between $0°$ and $30°$, which is within the permissible range of motion afforded by the commercially available spherical joints.

---

[6]Several choices for γ were tested and the said value was found to have minimum requirement on the joint range of motion.

Fig. 13 Variation of
spherical joint angle with
time and days on any given
year at Chennai

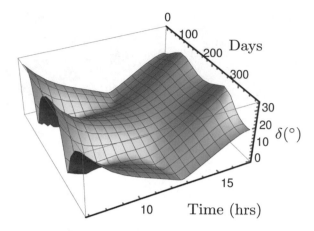

6   Conclusion and Future Work

A two-DoF R̲SSR-SS̲R manipulator is proposed for the sun-tracking application.
Closed-form expressions for the forward and inverse kinematic problems are presented. The *one-way coupling* of the kinematics of the two loops is exploited to
track the seasonal and diurnal motions of the sun in a nearly decoupled manner. The
actuator that carries most of the load, moves only through 20° on any given day,
which reduces the energy requirements significantly. The static analysis shows that
this architecture allows for shallower foundations, which can enable the installation
of trackers in areas with lower soil strength. When an array of trackers is deployed
in a solar farm, this architecture permits the use of a *line-shaft* layout, where a single
actuated shaft runs through the ground pivots. Such an arrangement replaces a series
of actuators by a single heavy actuator, saving on the multiplying cost of the motor
accessories.

The analysis in this work is restricted to one particular place, namely, Chennai.
It is of interest to investigate how this manipulator performs as one moves towards
the polar regions and the associated problems with the spherical joint in such cases.
Such studies are included in the plan for furthering this research.

Acknowledgements The authors would like to thank the second reviewer for their comments
concerning the practical issues with successively arranged spherical joints and also pointing to the
possibility of replacing one of them with a universal joint.

References

1. C.S. Solanki, *Solar Photovoltaics: Fundamentals, Technologies and Applications*, 3rd edn. (Prentice Hall India Learning Private Limited, New Delhi, India, 2015)
2. R.R. Rao, H. Swetha, J. Srinivasan, S.K. Ramasesha, Comparison of performance of solar photovoltaics on dual axis tracker with fixed axis at 13°N latitude. Curr. Sci. **108**(11), 2087–2094 (2015)
3. F.J.G. Gila, M.D.S. Martin, J.P. Vara, J.R. Calvo, A review of solar tracker patents in Spain, in *Proceedings of the 3rd WSEAS International Conference on Renewable Energy Sources* (Canary Islands, Spain, 2009)
4. R.A. Shyam, A. Ghosal, Three-degree-of-freedom parallel manipulator to track the sun for concentrated solar power systems. Chin. J. Mech. Eng. **28**(4), 192–202 (2015)
5. S. Pramanik, A. Ghosal, Development of a sun tracking system using a 3-UPU spherical wrist manipulator, in *Proceedings of the 2nd International and 17th National Conference on Machines and Mechanisms* (Kanpur, India, 2015)
6. D.M. Massala, Analysis and simulation of parallel robots for sun tracking using a CAD based approach. M.S. thesis, Instituto Superior Técnico, University of Lisbon, 2010
7. A. Cammarata, Optimized design of a large-workspace 2-DOF parallel robot for solar tracking systems. Mech. Mach. Theory **83**, 175–186 (2015)
8. J. Wu, X. Chen, L. Wang, Design and dynamics of a novel solar tracker with parallel mechanism. IEEE/ASME Trans. Mechatron. **21**(1), 88–97 (2016)
9. G. Quaglia, S.L. Maurino, Solar.q_1: a new solar-tracking mechanism based on four-bar linkages. Proc. Inst. Mech. Eng. Part C: J. Mech. Eng. Sci. **231**(15), 2855–2867 (2017)
10. A. Ghosal, *Robotics: Fundamental Concepts and Analysis* (Oxford University Press, New Delhi, India, 2006)
11. Hephaist Seiko Co., http://www.hephaist.co.jp/e/pro/ball.html. Accessed 15 Nov 2017

An Exact Synthesis of Pick-and-Place Mechanisms Using a Planar Four-Bar Linkage

Aravind Baskar and Sandipan Bandyopadhyay

Abstract For repetitive material-handling operations in various industries, fixed automation using single-degree-of-freedom mechanisms can often serve as a low-cost alternative to multi-degrees-of-freedom robots. Therefore, developing design procedures for inexpensive fixed automation solutions may be highly relevant in the context of developing as well as underdeveloped economies. A design methodology to analytically synthesise a planar pick-and-place system for displacement and velocity requirements using a planar four-bar mechanism is carried out in this work. A methodology to establish the availability of kinematic defect-free solutions in terms of two free design parameters is also proposed and illustrated with a numerical example.

Keywords Kinematic synthesis · Pick-and-place mechanism · Circuit defect
Branch defect

1 Introduction

The problem of kinematic path synthesis using planar four-bar linkage for positional requirements is well studied in the literature both analytically (see, e.g., [1]) and numerically using continuation techniques (for example, see [2, 3]). Holte et al. [4] presented a closed-form solution for a two precision-points problem with velocity requirements at one of the points and used the available free parameters for velocity approximations at several other positions, for assisting a technician in a laboratory environment. Robson and McCarthy [5] solved a synthesis problem matching three positions and two velocities by adjusting the velocity specifications iteratively to find

A. Baskar · S. Bandyopadhyay (✉)
Department of Engineering Design, Indian Institute of Technology Madras,
Chennai 600036, Tamil Nadu, India
e-mail: sandipan@iitm.ac.in

A. Baskar
e-mail: krishna.arvind91@gmail.com

© Springer Nature Singapore Pte Ltd. 2019
D N Badodkar and T A Dwarakanath (eds.), *Machines, Mechanism and Robotics*, Lecture Notes in Mechanical Engineering,
https://doi.org/10.1007/978-981-10-8597-0_13

defect-free solution. In this work, a closed-form solution to a pick-and-place application in an industrial setting is presented, for exact position and velocity requirements at two precision-points, in addition to a requirement of finite angular displacement of the end-effector by a desired angle. This problem falls under PP-PP category with two sets of two infinitesimally separated positions, as termed by Tesar [6]. A pair of infinitesimally separated positions represents a positional requirement and a velocity requirement at the same position.

Figure 1 depicts the problem schematically. The objective of this work is to design a pick-and-place system to transfer a component from a moving conveyor 1 to another moving conveyor 2, which is a common and highly repetitive task in many industries. While performing the pick-and-place operation, the following requirements are to be met:

1. The mechanism should include the pick and drop locations in the path of a designated coupler point, where a gripper would be attached.
2. The said coupler point (i.e., the gripper) should match the velocities of the corresponding conveyors as it picks and drops the object to reduce mechanical impact during operation.
3. The object to be handled should be rotated by a finite angle before the drop at the destination, as depicted with two different reference frames $p_1 - X_1Y_1$ and $p_2 - X_2Y_2$ at the pick and drop locations, respectively.
4. Additionally, the mechanism must be free of any kinematic defects such as the branch defect, circuit defect and order defect, and it should be of Grashof type.

Although kinematic synthesis of pick-and-place mechanisms have been discussed in the literature, only subsets of the requirements listed above have been addressed. For example, the requirements 1 and 2 are partially addressed in [4, 5] with little emphasis on kinematic defects. To the best of the authors' knowledge, all the four requirements are not addressed in an exact manner in the existing literature. The

Fig. 1 Schematic of a
two-conveyor system with a
pick-and-place mechanism

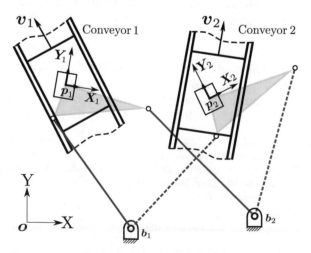

proposed comprehensive methodology to find a feasible design free of the defects can be potentially extended to other class of problems.

The rest of the paper is organised as follows: a closed-form solution to the aforementioned problem is proposed in Sect. 2. Feasibility analysis for obtaining defect-free solutions using the available free design parameters is carried out in Sect. 3. The solution methodology is illustrated with a numerical example of a pick-and-place problem in Sect. 4. Section 5 concludes the paper.

2 Problem Formulation

A planar four-bar mechanism is modeled as a combination of two vector-dyads, represented by the complex variables (z_1, z_2) and (z_3, z_4), with z_5 as the ground link, as shown in Fig. 2. The complex numbers r_1 and r_2 represent the position vectors of the pick and drop locations p_1 and p_2, respectively, in the global frame of reference $o - XY$. Let the conveyors be moving at constant velocities defined by v_1 and v_2, respectively[1] (refer to Fig. 1). Further requirement to rotate the object by a fixed angle λ, between the two positions, imposes an additional constraint. The angular velocity of the crank is considered to be a constant ω, which is the frequency of the operation cycle. This leaves the problem with two free real parameters, namely, the crank displacement, ϕ and the follower displacement, μ (see Fig. 2), of which the details are explained in the following. These parameters are utilised at a later stage to eliminate branch defects and to identify Grashof four-bars that are devoid of circuit defects, as classified by Chase and Mirth [7].

Formulation through complex variables enables easier computation of the solution in the closed-form. The procedure adopted is a hybrid one in that the complex variables are eliminated from the vector equations first and then the real variables are solved for by splitting the real and imaginary components of the residual equations. Loop-closure equations using complex numbers offer a concise way to pose the problem. First, the displacement constraints are posed mathematically. With z_6 as the reference vector of the base point b_1, the following equations can be written for the first precision-point in terms of its position vector r_1:

$$z_6 + z_1 + z_2 = r_1, \tag{1}$$
$$z_6 + z_5 + z_3 + z_4 = r_1. \tag{2}$$

Analogous equations can be written for the second position, r_2:

$$z_6 + z_1 e^{i\phi} + z_2 e^{i\lambda} = r_2, \tag{3}$$
$$z_6 + z_5 + z_3 e^{i\mu} + z_4 e^{i\lambda} = r_2, \tag{4}$$

---

[1] Vectors expressed as a pair of real numbers are represented in bold fonts, while those expressed as complex numbers are not.

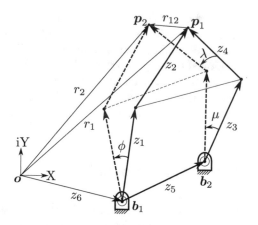

Fig. 2 Vector loop for two finitely separated positions p_1 and p_2, which represent the pick and drop locations, respectively

where i is the imaginary unit. As z_2 and z_4 are rigidly embedded in the coupler, they are displaced through the same angle λ between the two positions, thus completing the four-bar linkage architecture. Eliminating the variables z_5 and z_6 by subtracting Eqs. (1) and (2) from Eqs. (3) and (4), respectively, *the loop-closure conditions of the path* are obtained, with the *increment vector* [2] defined by $r_{12} = r_2 - r_1$:

$$z_1(e^{i\phi} - 1) + z_2(e^{i\lambda} - 1) = r_{12}, \tag{5}$$

$$z_3(e^{i\mu} - 1) + z_4(e^{i\lambda} - 1) = r_{12}. \tag{6}$$

The time derivative of the Eqs. (1)–(4) yields the velocity constraints, Eqs. (7)–(10), in terms of v_k, the conveyor velocity vector at position k, $k = 1, 2$:

$$z_1\omega + z_2\omega_{21} = -iv_1, \tag{7}$$

$$z_3\omega_{31} + z_4\omega_{21} = -iv_1, \tag{8}$$

$$z_1 e^{i\phi}\omega + z_2 e^{i\lambda}\omega_{22} = -iv_2, \tag{9}$$

$$z_3 e^{i\mu}\omega_{32} + z_4 e^{i\lambda}\omega_{22} = -iv_2. \tag{10}$$

where ω_{jk} refers to the angular velocity of the vector z_j, $j = 2, 3$ at the precision-point k, $k = 1, 2$.

The system of equations to be solved can be summarised as follows:

- Number of complex equations: 6 (Eqs. 5–10)
- Number of complex variables: 4 (z_1, z_2, z_3, z_4)
- Number of real variables: 4 ($\omega_{21}, \omega_{22}, \omega_{31}, \omega_{32}$).

Thus, the problem is formulated as $6 \times 2 = 12$ scalar equations and it can be solved for $4 \times 2 + 4 = 12$ scalar variables as listed. This leaves the designer with two free real design parameters, namely, ϕ and μ. From Eqs. (7)–(10), the complex variables z_1, z_2, z_3 and z_4 can be solved for linearly, in terms of the angular displacement variables ϕ and μ, and angular velocity variables $\omega_{21}, \omega_{22}, \omega_{31}$ and ω_{32}:

$$z_1 = -i(v_2\omega_{21} - e^{i\lambda}v_1\omega_{22})/(\omega(e^{i\phi}\omega_{21} - e^{i\lambda}\omega_{22})), \tag{11}$$

$$z_2 = -i(e^{i\phi}v_1 - v_2)/(e^{i\phi}\omega_{21} - e^{i\lambda}\omega_{22}), \tag{12}$$

$$z_3 = -i(v_2\omega_{21} - e^{i\lambda}v_1\omega_{22})/(e^{i\mu}\omega_{21}\omega_{32} - e^{i\lambda}\omega_{22}\omega_{31}), \tag{13}$$

$$z_4 = -i(v_2\omega_{31} - e^{i\mu}v_1\omega_{32})/(e^{i\lambda}\omega_{22}\omega_{31} - e^{i\mu}\omega_{21}\omega_{32}). \tag{14}$$

On substituting the solutions of Eqs. (11)–(14) in Eqs. (5) and (6), four scalar equations in terms of the four angular velocity variables are obtained by separating the real and imaginary parts of the equations. The variables ω_{21}, ω_{22}, ω_{31} and ω_{32} appear linearly, pairwise, in the resulting equations, which are not presented for the sake of brevity. They can be solved through Cramer's rule, in terms of the components of the increment vector $r_{12} = \delta_a + i\delta_b$ and the conveyor velocity vector $v_j = v_{ja} + iv_{jb}$, $j = 1$, 2, where δ_a, δ_b, v_{ja} and v_{jb} are real. The solutions to the angular velocity variables along with the dyadic solutions given by Eqs. (11)–(14) constitute a closed-form solution to the PP-PP problem parametrised in terms of the design parameters ϕ and μ. Since the problem has a unique solution for each point on the parameter space, the problem has ∞^2 solutions.

3 Parametric Analysis to Find Feasible Solutions

Although a closed-form solution is obtained for the problem, it is not guaranteed that the solution obtained is feasible. In other words, the mechanism may suffer from kinematic defects that are inherent to any synthesis problem. It has been well established in literature that, three types of defects can occur in kinematic synthesis, namely, branch defect, circuit defect (including Grashof defect) and order defect (see, for example, [8]). In problems of path synthesis, order defects occur only in problems with four precision-points or higher. In three precision-point problems, order defect can be circumvented by changing the direction of the input motion and in two-point problems, order defects do not occur at all. Thus, in the following sections, only branch and circuit defects are addressed for the pick-and-place problem using the two design parameters available to find a feasible solution.

3.1 Branch Defect

Branch errors cannot be avoided during synthesis, due to the inherent quadratic nature of trigonometric functions in the loop-closure constraints. A methodology is proposed here to identify branch transition linkages in the design parameter space, which mark the transition of a precision-point between the two branches of the four-bar mechanism. A two precision-point problem with points A and B can have the following branch behaviour regions:

1. $A_1 B_1$: Both precision-points lying on the first branch.
2. $A_1 B_2$: Point A lying in the first branch and point B in the second.
3. $A_2 B_1$: Point B lying in the first branch and point A in the second.
4. $A_2 B_2$: Both precision-points lying on the second branch.

Among the four cases listed, the first and the last cases represent the branch defect-free scenarios. For the problem at hand, the design parameters ϕ and μ represent the angular displacements of the crank and the follower, respectively, that vary from 0 to 2π radians. Since it is a PP-PP problem with only two finitely separated points and the design parameters can take any set of values in the continuous domain, the branch transition points occurring at the two design positions should split the two-dimensional parameter space into four distinct regions of branch behaviour as enumerated. Consequently, to find the corresponding branch transition points in the parameter space, the condition for collinearity of the vectors that represent the coupler and the follower at the design points are studied. For the first design point p_1, using the following identity for parallel vectors:

$$(z_2 - z_4)\bar{z}_3 = (\bar{z}_2 - \bar{z}_4)z_3, \tag{15}$$

and solving it in conjunction with the Eqs. (11)–(14) derived in the previous section, the condition for branch transition corresponding to the first precision-point p_1 is obtained, as shown below:

$$\omega_{21}\omega_{32} \sin(\phi - \mu) - \omega_{22}\omega_{31} \sin(\phi - \lambda) + \omega_{22}\omega_{32} \sin(\mu - \lambda) = 0. \tag{16}$$

Identical analysis at the second design point p_2 yields the transition condition for the second precision-point, given by Eq. (17):

$$\omega_{22}\omega_{31} \sin(\phi - \mu) - \omega_{21}\omega_{32} \sin(\phi - \lambda) + \omega_{21}\omega_{31} \sin(\mu - \lambda) = 0. \tag{17}$$

These two conditions divide the parameter space into four regions and facilitate identification of the feasible regions that are free of branch defect. There may be degenerate points in the parameter space where one or more link lengths become zero or tend to infinity. Hence, care must be taken to stay clear of these degenerate points while choosing a solution.

3.2 Circuit Defect

Elimination of branch error does not ensure mechanical feasibility, as the resulting mechanism can still encounter circuit defect. Chase and Mirth [7] termed a circuit as "all possible orientations of the links which can be realised without disconnecting any of the joints". Even if the precision-points lie on the same branch or phase of the mechanism, they may or may not lie on the same circuit. Murray et al. [9] showed that critical points in the parameter space, where the circuit behaviour changes, occur in a planar four-bar linkage when all the links are collinear. For identifying those critical points of the design parameter space that change the circuit behaviour, a formulation similar to the one presented in [10] is followed.

4 Numerical Results and Discussions

Consider the following specifications of a desired pick-and-place scenario,

$$\delta_a = -1 \text{ m}, \ \delta_b = -1 \text{ m}, \ v_{1a} = -1/\sqrt{2} \text{ ms}^{-1}, \ v_{1b} = -1/\sqrt{2} \text{ ms}^{-1},$$
$$v_{2a} = -\sqrt{3}/2 \text{ ms}^{-1}, \ v_{2b} = -1/2 \text{ ms}^{-1}, \ \lambda = 3\pi/4 \text{ rad}, \ \omega = 2 \text{ rad s}^{-1}.$$

For the above set of values, the parametric analysis to find feasible solutions is demonstrated for a test value of crank displacement[2] $\phi = 5\pi/3$ and the feasible regions are identified in the parametric space of μ. Without any loss of generality, the first precision-point p_1 is assumed to coincide with the origin o. Conditions for branch transition derived in the Sect. 3.1 yield the following points:

$$\mu_{p_1} = 1.648, \ \mu_{p_2} = 2.946,$$

where the subscripts denote the precision point with which each transition point is associated. Although the bounds are established, the directionality of the branch defect-free region can only be found by testing a sample value of μ. For this problem, (1.648, 2.946) forms the range of parameter values that avoids the branching problem. Some common degeneracies, where one of the link-lengths becomes zero, occur when μ takes the values 0, λ and ϕ, and also at 2.297 and 5.439 for this example.

The condition for circuit transition linkage (derived following [10]) yields eight non-degenerate roots for the parameter μ, with six real roots for the numerical example addressed. The six real roots of μ that alter the circuit behaviour are listed as follows:

$$\{1.185, \ 2.201, \ 2.269, \ 2.317, \ 5.397, \ 5.482\}.$$

Following the methodology explained in [9], it can be established that Grashof-type four-bar mechanisms occur for the values of μ represented by (1.185, 2.201). Thus, the intersection of the two domains, given by $\mu \in (1.648, 2.201)$, defines the range of values μ can take for defect-free Grashof four-bar solution. A sample plot for a feasible parameter value is shown in Fig. 3. The value of the parameter μ can be chosen so as to address secondary considerations such as foot-print and transmission capability.

---

[2]All the angles, namely, ϕ, λ and μ, are represented in radians and the units are omitted.

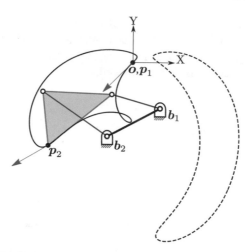

Fig. 3 Coupler-plot of defect-free four-bar mechanism for $\phi = 5\pi/3$ and $\mu = 2$. The numerical solution is given by $z_1 = -0.432 - 0.419i$, $z_2 = 0.098 + 0.968i$, $z_3 = 0.800 + 0.478i$, $z_4 = -0.502 + 0.408i$, $b_1 = [0.334, -0.549]^\top$ and $b_2 = [-0.299, -0.886]^\top$. The arrows indicate the direction of the conveyor velocity at the precision-points, scaled-down for representation

The methodology presented here does not take into account the angular velocity of the coupler at the pick and drop locations. However, the freedom in choosing the value of the parameter μ can be utilised to minimise the angular velocities at the pick and drop locations.

5   Contributions and Future Scope

This work presents a formulation for the exact synthesis of two sets of two infinitesimally separated points using a planar four-bar mechanism. The problem is formulated using complex variables to enable the derivation of the solution in the closed-form. Feasibility analysis using the available free design parameters, in the form of crank and follower angular displacements between two positions is carried out. Branch defect-free regions and degeneracies in the domain of the free parameter space are obtained. Circuit defect-free regions are identified through a characterisation scheme presented in [9]. Analytical formulation allows the user to design pick-and-place systems accurately using a single-degree-of-freedom mechanism. Once the feasible domains are identified, secondary objectives such as zero angular velocities at the pick-and-drop locations and foot-print considerations may be addressed. For double-dwell problems, the prescribed formulation breaks down and the classical solution involving double-cusp four-bar mechanisms could be considered (for example, see [11]). Using six-bar mechanisms for pick-and-place systems may offer additional variables to include acceleration constraints.

References

1. G. Sandor, A. Erdman, *Advanced Mechanical Design: Analysis and Synthesis*, vol. 2 (Prentice-Hall Inc, Englewood Cliffs, New Jersey, 1984)
2. B. Roth, F. Freudenstein, Synthesis of path-generating mechanisms by numerical methods. J. Eng. Ind. **85**(3), 298–304 (1963)
3. C. Wampler, A. Morgan, A. Sommese, Complete solution of the nine-point path synthesis problem for four-bar linkages. J. Mech. Des. **114**(1), 153–159 (1992)
4. J.E. Holte, T.R. Chase, A.G. Erdman, Approximate velocities in mixed exact-approximate position synthesis of planar mechanisms. J. Mech. Des. **123**, 388–394 (2001)
5. N.P. Robson, J.M. McCarthy, The synthesis of planar 4R linkages with three task positions and two specified velocities, in *ASME International Design Engineering Technical Conferences, 29th Mechanisms and Robotics Conference, ASME* (2005), pp. 425–432
6. D. Tesar, The generalized concept of four multiply separated positions in coplanar motion. J. Mech. **3**(1), 11–23 (1968)
7. T.R. Chase, J.A. Mirth, Circuits and branches of single-degree-of-freedom planar linkages. J. Mech. Des. **115**(2), 223–230 (1993)
8. K. Waldron, E. Stevensen, Elimination of branch, Grashof, and order defects in path-angle generation and function generation synthesis. J. Mech. Des. **101**(3), 428–437 (1979)
9. A.P. Murray, M.L. Turner, D.T. Martin, Synthesizing single DOF linkages via transition linkage identification. J. Mech. Des. **130**(2), 022301 (2008)
10. D.H. Myszka, A.P. Murray, C.W. Wampler, Computing the branches, singularity trace, and critical points of single degree-of-freedom, closed-loop linkages. J. Mech. Robot. **6**(1), 011006 (2014)
11. E.A. Dijksman, Symmetrical four-bar coupler curves, containing three cusps. Forsch. Ing. **57**(6), 198–202 (1991)

Forward Kinematics of the 3-RPRS Parallel Manipulator Using a Geometric Approach

Silla Pavan Santosh Kumar and Sandipan Bandyopadhyay

Abstract In this paper, the forward kinematics of the 3-RPRS manipulator is posed as an intersection problem of two plane algebraic curves. The manipulator is hypothetically decomposed into two kinematic sub-chains by dismantling one of the spherical joints. A pair of points, consisting of one each from the said sub-chains, are now constrained to individual loci, the points of intersection of which lead to the assembly modes of the manipulator. Computations of these points lead to the derivation of a 16-degree univariate polynomial equation, whose coefficients have been obtained as closed-form functions of the architecture parameters and the actuator variables. It is also found that this polynomial has only the even-powered terms, making it effectively an octic equation. The theoretical results are illustrated with the help of a numerical example and the results are validated numerically.

Keywords Forward kinematics · Coupler surface · 3-RPRS parallel manipulator
Planar algebraic circular curves · Forward kinematic univariate

1 Introduction

The 3-RPRS manipulator is a six-degrees-of-freedom spatial parallel manipulator, which is recently introduced in [1], where the inverse kinematics has been solved. In [2], the forward kinematic (FK) problem has been solved using a *joint-space* formulation where an 8-degree polynomial equation, namely, the *forward kinematic univariate* (FKU) (as defined in [3]), has been derived in terms of one of the joint-space variables. In the current work, a geometric approach has been followed to solve

S. P. Santosh Kumar
Systemantics India Pvt. Ltd., Bengaluru, India
e-mail: pavan.silla@gmail.com

S. Bandyopadhyay (✉)
Department of Engineering Design, Indian Institute of Technology Madras,
Chennai 600036, Tamil Nadu, India
e-mail: sandipan@iitm.ac.in

© Springer Nature Singapore Pte Ltd. 2019
D N Badodkar and T A Dwarakanath (eds.), *Machines, Mechanism
and Robotics*, Lecture Notes in Mechanical Engineering,
https://doi.org/10.1007/978-981-10-8597-0_14

the FK problem of the 3-RPRS manipulator in a similar manner as is done for the 3-RPS manipulator in [4]. The manipulator is hypothetically divided into two kinematic sub-chains. Once the input joint variables are fixed, the FK problem converts into an intersection problem of two plane algebraic circular curves corresponding to each of the sub-chains. To obtain the intersection points, a 16-degree FKU has been obtained and it is found that the FKU is even-powered, making it effectively a degree eight polynomial equation. A numerical example is used to illustrate the formulation.

The rest of the paper is organised as follows: in Sect. 2, the geometry of the 3-RPRS manipulator is discussed. Formulation of the FK problem leading to the derivation of the FKU is presented in Sect. 3.

The formulation is illustrated via a numerical example in Sect. 4. The conclusions are presented in Sect. 5.

2 Geometry of the 3-RPRS Manipulator

The *moving platform* of the 3-RPRS manipulator is in the form of an equilateral triangle, which is inscribed in a circle of radius a. Each vertex of the said triangle, denoted by $p_i, i = 1, 2, 3$, is connected to the fixed base of the manipulator through a RPRS leg. Only the first two joints, R (revolute) and P (prismatic) of each leg are *active* (i.e., actuated). The three prismatic joints are mounted on the fixed circular guide of rectangular cross-section, such that their axes intersect at the centre of the guide. A rigid strut of length l, connected to the moving platform via a spherical joint, joins the prismatic pair at the base of each leg via a rotary joint.

As shown in Fig. 1a, the fixed coordinate system {0}, given by o_0-$X_0 Y_0 Z_0$, is positioned at the centre of the circular guide fixed at the base platform. The coordinate system attached to the moving platform {1}, given by o_1-$X_1 Y_1 Z_1$, has its origin o_1, located at the centroid of the triangle $p_1 p_2 p_3$. The X_1 axis is directed towards the centre of the spherical joint at p_1. Consider another moving coordinate system {2}, denoted by o_2-$X_2 Y_2 Z_2$, which is obtained by rotating the fixed coordinate system {0} about its Z_0 axis through an angle θ_1 in the counter clockwise sense, such that the X_2 axis is always aligned with the first prismatic joint axis. The passive rotary joints are located at the points denoted by b_i, which are given in the frames {0} and {2}, respectively, as

$$^0 b_i = [d_i \cos \theta_i, d_i \sin \theta_i, 0]^\top, \tag{1}$$

$$^2 b_i = [d_i \cos \theta_{i1}, d_i \sin \theta_{i1}, 0]^\top, \text{ where, } \theta_{i1} = \theta_i - \theta_1, \quad i = 1, 2, 3, \tag{2}$$

and d_i is the ith prismatic joint extension (measured from the origin o_0), θ_i is the counterclockwise rotation of the ith prismatic joint axis, measured from the axis X_0 about the Z_0 axis.

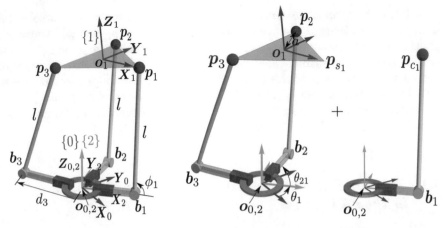

(a) Schematic representation of the manipulator.

(b) Decomposition of the 3-RPRS manipulator into kinematic sub-chains RSSR and RS.

Fig. 1 The 3-RPRS manipulator and its conceptual decomposition

The positions of the vertices of the top platform in terms of the active and passive variables are given by

$$^{0}\boldsymbol{p}_i = {}^{0}\boldsymbol{b}_i + \boldsymbol{R}_Z(\theta_i)[l\cos\phi_i, 0, l\sin\phi_i]^\top, \tag{3}$$

$$^{2}\boldsymbol{p}_i = {}^{2}\boldsymbol{b}_i + \boldsymbol{R}_Z(\theta_{i1})[l\cos\phi_i, 0, l\sin\phi_i]^\top, \quad i = 1, 2, 3, \tag{4}$$

where ϕ_i is the ith passive joint angle made by the strut, measured from the prismatic joint axis.

The position and orientation (or the *pose*) of the moving platform can be specified *uniquely*, once the variables, $\boldsymbol{q} = [\theta_1, \theta_2, \theta_3, d_1, d_2, d_3, \phi_1, \phi_2, \phi_3]^\top$ are known. Out of these, $\boldsymbol{\theta} = [\theta_1, \theta_2, \theta_3, d_1, d_2, d_3]^\top$ are the active (i.e. actuated) joint variables and $\boldsymbol{\phi} = [\phi_1, \phi_2, \phi_3]^\top$ are the *passive* (i.e., unactuated) joint variables.

3 Geometric Formulation of the FK Problem

In the FK problem, the actuator inputs $\boldsymbol{\theta}$, are known and the pose of the top platform is to be determined via the computation of the remaining configuration variables $\boldsymbol{\phi}$, from the kinematic constraint equations, that the manipulator needs to satisfy at all times. Towards this, the manipulator is hypothetically decomposed into two kinematic sub-chains at one of the three spherical joints. Consequently, the *loop-closure* constraints are formulated using the fact that the position of the endpoints of the said sub-chains should be *identical*.

In Fig. 1b, the manipulator is divided into two kinematic sub-chains at the spherical joint p_1 and this leads to two hypothetically distinct points p_{c_1} and p_{s_1}, where p_{c_1} is the point representing the tip of the serial kinematic chain $o_0 b_1 p_1$ and p_{s_1} is the coupler point of the spatial RSSR linkage $b_2 p_2 p_3 b_3$. Geometrically, the locus of the point p_{c_1}, which is the circle $C = 0$, should intersect the coupler surface $S = 0$, traced by the coupler point p_{s_1}. In order to identify the locus of the points p_{c_1} and p_{s_1} and to make those computations easier, all the calculations are performed in the coordinate system {2}.

3.1 Number of Assembly Modes of the 3-RPRS Manipulator in The FK Problem

As the name suggests, *assembly modes* in the FK problem are the different configurations in which the manipulator can be assembled while keeping the actuators fixed at a given set of inputs. The number of assembly modes possible can be found by identifying the various configurations in which the decomposed sub-chains can be assembled back. In other words, it is equal to the number of intersection points possible between the loci of p_{c_1} and p_{s_1}.

It is shown in [5, p. 433], that the degree of the surface traced by the coupler point of a general spatial RSSR link is 16. Further, in [6], the *circularity* of the said surface is stated to be 8. Consider the RSSR linkage $b_2 p_2 p_3 b_3$, as shown in Fig. 1b. The degree and the circularity of the coupler surface $S = 0$, traced by the point p_{s_1}, are $n_S = 16$ and $c_S = 8$, respectively.

Considering the other sub-chain $o_0 b_1 p_1$, in Fig. 1b. Point p_{c_1}, which is attached to a rotary joint at b_1 with a strut traces a circle $C = 0$, with its centre at b_1. Therefore, its degree $n_C = 2$ and circularity $c_C = 1$. The number of points of intersection of the coupler surface $S = 0$ with the circle $C = 0$ can be calculated by using the extension of the Bezout's theorem (see [7]):

$$n = n_S n_C - 2 c_S c_C = 16 \times 2 - 2 \times 8 \times 1 = 16. \tag{5}$$

Therefore, the maximum number of ways in which the 3-RPRS manipulator can be assembled is 16. This result is the same for the 3-RRS and 3-RPS manipulators because of their architectural similarity. All of these have moving triangular platforms connected to the rest of the respective manipulators via spherical joints located at the vertices of the triangle.

3.2 Derivation of the Circularity Constraint, $C = 0$

Given the input variables θ, one can determine the positions of the points b_1, b_2 and b_3. Let $^2p_{c_1} = {}^2p_{s_1} = {}^2p_1 = [x, y, z]^\top$. The locus of the point p_{c_1} is a circle of radius l, with its centre at b_1. The circle lies in the plane $o_0 b_1 p_1$, which contains the first limb. The algebraic equations representing the circle $C = 0$ in the coordinate system $\{2\}$ are derived from the constraint equations as follows:

- Leg-length constraint: The distance between the points p_{c_1} and b_1 is equal to l. This leads to the equation of a sphere centred at b_1:

$$\xi_1 \overset{\Delta}{=} (^2p_{c_1} - {}^2b_1) \cdot (^2p_{c_1} - {}^2b_1) = l^2. \tag{6}$$

- Planarity constraint: The strut $p_{c_1} b_1$ is always perpendicular to the axis of the rotary joint at b_1. This leads to the equation of the plane in which the point p_{c_1} is confined to move, which is obtained as follows:

$$\xi_2 \overset{\Delta}{=} (^2p_{c_1} - {}^2b_1) \cdot e_{Y_2} = 0, \text{ where } e_{Y_2} = [0, 1, 0]^\top; \tag{7}$$
$$\Rightarrow y = 0. \tag{8}$$

The equation of the circle $C(x, z) = 0$ is obtained by substituting the plane equation $y = 0$ in the leg-length constraint Eq. (6).

3.3 Derivation of the Coupler Surface, $S = 0$

The surface traced by the coupler point of the RSSR chain $b_1 p_1 p_2 b_2$, can be formulated in terms of the vector of the variables $\theta_s = [\phi_2, \phi_3, x, y, z, l_2, l_3, \theta_{21}, \theta_{31}]^\top$. Out of these variables $l_2, l_3, \theta_{21}, \theta_{31}$ are specified in the FK problem. Hence, the coupler surface can be expressed in terms of x, y, z after eliminating the passive variables ϕ_2, ϕ_3 from the constraint equations. The constraint equations are derived in the following:

- Loop-closure constraint: The first constraint is defined by closing the RSSR loop, the geometric condition being that the distance between the points p_2 and p_3 is a constant:

$$g_1(\phi_2, \phi_3) \overset{\Delta}{=} (^2p_2 - {}^2p_3) \cdot (^2p_2 - {}^2p_3) - 3a^2 = 0. \tag{9}$$

- Rigidity constraints: The remaining two constraint equations can be formulated by using the fact that the distance between the points p_{s_1} and p_j, $j = 2, 3$ are also fixed as the moving platform is rigid:

$$g_2(\phi_2, x, y, z) \overset{\Delta}{=} (^2p_{s_1} - {}^2p_2) \cdot (^2p_{s_1} - {}^2p_2) - 3a^2 = 0, \tag{10}$$
$$g_3(\phi_3, x, y, z) \overset{\Delta}{=} (^2p_{s_1} - {}^2p_3) \cdot (^2p_{s_1} - {}^2p_3) - 3a^2 = 0. \tag{11}$$

The passive variables ϕ_2, ϕ_3 are eliminated by the following procedure: Eqs. (9), (10) and (11) are linear in terms of $\cos\phi_2$, $\sin\phi_2$, $\cos\phi_3$, $\sin\phi_3$. Solving for $\cos\phi_2$, $\sin\phi_2$ from Eqs. (9), (10) and substituting these in the identity $\cos^2\phi_2 + \sin^2\phi_2 = 1$ gives an equation in terms of ϕ_3, x, y, z:

$$\left. \begin{array}{l} g_1(\phi_2, \phi_3) = 0 \\ g_2(\phi_2, x, y, z) = 0 \end{array} \right) \xrightarrow{\times\phi_2} h_1(\phi_3, x, y, z) = 0, \tag{12}$$

where the symbol '$\xrightarrow{\times\phi_2}$' denotes the elimination of the variable ϕ_2 from the equations preceding it. The solution of ϕ_2 can be uniquely identified by using the *two-argument inverse tangent function*, atan2$(\sin(\cdot), \cos(\cdot))$:

$$\phi_2 = \text{atan2}(\sin\phi_2, \cos\phi_2). \tag{13}$$

Equation (12) is not linear in terms of $\cos\phi_3$, $\sin\phi_3$. The variable ϕ_3 is eliminated after transforming the equations $h_1 = 0$, $g_3 = 0$ to their respective algebraic forms, via the tangent half-angle substitution: $t_3 = \tan\left(\frac{\phi_3}{2}\right)$. After the transformation, Eq. (12) becomes a polynomial equation, namely, $s_1 = 0$, of degree four in t_3 and Eq. (11) becomes a quadratic equation, $s_2 = 0$, in the variable t_3. The coupler surface can be obtained by finding the resultant of $s_1 = 0$ and $s_2 = 0$ with respect to the variable t_3. This elimination procedure is summarised schematically below:

$$\left. \begin{array}{l} h_1(\phi_3, x, y, z) = 0 \xrightarrow{\phi_3 \to t_3} s_1(t_3, x, y, z) = 0 \\ g_3(\phi_3, x, y, z) = 0 \xrightarrow{\phi_3 \to t_3} s_2(t_3, x, y, z) = 0 \end{array} \right) \xrightarrow{\times t_3} S(x, y, z) = 0. \tag{14}$$

The symbol '$\xrightarrow{\phi_3 \to t_3}$' denotes the conversion of an equation in ϕ_3 into their algebraic form in $t_3 = \tan(\phi_3/2)$. Equation $S(x, y, z) = 0$, which is in terms of the actuator variables and architecture parameters, defines the coupler surface of point $\boldsymbol{p}_{s_1}$ of the RSSR chain. The *size*[1] of the coupler surface is 218.053 MB.

The variable t_3 can be solved by equating the polynomial remainder obtained by dividing s_1 by s_2, with respect to the variable t_3 to zero. One can solve t_3 *uniquely* as the remainder is linear in t_3 and this solution is guaranteed to satisfy $s_1 = 0$ and $s_2 = 0$ simultaneously. Hence, the solution of the variable t_3 is obtained as follows:

$$s_1(t_3, x, y, z) = \alpha(t_3, x, y, z)s_2(t_3, x, y, z) + \beta(t_3, x, y, z) = 0,$$
$$\beta(t_3, x, y, z) = 0 \Rightarrow \beta_1(x, y, z)t_3 + \beta_2(x, y, z) = 0,$$
$$\Rightarrow t_3 = -\beta_2(x, y, z)/\beta_1(x, y, z), \text{ assuming } \beta_1(x, y, z) \neq 0. \tag{15}$$

Special cases such as $\beta_1(x, y, z) = 0$, need to be studied further, which fall outside the scope of the present paper.

---

[1] Here, the "size" of an expression indicates the amount of memory required to store the expression in the internal format of the computer algebra system (CAS) used, namely, Mathematica.

3.4 Derivation of the FKU

A real point of intersection of the coupler surface $S = 0$ with the circle $C = 0$ implies that the manipulator can be assembled, with the dismantled spherical joint re-established at that point. To identify the intersection points, one can eliminate two of the variables x, y, z and derive the FKU in terms of the remaining.

As the circle $C = 0$ lies in the plane $X_2 Z_2$, one can substitute $y = 0$ in $S = 0$. Tangent half-angle substitutions for θ_{21}, θ_{31} follow, to convert the resulting equation into its algebraic form.[2] This leads to the curve $C'(x, z) = 0$ in the $X_2 Z_2$ plane:

$$S(x, y, z) = 0 \xrightarrow{y \to 0, \theta_{21} \to t_{21}, \theta_{31} \to t_{31}} C'(x, z) = 0. \qquad (16)$$

The "size" of the curve $C'(x, z) = 0$ is 24.450 MB, after using the in-built symbolic simplification routine of Mathematica, namely, Simplify. The curve $C'(x, z) = 0$ is of degree 16 in x and z and the circularity of the curve is 8. The Bezout's limit for the number of intersections of this circular curve with the circle $C(x, z) = 0$ is 16. By eliminating the variable x from $C(x, z) = 0$ and $C'(x, z) = 0$ via their resultant yields the FKU:

$$\left. \begin{array}{c} C'(x, z) = 0 \\ C(x, z) = 0 \end{array} \right) \xrightarrow{\times x} \zeta(z) = 0. \qquad (17)$$

The FKU ζ, has only the even-powered terms and hence can be written as a polynomial of degree 8 in $m = z^2$:

$$\zeta = v_8 m^8 + v_7 m^7 + v_6 m^6 + v_5 m^5 + v_4 m^4 + v_3 m^3 + v_2 m^2 + v_1 m + v_0. \qquad (18)$$

The "size" of the FKU has been reduced from approximately 3 GB to 902.911 MB by using the Simplify routine, on each of the coefficients, (v_i, $i = 0, ..., 8$), individually.

Once the FKU equation $\zeta = 0$, is solved for z, after substituting architecture and actuator values in it, one can find the corresponding values of x. The value of x corresponding to each (real) value of z can be uniquely determined by equating the polynomial remainder obtained by dividing $C'(x, z)$ by $C(x, z)$ with respect to x to zero and solving for x in the same manner that was used for obtaining t_3 in Sect. 3.3.

---

[2] It is found that this tangent half-angle substitutions for θ_{21}, θ_{31} has made the algebraic computations in the later steps faster.

Table 1 Forward kinematic solutions of the 3-RPRS manipulator for the input variables: $d_1 = \frac{6}{5}, d_2 = \frac{3}{2}, d_3 = \frac{17}{10}, \theta_1 = 0, \theta_2 = \frac{7\pi}{12}, \theta_3 = \frac{7\pi}{4}$

Solution no.	x	y	z	ϕ_1	ϕ_2	ϕ_3
1, 2	0.353	0	±2.878	±1.857	±1.445	±2.683
3, 4	0.651	0	±2.949	±1.755	±2.677	±2.604
5, 6	−1.205	0	±1.794	±2.501	±1.603	±1.930
7, 8	−0.568	0	±2.424	±2.201	±2.755	±1.646

From the planarity constraint $y = 0$ for all the solutions of z and x, one can find all the passive angles ϕ_i as well. After the passive angles are computed for all the real solutions z, one can get the positions of the points $^0p_i, i = 1, 2, 3$ and the pose of the end-effector is determined uniquely.

4 Numerical Results

The above procedure is illustrated below via an example. The numerical values are adopted from [2], so as to compare the final results with the same. The architecture parameters considered are[3]: $l = 3$ and $a = 2$. All the numerical results are obtained in Mathematica, with a precision of 50 significant digits after the decimal point.

The numerical values of the active variables are chosen as: $d_1 = \frac{6}{5}, d_2 = \frac{3}{2}, d_3 = \frac{17}{10}, \theta_1 = 0, \theta_2 = \frac{7\pi}{12}, \theta_3 = \frac{7\pi}{4}$. The monic form of the FKU in this case, is shown below[4]:

$$\zeta = m^8 - 6.413m^7 - 534.433m^6 + 9911.630m^5 - 47703.189m^4 - 250740.961m^3$$
$$+ 3499560.799m^2 - 3096233.726m + 16559580.130 = 0, \text{ where } m = z^2.$$
(19)

Equation (19) admits 4 real solutions (tabulated in Table 1), each leading to a pair of poses of the manipulator which have a *mirror symmetry* about the base plane, X_0Y_0. The passive variables, ϕ_i, for each of the 8 poses, are enumerated in Table 1, which match those in Table 1 of [2] up to two digits after the decimal point.

In order to validate the solutions further, they are substituting back into the constraint equations, $\boldsymbol{\eta} = [g_1, g_2, g_3, \xi_1, \xi_2]^\top$. The *residual error*, defined as $\|\boldsymbol{\eta}\|$, is found to be of the order of 10^{-25}. The accuracy of the results can be improved by increasing the working precision albeit at the cost of additional computations.

The time taken to obtain the numeric monic polynomial Eq. (19) by substituting all the parameters and variables with their numerical values in Eq. (18) is around 34 s, whereas the same equation, when obtained by substituting the numerical values

---

[3]All the angles are measured in radians, and lengths in metres, unless mentioned otherwise explicitly.
[4]Though the coefficients are obtained with a precision of 50 significant digits, their real approximations are presented here for the want of space.

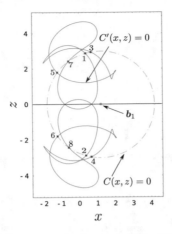

Fig. 2 Intersection of the constraint curves leading to the FK solutions

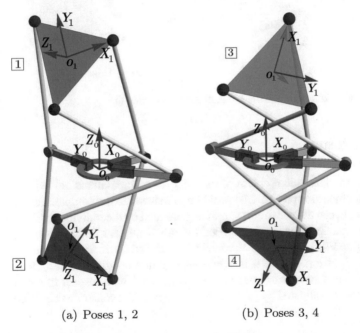

(a) Poses 1, 2   (b) Poses 3, 4

Fig. 3 Forward kinematic poses 1–4 (numbered as per Table 1)

at the stage of Eq. (17) is around 0.91 s. It is found that the accuracies of the results obtained are comparable in the two ways of computation.

The intersections of the coupler surface with the circle in the plane $X_2 Z_2$, for this example, are shown in Fig. 2 and the different poses of the manipulator are shown in Figs. 3 and 4.

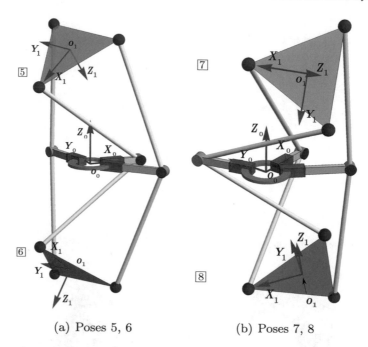

(a) Poses 5, 6   (b) Poses 7, 8

Fig. 4 Forward kinematic poses 5–8 (numbered as per Table 1)

5   Conclusion

The forward kinematic problem of the 3-RPRS manipulator is solved in this paper, using a geometric approach. The problem is reduced to the computation of the intersections between the constraint varieties generated by the individual sub-chains, into which the manipulator is decomposed hypothetically for the purpose of this work. A 16-degree FKU equation is obtained in the closed form, for a general architecture of the manipulator. The FKU is even-powered in the variable z and, therefore, half of the solutions are mirror images to the other half, with respect to the base plane. The results are validated by finding the residues of the constraint equations.

References

1. V. Venkatesan, Y. Singh, S. Mohan, Inverse kinematic solution of a 6-DOF(3-RPRS) parallel spatial manipulator, in *Proceedings of the 7th Asian Conference on Multibody System Dynamics* (Busan, South Korea), 29 June–3 July 2014
2. A. Nag, S. Mohan, S. Bandyopadhyay, Forward kinematic analysis of the 3-RPRS parallel manipulator. Mech. Mach. Theory **116**, 262–272 (2017)
3. R.A. Srivatsan, S. Bandyopadhyay, *Analysis of Constraint Equations and Their Singularities* (Springer International Publishing, 2014), pp. 429–436

4. T.K. Mamidi, A. Baskar, S. Bandyopadhyay, *A Novel Geometric Analysis of the Kinematics of the 3-RPS Manipulator* (Springer International Publishing, 2018), pp. 483–490
5. K.H. Hunt, *Kinematic Geometry of Mechanisms*, vol. 7 (Oxford University Press, Oxford, England, 1978)
6. J.-P. Merlet, Direct kinematics and assembly modes of parallel manipulators. Int. J. Robot. Res. **11**, 150–162 (1992)
7. K.H. Hunt, E.J.F. Primrose, Assembly configurations of some in-parallel-actuated manipulators. Mech. Mach. Theory **28**(1), 31–42 (1993)

Development and Performance Evaluation of Indigenous Control System of 500 Kg Payload Six-DOF Shake Table

Shiju Varghese, P. Ramakrishna, Jay Shah, P. K. Limaye and S. Raghunathan

Abstract Shake Tables are used to simulate the effects of earthquake loading on specimen structures and conduct experimental research in the areas of vibration, structural testing and safety assessment. In India, most high-capacity Shake Table installations are imported. Refuelling Technology Division, Reactor Design and Development Group, BARC has indigenously developed a 500 kg payload six-DOF Shake Table and commissioned at BARC. Synchronous control of all the eight actuators of the Table is required to control the Shake Table. Each actuator is provided with position, acceleration, differential pressure and load feedback sensors. A total of 40 feedback sensors are used in the Shake Table control algorithm with a control loop update rate of 1 kHz. It is required to acquire various parameters during Table control in order to do offline analysis and also to use in control strategies like experimental system identification and iterative tuning. The design and development of electronic control system for six-DOF Shake Table also includes implementation of various control methods such as Degrees of freedom (DOF) control, force balance control, and three-variable control (TVC) on a suitable electronic system. No generic hardware and software that satisfies all the control requirement of the Shake Table is readily available. Design and Development of an electronic control system that satisfies all the control requirements of the Shake Table is described in this paper. This development is based on four numbers of indigenously developed Double Actuator Controller with Dual CAN bus Interface (DACCI) networked through CAN bus. This paper describes Control and Instrumentation architecture, specifications and performance of the indigenously developed control system of the Shake Table.

Keywords Six-DOF Shake Table · Servo-hydraulic multi-axis controller
Parallel manipulator · CAN bus

S. Varghese (✉) · P. Ramakrishna · J. Shah · P. K. Limaye · S. Raghunathan
Refuelling Technology Division, Bhabha Atomic Research Centre, Mumbai,
Maharashtra, India
e-mail: shiju@barc.gov.in

S. Raghunathan
e-mail: raghu@barc.gov.in

© Springer Nature Singapore Pte Ltd. 2019
D N Badodkar and T A Dwarakanath (eds.), *Machines, Mechanism and Robotics*, Lecture Notes in Mechanical Engineering,
https://doi.org/10.1007/978-981-10-8597-0_15

171

1 Introduction

Six-DOF Shake Table is required to carry out safety studies of various systems to be used in nuclear reactors [1]. In India, most high-capacity Shake Table installations are imported. Key components of Shake Table are its control system and servo-hydraulic actuators. These are provided with limited engineering details to the users. Therefore, to implement specific requirements that arise during research, it requires support from the original manufacturer. Such support will be mostly limited by commercial terms and also, all maintenance and up gradation activities would be of proprietary nature. This leads to more downtime, high cost and also the scope of research becomes limited by these factors. In order to solve these issues, a 500 kg payload six-DOF Shake Table has been indigenously developed, installed, commissioned at BARC and is being used by a large number of satisfied users from various units of Department of Atomic Energy (DAE).

Input to the Shake Table is acceleration-time history. The acceleration waveform that simulates earthquake contains dominant frequencies up to 50 Hz. The servo-hydraulic system requires 50 Hz bandwidth for the generation of the earthquake acceleration waveforms on the Table as per guidelines provided in IEEE-344 standard. In order to achieve this bandwidth, in-house designed hydraulic servo actuators along with advanced control algorithms are used. These algorithms are implemented in an in-house developed electronic hardware platform named DACCI [2]. This paper describes Control and Instrumentation architecture, specifications and performance of the indigenously developed control system of the Shake Table.

1.1 Major Challenges for the Design of Electronic Control System for Six-DOF Shake Table

I. Control system for Shake Table should implement features like Degrees of freedom (DOF) control, force balance control, overturning moment compensation, offset moment compensation and three variable controls (TVC) [3]. For this, measured states of actuators have to be shared in real time with controllers of other actuators.

II. Shake Table is a complex Multiple Input Multiple Output (MIMO) system. Control algorithms require high order floating point matrix multiplications and the control loop update rate is 1 kHz. Hence, the processor should have sufficient computational power for the Table control.

III. Sensors such as MEMS accelerometer with SPI interface, LVDT with ±10 V output, pressure transmitters with 4–20 mA and load cells with Wheatstone bridge output are selected as feedbacks sensors. The electronic control system should have sufficient sensor interfaces suitable for the selected sensors with a sampling rate of 1 kHz.

IV. Fast and real-time methods for synchronizing the movement of all actuators.

V. Sufficient memory for storing the waveform history and control parameters of the actuators.

VI. Data acquisition facility for collecting various data during Table movement for further offline analysis and implementing offline system identification control schemes.

VII. Real-time display and modification for all the variables in the system, and Real-time plots with data points sampled at 1 kHz rate to visualize various parameters during tuning and operation of the system are major requirements of the system.

2 Control Requirements

In this six-DOF Shake Table, eight servo-hydraulic actuators are used. Four are installed horizontally and remaining four are installed vertically. The positions of horizontal actuators are defined as x1 and x2 in the longitudinal direction, y1 and y2 in transverse direction as shown in Fig. 1, and z1 to z4 (not visible in Fig. 1) in vertical direction.

Figure 2 shows servo control of a six-DOF Shake Table [4]. Position and acceleration sensor output of all the actuators (x1, x2, y1, y2, z1, z2, z3, z4) are read by the controller. The velocity is synthesized from the read position and acceleration.

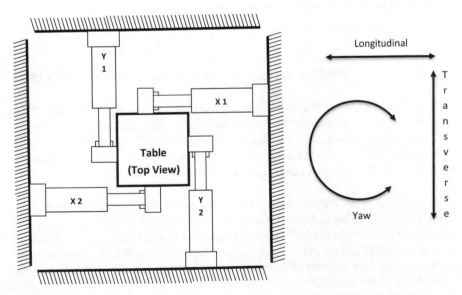

Fig. 1 Table top view. x1 and x2 actuators in longitudinal direction and y1 and y2 in transverse direction

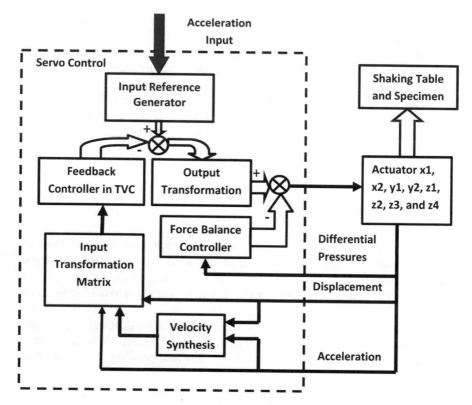

Fig. 2 Servo control of six-DOF Shake Table [4]

The velocity in the low-frequency band is estimated from the low pass filter of the position.

The velocity in the high-frequency band is obtained by the high pass filter of the acceleration. The input transformation matrix is used to calculate the DOF feedback.

"The control performance of a Shake Table is greatly affected by the interaction between the Table and the test specimen mounted on it. This is because the dynamic characteristics of large specimens impart significant force disturbances on the Table" [5].

Therefore, it is not appropriate to run the Table with conventional PID controllers. The TVC algorithm has been chosen as it can give a wide bandwidth required for this application as shown in Fig. 3. This requires measurement of various state feedbacks from the actuators and use of these in the control law execution [6]. Eight actuators are used to control the 6 Degrees of Freedom. When the number of actuators exceeds the controllable DOF small calibration errors of Table Position can cause generation of large Internal Table Forces by the actuators. Force Balance Compensation algorithm has to be in place in order to assure that forces are balanced on all the driving actuators. When several actuators are in the same degrees of freedom, it is necessary

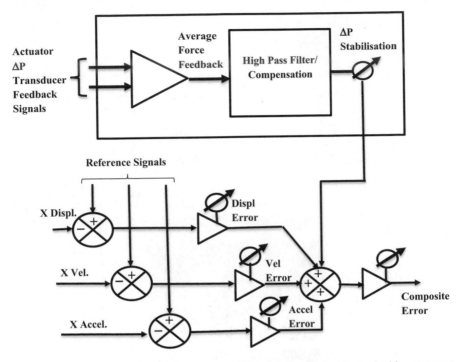

Fig. 3 Three-variable controller (TVC) servo stability function for longitudinal table movement with differential pressure compensation implemented in the Shake Table controller

to use the concept of DOF control. Seismic testing of large specimens with high velocity and acceleration demands for maximum gain setting for the control loop and still ensuring stability. This can be achieved by adding velocity and acceleration lead terms in the control algorithm.

3 Control and Instrumentation Architecture

Figure 4 shows the Control and Instrumentation architecture of the six-DOF Shake Table. Four numbers of indigenously developed Double Actuator Controller with Dual Can Bus Interface (DACCI) are used in this system. Specifications of the DACCI is given in Table 1. All the DACCIs are connected to a PC through CAN-A network. A custom protocol was developed to use in this network. The PC is updated with data from all the DACCIs every 200 ms using this protocol. Any variable on any DACCI can be modified from the PC software using a single CAN message. Also, a high speed plot of up to four floating point variables from each DACCI with 1 ms sampling interval is possible. Acceleration waveform download, configuration of internal data acquisition system, plot settings and transfer of acquired data from

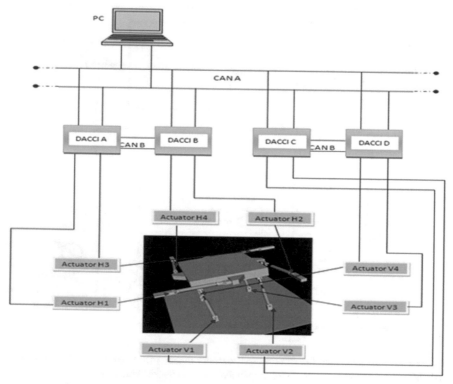

Fig. 4 Architecture of the Shake Table control system

MMC are possible with this protocol. DACCI-A and DACCI-B are interconnected through CAN-B network. Photograph of the electronic controller is shown in Fig. 5.

3.1 Firmware of DACCI

Following features are implemented in the firmware of DACCI

- Degrees of Freedom Control (DOF Control).
- Force Balance Controller to avoid Table warping.
- Control loop rate at 1 kHz.
- Ramping of inputs to avoid jerky steps.
- Sin, Cos, Sine sweep, Square functions in each degree of freedom.
- Playing random waveform from MMC pre-stored data (1 ms interval).
- 20 Channel Data Acquisition of user selectable data to the MMC card at 1 kHz rate.
- High-speed real-time plot data transfer of up to four floating point user-selected variables.

Table 1 Specifications of DACCI hardware

1.	**Digital signal controller**	
	150 MHz 32-bit Floating point processor (TI Delphino TMS320F28335)	
2.	**Analog inputs**	
	16-bit ADC channels for LVDT Interface with ±15 V sensor supply to LVDT	4 Nos
	12-bit ADC channels for 4–20 mA inputs with 24 V sensor supply	4 Nos
	12-bit ADC channels for configurable ±5 V or ±10 V	2 Nos
	12-bit ADC channels for all element varying Wheatstone bridge interface with 10 mA excitation current (for load cells)	2 Nos
3.	**Analog outputs**	
	PWM-based servo valve driver with 13-bit resolution	2 Nos
	DAC-based servo valve driver with 16-bit resolution	2 Nos
4.	**MEMS digital accelerometer interface**	4 Nos
5.	**Optically isolated digital input**	1 No
6.	**Digital output—NO/NC relay 24 V 1 A contact**	1 No
7.	**Quadrature encoder interface (QEI)**	1 No
8.	**Controller area interface (CAN)**	
	2 independent CAN networks: CAN-A and CAN-B	
	CAN-A network is configured at 1 Mbps speed and is used for networking all DACCI's with computer. A custom protocol is used for Read/Write operation of all the system variables from the computer	
	Fast data transfer for simultaneous plotting of up to four floating point variables from each DACCI is possible through CAN-A network	
	High-speed file transfer from PC to MMC and vice versa is also done though CAN-A	
	CAN-B is used for dedicated real-time inter-controller communication between DACCIs [7]	
9.	**Multimedia Card (MMC)**	128 MB
	• 20 channel data acquisition system with 1 kHz sampling rate • Earthquake waveform storage and play from MMC card	
10.	**Synchronization pulse input to DACCI-RS422 type**	1 No
11.	**External trigger for data acquisition (TTL)**	1 No

3.2 Graphical User Interface (GUI)

Major features of the GUI of the Shake Table control system are as follows:

- Real-Time display/edit of all the system variables.
- Real-time plot of selected variables (useful for online tuning of the controller).
- Table Run/Stop Command after setting the experimental parameters.
- Homing command.
- Sin, Cos, Sine sweep, and Square functions configuration.

Fig. 5 Photographs of the indigenous Shake Table and controller

- Play from MMC function, Upload of acquired data from MMC and Download of waveform data from PC.
- Response spectra conversion to acceleration-time history and vice versa.
- Selection and configuration of Plot and Data Acquisition Parameters.

4 Performance Validation

Standard waveforms such as step, sine and sine sweep were generated using the table for testing its performance which was found to be satisfactory.

In seismic qualification tests, acceleration-time history compatible to the Required Response Spectra (RRS) is required to be generated on the table. A 2% damping 0.2 g PGA OBE Response Spectrum was fed to an artificial motion generation algorithm to obtain the required acceleration-time history data. This acceleration data was played on the table. A MEMS accelerometer was used to acquire the actual acceleration achieved by the Shake Table. This data was used to obtain the Test Response Spectra (TRS) using the same algorithm. It is found that TRS is overlapping RRS as per the requirement of IEEE-344. Time history of measured acceleration, position, and velocity in longitudinal axis are shown in Fig. 6. The response spectra plotted for with and without inertial load experiments in longitudinal axis is shown in Fig. 7. It was observed that TRS overlaps RRS adequately. Figures 8, 9 and 10 is provided

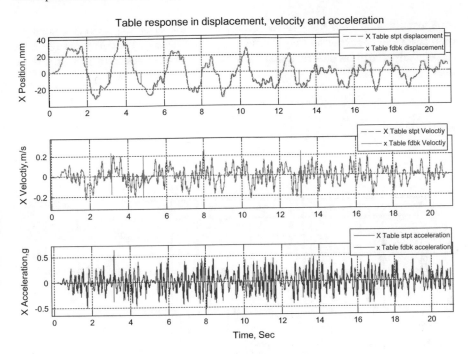

Fig. 6 Comparison of measured displacement, velocity and acceleration-time histories

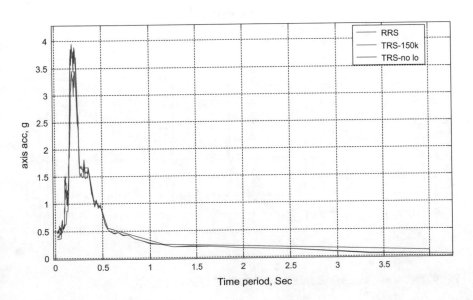

Fig. 7 TRS versus RRS: with load and without inertial load

in Appendix shows the RRS versus TRS comparison of an experiment conducted on a particular specimen in longitudinal (X), Transverse (Y) and Vertical (Z) axis, respectively. It can be observed that TRS adequately overlaps RRS in all the three axes.

Appendix

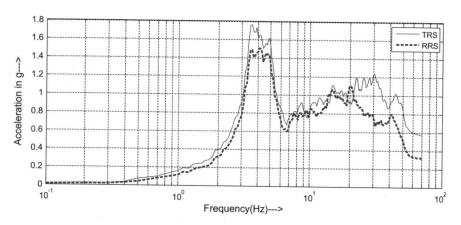

Fig. 8 RRS versus TRS comparison for an OBE-level spectra on X-axis

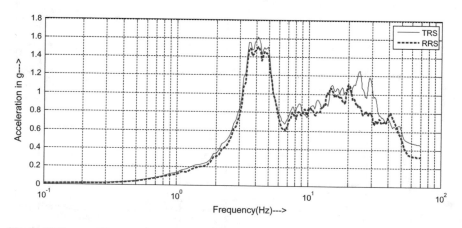

Fig. 9 RRS versus TRS comparison for an OBE-level spectra on Y-axis

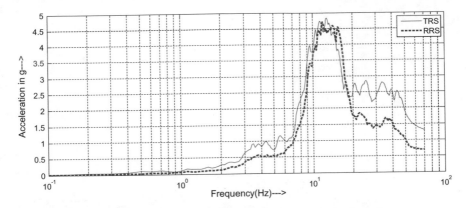

Fig. 10 RRS versus TRS comparison for an OBE level spectra on Z-axis

References

1. A.S. Pisharady, A.D. Roshan, V.V. Muthekar, *Seismic Safety of Nuclear Power Plants—A Monograph*, http://www.aerb.gov.in/images/PDF/SeismicSafety.pdf
2. S. Varghese, J. Shah, P. Ramakrishna, N.L. Soni, R.J. Patel, Double actuator controller with dual CAN bus interface for 6 DOF Shake Table, in *2013 International Conference on Control Communication and Computing (ICCC)*, Thiruvananthapuram (2013), pp. 86–89. https://doi.org/10.1109/iccc.2013.6731629
3. S. Ammanagi et al., Development of a digitally-controlled three-axis earthquake Shake Table. Curr. Sci. **91**(2), 190 (2006)
4. G. Guan, H. Wang, W. Xiong, J. Han, Vibration control of multiaxis hydraulic Shaking Table, in *Proceedings of 2011 International Conference on Fluid Power and Mechatronics*, Beijing (2011), pp. 179–184. https://doi.org/10.1109/fpm.2011.6045753
5. B.K. Thoen, P.N. Laplace, Offline tuning of shaking tables, in *13th World Conference on Earthquake Engineering* Vancouver, B.C., Canada (2004), Paper No. 960
6. P. Ramakrishna, S. Varghese, N.L. Soni, R.J. Patel, The effect of velocity feedback in position control of high performance servo hydraulic actuators, in *2013 International Conference on Control Communication and Computing (ICCC)*, Thiruvananthapuram (2013), pp. 440–445. https://doi.org/10.1109/iccc.2013.6731695
7. T.V. Unavane, M.S. Panse, S. Varghese, N.L. Soni, R.J. Patel, Development of CAN bus application layer protocol for 6 DOF Shake Table control system, in *2015 IEEE 2nd International Conference on Recent Trends in Information Systems (ReTIS)*, Kolkata (2015), pp. 285–289. https://doi.org/10.1109/retis.2015.7232892

Analysis of Dynamic Interaction Issues for Omnidirectional Mobile Robot

G. R. Nikhade, S. S. Chiddarwar and A. K. Jha

Abstract Omnidirectional welding mobile robot (Omni-WMR) consists of a manipulator mounted on the mobile platform equipped with omnidirectional wheel. Omnidirectional mobile robots have the capability to move in any direction and hence it is finding a prominent place in many applications in manufacturing and processing industries. This capability avoids the transportation of heavy and lengthy material to the workspace. As the manipulator mounted on the mobile platform while performing the task, it is necessary to study the effect of platform motion on the dynamic behavior of manipulator and vice versa. This paper is focused on the dynamic interaction between manipulator and platform. For this, coupled dynamic model of Omni-WMR is developed. To evaluate this approach, two different case studies are presented in this paper. Results show that there is a significant change in torque values developed at manipulator joints due to the platform motion and vice versa as well as change in position of the manipulator.

Keywords Dynamic interaction · Omnidirectional · Mobile robot
Coupled dynamic

G. R. Nikhade (✉) · A. K. Jha
Department of Mechanical Engineering, Shri Ramdeobaba College of Engineering and
Management, Nagpur, India
e-mail: grnikhade@rediffmail.com; nikhadegr@rknec.edu

A. K. Jha
e-mail: jhaak1@rknec.edu

S. S. Chiddarwar
Department of Mechanical Engineering, Visvesvaraya National Institute of Technology,
Nagpur, India
e-mail: s.chiddarwar@gmail.com

1 Introduction

Industrial robots are mainly classified as fixed and mobile robots depending on the nature of working. In industries, it is very difficult to transport lengthy and heavy structures to the workstation because of limited space on industrial floor. In such condition, a mobile robot finds the best alternative over the fixed base robots by mounting the robot on the moving platform. It obviously increases its workspace by moving the mobile robots to the workstation. The maneuverability of mobile robots mainly depends on the type of wheels used on the platform. To achieve the omnidirectional motion, special and omnidirectional wheels are used, namely ball wheels, universal wheels, and Mecanum wheels. Among these, Mecanum wheel is having an enormous omnidirectional capability due to its structure it can perform any task within least possible floor area [1]. Moreover, along with the various advantages of mobile robots, there are certain issues like dynamic stability, structural complexity and dynamic interaction between the manipulator and omnidirectional platform needs to be resolved. To resolve these issues, a SCORBOT ER-IV manipulator is considered which is mounted on the omnidirectional platform attached with Mecanum wheel. The kinematic and dynamic modeling of the manipulator and omnidirectional platform is performed to determine the torque variation at the joints of the manipulator with and without the platform motion as well as by mounting the manipulator at different locations. Finally, the proposed approach is implemented to two different case problems. In order to comprehend the current state of the art, a detailed literature review covering various issues of dynamic interaction is presented next.

Robert and Khatib [2] developed a dynamic model of a holonomic mobile robot with powered caster wheels. They claimed that the design of the powered caster vehicle provides smooth, accurate motion with the ability to traverse through the hazards of typical indoor environments.

Carter et al. [3] developed dynamic equations of motion by Newton's second law for omnidirectional RoboCup players, assuming that no slip occurs at the wheel in the spin direction. Whereas, Williams II et al. [4] presented a dynamic model for omnidirectional wheeled mobile robots, including wheel/motion surface slip. They experimentally measured the coefficient of friction and forces responsible for a slip in order to validate their friction model. Further, Yu and Chen [5] presented a dynamic model of a non-holonomic mobile manipulator consisting of multi-degree of freedom serial manipulator and an autonomous wheeled mobile platform. They have assigned a coordinate frame to each wheel to correlate their kinematic and dynamic parameters with a world coordinate frame to develop a combined dynamic model of mobile manipulators.

Bui et al. [6] developed a dynamic model of welding mobile robot (WMR) by assuming suitable constraints with no-slip condition for the wheel. They proposed an adaptive motion tracking algorithm for the two-wheeled WMR and implemented in simulation environment as well as a real-world model. A fully coupled dynamic model of the mobile manipulator system dealing with non-holonomic constraints was developed by Gomes and Ferreira [7] using a Lagrange–Euler formulation. Further, they have implemented it to control the end-effector position of a mobile manipulator having a differential-drive platform and two degrees of freedom manipulator mounted on it.

Amagai et al. [8] developed a dynamic model and control system for omnidirectional mobile manipulator with four driving wheels to determine the relationship between the torque of the wheel and driving force generated to the platform.

Williams II et al. [9] established a novel method of motion planning in the cluttered environment for three-wheeled omnidirectional mobile robots. The environment was considered to be dynamic, wherein the obstacles were moving with general velocities without previous knowledge of motion profiles. Wang et al. [10] developed a dynamic motion control algorithm for position control and trajectory tracking of the omnidirectional mobile platform equipped with four independent omnidirectional wheels equally spaced at 90° from one to another.

From the above discussion, it is evident that most researchers have limited their work toward the development of the dynamic model of either manipulator or mobile platform equipped with either conventional wheels or simple omnidirectional wheels like caster wheel, universal wheels. It is also observed that some researchers have worked on the dynamic coupling of a manipulator with non-omnidirectional mobile platform, but the attempts to exploit the benefits of robot manipulator mounted on the omnidirectional platform equipped with Mecanum wheel for industrial applications like welding, material handling, and service application are not significant.

2 Coupled Dynamic Modeling of Omnidirectional Mobile Robot

In this section, to study the dynamic interaction between manipulator and platform, firstly the equations of motion of a robot manipulator and wheeled mobile platform are described. Then based on these equations, a method for establishing the equations of motion of a mobile manipulator which incorporates the dynamic interactions between the mobile platform and the manipulator is developed.

2.1 Dynamic Model for SCORBOT ER-IV

The dynamic model for manipulator based on L-E formulation is presented as follows:

$$\tau_{ri} = \frac{d}{dt}\left(\frac{\partial L}{\partial \dot{q}_{r,i}}\right) - \frac{\partial L}{\partial q_{r,i}} \tag{1}$$

where L is the Lagrange function or Lagrangian which is the difference between the total kinetic energy K and the total potential energy P of a mechanical system,

Fig. 1 SCORBOT ER-IV
manipulator. *Source*
Intellitek user manual

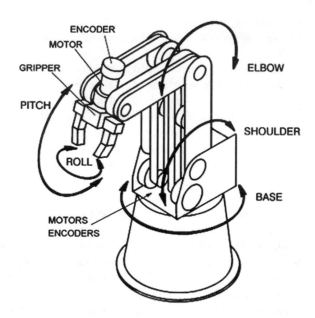

$q_r = [\theta_1(\text{base}), \ \theta_2(\text{shoulder}), \ \theta_3(\text{elbow}), \ \theta_4(\text{pitch}), \ \theta_5(\text{roll})]$ is the joint position or displacement variable of the manipulator as shown in Fig. 1. By substituting L and carrying out the differentiation, the generalized torque τ_{ri} applied to link i of an n-dof manipulator is expressed in (2) [11–13]:

$$M_r(q)\ddot{q}_r + C_r(q, \dot{q}) + G_r(q) = \tau_{ri} \tag{2}$$

where M_r is the inertia matrix of the manipulator, C_r Is the Coriolis and centrifugal term of the manipulator, G_r is the gravity loading force at joint due to link, $\dot{q}_r$ and $\ddot{q}_r$ is angular velocity and angular acceleration vector for the manipulator, respectively.

2.2   *Dynamic Modeling of Omnidirectional Platform*

Figure 2 shows the top view of omni-WMR platform with Mechanum wheel on which the manipulator will be mounted during the task.

To achieve the omnidirectional capability, the mobile platform is subjected constraint equation shown in (3):

$$\dot{x}cos\emptyset + \dot{y}sin\emptyset + (la)\dot{\emptyset} = R\dot{\beta}_j \tag{3}$$

where $\emptyset$ is the heading angle of the mobile robot measured from X_w axis of world coordinate system, $\dot{x}$ and $\dot{y}$ is the linear velocity of the mobile platform in x and y

Fig. 2 Top view of omni-WMR platform with heading angle Φ

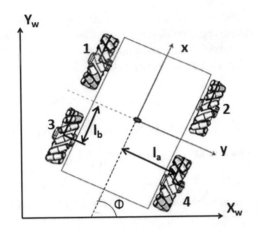

Table 1 Platform motion according to the direction and angular speed of the wheels

Direction	Wheel number			
	1	2	3	4
Forward	+	+	+	+
Backward	−	−	−	−
Right slide	−	+	−	+
Left slide	+	−	+	−
Clockwise rotation	+	−	−	+
Anticlockwise rotation	−	+	+	−
Forward–Right	0	+	0	+
Forward–Left	+	0	+	0
Backward–Right	0	+	0	+
Backward–Left	+	0	+	0

direction, respectively, R is the radius of wheel, l_a is the distance between driving wheel and vertical axis of symmetry, and $\dot{\beta}_j$ is the angular velocity of Mecanum wheels.

The constrained Eq. (3) is responsible for platform motion. The direction of platform motion depends on the direction of wheel rotation and angular speed of the wheels as shown in Table 1. '+' indicates clockwise rotation of wheel, '−' indicates anticlockwise rotation, and '0' indicates stationary wheel if seen from positive y direction.

Lagrange formulation is used to establish equation of motion for the mobile platform [14] as follows:

$$\frac{d}{dt}\left(\frac{\partial L}{\partial \dot{q}_{p,i}}\right) - \frac{\partial L}{\partial q_{p,i}} = Q_i - a_{1i}\lambda_1 - a_{2i}\lambda_2 - a_{3i}\lambda_3 - a_{4i}\lambda_4 \qquad (4)$$

where Q_i is the generalized force (torque at each wheel), $\lambda_1, \lambda_2, \lambda_3, \lambda_4$ are the Lagrange multipliers. a are the elements of the constrained matrix.

After substituting the Lagrange function, and carrying out the differentiation, the Eq. (4) can be arranged as

$$M_p(q)\ddot{q}_p + C_p(q, \dot{q}) = E(q)\tau_w - A^T(q)\lambda \tag{5}$$

where M_p is the inertia matrix of the platform, C_p represents Coriolis and centrifugal term of the platform, $\dot{q}_p = \begin{bmatrix} \dot{x} & \dot{y} & \dot{\beta}_1 & \dot{\beta}_2 & \dot{\beta}_3 & \dot{\beta}_4 \end{bmatrix}^T$ is linear and angular velocity vector for the platform, $\ddot{q}_p = \begin{bmatrix} \ddot{x} & \ddot{y} & \ddot{\beta}_1 & \ddot{\beta}_2 & \ddot{\beta}_3 & \ddot{\beta}_4 \end{bmatrix}^T$ is the linear and angular acceleration vector for platform, E is the constant matrix, A^T is the constraint matrix for the platform.

2.3 Dynamic Interaction Between Manipulator and Platform

The motion equations to distinguish the effect of platform motion on the manipulator and the effect of dynamics of manipulator on the platform are expressed in Eqs. (6) and (7), respectively.

$$M_r(q_r)\ddot{q}_r + C_r\left(q_r, \dot{q}_r\right) + C_{r1}\left(q_r, \dot{q}_r, \dot{q}_p\right) = \tau_{r/p} - R_r\left(q_r, q_p\right)\ddot{q}_p \tag{6}$$

where C_{r1} denotes Coriolis and centrifugal term caused by the angular motion of the mobile platform, $\tau_{r/p}$ is the input torque developed on the manipulator's joint due to platform motion, R_r is the inertia matrix which represents the effect of the platform dynamics on the manipulator.

$$M_p(q_p)\ddot{q}_p + C_p\left(q_p\ \dot{q}_p\right) + C_{p1}\left(q_r\ q_p\ \dot{q}_r\ \dot{q}_p\right)$$
$$= E\tau_{p/r} - A^T\lambda - M_{p1}\left(q_r\ q_p\right)\ddot{q}_p - R_p\left(q_r\ q_p\right)\ddot{q}_r \tag{7}$$

where M_{p1} and C_{p1} represents the inertial term and Coriolis and centrifugal terms due to the presence of the manipulator, respectively, $\tau_{p/r}$ is the input torque to the platform, and R_p represents the inertia matrix which reflects the dynamic effect of the arm motion on the platform [15, 16].

3 Application of the Proposed Approach

This section presents the two different case studies to estimate the effectiveness of the developed approach.

3.1 Case Study 1

This case study is formulated to see the effect of dynamics of the motion of the platform on the manipulator and vice versa while executing welding task along the straight path. For this, two sub-cases are considered. In first sub-case, trajectory tracking of the omni-WMR is considered for welding of two mild steel plates having 8 mm thickness and 440 mm length by keeping the platform stationary since the path length is within the workspace of the manipulator. In the second, two mild steel plates of 8 mm thickness and 860 mm length are supposed to be welded. Since the 860 mm length is beyond the reach of the SCORBOT ER-IV, the motion of omnidirectional platform is also considered. The time required to weld these plates is 72 s, which is calculated by considering the various welding parameters like voltage, current, feed rate, etc. [17].

To obtain the smooth joint trajectories for the SCORBOT ER-IV, a cubic spline as shown in (8) is fitted to the joint trajectory obtained from IK solutions [18].

$$\theta(t) = c_0 + c_1 t + c_2 t^2 + c_3 t^3 \tag{8}$$

where, c_0, c_1, c_2, and c_3 are the coefficient of the equations obtained from the initial and the final angular position of the manipulator joint and t is the time required to finish the task. Using the above expressions, the time history plot of displacement is obtained and it is shown in Fig. 3.

These joint trajectories and the physical parameters of the SCORBOT ER-IV and the omnidirectional platform with Mecanum wheels was given as an input to the

Fig. 3 Joint trajectory for straight path

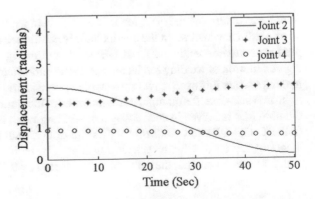

Fig. 4 Torque variations at
the joints of manipulator
mounted on stationary
platform

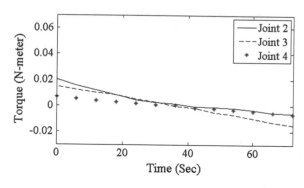

Fig. 5 Torque variations at
the joints of manipulator
mounted on mobile platform

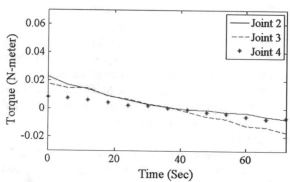

developed MATLAB® program to compute the torque required at each joint of the
SCORBOT ER-IV by using Eq. (6).

The torque required at each joint of the manipulator is obtained by this analysis
and same are plotted in Figs. 4 and 5.

3.2 Case Study 2

In order to determine the variation in torque developed at manipulator joints as well
as on platform wheel when the manipulator is positioned at different locations on the
platform, another weldment (ABCDE) as shown in Fig. 6. This weldment requires
zig-zag motion of welding torch attached to the end-effector of manipulator. In order
to demonstrate this aspect, two sub-cases are considered.

In first sub-case, the manipulator is mounted at the center of gravity of the platform.
Omni-WMR is moved in such a way that welding torch follows the double line path
(AB-BC-CD-DE) and platform follows the dotted path shown in Fig. 6. The total
length of the end—effector path is considered to be 600 mm and that of platform
path 200 mm. In second, the manipulator is shifted by 0.125 m (d) from the center of

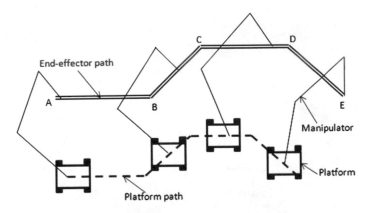

Fig. 6 Path followed by manipulator and platform to achieve weldment

gravity of the platform. Both paths are fitted with separate cubic splines and further analysis is done as discussed in Case Study 1 [19].

Temporal information of torque at various joints of the manipulator and wheels of the platform is obtained using Eqs. (6) and (7). Figure 7 shows the comparison of torque required at joint 2(shoulder), 3(elbow) and 4(pitch), respectively, at two different positions of the manipulator.

The welding time came out to be 50 s by the same methodology used in Case Study 1. The total distance traveled by the platform during the welding of the path is 200 mm in 50 s.

4 Results and Discussion

The analysis of case study 1 revealed that, even though displacement, velocity, acceleration and time were kept constant, the torque requirement was more for 860 mm weldment than for 440 mm weldment. It was observed that 15–30% more torque at manipulator joints is required when platform motion is also involved. From this fact, it can be inferred that the platform motion shows a considerable increase in the torque required at manipulator joints. These results justify the phenomenon of dynamic interaction between manipulator and platform. However, when the torque required for platform motion was computed, it came out to be constant. It signifies that the effect of dynamic interaction on platform wheel is uniform over all the four wheels. Moreover, when the torque requirement at the platform wheel is compared, it is found that average 53.4% more torque is required when the manipulator is mounted on platform as compared to platform without manipulator.

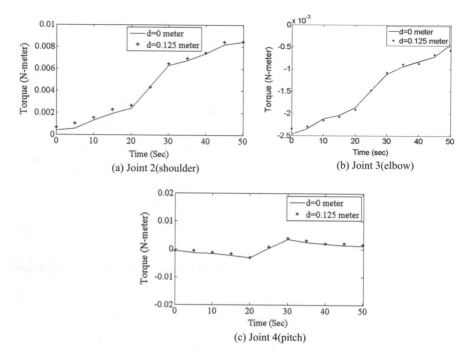

Fig. 7 Torque developed at the joints

From case study 2, it can be concluded that the torque requirements at manipulator joint do not change with a change in the position of the manipulator. However, a different scenario was observed for omnidirectional wheels. When torque requirement at platform wheels are compared, it is observed that the 9–12% more torque developed at front wheels and 2–3% less torque at the rear wheels when the manipulator is mounted away from the mass center of platform by distance 0.125 m compared to its location exactly at the mass center. This is because of shifting the manipulator towards the front wheels of the platform. Moreover, after comparing the torque at platform wheels for forward and diagonal motion of platform, it is seen that nearly 40–50% more torque developed during diagonal motion as compared to forward motion because another pair of wheels is stationary. These results clearly indicate that the effect of the position of the manipulator is more prominent on the torque requirement at omnidirectional wheels than on the joints of the manipulator.

5 Conclusions

In this paper, a coupled dynamic model for a omnidirectional mobile robot is developed to study the dynamic interaction between omnidirectional platform and SCOR-BOT ER-IV. To validate this model two different case studies were considered which included the welding of straight and zig-zag path. The study of dynamic interaction between omnidirectional platform and SCORBOT ER-IV revealed the effect of motion of platform on SCORBOT ER-IV and vice versa. The equations established for each condition of interactions are the function of joint/wheel velocity, which emphasizes the severity of effect of dynamic interaction at higher velocities. Moreover, the result obtained from the developed dynamic model is validated by MATLAB simulation environment but it is out of the scope of this paper.

References

1. I. Doroftei, V. Grosu, V. Spinu, Omnidirectional mobile robot: design and implementation, bioinspiration and robotics walking and climbing robots (InTech, 2007). ISBN: 978-3-902613-15-8
2. H. Robert, O. Khatib, Development and control of a holonomic mobile robot for mobile manipulation tasks. Int. J. Robot. Res. **19**(11), 1066–1074 (2000)
3. B. Carter, M. Good, M. Dorohoff, J. Lew, R.L. Williams II, P. Gallina, Mechanical design and modeling of an omni-directional robocup player, in *Proceedings RoboCup International Symposium* (2001), pp. 1–10
4. R.L. Williams II, B.E. Carter, P. Gallina, G. Rosati, Dynamic model with slip for wheeled omni-directional robots. IEEE Trans. Robot. Autom. **18**(3), 285–293 (2002)
5. Q. Yu, I. Chen, A general approach to the dynamics of nonholonomic mobile manipulator systems. J. Dyn. Syst. Meas. Control **124**, 512–521 (2002)
6. T.H. Bui, T.L. Chung, S.B. Kim, T.T. Nguyen, Adaptive tracking control of two-wheeled welding mobile robot with smooth curved welding path. KSME Int. J. **17**(11), 1682–1692 (2003)
7. M.D.S. Gomes, A.M. Ferreira, Manipulator control on a mobile robot, in *ABCM Symposium Series in Mechatronics*, vol. 1 (2004), pp. 428–435
8. S. Amagai, T. Tsuji, J. Samuel, H. Osumi, Control of omni-directional mobile platform with four driving wheels using torque redundancy, in *IEEE/RSJ International Conference on Intelligent Robots and Systems* (Acropolis Convention Center, Nice, France, 1996–2002, 2008)
9. R.L. Williams II, J. Wu, Dynamic obstacle avoidance for an omni-directional mobile robot. J. Robot. 1–14 (2010)
10. T. Wang, C. Tsai, D. Wang, Dynamic control of an omnidirectional mobile platform. J. Nankai **7**(1), 9–18 (2010)
11. A.A. Ata, M.A. Ghazy, M.A. Gadou, Dynamics of a general multi-axis robot with analytical optimal torque analysis. J. Autom. Control Eng. **1**(2), 144–148 (2013)
12. R. Dhaouadi, A.A. Hatab, Dynamic modelling of differential-drive mobile robots using Lagrange and Newton-Euler methodologies: a unified framework. Adv. Robot. Autom. **2**(2), 1–7 (2013)
13. Y. Wen, J. Rosen. A novel linear PID controller for an upper limb exoskeleton, in *IEEE 49th Conference on Decision and Control*, Atlanta, GA, USA (2010)
14. C.S. Tzafestas, S.G. Taffetas, Full-state modeling, motion planning and control of mobile manipulator. Stud. Inform. Control **10**(2), 1–22 (2011)
15. T. Fukao, H. Nakagawa, N. Adachi, Adaptive tracking control of a nonholonomic mobile robot. IEEE Trans. Robot. Autom. **16**(5), 609–615 (2000)
16. M.P. Cheng, C.C. Tsai, Dynamic modeling and tracking control of a nonholonomic wheeled mobile manipulator with two robotic arms, in *IEEE Proceedings of the 42nd Conference on Decision and Control*, Hawaii, USA (2003)
17. Wilhelmsen Ships Service, *Maritime Welding Handbook* (Norway, Edition 11, Revision 0)

18. R.K. Mittal, I.J. Nagrath, *Robotics and Control* (Tata McGraw-Hill, New Delhi, 2012). ISBN 10: 0070482934 / ISBN 13: 9780070482937
19. F. Adăscăliţei, I. Doroftei, Practical applications for mobile robots based on mecanum wheels—a systematic survey, in *Proceedings of International Conference on Innovations, Recent Trends and Challenges in Mechatronics, Mechanical Engineering and New High-Tech Products Development* (2011)

Dynamics of Articulated Landing Gear in Tail-Down Landing Condition

Mahesh Kadam, S. Sathish, Aditya Bujurke, Keertivardhan Joshi
and Balamurugan Gopalsamy

Abstract Articulated landing gears have relatively lower stowage volume and provide better taxiing characteristics when compared to telescopic gears. Unlike telescopic configuration, the articulated configurations do not have the same stroke for wheel axle and shock absorber travel. The objective of this work is to study and compare the dynamics of the articulated main landing gear, during level and tail-down landing conditions, using MSC/ADAMS software. The results are compared with the available landing gear analysis program, which has been experimentally validated by the drop tests. A 12.3% reduction in total vertical wheel axle travel is observed in tail-down condition when compared to level landing, due to the kinematic configuration. It results in 18.9% and 14.8% increase in dynamic load in limit and reserve landing respectively for tail-down condition. Also, the tire deflections are relatively higher and the shock absorber travel is relatively lower, in tail-down landing for both limit and reserve conditions.

Keywords Articulated landing gears · Landing gear dynamic analysis
Tail-down landing dynamics

M. Kadam (✉) · S. Sathish · A. Bujurke · K. Joshi · B. Gopalsamy
Structural Technologies Division, CSIR-National Aerospace Labaratories,
Bengaluru, Karnataka, India
e-mail: maheshkadam@nal.res.in

S. Sathish
e-mail: sathishs@nal.res.in

A. Bujurke
e-mail: adi9740@gmail.com

K. Joshi
e-mail: keerti.mj@gmail.com

B. Gopalsamy
e-mail: gbala@nal.res.in

© Springer Nature Singapore Pte Ltd. 2019
D N Badodkar and T A Dwarakanath (eds.), *Machines, Mechanism
and Robotics*, Lecture Notes in Mechanical Engineering,
https://doi.org/10.1007/978-981-10-8597-0_17

Nomenclature

LG	Landing Gear
MIL	Military Standard
FAR	Federal Aviation Regulations
MLG	Main Landing Gear
WA	Wheel Axle
SA	Shock Absorber
F_s	Total Shock Absorber Force (N)
F_a	Pneumatic Force (N)
F_h	Hydraulic Force (N)
n	Polytropic Index
N	Dynamic Load Factor or Reaction Factor
η_{sa}	Efficiency of Shock Absorber
η_t	Efficiency of Tire
P_e	Extended Pressure in the Shock Absorber (Pa)
V_e	Extended Volume in the Shock Absorber (m^3)
P_s	Static Pressure in the Shock Absorber (Pa)
V_s	Static Volume in the Shock Absorber (m^3)
P_r	Reserve Pressure in the Shock Absorber (Pa)
V_r	Reserve Volume in the Shock Absorber (m^3)
P_{ao}	Initial Pressure in the Shock Absorber (Pa)
V_{ao}	Initial Volume in the Shock Absorber (m^3)
A_{ao}	Pneumatic Area (m^2)
s/S_t	Shock Absorber Stroke (m)
S_{wa}	Wheel Axle Travel (m)
v	Velocity of Aircraft (m/s)
g	Acceleration due to gravity (m/s^2)
ρ	Density of hydraulic oil (kg/m^3)
A_h	Hydraulic Area (m^2)
A_n	Net Orifice Area (m^2)
C_d	Coefficient of Discharge
$\dot{s}$	Shock Strut Telescopic Velocity (m/s)
F_{ty}	Tire Force (N)
z	Tire Deflection (m)
L	Aircraft Lift (N)
W_1	Weight of Sprung Mass (N)
W_2	Weight of Unsprung Mass (N)
m_1	Sprung Mass (kg)
m_2	Unsprung Mass (kg)
F_{va}	Vertical Force on Wheel Axle (N)
F_{ha}	Horizontal Force on Wheel Axle (N)
F_{vg}	Vertical Ground Reaction (N)
F_{hg}	Horizontal Ground Reaction (N)

z_1 Deflection of Sprung mass (m)
z_2 Deflection of Unsprung mass (m)

1 Introduction

Aircraft Landing Gears (LG) serves to absorb energy during landing and ground handling conditions, so as to minimize the dynamic loads on the structure. The LG is both a mechanism (for extension and retraction) and a structure (for resisting the landing loads). LG design and testing should comply with regulatory standards (MIL, FAR, Def-stan, etc.) for airworthy requirements. The drop tests are carried out to establish the operational performance of the Landing Gear and to meet the regulatory requirements. With the development of reliable and efficient computer programs, virtual drop test can be simulated and gives the designer a leeway in plugging any performance lags while in the design stage, to prevent additional time and costs in the development cycle.

The paper presents virtual drop testing of an articulated type of landing gear in level and tail-down landing conditions. During tail-down landing, the vertical wheel axle travel gets reduced due to the kinematic configuration and results in increased dynamic load, in comparison with the level landing. According to MIL-T-6053C requirement, LG drop tests shall be conducted with sink velocity of 3.05 m/s (limit landing, with no plastic deformation) and 3.81 m/s (reserve landing, plastic deformation without LG structure disintegration).

2 Literature Survey

Tail-down landing dynamic analysis of an articulated landing gear has not been published much in the literature. As early as 1927, Temple [1] predicted the undercarriage forces using linear force–deflection model for the tire and characterized the shock strut using velocity squared damping and polytropic compression of air. In 1937, a linear spring-damper model was adopted by Franz [2]. In 1944, dynamic loads in the elastic structure were first calculated by Biot and Bisplinghoff [3]. In 1952, Flugge [4] worked on the dynamics by introducing non linearity in the spring and the damper characteristic. He derived the equations of motion of the wheel, tire and the shock absorber. Daughetee [5] in 1974 performed full scale aircraft landing simulations and reported that maximum load reached the peak in 0.2 s. Ghiringhelli [6] in 2000, conducted simulations on a landing gear to study the effects for different sink velocities. Chester [7] studied the effect of tail-down and heave motion on landing gear performance. Niezgoda et al. [8] proposed the numerical model to understand the statics and dynamics of landing gear. Kong et al. [9] conducted drop impact analysis on unmanned aerial vehicle landing gear using LS-DYNA in 2009. Zhang et al. [10] studied the dynamics of aircraft carrier-based landings using

MATLAB and VC software. Xue et al. [11] developed the drop test rig and compared the simulation and test results. Jakubowski and Tywoniuk [12] conducted the drop test of civil aircraft LG and found that separate tests should be conducted on level and tail-down conditions to get the optimized shock absorber (SA) performance. Along with these, two classical handbooks have comprehensively covered various design aspects of landing gear design, Conway [13] and Curry [14].

Hence, the main objective of this work is to study and compare the dynamics of the articulated main landing gear, during level and tail-down landing conditions.

3 Modeling Methodology

The details of the articulated main landing gear configuration, tire, and oleo-pneumatic shock absorber characteristics are defined in the following sections.

3.1 Articulated Main Landing Gear Configuration

An articulated main landing gear (Fig. 1) consists of an oleo-pneumatic shock absorber supported by spherical bearings at point C and point D. A retraction actuator is attached to the airframe at point A. The trailing arm is between points F and G and the point G receives one end of the axle, while the other end holds the wheel and tire assembly. Leg, which forms the primary support is hinged at point B. The kinematic details along with joint definition are as shown in Fig. 1. Upon touchdown, the trailing arm swivels about point F allowing the axle to move both in vertical and horizontal direction. The vertical movement of the axle will be referred to as wheel axle travel (WA Travel), the shock absorber telescopes between point C and point D. The displacement of the shock absorber piston will be referred to as Shock absorber stroke (SA Stroke).

A typical aircraft having a maximum take-off weight of 25 Tons and a landing weight of 16 Tons is considered for the study. In the present landing gear configuration, the maximum WA Travel is 300 mm which translates to 204.9 mm of the shock absorber stroke by the virtue of lever arms.

The shock strut considered for the study is of single stage oleo-pneumatic type. It comprises of an air spring and an oil damper. Total force (F_s) is given by pneumatic force (F_a) and the hydraulic force (F_h) as

$$F_s = F_a + F_h \tag{1}$$

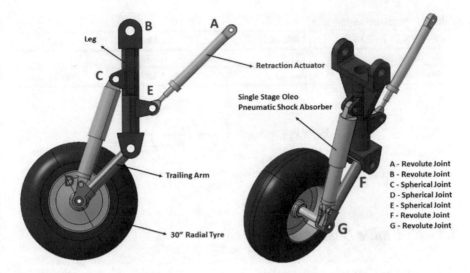

Fig. 1 Salient features of an articulated MLG configuration

Fig. 2 Aircurve for shock absorber

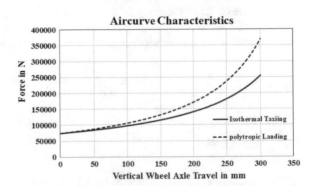

3.2 Air Curve Model

As shown in Fig. 2, there are two characteristic air curves, one of which represents the taxiing condition and is approximated by isothermal process (Eq. 2) with the value of $n = 1$. The other curve represents Landing condition and follows Polytropic process (Eq. 3) with the value of $n = 1.3$. Pneumatic Force, F_a and Dynamic Load Factor, N [14] is given by Eqs. (4) and (5), respectively. The efficiencies of the Shock absorber (η_{sa}) and the tire (η_t) are conservatively taken as 0.80 and 0.47, respectively, for preliminary estimation.

$$P_e \times V_e = P_s \times V_s \qquad (2)$$

$$P_e \times V_e^n = P_r \times V_r^n \qquad (3)$$

Table 1 Tyre parameters

Tire—30 × 11.5 –R14.5	Load (kN)	Deflection (mm)
Static condition	111.2	67.9
Bottoming condition	300.25	139.7

$$F_a = P_{ao} \times A_{ao} \times \left(\frac{V_{ao}}{V_{ao} - A_{ao}s} \right)^n \tag{4}$$

$$N(S_t \times \eta_t + S_{wa} \times \eta_{sa}) = \frac{v^2}{2g} \tag{5}$$

3.3 Hydraulic Damper Model

The shock absorber telescopic motion, forces the oil through an orifice to provide hydraulic damping. The damping force is nonlinear and is found to be proportional to the square of the telescoping velocity [15] as given by Eq. (6). The coefficient of discharge (C_d) of the knife edge orifice is treated as a constant value of 0.65. The oil compressibility effects are neglected in the current simulations.

$$F_h = \frac{\rho \times A_h^3}{2(C_d \times A_n)^2} \times \dot{s}^2 \tag{6}$$

3.4 Tire Model

A 30 in. diameter radial tire (Michelin) is used for MLG to meet the static and dynamic load requirements. Tire Force (F_{ty}) in Z-direction (aircraft coordinate system) is represented by the power law (Eq. 7), where "m" and "r" are constants determined from the data in Table 1. The constants "m" and "r" are found to be 4,173,399 and 1.352, respectively. Power law relation for tire stiffness [15] is given by

$$F_{ty} = m * z^r \tag{7}$$

where "z" is tire deflection.

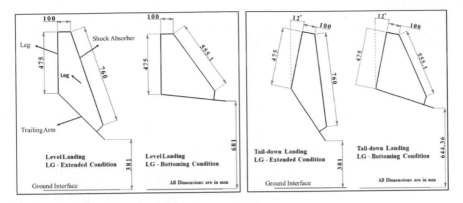

Fig. 3 Comparison of kinematics between level and tail-down landing configurations

3.5 Friction Model: Tire–Ground Interaction

The coefficient of friction is assumed to be a constant value of 0.55 at tire–ground interface, conservatively based on MIL-A-8862 standard. The variation of coefficient of friction with respect to slip has not been considered in this simplified model.

3.6 Level and Tail-Down Landing Kinematics

A maximum tail-down angle of 12° is considered for the analysis. The vertical wheel axle travel is significantly reduced in tail-down landing when compared to level landing condition as shown in Fig. 3. It has considerable implication on the dynamic loads, which will be discussed in the results section. For a total shock absorber travel of 204.9 mm, the total wheel axle vertical travel is 300 mm in level landing condition and 263.4 mm in 12° tail-down condition. A 36.6 mm loss in vertical wheel axle travel is observed in the chosen MLG kinematic configuration. Also, the kinematic relationship between the wheel axle and shock absorber travel changes between level and tail-down landing condition as shown in Fig. 4.

The kinematic relationship between vertical WA travel and SA stroke is given by the following equations (Eqs. 8 and 9), for level and tail-down landing, obtained from curve fitting.

$$y = 0.00004x^2 + 0.6666x + 0.5282 \text{ (Level Landing)} \tag{8}$$

$$y = -0.0002x^2 + 0.8303x + 1.1045 \text{ (Tail-down Landing)} \tag{9}$$

where "y" is shock absorber travel and "x" is vertical wheel axle travel.

Fig. 4 Relationship between vertical wheel axle and shock absorber travel

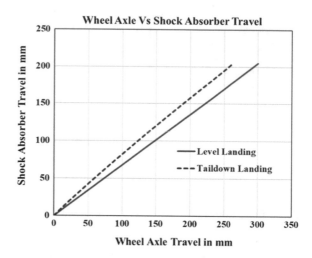

4 Simulation

The landing gear elements considered in the model for the dynamic analysis are the air spring, oil damper, and tire vertical stiffness. Simulations are carried out in MSC-ADAMS software by using GSTIFF solver with SI2 formulation. Wheel, Tire, and brakes are represented as unsprung mass and remaining structure is represented as a sprung mass in ADAMS as shown in Fig. 5. A standard Fiala Tire Model and 2D Flat Road Model available in MSC-ADAMS are used to represent tire and road characteristics, respectively. Virtual drop test simulations are carried out with constant sink velocity as the initial condition, until the recoiling point (where vertical sink velocity of aircraft becomes zero). Lift is assumed to be equal to the total weight of the aircraft at the instant of touch down as per MIL-A-8862 standard guideline. The recoil dynamics are not simulated, as the peak ground reaction is captured during the initial compression phase, for estimating the reaction factor.

Initially, the aircraft is assumed to be in level condition as shown in Fig. 6 and the dynamic analysis is carried out for limit landing (3.05 m/s sink velocity) for different orifice diameters to attain the maximum landing gear efficiency. Then, with the optimized orifice diameter, reserve landing study (3.81 m/s sink velocity) is carried out to evaluate the landing gear performance. The level landing MSC/ADAMS results are compared with the results of experimentally validated landing gear program [14]. Once the level landing model is validated, tail-down landing for limit and reserve conditions are carried out.

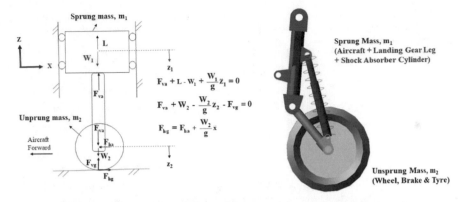

Fig. 5 Representation of landing gear dynamic model in LG program and ADAMS

Fig. 6 Level and tail-down landing models in MSC/ADAMS

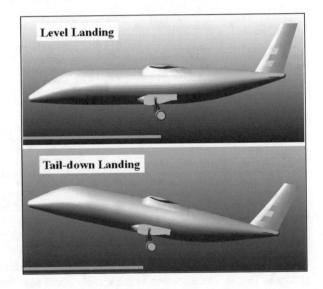

5   Results and Discussion

Landing gear efficiency is estimated for various orifice diameters under level landing condition. It is found that maximum landing gear efficiency of 88.3% is obtained with the orifice diameter of 21.4 mm as shown in Fig. 7.

With the optimized orifice diameter (in level landing), the ground reaction transient for limit and reserve conditions are validated with the results from LG program as shown in Fig. 8. The LG program [15] adopts Runge–Kutta fourth-order method for solving the dynamic model (Fig. 5) of articulated landing gear. The results are in agreement within 1%. Tail-down landing is simulated on the 12° tail-down aircraft model with an orifice diameter of 21.4 mm. The comparison of ground reaction

Fig. 7 Landing gear
efficiency for various orifice
diameter in level landing
condition

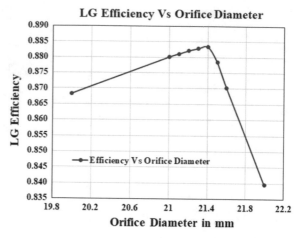

Fig. 8 Validation of level landing results with landing gear program results

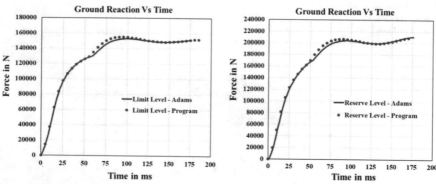

transients between level and tail-down landing for limit and reserve conditions are
shown in Fig. 9. The Shock absorber travel, wheel axle travel, reaction factors, etc.,
are compared between level and tail-down landing condition and shown in Table 2.

A 12.3% reduction in total vertical WA travel is observed in tail-down condition
when compared to level landing. It results in 18.9% and 14.8% increase in dynamic
load in limit and reserve landing respectively for tail-down condition. A maximum
shock absorber travel of 187 mm is observed out of total stroke of 204.9 mm in level
landing condition, showing adequate margin (18 mm) to prevent the bottoming of
the piston. A drop in landing gear efficiency of 2.2% and 3.2% for limit and reserve
landing respectively in tail-down condition has been observed when compared to
level landing condition. The shock absorber travel in tail-down condition is 3 mm
lesser than the level landing condition (Table 2). On the contrary, the tire deflection is relatively higher in tail-down condition indicating a relatively higher energy
absorption by the tire. A maximum tire deflection of 121.5 mm is observed in Tail-
down reserve case against the tire bottoming deflection of 139.7 mm. The maximum

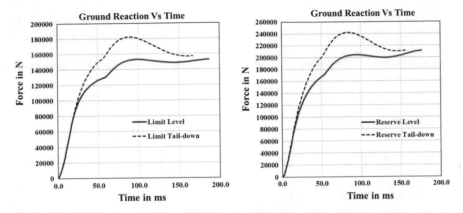

Fig. 9 Comparison of level and tail-down ground reaction transients

Table 2 Comparison results between level and tail-down landing

Parameter	Level landing: Adams		Tail-down landing: Adams	
	Limit	Reserve	Limit	Reserve
Max. wheel travel (mm)	238	278	201	237
(% of total travel)	(79.3)	(92.7)	(76.3)	(90)
Max. SA travel (mm)	161	187	158	184
Max. LG efficiency (%)	88.3	83.7	86.1	85.1
Max. reaction factor	1.95	2.69	2.32	3.09
Max. tire deflection (mm)	87.4	110.4	99.3	121.5

value of reaction factor is 2.32 in limit, tail-down landing condition. It will be used in the generating the ground loads in accordance with MIL-A-8862 standard and subsequently in the structural design of landing gear members.

6 Conclusions

Simulations have been carried out to understand the dynamics of articulated landing gear in 12° Tail-down condition. The analysis has provided deeper insights on the operational and performance aspects of the LG in level and tail-down conditions (as seen from Sect. 5). A more robust model can be built by including the effects of oil compressibility, gland friction, tire-ground interface friction as a function of percentage slip, the coefficient of discharge of damper orifice with respect to

Reynolds number, etc., to represent practical operational conditions. As a preparatory activity, it helps in reducing the cost and time in performing the actual drop tests.

Acknowledgements The authors would like to thank Mr. P. Jayarami Reddy, for his kind support.

References

1. G. Temple, *Prediction of Undercarriage Reactions*, R & M No. 1927, 1944. (RAE Report, S.M.E. 3298, 1945)
2. M. Franz, Theoretical and experimental principles of landing gear research and development. Luftfahrtforschung **14**(8), 387–419 (1937)
3. M.A. Biot, R.L. Bisplinghoff, Dynamic loads on airplane structures during landing, NACA Wartime Report, W-92 (1944)
4. W. Flugge, Landing gear impact, NACA TN 2743 (1952)
5. C.C. Daughetee, Drop testing naval aircraft and the VSD landing gear dynamic test facility, in *15th ASME Structures, Structural Dynamics and Materials Conference* (AIAA Paper, 1974)
6. G.L. Ghiringhelli, Testing of semiactive landing gear control for a general aviation aircraft. J. Aircr. **37**(4), 606–616 (2000)
7. D.H. Chester, A parametric study of aircraft landing-impact, with emphasis on nose gear landing conditions, in *ICAS Congress* (2000)
8. T. Niezgoda, J. Malachowski, W. Kowalski, *Numerical Simulation of Landing Gear Dynamics* (XXI, Mecanica Computacional, 2002), pp. 2579–2586
9. J.P. Kong, Y.S. Lee, J.D. Han, O.S. Ahn, Drop impact analysis of smart unmanned aerial vehicle (SUAV) landing gear and comparison with experimental data. Materialwiss. Werkstofftech. **40**(3), 192–197 (2009)
10. Z. Wen, Z. Zhi, Z. Qidan, X. Shiyue, Dynamics model of carrier-based aircraft landing gears landed on dynamic deck. Chin. J. Aeronaut. **22**, 371–379 (2009)
11. C.J. Xue, Y. Han, W.G. Qi, J.H. Dai, Landing gear drop test rig development and application for light airplanes, J. Aircr. **49**(6) (2012)
12. R. Jakubowski, A. Tywoniuk, An energy absorption dynamic test of landing gear for 1400 Kg general aviation aircraft. J. KONES Powertrain Transp. **23**(4), 159–165 (2016)
13. H.G. Conway, Landing Gear Design (Chapman & Hall Ltd., 1958)
14. N.S. Curry, *Landing Gear Design Handbook* (Lockheed-Georgia Company, Marietta, Georgia, 1982)
15. P. Jayarami Reddy, V.T. Nagaraj, V. Ramamurti, Analysis of a semi-levered suspension landing gear with some parametric study. J. Dyn. Syst. Meas. Contr. **106**(3), 218–224 (1984)

Self-synchronization of Two Unbalanced DC Motor-Driven Rotors on a Common Movable Platform

Anubhab Sinha, A. K. Samantaray and R. Bhattacharyya

Abstract A pair of identical unbalanced rotors, independently driven by two separate DC motors, is placed on a common movable platform. The assembly is designed as an SDOF spring-mass-damper system and the modeling is done entirely on MSC Adams. For a set of predefined system parameters, the voltage values for both motors are operated manually and separately. Both motors are defined as nonideal drives with inadequate power supply. With the help of simulated responses, the Sommerfeld effect along with the phenomenon of self-synchronization is studied numerically, with an aim to attenuate large amplitude vibrations for the movable platform.

Keywords Self-synchronization · Sommerfeld effect · Jump phenomena
Nonideal drive

1 Introduction

The synchronization phenomenon is well known in the scientific community as a spontaneous move towards order and uniformity in a system. It can be defined as the propensity for different entities in a system to act in coordinated unison and harmony, even without the need for an external choreographer. This natural tendency to synchronize has been described as '*one of the most mysterious and pervasive driving forces in all of nature*' [1]. At its core, it stands as a countervailing force to the thermodynamic law of entropy or general disorderness of the universe. In a mysterious fashion, synchronization permeates most of nature's dynamics—from

A. Sinha (✉) · A. K. Samantaray · R. Bhattacharyya
Department of Mechanical Engineering, Indian Institute of Technology Kharagpur, Kharagpur
721302, India
e-mail: sinhaanubhab@gmail.com

A. K. Samantaray
e-mail: samantaray@mech.iitkgp.ernet.in

R. Bhattacharyya
e-mail: rbmail@mech.iitkgp.ernet.in

© Springer Nature Singapore Pte Ltd. 2019
D N Badodkar and T A Dwarakanath (eds.), *Machines, Mechanism and Robotics*, Lecture Notes in Mechanical Engineering,
https://doi.org/10.1007/978-981-10-8597-0_18

choreographed motion of birds, shoals of fish, and synchronized flashing of hordes of fireflies to interaction between atoms, molecules, even the cells within the pacemaker of human heart, heartbeats and circadian rhythms (biological sleep-wake cycles) etc.; in essence, affecting everything to everyone, living and nonliving alike. It has been observed that nonliving objects can also synchronize; although they communicate strictly via 'mechanical means'. This was first described by Dutch physicist Christiaan Huygens in the seventeenth century, for two mechanical pendulum clocks hanging from the same wall, which reportedly went in and out of sync periodically [2]. Thereafter, more such synchronized mechanical systems were studied—such as clocks, metronomes, and engineering-based rotating systems [3–5]. The phenomenon of synchronization may manifest in any kind of unbalanced multi-rotor systems that share a common interacting vibrational support. As such, the study of synchronization is important from the perspective of component safety and stability for any industrial structure with multi-shaft components having some kind of unbalances, for example—a gas turbine engine with multiple shafts [3]. The phenomenon also finds its application while designing various kinds of shakers or exciters for deliberate and purposeful vibration of objects [6–10].

On that basis, an Adams model for a dynamical system comprising two unbalanced rotor-motors placed on a flexible foundation will be constructed. For specific inputted parameters, the simulated responses from the model will be inspected to study self-synchronization via mechanical means. The DC motors powering the two unbalanced rotors will be assumed to be nonideal, i.e., having limited power supply capabilities. Due to the presence of nonideal drives in a vibrating system, the motor dynamics is counter-influenced by the response of the vibrating system and thereby, the so-called Sommerfeld effect is manifested within the system [11–14]. This is characterized by the jump phenomenon, which is encountered when a nonideal system is operated near resonance. Upon approaching the structure's natural frequency, the rotor speeds get arrested at resonance for a prolonged length of time accompanied by an ominous rise in the foundation vibrations. In other words, around resonance, the supply power is used to vibrate the base structure rather operate the actual machinery. This invariably causes a delay in the passage time through resonance; and furthermore, certain intermediate motor speeds are rendered unattainable. Afterward, even with a small increment in voltages, the rotor speeds attain instantaneous jump to higher values, accompanied by simultaneous fall in vibration amplitudes [15–17].

2 System Description

Two unbalanced rotors (Rotor 1 and Rotor 2) with identical configurations (i.e., having the same mass, diameter, moment of inertia, eccentricity, etc.) are installed on a common movable platform (Fig. 1). The platform is supported with flexible mounts, which has been modeled with stiffness parameter K and damping parameter C. For the present scenario, the vertical and pitch vibrating modes of the platform are not taken into consideration and thereby, only horizontal motions are allowed. In

Fig. 1 Schematic representation of the nonideal self-synchronizing system

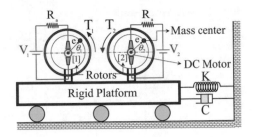

essence, the eccentric twin-rotor system along with the movable platform basically represents a single degree of freedom (SDOF) vibrational system. Although both rotors (1 and 2) are structurally identical, they are individually powered by two DC motors (of the permanent magnet type), each having different operating source voltages. Both motors are operated separately and develop output torques directly on their respective rotor shafts, thus allowing them to rotate independently on their own.

For simulation purposes, the above twin-rotor system is constructed in MSC Adams, a multi-body dynamics and motion analysis software (with the help of appropriate Points, Markers, Solid bodies, Connective Joints, Measures and Force parameters). An isometric solid frame version of the Adams model, as seen in Adams GUI (Graphical User Interface), is shown in Fig. 2. The supporting flexible mount for the platform is designed as a single-component spring-damper-force along the horizontal direction. In an ad hoc fashion, the nonideal drives are introduced within the model with the help of two single-component torque forces on both rotor bodies. These applied torque forces are stand-in for the actual motor generated torque, T on the rotor shafts; the expression for which is

$$T = \frac{\mu_m}{R_a}(V - \mu_m\omega) \tag{1}$$

where V is the operating voltage, μ_m is the motor characteristic constant, R_a is the armature resistance, and ω is the measured rotor speed which is fed back into the torque expression.

Fig. 2 Adams model for the system

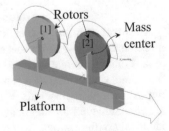

Table 1 System parameters

Parameters				Description	Value
Motor specifications	μ_m			Motor characteristic constant	0.5 Nm/A
	R_a			Armature resistance	0.1 Ω
Rotor 1	V_1	Rotor 2	V_2	Operating voltage (different)	<Variable>
	m_1		m_2	Rotor mass (same)	70 kg
	e_1		e_2	Rotor eccentricity (same)	0.0095 m
	J_1		J_2	Moment of inertia (same)	0.10 kg m^2
Movable platform	m_p			Mass of platform	45 kg
Total assembly	M			Mass of the entire assembly	185 kg
Flexible mount	K			Stiffness parameter	1.85×10^6 N/m
	C			Damping parameter	3350 Ns/m

With reference to Fig. 1, let $\dot{\theta}_1$, $\dot{\theta}_2$ be the instantaneous angular velocities and ω_1, ω_2 be the steady state angular velocities of the respective rotors; subscript 1 and 2 representing Rotor 1 and Rotor 2, respectively. To simulate the Adams model, suitable test input parameters are now considered, as shown in Table 1. For simulation purposes, both rotors are operated simultaneously with no time lag between their start-ups and furthermore, it is assumed that they have same initial eccentric positions of their respective mass centers.

3 Response Plots and Discussions

Simulated responses demonstrate that even in the absence of any direct kinematic couplings between them, the two rotors enter into a state of '*self-synchronization*' simply under the influence of the common movable platform. The rotor speeds are actually entrained by one another and either one tries to speed up or slow down with respect to other, with a combined aim to enter a state of mutual interaction characterized by a common attainable speed. At steady state, this common attainable speed is called the 'synchronized speed' and is marked by a characteristic phase lead/lag between the two rotors.

However, it must be mentioned that such synchronization is achieved only for a reasonable voltage difference value between the two motors and is subsequently lost, if this difference becomes too high. When synchronized, the rotors along with the foundation bring out a sense of coordination amongst themselves, thus behaving as a single family unit. It is further observed that such speed-synchronization is better achieved for identical rotor systems. In other words, when two rotors have identical configurations, they synchronize their speeds over wider ranges of voltage differences. Conversely, for rotors with dissimilar masses and geometric configurations, synchronization is attained only over narrow ranges of voltage differences and is lost, once that range is exceeded. The ease with which the rotors synchronize is deduced from the transient nature of the responses, i.e., shorter transient means faster synchronization and vice versa.

3.1 Self-synchronization Characteristics

For the present problem, it is observed that for lower operating voltages, the rotors show no sign of entrainment or synchronization (Fig. 3a). This happens even when the input voltage difference between both motors is kept very low. It is attributed to the fact that the common platform/foundation is the only form of 'communication channel' between the two rotors. For proper communication, the foundation must be suitably excited to serve the aforesaid purpose. Now, the exciting force amplitude for the foundation comes from the unbalanced force component (i.e., the term—$me\omega^2$) of the rotors. In a way, the mass, eccentricity, and speed of both rotors indirectly contribute to the possibility of synchronization. Taking that into consideration, it can be reasoned that at lower voltages, the rotor speeds are possibly too low to appropriately excite the foundation. Accordingly, no synchronization is possible and the obtained foundation response is akin to a beat phenomenon (Fig. 3b).

Afterward, higher operating voltages are applied and the foundation is duly excited during the transient phases. As a result, the rotors start communicating early on, which eventually leads to synchronization at steady state conditions. Depending on the operating conditions, two distinct modes of synchronization emerge—(a) In-phase synchronization and (b) Out-of-phase synchronization.

The in-phase synchronization is strictly observed before and around the resonance zone. It is characterized by the synchronized rotor speeds oscillating around a mean value with a distinct phase lead/lag between them (Fig. 4a). The phase difference (in radians) is usually small and may range anywhere between $\pm(0, \frac{\pi}{2})$ or $\pm(\frac{3\pi}{2}, 2\pi)$, depending upon the voltage difference values. The less is the difference in voltages, the less is the phase difference. Due to the state of synchronization, the steady-state foundation response is strictly SHM (Simple Harmonic Motion). The

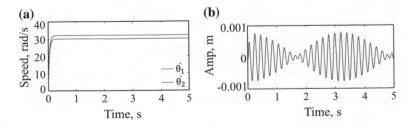

Fig. 3 Response characteristics for $V_1 = 15$ V, $V_2 = 16$ V (*No synchronization*)

vibrational amplitudes for in-phase synchronization have very high magnitudes since the unbalanced force components from both rotors add up (as a form of constructive interference). The response for in-phase synchronization is shown in Fig. 4b.

Contrarily, the out-of-phase synchronization (Fig. 5a) is featured prominently when the system is operated away from resonance. In this case, the synchronized rotor speeds have phase difference value ranging between $\pm(\frac{\pi}{2}, \pi)$ or $\pm(\pi, \frac{3\pi}{2})$. For lesser voltage differences, the rotor speeds are distinctly out of phase with each other. The foundation executes SHM with bare minimal amplitudes (Fig. 5b). This is due to the canceling out nature of the two out-of-phase rotors (i.e., destructive interference), which weakens the foundation motions considerably.

Now, for very large differences in input voltages, said synchronizations are effectively lost. Even if the foundation is reasonably excited, due to the high difference in generated torques, the rotor speeds can't keep up with each other. Eventually, the rotors fall out of entrainment and are forced to operate independently (Fig. 6a). The resulting steady-state foundation motions are not harmonic; instead, they are quasi-periodic in nature (Fig. 6b).

From the above four scenarios, it can be claimed that the foundation response is harmonic strictly when the rotor speeds are synchronized (i.e. both in-phase and out-of-phase sync conditions). For high-speed operations, in terms of vibration reduction of the base foundation, the out-of-phase synchrony is easily the most favorable scenario.

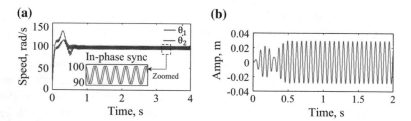

Fig. 4 Response characteristics for $V_1 = 65$ V, $V_2 = 57$ V (*In-phase synchronization*)

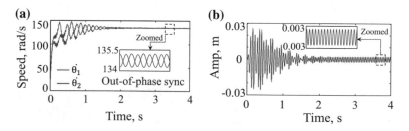

Fig. 5 Response characteristics for $V_1 = 65$ V, $V_2 = 70$ V (*Out-of-phase synchronization*)

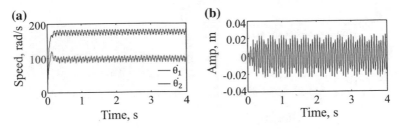

Fig. 6 Response characteristics for $V_1 = 60$ V, $V_2 = 90$ V (*Failed synchronization*)

3.2 Jump Phenomenon Features

As per the inputted parameters in Table 1, the natural frequency and the damping factor of the system is obtained as $\omega_n = 100$ rad/s and $\xi = 0.09$, respectively. Based on the motor torque expression (Eq. 1), when torque input at steady state becomes zero, the steady state rotor speed will be twice the value of input voltage. Going by that, it can be deduced that resonance conditions will be encountered when the motors are operated around 50 V. The jump phenomenon features at resonance will be considered for two separate cases—(a) when only one of the two rotors is operated (b) when both rotors are simultaneously operated. Since the synchronized speeds are oscillating around a mean value, their steady-state RMS values are considered.

At first, only rotor 1 is operated and no voltage is applied to rotor 2 (Fig. 7a, b). As the system approaches resonance, the rotor speed gets stuck at the system's natural frequency. As the voltage V_1 is increased, for some time, there seems to be no apparent increase in the speed value. Adjacently, vibration amplitudes for the foundation continue to increase. Afterward, at $V_1 = 63.7$, even with the slight change in voltage input (=0.1 V), the rotor speed suddenly jumps to a high value (RMS speed value jumps from 100.5 to 117.7 rad/s) almost instantaneously. Moreover, this jump in speed is simultaneously accompanied by a decrease in vibration amplitudes. Overall, the jump actually signifies a delayed passage through resonance and subsequent

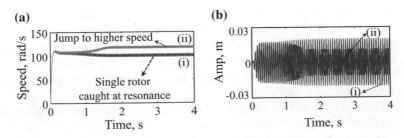

Fig. 7 Response characteristics for single Rotor; (i) when $V_1 = 63.7$ V, $V_2 = 0$ V (*Pre-jump condition*) and (ii) when $V_1 = 63.8$ V, $V_2 = 0$ V (*Post-jump condition*)

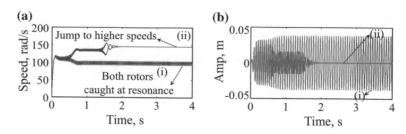

Fig. 8 Response characteristics for both Rotors; (i) when $V_1 = V_2 = 72.5$ V (*Pre-jump condition*) and (ii) when $V_1 = V_2 = 72.6$ V (*Post-jump condition*)

unattainability of intermediate rotor speeds (i.e., speeds ranges in between 100.5 and 117.7 rad/s).

The aforementioned jump becomes more prominent when both rotors are operated together (Fig. 8a, b). In this case, the jump is postponed to a higher voltage value. Around resonance, both rotors are stuck together and collectively undergo in-phase synchronization. Up until $V_1 = 72.5$, $V_2 = 72.5$, the rotors are exactly in-phase with each other. In other words, stuck at resonance, the in-phase rotors keep reinforcing each other, which contributes to very large vibrational amplitudes. Afterward, when both voltages are slightly increased to $V_1 = 72.6$, $V_2 = 72.6$, there is a complete changeover in the response characteristics. The small increase in voltage values triggers the simultaneous jump in rotor speeds (RMS speed values jump from 97.8 to 145.11 rad/s) and the synchronization mode suddenly switches from complete in-phase to complete out-of-phase. The changes appear very abruptly and distinctly and the switch from in-phase to out-of-phase sync wholly annihilates the vibrational amplitudes. The foundation motion comes to a complete stand-still, even with both unbalanced rotors operating at high speed. This synchronized jump, for both rotors together, signals that no in-phase synchronizations are possible for rotors operating beyond 72.6 V.

It must be noted that the post-jump scenario for a single rotor is characterized by a noticeable fall in vibration amplitudes; whereas, the same for a pair of synchronized rotors is characterized by near annihilation of foundation vibrations. Hence, in terms of structural integrity and component safety, it is recommended that two heavy unbalanced rotors installed on a common foundation be permitted to synchronize in an out-of-phase manner. This allows major attenuation of any potentially dangerous large amplitude vibrations (albeit achieved at the expense of additional power).

As mentioned above, the rotors undergo in-phase synchronizations predominantly around the resonance. Therefore, an attempt is made to determine the modes of synchronization over varying voltage differences in the resonance conditions. The aim is to check for a pair of operating voltages (V_1, V_2) that can possibly avoid in-phase synchronization and instead, promote out-of-phase synchronization. To that end, a chart representation of the ranges of V_2 value for which a fixed set of V_1 values can synchronize is shown in Fig. 9. It is observed that near the resonating conditions, where synchronization takes place, there can be alternating regions for

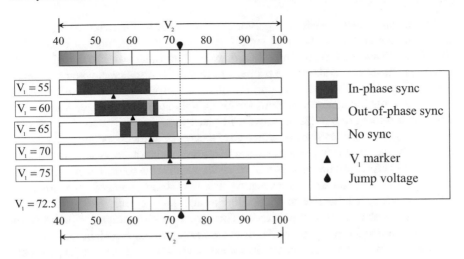

Fig. 9 Synchronization modes over varying ranges of voltage differences

in-phase and out-phase modes. On the outer peripheries, synchronization fails due to large voltage differences.

For $V_1 = 55$, the rotors can only attain in-phase synchronization and there is no provision for out-of-phase synchrony. But for $V_1 = 60$, a small region appears, where out-of-phase synchronization is possible (V_2 values ranging from 64.1 to 65.9 V). This out-of-phase region is sandwiched in between two adjacent in-phase regions. As one moves further down the chart, for $V_1 = 65$, two alternating regions of in-phase and out-of-phase sync are encountered. It is observed that as the system progressively operates away from resonance, the in-phase regions keep shrinking size-wise; for example—the in-phase region for $V_1 = 70$ is essentially reduced to a thin strip as compared to the ones for $V_1 = 65$ and $V_1 = 60$. Overall, the in-phase synchronization persists till $V_1 = 72.6$ (i.e., the jump voltage for both rotors, which signals that resonance has been passed), after which there can be no in-phase synchrony.

In contrast to that, the domains for out-of-phase regions keep on expanding as one moves away from resonance; for example, with $V_1 = 250$, out-of-phase synchronization is obtained for V_2 values ranging all the way from 200 to 322 V i.e. over a span of 122 V (not shown here).

4 Conclusions

The work presented here is purely a simulations based approach to investigate non-ideal self-synchronization in rotating systems. To that end, an unbalanced twin-rotor SDOF system, excited by two separate nonideal drives is constructed on MSC Adams. At first, for low voltages, foundation is not excited enough and there is no scope for synchronization. Afterwards, at high voltages, even for distinct voltage inputs, the two rotors attain a common speed simply via communication through the excited foundation. Two main modes of synchronization transpire—in-phase and out-of-phase. The in-phase mode occurs primarily around the resonance, when the rotors get stuck together at the system's natural frequency. The passage through resonance is delayed and the foundation vibrations are alarmingly large at this stage. Afterwards, when both rotors jump to higher speeds, in-phase is replaced by out-of-phase synchrony, which is characterized by a near disappearance of the foundation vibrations. Effectively, too large voltage differences will eventually cause the synchronization to fail. A chart representation is prepared to visualize how the rotors synchronize over varying voltage ranges around resonance. For two rotors mounted on a common base, it is strongly advisable to opt for the voltage pairs corresponding to regions depicting out-of-phase synchronization. This would ensure minimal vibrations for the foundation and thereby, prevent unforeseen structural damage/failure.

When operated around resonance, a preferential selection of the voltage pairs corresponding to out-of-phase sync regions is deemed to be most favorable. For a given system and motor characteristic constant, the above chart can be used to decide voltage values for which the two motors are out-of-phase with each other. Nevertheless, the target is to drive the system away from resonance which promotes out-of-phase synchrony naturally and over wider ranges of voltage difference, with no possibility of in-phase synchrony. As with any vibrating system, quick passages through resonance is a welcome feature, whose importance cannot be emphasized enough. This is particularly true for nonideal systems, where inadequate power supply manifests as a tendency to get stuck at resonance. To ensure quicker, unrestricted passages through resonance, an exhaustive theoretical assessment of the minimum power requirement for the nonideal motors is supposedly necessary [17]. The complete passage through resonance will promote the desirable switch from in-phase sync to out-of-phase sync. Once the resonance is crossed, and the rotors start functioning at higher speeds, out-of-phase synchronization is achieved with greater ease. An analytical study to investigate the critical power input conditions for both motors to navigate resonance will be the focus of future work. Prototypical experimental setup for the synchronizing system may also be constructed to validate the numerically simulated results. The problem may be further expanded to explore complex systems with more number of rotors or foundations that allow other modes of vibrations.

References

1. S. Strogatz, A.W.F. Edwards, Sync—How order emerges from chaos in the universe, nature, and daily life. Math. Intell. **27**(1), 89 (2005)
2. J. Pantaleone, Synchronization of metronomes. Am. J. Phys. **70**(10), 992–1000 (2002)
3. M. Dimentberg, E. Cobb, J. Mensching, Self-synchronization of transient rotations in multiple shaft systems. J. Vib. Control **7**(2), 221–232 (2001)
4. A.A. Nanha Djanan, B.R. Nana Nbendjo, P. Woafo, Self-synchronization of two motors on a rectangular plate and reduction of vibration. J. Vibr. Control **21**(11), 2114–2123 (2015)

5. M.F. Dimentberg, L. McGovern, R.L. Norton, J. Chapdelaine, R. Harrison, Dynamics of an unbalanced shaft interacting with a limited power supply. Nonlinear Dyn. **13**, 171–187 (1997).
6. I.I. Blekhman, *Synchronization in Science and Technology* (ASME, New York, 1988)
7. C.Y. Zhao, H.T. Zhu, R.Z. Wang et al., Synchronization of two identical coupled exciters in a non-resonant vibrating system of linear motion Part I: Theoretical analysis. Shock Vibr. **16**, 505–516 (2009)
8. C.Y. Zhao, H.T. Zhu, T.J. Bai et al., Synchronization of two identical coupled exciters in a non-resonant vibrating system of linear motion Part II: Numeric analysis. Shock Vibr. **16**, 517–528 (2009)
9. C.Y. Zhao, H.T. Zhu, Y.M. Zhang et al., Synchronization of two coupled exciters in a vibrating system of spatial motion. Acta Mech. Sin. https://doi.org/10.1007/s1040900903111
10. C.Y. Zhao, Y.M. Zhang, B.C. Wen, Synchronization and general dynamic symmetry of a vibrating system with two exciters rotating in opposite directions. Chin. Phys. B **19**, 030301 (2010)
11. L. Cveticanin, Dynamics of the non-ideal mechanical systems: a review. J. Serb. Soc. Comput. Mech. **4**, 75–86 (2010)
12. J.M. Balthazar, D.T. Mook, H.I. Weber, R.M.L.R.F. Brasil, A. Fenili, D. Belato, J.L.P. Felix, An overview on non-ideal vibrations. Meccanica **38**, 613–621 (2003)
13. A.H. Nayfeh, D.T. Mook, *Nonlinear Oscillations* (Wiley, 1979)
14. M. Eckert, The Sommerfeld effect: theory and history of a remarkable resonance phenomenon. Eur. J. Phys. **17**(5), 285–289 (1996)
15. A.K. Samantaray, S.S. Dasgupta, R. Bhattacharyya, Sommerfeld effect in rotationally symmetric planar dynamical systems. Int. J. Eng. Sci. **48**(1), 21–36 (2010)
16. A.K. Samantaray, On the non-linear phenomena due to source loading in rotor-motor systems. Proc. Inst. Mech. Eng. C: J. Mech. Eng. Sci. **223**(4), 809–818 (2009)
17. M. Karthikeyan, A. Bisoi, A.K. Samantaray, R. Bhattacharyya, Sommerfeld effect characterization in rotors with non-ideal drive from ideal drive response and power balance. Mech. Mach. Theory **91**, 269–288 (2015)

Six DOF Mirror Alignment System for Beamline Applications

Sumit Kumar Sinha, T A Dwarakanath and Abhishek Jaju

Abstract The paper deals with the design and implementation of a high-precision six DOF parallel mechanism based system for mirror alignment inside a high vacuum chamber. Analysis and synthesis are carried out in order to meet the desired range of mirror mobility in six dimensions in the presence of cylindrical constraints due to the two-column support of the mirror. The beam alignment system should have a translation resolution of 1 μm and rotational resolution of 1 arc-sec about a remote mirror coordinate axis. This paper discusses in detail the design and development of a Mirror Positioning Mechanism System (MPMS) meeting the above requirements.

Keywords Six DOF parallel mechanism · Beam alignment · Mirror positioning system · Calibration

1 Introduction

A synchrotron is a particular type of cyclic particle accelerator, descended from the cyclotron, in which the accelerating particle beam travels around a fixed closed-loop path. As the charged particles are deflected through magnetic fields, they create extremely bright light. The light is channeled down beamlines to experimental workstations where it is used for material characterization and other research applications. Beam alignment is carried out in a synchrotron to incident the high-energy beam on the target. Ultrahigh vacuum (in the range of 10^{-9} mbar) is required throughout the beamline. There are frequent significant deviations from the prescribed path of the

S. K. Sinha (✉) · T A Dwarakanath (✉) · A. Jaju (✉)
Division of Remote Handling & Robotics, Bhabha Atomic Research Centre,
Trombay, Mumbai 400085, India
e-mail: sinhask@barc.gov.in; sumitksinha@yahoo.com

T A Dwarakanath
e-mail: tad@barc.gov.in

A. Jaju
e-mail: ajaju@barc.gov.in

© Springer Nature Singapore Pte Ltd. 2019
D N Badodkar and T A Dwarakanath (eds.), *Machines, Mechanism
and Robotics*, Lecture Notes in Mechanical Engineering,
https://doi.org/10.1007/978-981-10-8597-0_19

beam. As the location of the target is predefined and fixed, it is required to reflect the high-energy beam toward the target with the help of a highly polished mirror. A very high-precision system is required for positioning and orienting the mirror assembly for beam alignment with respect to the target. Various methodologies have been adopted worldwide to align the beam with respect to the target [1–3]. One method for beam alignment is to position and orient the complete chamber housing with the mirror assembly. The advantage of this method is that the manipulating system can be external to the vacuum space. The problem is that the payload of the chamber is quite high. Also manipulating chamber in an isolated fashion without disturbing the connected pipes and devices is a bulky proposition, and it becomes quite difficult to precisely orient and control the chamber for beam alignment. The other method for beam alignment is by mounting mirror assembly on independent linear actuators along various axes in such a way that each desired degree of freedom is achieved by an individual motor mounted outside the chamber. Each motor is connected through the mirror assembly through cylindrical conduits and bellows such that the vacuum inside the chamber can be maintained. This method is having a disadvantage of a bigger chamber size and difficulty of coordinated control of axes to synchronize the motion of motors to position and orient the chamber. The present development addresses a highly compact and high-precision six-dimensional posturing mirror alignment system. The six DOF parallel mechanism is a right choice in order to provide required high accuracy, stiffness, and payload capacity [4–8]. A compact six DOF parallel mechanism based Mirror Positioning Mechanism System (MPMS) has been designed, developed, and implemented for aligning the mirror with the incident beam. This paper describes in detail the methodology, kinematic arrangement, control features, accuracy, and repeatability analysis of the MPMS unit.

2 Beam Alignment System

Figure 1 shows the schematic arrangement of beam alignment system. As per the accuracy and repeatability requirements, a high-precision six DOF MPMS unit has been developed for mirror alignment inside a vacuum chamber to align the high-energy beam on the target. The high-energy beam will enter through beam-in cylindrical tube, and the mirror is postured at the center of the chamber so as to get the beam reflected through the beam-out cylindrical tube. The mirror has to be micro-manipulated to focus the beam to strike on the predetermined spot on the target. A coordinate system $O_m(X_m, Y_m, Z_m)$ is defined at the center point of the mirror. The reference point O_m can be positioned with respect to the base coordinate system and the mirror can be oriented about any axis passing through mirror coordinate system with the help of the six DOF MPMS. The mirror is housed to the MPMS platform through the cylindrical columns. The platform surface is connected with the bellows to chamber to isolate and provide cylindrical conduits for the two cylindrical columns supporting the mirror. The design should accommodate an invisible load that comes on the platform due to the vacuum which causes compression of the bellows. The

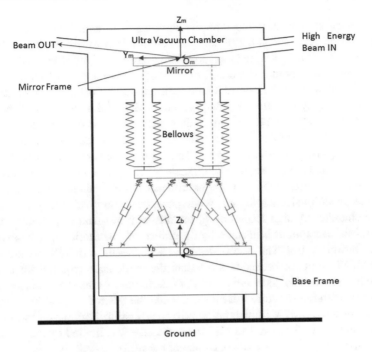

Fig. 1 Schematic layout for beam alignment system

vacuum load and the payload due to the weight of the mirror and attachments may act as neutralizing forces or summing up forces depending on how the mirror is housed with respect to gravity axis. Second, the workspace and resolution should meet the user requirement specification.

Load distribution on the MPMS platform is optimized in such a way that the weight of the mirror assembly and the spring load provided by the bellows are compensated by the vacuum load during the beam operation.

$$L_P = L_V - L_M - L_S = 97-12-12 = 73\,\text{Kgf},$$

where

L_P Maximum load for which platform needs to be designed.
L_V Load on platform due to ultrahigh vacuum (upward direction).
L_M Weight of the mirror (downward direction).
L_S Load due to compression of bellows (downward direction).

In this case, maximum payload on the platform is 73 Kgf. The system has been designed for 80 Kgf payload. The nominal height of the mirror surface is 464 mm above the nominal height of the hexapod. The nominal height of the MPMS unit is defined at the sweet point, which is the center of the workspace of the platform. It has been calculated by the system's kinematic model. To avoid the interference of the mirror assembly with the chamber's conduits, the total mobility of the beamline alignment mirror is limited to ±10 mm at the center of the mirror along three mutually perpendicular directions and ±2° in rotation about three mutually perpendicular axes passing through the center of the mirror. The bellows are concentric with the mirror assembly rods in an initial setup. The diameter of the rod is 18 mm, and the conduit cylinder inner diameter is 54 mm. These dimensions are evaluated to ensure that for the given translational and rotational workspace, the cylindrical rods do not interfere with the chamber. A high resolution of the mirror movement (1 μm in translation and 1 arc-sec in rotation) is ensured by the choice of fine motion measurement and high-resolution control. The system designed achieves the required specification.

The MPMS unit workspace is more than the workspace required for the beam alignment system. Also, there is a chance of interference of the rods connected to the MPMS unit with the structure if it moves outside the desired workspace. Therefore, the workspace of the MPMS unit is curtailed by readjusting the photosensors to ensure that there is no interference. The MPMS workspace was limited by readjusting the photosensors to suit the desired workspace of the mirror assembly.

3   Kinematic Design of a Six DOF MPMS Unit

The beam alignment system is a well-known semi-regular Stewart platform manipulator. It consists of two rigid bodies and six legs. One end of each leg is connected to a rigid body through a universal joint and another end of each leg is connected to second rigid body through a spherical joint. In order to simplify modeling, design, and manufacture, the six connecting points of the joints on each of the two rigid bodies are considered to lie in a plane. The planar rigid surface, which translates and rotates in three dimensions with respect to the other rigid planar surface, is termed as the platform and the reference fixed surface is termed as the base. To eliminate the interference of legs, the connecting points are suitably separated. Each of the six legs is a serial UPS (Universal-Prismatic-Spherical) chain and the six connection points form a semi-regular hexagon both at the platform and at the base.

The schematic sketch of the hexapod is shown in Fig. 2. The front view and the top view are shown in Figs. 3 and 4, respectively. The spherical and the universal joints are passive composite joints, whereas the prismatic joint is integrated with the actuator and is referred to as the active joint. The coordinates of all the points are defined with respect to a global coordinate system fixed at the geometrical center of the base $O(XYZ)$ as shown in Figs. 2 and 4. The height of the manipulator is described

Fig. 2 MPMS unit isometric view

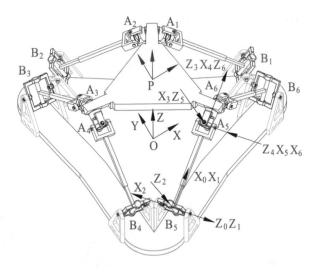

Fig. 3 MPMS unit front view

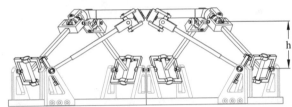

as the distance from the geometrical center of the base to the geometrical center of the platform. Both the base and the platform are designed as equilateral triangular plates. The design parameters denoted as "b" is the side of the base equilateral triangle, and "a" is the side of the platform equilateral triangle. B_i and A_i ($i=1, \ldots, 6$) are the six connection points at the base and at the platform, respectively. Let "b_1" be the offset of the base connection points from its nearest vertex (equal to smaller semi-hexagonal side at the base), and "a_1" be the offset of the platform connection points from its nearest vertex (equal to smaller semi-hexagonal side at the platform). l_i are the leg lengths connecting base connection point B_i to the corresponding platform connection point A_i, ($i=1, \ldots, 6$). A coordinate system is fixed at the center (of the semi-regular hexagon) of the base plate formed by the six connection points ($B_i, i = 1, \ldots, 6$). The **X-Y** axes are defined along the plane of the base plate. The **X**-axis is directed from the center of the base plate to the midpoint of line connecting B_1 & B_6 (Fig. 4), the **Z**-axis is perpendicular to the plane of the base plate, and the **Y**-axis completes the right-handed coordinate system. $\hat{i}, \hat{j}, \hat{k}$ are the unit vectors along the **X**-, **Y**-, and **Z**-axes. At the minimum height of mechanism, "h", the coordinates of the geometrical center of the platform with respect to the geometrical center of the base at zero translation are $(0, 0, h)$. The translation of the platform from its minimum height is given by ($tx, ty,$ and tz) and hence ($tx, ty,$ and $tz + h$) are the coordinates of

Fig. 4 MPMS unit top view

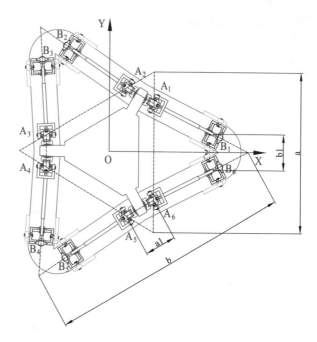

the center of the platform from $O(XYZ)$ after the translation. $R_{3\times3}$ is the rotation of the platform with respect to the platform coordinate frame [9].

The homogeneous coordinates of the leg connection points at the base with respect to $O(XYZ)$ are given by

$$B_1 = \left[\frac{b}{\sqrt{3}} - \frac{b_1\sqrt{3}}{2}, \frac{b_1}{2}, 0, 1\right]^T, B_2 = \left[-\frac{b}{2\sqrt{3}} + \frac{b_1\sqrt{3}}{2}, \frac{b}{2} - \frac{b_1}{2}, 0, 1\right]^T,$$

$$B_3 = \left[-\frac{b}{2\sqrt{3}}, \frac{b}{2} - b_1, 0, 1\right]^T, B_4 = \left[-\frac{b}{2\sqrt{3}}, -\frac{b}{2} + b_1, 0, 1\right]^T,$$

$$B_5 = \left[-\frac{b}{2\sqrt{3}} + \frac{b_1\sqrt{3}}{2}, -\frac{b}{2} + \frac{b_1}{2}, 0, 1\right]^T, B_6 = \left[\frac{b}{\sqrt{3}} - \frac{b_1\sqrt{3}}{2}, -\frac{b_1}{2}, 0, 1\right]^T \quad (1)$$

The homogeneous coordinates of the leg connection points at the platform with respect to $O(XYZ)$ after the translation (tx, ty, tz) and rotation $R_{3\times3}$ are given by

$$A_1 = \begin{bmatrix} & & tx \\ R_{3\times3} & & ty \\ & & tz+h \\ 0\ 0\ 0 & & 1 \end{bmatrix} \begin{bmatrix} \frac{a}{2\sqrt{3}}, \frac{a}{2} - a_1, 0, 1 \end{bmatrix}^T,$$

$$A_2 = \begin{bmatrix} & & tx \\ R_{3\times3} & & ty \\ & & tz+h \\ 0\ 0\ 0 & & 1 \end{bmatrix} \begin{bmatrix} \frac{a}{2\sqrt{3}} - \frac{a_1\sqrt{3}}{2}, \frac{a}{2} - \frac{a_1}{2}, 0, 1 \end{bmatrix}^T,$$

$$A_3 = \begin{bmatrix} & & tx \\ R_{3\times3} & & ty \\ & & tz+h \\ 0\ 0\ 0 & & 1 \end{bmatrix} \begin{bmatrix} -\frac{a}{\sqrt{3}} + \frac{a_1\sqrt{3}}{2}, \frac{a_1}{2}, 0, 1 \end{bmatrix}^T,$$

$$A_4 = \begin{bmatrix} & & tx \\ R_{3\times3} & & ty \\ & & tz+h \\ 0\ 0\ 0 & & 1 \end{bmatrix} \begin{bmatrix} -\frac{a}{\sqrt{3}} + \frac{a_1\sqrt{3}}{2}, -\frac{a_1}{2}, 0, 1 \end{bmatrix}^T,$$

$$A_5 = \begin{bmatrix} & & tx \\ R_{3\times3} & & ty \\ & & tz+h \\ 0\ 0\ 0 & & 1 \end{bmatrix} \begin{bmatrix} \frac{a}{2\sqrt{3}} - \frac{a_1\sqrt{3}}{2}, -\frac{a}{2} + \frac{a_1}{2}, 0, 1 \end{bmatrix}^T,$$

$$A_6 = \begin{bmatrix} & & tx \\ R_{3\times3} & & ty \\ & & tz+h \\ 0\ 0\ 0 & & 1 \end{bmatrix} \begin{bmatrix} \frac{a}{2\sqrt{3}}, -\frac{a}{2} + a_1, 0, 1 \end{bmatrix}^T \qquad (2)$$

The inverse kinematics of the MPMS unit can be written as

$$\left\| \vec{l_i} \right\| = \left\| \vec{A_i} - \vec{B_i} \right\|, \quad i = 1, 2, \ldots, 6 \qquad (3)$$

Figure 5 shows the translational workspace of six DOF MPMS unit based on the minimum and maximum permissible leg lengths for the MPMS unit. The workspace is also verified by the actual motion of the unit on the CMM table. The beamline workspace requirement was less as compared to the translational workspace stated above. The restrictions in the leg lengths were further provided to satisfy the restricted

Fig. 5 3D translation
sub-workspace of MPMS
unit

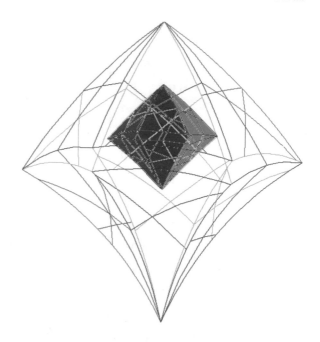

workspace required for the beamline application. Sub-workspace shown as the solid
volume is the restricted workspace for beam alignment purpose as shown in Fig. 5.

The system was designed to meet the general requirements of the beamline alignment. As per the workspace and payload requirements, the kinematic parameters
(a, a_1, b, b_1, h) were selected. The structural member's cross-section, power rating
of the motors, etc. are determined based on the payload requirements as discussed
in the previous section. The commercially available universal and spherical joints
do not satisfy the passive mobility requirement for the given workspace. Hence, the
novel design solution is undertaken for the universal joint connected at the base side
and the spherical joint connected at the platform side of each leg of the MPMS unit
[9].

4 Determination of Kinematic Parameters and Control Algorithm of Beam Alignment System

To account for the manufacturing inaccuracies, the exact values of kinematic parameters of the mechanism are measured. It includes the leg connection points at base
$(\overrightarrow{B_i})$ with respect to base coordinate system, and platform connection points $(\overrightarrow{A_i})$
with respect to platform coordinate system, minimum and maximum leg lengths
$(l_{min} \& l_{max})$ of each leg, and position of mirror assembly w. r. t. platform coordinate system. The values of the various kinematic parameters of the MPMS unit are

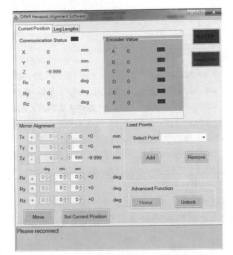 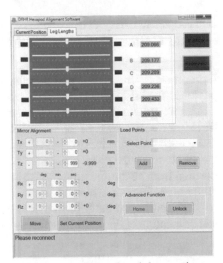

(a): Position and orientation of platform along with encoder valued displayed

(b): Leg lengths of each leg getting displayed

Fig. 6 GUI for beam alignment system

measured using a high-precision Coordinate Measuring Mechanism (CMM) in an accredited metrological laboratory. The measured value of the kinematic parameters is used to solve inverse kinematic solution to determine the leg lengths of each leg for a given position and orientation of the mirror assembly with respect to the base.

Control interface for MPMS unit (comprising of actuators, position, and photo sensors with multiaxis motion controller) is developed and is systematically tested for all the control functions of the MPMS unit. A control algorithm and a Guided User Interface (GUI) (Fig. 6) are developed to home (predefined position) the mechanism and to move the mirror assembly for any given position and orientation. Photosensors are mounted at both the leg ends and integrated with motion controller, which are used for homing of the system and to limit the leg lengths. Features like emergency stopping of the mechanism and "Homing" the mechanism have been integrated in the GUI. The GUI displays current position and orientation of the mirror assembly, current leg lengths, current encoder values, and connection status of controller with computer. The desired position of mirror can be given as an input in the "Mirror Alignment" window and by clicking the "Move" button in the GUI, the inverse kinematics is solved to determine the desired leg lengths which are sent to the motion controller to move the mechanism to the new position. After reaching the new position, the current position would be updated and "Position Reached" message will be displayed in message window. The reached position can be stored by a command in "Load Points" window by a specific name for future reference. The mechanism can be moved to the predefined stored position any time by selecting stored point directly.

5 Repeatability Analysis, Accuracy Analysis, and Calibration of MPMS Unit

Experiments were carried out to evaluate the repeatability and accuracy at various payloads for MPMS unit. The repeatability of MPMS unit in achieving a position along three mutually perpendicular axes is measured individually using a standard CMM in a metrological laboratory (Fig. 7). The MPMS unit is fed with an input along each axis to achieve a predefined position several times. The repeatability of the unit to reach the given position is evaluated. The deviation if any to reach a given position from all the directions is also evaluated. Figure 8 shows that the repeatability of the MPMS unit is within 14 μm.

The accuracy of the MPMS unit is carried out by measuring the actual position and orientation of the platform with respect to rigid base frame for a given theoretical

Fig. 7 MPMS unit in CMM lab

Fig. 8 Repeatability of MPMS unit

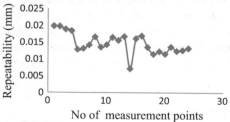

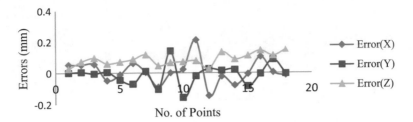

Fig. 9 Accuracy of MPMS unit in X-, Y-, and Z-axes (before calibration)

position and orientation of the platform. The platform of MPMS unit is commanded to move at various positions using motion controller attached to it to determine the actual position and orientation. The absolute average errors in X-, Y-, and Z-axes are 55 μm, 45 μm, 86 μm, respectively, before the calibration (Fig. 9).

Calibration procedure of beam alignment system:

1. The exact values of kinematic parameters of the mechanism $\overrightarrow{B_i}$, $\overrightarrow{A_i}$, l_{min} & l_{max} were measured with CMM and fed into the control algorithm.
2. For a given position and orientation of the platform, the inverse kinematics problem is solved to determine the corresponding leg lengths l_i of MPMS unit.
3. The leg lengths are fed into the MPMS unit trajectory code to reach to the desired position and orientation.
4. The actual position and orientation was measured. High-accuracy CMM is used to measure actual readings. The position and orientation error, difference in desired, and the actual value are established for the location.
5. Again by using the inverse kinematics equations, actual leg lengths la_i are calculated for the achieved orientation of platform measured through CMM.
6. The ratio of leg lengths will give the pitch correction factor (PCF_i)

$$PCF_i = \frac{l_i}{la_i}, \quad \text{where,} \quad i = 1, 2, \dots, 6 \tag{4}$$

7. The pitch correction factors are implemented in inverse kinematics module.
8. To evaluate the backlash error, the legs are traversed in forward direction and again traversed back to reach the same position again. The actual leg lengths $la_i(initial)$ & $la_i(final)$ for the same position are measured.
9. The deviation $la_i(initial) - la_i(final)$ gives a measure of backlash error. The backlash error is implemented in the inverse kinematics module.

The platform of MPMS unit is made to move to a given position and orientation from all the directions. The accuracy of MPMS unit is again evaluated after calibration procedure (Fig. 10). The absolute average errors in X-, Y-, and Z-axes are 54 μm, 31 μm, and 16 μm, respectively, after the calibration. The average volumetric accuracy of the MPMS unit had improved from 132 to 67 μm after calibration of the

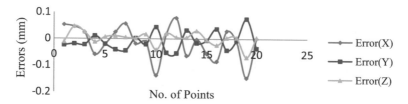

Fig. 10 Accuracy of MPMS unit in X-, Y-, and Z-axes (after calibration)

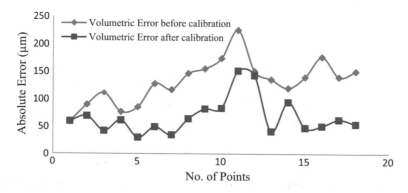

Fig. 11 Volumetric error of MPMS unit before and after calibration

Fig. 12 MPMS unit with bellows

system (Fig. 11). The achieved accuracy is in accordance with the desired accuracy for beam alignment system.

Bellows were fixed with each leg of MPMS unit to safeguard against outside environment (Fig. 12). Figure 13 shows the MPMS unit that has been installed for the purpose of beam alignment.

Fig. 13 MPMS unit placed
in beam alignment system

6 Conclusion

This paper discusses in detail the design and development of a Mirror Positioning Mechanism System (MPMS) for beam alignment for synchrotron application. The resolution of 1 μm in translation and 1 arc-sec in rotation about the remote mirror coordinate axes for successful beam alignment has been achieved. The MPMS unit has been calibrated to achieve a multi-direction approach to a target point repeatability of 14 μm and an accuracy of 67 μm. The achieved accuracy is in accordance with the desired accuracy for beam alignment system. The system was tested with a load of 80 Kgf. The MPMS unit has been demonstrated at laboratory for its accuracy and repeatability, and has been successfully delivered for synchrotron beam alignment application.

References

1. M.R. Sullivan, S. Rekhi et al., Installation and testing of a focusing mirror at beamline X28C for high flux X-ray radiolysis of biological macromolecules. Rev. Sci. Instrum. (Published by American Institute of Physics) **79**, 025101 (2008)
2. E. Johnson, A. Lyndaker et al., Synchrotron radiation instrumentation, in *9th International Conference (Korea)*, vol. 879 (2007) pp. 675
3. RRCAT Indore, India, www.cat.ernet.in/technology/accel/indus/actrep03/4_2.html. Accessed 10 Nov 2017
4. B. Dasgupta, T. Mruthyunjaya, The Stewart platform manipulator: a review. Mech. Mach. Theory **35**, 15–20 (2000)

5. J.P. Merlet, *Parallel Robots*, 2nd edn. (Springer Publications, 2006)
6. J. P. Merlet, Parallel manipulators. Part I: Theory design, kinematics, dynamics and control, in *INRIA Research Report* No. 646 (1987)
7. G. Bhutani, T.A. Dwarakanath, Novel design solution to high precision 3 axes translational parallel mechanism. Mech. Mach. Theory **75**, 118–130 (2014)
8. S. Bandyopadhyay, A. Ghosal, Analysis of configuration space singularities of closed loop mechanisms and parallel manipulators. Mech. Mach. Theory **39**(5), 519–544 (2004)
9. G. Bhutani, Modeling, design and development of frameless stereotaxy in robot assisted neuro-surgery. Ph.D. Thesis, Homi Bhabha National Institute, July 2015

Modeling, Design, Identification of D-H Parameters and Calibration of Surgical Coordinate Measuring Mechanism

Gaurav Bhutani, T A Dwarakanath and D N Badodkar

Abstract A portable Surgical Coordinate Measuring Mechanism (SCMM) is designed and developed to measure the 3D coordinates of a point and a line vector passing through a point in its workspace. The synthesis of the mechanism is done to localize a neuro-anatomical reference frame with respect to the robot reference coordinate system. The SCMM is an articulated serial chain and is an important constituent of the neurosurgical suite being developed by DRHR, BARC, Mumbai. Dimensional synthesis of the SCMM is carried out by optimizing the mechanism footprint and manipulability of the neuro-registration. Design, development, calibration, and demonstration of SCMM are discussed in the paper. The paper emphasizes that the measured values of the D-H parameters are most often not practically feasible for implementation. It is shown that calibration-based methods are useful for improving the accuracy of system.

Keywords Neuro-registration · Neuronavigation · D-H parameters · Design Calibration · Point and line coordinate measuring mechanism

1 Introduction

The stereotactic surgery is a minimally invasive form of surgical intervention which makes use of a three-dimensional frame of reference outside the body to locate the tumor within the body. The geometric center of the tumor should be known with respect to the three-dimensional body frame of reference. Also, the position of the

G. Bhutani (✉) · T A Dwarakanath (✉) · D N Badodkar
Division of Remote Handling & Robotics, Bhabha Atomic Research Centre, Trombay,
Mumbai 400085, India
e-mail: bhutani@barc.gov.in

T A Dwarakanath
e-mail: tad@barc.gov.in

D N Badodkar
e-mail: badodkar@barc.gov.in

© Springer Nature Singapore Pte Ltd. 2019
D N Badodkar and T A Dwarakanath (eds.), *Machines, Mechanism and Robotics*, Lecture Notes in Mechanical Engineering,
https://doi.org/10.1007/978-981-10-8597-0_20

233

surgical tool should be known with respect to the same body frame of reference. The current practice of neuro-registration is by frame-based stereotaxy, where a rigid frame is attached to the patient prior to CT/MRI and the coordinates of tumor are measured with respect to the external frame. When the patient is moved to the surgical table, a stereotactic arc is connected on the stereotactic frame to guide the surgical tool [1–4]. Although the frame-based systems provide high accuracy, wearing it induces discomfort to the patient and offers restricted manipulability of the surgical tool during neurosurgery. Research into frameless stereotaxy gathered momentum with the advances in measurement technology to circumvent the problems faced in frame-based stereotaxy. Presently, two frameless stereotaxy methods are being practiced. One is the marker-based frameless stereotaxy and another is the marker-less frameless stereotaxy. In marker-less point registration, a set of three or more MRI image data and the corresponding actual anatomical landmark positions are matched. In marker-based pair point registration, skin-based fiducials are fixed to the skull before the pre-operative imaging. Camera-based optical tracking is well accepted for the use in frameless stereotaxy/neuronavigation systems. Although optical tracking is well accepted, it has some inherent limitations of accuracy and "line of sight" problem as compared to frame-based stereotaxy [5–8]. The "line of sight" refers to the condition that the camera system cannot "see" the markers; hence, the surgical tool tracking is not feasible.

In this paper, various developmental stages of Surgical Coordinate Measuring Mechanism (SCMM)-based frameless stereotaxy are discussed in detail. The synthesis of SCMM to measure the 3D coordinates of a point and also a line vector through a point in its workspace is discussed. The SCMM features (i) accuracy analogous to frame-based stereotaxy, (ii) comfort levels for the patient equivalent to frameless stereotaxy, and (iii) eliminates the "line of sight" problem in registration and in navigation, in comparison with optical-based frameless stereotaxy are highlighted through the paper. This paper also presents the solid modeling, design, calibration, and experimental results of SCMM.

Section 2 discusses the mathematical formulation to determine the transformation from fiducial frame to robot frame. Section 3 discusses the design aspects taken into consideration during development of SCMM. Sections 4 and 5 present the calibration and experimental results of SCMM, respectively. Section 6 concludes the paper.

2 Fiducial Frame to Robot Frame Transformation

From the image, using the DICOM viewer, the coordinates of the fiducial points with respect to the fiducial frame are measured (see Fig. 1).

$$^f P_A = \{X_A, Y_A, Z_A, 1\}, \ ^f P_B = \{X_B, Y_B, Z_B, 1\}, \ ^f P_C = \{X_C, Y_C, Z_C, 1\} \text{ and } ^f P_D = \{X_D, Y_D, Z_D, 1\}$$

The coordinates of the fiducial points A, B, C, and D with respect to the robot frame (SCMM base frame) of reference are measured using the measuring device.

Fig. 1 Sketch showing
fiducial frame, fiducial
points A, B, C, and D on the
scalp and tumor point P

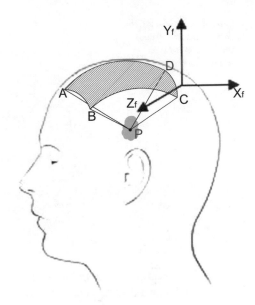

$${}^R P_A = \{X_A, Y_A, Z_A, 1\}, \quad {}^R P_B = \{X_B, Y_B, Z_B, 1\}, \quad {}^R P_C = \{X_C, Y_C, Z_C, 1\} \text{ and } {}^R P_D = \{X_D, Y_D, Z_D, 1\}$$

The transformation matrix, ${}^R[T]_f$ which transforms the points that are known in the fiducial frame to the robot frame, is obtained.

$${}^R(P_A, P_B, P_C, P_D)_{4\times4} = {}^R [T]_{f(4\times4)} {}^f (P_A, P_B, P_C, P_D)_{4\times4}$$

Writing the above equation in short form, we have

$${}^R(P) = {}^R [T]_f {}^f (P) \tag{1}$$

The solution of ${}^R[T]_f$ for a general case (fiducial points more than 4) is given as

$${}^R[T]_f = {}^R (P)^f (P)^T \left[{}^f (P)^f (P)^T \right]^{-1} \tag{2}$$

The expression ${}^f (P)^T \left[{}^f (P)^f (P)^T \right]^{-1}$ in Eq. (2) would simplify to $\left[{}^f (P) \right]^{-1}$ for the case when fiducial points are four. Equation (2) is still valid if the number of fiducial points selected for neuro-registration is more than four. The tumor point is obtained in the robotic frame of reference using the transformation

$${}^R(P)_p = {}^R [T]_f {}^f (P)_P \tag{3}$$

where ${}^f (P)_P$ is the position of the tumor point in the fiducial frame of reference. All the fiducial points, tumor point, surgical tool, and surgical path of the tool, are determined with respect to the robot frame of reference. The various points are labeled

Fig. 2 Sketch showing the
registered fiducial (blue)
points, which form a
reference frame

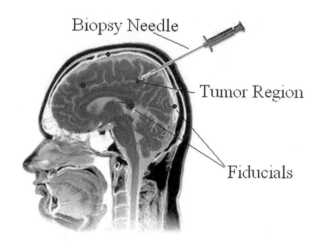

in Fig. 2. The position of the tumor is established with respect to the fiducial frame
from the MRI image data and later transformed to the robot frame of reference. The
rigid body motion of a surgical tool is localized with respect to the robot frame.

3 Solid Modeling and Design of SCMM

Synthesis of the Surgical Coordinate Measuring Mechanism (SCMM) has been done
such that it can be positioned in the desired measurement space and satisfies the neurosurgical manipulability requirements. The geometry of SCMM workspace resembles
a spherical segment with reachable space more than a hemisphere of radius 300 mm.
The SCMM satisfies the required accuracy, portability, and comfort requirements of
the neuro-registration system. The SCMM is made of high-strength aluminum alloy
to reduce the weight of the mechanism. It is a passive four degree of freedom serial
mechanism with encoders mounted at each joint and with a base fixture. The SCMM
has a four DOF to give neurosurgeon flexibility to approach and measure angle of
approach to the fiducial points from various directions. Three parallel axes of SCMM
are used for much desired redundancy and ease of operation. It is to be noted that
SCMM falls under the category of Articulated Arm Coordinate Measuring Mechanism (AACMM). Although AACMMs are commercially available [9, 10], none suits
the neurosurgical requirements.

The end link of the SCMM is equipped with an end probe to suit the circumference
contact nesting measurements. The solid model of the mechanism along with its joint
axes orientations is as shown in Fig. 3. A secure housing design for the end-effector
homing reference is shown in Fig. 4. The joint angular displacements sensed at the
corresponding rotary joint encoders serve as the input for a Direct Kinematic Problem
(DKP). The DKP is solved to compute the coordinates of the reference point on the

Fig. 3 Solid model of four
DOF SCMM

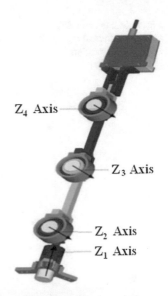

Fig. 4 SCMM in homing
position

end probe with respect to the base frame of the SCMM. The base frame of the SCMM
is fixed and is in constant relation with the robot frame.

The measurement can be conducted by resting the end stylus of the probe at the
last link on at least three non-collinear fiducial points to establish the relation of the
fiducial frame with the robot frame. The last link of the SCMM carries a spring-
loaded electrode along with the spherical stylus at the end as shown in Figs. 5 and 6.
The switch of a probe in open condition is shown in Fig. 5, and the switch in closed
condition is shown in Fig. 6. The rigid contact of electrodes ensures exact length
of the last link of the SCMM in switch-off condition. On contact, it sends a signal

Fig. 5 SCMM end link
showing spherical stylus in
non-pressed position

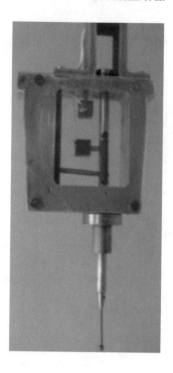

to the attached computer to record the encoder readings. The accurate coordinate measurements are obtained by resting a stylus in the fiducial and with a gentle push to bring the spring-loaded electrode in contact with the rigid conducting surface to close the switch.

Instant registration of the spatial point in order to avoid uncertainty for a range of points has been considered carefully. The end probe mechanism and the circuitry are designed in such a manner that the configuration remains same and it results in a single instance of a position. At the instant of closing the switch, the encoder values are recorded and the coordinates of the end reference point are computed. However, on track mode (switch is in closed condition), the encoder values are polled at a high frequency and the coordinates of the end point path are computed continuously in high resolution. Figure 4 represents the prototype of the SCMM system with a homing fixture. The SCMM is used to measure the coordinates of the fiducial points with respect to the robot frame of reference. The coordinate measurements are utilized to establish a relation between the fiducial frame and the robot frame [11].

Fig. 6 SCMM end link
showing spherical stylus in
pressed position and
electrodes in activated
position

4 Identification of D-H Parameters and Calibration of SCMM

The D-H parameters are used to determine the coordinates of the tip point of SCMM
at different orientations. The coordinates of the end probe point of SCMM with
respect to base frame of reference of the SCMM are given as

$$_P^B P = {_0^B T}\, {_1^0 T}\, {_2^1 T}\, {_3^2 T}\, {_4^3 T}\, {_P^4 P}$$

$_P^B P$ End probe point of SCMM w. r. t. base frame coordinate system of SCMM.
$_0^B T$ Transformation matrix of 0th frame of reference w. r. t. base frame of reference
of SCMM.
$_P^4 P$ End probe point of SCMM w. r. t. 4th link frame coordinate system of SCMM.
$_{i+1}^i T$ Transformation matrix relating $(i + 1)$th link of SCMM w. r. t. ith link of
SCMM.

The D-H parameters are used to determine the transformation $_{i+1}^i T$. Theoretical
values of D-H parameters (at home position) are given in Table 1.

$$_0^B T = \begin{bmatrix} 1 & 0 & 0 & 0 \\ 0 & 1 & 0 & 0 \\ 0 & 0 & 1 & 0 \\ 0 & 0 & 0 & 1 \end{bmatrix}, \quad _P^4 P = \begin{bmatrix} 163 \\ 0 \\ 0 \\ 1 \end{bmatrix}, _P^B P(calculated\ at\ home\ position) = \begin{bmatrix} 119.802 \\ 0.0576 \\ 19.619 \\ 1 \end{bmatrix}$$

Table 1 Theoretical value of D-H parameters

Link no i	α_{i-1} (rad)	a_{i-1} (mm)	d_i (mm)	θ_i (rad) (home)
1	0	0	92	0
2	−1.57	0	0	−1.37
3	0	100	0	1.444
4	0	100	0	1.496

Table 2 Measured value of D-H parameters in a CMM lab

Link no i	α_{i-1} (rad)	a_{i-1} (mm)	d_i (mm)	θ_i (rad) (home)
1	0.004	0.027	49.655	2.2
2	−1.527	0.033	1890.433	−2.649
3	0.041	63.574	1155.623	−1.913
4	−3.109	21.941	3041.377	0.145

The measurement of D-H parameters was carried out on a high-precision Coordinate Measuring Machine (CMM) at homing location of SCMM (Table 2). It is noticed that the small dimensional deviations in the manufacturing of the SCMM largely alter the D-H parameters of the SCMM.

$$
{}^{B}_{0}T = \begin{bmatrix} 0.576 & -0.817 & 0 & 0 \\ 0.817 & 0.576 & 0 & 0 \\ 0 & 0 & 1 & 42.708 \\ 0 & 0 & 0 & 1 \end{bmatrix}, \quad {}^{4}_{P}P = \begin{bmatrix} 163.341 \\ 0 \\ 0 \\ 1 \end{bmatrix},
$$

$$
{}^{B}_{P}P(calculated\ at\ home\ position) = \begin{bmatrix} 119.909 \\ -0.190 \\ 19.863 \\ 1 \end{bmatrix}
$$

When the Direct Kinematics Problem (DKP) was solved using the measured value of D-H parameters of SCMM, it shows a large deviation of actual from calculated end-effector position at different orientations of the SCMM throughout the workspace. The set of D-H parameters determined from measurement gives the position of probe point correct only at the home position. It is concluded that the measured values of D-H parameters cannot be used for practical implementation and utmost serve as guidance values for calibration.

The calibration of SCMM was carried out for improving the accuracy of the system, using the theoretical D-H parameters as the initial value. The joint variables at home position are taken as reference and are to be measured with high accuracy. For calibration, the SCMM is positioned at various orientations in its workspace. At each position, the joint angles (θ_i) are measured along with the end probe point ${}^{B}_{P}P$ with respect to the home position of SCMM by a standard CMM. The SCMM

Table 3 Calibrated D-H parameters (for $-85° \ll \theta_i \ll +90°$)

Link no i	α_{i-1} (rad)	a_{i-1} (mm)	d_i (mm)	θ_i (rad) (home)
1	0.006	−0.3	92.393	0.00722
2	−1.572	0.089	0	−1.369
3	−0.001	99.971	0	1.44
4	−0.007	100.442	0	1.499

Table 4 Calibrated D-H parameters (for $-180° \ll \theta_i \ll -85°$ and $+90° \ll \theta_i \ll +180°$)

Link no i	α_{i-1} (rad)	a_{i-1} (mm)	d_i (mm)	θ_i (rad) (home)
1	0.008	−0.474	92.393	0.018
2	−1.547	−1.272	0	−1.387
3	−0.001	100.931	0	1.462
4	−0.022	99.925	0	1.5

configurations are selected in a way that effects of some of the D-H parameters are more pronounced than the other parameters. Then by a least squares optimizing method, the error between the actual positions achieved and theoretical positions obtained from D-H parameters is minimized.

$$Positional\ Error = {}^B_P P_{(Theroretcal)} - {}^B_P P_{(CMM)} = fxn(\alpha_i, a_i, d_i, \theta_i)$$

The D-H parameters are optimized to minimize the errors in all directions. Rather than optimizing all the D-H parameters altogether, some of the configurations in which the effect of those D-H parameters is predominant are first taken for optimization. The calibration procedure is repeated to optimize all the D-H parameters to minimize the positional error. The partial derivatives $\frac{\partial_P^B P}{\partial \theta_i}$, $\frac{\partial_P^B P}{\partial \alpha_i}$, $\frac{\partial_P^B P}{\partial a_i}$, and $\frac{\partial_P^B P}{\partial d_i}$ are used for establishing the optimizing function.

The calibration shows a large improvement in the measurement accuracy of SCMM. The calibration-based methods seem to be a good solution for improving the accuracy of the system. Tables 3 and 4 show the calibrated values of the D-H parameters. Figure 7 gives the error of the SCMM before and after the calibration procedure. It is noticed that the average error of SCMM has reduced from 2.80 to 1.19 mm after calibration.

$$
{}^B_0 T = \begin{bmatrix} 1 & 0 & 0 & 0 \\ 0 & 1 & 0 & 0 \\ 0 & 0 & 1 & 0 \\ 0 & 0 & 0 & 1 \end{bmatrix}, \quad {}^4_P P (\text{for} -85° \ll \theta_i \ll +90°) = \begin{bmatrix} 163.248 \\ 0.007 \\ 0.114 \\ 1 \end{bmatrix},
$$

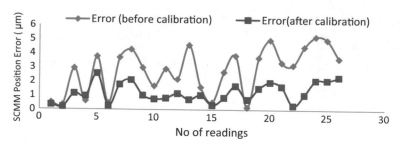

Fig. 7 Error of SCMM before and after calibration

$$
{}_{P}^{4}P(-180° \ll \theta_i \ll -85° \text{ and } +90° \ll \theta_i \ll +180°) = \begin{bmatrix} 163.341 \\ 0 \\ 0 \\ 1 \end{bmatrix},
$$

$$
{}_{P}^{B}P(\textit{calculated at home position}) = \begin{bmatrix} 120.03 \\ -0.51 \\ 19.91 \\ 1 \end{bmatrix}
$$

5 Experimental Evaluation of SCMM

Experiments are conducted to evaluate the performance characteristics of the SCMM. The SCMM is evaluated for pair point registration. The results are in concurrence with the registration techniques which are currently being used for stereotactic neurosurgery. An acrylic block is chosen as a phantom on which the fiducials are affixed in predefined positions. The SCMM along with the acrylic block is shown in Fig. 8. The phantom is prepared (with fiducials affixed) and by imaging techniques the relationship of a fixed point on the phantom with respect to the fiducial frame is established. The phantom is subjected to a CT scan; DICOM images are analyzed and from there the coordinates of the fiducials and the fixed point on the phantom with respect to the fiducial frame of reference are determined.

The coordinates of the fiducials affixed to the acrylic block are determined with respect to the SCMM base frame. Then, using the transformation relationship between the fiducial frame and the SCMM base frame, the coordinates of the fixed point on the phantom are determined with respect to the SCMM base frame. Thus, the pair point registration procedure using the SCMM is established.

Using the same phantom, the accuracy analysis of the SCMM is carried out. To check the accuracy of the SCMM, the first set of distances between the fiducials already pasted on the acrylic block is measured with it. The same distances are measured separately by using a high-precision coordinate measuring machine. The two

Fig. 8 SCMM along with a
acrylic block

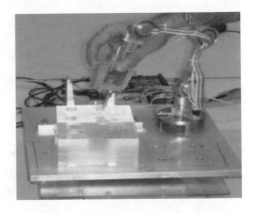

sets of readings are compared to determine the accuracy of SCMM. The difference in reading is found to be less than 1 mm.

A point-to-point fiducial-based neuro-registration and neuronavigation is demonstrated in the laboratory. Neuronavigation experiments are conducted using a human skull phantom to evaluate the performance characteristics of the SCMM. The human skull phantom is prepared for a CT scan by affixing the fiducials on the surface of the skull. The phantom is subjected to a CT scan, and the relation of the fiducials with respect to the fiducial frame is established using DICOM images. The relation between the tumor (a fixed point on the skull phantom) with respect to the fiducial frame is established. Using the transformation formulated, the coordinates of the tumor with respect to the SCMM base frame are determined. Subsequent to the registration, the neuronavigation procedure is performed.

In the neuronavigation procedure, the passive SCMM is used to navigate the surgical tool. When the user manually navigates the end tool fixed to the SCMM (Fig. 9), he can visualize on the computer screen: the actual configuration of the SCMM, tool movement relative to the 3D model of the actual skull built using a CT image, and also the tip of the tool with respect to the tumor region. SCMM not only measures the 3D coordinates of the point but also determines a line vector passing through the point in its workspace (Fig. 10). SCMM-based neuronavigation guides the neurosurgeon how to position and orient the surgical tool such that it traverses in a straight line path from entry point to tumor point. The neuronavigation software generates the real-time axial, coronal, sagittal, and an oblique view (normal to axis of the surgical tool) of the brain as SCMM approaches the tumor. The implementation of the SCMM-based neuronavigation is illustrated in Fig. 9, where SCMM and its simulated model are shown when the user is traversing the surface of the skull.

Fig. 9 Neuronavigation
procedure demonstrated
using SCMM

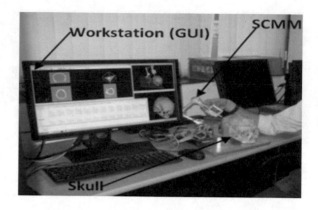

Fig. 10 SCMM guiding
surgical tool to approach
tumor point

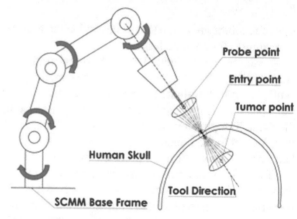

6 Conclusion

The SCMM-based neuronavigation procedure presented eliminates the "line of sight" problem which is a constraint of the current neuronavigation procedures. SCMM-based neuronavigation guides the neurosurgeon how to orient the surgical tool so that it approaches in a straight line path from entry point to the tumor point. The SCMM-based frameless stereotaxy system has an accuracy comparable to the frame-based stereotaxy system and at the same time patient comfort levels equivalent to the optical tracking-based frameless stereotaxy systems. The SCMM-based neuro-registration and neuronavigation is an economical and a promising substitute over the current optical tracking-based neuronavigation systems. The important conclusion is that the measured values of the D-H parameters are not feasible for implementation. The calibration-based methods should be used for improving the accuracy of the system. It shows the large improvement in the measurement accuracy of SCMM.

References

1. J. Zheng, An accurate and efficient target localization method for stereotactic neurosurgery of Parkinson's disease, Ph.D. Thesis, The State University of New Jersey, October 2006
2. P.L. Gildenberg, General concepts of stereotactic surgery, in *Modern Stereotactic Neurosurgery* (Lunsford LD, Ed. Martinus Nijhoff Publishing, Boston, 1988)
3. P.L. Gildenberg, Stereotactic surgery: present and past, in *Stereotactic Neurogurgery* (Heilbrun MP, Ed. Baltimore, Williams & Wilkins, 1988)
4. L. Leksell, Stereotactic apparatus for intercerebral surgery. Acta Chir Scand **99**, 229–233 (1949)
5. G. Eggers, J. Muhling, R. Marmulla, Image-to-patient registration techniques in head surgery. Int. J. Oral Maxillofac. Surg. **35**, 1081–1095 (2006)
6. Brainlab Surgery Products, http://www.brainlab.com/. Accessed 10 Nov 2017
7. S. Frey, R. Comeau, B. Hynes, S. Mackey, M. Petrides, Frameless Stereotaxy in the nonhuman primate. NeuroImage **23**, 1226–1234 (2004)
8. N.L. Doward, Frameless Stereotactic biopsy with the EasyGuide. Medicamumdi **42**(1) (1998)
9. Faro India, http://www.faro.com/en-in/products/metrology/faroarm/overview. Accessed 10 Nov 2017
10. Cimtrex Systems, http://www.cimtrix.com/baces-3d.htm. Accessed 10 Nov 2017
11. G. Bhutani, Modeling, design and development of frameless stereotaxy in robot assisted neurosurgery. Ph.D. Thesis, Homi Bhabha National Institute, July 2015

Kinematic Analysis of Carrier Mechanism for In-service Inspection of Sodium-Cooled Fast Reactor Internals

Sudheer Patri, Varun Kaushik, C. Meikandamurthy, B. K. Sreedhar, V. Prakash and P. Selvaraj

Abstract In-service inspection requirements of reactor internals of sodium-cooled fast reactors offer challenges in the design and successful deployment of carrier mechanisms. A single-carrier mechanism consisting of inter-connected rigid links having multiple ultrasonic transducers is envisaged for carrying out all the necessary inspections. The kinematic analysis of the chain assembly of the proposed carrier mechanism is the main focus of the present paper. Initially, a base design of the chain assembly was proposed and the same is analysed with respect to the linearity and smooth motion transmission. The kinematic chain of the base design was modified to improve the motion transmission characteristics. Parametric studies were done to fine-tune the design parameters of modified design. The analysis has given valuable insights into the performance of chain assembly and provided necessary data for the smooth operation of chain assembly.

Keywords Sodium-cooled fast breeder reactors · In-service inspection
Kinematic design of chain assembly

S. Patri (✉) · C. Meikandamurthy · B. K. Sreedhar · V. Prakash · P. Selvaraj
Indira Gandhi Centre for Atomic Research, Kalpakkam, Tamil Nadu, India
e-mail: patri@igcar.gov.in; sudheerpatri@gmail.com

C. Meikandamurthy
e-mail: cmm@igcar.gov.in

B. K. Sreedhar
e-mail: bksd@igcar.gov.in

V. Prakash
e-mail: prakash@igcar.gov.in

P. Selvaraj
e-mail: pselva@igcar.gov.in

V. Kaushik
Birla Institute of Technology and Science, Pilani, Rajasthan, India
e-mail: varunkaushik43@gmail.com

© Springer Nature Singapore Pte Ltd. 2019
D N Badodkar and T A Dwarakanath (eds.), *Machines, Mechanism and Robotics*, Lecture Notes in Mechanical Engineering,
https://doi.org/10.1007/978-981-10-8597-0_21

1   Introduction

Sodium-cooled fast reactors (SFR) promise to be the energy workhorses of the future. Although SFR technology has been convincingly demonstrated in the last five decades, scope exists for further technological improvement in the area of in-service inspection of SFR internals. In-service monitoring is difficult in SFRs mainly because of the opacity of sodium and the high temperature radioactive operating environ-ment. Ultrasonic techniques offer a solution to the problems of inspection, and ultrasonic technology for under-sodium visualisation has been actively pursued to meet the challenges of in-service inspection of reactor internals.

Design of carrier mechanisms for ultrasonic inspection of reactor internals is important because of constraints from complex geometries and the importance of safe retrieval of the mechanism from the reactor in the event of a mechanical snag.

The in-service inspection of reactor internals involves system-level measurements on multiple components such as core sub-assemblies, above core structure, grid plate, etc. A single-carrier mechanism consisting of inter-connected rigid links, called chain assembly, having multiple ultrasonic transducers is envisaged for carrying out all the necessary inspections. Similar mechanism was proposed to be used in prototype fast reactor [1]. Figure 1 shows the schematic of the mechanism along with the scheme of its deployment. It also shows various motions of the mechanism.

The kinematic analysis of the chain assembly of the carrier mechanism is the main focus of the present paper. A mathematical programme is developed to calculate the displacement characteristics, velocity analysis and acceleration analysis for different designs of chain assembly. The programme also provides graphical display of results to aid for visualisation.

Initially, a base design of the chain assembly was proposed and the same is anal-ysed with respect to the linearity and smooth motion transmission. The kinematic chain of the base design was modified to improve the motion transmission character-istics. The mathematical programme, as mentioned above, was used to finalise the various parameters for optimising the performance of modified design.

2   Description of Carrier Mechanism

The mechanism consists of a chain carrying ultrasonic transducers. The chain is inserted via a 'housing' into the primary circuit of the reactor. The housing is the main body of mechanism that accommodates all the components of the mechanism as well as the different sub-assemblies required for their operation. A supporting arm is mounted at the lower part of the housing. The supporting arm can be folded in vertical position or opened up in horizontal position. In horizontal position, supporting arm provides the sweeping motion required to scan as well as to guide and support the links. The housing can be raised/lowered and rotated and similarly, the chain can be extended as a stiff cantilever. This gives the opportunity to carry out various

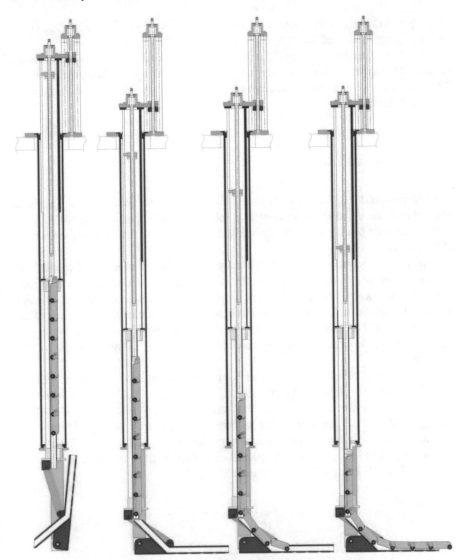

Fig. 1 Schematic of the carrier mechanism and its deployment

inspection tasks within the reactor internals. An articulated section is provided at the end of the chain to facilitate greater flexibility of operation. The articulated section consists of pneumatic motors using argon as working fluid.

There are four independent motions that must be achieved for complete operation of the carrier mechanism, viz., (i) vertical motion of the main housing through the roof opening (during insertion and retrieval), (ii) vertical motion of an inner pipe for opening and closing of the support arm, (iii) vertical motion of the chain assembly and (iv) rotary motion of the support arm to scan the reactor core.

All the prime movers, except the articulated section, are located above the reactor so as to ensure access for servicing and replacement in the event of malfunction. The prime movers of articulated section are protected from sodium environment by metallic bellows.

3 Chain Assembly

The chain consists of 7½ links, the half link being the rear link where the chain is connected to the drive shaft. To complete the chain, each link was connected to its neighbours with bearings, which joined the front end of the one link to the rear end of the adjacent link.

The hinges joining two successive links of the chain are arranged above butting faces at the bottom of the links so that the chain can be extended beyond the tracks in the supporting arm and remain as a rigid link. Ultrasonic transducers are mounted in the links so as to 'beam' ultrasound downwards towards the core top. Other transducers may be positioned to beam ultrasound upwards towards the above core structure, forwards along the axis of the chain and possibly sideways perpendicular to the chain.

Wheels are provided at the front of each link for guiding and controlling the links during their deployment beyond the supporting arm. Each link has two wheels instead of four. When a link will move from vertical arm to horizontal position, incompatibility arises between pivots and wheels, which may result in jamming of the link. Hence, only one set of wheels is provided. Some space is provided in each link for the electrical components (transducers, cables, etc.) that will be used for imaging. The schematic of a link is shown in Fig. 2.

Fig. 2 Schematic of a link in the chain assembly

In the preliminary design, the extended length (viewing length) of the carrier mechanism is selected as 1 m and the length of each link is finalised as 150 mm. The diameter of the wheels is selected as 20 mm. Magnitude of link length is a compromise between the manoeuvrability and higher number of bearings in sodium operation, which reduce the reliability. The size of each ultrasonic transducer is also a constraint in deciding the link length.

4 Kinematic Analysis of Chain Assembly

As indicated in Sect. 2, the drive shaft drives down the rear link and the motion is transmitted to all other links. Thus, the transmitted vertical motion is converted to horizontal movement of the front link by the inclined link travelling between the vertical support and the arm.

Displacement, velocity and acceleration analysis of chain assembly was carried out to validate the design choices made. Smooth transmission of motion with linear relationship between input and output motions is the main aim of the kinematic design. The downward motion of the drive shaft is the input motion, and the horizontal displacement of the tip of the link is the output motion in the analysis.

The analysis is restricted to the motion of a typical link as it passes through the inner pipe to the arm, as the same characteristics would be repeated for each subsequent link. Initially, calculations were done for the base design where the arm is straight, Fig. 3a shows the schematic of base design. Due to highly nonlinear characteristics obtained in displacement analysis, the design of supporting arm is modified to include an inclined portion as shown in Fig. 3b. Kinematic analysis of the modified design is carried out to obtain various characteristics.

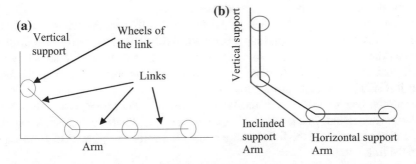

Fig. 3 **a** Schematic of base kinematic design of chain assembly. **b** Modified kinematic design of chain assembly

Fig. 4 Initial condition

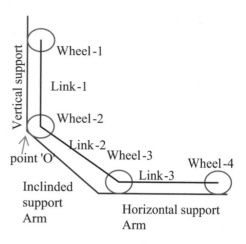

4.1   Methodology [2]

Displacement analysis is carried out by calculating the position of front end of the output link for the given input motion using analytical geometry. The methodology for displacement analysis of modified design is more general and applicable to the base design as well and hence the same is given below:

- Three links fall into the analysis domain. The links are named as Link-1, 2 and 3 as shown in Fig. 4. The wheels of the, respectively, links are also named as shown in figure.
- The initial condition is chosen in such a way that Wheel-2 is touching both vertical and supporting arm. The centre coordinates of all the wheels are calculated using simple geometry, considering the origin 'O' as the point of intersection of the vertical arm and the inclined support arm.
- Further, downward displacement of the Wheel-1 will move the Wheel-2 such that it now lies completely on the supporting arm, while Wheels-3 and 4 will displace along the horizontal arm, as shown in Fig. 5. The movement of Wheel-1 can be effected mathematically by changing its 'ordinate' (its abscissa remains the same as it is still on the vertical support).
- From the new coordinates of the Wheel-1, the new coordinates of other wheels can be calculated. The constraint between their coordinates is in such a way that the distance between the links' centre is always a constant value of 150 mm, equal to the link length.
- From the new and initial coordinates of the wheels, displacement of different wheels can be calculated with simple mathematics. Thus, the output displacement of front wheel (Wheel-4) for the given input displacement of rear wheel (Wheel-1) is obtained.
- After the downward displacement of the Link 1 by 150 mm, a situation similar to the initial condition will arise again. Thus, the same cycle will repeat.

Fig. 5 Displaced position

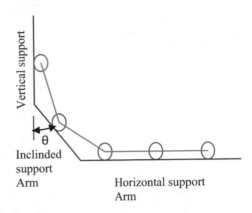

- Depending upon the length of support arm, a situation may arise wherein the Wheel-2 moves from the supporting arm to the horizontal arm. New set of equations is used to describe the link positions. The constraint for this situation will be that the distance between the centres will again remain the same and the ordinate of the Wheel-2 will remain a constant thereafter.

'Velocity diagram technique' is used for calculating the velocities. Based on the geometric configuration of the chain assembly for different input displacements, as obtained in displacement analysis above, the velocity diagrams are mathematically created and the velocity of the output link is calculated for the given input displacement. Since the mathematical implementation is straightforward, it is not presented here. Similar to velocity analysis, 'acceleration diagram technique' is used for calculating the accelerations of various links.

5   Results and Discussion

The displacement characteristics, defined as the variation of output displacement with respect to the input displacement, for the base design are shown in Fig. 6. It can be seen that the characteristics are highly nonlinear. Linear characteristics are also shown for the sake of comparison in all the graphs.

The displacement characteristics of modified design depend upon the length of inclined supporting arm (L) and the inclination of the supporting arm with the vertical (θ). Parametric studies are carried out with 'L' and 'θ' as parameters. Figure 7 shows the displacement characteristics for different values of 'θ' for L = 150 mm. It is clear that the deviation from linearity is almost same for $\theta = 30°$ and 45°. However, similar analysis for different values of 'L' revealed that the characteristics are better for $\theta = 45°$. Figures 8 and 9 show the displacement characteristics for different values of 'L' with $\theta = 45°$. The characteristics are identical for L = 150 and 300 mm. The nonlinearity decreases as the magnitude of 'L' is increased from 150 mm up to

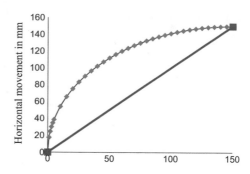

Fig. 6 Displacement characteristics for the base design of chain

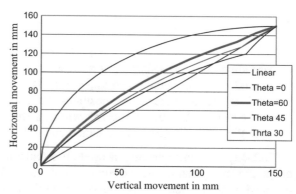

Fig. 7 Displacement characteristics for different angles of inclinations of the arm

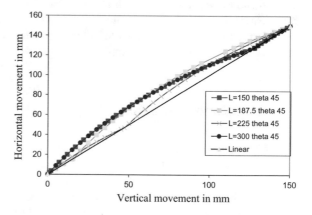

Fig. 8 Displacement characteristics for various lengths of support arm

225 mm and then increases thereafter. However, the behaviour is slightly different while the 'L' is decreased from 150 mm. The smaller the value of 'L', the early the Wheel-2 touches the horizontal portion of the arm and subsequent characteristics are similar to the base case, with high nonlinearity. Thus, the characteristics with L = 75 mm are highly nonlinear. In summary, it is found that nonlinearity is minimum for L = 225 mm and θ = 45°.

Fig. 9 Displacement characteristics for various lengths of support arm

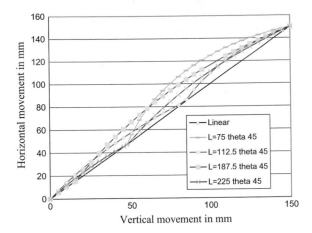

Fig. 10 Velocity characteristics of the chain assembly for the reference design

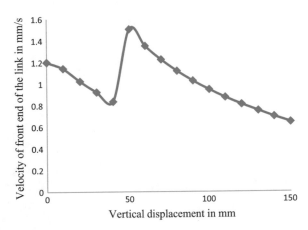

Thus, this configuration is taken as reference design and both the velocity and acceleration analyses of the chain assembly are carried out when the vertical link is translating with a constant velocity of 1 mm/s. Figure 10 shows the velocity characteristics of the reference design. The variation in velocity is small throughout the travel. Similarly, it is found from acceleration analysis that the acceleration of all the links is negligibly small and changes smoothly during the chain deployment.

6 Conclusion

The kinematic analysis of the chain assembly of the proposed carrier mechanism is the main focus of the present paper. The analysis has given valuable insights into the performance of chain assembly and provided necessary data for the smooth operation of chain assembly. It is also planned to experimentally verify the performance of chain assembly in a full-scale mock-up facility and the same is under manufacturing.

References

1. S.D. Brayant, P. Fenemore, G. Chesworth, Under sodium diagnosis and imaging. CEC study contract RA1/CT 94-0233 UK; C9672/TR/001, April 1997
2. V. Kaushik, Kinematic analysis of carrier mechanism for in-service inspection of FBR internals. Report of BITS practice school-1 at IGCAR, Kalpakkam

Dynamic Analysis of Partially Compliant Planar Slider–Crank Mechanism with Joint Clearance

S. Basumatary, J. Srinivas, Penta Akhil and Adhil Basheer

Abstract In practical operation of mechanisms, joint clearances and compliance influence the overall performance drastically. Excessive clearances induce extra degrees of freedom at the joint, while compliance provides an additional torque. This paper presents the dynamic analysis of partially compliant planar slider–crank mechanism with joint clearance. When joint clearance is considered, an additional intermittent impact force acts on the system and velocity and acceleration as well as forces at the joints change drastically. Therefore, mechanisms are often made compliant with limited number of joints. In order to model compliant linkage, equivalent torque is introduced at the joint using pseudo-rigid-body modeling. Initially, the turning moment and force equations of crank, coupler, and slider are obtained in terms of contact forces at the clearance joint. Effect of clearance at the crank pin on the kinematic and dynamic characteristics is studied in detail.

Keywords Dynamic analysis · Motion simulator · Partially compliant · Passive joint clearance · Slider–Crank linkage

S. Basumatary · J. Srinivas (✉) · P. Akhil · A. Basheer
Department of Mechanical Engineering, National Institute of Technology
Rourkela, Rourkela 769008, Odisha, India
e-mail: srin07@yahoo.co.in

S. Basumatary
e-mail: sbasumatary789@gmail.com

P. Akhil
e-mail: akhilpenta007@gmail.com

A. Basheer
e-mail: adhilkb8@gmail.com

© Springer Nature Singapore Pte Ltd. 2019
D N Badodkar and T A Dwarakanath (eds.), *Machines, Mechanism and Robotics*, Lecture Notes in Mechanical Engineering,
https://doi.org/10.1007/978-981-10-8597-0_22

257

1 Introduction

Slider–crank mechanisms are widely used to convert the translatory motion of piston into rotary motions of crank or vice versa. In internal combustion engines, with a gas pressure arising from combustion of fuel, often output torque at crankshaft is measured. In kinematic analysis of such constrained (one-degree of freedom) mechanism, the displacement of slider along with corresponding velocity and accelerations are required. Dynamic analysis further makes use of the kinematic results to obtain the time-dependent joint forces including the torque on the crankshaft and link forces. A wide literature is available on kinematic and dynamic modeling procedures of the slider–crank linkage [1–4]. Recently, compliant mechanisms with few joint pairs have attracted research community due to their several advantages like reduced backlash, joint clearances, and overall weight of linkage. Often compliant mechanisms are simulated with pseudo-rigid-body models, where a torsional spring of finite stiffness replaces a joint. Two-dimensional compliant mechanisms were studied earlier to predict resulting transmission angle [5], to improve the fatigue life of linkage [6], etc. Compliance in spatial slider–crank linkage was presented by Parlaktas and Tanik [7, 8]. In a macroscopic scale, workability of fully compliant linkage is difficult in a plane due to several reasons. Therefore, linkages are considered with partially compliance allowing certain joints to remain as articulated.

Conventionally, joints have a journal (at one link terminal) and bearing (at other link terminal) arranged with certain initial clearance. Due to repeated usage, the clearance increases slowly with wear and tear, leading to additional degrees of freedom of the mechanism. It may result in free flight and impact movements at the joint. Such movements give rise to uncertainties with additional joint forces. Effect of joint clearance on the accuracy of slider–crank linkage was studied over the last two decades [e.g., 8–12]. Effects of multiple joint clearances on the slider acceleration were studied in some works [e.g., 13] and a constrained optimization problem was solved to smoothen the effects of joint clearances. In recent years, studies relating to partial compliant slider–crank linkages with one or two joint clearances have also been found [14]. Notably, Erkaya and his colleagues [15, 16] shown that the undesired output of joint clearance could be minimized by providing suspension effect to the flexural joint of any compliant mechanism. Although wide amount of work was done, still the dynamics of compliant linkage with joint clearance is not fully understood.

Present work deals with dynamic analysis of slider–crank mechanism with partial compliance along with a joint clearance effect. Initially, kinematic analysis of a constant speed slider–crank mechanism is carried. Dynamic analysis is performed with a pseudo-rigid-body model, and the modified dynamic equations obtained by introducing additional torque term obtained from compliant joint are solved. Effect of joint clearance at the crank pin on the kinematic and dynamic characteristics of resultant linkage is illustrated. Additional impact force due to clearance effect drastically influences the velocities and accelerations as well as forces at the joints.

2 Compliant Linkage with Joint Clearance

The compliant planar slider crank mechanism considered is shown in Fig. 1. The linkage has a crank of radius l_2 and coupler of length l_3 up to flexure hinge connecting the coupler with the slider (link-4).

If effective link length remains the same, the kinematic quantities like velocity and acceleration do not change from conventional rigid slider–crank mechanism. For dynamic analysis of the linkage, the joint is treated as an external torsional spring of stiffness $K = E_n I / l_n$, where E_n is the elastic modulus of the flexure hinge material, $I = \frac{bh^3}{12}$ is area moment of inertia of rectangular narrow section ($b \times h$) of flexure hinge, and l_n is the length of narrow region. With equivalent rigid body treatment, it produces a torque $M_{ext} = K(\theta_3 - \theta_{30})$, where θ_3 is displaced joint angle from initial position θ_{30}. Figure 2 shows the joint configuration with a journal bearing pair during the clearance condition.

The difference between the radii of bearing and journal is called clearance (c). Due to excessive motion of the journal, sometimes the journal impacts with the bearing surface. Contact between the journal and bearing surfaces is obtained when the penetration depth $\delta = e - c \geq 0$. It leads to vibration and affects the performance of mechanism. By using modified Hertz contact law [17], it is possible to calculate the normal contact force between journal and bearing accordingly as

$$F_N = C_N \delta^n + D\dot{\delta} \tag{1}$$

where C_N is contact stiffness and $n = 1.5$ for metals. For spherical contact surfaces,

$$C_N = \frac{4/3}{\left(\frac{1-v_b^2}{E_b} + \frac{1-v_j^2}{E_j}\right)} \left(\frac{r_b r_j}{(r_b + r_j)}\right)^{0.5} \tag{2}$$

Fig. 1 Compliant link in slider–crank mechanism

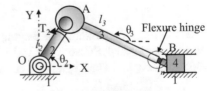

Fig. 2 Joint clearance representation

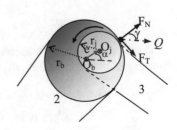

with ν and E representing Poisson ratio and elastic modulus of contacting surfaces, and suffices b and j are bearing and journal, respectively. In order to account the amount of energy lost during impact process, the hysteresis damping force shown as a second term in Eq. (1) is considered. Here, $D = \chi \delta^{1.5}$ is damping coefficient, while $\chi = \frac{3C_N(1-c_e^2)}{4\dot{\delta}^*}$ is hysteresis factor with c_e and $\dot{\delta}^*$ are, respectively, the restitution coefficient and initial impact velocity. By considering tangential friction force as $F_T = -\mu F_N$, the magnitude of resultant contact force Q at bearing is obtained.

2.1 Dynamic Modeling

In the present analysis, the crank and coupler are considered to be connected by a revolute joint with clearance. From Fig. 1, loop-closure equation can be written as [18]

$$O\vec{A} + \vec{r} + A\vec{B} = x_4\hat{i} \tag{3}$$

where $O\vec{A} = l_2 \cos\theta_2 \,\hat{i} + l_2 \sin\theta_2 \,\hat{j}, \vec{r} = e \cos\alpha\hat{i} + e \sin\alpha\hat{j}, A\vec{B} = l_3\cos\theta_3 \,\hat{i} + l_3 \sin\theta_3 \,\hat{j}$, and x_4 is the slider position in horizontal direction. Here, $\hat{i}$ and $\hat{j}$ are unit vectors in X and Y directions, respectively. The kinetic energy of the linkage in terms of link masses (m_2, m_3, m_4) and moments of inertia (I_{G2}, I_{G3}) is given as

$$T = \frac{1}{2}(I_{G2} + m_2(b_2l_2)^2 + m_3l_2^2)\dot{\theta}_2^2 + \frac{1}{2}(I_{G3} + m_3(b_3l_3)^2)\dot{\theta}_3^2$$
$$+ m_3b_3l_2l_3\dot{\theta}_2\dot{\theta}_3 \cos(\theta_2 - \theta_3) + \frac{1}{2}m_4\dot{x}_4^2 \tag{4}$$

Similarly, the potential energy of the system is

$$U = m_2gb_2l_2 \sin\theta_2 + m_3g(l_2 \sin\theta_2 + b_3l_3 \sin\theta_3) \tag{5}$$

where b_2 and b_3 are fraction of lengths of links 2 and 3, respectively, where centers of mass are located. Subscripts 2 and 3 refer to the links 2 (crank) and 3 (connecting rod), respectively. The Lagrange's equation of motion is expressed as

$$\frac{d}{dt}\left(\frac{\partial T}{\partial \dot{q}_i}\right) - \frac{\partial T}{\partial q_i} + \frac{\partial U}{\partial q_i} = Q_{1i}, i = 1, 2, 3 \tag{6}$$

Here, Q_i are the set of nonconservative forces. It results in the following equations in terms of the variables: θ_2, θ_3, and x_4:

$$m_3b_3l_3l_2\ddot{\theta}_3 \cos(\theta_2 - \theta_3) + m_3b_3l_3l_2\dot{\theta}_3^2 \sin(\theta_2 - \theta_3)$$
$$+ m_2gb_2l_2 \cos\theta_2 + m_3gl_2 \cos\theta_2 = M_2 - Ql_2 \sin(\theta_2 - \gamma) \tag{7}$$

$$(I_{G3} + m_3(b_3l_3)^2)\ddot{\theta}_3 + m_3b_3l_3l_2\dot{\theta}_2^2 \sin(\theta_3 - \theta_2)$$
$$+ m_3b_3l_3g \cos \theta_3 = Q(r_b \sin \gamma - l_3 \sin(\theta_3 - \gamma)) + M_{ext} \tag{8}$$
$$m_4\ddot{x}_4 = -F_{43x} - \mu_1 F_{43y} \tag{9}$$

Here, $F_{43\,x,y}$ are the component forces exerted on link 3, Q and γ are the contact force and angle, respectively, as depicted in Fig. 2. Also, if crank speed ω is assumed constant, then $\theta_2 = \omega t$. The coefficient of friction μ_1 between slider and guides is taken as 0.3. The force Q exists only when $\delta > 0$ in every time step.

3 Proposed Methodology

Interactive computer programs are implemented in Matlab to perform the kinematic analysis and for solving the dynamic equations with clearance parameters. Kinematic analysis of linkage without clearance conditions is first conducted. This initial condition is given to the solver for computing e and α values using Eq. (3). Further, the dynamic Eqs. (8) and (9) are solved in every time step using Runge–Kutta fourth-order explicit time-integration method. Figure 3 shows the flowchart of implemented methodology. In every time step, the radial deformation e changes and the value of δ is estimated. If it is found positive, the contact force is computed and the time-dependent compliance torque M_{ext} is accounted before solving the equations in current time step. Thus, both the contact force and compliance torque are considered.

4 Results and Discussion

Table 1 depicts the geometric and mass parameters of the mechanism under consideration. Initially, the crank and coupler are considered as collinear in horizontal direction. That is, initial crank angle is set to zero.

The initial positions and velocities necessary to start the dynamic analysis are obtained from kinematic simulation of the slider–crank mechanism in which all joints considered as ideal. Figure 4 shows the kinematic parameters of the slider at constant crank speed of 200 rpm over five crank revolutions.

Table 1 Dimensions and mass parameters of slider–crank mechanism

Part	Length (m)	Mass (kg)	Moment of inertia (kgm^2)
Crank	0.05	0.3	0.0001
Coupler	0.12	0.21	0.00025
Slider	–	0.14	–

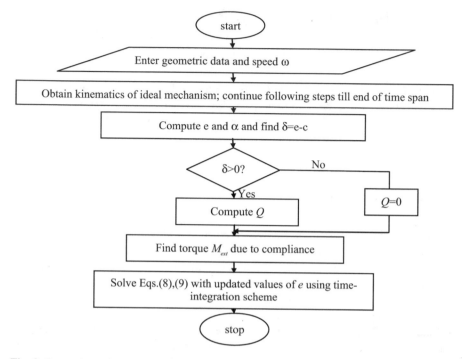

Fig. 3 Dynamic modeling procedure with clearances and compliance

The corresponding turning moment on the crankshaft is shown in Fig. 5. It is obtained from conventional joint force analysis of the linkage with constant angular velocity of the crankshaft. The results are initially validated with ADAMS solution.

Following parameters of contact surfaces are used in the dynamic model: $c_e = 0.9$, $r_b = 10$ mm, $r_j = 9.5$ mm, $E_b = E_j = 207$ GPa, $v = 0.3$, and $\mu = 0$. Also, the factors are set as $b_2 = b_3 = 0.5$. The dynamic response of the slider–crank mechanism is represented in terms of the turning moment on the crank and the journal center trajectory relative to the bearing center. The narrow rectangular section idealizing the compliant joint has the following parameters: $l_n =$ length of small segment of pivot $= l_3/10 = 12$ mm, width b $= 10$ mm, and height h $= 4$ mm. Further, the elastic modulus of this segment is taken as $E_n = 953$ MPa. The initial value $\theta_{30} = 0°$. Without considering the compliance effect, Fig. 6a shows the orbit of journal relative bearing for 10 s. Figure 6b shows the variation of angular velocity of coupler. As seen due to clearance, the system is unstable.

As the compliant joint torque T_{ext} is considered to avoid the revolute joint between coupler and slider, the changes in the angular velocity of coupler as a function of time are shown in Fig. 7.

As an extension of this study, it is possible to develop an inverse identification model that can predict the joint clearance levels from the response data.

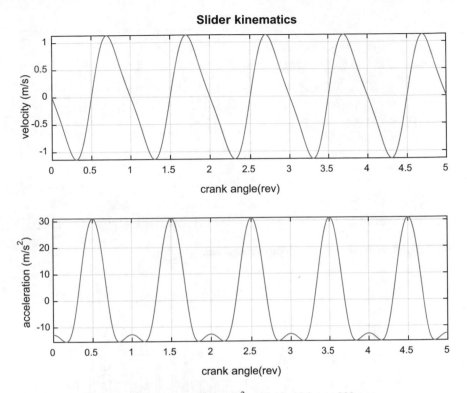

Fig. 4 Slider velocity (m/s) and acceleration (m/s^2) with ideal joints at 200 rpm

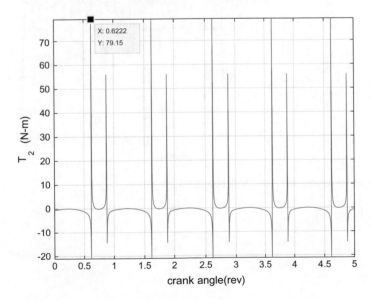

Fig. 5 Variation of turning moment on crankshaft

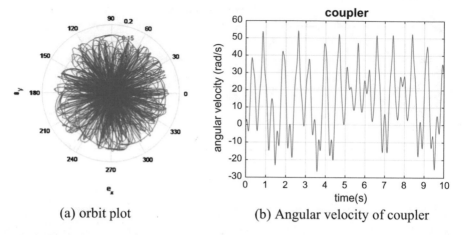

(a) orbit plot	(b) Angular velocity of coupler

Fig. 6 Dynamic response obtained without compliance

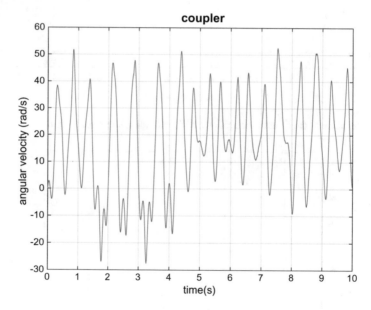

Fig. 7 Angular velocity of coupler with compliant joint

5 Conclusions

A simplified dynamic model of slider–crank linkage with joint clearances has been presented in this paper. As reported in earlier works, the effect of joint clearances on the piston kinematics and mechanism dynamics depends on several factors. By considering, compliance at other joint with a narrow hinge configuration, it is possible to minimize the joint clearance effect slightly. An experimental work is planned to be carried out on a scaled model with joint clearance and compliance together by measurement of accelerations of piston at varied joint clearances. Using such a data, it is possible to predict the magnitude and location of clearances in mechanism with the help of inverse modeling via fuzzy/neural networks.

References

1. R.F. Fung, Dynamic analysis of the flexible connecting rod of a slider-crank mechanism. J. Vib. Acoust. **118**, 687–689 (1996)
2. E. Soylemez, Classical transmission angle problem for slider–crank mechanisms. Mech. Mach. Theory 37(4), 419–425 (2002)
3. J.L. Ha, R.F. Fung, K.Y. Chen, S.C. Hsien, Dynamic modeling and identification of a slider–crank mechanism. J. Sound Vib. **289**(4–5), 1019–1044 (2006)
4. S. Erkaya, S. Su, I. Uzmay, Dynamic analysis of a slider-crank mechanism with eccentric connector and planetary gears. Mech. Mach. Theory **42**, 393–408 (2007)
5. E. Tanik, Transmission angle in compliant slider-crank mechanism. Mech. Mach. Theory **46**(11), 1623–1632 (2011)
6. T.P. Dao, S.C. Huang, Design and analysis of flexible slider crank mechanism. World Academy of Science, Engineering and Technology, Int. J. Mech. Aerosp. Ind. Mechatron. Manuf. Eng. **8**, 836–843 (2014)
7. V. Parlaktas, E. Tanik, Partially compliant slider-crank mechanism. Mech. Mach. Theory **46**(11), 1707–1718 (2011)
8. V. Parlaktas, E. Tanik, Single-piece compliant slider-crank mechanism. Mech. Mach. Theory **81**, 1–10 (2014)
9. I. Khemili, L. Romdhane, Dynamic analysis of a flexible slider crank mechanism with clearance. Eur. J. Mech. A/solids **27**, 882–898 (2008)
10. S.P. Flores, C.S. Koshy, H.M. Lankarani, J. Ambrósio, J.C.P. Claro, Numerical and experimental investigation on multibody systems with revolute clearance joints. Nonlinear Dyn. **65**, 383–398 (2011)
11. G.B. Daniel, K.L. Cavalca, Analysis of the dynamics of a slider-crank mechanism with hydrodynamic lubrication in the connecting rod–slider joint clearance. Mech. Mach. Theory **46**, 1434–1452 (2011)
12. V.L. Reis, G.B. Daniel, K.L. Cavalca, Dynamic analysis of a lubricated planar slider–crank mechanism considering friction and Hertz contact effects. Mech. Mach. Theory **74**, 257–273 (2014)
13. S.M. Varedi, H.M. Daniali, M. Dardel, Dynamic synthesis of a planar slider-crank mechanism with clearances. Nonlinear Dyn. **79**, 1587–1600 (2015)
14. Y. Li, G. Chen, D. Sun, Y. Gao, K. Wang, Dynamic analysis and optimisation design of a planar slider-crank mechanism with flexible components and two clearance joints. Mech. Mach. Theory **99**, 37–57 (2016)
15. S. Erkaya, S. Dogan, A comparative analysis of joint clearance effects on articulated and partly compliant mechanism. Nonlinear Dyn. **81**(1–2), 323–341 (2015)

16. S. Erkaya, S. Dogan, S. Ulus, Effects of joint clearance on the dynamics of partly compliant mechanism: numerical and experimental studies. Mech. Mach. Theory **88**, 125–140 (2015)
17. H. Lankarani, P. Nikravesh, A contact force model with hysteresis damping for impact analysis of multibody systems. J. Mech. Des. **112**, 369–376 (1990)
18. L. Robert, *Design of Machinery* (McGraw-Hill Higher Education, Norton, 2004)

Mathematical Model for Pressure–Deformation Relationship of Miniaturized McKibben Actuators

K. P. Ashwin and Ashitava Ghosal

Abstract A McKibben actuator/Pneumatic Artificial Muscle (PAM) is a soft actuator which has great potential in the field of bioinspired robotics. Miniaturized versions of PAMs or MPAMs of less than 1.5 mm diameter are ideal actuators for developing surgical devices due to their compliance and high power-to-weight ratio. Accurate mathematical model to represent the mechanics of PAM is an ongoing research. This paper develops a mathematical model which relates the input pressure to end-point deformation of a fabricated MPAM without external loading. The developed theoretical model is validated against experimental data for MPAM of lengths 60 and 70 mm. The model predicts the deformation of MPAM with standard error of less than 10%. The model is also able to predict the locking angle of 54.7° at higher pressures which is a distinct characteristic of McKibben actuators.

Keywords Miniaturized McKibben actuators · Pneumatic muscles · Actuated endoscopic instruments

1 Introduction

McKibben actuators or Pneumatic Artificial Muscles (PAM) are linear actuators which are gaining popularity in the field of flexible robotics. The device consists of a flexible inner tube (usually made of silicone) which is braided on the outside using sets of inextensible fibers woven in the form of a helix [1]. One end of the tube is sealed, while compressed air is input to the tube through the other end. When

K. P. Ashwin · A. Ghosal (✉)
Indian Institute of Science, Bengaluru, India
e-mail: asitava@iisc.ac.in; asitava@mecheng.iisc.ernet.in

K. P. Ashwin
e-mail: ashwinkp@iisc.ac.in

© Springer Nature Singapore Pte Ltd. 2019
D N Badodkar and T A Dwarakanath (eds.), *Machines, Mechanism and Robotics*, Lecture Notes in Mechanical Engineering,
https://doi.org/10.1007/978-981-10-8597-0_23

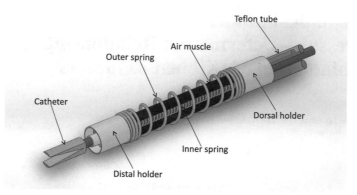

Fig. 1 End effector

the tube is pressurized, the entire device contracts or expands along the axis of tube depending on the geometric and material properties of the helix. Miniaturized versions of PAM (MPAM) of diameter less than 1.5 mm as shown in references [2, 3] can be used for developing surgical devices since they offer high power-to-weight ratio and compliance in its actuated state. In an earlier work [4], a flexible end effector using three MPAMs that can deflect an endoscopic catheter tip up to 15 mm within an approximately hemispherical surface is presented. The design is similar to a tendon-driven continuum robot [5] where tendons are replaced by MPAMs to provide flexibility (see the CAD model shown in Fig. 1). Figure 2 shows the in-house fabricated MPAM used to develop the end effector. In order to study the kinematics of the end effector developed using MPAMs and to apply model-based control strategies, understanding the relationship between applied pressure and deformation of MPAM is essential and this is the focus of this work.

Development of accurate models to predict this relationship based on the geometric and material parameters of PAM is an active topic of research. The first model to describe the statics of PAM, developed by Schulte [6], equated the input work done by applied pressure to the work done by an end force to displace the actuator tip

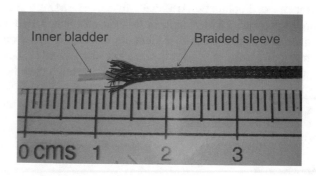

Fig. 2 MPAM

through a particular distance. A review paper by Tondu [7] lists the major improvements made by researchers on this basic model in subsequent years. However, with the inclusion of details such as nonlinear material modeling, friction modeling as well as the variation of MPAM profile at the ends, these models become complex, computationally expensive to simulate or vary considerably when applied on miniaturized PAMs. Hence, most of these models are not suitable for real-time control of the developed end effector.

In this paper, a new model describing the pressure–deformation relationship of MPAM is developed. Section 2 details the proposed mathematical model starting from the equilibrium equations of a thick cylinder under inflation. In Sect. 3, the theoretical model is compared against experimental results for validation. It is also shown that the model is able to predict the locking angle of 54.7°. Conclusions are presented in Sect. 4.

2 Mathematical Model of MPAM

In this section, we present the developed mathematical model of an MPAM. We start by mentioning the two main assumptions on use of linear elasticity and ignoring the hysteresis present in a PAM. In reference [8], the authors describe two derivations using energy method as well as force balance method to model the statics of PAM. It is shown that the force balance method which considers the bladder as linear elastic material gives better accuracy and is simpler to implement compared to energy method which considers the inner bladder as a nonlinear Mooney–Rivlin material. Hence, in the derivations presented in this work, we assume linear elastic thick cylinder model for the silicone bladder in MPAM. It may also be noted that as in the case of PAMs in general, the developed MPAM also shows hysteresis. In reference [7], it is shown that the major reason for hysteresis in a PAM is the static friction between braid strands as well as the friction between the braid strands and the bladder. Though hysteresis effects are prominent in PAMs, in the case of MPAM used in this work, the hysteresis width between the inflation and deflation phase is of same order of magnitude as the measurement error band (shown in later plots). Also, since accurate friction modeling of PAM is particularly hard [7], we neglect the same in subsequent formulation.

Figures 3 and 4 show the schematic of MPAM as well as the nomenclature which will be followed in this paper. The silicone tube has initial length l_0, outer radius r_o, and inner radius r_i. The symbols δl_0 and δr_o denote the changes in length and outer radius, respectively, after applying the input pressure P_i. The initial angle of winding of MPAM, α, changes to β upon pressurization, b represents the length of a single strand of braid, and N represents the number of turns in the helix.

The inflation problem of the silicone tube is solved using linear elastic equilibrium equations for thick cylinder [9] which are given as

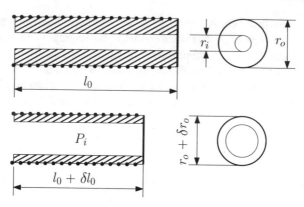

Fig. 3 MPAM nomenclature

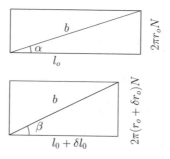

Fig. 4 Braid kinematics

$$\frac{\partial}{\partial r}\left[\frac{1}{r}\frac{\partial}{\partial r}(ru_r)\right] + \left(\frac{\mu}{\lambda + 2\mu}\right)\frac{\partial^2 u_r}{\partial z^2} + \left(\frac{\lambda + \mu}{\lambda + 2\mu}\right)\frac{\partial^2 u_z}{\partial r \partial z} = 0$$

$$\frac{\partial^2 u_z}{\partial z^2} + \left(\frac{\mu}{\lambda + 2\mu}\right)\left[\frac{1}{r}\frac{\partial}{\partial r}\left(r\frac{\partial u_z}{\partial r}\right)\right] + \left(\frac{\lambda + \mu}{\lambda + 2\mu}\right)\left[\frac{\partial}{\partial z}\left[\frac{1}{r}\frac{\partial}{\partial r}(ru_r)\right]\right] = 0 \quad (1)$$

where λ, μ are Lame's parameters, and the radial and axial displacements u_r, u_z are assumed to be functions of both r and z. The displacement in tangential direction is assumed to be zero. The boundary conditions on the radial and axial stresses, τ_{rr} and τ_{zz}, as well as the displacements on boundaries are given as

$$\tau_{rr}|_{r=r_i} = -P_i, \qquad \tau_{rr}|_{r=r_o} = -P_o, \qquad \tau_{zz}|_{z=l_0} = P_s \qquad (2)$$

$$u_z(r, 0) = 0, \qquad u_r(r, 0) = u_r(r, l_0) = 0 \qquad (3)$$

where P_o, P_s are the radial pressure on the outer surface and pressure on the axial end, respectively. The above differential equations and boundary conditions do not have analytical solutions and can only be solved using numerical techniques. However, since the length of tube is much larger compared to the radial dimensions (length to radius ratio is >70), the variation in curvature is apparent only at far ends of MPAM.

Ignoring the curvature effects[1] and assuming that u_r and u_z are only functions of r and z, respectively, Eq. (1) can be simplified to

$$\frac{\partial}{\partial r}\left(\frac{1}{r}\frac{\partial (ru_r)}{\partial r}\right) = 0$$

$$\frac{\partial^2 u_z}{\partial z^2} = 0 \qquad (4)$$

Equation (4) refers to a standard problem of thick cylinder subjected to internal pressure and can be analytically solved to obtain the displacements as

$$u_r = c_1 r + \frac{c_2}{r}, \quad u_z = c_3 z + c_4$$

where c_i, $i = 1, 2, 3, 4$ are constants whose values can be calculated using the boundary conditions given by Eqs. (2) and (3). We next consider the effect of the nylon braids and include the effect of braid with the thick cylinder model.

The expression relating axial tension on the actuator and applied pressure required to maintain equilibrium of the actuator can be found in [10]

$$P_i = \frac{F}{\pi r_o^2}\frac{\sin^2 \alpha}{(3\cos^2 \beta - 1)} \qquad (5)$$

where F is the axial end load. In the case of free contraction of MPAM, the term $\dfrac{F}{\pi r_o^2}$ is essentially the pressure applied on the sidewall of silicone tube, P_a^b. Rearranging the above equation, we can write

$$P_a^b = P_i\frac{(3\cos^2 \beta - 1)}{\sin^2 \alpha} \qquad (6)$$

The total pressure acting on the axial end of silicone tube can be written as

$$P_s = P_a^b + P_a^{P_i} \qquad (7)$$

where $P_a^{P_i} = P_i\dfrac{r_o^2}{r_o^2 - r_i^2}$ is the component due to internal pressure.

A common modeling strategy for braid kinematics is to consider the helix as an array of pantographs [11]. From the pantograph model, the kinematics of single strand of braid can be described by

$$l_0 = b\cos \alpha, \quad l_0 + \delta l_0 = b\cos \beta \qquad (8)$$

$$2\pi r_o N = b\sin \alpha, \quad 2\pi (r_o + \delta r_o)N = b\sin \beta \qquad (9)$$

---

[1]The curvature effect at the end of the silicone tube is considered separately and discussed later.

The above expressions assume that the MPAM remains cylindrical even after pressurizing. However, once pressurized, the ends of the MPAM will not be perfectly cylindrical since the diameter of middle section of MPAM and the diameter of ends will be different. In reference [3], this curvature effect at ends is accounted for by modifying the second expression of Eq. (8) as

$$l_0 + \delta l_0 = b \cos \beta k_1 + k_2 \tag{10}$$

where k_1 and k_2 are constants which are experimentally determined. From Eqs. (8), (9) and (10), we get

$$\delta r_0 = r_o \left(\frac{\sin \beta}{\sin \alpha} - 1 \right), \quad \delta l_0 = l_0 \left(k_1 \frac{\cos \beta}{\cos \alpha} - 1 \right) + k_2 \tag{11}$$

Since the braid and sleeve are in contact during contraction of MPAM, we can write the constraint equations $u_r|_{r_o} = \delta r_o$ and $u_z|_{l_0} = \delta l_0$. Then

$$c_1 r_o + \frac{c_2}{r_o} = r_o \left(\frac{\sin \beta}{\sin \alpha} - 1 \right) \tag{12}$$

$$c_3 l_0 + c_4 = l_0 \left(k_1 \frac{\cos \beta}{\cos \alpha} - 1 \right) + k_2 \tag{13}$$

Equations (12) and (13) give two equations in two unknowns β and P_o which are solved numerically. Then using the second expression of Eq. (11), we can find the displacement at the free end of MPAM.

It may be noted that contraction of MPAM does not start until a particular value of pressure. This is due to a small gap between the braided sleeve and silicone tube resulting from fabrication. Hence, at the initial stage of pressurization, the silicone tube expands till a contact between tube and sleeve is established. In this stage, the pressure on the side wall, P_s, in only $P_a^{P_i}$ and the pressure on the radial surface P_o is zero. Hence, only Eq. (13) is to be solved to obtain the value of deformed angle β and subsequently, the end-point displacement.

3   Model validation

In order to validate the proposed mathematical model for MPAM, results from theoretical model are compared with experimental data. Figure 5 shows the experimental setup which is used to validate the model characteristics. The setup consists of an air reservoir of 1-liter capacity which supplies compressed air to the MPAM at a maximum of 1.03 Mpa (150 psi) pressure. The MPAM is connected to two pressure lines, one for pressurizing and the other for bleeding the air from MPAM; each controlled by individual proportional solenoid valves. An ATmel ATMEGA2560 controller board

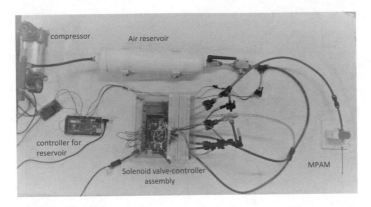

Fig. 5 Experimental setup

reads the pressure inside MPAM using a Honeywell pressure transducer and controls the opening or closing of the solenoid valves. The controller board is interfaced with MATLAB so that user can specify the required pressure inside the MPAM. Another controller circuit is used to sense the pressure inside reservoir and run the compressor to maintain compressed air inside reservoir at 1 MPa at all times. A high-resolution camera is used to take images of contracted MPAM and the changes in length are measured using image processing. The maximum error due to measurement is approximately 0.1 mm. The experimental plots show error bars obtained from at least five sets of experiments. In these plots, hysteresis is not shown, and the mean value between inflation and deflation is used.

Variation of displacement according to applied pressure is determined experimentally for a MPAM of length 60 mm and is compared with the numerical simulation results obtained by solving Eqs. (12) and (13) using MATLAB. The parameters used are $E = 0.9$ MPa, $v = 0.4999$, $\delta = 0.015$ mm, $\alpha = 36°$, $r_i = 0.25$ mm, and $r_b = 0.55$ mm. The values of k_1 and k_2 for the MPAM are determined by linearly interpolating the values mentioned in reference [3] for the length of MPAM used in this study. From Fig. 6, we can see that the theoretical results match with experimental values with good accuracy (standard error of maximum 2%). Using the same parameter values, theoretical results obtained for a 70 mm MPAM in comparison with experimental values give a standard error of 8%. This shows that the model is consistent with changes in initial length of the MPAM (refer Fig. 7). It may be noted that the error bars in the range of 100–400 kPa are larger than the rest of the curve due to the averaging of inflation and deflation data. The discrepancy between the theoretical and actual plots in the onset of contraction may be attributed to the fact that the developed model does not take into account the energy losses due to friction and hence predicts only the inflation characteristics.

From the literature, we know that the actuator contracts when the initial angle of winding is less than 54.7°, while it elongates when the winding angle is more than 54.7° [10]. Additionally, as the pressure increases, the final angle of winding

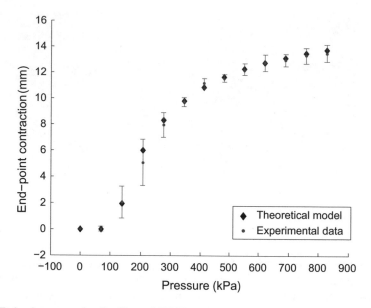

Fig. 6 End-point contraction for 60 mm MPAM

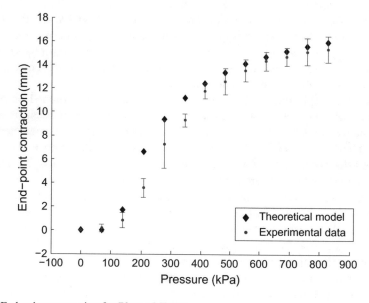

Fig. 7 End-point contraction for 70 mm MPAM

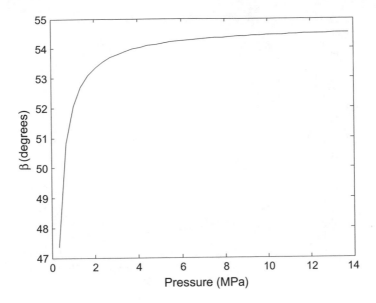

Fig. 8 β versus P_i for $\alpha = 35°$

approaches these limiting values. The results of the theoretical model for a MPAM
with a winding angle of 35°, when subjected to higher pressure, are shown in Fig. 8.
It can be seen that the angle approaches 54.7° at higher pressure. It may also be noted
that the pressure required to reach the locking angle with initial $\alpha > 54.7°$ is much
higher than when the initial starting angle is less than 54.7° (Refer Fig. 9, $\alpha = 70°$).
This result may be explained by considering the rate of change of volume of MPAM.
The volumetric strain for a volume $V = \pi r_o^2 l_0$ is

$$\frac{\delta V}{V} = 2\frac{\delta r_o}{r_o} + \frac{\delta l_0}{l_0} \tag{14}$$

For the linear elastic material used in the formulation,

$$\frac{\delta r_o}{r_o} = C_1 + \frac{C_2}{r_o^2} \text{ and } \frac{\delta l_0}{l_0} = C_3 \tag{15}$$

For a given pressure, the radial strain given by the first term increases by a magnitude of three orders higher than the magnitude of axial strain which is the second term.
It means that the compliance of tube in radial direction is much higher compared to
the axial direction. Hence, the silicone tube tends to expand radially at a faster rate
when subjected to pressurization. For the case of MPAM with $\alpha > 54.7°$, the tube
has to contract radially due to the kinematics of braided sleeve which is achieved
only by working against the applied pressure. Hence, locking angle is reached only
at larger pressures for elongation of the MPAM, while it is achieved easily in the

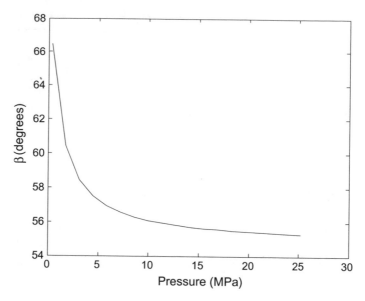

Fig. 9 β vs P_i for $\alpha = 70°$

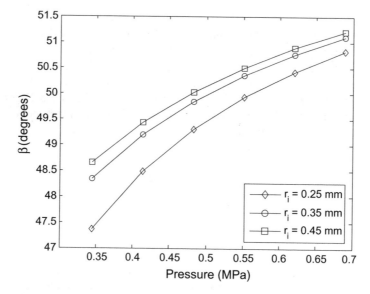

Fig. 10 Variation of β w.r.t change in thickness, $r_o = 0.55$ mm

case of contraction. This observation is further verified from the experimental data mentioned in references [12] and [13] where the limiting angle is not achieved even for high pressure values.

The response to change in thickness of silicone tube is plotted in Fig. 10. We see that as the thickness increases, the initial slope of curve decreases so that the limiting value of β is reached only at high pressure. This is because the applied pressure now works against the increased elastic force due to added material. This observation is also consistent with other models available in literature.

4 Conclusions

A mathematical model representing the relationship between applied pressure and deformation of miniaturized pneumatic artificial muscles is successfully developed. Unlike the existing models in literature for PAM, the developed model is considerably simple even after taking into account material properties of the tube as well as the curvature effects at the ends, making it ideal for implementing model-based control strategies in real time. The numerically simulated results show very good agreement with experimental results for a 60-mm- as well as 70-mm-long MPAM. The model shows increase in the value of braid angle when the initial angle of winding is less than 54.7° and decrease in braid angle when the initial angle is more than 54.7°. In both cases, for higher value of applied pressure, the braid angle reaches the locking angle which further confirms the consistency of the model with the observations reported in the literature. From the developed theoretical model for the pressure–deformation relationship of MPAM, kinematics of the flexible end effector corresponding to the values of pressure applied on MPAMs can be developed. The authors are presently working toward achieving this goal.

Acknowledgements This work was funded in part by the Robert Bosch Center for Cyber Physical Systems (RBCCPS) at the Indian Institute of Science, Bangalore.

References

1. R.H. Gaylord, Fluid actuated motor system and stroking device, 22 July 1958. US Patent 2,844,126
2. M. De Volder, A. Moers, D. Reynaerts, Fabrication and control of miniature McKibben actuators. Sens. Actuators A Phys. **166**(1), 111–116 (2011)
3. S. Chakravarthy, K. Aditya, A. Ghosal, Experimental characterization and control of miniaturized pneumatic artificial muscle. J. Med. Devices **8**(4), 041011 (2014)
4. K.P. Ashwin, D.P. Jose, A. Ghosal, Modeling and analysis of a flexible end-effector for actuating endoscopic catheters, in *Proceedings of the 14th IFToMM World Congress* (IFToMM, 2015), pp. 113–120

5. I.A. Gravagne, I.D. Walker, On the kinematics of remotely-actuated continuum robots, in *Proceedings of the 2000 IEEE International Conference on Robotics and Automation, ICRA'00* vol. 3 (IEEE, 2000), pp. 2544–2550

6. H. Schulte, The application of external power in prosthetics and orthotics, *The Characteristics of the McKibben Artificial Muscle, National Research Council*, vol. 874 (1961)

7. B. Tondu, Modelling of the McKibben artificial muscle: a review. J. Intell. Mater. Syst. Struct. **23**(3), 225–253 (2012)

8. C.S. Kothera, M. Jangid, J. Sirohi, N.M. Wereley, Experimental characterization and static modeling of McKibben actuators. J. Mech. Des. **131**(9), 091010 (2009)

9. C.S. Jog, *Continuum Mechanics*, vol. 1 (Cambridge University Press, 2015)

10. C.-P. Chou, B. Hannaford, Measurement and modeling of McKibben pneumatic artificial muscles. IEEE Trans. Robot. Autom. **12**(1), 90–102 (1996)

11. B. Zhou, M. Accorsi, J. Leonard, A new finite element for modeling pneumatic muscle actuators. Comput. Struct. **82**(11), 845–856 (2004)

12. D. Chen, K. Ushijima, Prediction of the mechanical performance of McKibben artificial muscle actuator. Int. J. Mech. Sci. **78**, 183–192 (2014)

13. G. Krishnan, J. Bishop-Moser, C. Kim, S. Kota, Kinematics of a generalized class of pneumatic artificial muscles. J. Mech. Robot. **7**(4), 041014 (2015)

Wrench Guided Task Space Trajectory Control of Parallel Manipulators

Anirudh Krishnan Komaralingam, T A Dwarakanath and Gaurav Bhutani

Abstract Wrench guided task space trajectory motion control is described in the paper. Serving the change in task space trajectory frequently through code is insurmountable. An easily induced wrench trajectory at the task space as the input to generate proportional six DOF motion output is looked into as an alternative to conventional motion programming. The paper also discusses the implementation of joint force-based homing, task space force–torque estimation, and force-assistive task space motion. Each of the modules has been implemented on six DOF parallel mechanism-based manipulator.

Keywords Force control · Parallel robot · Wrench guidance · Force guidance
Parallel kinematic manipulator

1 Introduction

Force control in parallel robots is an interesting prospect due to its parallel architecture. In serial mechanisms, the inertial forces have a cascading effect starting from the free link to the lower links. The position vector of the end point and orientation vector of end frame depend on positions and orientations of all the preceding joint axis of the serial manipulator. On the other hand, the mapping of instantaneous kinematics of parallel mechanism from task space to joint space is formed by the line coordinates of the six connectors. The six connectors acting independently support

A. K. Komaralingam (✉)
Manipal University, Jaipur, India
e-mail: anirudhkrishnanisavailable@gmail.com

T A Dwarakanath (✉) · G. Bhutani (✉)
Division of Remote Handling & Robotics, Bhabha Atomic Research Centre,
Trombay, Mumbai 400085, India
e-mail: tad@barc.gov.in

G. Bhutani
e-mail: bhutani@barc.gov.in

© Springer Nature Singapore Pte Ltd. 2019
D N Badodkar and T A Dwarakanath (eds.), *Machines, Mechanism and Robotics*, Lecture Notes in Mechanical Engineering,
https://doi.org/10.1007/978-981-10-8597-0_24

the inertia of the platform and the external wrench acting on the platform. Therefore, the in-parallel mechanism is ideally suited for active wrench sensing and manipulation. There are successful implementations of in-parallel mechanism-based stiff and compliant wrench sensors [1–7].

The objective of this paper is to generate a six DOF motion, the twist in response to the six-axis force and torque, i.e., wrench applied at the platform (end effector) of a six Degree of Freedom Parallel Kinematic Mechanism (6D-PKM). Specifying the posture coordinates for alignment is often not possible. A scheme has been developed to sense the instantaneous wrench and to generate proportional instantaneous response twist. The proposed scheme also serves as a parallel mechanism-based wrench Sensor-Cum-Manipulator (SCM). This paper proposes to introduce human in loop to apply wrench and describes how small underlying motion iterations can be perceived to affect the successful segment of motion for the docking. Section 2 of the paper describes the mathematical model of the transformation for the applied wrench and the twist at the given configuration. Section 3 discusses the algorithm and results of setting high-precision homing using torque and position error limit conditions. Section 4 presents the control scheme, algorithm, and implementation of wrench guided task space trajectory control. The paper is concluded in Sect. 5.

2 Task Space Wrench to Joint Space Axial Force Transformation

The schematic sketch of the six-axis parallel mechanism structure that was used is shown in Fig. 1. A rigid, suspended platform is constrained with respect to the fixed base by six linearly independent line constraints. The lines connecting platform and base are called connectors or legs. The line constraint is formed by passive Spherical and Universal (S-U) kinematic chain or S-S chain. Any wrench applied on the platform will be transmitted to the fixed base through the six lines formed by the six line constraints. In other words, the applied wrench is transmitted to the fixed base axially through the connectors. A set of reaction forces is generated along six lines (axes of the connectors) with coordinates $\{\hat{s}_1, \hat{s}_2, \ldots, \hat{s}_6\}$. To make a static force analysis, an external wrench $\vec{W} = [Fx, Fy, Fz, Mx, My, Mz]$ (a force, F acting through the origin, together with a general couple M) is applied to the movable platform. The external wrench is in static equilibrium with the six-connector forces, the equation representing this is given by

$$[\vec{w}] = f_1 \begin{bmatrix} \hat{s}_1 \\ \vec{b}_1 \times \hat{s}_1 \end{bmatrix} + f_2 \begin{bmatrix} \hat{s}_2 \\ \vec{b}_2 \times \hat{s}_2 \end{bmatrix} + f_3 \begin{bmatrix} \hat{s}_3 \\ \vec{b}_3 \times \hat{s}_3 \end{bmatrix} + f_4 \begin{bmatrix} \hat{s}_4 \\ \vec{b}_4 \times \hat{s}_4 \end{bmatrix} + f_5 \begin{bmatrix} \hat{s}_5 \\ \vec{b}_5 \times \hat{s}_5 \end{bmatrix} + f_6 \begin{bmatrix} \hat{s}_6 \\ \vec{b}_6 \times \hat{s}_6 \end{bmatrix} \quad (1)$$

where $f_{i(i=1,\ldots,6)}$ are the axial reaction forces generated in the connectors. $\hat{s}_{i(i=1,\ldots,6)}$ is the unit vector along the ith connector and $\vec{b}_i$ is the ith connector connection point

Fig. 1 6–6 In-parallel
structure

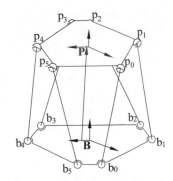

Fig. 2 6–6 In-parallel
manipulator

Fig. 3 6D-PKM prototype

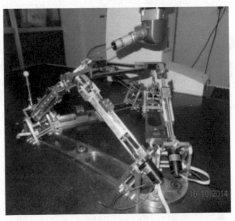

at the base with respect to the base frame B (see Figs. 1 and 2). Figure 3 shows the
6D-PKM designed and developed at author's laboratory.

The sensors at the connectors can bypass the dead wrench load, so as to sensitize
them to only active wrench.

The active wrench experienced by the platform is distributed to the six legs connecting the platform and base plates. The external wrench applied is statically balanced by the six leg forces of the platform and it is important that these six leg forces are linearly independent. Though the wrench measurement fundamentally relies on Eq. (1), it is seen that there are many contributory factors that are to be assessed practically. Subsequent sections deal with those factors and experiments are conducted to show wrench guided task space trajectory control of the parallel manipulators under continuously changing manipulator configurations.

3 Method of Setting High-Precision Homing Using Torque and Position Error Limit Conditions

In order to generate motion of the platform in response to a guiding force, it is required to measure the force sensed by the platform, and therefore the forces on the connectors or legs of the mechanism. Each leg of the mechanism is constructed by coupling a high-precision ball screw to a servomotor equipped with a position encoder (see Fig. 3). This allows the axial load to be transformed to motor torque, which corresponds to current draw, a quantity that can be measured directly. Since measurement of torque is fundamental to force control, this type of measurement was first used in a software module which performs the task of bringing the mechanism to its dead-end or home position, dead-end homing. This involved jogging the motors to decrease the extension of all connectors until the moving parts on the connector and the base met, causing an abrupt increase of motor torque that would signal a stop. The values of "torque" obtained from the controller are a function of current drawn and vary from $-32,768$ to $32,767$ corresponding to maximum torque and 0 being no torque. In Fig. 4, time is shown in counts where 100 counts are 1 s. Sample data of motor torque for a single actuator running when unloaded and with intermittent loading (sufficient to stall) is shown in Figs. 4 and 5.

The torque values for a freely jogging (unloaded running) motor oscillate significantly as compared to the average torque to jog at the desired speed (indicated in

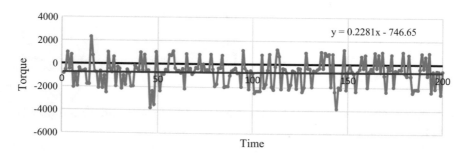

Fig. 4 Torque versus time for unloaded motor

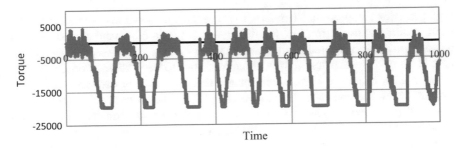

Fig. 5 Torque versus time for motor with intermittent loading

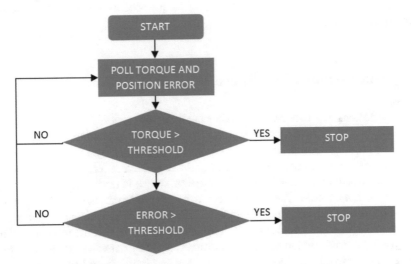

Fig. 6 Flowchart of torque and position error homing

red in Fig. 4). Nevertheless, the motor under load yields a clearly measured response which makes this signal suitable for use to stop the motor (Fig. 5). The raw data was refined by real time averaging of every 5 data points before further processing. The peak torque value when motor jogging speed is 10,000 counts/s (2.5 rpm) is approximately 2800 (Fig. 4). A fixed stopping torque limit of 3000–3500 to indicate an encounter with an obstacle was assumed for initial testing. The flowchart for the logic used in the homing module that was implemented is shown in Fig. 6.

When implemented on an isolated free running motor, with redundant load applied by hand, it worked well. When applied to a single leg of the mechanism occasional torque spikes above the limit caused the homing to stop prematurely. A stop condition using a static limit did not provide reliable results to compensate for random errors. The increase of torque relative to previous values was considered, i.e., a surge in torque had to be detected for stopping. A surge in torque of 20% over the last measured value was found to be sufficient to indicate that an obstacle was encountered. This worked well with few exceptions due to random wear of the otherwise high-precision components. Therefore, to prevent the usage of an even higher torque limit, motor position error, i.e., the difference between commanded position and actual position as measured by the encoders, was introduced as a secondary parameter to be used with motor torque along with the torque "surge" condition. The position error condition was ignored for the first 50 counts of displacement (4000 the ball screw had counts/lead) because of the difference caused when starting the motor. The optimal amount of position error for the homing condition to function reliably was 45 counts, i.e., when a difference of 45 counts was measured; it provided supporting evidence that an obstacle was encountered. The dead-end homing of the mechanism helped to serve as confirmation that force on the nut/housing of the ball screw translated efficiently to motor torque load and was measurable with high repeatability.

4 Wrench Guided Task Space Trajectory Control

The expectations of "force control" is that the trajectories along which the robot is to be moved will be defined using a nominal guiding force applied to the robot's platform. The guiding wrench (force and twist) will be provided by a human in loop (the human operator) which essentially removes the requirement for preplanning motion trajectories based on inverse kinematic solution, which is useful when planning the trajectory is not feasible. The operator can not only guide the manipulator along the desired trajectory but can "feel" the loss of structural rigidity when approaching singularity configurations while controlling the robot and can guide the robot away from such configurations, which solves a significant issue of conventional motion planning. Force control is implemented as software and requires no hardware changes; it only needs to be enabled/disabled. The motion of the parallel robot is completely tracked at all times using feedback provided by encoders connected to each motor. Once the major part of unplanned trajectory has been traversed using force control, conventional preplanned motion can be resumed if the robot needs to perform a specific task relating to its end effector that may benefit from the inherent precession of the parallel robot under preprogrammed motion.

Force on the platform, which is transformed to motor torque as described previously, is used as the input to the force control software module, which then instructs the motors to generate the motion response of the platform. The approach to force control is to use the 6D-PKM as a force–torque sensor which is possible due to the nature of its construction and the actuation method. It is also used to demonstrate that parallel robots can be used for force-assisted motion through variations in basic force control. Force control allows heavy loads on the platform to be manipulated with small force from the operator.

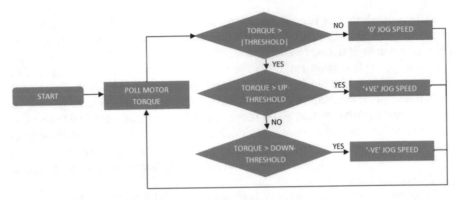

Fig. 7 Flowchart of force control in joint space

4.1 Development of the Force Control Module

In dead-end homing, torque helped to decide how to stop but for force control, it will decide how to start motion. Consider a situation in which the platform is to be held stationary. The motors of the legs provide torque of magnitude and direction to sustain its weight at a particular configuration. Now, if force is applied to move the platform in a certain direction, say in the upward direction, the upward force applied on the platform causes the motors of the legs to produce torque in the direction to prevent a change of configuration. The torque sensed by the platform when wrench is applied is the torque generated to maintain its current state. Therefore, torque generated this way is used to set the threshold for enabling motion in the direction of the applied force. The force control algorithm seeks to maintain the measured torque within a threshold. When the measured torque load on the motor exceeds this threshold, the motors rotate in the direction so as to bring the torque within the threshold. The feedback response when the threshold is exceeded is to indefinitely jog the motor in the appropriate direction and at a fixed rate. Polling for torque continuously tells the program when the torque has fallen inside the threshold and the module sets the jogging speed to 0, bringing the motors/platform to rest. The flowchart for the logic of the program is shown in Fig. 7.

4.2 Implementation on 6D-PKM

Force control algorithm was executed on a motor (not coupled to the mechanism), one individual leg of the 6D-PKM, and then on all the legs and platform of 6D-PKM.

The first successful trials of force control that were done on a single motor (that was not connected to the mechanism) were implemented with a torque threshold in one direction only. This means the motor starts from rest when activated, because there is a threshold that has not been crossed. When twisted by hand beyond the torque threshold, it begins rotating in the direction of applied force. When trying to stop the rotation, it started rotating the other direction because there was no torque threshold (zero) to contain motion in the opposite direction. This was done to find a suitable range for the torque threshold. The initial threshold values that were tried were based on the stopping value from dead-end homing (3000–4500 range) and the speed of jogging/rotation was 10,000 counts/s (2.5 rpm) that is identical to homing, and the acceleration and deceleration values were 10,000 (count/s^2) which becomes significant later. Next, both jogging directions were checked for torque threshold in both directions, which allowed the motor to stop when twist was removed instead of perpetually turning.

Force control was then executed on one leg of the 6D-PKM. Higher jogging speed of 14,000 counts/s and the same acceleration and deceleration values were used. Force was applied to the nut of the screw shaft, so torque was not applied as directly as twisting the motor shaft. This required the torque limits to be lowered (1200–2000) which was apparent due to the excessive force required and the irregular motion under force control. The acceleration of 10,000 counts/s^2 was also insufficient because the time the applied force satisfies the torque limit condition; there was a 1.4 s delay to accelerate to the set jogging speed, which is very uncomfortable when trying to move the leg. Increasing the value of acceleration to 20,000, 40,000 counts/s^2 made motion easier, and more responsive to applied force. Increasing the jogging speed with the increased acceleration reduced the effort to sustain motion after crossing the initial threshold. However, the motor was unable to stop without applying force in the opposite direction to bring the measured torque under the threshold. This was solved by increasing deceleration to a value similar to acceleration. When the deceleration was within a range of 60–80% of the acceleration, the motion in response to applied was controlled and smooth. If the deceleration was higher than this, the impact of increasing acceleration was lost. This is because the measured torque had fluctuations which were significant in the range of operation (Fig. 4) and frequent strong deceleration did not allow the motor to achieve its jogging speed. If it was lower than 60%, force control is unable to reliably stop motion after applied force was removed.

When the acceleration was above 3,00,000 counts/s^2 and the jogging speed was above 80,000 counts/s, the behavior under force control became unpredictable. When the applied force was lifted, the rotation of the motor persisted and the leg extended to the limit switch at the top/bottom dead end of leg. This was because the torque needed to respond to the applied force was more than the torque threshold and could not stop due to positive feedback; hence, there was a need for appreciable deceleration. It was also observed that a small time delay ~50 ms was required after providing the signal to start motion or change direction in order to avoid responding to irregular torque behavior near inflection points.

Torque limit parameter determines how much force is required to actuate the legs of the mechanism. It can also make the system more stable because it filters torque fluctuations below a certain level. This reduces the number of times the motor has to change direction, reducing the oscillations during motion. However, if the torque threshold is too high the leg becomes difficult to actuate and requires excessive force

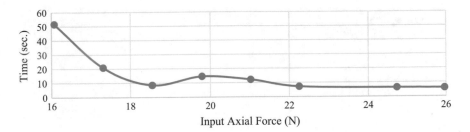

Fig. 8 Axial force versus traversal time for single leg in force control

to produce motion. Torque limit is important for robot-assisted motion as it helps force control to be independent of the self-weight of the platform, i.e., torque needed to sustain the dead weight of the platform. This is done by setting the torque as follows:

$$torque\,limit = self\,weight \pm threshold \tag{2}$$

For example, if the torque threshold for upward motion of the leg is +1700 and in for downward motion is −300 (when the platform is not carrying weight), the $torque\,limit = 700 \pm 1000$. This allows large loads to be maneuvered with the same force needed to move the unloaded platform without changing the code.

Force control with speed of motion dependent on input force was also executed. This is realized by changing the jogging speed of motion from a static value to the expression below:

$$jogging\,speed = [abs(axis\_torque) \times 10] + 40,000 \tag{3}$$

This allowed the jogging speed to change depending on the torque detected at the legs. The performance of force control algorithm was evaluated by measuring the time that a single leg took to travel from the bottom dead end to the top limit switch/top dead end with various constant force values. The results show that once the torque threshold was overcome, there was a drop in traversal times for a fixed acceleration and maximum speed (when the speed of the leg was made dependent on the input force applied on the leg). The results of axial force versus traversal time are plotted for clarity (Fig. 8).

The result shows that the force control is able to reliably provide additional speed for an additional applied force. The final values show less improvement because of a maximum speed limit which is implemented for safety.

Force control was then implemented on the 6D-PKM. Figure 9 illustrates how force was applied to change the configuration of the 6D-PKM under force control. Motion in the three orthogonal directions and rotation about these axes was successfully accomplished. The degree to which the motion was coordinated was completely dependent on the application of force by the user.

Fig. 9 Demonstration of force control on the 6D PKM

5 Conclusions

The dead-end-based homing and force control algorithm was successfully executed
on the 6D-PKM. The task of generating six degree of freedom motion in response
to applied wrench on the platform of a 6D-PKM was successful. Considerable effort
was channeled toward establishing effective ways of measuring and using the raw
data. The torque data obtained through direct measurement was oscillatory in nature
which made its use challenging. However, the data was highly usable for signaling
purposes as demonstrated in the "Dead-End Homing" module. This involved using
measured torque and supporting data to bring the mechanism to its dead-end reference by sensing when a dead end was encountered. Torque data alone was sufficient
for the force control algorithm to function. The performance was highly dependent
on the speed, acceleration, and deceleration of the motion. The ease of manipulation was benefited from high jog speed and acceleration. Comparable deceleration
helped to keep motion controlled when the mechanism was being guided. A minor
time delay was introduced after signaling a change in motion as torque fluctuations
immediately after starting or changing direction were noticeably higher and tended
to cause instability and hence were left out of detection scope in this way. Finally,
the scope of robot-assisted motion was explored by parameterizing the module in a
way that made the torque limits equally spaced from a self-weight parameter which
represented the weight carried by the platform.

References

1. R.W. Daniel, P.R. McAree, Fundamental limits of performance for force reflecting teleoperation.
   The Int. J. Robot. Res. **17**, 811–830 (1998)
2. T.A. Dwarakanath, G. Bhutani, D. Venkatesh, Modeling and simulation of very small in-parallel
   wrench sensor cum manipulator (SCM), in *11th National Conference on Machines and Mechanisms*, IIT Delhi, December 2003
3. B. Dasgupta, T.S. Mruthyunjaya, A Newton-Euler formulation for the inverse dynamics of the
   Stewart platform manipulator, Mech. Mach. Theory **3**, 1135–1152 (1998)

4. R.A. Freeman, D. Tesar, Dynamic modeling of serial and parallel mechanisms/robotic systems: part 1—methodology, trends and development in mechanisms. Mach. Robot. ASME Publications **15**, 7–18 (1988)
5. Friction modeling and compensation, in *The Control Handbook*, ed. by W.S. Levine (CRC Press, 1996), pp. 1369–1382
6. T.A. Dwarakanath, C.D. Crane, J. Duffy, C. Tyler, Implementation of in-parallel mechanism based compliant coupler for robot force control, in *ASME Mechanisms Conference* (2000)
7. T.A. Dwarakanath, B. Dasgupta, T.S. Mruthyunjaya, Design and development of Stewart platform based force-torque sensor. Mechatronics **1**, 793–809 (2001)

Heuristic for Selection of Grasp Surfaces for Form-Closure on Polyhedral Objects

Tejas Tamboli and Sourav Rakshit

Abstract This paper proposes a novel heuristic for searching a set of surfaces eligible for providing form-closure grasp of robotic fingers on a rigid polyhedral 3-D object. The key idea that drives the search of eligible surfaces is the formal definition of a convex hull which describes convex hull of a set of points as the smallest convex polygon containing all the points of that set. Eligibility determination of a set of surfaces is carried out by the test based on ray-shooting algorithm (Liu IEEE Trans Robot Automat 15(1):163–173, 1999, [1]), which is formalization of the necessary and sufficient condition for form-closure grasps requiring that the origin of the wrench space lies inside the convex hull of the primitive contact wrenches (Algorithm Spec Issue Robot 2(4):541–558, 1987, [2]). The implementation of three numerical examples demonstrates the usefulness and efficiency of the proposed heuristic.

Keywords Grasping · Form-closure · Convex hull · Vertex contact wrench

1 Introduction

Owing to their potential in performing dextrous and fine manipulation tasks, multi-fingered robotic hands have been an area of extensive research work since the work of Salisbury and Roth [3]. Several aspects of robotic grasp are studied in [3–11]. This paper focuses on fundamental problem of grasp stability.

Form-closure and force-closure properties are means for characterizing the stability of a grasp. Form-closure grasp is characterized by its ability to balance any

T. Tamboli (✉) · S. Rakshit (✉)
Department of Mechanical Engineering, Indian Institute of Technology Madras,
Chennai, India
e-mail: tejastamboli1@gmail.com

S. Rakshit
e-mail: srakshit@iitm.ac.in

© Springer Nature Singapore Pte Ltd. 2019
D N Badodkar and T A Dwarakanath (eds.), *Machines, Mechanism and Robotics*, Lecture Notes in Mechanical Engineering,
https://doi.org/10.1007/978-981-10-8597-0_25

externally applied wrench at the grasped object by grasp forces of the robot hand. Salisbury and Roth [3] have proved that a necessary and sufficient condition for form-closure is that the primitive contact wrenches resulted by contact forces at the contact points positively span the entire wrench space. This condition is equivalent to that the origin of the wrench space lies strictly inside the convex hull of the primitive contact wrenches [2, 12, 13]. The qualitative test based on ray-shooting algorithm, for 3-D frictional form-closure grasps of n robotic fingers, was formalized by Liu [1]. Due to significant progress in the advanced machine learning techniques and their applications, there has been paradigmatic shift in the approach toward grasp synthesis problem in the last decade. Instead of relying on 3-D model of the object, the contemporary approach tries to directly predict, as a function of the object images, the grasping points at which to grasp the object [14]. The current state-of-the-art technique based on deep learning, as described in [15], further enhances the efficiency of the approach and overcomes the limitations of earlier work [14].

This paper addresses an important practical problem of selecting a set of surfaces (referred to as *eligible set* hereafter) capable of providing form-closure property on a rigid polyhedral 3-D object. A brute force approach is combinatorially formidable. Ding et al. [16] proposed a heuristic method whose initialization step itself suffers from the very problem that the heuristic was meant to cure. Their heuristic depends on a random choice of an initial set of surfaces, which potentially can lead to a large number of unsuccessful iterations of the algorithm especially when the polyhedral object has very large number of surfaces. We propose a new heuristic method which does not rely on user to provide an initial set and is capable of providing a large number of different eligible sets of surfaces for the same object as demonstrated by three numerical examples. The utility of the heuristic assumes greater significance when the polyhedral object has a very large number of surfaces. In order to determine the eligibility of a candidate set, the well-known qualitative test based on ray-shooting algorithm [1] is used. The application of heuristic is limited to rigid polyhedral object geometry.

2 Finding Eligible Set of Grasping Surfaces on Polyhedral Object

2.1 Preliminaries and Assumptions

The fundamental concept underlying the development of the heuristic is stated in the following proposition (for proof, refer [16]).

Proposition 1 *Assume that n grasp locations on an object are given. The grasp is eligible if and only if the convex hull of the corresponding primitive contact wrenches strictly contains the origin of $\mathbb{R}^6$.*

Here, we restrict our attention to three-dimensional polyhedral objects having k convex surfaces. A polyhedral object is made up of convex as well as concave faces.

A concave surface can be decomposed into convex ones. We assume that a geometric model of the object is available with sufficient accuracy and that all contacts are point contacts and frictionless. This leads to conservative results, as any grasp that achieves form-closure under frictionless case will also achieve form-closure with nonzero friction. It is known that seven frictionless contacts are necessary [2] to hold a 3-D object in form-closure and are sufficient [17] for a 3-D object without rotational symmetries. In this paper, we assume that each surface will have exactly one grasping location on it and therefore, an eligible set of seven distinct grasping surfaces is to be determined. We use the qualitative test based on ray-shooting algorithm, as described in [16], as criteria for determining eligibility of a set of grasping surfaces for form-closure. This test is formalization of Proposition 1.

2.2   Problem Statement

Problem: Given a geometric model of a 3-D polyhedral object with well-defined surface normal vectors and vertices information, objective is to

- Find at least one eligible set of grasping surfaces on which grasping locations satisfying form-closure property exist.

2.3   Background

Under the assumptions mentioned at the beginning of this section, interpretation of Proposition 1 in the special case of frictionless grasp of polyhedral object leads us to the search of set of seven convex surfaces of the given object with a view of ensuring that the convex hull made up by vertex contact wrenches of those surfaces will strictly enclose origin inside it. A brute force approach involves checking all $\binom{k}{7}$ combinations (k is total number of convex surfaces of the object.).

Observe in Fig. 1 that in six-dimensional wrench space, each of k convex surfaces has associated with it, a set of vertex contact wrenches (existing as points of 6-D Euclidean space). Imagine each set of vertex contact wrenches associated with a particular face, to be a set of pegs fixed on the ground having a unique color (identical for all pegs within a set, but different from every other $k - 1$ sets of vertex contact wrenches). Therefore, the 6-D wrench space is imagined to have a total of k distinctly colored sets of pegs(In Fig. 1, $k = 11$). Convex hull made up by a particular subset from among these k sets can be thought of as a shape of a rubber band stretched around the pegs involved in that subset. Toward solving the problem statement, the objective is to choose such a subset of size 7 from among these k sets that ensures strict enclosure of origin inside the convex hull made up by the subset. Define *extremity* of each of these k sets to be that peg of the set which is

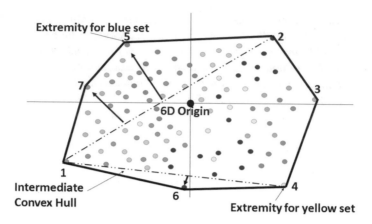

Fig. 1 Schematic illustration of a single iteration of the algorithm. Different colored dots indicate vertex contact wrenches of different faces of the polyhedral object. The final convex hull in 6-D wrench space is indicated using a bold line (rubber band tied around extremities). The three arrows inside final convex hull indicate the growth direction of the algorithm

located farthest from origin (For illustration, *extremity* of blue and yellow sets are shown in Fig. 1). Toward achieving the stated objective, the *extremities* of the sets will play the most critical role because they will determine the shape of the convex hull. Therefore, in order to achieve the objective, if we start with a set of pegs having its *extremity* to be globally farthest among k sets, and gradually include sets whose *extremities* have negative inner product (Note: Inner product is between position vectors of the corresponding vertex contact wrenches in 6-D Euclidean space.) with the *extremity* of starting set, then we are closely simulating the process of gradual stretch of rubber band around distinct sets of pegs fixed on ground with a view of enclosing a prespecified point inside the boundary of the rubber band. This procedure can be repeated iteratively by starting with a set having its *extremity* to be globally second farthest among k sets, then starting with third farthest, and so on. The vertex numbering in Fig. 1 describes the order in which corresponding surfaces were chosen by the algorithm in one successful iteration.

This intuition is used in the development of the heuristic strategy.

2.4 Preprocessing

Why is preprocessing needed?
The objective behind preprocessing the available data is to transform it into a structured form that is amenable to the direct usage by the fundamental working mechanics of the proposed algorithm as described in Sect. 2.3. As described in Sect. 2.3, algorithm tries to search iteratively through the set of faces starting with a face having its *extremity* to be globally farthest and parallelly maintains for each face, a list of

faces whose *extremities* have negative inner product with the face in question. This necessitates that the data fed to the algorithm is in such a way that the algorithm can quickly work with.

Terminology:

1. Point := A six-dimensional vertex contact wrench.
2. $RS == T$:= Eligibility checking condition based on ray-shooting based test.

With each face S_i, $i = 1, ..., k$, there is an associated set of points, $J_i = \{P_1^{(i)}, ..., P_{t_i}^{(i)}\}$, where t_i = Number of vertices associated with S_i.

Define $d_j^{(i)}$:= Euclidean distance of $P_j^{(i)}$ from origin of 6-D space.

Do the following, for $i = 1, ..., k$.

Define $P_i^* = \{P_j^{(i)} | d_j^{(i)} = max\{d_1^{(i)}, ..., d_{t_i}^{(i)}\}\}$. Note : If there is tie, break it arbitrarily. Define v_i^* := Coordinates of P_i^*; d_i^* := Distance of P_i^* from origin;

n_i^* := No. of negative dot products of v_i^* with v_j^*, $\forall j = 1, ..., k, j \neq i$

Construct set, $D_i = \{S_j | (v_i^*)^T (v_j^*) < 0, j \neq i, \forall j = 1, ..., k\} \cup \{S_i\}$

Sort the set of surfaces $\{S_1, ..., S_k\}$ in the descending order of d_i^* in order to get sorted set $\{S_{l_1}, S_{l_2}, ..., S_{l_k}\}$. If there is tie, give higher preference to S_i having higher n_i^*. If tie persists, break it arbitrarily.

Make the following table:

Row no.	Sorted surfaces	Corresponding D_{l_i}	Set size
1	S_{l_1}	D_{l_1}	$|D_{l_1}|$
2	S_{l_2}	D_{l_2}	$|D_{l_2}|$
:	:	:	:
k	S_{l_k}	D_{l_k}	$|D_{l_k}|$

where, $|D_{l_i}|$:= No. of elements of in set D_{l_i}

For each row of the table, one of the following possibilities exists, and the step that should be taken in each is mentioned :

1. $|D_{l_i}| = 7$: Directly subject D_{l_i} to eligibility check.
2. $|D_{l_i}| > 7$: Keeping first 6 surfaces of D_{l_i} to be fixed, add 1 surface starting from 7th till $|D_{l_i}|$th to get total $|D_{l_i}| - 6$ different sets of seven surfaces. Subject each of them to eligibility check.
3. $|D_{l_i}| < 7$: Pick all the surfaces starting from last row of the table till the current row and subject the constructed set to eligibility check.

2.5 Algorithm to Find Eligible Set of Surfaces for Grasp

Block diagram illustrating methodology of the algorithm (Fig. 2):
   Steps of algorithm:
   Note: i is counter for row number in aforementioned table.

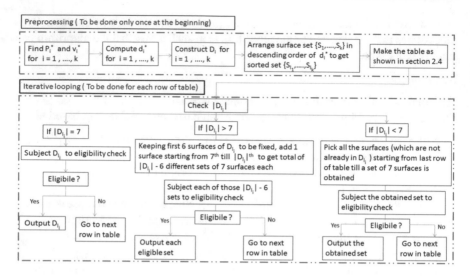

Fig. 2 Block diagram to illustrate the algorithm

1: Initialize $cnt \leftarrow 0$
2: **for** i=1,...,k **do**
3:    $cdn \leftarrow |D_{l_i}|$
4:    **if** $cdn > 7$ **then**
5:      **for** $j = 1, ..., (|D_{l_i}| - 6)$ **do**
6:        Define: $D'_{l_i} :=$ {First 6 surfaces of D_{l_i} } $\cup$ {$(6+j)^{th}$ surface of D_{l_i} }
7:        **if** $RS == T$ **then**
8:          **print** Eligible set found: D'_{l_i}
9:          $cnt \leftarrow cnt + 1$
10:        **end if**
11:      **end for**
12:    **else if** $cdn = 7$ **then**
13:      **if** $RS == T$ **then**
14:        **print** Eligible set found: D_{l_i}
15:        $cnt \leftarrow cnt + 1$
16:      **end if**
17:    **else if** $cdn < 7$ AND $i \neq k$ **then**
18:      Define: $E :=$ {Starting from k^{th} row till $(i+1)^{th}$ row, set of all surfaces which are not in D_{l_i} }
19:      Define: $E^* := E \cup D_{l_i}$, $c =$ no.of elements in E^*,
20:      **if** $c > 7$ **then**
21:        **for** $t = 1, ..., (c - 6)$ **do**
22:          Define: $E' :=$ {First 6 surfaces of E^* } $\cup$ {$(6+t)^{th}$ surface of E^* }
23:          **if** $RS == T$ **then**
24:            **print** Eligible set found: E'

```
25:              cnt ← cnt + 1
26:           end if
27:         end for
28:      else
29:        if RS == T then
30:           print Eligible set found: E*
31:           cnt ← cnt + 1
32:        end if
33:      end if
34:    end if
35:    if i = k AND cnt = 0 then
36:      print Heuristic unable to find an eligible set.
37:    end if
38: end for
```

Drawback: Since it is a heuristic strategy, it may be possible that even though there exist eligible sets for the given object, yet heuristic fails to find any one of them.

3   Results

The proposed approach is implemented for finding eligible set of grasp surfaces using MATLAB. Performance of the algorithm is verified by three examples.

Example 1:
The first test object is dodecahedron. It has 12 convex surfaces.
   The algorithm returns a total of 23 eligible sets of seven surfaces each. One of the 23 eligible sets is shown in Fig. 3.

Example 2:
The second test object is icosahedron. It has 20 convex surfaces.

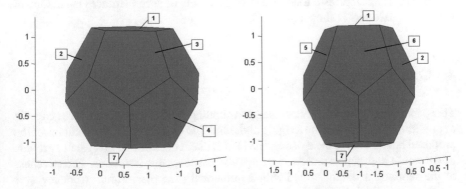

Fig. 3 An eligible surface set for dodecahedron

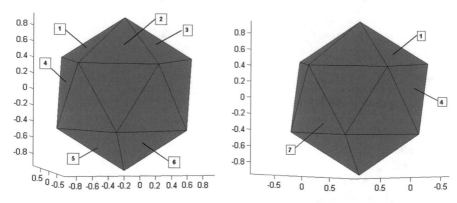

Fig. 4 An eligible surface set for icosahedron

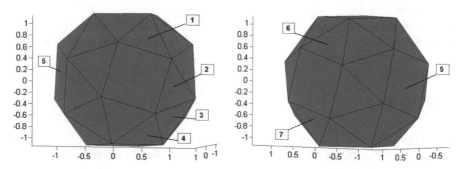

Fig. 5 An eligible surface set for snub cube

The algorithm returns a total of 80 eligible sets of seven surfaces each. One of the 80 eligible sets is shown in Fig. 4.

Example 3:
The third test object is snub cube. It has 38 convex surfaces.

The algorithm returns a total of 231 eligible sets of seven surfaces each. One of the 231 eligible sets is shown in Fig. 5.

4   Conclusion

This paper provides a heuristic strategy for finding a set of eligible surfaces capable of providing form-closure on a rigid polyhedral 3-D object. The key advantage of the proposed heuristic over the existing one [16] is that it does not rely on user to provide initial guess and hence more robust against unsuccessful iterations. Effectiveness of the heuristic is demonstrated with 3 numerical examples. Future work involves development of a technique for determination of exact grasp locations on the eligible grasp surfaces (as chosen by the proposed heuristic) based on an optimality criterion characterizing a useful physical requirement.

References

1. Y. Liu, Qualitative test and force optimization of 3-d frictional form-closure grasps using linear programming. IEEE Trans. Robot. Automat. **15**(1), 163–173 (1999)
2. B. Mishra, J.T. Schwartz, M. Sharir, On the existence and synthesis of multifinger positive grips. Algorithm. Spec. Issue Robot. **2**(4), 541–558 (1987)
3. J.K. Salisbury, B. Roth, Kinematic and force analysis of articulated hands. ASME J. Mech. Transm. Autom. Des. **105**(1), 33–41 (1982)
4. M.R. Cutcosky, On grasp choice, grasp model, and the design of hands for manufacturing task. IEEE Trans. Robot. Automat. **5**(3), 269–279 (1989)
5. Z. Li, P. Hsu, S. Sastry, Grasping and coordinated manipulation by a mutlifingered robot hand. Int. J. Robot. Res. **8**(4), 33–50 (1989)
6. D.J. Montana, The kinematics of contact and grasp. Int. J. Robot. Res. **7**(3), 17–32 (1988)
7. J.R. Kerr, B. Roth, Analysis of multifingered hands. Int. J. Robot. Res. **4**(4), 3–17 (1986)
8. V. Kumar, K. Waldron, Suboptimal algorithms for force distribution in multifingered grippers, in *Proceedings of IEEE International Conference Robotics and Automation*, pp. 252–257 (1987)
9. J. Ponce, B. Faverjon, On computing three finger force-closure grasp of polygonal objects. IEEE Trans. Robot. Automat. **11**(6), 868–881 (1995)
10. L.A. Munoz, C. Bard, and J. Najera, Dextrous manipulation: a geometrical reasoning point of view, in *Proceedings of IEEE International Conference Robotics and Automation*, pp. 458–463 (1995)
11. H. Zhang, K. Tanie, H. Maekawa, Dextrous manipulation planning by graph transformation, in *Proceedings of IEEE International Conference Robotics and Automation*, pp. 3055–3060 (1996)
12. D.J. Montana, The condition for contact grasp stability, in *Proceedings of IEEE International Conference Robotics and Automation*, pp. 412–417 (1991)
13. R.M. Murray, Z. Li, S.S. Sastry, *A Mathematical Introduction to Robotic Manipulation* (CRC, Orlando, FL, 1994)
14. A. Saxena, J. Driemeyer, J. Kearns, and A. Y. Ng, Robotic grasping of novel objects, in *Neural Information Processing Systems (NIPS 19)* (2006)
15. I. Lenz, H. Lee, A. Saxena, Deep learning for detecting robotic grasps. Int. J. Robot. Res. **34**(4–5), 705–724 (2015)
16. D. Ding, Y. Liu, M. Wang, S. Wang, Automatic selection of fixturing surfaces and fixturing points for polyhedral workpieces. IEEE Trans. Robot. Automat. **17**(6), 833–841 (2001)
17. X. Markenscoff, L. Ni, C.H. Papadimitriou, The geometry of grasping. Int. J. Robot. Res. **9**(1), 61–74 (1990)

Building Autonomy in Outdoor Mobile Robots for Radiation and Video Survey

Shishir Kumar Singh, Namita Singh, Jagadish Kota and P. V. Sarngadharan

Abstract In this paper, we describe a LIDAR-based autonomous navigation approach applied at tracked mobile robot and a software tool developed for managing the mobile robots' outdoor radiation survey missions. A mission to do radiological survey around the scrap yard of lab premises has been considered as a concrete instance to build the system. Mission management tool is designed to plan autonomous radiation survey missions in affected areas. The robot carries radiation sensor packs suitable for the survey to record and transmit radiological measurements to the control centre. Additionally, the scheme implemented has provision to monitor the real-time progress of the survey mission and to switch between various autonomy levels built into the system.

Keywords Mobile robot · Radiation survey · Mission planning · Autonomy
Teleoperation · Obstacle detection · Obstacle avoidance · Occupancy grids

1 Introduction

Outdoor radiation survey with mobile robot is not routine in nuclear plants. However, it becomes inevitable during the post-nuclear incidents for gathering vital inputs to plan rescue operations or restoration activities at affected sites. In general, radiation monitoring systems in nuclear plants consist of several stationary radiation measuring

S. K. Singh · N. Singh · J. Kota · P. V. Sarngadharan (✉)
Division of Remote Handling and Robotics, Bhabha Atomic Research Centre,
Mumbai 400085, Maharashtra, India
e-mail: sarang@barc.gov.in

S. K. Singh
e-mail: shishir@barc.gov.in

N. Singh
e-mail: namita@barc.gov.in

J. Kota
e-mail: jkota@barc.gov.in

© Springer Nature Singapore Pte Ltd. 2019
D N Badodkar and T A Dwarakanath (eds.), *Machines, Mechanism and Robotics*, Lecture Notes in Mechanical Engineering,
https://doi.org/10.1007/978-981-10-8597-0_26

equipments and a number of portable-type equipments to supplement them. In the event of nuclear incident, many of these infrastructures may fail; several parts of the site may become inaccessible due to extreme conditions in terms of high levels of radiation, toxicity or temperature. In such circumstances, robots are preferred to conduct preliminary survey instead of humans.

Such robots shall be suitable to operate under different 'degrees of autonomy' ranging from teleoperation to fully autonomous operation. Practical configurations especially in nuclear plant environment are somewhere in between these extremes. A typical survey mission consists of long stretches of large-scale autonomous navigation and inevitable stretches of teleoperated navigation or semi-autonomous navigation of the mobile robot. A satisfactory solution to localise mobile robots in outdoor [1–3] is the fundamental building block for autonomous navigation. Although quite complex approaches exist to solve localization [4–9] problem, they generally rely on the map-building approaches [2, 3, 10, 11]. But in the case of nuclear accidents many known structures at the site may get deformed, as a result a priory map of the site becomes invalidated. SLAM [1, 12–16]-based solution for outdoor environment is more complex and challenging. Tentacle-based navigation solution as discussed in [17] is as it deals with safe navigation to reach destination without making a thorough map of the environment. For autonomous navigation, obstacle detection and avoidance are also a necessary requirement. Therefore, autonomous survey in a nuclear plant like environment requires a blend of various strategies. The solution we have implemented with a combination of autonomous navigation and teleoperation is relatively simple. We considered the tentacle-based approach as given in [17]. In [17], they dealt with fast moving vehicles like cars, and on the other hand, our platform's speed is approximately 0.5 m/s with a capability of in-place turning. High-level mission management software having satellite map-based interface has been developed to automate the entire process of radiation and video survey. This has been equipped with a user-friendly GUI for mission planning, real-time mission progress and configuring modes.

2   Mobile Platform

The modular robotic platform used for building the radiation survey robot has a robot chassis with track packs on either side (Figs. 1 and 2). Overall size of the platform is around 550 mm × 750 mm. The platform is designed to achieve 0.5 m/s speed.

Laser range sensor (3D-LIDAR) and GPS/INS sensor are the two important onboard sensors. The range sensor has 32 lasers uniformly distributed across 40° vertical field of view. Each laser has 100 m range and has 360° horizontal field of view. It gives out 700,000 range data points per second with ±2 cm accuracy. The GPS/INS sensor is capable of giving GPS-enhanced 3D orientation and AHRS (Attitude and Heading Reference System)-augmented 3D position and velocity. An integrated real-time gamma radiation monitoring device for ambient gamma activity over wide range has been provided as onboard radiation sensor. Sensors provide

Fig. 1 Robot platform with sensors

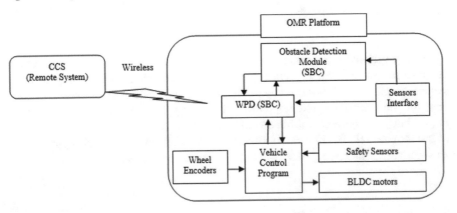

Fig. 2 System architecture

data over high-speed Ethernet TCP/IP network. Dose rate, integrated dose and status information are communicated over TCP/IP Ethernet.

3 Large-Scale Autonomous Navigation

Many life forms including human beings navigate elegantly in unknown environments. They have gross awareness of their position in the environment but not precise. Analogously, the robot we developed has GPS/INS system to give gross awareness of its position in relation with the path it must follow. It has an egocentric

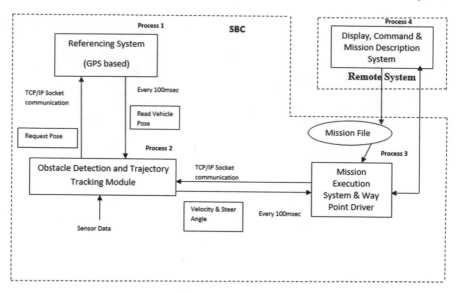

Fig. 3 Software system overview

occupancy grid-based representation of terrain and a tentacle-based mechanism to perceive parameters which influence selection of tentacle to drive on. With these systems in place, the robot is ready to undertake large-scale autonomous navigation (Fig. 3). The scheme we have implemented is largely in line with the ideas presented in [17] but with significant difference. Paper [17] discusses the approach in context to fast moving vehicles like car. Here, we need to adapt and modify the approach for slow-moving vehicles, e.g. less than a metre per second speed.

3.1 Mission Trajectory

The mission trajectory encoded in the mission plan is a series of line segments with nodes at either ends (Fig. 4). In a mission, larger part of the travel is covered by autonomous navigation. An aerial view of the mission site is presented to the technician through the GUI of the mission tool to mark the trajectory. The trajectory marked by the technician is only a guideline; precise tracking of trajectory is not envisaged. Mobile robot is expected to take several real-time decisions on its journey to avoid obstacles on the way, to travel on flatter surfaces and to grossly follow predefined trajectory. The trajectory nodes marked by technicians are GPS waypoints. If the waypoints are far apart, software tool automatically introduces additional waypoints.

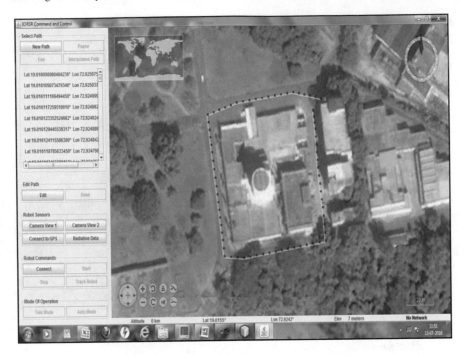

Fig. 4 Operator interface

3.2 Obstacle Detection

Scheme uses occupancy grid-based obstacle detection and this is an imaginary grid in front of the mobile robot with 125×125 cells each of which has a size of 25×25 cm (Fig. 5). The size of cell and grid is configurable. In a sensor rotation, several data points in the form of scan lines get projected into a cell. Thresholding based on z-difference combined with slope [18] is used to decide whether the point being mapped onto a cell is an obstacle point or traversable point. We have considered an urban scenario in our experiments for which we arrived at a threshold in z as 8 cm and a slope threshold of 30° after tuning. With this, a point is treated as an obstacle if and only if it is having a discontinuity in height and slope exceeding above constants. The strategy relies on finding an initial ground point which is continuously updated throughout the scan lines. We assume that the ground point is always available in the scan. Each cell holds a numerical value called 'cell status' which relates to the degree of obstacle occupancy of the cell and an 'occupancy value' which stores the absolute z-difference in the cell. Cell status signifies whether the cell is free (cell status 0), and is occupied (cell status 1) or unknown (cell status 2). A single obstacle point being mapped to a cell changes its status to be occupied. For every rotation of LIDAR, a new occupancy grid is created and the old one is discarded.

Fig. 5 Gridpbased
representation of terrain

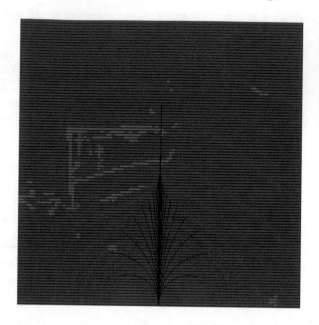

3.3 *Tentacles*

The virtual tentacles have the shape of circular arcs. All of them are defined to have
their starting points at the geometrical centre of the mobile robot. The vertical axis of
the mobile robot is tangential to the entire tentacles at geometric centre of the robot.
Therefore, the tentacles become natural options for the robot to move on. Choosing
the 'best' option for motion from the choices available is a two-step process.

The first step classifies the tentacles into drivable and non-drivable groups. Second step is to select the 'best' tentacle from the group of drivable tentacles at the
given instance based on certain parameters. The parameters influencing selection are
explained under the head tentacle selection.

3.3.1 Tentacle Classification

In every sensor cycle, tentacles are classified into drivable or non-drivable groups.
For this, a longitudinal histogram for each tentacle with its bins aligned along the
curve is envisaged. A fixed number of bins, in this case one hundred numbers, are
used to discretise tentacles irrespective of their length. Area on both sides, closer
to the tentacle, is marked as support area. For low speeds (0.15 m/s), the support
area is only slightly wider than the vehicle, allowing driving along narrow roads or
through narrow gates. If orthogonal projection of a cell in support area falls on a bin,
then the cell contributes to the value of the bin. If the occupancy status in the cell
is 1, histogram bin value is incremented. An obstacle is detected if the sum of all

Fig. 6 Selected tentacle for
motion in white

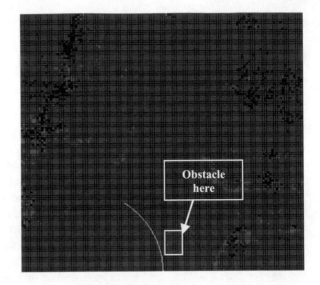

bins within a sliding window exceeds a threshold (in our case 1). In case the bin is
occupied, compute the distance to the first obstacle (lo) along the tentacle. If lo is
more than the safe distance l, then the tentacle is drivable (Fig. 6). $l\ \psi$ is evaluated
experimentally to be 1.8 m in our case. For detailed computational steps, refer to the
paper [17].

3.3.2 Tentacle Selection

Several parameters influence tentacle selection. However, a single decision value is
necessary to judge all drivable tentacles to select the 'best' one. The first parameter
influencing tentacle selection is '*clearance value*'. This is a measure of how far
the robot could drive along a tentacle before hitting an obstacle. To make the values
comparable, they are normalised to the range [0, …, 1], where a value of 0 designates
a preference for such a tentacle. The second parameter '*flatness value*' is to give
preference to the tentacle leading over smooth terrain. Another purpose of second
parameter is to help robot to exploit the free space along the trajectory. Care has been
taken to normalise flatness value to make it comparable among tentacles. The third
parameter affecting selection of tentacle is '*trajectory value*', a measure of ability
of tentacle to bring the robot towards following a given trajectory. Finally, all these
parameters computed are linearly combined to generate a single decision-making
value 'υ'.

$$\upsilon = a_0 * clearance\,value + a_1 * flatness\,value + a_3 * trajectory\,value \qquad (1)$$

The tentacle which has the minimum computed single decision value 'υ' is chosen to drive the robot during next sensor cycle.

4 Mission Management

The need of software for describing mission of robots increases with the expansion of robotic applications. We have adopted a very simple format suggested here as 'Mission Plan String' (Fig. 7). A radiation worker can take high-level orders such as 'Conduct a spot survey' or 'Survey a specified area', etc. However, mobile robots at present can only understand direct controls. Workers can operate on high-level orders because they have been told the mission plan ahead of time and have been trained on standard practices for doing radiological survey. To encode above-described survey mission, a domain-specific mission plan descriptor tool has been developed. The survey mission can be completely specified by a series of waypoints and activities in the form of 'string'. Waypoints are represented by its identity number and activities are represented by appropriate acronyms.

Mobile robot will perform a specified activity as and when the closest point (between trajectory and mobile robot) on predefined trajectory crosses the associated waypoint. This tool displays an aerial view of the mission site. Operator can zoom and pan the image to mark waypoints at intervals from launch point to goal point. Operator can select waypoint to add associated activity. The sequence of waypoints along with activity acronym will form the mission plan string for large-scale autonomous navigation. The mission plan encoding software has the following capabilities:

a. display an aerial view of the specified mission site;
b. interactively place waypoints on aerial view image;
c. insert more points, if waypoints are sparsely placed;
d. interactively align/move the waypoints;

Fig. 7 Mission plan string—specimen

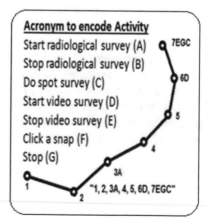

e. select a waypoint and add an activity;
f. create a string of mission plan in the form of a packet; and
g. send commands to stop, proceed or abort a mission.

4.1 Execution Management

Mission execution management software interprets mission plans and executes it within the capabilities of the platform. This software residing onboard decodes the mission plan string to uncover the underlying large-scale autonomous navigation command and take the service of navigation control software described in section three for its execution. Another important feature of 'Mission Execution Management Software' is that it will monitor activities encoded in the mission string and initiate corresponding actions as and when closest point on trajectory from robot cross the associated waypoint.

4.2 In-Mission Decision Support

Realistic missions rarely go exactly as planned. As robots take more active and autonomous roles in missions, they must have the ability to adapt to dynamically changing scenarios. Mission management software shall allow specifying 'plan of actions' (contingency or emergency operations) and facilitate storage and retrieval of these plans. When a deviation from scripted mission arises, in-mission decision support module shall retrieve a suitable plan for execution. Contingency or emergency operation can be as simple as aborting the mission and waiting for the next mission plan from the supervisor.

5 Results

An obstacle detection algorithm in support of the rough terrain conditions has been tested, and its results are shown for positive and negative obstacles. The algorithm used is grid-based obstacle detection and avoidance based on 3D lidar data coming at a high frame rate.

We make use of tentacle-based approach for drivability in an unstructured and complex environment. Tentacle-based approach has been customised to suit our vehicle configuration. Finally, the performance of the system has been evaluated in both simulation and real environment (Figs. 8 and 9), and results are presented and discussed here.

We used artificial obstacles to evaluate the algorithm's ability to detect obstacles of known sizes and to determine the maximum range at which different size obstacles

Fig. 8 Experimental setup for obstacle detection and driving

could be detected. We used five different blocks of varying dimensions and kept them at known distances on the road. Figure 10 shows detection state on y-axis and range in metres on x-axis. Graph is plotted to show different blocks being detected as obstacles till a particular range, and then getting detected but not as obstacles and finally no detection.

The block with dimensions 30 cm × 30 cm is detected as obstacle till 22 m, detected but not as obstacle by the sensor till 28 m and stops getting detected after 30 m.

Negative obstacles are always challenging to handle because of lack of sensor data in the region. They are nearly impossible to detect from far away. Loss of data in a wide range along the driving direction suggests a potential negative obstacle. We conducted experiments using three ditches (Fig. 11) of sizes (a) 50 cm × 30 cm × 30 cm, (b) 25 cm × 20 cm × 30 cm and (c) 16 cm × 16 cm × 30 cm. The viewing direction was along the direction of approach. Largest ditch could be detected from as far as 5.5 m, while the smallest was detected from as far as 3 m (Fig. 12). Figure 16 depicts the performance of solution for a closed path on road around a building (Fig. 15). It plots raw readings of the GPS during the experiment. One can observe in the plot some spike like variations as seen in purple trajectory. These are actually spurious GPS readings extending even into the area of the building and can easily make the robot to go out of the road. Despite all these variations in GPS data, robot continued its smooth travel on flat surfaces seeking road like conditions in all our experiments (Figs. 13, 14, 15 and 16).

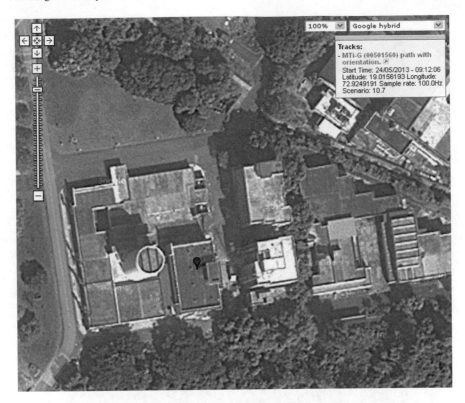

Fig. 9 Raw GPS readings on the traversed path. *Courtesy* Google Map

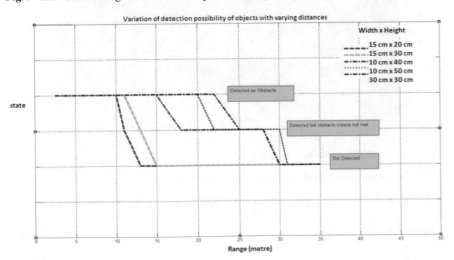

Fig. 10 Positive obstacle detection performance

Fig. 11 Camera view of negative obstacle

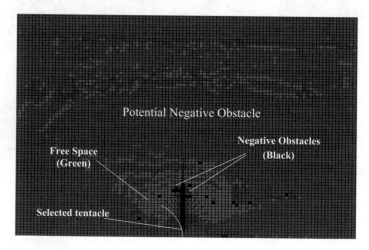

Fig. 12 Occupancy grid view of negative obstacle and chosen tentacle

Fig. 13 Path with waypoints in an open ground with good GPS fix

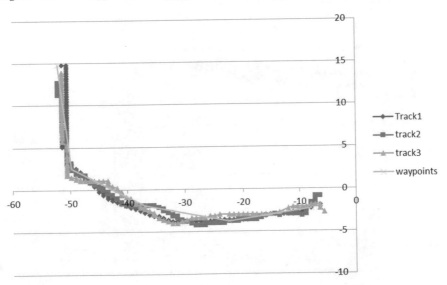

Fig. 14 Tracking performance for open ground

Fig. 15 A closed path around the building

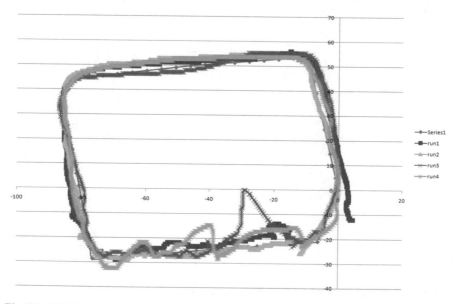

Fig. 16 RAW GPS data plot during multiple successful runs of the solution shows effectiveness of the method

6 Conclusion and Future Work

A radiation survey robot which safely follows GPS waypoints in previously unknown terrains has been developed successfully. Obstacle detection algorithm has been evaluated using the offline extensive sets of Lidar data before taking real trials. It is capable of detecting both positive and negative obstacles. During trials, it has been observed that this scheme has imparted improvement in the behaviour of basic GPS waypoint follower by giving preference to smoother surfaces while avoiding obstacles aside. The mission management tool presented here has features to prepare a mobile robot to take-up high-level orders and execute it. The basic GPS waypoint follower is to be augmented with other techniques to make the navigation system suitable for GPS-denied environments.

References

1. R. Kümmerle, B. Steder, C. Dornhege, A. Kleiner, G. Grisetti, W. Burgard, Large scale graph-based SLAM using aerial images as prior information, in *Proceedings of Robotics: Science and Systems (RSS)* (2009)
2. J.E. Guivant, Efficient simultaneous localization and mapping in large environments, Doctor of Philosophy thesis, The University of sydney, 2002
3. T. Bailey, Mobile Robot localisation and mapping in extensive outdoor environments, Doctor of Philosophy thesis, The University of Sydney (2002)
4. P. Pfaff, W. Burgard, D. Fox, Robust monte-carlo localization using adaptive likelihood models, in *European Robotics Symposium* (2006)
5. D. Fox, W. Burgard, F. Dellaert, S. Thrun, Monte carlo localization: efficient position estimation for mobile robots, in *Proceedings of the National Conference on Artificial Intelligence (AAAI)* (1999)
6. S. Thrun, W. Burgard, D. Fox, *Probabilistic Robotics*, 01 edition (MIT Press)
7. J. Borenstein, H. Everett, L. Feng, D. Wehe, Mobile robot positioning: sensors and techniques. J. Robotic Syst. **14**(4), 231–249 (1997)
8. A. Martinelli, N. Tomatis, A. Tapus, R. Siegwart, Simultaneous localization and odometry calibration for mobile robot, in *Procceedings of IEEE International Conference on Intelligent Robots and Systems*, vol. 2, pp. 1499–1504, February 2003
9. F. Dellaert, D.Fox, W. Burgard, S. Thrun, Monte Carlo localization for mobile robots, in *Proceedings of ICRA-99* (1999)
10. S. Thrun, Robotic mapping: a survey, exploring artificial intelligence in the new millenium (Morgan Kaufmann, 2002)
11. N. Tomatis, I. Nourbakhsh, R. Siegwart, Hybrid simultaneous localization and map building: a natural integration of topological and metric. Robot. Auton. Syst. **44**, 3–14 (2003)
12. D. Hähnel, W. Burgard, D. Fox, S. Thrun, An efficient FastSLAM algorithm for generating maps of large-scale cyclic environments from raw laser range measurements, in *Proceedings of the International Conference on Intelligent Robots and Systems (IROS)*, 206–211 (2003)
13. W. Burgard, C. Stachniss, G. Grisetti, B. Steder, R. Kümmerle, C. Dornhege, M. Ruhnke, A. Kleiner, J.D. Tardós, A comparison of slam algorithms based on a graph of relations, in *Proceedings of the International Conference on Intelligent Robots and Systems (IROS)* (2009)
14. A. Garulli, A. Giannitrapani, A. Rossi, A. Vicino, Mobile robot SLAM for line-based environment representation, in *44th IEEE Conference on Decision and Control, 2005 and 2005 European Control Conference (CDC-ECC 05)*, pp. 2041–2046, December 2005

15. A. Diosi, L. Kleeman, Laser scan matching in polar coordinates with application to SLAM, in *IEEE/RSJ International Conference on Intelligent Robots and Systems (IROS 2005)*, pp. 3317–3322, August 2005
16. S. Thrun, Y. Liu, D. Koller, A.Y. Ng, Z. Ghahramani, H. Durrant-Whyte, Simultaneous localization and mapping with sparse extended information filters. Int. J. Robot. Res. **23**(7/8), 693–716 (2004)
17. F. von Hundelshausen, M. Himmelsbach, F. Hecker, A. Mueller, H.-J. Wuensche, Driving with tentacles: integral structures for sensing and motion, in *Autonomous Systems Technology* (Department of Aerospace Engineering, University of the Federal Armed Forces, Munich 85579, Neubiberg, Germany); J. Field Robot. **25**(9), 640–673 (2008)
18. T. Chang, T.-H. Steve Legowik, M.N. Abrams, Concealment and obstacle detection for autonomous driving, in *Submitted to International Association of science and Technology for Development-Robotics and Applications Conference* (1999)

Workspace of Multi-fingered Robotic Hands Using Monte Carlo Method

Arkadeep Narayan Chaudhury and Ashitava Ghosal

Abstract Multi-fingered hands enable significantly enhanced manipulation capabilities to the robot where it is attached. As a consequence, analysis, design and development of multi-fingered hands has been of continuing interest in the robotics community. In this work, we propose a probabilistic Monte Carlo based approach to obtain the workspace of a well-known multi-fingered hand, the three-fingered Salisbury hand, modeled as a hybrid parallel manipulator. It is shown that Monte Carlo method can be used to obtain the volume of the well conditioned workspace of the hybrid manipulator in $\Re^3$ and SO(3). One of the obtained novel results is that with realistic constraints on the motion of the joints, the well-conditioned workspace of the hybrid manipulator is the largest when the grasped object area is approximately equal to the palm area. We also obtain and discuss the dependence of the workspace of the manipulator on it's geometry and other link and joint variables.

Keywords Multi-fingered hand · Monte Carlo method · Well-conditioned workspace

1 Introduction

The use of multi-fingered hands in robots enable it to perform dexterous manipulation of object and thus enhance it's capabilities. Due to this reasoning several human hand inspired multi-fingered hands have been studied and built by the robotics research community. Some of the early (c.1980–90) major advances in multi-fingered hand design were robotic hands with elastic fingers [1], the Stanford-JPL hand [2], the Utah-MIT hand [3] and the Styx hand [4]. In a class of works, see e.g. the works [2]

A. N. Chaudhury · A. Ghosal (✉)
Department of Mechanical Engineering, Indian Institute of Science,
Bengaluru, India
e-mail: asitava@iisc.ac.in; asitava@mecheng.iisc.ernet.in

A. N. Chaudhury
e-mail: arkadeepc@iisc.ac.in

© Springer Nature Singapore Pte Ltd. 2019
D N Badodkar and T A Dwarakanath (eds.), *Machines, Mechanism and Robotics*, Lecture Notes in Mechanical Engineering,
https://doi.org/10.1007/978-981-10-8597-0_27

317

and most recently [5], researchers have explored dexterous manipulation from the context of a parallel manipulator focusing on dexterity, precision of manipulation of a given object in a given workspace by considering a lower degree of freedom ($\sim$6) approximation of the human hand. In this work, we study the well known three-fingered Stanford-JPL hand, originally proposed by Salisbury and Craig [2], as a hybrid parallel manipulator. The details of the modeling of the three-fingered Salisbury hand as a parallel hybrid manipulator, it's forward and inverse kinematics equations are well-known (see, for example, Ghosal [6]). In this work, we define the well-conditioned workspace of the manipulator by setting realistic constraints on the actuated and passive joints and by restricting the condition numbers of the equivalent Jacobians (relating the linear and angular velocities of the end effector separately with the joint rates) to be less than 1000 at all times. Next, using the definition of the well conditioned workspace, we formulate the problem of obtaining the well conditioned workspace of the parallel manipulator as an integration problem in the task space (in $\Re^3$ for the linear component of the motion and in $SO(3)$ for the angular component of motion of the end effector). We finally use the Monte Carlo method to evaluate the integral and obtain the workspace.

2 Description of the Stanford-JPL Hand

The kinematic model shown in Fig. 1 represents a three-fingered hand grasping an object. The grasping of the object is assumed to be achievable by three point contacts with friction—we have modeled them as spherical (S) joints. The manipulator, modeled as a 6-DoF hybrid parallel mechanism has been shown schematically in Fig. 1. In Fig. 1, the "gripped object" is represented by the moving platform $\{S_1, S_2, S_3\}$ connected to a "fixed base" $\{B_1^0, B_2^0, B_3^0\}$ by three 3R serial manipulators of link lengths $\{l_{i1}, l_{i2}, l_{i3}\}$ $\forall i = 1, 2, 3$. The contacts between the gripped object and the distal ends (from the base) of the serial manipulators are modeled as 3 unactuated "S" joints (S_1, S_2 & S_3) with three rotational degrees of freedom. It may be observed that the last "R" joint from the base towards the object shown by $\{B_1^2, B_2^2, B_3^2\}$ in Fig. 1 is un-actuated[1]—with this assumption the degree of freedom, by using the Grübler-Kutzbach criterion, is obtained as six. In the figure, the first joint axis of the "index" and "middle" finger are shown as parallel and the first "thumb" joint axis is at an angle of γ to the Y axis. From the figure, the position vectors of $\{B_1^0, B_2^0, B_3^0\}$ from the origin of the fixed co-ordinate system $\{O\}$ can be written as

$$^O B_1^0 = \{0, -d, h\}^T; \quad ^O B_2^0 = \{0, d, h\}^T; \quad ^O B_3^0 = \{0, 0, 0\}^T \qquad (1)$$

and the point of contact of the fingers with the object, namely $\{S_1, S_2, S_3\}$, form the origin of $\{O\}$ can be written as

---

[1]Joints with the least motion have been chosen to be passive.

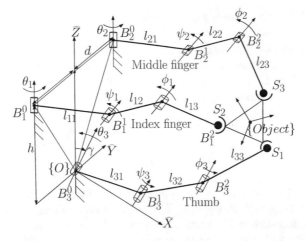

Fig. 1 Schematic of the Salisbury hand (from Ghosal [6])

$$^{O}S_i =^{O} B_i^0 + R[\hat{Y}, \gamma_i] \begin{bmatrix} \cos{(\theta_i)}\,[l_{i1} + l_{i2}\cos{(\psi_i)} + l_{i3}\cos{(\psi_i + \phi_i)}] \\ \sin{(\theta_i)}\,[l_{i1} + l_{i2}\cos{(\psi_i)} + l_{i3}\cos{(\psi_i + \phi_i)}] \\ l_{i2}\cos{(\psi_i)} + l_{i3}\cos{(\psi_i + \phi_i)} \end{bmatrix} \quad (2)$$

$$\forall i = \{1, 2, 3\}; \ \gamma = [0, 0, \pi/4]$$

Equation (2) along with the constraints imposed on the manipulator by the 3 spherical joints will be used to formulate and solve the inverse kinematics problem, obtain expressions for linear and angular velocity of the gripped object and, from the linear and angular velocity Jacobians, define the well-conditioned workspace of the manipulator. Appendices 1 and 2 briefly outline the formulation and solution of the inverse kinematics problem and the definition of the condition number of the manipulator Jacobian respectively.

2.1 Well-Conditioned Workspace of the Manipulator Using Monte Carlo Method

In this section we present a brief overview of the Monte Carlo method and how it can be used to quantify and obtain a representation of the workspace of a manipulator in $\Re^3$. For a more detailed discussion on the Monte Carlo method in general, one may refer to any standard textbook of Monte Carlo method (see, for example, Dunn and Shultis [7]). For literature on using Monte Carlo method on design and optimization of parallel manipulators one may refer to the works by Stamper et al. [8] and the references contained therein. For a comprehensive review on the usage of Monte Carlo method for obtaining the workspace volume of parallel manipulators and it's comparison with similar methods, and further implications of using it for design of parallel manipulators one may refer to [9].

We assume that the well-conditioned workspace $\mathcal{W}$, ($\mathcal{W} \in SE(3)$), of a parallel manipulator is a collection of a finite number or closed sets in $SE(3)$ bounded by surfaces $\mathcal{S}_w^i$, $\forall i = 1, 2, \ldots, n$. We formulate an *in-out* function $\mathcal{F}$ for $\mathcal{S}_w^i$s which takes input of the position and orientation of the end effector of the manipulator. This function can be represented as

$$\mathcal{F}(\mathbf{X}) = \left\{ \begin{array}{l} 1 \ \text{if} \ \mathbf{X} \in \mathcal{W} \\ 0 \ \text{if} \ \mathbf{X} \notin \mathcal{W} \end{array} \right\} \tag{3}$$

The inclusion(or exclusion) of a given position and orientation of the manipulator (given by $\mathbf{X} = \{x, y, z, \theta, \phi, \psi\}^T$ i.e., $\mathbf{X} \in SE(3)$ is determined by the fact that (a) for a given $\mathbf{X}$ the inverse kinematics problem ($\mathcal{IK}(\mathbf{X})$ see Appendix 1) has real solutions, (b) the active and passive joint values are within prescribed limits, and (c) the manipulator Jacobian is well conditioned (see Appendix 2). The well-conditioned workspace is quantified by the union of all the sets $\mathcal{S}_w^i$, $\forall i = 1, 2, \ldots, n$. To obtain the well-conditioned workspace, we randomly generate N vectors $\mathbf{X}$ and evaluate $\mathcal{F}(\mathbf{X})$ for each of these points. If a randomly chosen position and orientation is in the well conditioned workspace, it is saved and at the end of the simulation, the total number of randomly generated configurations that were found to be inside the well conditioned workspace, denoted by N_{in}, is obtained. To determine the well-conditioned workspace, we define the search space $\mathcal{V}$ as the span of $\mathbf{X}$ (in Cartesian or angular coordinates) and obtain $\widehat{\mathcal{W}}$, an estimate of the well-conditioned workspace $\mathcal{W}$ of the chosen parallel manipulator as

$$\widehat{\mathcal{W}} = \frac{N_{in}}{N} \times \mathcal{V} \tag{4}$$

For a detailed discussion on the topic, one may refer to the work by Chaudhury and Ghosal [9]. Figures 2 and 3 represent the workspace of the manipulator in $\mathfrak{R}^3$ and angular coordinates respectively.

3   Results

Using the method described above, we can obtain separate representations of the workspace in $\mathfrak{R}^3$ and $SO(3)$. Figure 2 shows the representation of the workspace in $\mathfrak{R}^3$ as a triangulated domain, enveloping the cloud of points inside the well-conditioned workspace. Figure 3 shows the well-conditioned workspace of the parallel manipulator in $SO(3)$ as a cloud of points. The dimensions of the hand segments were taken from Table 1 and the object size (circum-radius of $\triangle S_1 S_2 S_3$ in Fig. 1) was taken as 20 mm. The volume of the obtained workspace is 1.83×10^3 mm^3. Figure 6 shows the variation of the workspace of the hand across varying hand and object sizes. For

Table 1 Sample finger and hand segment lengths (refer Fig. 1 for symbols)

Hand part	Symbols	Values (mm)
Index finger	$\{l_{11}, l_{12}, l_{13}\}$	$\{35, 23, 28\}$
Middle finger	$\{l_{21}, l_{22}, l_{23}\}$	$\{41, 22, 28\}$
Thumb	$\{l_{31}, l_{32}, l_{33}\}$	$\{45, 36, 34\}$
Palm	$\{d, h\}$	$\{13, 82\}$

this, we considered 7 data sets (like the ones shown in Table 1) from the hand dimensions of 1 female and 6 male subjects. The horizontal axis in Figs. 4 and 6 denotes the quantity r_{po} given by $\dfrac{\mathcal{A}_{Object}}{\mathcal{A}_{Palm}}$ where $\mathcal{A}_{Object}$ is the area of the circum-circle of $\triangle S_1 S_2 S_3$ and $\mathcal{A}_{Palm}$ is the area of $\triangle B_1^0 B_2^0 B_3^0$ in Fig. 1 (Table 2). It may be noted that the hand workspace is the largest when the area of the palm is approximately equal to the object area—the mean $\bar{r}_{po}$ is found to be 1.043 with a standard deviation $\sigma(r_{po})$ of 0.05.

Since the method of obtaining the workspace is an iterative one, we demonstrate the convergence of our algorithm in Fig. 7. The plot shows that the algorithm gives the similar results for 40 different object sizes varying between 2 and 40 mm across 6 different executions of the algorithm. Figure 4 demonstrates that the mean $\bar{r}_{po}$ is independent of the upper bound on the condition number set in Eq. (15). To understand the dependence of the workspace of the manipulator on the geometric parameters of the manipulator we parametrize the hand as

$$\mathbf{P} = \left\{ d, h, l_{11}, l_{12}, l_{13}, r_m = \sum_{i=1}^{3} l_{2i} / \sum_{i=1}^{3} l_{1i}, r_t = \sum_{i=1}^{3} l_{3i} / \sum_{i=1}^{3} l_{1i} \right\} \qquad (5)$$

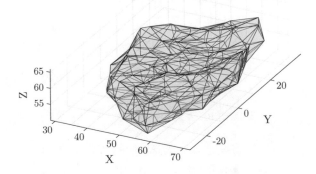

Fig. 2 Workspace of the Salisbury hand (all dimensions in mm)

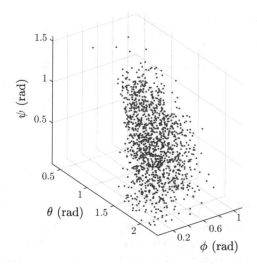

Fig. 3 Angular workspace of the Salisbury hand

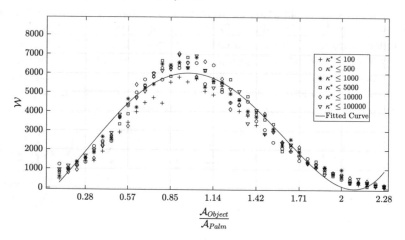

Fig. 4 Independence of the result in Fig. 6 to upper bounds on κ^*

Next, we formulate the following optimization problem as shown below.

$$\underset{\mathbf{P}}{\text{Maximize}} \; \mathcal{W}(\mathbf{P}) \tag{6}$$

$$\text{Subject to} \quad h \times d \leq 1000, \; \sum_{i=1}^{3} l_{1i} = 80$$

$$r_m < 2, \; r_t < 2, \; l_{1i} \geq 20, \; \forall i = 1, 2, 3$$

$$d > 0, \; h > 0, \; d \leq 20, \; h \leq 80 \; \& \; d \leq 0.3h$$

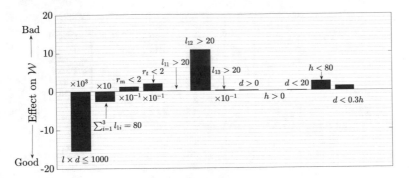

Fig. 5 Scaled constraint Lagrange multipliers at an optimum

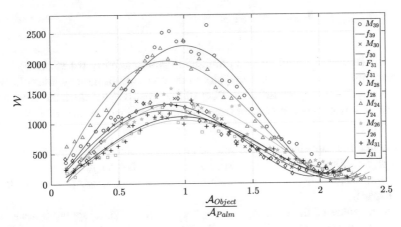

Fig. 6 Variation of the workspace with varying object size

Table 2 Joint notations in Fig. 1 and maximal permissible motions

Joint center	Joint variable	Type	Value/range
B_1^0 and B_2^0	θ_1 and θ_2	Active	$-45°$ to $45°$
B_3^0	θ_3	Active	$-45°$ to $45°$
B_1^1 and B_2^1	ψ_1 and ψ_2	Active	$0°$ to $90°$
B_3^1	ψ_3	Active	$0°$ to $90°$
B_3^2	ϕ_3	Passive	$0°$ to $30°$
B_1^2 and B_2^2	ϕ_1 and ϕ_2	Passive	$0°$ to $30°$
B_3^0	γ	Fixed	$\gamma = 45°$
S_1, S_2 and S_3	$\{\xi_X^i, \xi_Y^i\}$	Passive	$\pm45°$

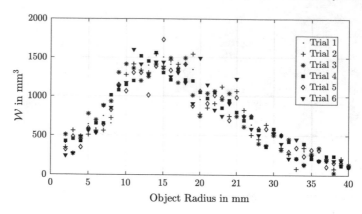

Fig. 7 Convergence of algorithm over 6 trials

The constraints imposed on the optimization problem in Eq. (6) are based on the 95th percentile human hand. A scaled plot of the constraint Lagrange multipliers are given in Fig. 5, at an optimum. The effect of the sensitivity of the hand workspace to the hand dimensions can be seen from the figure, and we can draw the following conclusions[2]:

- The constraints limiting the hand size i.e., palm area and index finger length given by $l \times d < 1000$ and $\sum_{i=1}^{3} l_{1i} = 80$, have negative Lagrange multipliers associated with them, which signifies the obvious result that a *larger hand* has a larger workspace.
- From the value of the Lagrange multipliers for the constraints we observe that the workspace is more sensitive to a change in palm area than a change in finger length.
- The workspace is not very sensitive to the upper limits on r_m and r_t. Also, at an optimum we obtain $r_m = 1.1$ and $r_t = 1.35$ which are quite close to the values suggested by [11, 12].
- The workspace is quite sensitive to lower bounds on the fingers segments, however, the workspace is not sensitive to the lower limits on d and h.
- Values of the Lagrange multipliers associated with constraints on the upper limits on d and h suggest that the workspace is equally sensitive to these constraints.

4   Conclusion

The current work deals with quantifying and obtaining a representation of the well-conditioned workspace of the 6-DoF hybrid parallel manipulator modeling the well-known Salisbury hand. We began by outlining the geometry of the manipulator in

---

[2]For a detailed discussion on constraint sensitivity analysis see Arora [10].

Sect. 2. Following which, in Sect. 2.1 we have outlined the use of Monte Carlo method to obtain the well-conditioned workspace of the manipulator. In Sect. 3 we have given representations of the workspace in $\Re^3$ and $SO(3)$, and a new result indicating the the workspace of the hand is the largest when the object area is approximately equal to the palm area of the manipulator. Finally, we have outlined the dependence of the workspace of the manipulator on it's geometric dimensions.

Appendix 1:   Inverse Kinematics Problem Solution [6]

For a given position vector of the point S_1, (see Fig. 1), the expressions of the X, Y and Z coordinates of the point S_1 are given as the rows of Eq. (2). From which, by simplifying $X^2 + (Y + d)^2 + (Z - h)^2$ we can obtain the expression with only ϕ_1, given in Eq. (7).

$$4l_{11}^2 (l_{12}^2 + l_{13}^2 + 2l_{12}l_{13} \cos(\phi_1)) = C_1^2 + 4l_{11}C_2^2 \tag{7}$$

where $C_1 \equiv C_1(l_{11}, l_{12}, l_{13}, d, h, \phi_1)$ and $C_2 = h - Z$. Substituting $\cos(\phi_1)$ with its tangent half angle equivalent in Eq. (7) we can obtain a quadratic expression for ϕ_1. The angle ψ_1 can be solved from the eliminant obtained by using Sylvester's dialytic method and θ_1 is obtained as $\theta_1 = \mathrm{atan2}(Y + d, X)$. The inverse kinematics problem for the middle finger and the thumb can be solved in a way similar to index finger shown above.

Appendix 2:   Definition of Condition Number

The position vector of the center of the object in Fig. 1 is given by,

$$^OP_{Obj} = \frac{1}{3} \sum_{i=1}^{3} {}^OS_i \tag{8}$$

and the orientation of the top platform with the base may be given as in

$$^O[R]_{Obj} = \left[\frac{^OS_1 - {}^OS_2}{|^OS_1 - {}^OS_2|} \quad \hat{Y} \quad \frac{(^OS_1 - {}^OS_1) \times (^OS_1 - {}^OS_3)}{|(^OS_1 - {}^OS_1) \times (^OS_1 - {}^OS_3)|} \right] \tag{9}$$

where $\hat{Y}$ is obtained by the cross product of the third and first column of the matrix in Eq. (9). The 3 constraint equations ensuring that the distance $\|S_i - S_j\|$, $\{i, j\} \in [1, 2, 3]$, $i \neq j$, are always constant, may be differentiated to obtain Eq. (10).

$$[\mathbf{K}(\theta, \phi)]\{\dot{\theta}\} + [\mathbf{K}^*(\theta, \phi)]\{\dot{\phi}\} = 0 \tag{10}$$

It is easily seen that $[\mathbf{K}^*]$ is a square matrix of dimension 3×3. Equation (10) can be solved for $\dot{\gamma}$, given $\det(\mathbf{K}^*) \neq 0$,[3] and we can obtain $\dot{\phi} = -[\mathbf{K}^*(\theta, \phi)]^{-1}[\mathbf{K}(\theta, \phi)]\dot{\theta}$. Differentiating equations (8) and (9) with respect to time we obtain the expressions for the linear and angular velocities of the manipulator and these can be written as

$$^0V_{Obj} = [\mathbf{J}_V]\{\dot{\theta}\} + [\mathbf{J}_V^*]\{\dot{\phi}\} \tag{11}$$

$$^0\omega_{Obj} = [\mathbf{J}_\omega]\{\dot{\theta}\} + [\mathbf{J}_\omega^*]\{\dot{\phi}\} \tag{12}$$

Following [6] and using Eqs. (10)–(12) we define the square, nonsingular, equivalent Jacobian matrices for both linear and angular velocity parts as

$$\mathbf{J}_{eqv}^V = (\mathbf{J}_V - \mathbf{J}_V^*[\mathbf{K}^*]^{-1}[\mathbf{K}]) \tag{13}$$

$$\mathbf{J}_{eqv}^\omega = (\mathbf{J}_\omega - \mathbf{J}_\omega^*[\mathbf{K}^*]^{-1}[\mathbf{K}]) \tag{14}$$

The equivalent, dimensionless condition number of Jacobian for the manipulator, undergoing both linear and angular motions are given as κ_V and κ_ω for $\mathbf{J}_{eqv}^V$ and $\mathbf{J}_{eqv}^\omega$ respectively where we find the 2-norm condition number of a matrix $\mathbf{A}$ as $\kappa_A = \| \mathbf{A} \|_2 \| \mathbf{A}^{-1} \|_2$. To ensure that a given configuration of the end effector is well conditioned we ensure that

$$\max\{\kappa_V, \kappa_\omega\} \leq \kappa^* \tag{15}$$

where κ^* is chosen as 1000.

References

1. H. Hanafusa, H. Asada, A robot hand with elastic fingers and its application to assembly process, in *Proceedings of IFAC First Symposium on Information Control Problems in Manufacturing Technology* (1977), pp. 127–138
2. J.K. Salisbury, J.J. Craig, Articulated hands: force control and kinematic issues. Int. J. Robot. Res. **1**(1), 4–17 (1982)
3. S. Jacobsen, E. Iversen, D. Knutti, R. Johnson, K. Biggers, Design of the Utah/MIT dextrous hand, in *Proceedings of the 1986 IEEE International Conference on Robotics and Automation*, vol. 3 (IEEE, 1986), pp. 1520–1532
4. R.M. Murray, S.S. Sastry, Control experiments in planar manipulation and grasping, in *Proceedings of the 1989 IEEE International Conference on Robotics and Automation* (IEEE, 1989), pp. 624–629
5. J. Borràs, A.M. Dollar, Dimensional synthesis of three-fingered robot hands for maximal precision manipulation workspace. Int. J. Robot. Res. **34**(14), 1731–1746 (2015)
6. A. Ghosal, *Robotics: Fundamental Concepts and Analysis* (Oxford University Press, 2006)
7. W.L. Dunn, J.K. Shultis, *Exploring Monte Carlo Methods* (Elsevier, 2011)
8. R.E. Stamper, L.-W. Tsai, G.C. Walsh, Optimization of a three DOF translational platform for well-conditioned workspace, in *Proceedings of the 1997 IEEE International Conference on Robotics and Automation*, vol. 4 (IEEE, 1997), pp. 3250–3255

---

[3]In the simulation, it was ensured that $\det(\mathbf{K}^*) \neq 0$ and the condition number of $\mathbf{K}^*$ was $\leq 10^4$ at all points inside the obtained workspace.

9. A.N. Chaudhury, A. Ghosal, Optimum design of multi-degree-of-freedom closed-loop mechanisms and parallel manipulators for a prescribed workspace using Monte Carlo method. Mech. Mach. Theory **118**, 115–138 (2017)

10. J. Arora, *Introduction to Optimum Design* (Chapter 4) (Academic Press, 2004), pp. 154–157

11. R.M. White, Comparative anthropometry of the hand. Technical report, DTIC Document, 1980

12. J.T. Manning, Sex differences and age changes in digit ratios: implications for the use of digit ratios in medicine and biology, in *Handbook of Anthropometry* (Springer, 2012), pp. 841–851

Modular Mission Control for Automated Material Handling System and Performance Analysis—A Case Study

Namita Singh, Vaibhav Dave, Jagadish Kota, Shishir Kumar Singh, Rahul Sakrikar and P. V. Sarngadharan

Abstract The paper describes the design of mission planning and control architecture for an autonomous material handling system which perceives the live requirements of material movement on a factory floor and does judicious deployment of autonomous guided vehicles (AGVs) to service them. The system has a novel methodology to perceive prevailing situation on factory floor in terms of material transportation and fetching suitable mission, from a predefined set, for execution. This research effort is part of a long-term project that aims to enable AGV to carry out loading and delivery missions in hazardous areas of fuel fabrication facility, in a completely autonomous mode. The system is being used as an advanced test bed to test developments in mission planning and real-time mission execution system for AGVs. The system consists of single or multiple AGVs transporting material between

N. Singh (✉) · V. Dave · J. Kota · S. K. Singh · R. Sakrikar · P. V. Sarngadharan (✉)
Division of Remote Handling and Robotics, Bhabha Atomic Research Centre,
Mumbai, Maharashtra, India
e-mail: namita@barc.gov.in

P. V. Sarngadharan
e-mail: sarang@barc.gov.in

V. Dave
e-mail: vdave@barc.gov.in

J. Kota
e-mail: jkota@barc.gov.in

S. K. Singh
e-mail: shishir@barc.gov.in

R. Sakrikar
e-mail: rsakrikar@barc.gov.in

© Springer Nature Singapore Pte Ltd. 2019
D N Badodkar and T A Dwarakanath (eds.), *Machines, Mechanism and Robotics*, Lecture Notes in Mechanical Engineering,
https://doi.org/10.1007/978-981-10-8597-0_28

several loading and delivery points, through a structured environment. It modularizes all aspects of factory automation like floor configuration, individual vehicle control, mission execution, high-level mission planning, and coordination. We present a methodology of building complex missions in terms of unique operations. In the later part, we present a case study based on a real scenario for evaluating the performance of indigenously developed AGV in simulation.

Keywords Autonomous guided vehicles · Transfer plans · Supervisory control Trajectory editor · Mission planner

1 Introduction

Intelligent material handling solutions involving AGVs are ideally suited in manufacturing scenario where simultaneous production of different parts being produced at different rates in varying quantities while maintaining high quality. In the production environment, an AGV needs to perform number of trips between loading and delivery points to meet the production schedule. In this process, the system needs to select the AGV, assign the task (mission) which is called *Dispatching*, determine specific routes to be taken by the AGV known as *Routing,* and schedule the jobs efficiently [1–3]. Design of control architectures and mission planning for autonomous solutions remains a challenge involving use of wide domains like artificial intelligence and operational research. Owing to the involved complexity, they require extensive testing to verify safety and correctness of behavior [4, 5]. Though great amount of efforts have been devoted to route optimization and traffic management of AGVs, mission configuration has not yet received desired attention [6]. Horst et al. [7] presented a logic action model to defining plans under uncertainty with a notion of limited correctness for an unstructured environment. The industrial environments are inherently structured with a well-defined job to be handled by the mobile robots. The mission description and planning can then be designed by exploiting the inherent structured information. Efficiency of mission planning depends greatly on situation awareness which covers AGV knowledge of the system and the operator knowledge of the current status of AGV. Endsley [8] described a well-accepted definition of situation awareness. The challenge is to efficiently communicate the operator intent to the AGV in the system to maximize the availability of AGV in the system, thus maximizing the production rate.

In the remaining paper, we shall discuss a typical material handling scenario with a set of requirements in Sect. 2. In Sect. 3, the design of the control architecture is discussed along with the AGV for material transfer. In Sects. 4 and 5, various software modules are discussed for integrating the control architecture including the vehicle state management, mission specification, and validation. Section 5 also deals with the considerations for analysis, development, and modeling for validation. Finally, conclusive remarks are presented.

2 Mission Scenario and Performance Requirements

This section deals with one possible scenario for the system deployment. The material handling scenario considered here for performance evaluation is based on the requirements of a typical fuel fabrication facility where a series of transfers are required among designated isolated areas. The full cycle consists of the following:

- Loading of boats from the compacting area.
- Delivery of the boats to the input of the sintering furnaces in the sintering area.
- Collecting the processed boats from the output of the sintering furnaces.
- Delivering the processed boats to the boat disassembly station.
- Collecting empty boats from the boat disassembly station and delivering them back to the compacting stations.

In Fig. 1, a sample layout of the workspace is shown where there are four compacting stations shown as C1, C2, C3, and C4 in the compacting area each having a drop-off and pick-up points. In the sintering area, there are six furnaces F1, F2, F3, F4, F5, and F6 each having a drop-off point at the entry side and pick-up point at the exit side. There is a boat disassembly area (BD) which is having one drop-off point for transferring the processed boats and one pick-up point for picking the empty boats. All these pick-up and drop-off points are having conveyers with finite buffer capacity. The compacting and the sintering area are physically isolated from each other to control the particulate contamination from the compacting area. The two areas are connected by double door unit for material movements (Fig. 1).

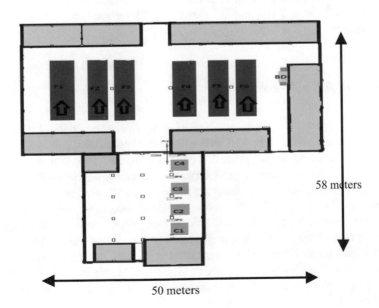

Fig. 1 A sample layout of environment

Fig. 2 Graphical layout of trajectories

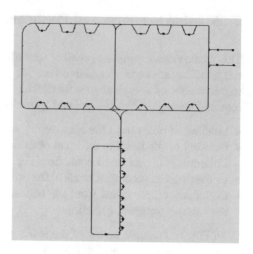

The floor plan is provided a priori to the supervisory controller in the form of a floor plan project (Fig. 2) having a map file along with the database file. Missions can be stored prior at the time of configuration or can be given online. A mission consists of description of trajectories to be followed along with the activities to be completed at selected nodes along the trajectories. The overall requirement specifications include (i) complete all the jobs in a mission in the shortest possible time while respecting the delivery order specified in the mission, (ii) robust against plant parameter changes, (iii) recovery from fault and in case of inability to recover on its own, provide guidance for operator-assisted recovery, and (iv) user-friendly interface for operator interaction with the system.

3 Control Architecture

Designing a fully autonomous system requiring minimal or no operator intervention is a complex job. In addition, lack of well-established methodology motivates to consider some fundamental architectural designs based on set of proposed requirements. A modular and layered design approach proves a boon for managing this complexity [9]. Each module has well-defined scope of tasks and communicates with other modules using its interface. This has facilitated the development, testing, and performance evaluation of the system. Each module can be independently developed and tested. The overall architecture has been shown in Fig. 3. The main components are trajectory editor, supervisory controller, mission planner, device interface module, plan executor, and motion control program. Mission planner represents the core of the control system which is higher level management logic responsible for specification of mission, error handling, and recovery.

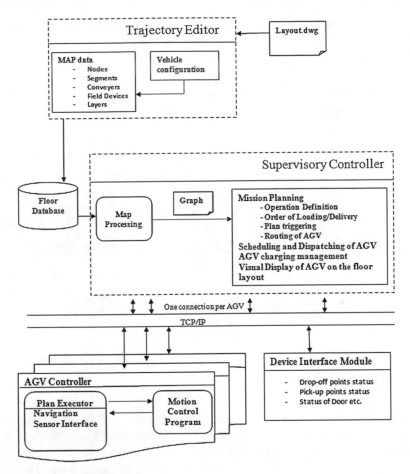

Fig. 3 Control architecture overview

For deploying AGV to move autonomously in the surrounding environment, a precise and compact representation of the environment is required. This task is carried out by the module trajectory editor which uses the CAD drawing of the floor as input. There are many approaches to represent the environment [10]. We have used a topological model in which the environment is represented as a graph structure where nodes correspond to distinct locations. They are connected by edge if there is a direct path between them. This is used by mission planner module and plan executor module. We are currently using modified A-star algorithm for routing the AGV. It is a heuristic algorithm which takes into account the cost involving turn in place by AGV.

This architecture has been designed so that it is scalable to multi-AGV solution and modules like deadlock avoidance can be easily incorporated.

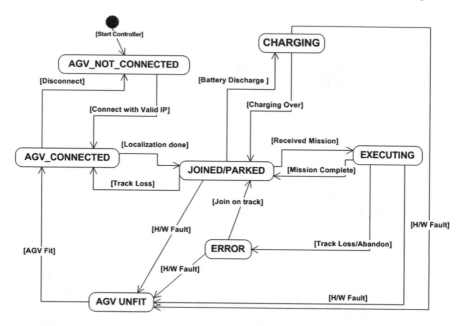

Fig. 4 States of AGV

3.1 AGV Description

This portion contains a short description about the AGV. For complete details, the reader is referred to [11]. The vehicle is battery-powered mobile platform with onboard-powered roller conveyers for material transfer. It has two bays consisting of two conveyers each. It is using a laser-guided system for navigation and reaching the material transfer points with great precision. The physical parameters related to AGV are detailed in the appendix at the end.

4 Supervisory Controller

The supervisory controller is responsible for processing the demand and supply of bins at various locations seamlessly. It needs to maintain communication with the AGV controllers and the field device interface module. It keeps a track of current AGV state as per its state diagram (shown in Fig. 4). Also, it manages the decision when AGV should go for charging. As per charging policy, if AGV needs charging, it commands AGV to charge at the nearest available charging point. Based on continuous feedback regarding current state of AGV, the software provides recovery options and logic flow control.

5 Mission Definition and Validation

A methodology has been designed for intuitive mission encoding which aims to have mission structure which can be easily composed, decomposed, and extended on the introduction of new field devices. It allows for independent module design. The mission is specified in terms of *operations*. An *operation* is the smallest atomic task which an AGV has to perform on field devices. We define operation format as

Operation format					
Device ID	Activity	Direction	Bay	Number	Material type (reserved for future)

Device ID is the index of the corresponding field device, activity corresponds to the loading/unloading which needs to be carried out when AGV reaches that device. This way the activity also signifies the event associated with the device. The interface supports creation of user-defined activity during the configuration. Additional fields are only valid if the corresponding device is conveyer. The third field *Direction* = {left, right} signifies the direction of activity on AGV, fourth field is the *bay* of AGV on which the bin will be transferred, fifth field is number of bins to be transferred, and the last field is reserved and is relevant in case there are multiple types of materials being handled by the system.

This information is encapsulated in the mission given to AGV. A mission M constitutes of sequence of such operations.

$M = \{O_1, O_2, …, O_n\}$ where n is the total operations in the mission M. These missions can be stored a priori and are automatically invoked based on the situation. An appropriate mission is selected out of several missions when AGV becomes idle.

All the conveyors on the AGV are assumed to be vacant or empty at the start of a plan. An activity performed on a specific conveyor by AGV needs to be in proper order, e.g., unloading from a conveyor is not possible before loading is performed on it. All the operations enter and leave the system through pick-up and drop-off points. Incomplete mission is not allowed. Mission is validated and verified for correctness and completeness at the time of its creation. Onboard AGV conveyers can be considered as a matrix V ($b \times c$) with b bays and c conveyers in each bay. Each cell of V holds current state specified by occupancy. At the start and end of mission, the cells should have a default value 0; this verifies the completeness of the mission plan. Also, every consecutive operation in a mission must leave the AGV conveyer matrix V into a valid state. A cell in V can only be loaded if it is 0 till the previous operation. Similarly, a cell in V can only be unloaded if it is 1 till the previous operation.

Table 1 Sample order of missions

Stage	Pick-up point	Drop-off point	Order
I	{CL1, CL2, CL3, CL4}	{FD1, FD2, FD3, FD4, FD5, FD6}	0
II	{FL1, FL2, FL3, FL4, FL5, FL6}	{EBD}	1
III	{EBL}	{CD1, CD2, CD3, CD4}	2

6 Mission Modeling and Simulation

A mission can be selected in various ways in order to optimize parameters like AGV performance, load on various pick-up and drop-off points, throughput of the system, etc. Spatial distribution of processing units in the material handling scenario under consideration provides cues to divide missions into three different groups. Physically, all compaction units are adjacent to each other at one location and furnaces are kept close to each other at another location. This suggests that all feeder route missions to furnaces have similar trajectory lengths and similar parameters and hence they are grouped as stage-I missions. On same logic, all product transfer missions from furnace are grouped as stage-II and all empty boat transfer missions are grouped as stage-III. Production rate of all compaction units put together is six boats per hour. This is equal to the aggregate consumption rate of all sintering furnaces in the system. Goal is to find such an order of preference for selecting the mission which satisfies the following objectives: (i) Maximize the utilization of important machines, viz., compacting units and sintering units by maintaining required material flow rate in each stage; and (ii) Minimize the usage of AGV to attain above objective.

While developing the solution, we evaluated various strategies including simple cyclic selection and first available selection. We have found that prioritizing the missions based on the stages of transfer combined with first come first serve greatly improves AGV performance and throughput of the system. The three-stage transfers can be prioritized by assigning orders 0, 1, and 2 as shown in Table 1 with 2 being the highest priority. This order can be configured on the fly and given to the controller.

6.1 Simulation Parameters

The number of jobs which can be simultaneously carried out is limited in the given scenario because of the serial nature of production process. Here, the total processing time is more or less constant and can be predetermined upon the arrival of job so the only way to optimize the throughput is to reduce the waiting times due to unavailability of required resources at processing units.

Table 2 Flow parameters in six scenarios

Flow parameters	Stage priority (I-II-II)					
	0-1-2 (scenario 1)	0-2-1 (scenario 2)	1-0-2 (scenario 3)	1-2-0 (scenario 4)	2-0-1 (scenario 5)	2-1-0 (scenario 6)
MFR I						
MFR II	2.99	3.15	2.94	6.00	3.62	6.00
MFR III	3.00	3.10	2.93	0.50	3.63	1.81
Flow variance	0.19	0.32	1.22	10.08	1.88	5.85
BS I	<600	<600	<400	≤2	≤1	≤1
BS II	≤2	≤1	<300	≤1	<500	≤2
BS III	≤3	≤4	≤3	<1000	≤6	<1000

Mean flow rate (MFR) is defined as the AGV output per hour in each stage averaged over a number of simulation runs.

$$\text{MFR} = \left(\sum \frac{\text{Boats transferred by AGV in a stage}}{total\ time} \right) / n$$

where n is the number of independent simulation runs.

Buffer status, BS, is defined as the number of boats at any time lying in the buffer waiting for the AGV service. Flow variance is defined as the variance of mean flow rates observed in different stages.

7 Performance Evaluation Using Simulation

Simulation can give a more detailed picture of system behavior in a scenario like the one being discussed here where there is a constrained flow of material involving multiprocessing units. As we grouped missions into three, there are six ways of assigning the order of preference among missions for evaluation. During the start of the simulation, AGV is bound to serve the first stage solely as there is no demand for AGV in stage 2 and 3, after some time demand for the AGV is seen in the second stage and then in the third stage. We assume the time lapsed till demand for AGV is generated in all the three stages as the warm-up period. All the statistics of system parameters are collected after this period to eliminate the bias. The data has been collected assuming 24 × 7 operation of AGV for 45 days.

The flow rate of boats achieved in each stage is a clear parameter of whether the AGV can meet the demands at all stages. From Table 2, it can be seen from the buffer status that AGV cannot meet the desired flow rate in any of the scenarios.

Table 3 AGV speed-up performance using scenario-1

Speedup	Flow parameters					
	MFR I	MFR II	MFR III	BS I	BS II	BS III
2	5.72	5.09	5.09	<150	≤1	≤2
2.2	5.82	5.45	5.4	<100	≤1	≤2
2.4	5.97	5.84	5.8	<30	≤1	≤2
2.45	5.98	5.89	5.85	<25	≤1	≤2
2.5	6.00	6.00	6.00	≈0	≈0	≈0

Table 4 Increasing empty bin flow rate by stacking

Scenario-6 with stacking of four bins	MFR I	MFR II	MFR III	BS I	BS II	BS III
	6.00	6.00	5.98	≤1	≤2	<35

Scenario-1 found to be promising in terms of flow variance with a variance of 0.19 among the three stages. Approximately, half of the required flow rate of material can only be achieved in every stage with the given AGV. As there is scope for improvement in the speed of the AGV, we have further analyzed scenario-1 at higher speeds of the AGV.

Table 3 shows the flow rates and buffer status in each stage after speeding up the AGV by 2, 2.4, 2.45, and 2.5 times the present speed. It is seen that a speedup of 2.5 is required for meeting the desired flow rate while maintaining a good buffer status.

Empty bins are several folds lighter than the loaded bins. AGV can carry a stack of bins in every conveyor and easily increase the empty bin flow rate by several folds. A fourfold increment in empty bin flow rate will make scenario-6 an apt case to meet required flow rate of materials in all stages. This case is analyzed and values are tabulated in Table 4.

8 Conclusions and Future Work

In this paper, we presented design of modular mission control architecture, mission specification, and its validation for a conveyer-based AGV in an automated material handling system. The mission definition has been formed focusing on composability, decomposability, and validation at the time of creation mission itself. Mission has been defined in terms of sequence of operations to be carried out at nodes and presented a scheme to validate the mission wherein single material type is being handled. In future, this will be extended to multiple material types and the operation will be validated for loading/unloading sequences. In the latter part, requirements from a typical fuel fabrication facility have been modeled using our software to evaluate the AGV performance. The analysis has been done with the assumption that a standby AGV is available to service the mission requests throughout the period of the operation. Achieved flow rate and the buffer status in each stage suggest that AGV needs higher speed, as high as 2.5 times the present speed, to attain a required rate of material transfer. An alternate solution surfaced in this analysis is the usage of stacked empty bins in conjunction with stage priority as described in scenario-6. As the present AGV design allows transportation of stacked empty bins, the suggested alternate solution seems more attractive.

Appendix

A.1 AGV Related Data
See Tables 5, 6, 7, and 8.

Table 5 AGV dimensions

Length (m)	Width (m)	Height (m)	Payload (kg)	Weight (Kg)	Speed (m/s)	Capacity
1.39	0.91	1.0	200	400	1.00	4 bins

Table 6 Assumed AGV parameters

Condition	Acceleration (m/s²)	Deceleration (m/s²)	Speed at straight segment (m/s)	Speed at curved segment (m/s)
Empty	0.50	0.50	0.5	0.2
Loaded	0.5	0.5	0.3	0.15

Table 7 Delay assumptions

MTBF/MTTR	Uptime	Downtime
Function	Exp(0,1000)	Uniform(50,100)

Table 8 Machines rate of production and buffer

Stations	Production rate	Buffer accumulation (assumed)
Compacting unit	1.5 boat/h	Unlimited buffer
Sintering unit	1 boat/h with a capacity of 12 boats at a time in furnace	Unlimited buffer
Empty boat station	6 min/boat	Unlimited buffer

References

1. P.K. Pal, R. Sakrikar, P.V. Sarngadharan, S. Sharma, V.K. Shrivastava, V. Dave, N. Singh, A.P. Das, Development of an AGV-based intelligent material distribution system. Current Sci. **101**(8), 2011, 1028–1035
2. N. Singh, P.V. Sarngadharan, P.K. Pal, AGV scheduling for automated material distribution: a case study. J. Intell. Manuf. **22**(2), 219–228 (2011)
3. P. Lacomme, N. Tchernev, C. Chu, An efficient framework for job input sequencing and vehicle dispatching in a flexible manufacturing system based on AGV transport (IEEE 1999)
4. S. Berman, E. Schechtman, Y. Edan, Evaluation of automatic guided vehicle systems. Robot. Comput. Integr. Manuf. **25**, 522–528 (2009)
5. M. Shneier, R. Bostelman, Literature review of mobile robots for manufacturing, May 2015, http://dx.doi.org/10.6028NIST.IR.8022
6. R. Yan, L.M. Jackson, S.J. Dunnett, Automated guided vehicle mission reliability using a combined fault tree and Petri Net approach. Int. J. Adv. Manuf. Technol. **92**(5–8), 1825–1837 (2017)
7. B. Horst, N. Hartmut, K. Takeo, *Book Series: Modelling And Planning for sensor based Intelligent Robot Systems* (1995)
8. M.R. Endsley, Toward a theory of situation awareness in dynamic systems. Hum. Factors J. **37**(1), 32–64 (1995)
9. D. Miklic, T. Petrovic, M. Coric, Z. Piskovic, S. Bogdan, A modular control system for warehouse automation—algorithms and simulations in USARSim, in *IEEE International Conference on Robotics and Automation* (2012)
10. C. Wang, L. Wang, J. Qin, Z. Wu, L. Duan, Z. Li, M. Cao, X. Ou, Path planning of automated guided vehicles based on improved a-star algorithm, in *IEEE International Conference on Information and Automation* (2015)
11. V. Dave, S. Singh, J. Kota, N. Singh, R. Sakrikar, V.K. Shrivastava, P.V. Sarngadharan, Tuning procedure for correcting systematic errors in a quad configuration AGV, in *iNaCoMM* (2017, Appearing)

On-Power Fuelling Machine
for Advanced Heavy Water Reactor

Monesh Chaturvedi, M. Dev and S. Raghunathan

Abstract Advanced Heavy Water Reactor (AHWR) is a thorium-based vertical, pressure tube type reactor. The reactor needs to be refuelled periodically mainly to maintain requisite reactivity in reactor. A dedicated, remotely operated on-power Fuelling Machine (FM) is used for this purpose. The FM removes spent fuel from reactor, replaces it with new fuel and finally transfers the spent fuel to fuel transfer system of reactor. During refuelling, the FM interacts with high temperature and high-pressure coolant channel and maintains the pressure boundary during refuelling. The FM consists of various innovative design features like limiting load on coolant channel during refuelling, maintaining isolation between V1 and V2 volumes, handling of long fuel assembly, maintaining cooling and shielding of fuel, compact configuration, etc. Safe handling of fuel is ensured by incorporating adequate safety features to avoid fall of fuel during handling. This paper covers the design requirements, challenges and features of AHWR FM.

Keywords AHWR · On-power fuelling · Refuelling · Fuelling machine
Fuel handling

1 Introduction

Fuel handling system is provided in nuclear reactors to refuel the reactor periodically. Reactors like PWR and BWR are provided with shut down fuelling system, whereas reactors like PHWR and AHWR are provided with on-power fuelling system.

M. Chaturvedi (✉) · M. Dev · S. Raghunathan
Refuelling Technology Division, Bhabha Atomic Research Centre, Mumbai, Maharashtra, India
e-mail: moneshc@barc.gov.in

M. Dev
e-mail: mdev@barc.gov.in

S. Raghunathan
e-mail: raghu@barc.gov.in

© Springer Nature Singapore Pte Ltd. 2019
D N Badodkar and T A Dwarakanath (eds.), *Machines, Mechanism and Robotics*, Lecture Notes in Mechanical Engineering,
https://doi.org/10.1007/978-981-10-8597-0_29

Advanced Heavy Water Reactor (AHWR) is a Th-^{233}U fuelled 300 MWe vertical, pressure tube type, boiling light water, natural circulation cooled reactor. The reactor is having 452 coolant channels with coolant at 558 K temperature and 7 MPa pressure. A remotely operated on-power Fuelling Machine (FM) is provided in reactor to remove the spent fuel from reactor core and to replace it with new fuel. The spent fuel removed by the FM is then discharged to fuel transfer system for transferring it outside reactor building to fuel storage bay. The on-power refuelling ensures efficient utilization of fuel, maintaining requisite reactivity in reactor and improves availability factor of reactor. It also facilitates quick removal of failed fuel from coolant channel.

On-power fuelling of natural circulation-based vertical reactor poses various design challenges like avoiding entry of hot water from coolant channel to FM, ensuring cooling of spent fuel in FM and use of fail-safe mechanisms with mechanical interlocks to prevent fall of fuel. Other engineering challenges are alignment of FM with coolant channel, making leak tight connection with coolant channel, limiting load imposed on coolant channel by FM during clamping, avoiding accidental unclamping of FM from coolant channel, separating/joining of fuel assembly parts using reliable joining mechanism during refuelling, accessibility of different mechanisms for retrieval from emergency situation, maintaining isolation of V1 (high enthalpy) and V2 (low enthalpy) volumes, addressing seismic considerations, compact configuration, etc. The design of FM is worked out to meet functional requirement and meeting above mentioned challenges. The interface components to fuel handling system like fuel assembly, sealing plug and coolant channel are also described.

2 Coolant Channel Components

The coolant channel of AHWR is a vertical assembly filled with pressurized light water coolant at high temperature. The coolant channel is provided with natural circulation flow from bottom to top, i.e. cold water enters at bottom and comes out from top. Fuel assembly is hanging inside the coolant channel from top and top end of the coolant channel is closed by a removable-type sealing plug.

2.1 Fuel Assembly

The fuel assembly of AHWR is a 10.2-m-long assembly. One fuel assembly is provided in each coolant channel. The fuel assembly is made up of three parts, viz., shield 'A', shield 'B' and fuel cluster. The top two parts are the shielding portion (shield 'A' and shield 'B') and bottom-most part is fuel cluster which contains the nuclear fuel material (Fig. 1). All the three parts of fuel assembly are kept joined together using a detachable collet joint.

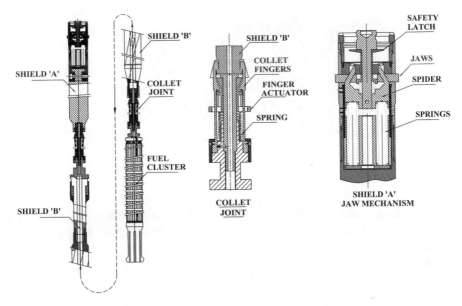

Fig. 1 AHWR fuel assembly

The fuel assembly is hanged inside the coolant channel using a jaw mechanism provided at top of the shield 'A'. During refuelling, the spent fuel assembly is removed from the core by unlocking the shield 'A' jaw mechanism. On removal, the fuel assembly is taken inside the FM and the collet joint is detached inside the FM to separate the shield 'A' from shield 'B' and shield 'B' from spent fuel cluster. During refuelling, the shield 'B' and shield 'A' are attached with fresh fuel using collet joint and inserted back into the coolant channel. The feature of attaching and separating parts of fuel assembly facilitates reuse of shield 'A' and shield 'B' and storing these parts in compact space.

2.2 Sealing Plug

Sealing plug is (Fig. 2) provided at top of the coolant channels to maintain the pressure boundary of the coolant channels. Each coolant channel is provided with one sealing plug. During refuelling, the FM clamps onto the coolant channel and removes the sealing plug. On removal of sealing plug, pressure boundary of coolant channel is extended to FM.

Sealing plug is provided with jaws to remain engaged in coolant channel end fitting. A self-energizing radial seal made of Ti alloy is provided to maintain pressure boundary with leak tightness within permissible limit. For removal of sealing plug from coolant channel, FM facilitates collapse of the jaws to detach the sealing plug

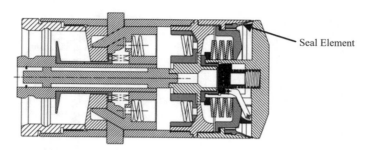

Fig. 2 Sealing plug

from end fitting groove. The lateral expansion of radial seal in this condition is relaxed and any damage to the seal is avoided during movement of sealing plug from end fitting to FM for storage in magazine.

3 Fuelling Machine

The FM consists of various subsystems/assemblies to perform different functions. Following are the major assemblies/subsystems of the FM.

3.1 FM Carriage and Trolley

FM is required to be moved and aligned with three locations, viz., identified coolant channel in reactor pile, FM maintenance area and fuel discharge location of fuel transfer system. To meet this objective, FM along with shielding is supported on a carriage and trolley which moves on rails laid on the reactor deck. Carriage provides long travel (X-direction) and trolley provides cross travel (Y-direction). With the help of X–Y travel of carriage and trolley, the FM is aligned to any designated position within ±5 mm. Further alignment is achieved using fine-X and fine-Y drives of FM support system. To avoid skidding of FM in seismic condition, the FM carriage and trolley is locked using seismic arrester after coarse alignment to designated position. The carriage and trolley is provided with guiding wheel to prevent its derailment. Carriage and trolley is driven by drive system consisting of oil hydraulic motors, gear boxes, EM brake, synchronizing shafts, etc. Drive system facilitates the movement at coarse and fine speed to achieve required alignment accuracy.

3.2 FM Shielding

FM of AHWR is provided on reactor deck which is categorized as accessible area from radiation point of view. To keep the area accessible for limited occupancy, a shielding is provided around the FM to maintain the dose rate within acceptable limit. The shielding is made of layers of various shielding materials, viz., steel, wax and lead. The shielding is supported on FM trolley and made of two parts, i.e. fixed shield and movable shield provided at bottom of fixed shield. The fixed shield remains fixed outside FM, whereas moveable shield can be moved vertically up/down w.r.t fixed shield. This feature facilitates lifting of movable shield during movement of FM from one location to another location. During refuelling, the movable shield is lowered to rest on the deck and protects against radiation streaming during refuelling.

3.3 Fuelling Machine Head

The FM head interacts with coolant channel during refuelling and houses all the mechanisms to perform the refuelling operation safely. The FM head has four major assemblies, viz., Snout assembly, separator assembly, magazine assembly and Ram assembly. Putting together, these assemblies perform the functions of clamping with coolant channel, making leak tight joint with coolant channel, removing sealing plug and fuel assembly from coolant channel, separating fuel assembly parts during refuelling, storage of different components, movement of components within FM head during different stages of refuelling, etc. FM head is the pressure boundary component of FM and always remain filled with water. Oil hydraulic motors are used in the assemblies to perform various operations, and a dedicated oil hydraulic system is used for this purpose. Following are the details of each assembly.

3.3.1 Snout Assembly

Snout assembly (Figs. 3 and 4) is the bottom-most part of the FM head. The main functions of snout assembly are to sense the misalignment of FM head with coolant channel before clamping, making leak tight connection with end fitting, ensuring safety against accidental unclamping of FM head from coolant channel, limiting load on end fitting and checking of leak tightness of sealing plug before unclamping the FM head on completion of refuelling.

During refuelling, the FM head is grossly aligned with coolant channel within ±5 mm using carriage and trolley. The FM head is then lowered (Z-direction) by 1400 mm towards coolant channel. At this condition, FM head remain around 150 mm away from coolant channel. The misalignment of FM head with coolant channel is sensed using sensing fingers attached at front of snout assembly. The FM head misalignment is corrected using FM support assembly. On fine alignment of

FM head, the snout assembly piston is actuated to further advance the snout front portion towards coolant channel. Dedicated water hydraulic circuit for this purpose ensures that the front portion is advanced with predefined force to ensure that load on end fitting does not exceed the permissible level. A metallic skinner seal is provided at front butting face of snout assembly to ensure sealing between FM head and coolant channel. Clamping on the snout assembly with end fitting is done by a cam-based lever operated by irreversible nut and screw mechanism. The nut and screw mechanism is operated by worm–worm wheel gears driven by oil hydraulic motor. To avoid accidental unclamping of snout assembly during refuelling, locking mechanism operated by FM water pressure is provided. This ensures that FM remains clamped till the time FM pressure is high. Dedicated water hydraulic circuits are provided in snout assembly to check leak tightness of metallic face seal before removing sealing plug and checking of leak tightness of sealing plug after installing sealing plug during channel normalization after refuelling.

3.3.2 Separator Assembly

Separator assembly is located above the snout assembly. The main function of this assembly is to enable attachment/detachment of fuel assembly parts (Shield 'A', shield 'B' and fuel cluster) using collet joint and hold them in FM during different stages of refuelling operation. The separator assembly also actuates the collet joint to flare/collapse the collet fingers to unlock/lock the collet joint. To perform these functions, water hydraulic based piston cylinder type linear actuators are provided in the assembly. Linear movement of these actuators is converted into rotary motion using rack and pinion mechanism to perform the intended functions. Safety feature is provided in separator assembly to prevent accidental release of fuel assembly components by providing suitable locking arrangement to the linear actuators. Also, suitable design features are provided to protect the fuel assembly from any damage in the condition when groove provided in the fuel assembly components for holding these components is not properly aligned to separator finger. The linear actuators are designed to operate using water hydraulic system and normally remain retracted due to FM pressure and hence provide free passage to components for passing through this assembly.

3.3.3 Magazine Assembly

Magazine assembly is provided in FM to store different fuel assembly components/plugs during different stages of refuelling. The magazine is having seven stations provided on a rotor. The stations are assigned one each to store snout plug, sealing plug, spare sealing plug, shield 'A', shield 'B', fresh fuel cluster and spent fuel cluster. To store the components in the magazine stations, an annular groove is provided at top portion of each station. The components like sealing plug, shield 'A' and snout plug are having jaws type mechanism to engage into the groove of stations

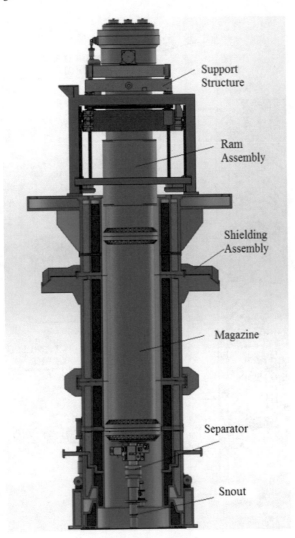

Fig. 3 Fuelling Machine

for storage. Shield 'B' and fuel cluster are not having any jaws to engage into the groove, and hence, they are first attached with a Ram Adaptor which is having jaws to facilitate their storage in magazine stations. During refuelling, the magazine rotor is rotated as per refuelling sequence to align designated station with the snout centre so that the identified component/plug can be picked and placed from one location to other location of FM/coolant channel. To achieve required alignment accuracy of magazine station with snout centre during refuelling, the magazine rotor is driven using 4-stage parallel indexer and suitable gearing arrangement. This arrangement provided one-seventh of the rotation to the magazine rotor on one rotation of input

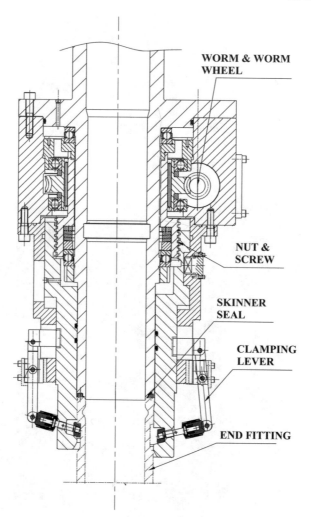

Fig. 4 Snout assembly

shaft of indexer. The indexer is connected to planetary gear box and oil hydraulic motor to rotate the magazine rotor. In case of emergency, when hydraulic motor becomes unavailable during any intermediate stage of refuelling, provision has been kept to drive the magazine rotor manually. The magazine is provided with water hydraulic connections for supply of water in FM for cooling of spent fuel cluster.

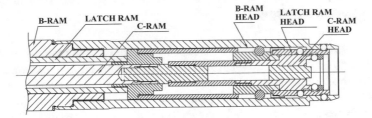

Fig. 5 Ram Head

3.3.4 Ram Assembly

Ram assembly is provided above magazine assembly to pick plugs and fuel assembly during refuelling and moving them axially from one location to other location within FM as per refuelling sequence.

To perform these operations, Ram assembly is provided with three concentric rams. The outer most ram is called Ram-B, middle ram is called Latch Ram and innermost ram is called Ram-C. The front portions of these rams are connected to a latching mechanism called Ram Head. The Ram Head is having three concentric sleeves. The outer sleeve is connected to Ram-B, inner sleeve is connected to Ram-C and middle sleeve is connected to Latch Ram. The outer and inner sleeves are provided with balls on their circumference. These balls of Ram Head are actuated by movement of Latch Ram for latching Ram Head with different plugs/Ram Adaptors. On picking the plugs/Ram Adaptors by Ram Head, the gross movement of these components from one location to other location within FM is done by moving the Ram-B. Mechanical interlocks of Ram Head and internal design of jaw mechanism of plugs/ram adaptors ensures that these components, can be latched or unlatched in locations of annular groove. This feature ensures safety during different refuelling sequences by avoiding unintended release of these components in other locations.

The total travel required by RAM-B is 7500 mm and latch ram & C-ram travel is 50 mm. To provide movement to these rams, two ball screws compatible with water environment are used. One ball screw is provided with three ball nuts, whereas other ball screw is provided with one ball nut. The bottom-most ball nuts of both the ball screws are connected to Ram-B, middle ball nut is connected to Latch Ram and top-most ball nut is connected to Ram-C. Rotation of ball screws provides simultaneous movement to Ram-B, Latch Ram and Ram-C, whereas independent rotation of ball nut of Latch Ram and Ram-C provides independent movement to these rams for which two drive shafts with independent drive system are provided. At top of the Ram Assembly, oil hydraulic motor based drive system is provided for synchronized rotation of both the ball screws for Ram-B movement and independent rotation of Latch Ram and Ram-C nut using suitable spline and gearing arrangement. Balanced shaft seals are used for sealing the driveshafts penetrating through pressure housing. Movements of rams are monitored using potentiometers provided in respective drive systems (Fig. 5).

3.4   Support Assembly

The entire FM head is supported on a support assembly. The function of support assembly is to provide Z-movement (vertical) to FM head for approaching towards coolant channel for clamping. The support assembly is also provided with Fine-X and Fine-Y drives to precisely align the FM with coolant channel. The support assembly is provided with two ball screws to provide the Z-movement. Two linear guides are also provided to prevent any eccentric load on ball screws. The ball screws are connected to oil hydraulic motor based drive system including irreversible gear reducer, EM brake and synchronizing shafts to provide the Z-motion.

3.5   V1-V2 Isolation

The FM is located at reactor deck which is a low enthalpy area called V2 area. During refuelling, the snout of FM head clamps to coolant channel which is located in high enthalpy area is called V1 area. As per reactor design requirement, the V1 and V2 areas shall be kept isolated from each other. To meet this requirement, inflatable seal based V1–V2 isolation arrangement is provided at two places in FM shielding: First between fixed shield and movable shield and second between fixed shield and Ram assembly pressure housing outer surface. During relative movement between these components, the pressure of inflatable seal is lowered to reduce the friction between the components and in static condition, the pressure is restored to achieve the desired sealing.

3.6   FM Water Hydraulic System

Dedicated water hydraulic system is provided in the FM to achieve cooling of spent fuel cluster, to maintain pressure in FM head, to avoid entry of hot water from coolant channel to FM head, to provide cooling to various mechanical seals and also to operate various water hydraulic actuators like separator assembly linear actuators and snout emergency lock. The water hydraulic system takes feed from reactor main heat transport system through a tank and returns the water to same tank. The water hydraulic system consists of positive displacement pump, filters, valve station, catenaries, etc. Adequate redundancy & design provisions are provided in the system to ensure that failure of any components does not hamper the supply of water to FM.

4 Emergency/Off-Normal Conditions

During refuelling, the FM interacts with coolant channel and exchanges new fuel with spent fuel. During this exchange operation, design basis events leading to off-normal condition of the system have been postulated. A systematic evaluation of each event is carried out to ensure that cooling of fuel cluster is available at all the time and system is able to restore to safe state. Built-in safety features/design provisions are made available in the system to take care of such situations. Various emergency/off-normal conditions like station blackout (Class IV and class III power supply not available), hot water backup in fuelling machine, unavailability of oil hydraulic system to operate various actuators, failure of magazine water supply line, failure of magazine return line, sealing plug leakage, failure of control computers/operator interface system, failure of control power supplies, etc. are considered in design of the system and ensured that mitigation & retrieval from any scenario at any intermediate stage of refuelling is possible.

5 Conclusion

On-power refuelling of reactor is a critical task in AHWR considering requirement of safe operation during refuelling. This becomes further complicated due to vertical configuration of reactor, and innovative provisions are required to meet the challenges. FM is designed using reliable mechanical systems/components, ease of handling during maintenance, design optimization for compactness of the system, approachability to different components during emergency condition and use of adequate redundancy in critical systems related to controls, instrumentation, hydraulic system for safe fuel handling operation. Design uses indigenously manufactured components to ensure long-term availability. Experience of fuel handling system of previous generation reactors has been useful in working out of the design of FM.

Acknowledgements Design of fuelling machine is a multidisciplinary activity requiring involvement of different domain experts related to equipment design, design analysis, water and oil hydraulic system, sensors and control, QA, experimentation, etc. Authors would like to express their sincere thanks to different domain experts actively involved in design and development of FM.

Effect of Whole-Body Flexibility of Caudal Fin on Propulsion Performance

N. Srinivasa Reddy, Soumen Sen, Chandan Har
and Sankar Nath Shome

Abstract Naturally evolved fish fins display superior qualities over conventional man-made thrusters by offering better maneuverability, less or no noise, and better efficiency. Caudal fin of a fish contributes most of the thrust force in fish swimming through body and fin undulations. Fish fins naturally happen to be flexible. The present work investigates the effect of whole-body flexibility of caudal fin on thrust production. A flexible trapezoidal fin is modeled as series of rigid segments connected with torsion springs and the governing equations of motion are obtained through multi-body dynamics approach. The hydrodynamic force acting on the fin segments is calculated as summation of drag and added mass force components. Simulations are carried out with different stiffness profiles for different motion parameters. The results show that flexible fins perform better than the rigid fin and different motion parameters require different stiffness profiles for higher thrust production and better efficiency.

Keywords Underwater propulsion · Flexible fin · Multi-body dynamics
Thrust force · Fin efficiency

N. Srinivasa Reddy (✉)
Academy of Scientific and Innovative Research, Chennai, Tamil Nadu, India
e-mail: nsreddy@cmeri.res.in

N. Srinivasa Reddy · S. Sen (✉) · C. Har · S. N. Shome (✉)
CSIR-Central Mechanical Engineering Research Institute,
Durgapur 713209, West Bengal, India
e-mail: soumen_sen@cmeri.res.in

C. Har
e-mail: c_har@cmeri.res.in

S. N. Shome
e-mail: snshome@cmeri.res.in

© Springer Nature Singapore Pte Ltd. 2019
D N Badodkar and T A Dwarakanath (eds.), *Machines, Mechanism and Robotics*, Lecture Notes in Mechanical Engineering,
https://doi.org/10.1007/978-981-10-8597-0_30

1 Introduction

Aquatic animals widely use fins or webbed feet to move around in waters. Fishes are good swimmers with impeccable maneuverability, stealth, and efficiency. Man-made conventional underwater actuators like thrusters are noisy which make them unfit for stealth operations and can potentially disturb the surrounding aquatic environment. The noise of the thrusters can cause interference in the communication between different aquatic species and may also cause trauma [1, 2]. Biomimetic propulsive devices are thought to be better alternative to solve some aforementioned problems. Biomimicking of fish propulsion, to make fin-like propulsive devices suitable for small size aquatic robots, require reasonable knowledge and understanding of the fish fins from their design to the functionality. The potential applications of flexible fins include small underwater swimming robots, underwater vehicles, fin-based wave energy harvesting devices, etc.

Fish swim in two distinct modes—BCF (body and/or caudal fin) and MPF (median and/or paired fins) [3]. In BCF mode, thrust is generated by body and caudal fin (tail) undulations. Motion parameters (amplitude and frequency), geometry, and stiffness of the fin are the main factors that influence the propulsion performance. While it is very difficult to asses these factors by experimentation with live fishes, robotic fins and simulations offer better test platform and can be made to suit the purpose. Many robotic fin designs reported in literature include rigid flat plate fins [4], foils [5, 6], and multi-joint fin-ray models [7, 8]. The hydrodynamic effects of the different fin shapes remain inconclusive and not fully understood [9]. The shape effect shares a complex relationship along with stiffness in determining the swimming performance [10]. The optimum aspect ratio of the fin may depend on the swimming speed. Simulation results in [9] with flexible rectangular fins of different aspect ratios show that fins of low aspect ratio encounter less drag leading to higher swimming speed and are more economical. Also, the swimming velocity peaks at first natural frequency regardless of the aspect ratio. Fin compliance and bending pattern are important for vectoring hydrodynamic forces to generate thrust and maintaining high swimming economy by minimizing energy dissipation [9, 11].

Fish fins are flexible and also they actively control the fin-ray curvature by differential muscle activity [11]. Inspired by the variable flexural stiffness profile of the fish fin rays, this work investigates the effect of whole-body flexibility of the trapezoidal fins on propulsion performance. For the analysis, flexible fins are considered as series of rigid segments connected with torsion springs. The dynamics of the flapping flexible fin are modeled through multi-body dynamics approach by considering the hydrodynamic force acting on the fin as an external force.

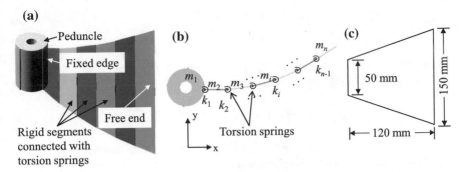

Fig. 1 **a** Multi-segment model—isometric view **b** top view **c** trapezoidal fin dimensions considered in this work

2 Dynamic Model of the Flexible Fin

The hydrodynamic loads acting on the flapping flexible fin can cause large deformation. It is accepted in the literature that multi-segment approximation method predicts the flexible fin behavior better than linear Euler–Bernoulli beam theory in case of large deformation [12]. In multi-segment approximation, a continuous flexible fin is considered as a series of rigid segments connected with passive torsion springs as shown in Fig. 1 and can be modeled through multi-body dynamics approach [13]. The governing equation of motion of the flexible fin with N segments is given in the matrix form as

$$[a]\{\ddot{x}\} + [b]\{\dot{x}\} + [c]\{\dot{x}\} = \{F\} \tag{1}$$

where $\{x\}^T = \{\theta_1 \ \theta_2 \ \theta_3 \ ... \ \theta_N\}$ is the generalized coordinate vector consisting of all joint rotations. The matrix $[a]$ is the generalized inertia matrix, the matrices $[b]$, $[c]$ account for the quadratic velocity terms and Coriolis effects, respectively, and $\{F\}$ is the generalized active force consisting of hydrodynamic forces and torsion spring torques. Detail description and automated procedure to compute these matrices can be found in [13]. The hydrodynamic force acting on each fin segment is calculated through blade element approach [14, 15] as the summation of acceleration-dependent added mass force and velocity dependent drag force.

A sinusoidal motion constraint, Eq. (2), is imposed on the peduncle to simulate the flapping fin behavior.

$$\theta_1 = \sigma \ \sin(2\pi f t) \tag{2}$$

where σ is the amplitude, f is the flapping frequency, and t is the time. The velocity and acceleration level constraints are obtained by differentiating the position level constraint, Eq. (2), as

$$[B]\{\dot{x}\} = \{g\} \tag{3}$$

$$[B]\{\ddot{x}\} = \{\dot{g}\} \tag{4}$$

where $[B]=[1\ 0\ 0\ 0\ ...0]_{1 \times N}$ and $\{g\} = 2\pi f \sigma \cos(2\pi f t)$. The constraint force is taken in to account in the equations of motion as

$$[a]\{\ddot{x}\} + [b]\{\dot{x}\} + [c]\{\dot{x}\} = \{F\} - [B]^T\{\lambda\} \tag{5}$$

where λ is the Lagrange undetermined multiplier and it is eliminated by multiplying Eq. (5) with the orthogonal complement of $[B]$.

$$[W]([a]\{\ddot{x}\} + [b]\{\dot{x}\} + [c]\{\dot{x}\} - \{F\}) = 0 \tag{6}$$

where $[W]_{(N-1) \times N}$ is the orthogonal complement of $[B]$ which satisfies $[W][B]^T = 0_{(N-1) \times 1}$. Now, Eqs. (6) and (4) are clubbed and represented in simple form as

$$[A]\{\ddot{x}\} - [D] = 0 \tag{7}$$

where $[A] = \begin{bmatrix} [W][a] \\ [B] \end{bmatrix}$ and $[D] = \begin{bmatrix} [W]([F] - [b]\{\dot{x}\} - [c]\{\dot{x}\}) \\ [\dot{g}] \end{bmatrix}$. The behavior of the constrained multi-segment fin model is governed by Eq. (7).

3 Effect of Whole-Body Flexibility

Four trapezoidal fins of same size and different stiffness profiles of biologically relevant magnitudes are considered for comparative analysis. Of these, three fins are flexible with different stiffness profiles and fourth one is rigid which does not deform, in any practical sense, under any loading conditions. The assumed stiffness profiles of the flexible fins are as shown in Fig. 2. Stiffness profile of flexible fin 1 and flexible fin 3 is considered to be linearly increasing and decreasing, respectively, from fixed edge toward free end. A uniform stiffness profile is considered for the flexible fin 2. While flexible fin 1 corresponds to the scenario of a uniform thickness trapezoidal fin, flexible fin 3 reflects the scenario of a biological fish fin with tapered fin rays.

The effect of whole-body flexibility is analyzed by utilizing the developed dynamic model. The pseudo-upper triangular decomposition (PUTD) method [16] is used to compute the orthogonal complement $[W]$. Equation (7) is solved by using standard ODE solver in Matlab software package (Mathworks, Natick, MA, USA) with error tolerance of 1e−3 for different motion parameters and stiffness profiles.

Mean thrust force and mean thrust-to-input power (T/P) ratio are the two important parameters considered for comparative analysis of the aforementioned flexible fins and rigid fin. Thrust force is the component of hydrodynamic force acting on

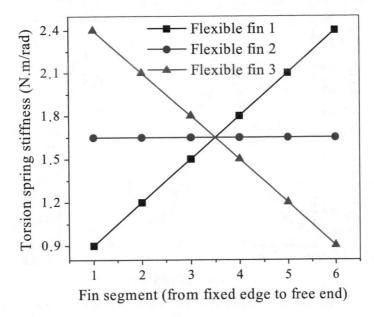

Fig. 2 Stiffness profiles of three trapezoidal flexible fins

the fin along the negative x-axis. Input power is the energy consumed per unit time for making the fins oscillate under the influence of the hydrodynamic force. A high thrust-to-power ratio is desirable for better performance in terms of energy efficiency.

Figure 3 shows the nature of the thrust force produced by all the four fins for one cycle of flapping motion with 15° amplitude and 1.0 Hz frequency. The flapping motion of the fins produces time-varying thrust force with two peaks of positive thrust and little negative thrust. Although the nature of the thrust force generated by the flexible and rigid fins is same, it differs in magnitude. Figure 4a, b show mean thrust for amplitudes $\sigma = 15°$ and 30°, respectively, for flapping frequencies $f = $ 1.0, 1.5, 2.0, and 2.5 Hz. It can be observed from Fig. 4 that the rigid fin generated relatively lower thrust force for lower motion frequencies and higher thrust force than the flexible fin 1 and flexible fin 2 at higher frequencies. However, flexible fin 3 which resembles the biological fish fin generated higher thrust force for all simulated motion parameters. It is evident from Fig. 4, in the case of flexible fin 1 and flexible fin 2, that the mean thrust gradually increases with increase in frequency till it reaches a peak value and then drops slowly with further increment in frequency. The frequency range considered in this work may be insufficient to observe the same phenomenon in the case of flexible fin 3. However, in the case of rigid fin, the mean thrust consistently increased with increase in frequency. This shows that there exists an optimum motion frequency for a flexible fin with given stiffness profile which results in maximum thrust force generation.

Figure 5 shows T/P ratio for different motion parameters, $f = $ 1.0, 1.5, 2.0, 2.5 Hz and amplitudes $\sigma = 15°$, 30°. While the flexible fin 1 achieved higher T/P

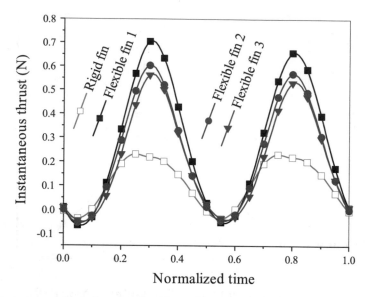

Fig. 3 Instantaneous thrust force generated for motion parameters $\sigma = 15°$ and $f = 1.0$ Hz

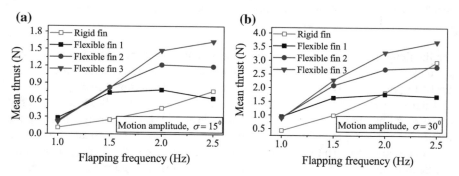

Fig. 4 Mean thrust force generated by the rigid and flexible fins for different motion amplitudes and frequencies

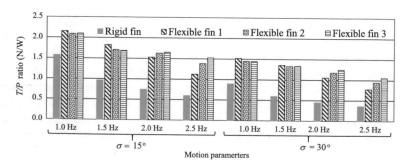

Fig. 5 Mean thrust-to-power ratio

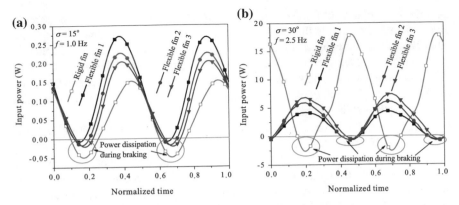

Fig. 6 Input power for the rigid and flexible fins executing flapping motion with **a** $\sigma = 15°$, $f = 1.0$ Hz and **b** $\sigma = 30°$, $f = 2.5$ Hz

ratio at lower motion frequencies, flexible fin 3 achieved higher T/P ratio at higher frequencies. The flexible fin 2 exhibited medium performance in terms of thrust force generation and T/P ratio for all the motion parameters. It can be noticed from Fig. 5 that the T/P ratio of the rigid fin is lesser compared to that of all the three flexible fins for all the motion parameters. The difference among the four fins in mean thrust generation and T/P ratio is less for slower motion ($\sigma = 15°$, $f = 1.0$ Hz) and high for faster motion ($\sigma = 30°$, $f = 2.5$ Hz). The instantaneous power input for one cycle of motion corresponding to these two cases is as shown in Fig. 6. The negative power represents the dissipated power during braking where the reversal of motion occurs in oscillatory motion. Higher levels of efficiency can be achieved by minimizing the power dissipation. It can be noticed from Fig. 6 that more energy get dissipated for the case of rigid fin compared to flexible fins. Flexible fins store the energy while braking and release when required during flapping motion. This clearly shows the advantage of using flexible fins, similar to those found in nature, over rigid fins to achieve better efficiency levels. However, optimum stiffness profiles for different swimming conditions are to be found in order to derive complete benefits of using flexible fins.

4 Conclusion and Future Work

In the present work, a multi-segment model of the flexible trapezoidal caudal fin is formulated through multi-body dynamics approach. To analyze the effect of whole-body flexibility of the fin on its propulsion performance, three different stiffness profiles (increasing stiffness from fixed edge to free end, uniform stiffness, and decreasing stiffness) are considered. Mean thrust force and mean thrust-to-power ratio are the two important performance parameters considered for comparative analysis of flexible fins and a rigid fin. The simulation results with different motion parameters show that the flexible fins could generate higher thrust forces than the rigid fin. Also, the results show that there exist an optimum frequency for the flexible fin with given stiffness which results in maximum thrust production. The mean thrust-to-power ratio of the fins shows that flexible fins are more energy efficient than the rigid fin. Among all the considered flexible fins, the flexible fin 1 with increasing stiffness profile exhibits slightly higher thrust-to-power (T/P) ratio at lower motion frequencies and the flexible fin 3 with decreasing stiffness profile exhibits higher thrust-to-power ratio at higher frequencies. These results show that the whole-body flexibility of the fin greatly effects the thrust generation and energy efficiency of the fin. The developed dynamic model of the caudal fin serves as prerequisite to the numerical optimization studies. A comprehensive study on numerical optimization of stiffness distribution of the caudal fin for thrust as well as efficiency maximization and experimental validation of the results obtained will constitute the future work.

Acknowledgements This work has been carried out at CSIR-CMERI, Durgapur, India under the activities of the project (GAP-152812) funded by Department of Science and Technology, Govt. of India.

References

1. J.A. Hildebrand, Impacts of anthropogenic sound, in *Marine Mammal Research: Conservation Beyond Crisis*, pp. 101–124 (2005)
2. L.E. Wysocki, J.P. Dittami, F. Ladich, Ship noise and cortisol secretion in european freshwater fishes. Biol. Conserv. **128**(4), 501–508 (2006)
3. M. Sfakiotakis, D.M. Lane, J.B.C. Davies, Review of fish swimming modes for aquatic locomotion. IEEE J. Ocean. Eng. **24**(2), 237–252 (1999)
4. H. Suzuki, N. Kato, K. Suzumori, Load characteristics of mechanical pectoral fin. Exp. Fluids **44**(5), 759–771 (2008)
5. M.B. Read, Performance of biologically inspired flapping foils. Ph.D. Thesis, Massachusetts Institute of Technology (2006)
6. S. Licht, V. Polidoro, M. Flores, F.S. Hover, M.S. Triantafyllou, Design and projected performance of a flapping foil auv. IEEE J. Ocean. Eng. **29**(3), 786–794 (2004)
7. Y. Cai, S. Bi, L. Zheng, Design optimization of a bionic fish with multi-joint fin rays. Adv. Robot. **26**(1–2), 177–196 (2012)
8. C.J. Esposito, J.L. Tangorra, B.E. Flammang, G.V. Lauder, A robotic fish caudal fin: effects of stiffness and motor program on locomotor performance. J. Exp. Biol. **215**(1), 56–67 (2012)
9. P.D. Yeh, A. Alexeev, Effect of aspect ratio in free-swimming plunging flexible plates. Comput. Fluids **124**, 220–225 (2016)
10. K.L. Feilich, G.V. Lauder, Passive mechanical models of fish caudal fins: effects of shape and stiffness on self-propulsion. Bioinspir. Biomim. **10**(3), 036002 (2015)
11. G.V. Lauder, P.G. Madden, Learning from fish: kinematics and experimental hydrodynamics for roboticists. Int. J. Autom. Comput. **3**(4), 325–335 (2006)
12. J. Wang, P.K. McKinley, X. Tan, Dynamic modeling of robotic fish with a flexible caudal fin," in *Proceedings of the ASME 2012 5th Annual Dynamic Systems and Control Conference joint with the JSME 2012 11th Motion and Vibration Conference, Oct*, pp. 17–19, 2012
13. F. Amirouche, *Fundamentals of Multibody Dynamics: Theory and Applications* (Springer Science & Business Media, 2007)

14. J.M. Gal, R. Blake, Biomechanics of frog swimming: I. Estimation of the propulsive force generated by hymenochirus boettgeri. J. Exp. Biol. **138**(1), 399–411 (1988)
15. J.M. Gal, R. Blake, Biomechanics of frog swimming: II. Mechanics of the limb-beat cycle in hymenochirus boettgeri. J. Exp. Biol. **138**(1), 413–429 (1988)
16. F. Amirouche, T. Jia, Pseudouptriangular decomposition method for constrained multibody systems using Kane's equations. J. Guid. Control. Dyn. **11**(1), 39–46 (1988)

Comparative Evaluation of Steering Configurations for a 6 × 6 Wheeled Armoured Vehicle

V. V. Jagirdar, V. P. Maskar and M. W. Trikande

Abstract Mechanized forces of armies world over tend to use multi-axle vehicles for their versatile capability of deployment on-road and off-road operations. Manoeuverability on-road requires good high-speed control defined by handling characteristics and manoeuverability off-road required ability to overcome hairpin bends; this requires smaller turning circle radius. Studies pertaining to the selection of appropriate steering strategy are very limited. One of the approaches is utilizing a bicycle model of the vehicle. Bicycle model assumes the same magnitude for angle of left and right wheels; this holds good for large turning radii. Further to this, all steering strategies are evolved and those apt for practical implementation are considered in study. A worldwide survey of vehicles of similar class was also carried out. Four strategies were found after this exercise: first axle steer, first two-axle steer, first and last axle steer and all axle steer. An combined nonlinear ride and handling model developed using Simulink is used for carrying out the study. Physical parameters considered are lateral acceleration, yaw angle and vehicle side slip angle. If forward speed of the vehicle is assumed constant, higher magnitudes of lateral acceleration and yaw angle indicate vehicle ability to take a sharp turn or in other words better manoeuverability. Side slip angle is the difference between vehicle axis and the wheel axis. Vehicle designers strive to achieve near zero side slip angle. Apart from steering, other inputs considered are drive torque and road undulations. Longitudinal vehicle dynamics is of little consequence to this study and hence, equal and constant drive torque to all wheels is applied. Road undulations are provided as an input to the model from smoothened power spectral density (PSD) hyperbolic curve. The road undulation is defined by 'C' and 'N' values from ISO: 8608. For rough runway, the values of C and N are 8.1×10^{-06} and 2.1, respectively. The simulations were carried out at various constant speeds, and results were obtained.

V. V. Jagirdar (✉) · V. P. Maskar (✉) · M. W. Trikande
Vehicles Research and Development Establishment (VRDE), Ahmednagar, India
e-mail: vinit.jagirdar@gmail.com

V. P. Maskar
e-mail: maskarvikasp@gmail.com; vikaspmaskar@gmail.com

M. W. Trikande
e-mail: mukund.trikande@gmail.com

© Springer Nature Singapore Pte Ltd. 2019
D N Badodkar and T A Dwarakanath (eds.), *Machines, Mechanism and Robotics*, Lecture Notes in Mechanical Engineering,
https://doi.org/10.1007/978-981-10-8597-0_31

Keywords Mathematical modelling · Multi-axle steering · Random road · Ride
Handling · Multi-body simulation

Notations

F_{xi} Longitudinal force generated by the tyre [N]
F_{yi} Lateral force generated by the tyre (N)
M_s Sprung mass (kg)
m_u Unsprung mass (kg)
C_1 Cornering stiffness of tyres on first axle (N/rad)
C_2 Cornering stiffness of tyres on second axle (N/rad)
C_3 Cornering stiffness of tyres on third axle (N/rad)
C_4 Cornering stiffness of tyres on fourth axle (N/rad)
C_α Nominal cornering stiffness (N/rad)
C_s Longitudinal stiffness of tyres on all tyres (N/slip)
C_{yl} Lateral force lag coefficient
I_x Mass moment of inertia, X-axis (kg m^2)
I_y Mass moment of inertia, Y-axis (kg m^2)
I_z Mass moment of inertia, Z-axis (kg m^2)
I_{wi} Moment of inertia for all wheels (kg m^2)
V_x Vehicle speed (m/s^2)
T_i Input torque on each wheel (N m)
R_i Rolling resistance coefficient (N m)
B_s Damping coefficient of suspension (N s/m)
l_1 Distance from centre of gravity to first axle(m)
l_2 Distance from centre of gravity to second axle (m)
l_3 Distance from centre of gravity to third axle (m)
l_4 Distance from centre of gravity to fourth axle (m)
S_i Longitudinal slip for each tyre
ε_r Road adhesion reduction factor (s/m)
k_s Spring stiffness (N/m)
F_x Force in longitudinal direction (N)
F_y Force in lateral direction (N)
F_z Force in vertical direction (N)
M_x Rolling moment (N/m)
M_y Pitching moment (N/m)
M_z Yaw moment (N/m)
k_t Tyre stiffness (N/m)
k_r Rollbar stiffness (N/m)
R_w Wheel radius (m)
μ Friction coefficient
t Track (m)
α_i Slip angle

r	Yaw velocity
β	Sideslip angle
δ_i	Steer angle
θ	Pitch angle
$\emptyset$	Roll angle
φ	Yaw angle

1 Introduction

Multi-axle wheeled vehicles are widely used by mechanized forces of armies world-wide for their suitability on-road and off-road mobility. There are multiple possibilities in terms of steering configuration, and a variety of those have been implemented by armies. There is dearth of technical literature on selection of suitable steering configuration for multi-axle vehicle. Multi-axle trucks have been in use for long, and selection of the steering configuration is driven by simplicity of design, required manoeuverability on roads and utilization of availability of under chassis space. Commercial multi-axle trucks tend to lift off one of the intermediate axles to avoid tyre scrub while turning. Application of steering strategy of multi-axle trucks to wheeled armoured vehicles is not valid approach. Wheeled armoured vehicles are equipped with independent suspension with to achieve higher cross-country speed and springs with rising rate characteristics such as hydro-pneumatic struts. Load distribution on axles is almost uniform. However, there is scarcity of studies related to steering configuration and handling studies of armoured vehicle. Among these, design variations of existing vehicle were studies using vehicle dynamic simulations define best axles configuration for a 6×6 military vehicle by Franco [1]. Bayar and Samim Unlusoy [2] used the strategies from four-wheel steering in two-axle vehicles and applied to three- and four-axle vehicles. An integrated nonlinear ride and handling model in Matlab and Simulink environment is used for simulations. It is shown that lateral acceleration and yaw velocity responses can be improved while keeping zero vehicle sideslip angle by steering wheels on intermediate axles. Huh et al. [3] investigated handling performance of six-wheeled special-purpose vehicles. Vehicle model is built using Matlab/Simulink such that effect of change in input and vehicle parameters is seen. It is demonstrated from simulation that effect of middle-wheel steering on handling characteristics such as yaw rate, lateral acceleration, etc. is noticeable. Qu et al. [4] carried out three-axle vehicle with only front and rear wheel steering strategies, and steered wheels on intermediate axles were not considered. Nalecz et al. [5] reported that four-wheel steering systems are being developed to enhance the dynamic response characteristics of passenger vehicles. Control methodology used to steer the rear wheels varies with manufacturer. These systems enhance the response of the vehicles at high speed by steering the rear wheels in the same direction as the front wheels in order to reduce vehicle sideslip and the time required by the vehicle to achieve steady state.

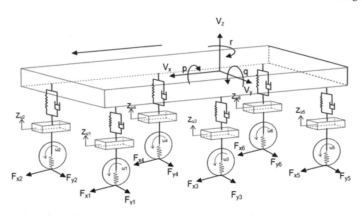

Fig. 1 6 × 6 vehicle model (illustrated) wheel rotation

1.1 Modelling of Six-Wheeled Vehicle

Vehicle Dynamics Model

The six-wheeled vehicle model is represented in Fig. 1. A mathematical model of the vehicle as shown in the figure is developed. The sprung mass has three translations, and three rotations along X−, Y− and Z− axes, respectively. F_x, F_y and F_z are forces in longitudinal, lateral and vertical directions. M_x, M_y and M_z are the resultant moments about X−, Y− and Z− axes, respectively. The equations of motion are written as follows:

Longitudinal motion

$$\sum F_x = M_s\left(\dot{V}_x + V_z q - V_y r\right) \tag{1}$$

Lateral motion

$$\sum F_y = M_s\left(\dot{V}_y + V_x r - V_z p\right) \tag{2}$$

Vertical motion

$$\sum F_z = M_s\left(\dot{V}_z + V_y p - V_x q\right) \tag{3}$$

Roll motion

$$M_x = (I_x \times \dot{p}) + \left(I_z - I_y\right)r \times q \tag{4}$$

Pitch motion

$$M_y = \left(I_y \times \dot{q}\right) + (I_x - I_z)r \times p \tag{5}$$

Fig. 2 Wheel dynamics

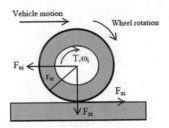

Yaw motion

$$M_z = (I_z \times \dot{r}) + (I_y - I_x)p \times q \tag{6}$$

Unsprung mass motion is represented by equation

$$M_u\ddot{Z}_u = \left(k_s(Z_s - Z_u) + B_s(\dot{Z}_s - \dot{Z}_u) - k_t(Z_u - Z_g) - k_r t\right) \tag{7}$$

From Fig. 2, the following equation can be written for traction:

$$w_i = \frac{1}{I_{wi}}(T_i - r_{wi}F_{xi} + r_{wi}R_i) \tag{8}$$

where ωi denotes rotational speed, F_{xi} longitudinal force and Ri rolling resistance. T is the drive torque coming to the wheel.

Tyre model, a mathematically simple Dugoff 1970 tyre model, is used to calculate longitudinal force generated by tyre (F_{xi}) using equations given below.

F_{xi} is longitudinal force generated by the tyre.

$$F_{xi} = \frac{C_s S_i}{(1 - S_i)}X_i(2 - X_i) \tag{9}$$

F_{yi} is lateral force generated by the tyre.

$$F_{yi} = \frac{C_\alpha \tan \alpha_i}{(1 - S_i)}X_i(2 - X_i) \tag{10}$$

Longitudinal slip for each tyre is expressed as

$$S_i = \begin{cases} \frac{r_w \omega_i - V_i}{r_w \omega_i} & \text{if } r_w \omega_i \leq V_i \text{ (in acceleration)} \end{cases} \tag{11}$$

$$X_i = \begin{cases} X_i & \text{if } X_i \leq 1 \\ 1 & \text{if } X_i > 1 \end{cases}$$

Total slip coefficient considering the slip angle and the slip ratio

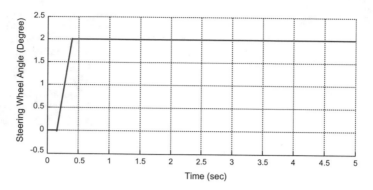

Fig. 3 Shows ramp steering wheel input used for the simulation

$$X_i = \frac{\mu F_{zi}(1 - S_i)\left(1 - \varepsilon_r V_i \sqrt{S_i^2 + \tan^2 \alpha_i}\right)}{2\sqrt{C_s^2 S_i^2 + C_\alpha^2 \tan^2 \alpha_i}} \tag{12}$$

Bicycle model has been considered, assuming left and right wheels steer at almost equal angles for large turning radius. No longitudinal or lateral motion is allowed for unsprung mass, and pure vertical motion along Z-axis is assumed. It is also assumed that there is no longitudinal load transfer due to traction or braking and no change in steering angle due to bump, body roll steer and change in wheel camber angle. Three inputs have been considered for this model, viz., tractive effort in the form for torque on wheels, road undulations and steering angle at wheels. Equal and constant drive torque to all wheels is applied, since the objective of this work is vehicle handling, and longitudinal dynamics of the vehicle is neglected. The road undulation is given below and is defined by 'C' and 'N' values from ISO: 8608.

1.2 Steering Wheel Input

See Fig. 3

$$G(\Omega) = \frac{C}{\Omega^N} \tag{13}$$

For rough runway, the values of C and N are 8.1×10^{-06} and 2.1, respectively. Figure 4 shows road profile generated for rough runway using above-defined relationship..

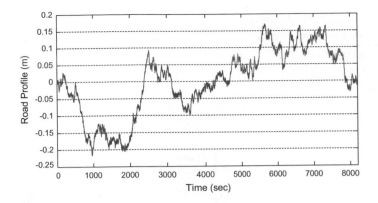

Fig. 4 Road profile representing rough runway

1.3 Steering Strategies

Yaw rate and lateral acceleration affects handling behaviour of vehicle. Simple single track model, i.e. bicycle model, has been used for comparison of steering strategies, where β is the vehicle sideslip angle, r is the yaw velocity, δ_i is the steering angle of axles, C is the cornering stiffness of the tyres, M is the mass of the vehicle, I_z is the mass moment of inertia of the vehicle along the Z-axis, V_x is vehicle velocity in longitudinal direction and l is the distance from centre of gravity. Equation 14 is derived from bicycle model of the vehicle as shown in Fig. 5.

$$
= \begin{bmatrix} \dfrac{-2(C_1+C_2+C_3)}{M_s V_x} & -1 - \dfrac{(2(l_1 C_1 - l_2 C_2 - l_3 C_3))}{M_s V_x^2} \\[2mm] \dfrac{-2(l_1 C_1 - l_2 C_2 - l_3 C_3)}{I_z} & \dfrac{-2(l_1^2 C_1 + l_2^2 C_2 + l_3^2 C_3)}{I_z V_x} \end{bmatrix} \begin{Bmatrix} \beta \\ r \end{Bmatrix}
$$

$$
+ \begin{bmatrix} \dfrac{2C_1}{M_s V_x} & \dfrac{2C_2}{M_s V_x} & \dfrac{2C_3}{M_s V_x} \\[2mm] \dfrac{2l_1 C_1}{I_z} & \dfrac{-2l_2 C_2}{I_z} & \dfrac{-2l_3 C_3}{I_z} \end{bmatrix} \begin{Bmatrix} \delta_1 \\ \delta_2 \\ \delta_3 \end{Bmatrix} \tag{14}
$$

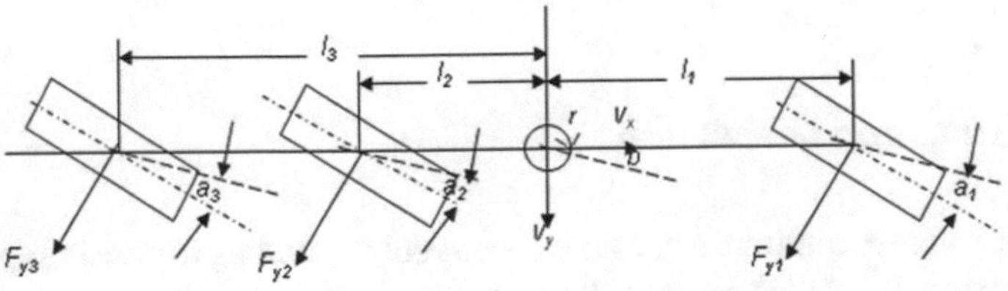

Fig. 5 Bicycle model for a three-axle vehicle

Table 1 Steering angle relationship

Steering angle on Steerable axles	First axle	Second axle	Third axle
Front axle steerable (1)	δ	0	0
Front and middle axle steerable (1 + 2)	δ	0.61δ	0
Front and rear axle steerable (1 + 3)	δ	0	δ
Front, middle, rear axles steerable (1 + 2 + 3)	δ	0.13δ	δ

$$\alpha_1 = \frac{(V_y - rl_1)}{V_x} - \delta_1 \tag{15}$$

$$\alpha_2 = \frac{(V_y - rl_2)}{V_x} - \delta_2 \tag{16}$$

$$\alpha_3 = \frac{(V_y - rl_3)}{V_x} - \delta_3 \tag{17}$$

This study has been carried out for four steering configurations as mentioned in Table 1. These steering configurations were evaluated and compared. These steering configurations evolved are a combination of front wheel steer (FWS), intermediate wheel steer (IWS) and rear wheel steer. For a large turning radius, wheels on left and right will turn at almost equal angles. Front wheel steer is common across all configuration and wheels on intermediate and rear axle turn in proportion with front wheel steering angle. If forward speed of the vehicle is assumed constant, higher magnitudes of lateral acceleration and yaw angle indicate vehicle ability to take sharp turn or in other words better manoeuverability. Side slip angle is the difference between vehicle axis and the wheel axis. Vehicle designers strive to achieve near zero side slip angle. Simulation flowchart followed in this study is shown in Fig. 6. Table 1 shows steering angle relationship of the axles with respect to first axle for the steering strategies. A ramp input of 2° was given to front steering wheels (Fig. 4). Forward speed of 40 kmph has been maintained constant throughout simulation to ascertain that the effect on vehicle dynamic parameters is on account of steering configuration. The simulation was repeated at constant speeds of 60, 80 and 100 kmph. Effect of change in steering configuration on handling parameters, viz., side slip angle, yaw velocity and lateral acceleration, is carried out in this study. Each steering strategy is indicated by the number of steerable axle.

1.4 Results and Discussion

Simulations were carried out at constant speeds corresponding to cruising speed up to vehicle maximum speed in steps of 20 kmph. Constant driving torque as acceleration performance is of little significance in this study. A ramp steer input in terms of magnitude, slope and time is kept same for all the simulation at constant speeds.

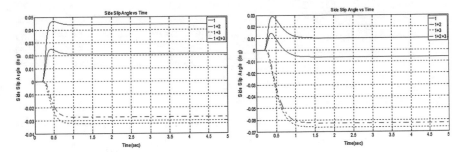

Fig. 6 Side slip angle at 40, 60, 80 and 100 kmph

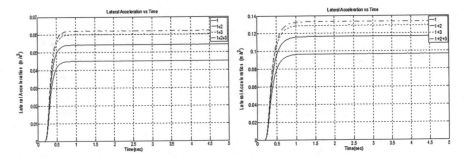

Fig. 7 Lateral acceleration at 40, 60, 80 and 100 kmph

Road surfaces are classified in based upon the power spectral density functions. Road undulations have been considered in the form of random road profile. Using Fourier transforms, it is possible to generate the road surface elevations as a function of time. Although this study was carried out for different terrain results, only rough roads are presented in this paper. Same ramp steer input of 2° is given to wheels on front axle and steering angles on intermediate and rear axles turn at angles in proportion to the front axle. Details are provided in Table 1. It can be seen from Figs. 6, 7 and 8 that steady state is reached in about 1 s at speed of 40 kmph and steadily increases with increases in speed. Time required to attain steady state increases with increase in speed.

Time required achieving steady state increases with number of steerable axles. Front and rear axles have more effect on reaching steady state as compared to effect of intermediate axle. For constant forward speed of the vehicle, higher magnitudes of lateral acceleration and yaw angle indicate vehicle ability to take sharp turn or in other words better manoeuverability. On careful examination of figures, it can be seen that higher yaw velocity and higher lateral acceleration result in undesirably large side slip angle. Side slip angle is the difference between vehicle axis and the wheel axis. Vehicle designers strive to achieve near zero side slip angle. There is no single best steering configuration to achieve higher yaw velocity and lateral acceleration with near zero side slip angle. Front and middle steerable axles allow smaller turning circle radius with good stability and manoeuverability. The performance presented

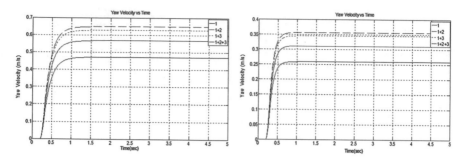

Fig. 8 Yaw velocity at 40, 60, 80 and 100 kmp

Table 2 Comparison of steering strategies

Steering strategy	(1)	(1+2)	(1+2+4)	(1+2+3)
Turning circle diameter	***	***	****	*****
Tyre scrub	*	***	****	*****
Packaging	*****	****	**	*
Yaw velocity and lateral acceleration	*	**	***	*****
Side slip angle	*****	*****	***	*

Note (i) Nos in () indicate no. of steerable axles (ii) More nos. of '*' means better in that parameter
crew compartment of this vehicle is to be placed at rear of the vehicle, and hence any steering
configuration with rear wheel steer will result in some compromise of space in crew compartment.
At higher speeds stability of vehicle decreases in case of steering configuration with rear wheel steer
(RWS) magnitude of side slip angle is almost double that of other two steering configurations with
non-steerable rear wheels. Taking into consideration, all the factors like vehicle manoeuverability,
stability, turning circle radius, tyre scrub and packaging front and middle axle steerable (1+2)
configuration has been finalized

by the oldest arrangement, with non-steerable rear axles, is unsatisfactory. It is more
difficult to handle in small spaces due to its higher turning circle radius and lowest
lateral acceleration and yaw velocity values. Magnitude of side slip angle at lower
speed indicates poor manoeuverability (Table 2).

2 Steady State Handling Test

Multi-body dynamics (MBD) has played a significant role in the analysis of vehicle motions. Software like ADAMS (Automatic Dynamic Analysis of Mechanical
Systems) is able to perform wide range of simulations including handling, obstacle
crossing and ride evaluation optimization. The process of constructing and testing
multiple physical prototypes is time-consuming. In this approach, the layouts are
created and tested virtually in order to reduce the product development time and
reduce the cost. Complete vehicle model for the steering configuration was built

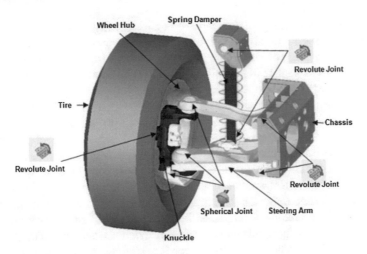

Fig. 9 Suspension corner module

in multi-body environment. Basic suspension stiffness, damping and double wishbone independent suspension mechanism, and wheel travel at all wheels were kept same. All kinematics and dynamical systems of vehicle are implemented in an MBD environment using MSC-ADAMS. Mass and inertia properties are assigned to each component of the vehicle in the MBD model.

These models have more than 200 degrees of freedom. Joints and constraints are added between components. Pac 2002 tyre model is used for dynamic analysis. MBD model consists of vehicle body or hull, chassis (suspension mounting brackets), front and rear suspension system, steering system, and road. Topology map showing joints and constraints of individual axle has also been described. Simulation studies related to the selection of suspension stiffness, damping and wheel travel was carried out separately, though this work will not be covered in this paper. Vehicle axle spacing, track width, centre of gravity and main vehicle inertia moments were incorporated in the model. Turning circle diameter manoeuver was performed to analyse the effect of steering configuration. Rolling resistance, tyre slippage was the parameters obtained and compared. Vehicle handling evaluation was carried out by carrying out steady state cornering test on constant radius curve. The objective of this study is to analyse vehicle 'understeer/oversteer' tendencies and vehicle stability. In addition to this vehicle dynamic behaviour, transient behaviour was carried out using lane change manoeuver (Fig. 9).

On finalization of steering strategy, a multi-body model of the vehicle was built to study the vehicle steady state cornering performance using constant speed test. The directional control response characteristics are determined from data plotted against lateral acceleration. A constant speed test was selected, and the vehicle was initially driven in straight line till it achieved the test speed; a predefined input to steering wheel was applied. It was maintained at that value until the measured vehicle motion variables reached a steady state. When the steering was applied, the throttle opening was increased to a setting sufficient to maintain essentially constant speed at steady state and held constant at this setting throughout the remainder of the run. The test was repeated for range of steer angles at constant speeds. In this test, the steering wheel angles were kept at $360°$, $540°$, $720°$ and $900°$, and the data was collected for a steady state response at constant speed. Figure 10 shows one of the handling simulations carried out at vehicle speed of 10 m/h speed at $900°$ steering angle. Top right quadrant shows the steering wheel input of $900°$ and bottom left and right quadrant show vehicle speed and turning circle diameter, respectively. Understeer can be measured at constant speed by varying the steer angle. This method closely duplicates real driving situation since vehicles are normally driven at near constant speed. With this method, the radius of turn varies continuously and requires extensive data collection to determine the steer gradient. In addition to measurement of speed and steer angle, the radius of turn must be determined for each condition as well. However, with simulation, this can be done in much shorter time. The Ackerman steer angle gradient indicating neutral steer is a straight line of constant slope. In region where the steer angle gradient is greater than that of Ackerman, the vehicle is understeer, and where the steer angle gradient is less than that of Ackerman, the vehicle is oversteer. The simulation results plotted are shown in Fig. 11 and handling behaviour of the vehicle is determined from the slope of the steer angle lateral acceleration curve. The slope of the curve represents the value of the understeer gradient 'K' of that curve. The handling characteristics of any vehicle are affected by vehicle weight and its distribution, road surface conditions, tyre characteristics, suspension properties and steering angle. Multi-axle armoured vehicles require more stability. More time and money is also required to carry out experiments on prototype.

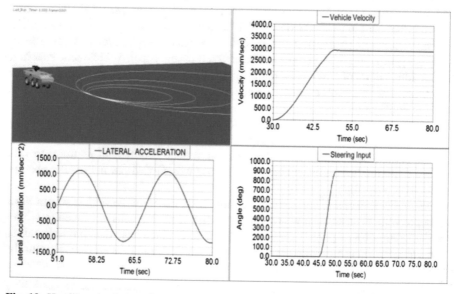

Fig. 10 Handling simulation of 10 km/hr speed at $900°$ steering angle

Fig. 11 Steer angle versus lateral acceleration curve for constant speed simulation and experimental data

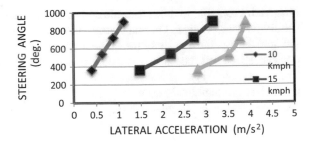

A comprehensive multi-body dynamics handling model was created, and constant speed test as per SAEJ266 was simulated. The results so obtained from simulation of steer angle versus lateral acceleration were plotted, and it is concluded that understeer characteristics are achieved.

3 Conclusions

A combined nonlinear ride and handling model is developed using Simulink software for comparing the performances of steering configurations. All theoretically possible steering configurations were evolved, and only those apt for practical implementation were considered in this study. For this purpose, a worldwide survey of vehicles of similar class was also carried out and four strategies were found after this exercise: first axle steer, first two-axle steer, first and last axle steer and all axle steer.

A combined nonlinear ride and handling model developed using Simulink is used for carrying out the study. Bicycle model was considered, it assumes same magnitude for angle for left and right wheels and this holds good for large turning radii. Steering angles at intermediate and rear wheels are considered in proportion with front wheel steer angles. Physical parameters considered were lateral acceleration, yaw angle and vehicle side slip angle. If forward speed of the vehicle is assumed constant, higher magnitudes of lateral acceleration and yaw angle indicate vehicle ability to take sharp turn or in other words better manoeuverability. Side slip angle is the difference between vehicle axis and the wheel axis. Vehicle designers strive to achieve near zero side slip angle. Apart from steering, other inputs considered are drive torque and road undulations. Longitudinal vehicle dynamics is of little consequence to this study; hence, equal and constant drive torque to all wheels is applied. Road undulations are provided as an input to the model from smoothened power spectral density (PSD) hyperbolic curve. Simulations have been carried out for step-steer input at constant forward speeds on a random road profile. It is observed that time required to attain steady state increases with increase in speed and increase in number of steerable axles. However, first and last axle has more effect achieving steady state than intermediate axle. High yaw velocity and lateral acceleration responses are obtained for strategies with RWS, but large vehicle sideslip angles were observed. Front and middle steerable and rear non-steerable axles were selected for the six-wheeled vehicle. On finalization of steering strategy, a multi-body model of the vehicle was built to study the vehicle steady state cornering performance using constant speed test. The directional control response characteristics were determined from data plotted against lateral acceleration. It is observed from the plot that as the understeer gradient increases with increase in vehicle forward speed, positive slope, i.e. understeer, is achieved and it indicates better directional control.

References

1. J.M.V. Franco, E.G.F. Pinto, G. Schaefer, Use of vehicle dynamic simulations to define the best axles configuration for a 6 × 6 military vehicle. SAE Technical Paper 2008-36-0144 (2008)
2. K. Bayar, Y. Samim Unlusoy, Steering strategies for multi-axle vehicles. Int. J. Heavy Veh. Syst. https://doi.org/10.1504/ijhvs.2008.022243
3. K. Huh, J. Kim, J. Hong, Handling and driving characteristics for six-wheeled vehicles. J. Automob. Eng. (2000), https://doi.org/10.1177/095440700021400205
4. Q.Z. Qu, Y.Z. Liu, J.W. Zhang, Control strategies of steering characteristic of commercial three-axle vehicle for front and rear wheel steering. Int. J. Veh. Design 6(2–3), 239–248 (2001)
5. A.G. Nalecz et al., Investigation into the stability of four wheel steering vehicles. Int. J. Veh. Des. 9(2) (1988), https://doi.org/10.1504/ijvd.1988.061479

An Approach to Trajectory Planning for Underwater Redundant Manipulator Considering Hydrodynamic Effects

Virendra Kumar, Soumen Sen, Sankar Nath Shome and Shibendu S. Roy

Abstract This article considers motion planning of a redundant serial link manipulator in fully submerged underwater scenario in the presence of obstacles, modelled as point objects. The proposed trajectory planning is based on minimizing the energy required in overcoming the hydrodynamic effects, and in the same time avoiding both obstacles and singularities. The presence of redundancy in joint space enables to choose optimal sequence of configurations and associated motion rates. The proposed approach is applied for motion planning of a three degrees-of-freedom planar manipulator avoiding a point obstacle and solved.

Keywords Underwater manipulator · Hydrodynamic forces · Hydrodynamic drag · Added mass · Redundant manipulator · Trajectory/motion planning

1 Introduction

Use of underwater robotic manipulators (either on ROV or mounted on stationary structure) in hazardous and inaccessible underwater environment is becoming inevitable, such as in applications like underwater pipeline maintenance, underwater welding, assembly and repair, material handling, rescue and recovery of sunk objects, operations in nuclear reactor pool, etc. In some of such applications, keeping joint space redundancy is essential in reaching intricate or narrow areas. Also,

V. Kumar (✉) · S. Sen · S. N. Shome
CSIR-Central Mechanical Engineering Research Institute, Durgapur, West Bengal 713209, India
e-mail: vkumar@cmeri.res.in

S. Sen
e-mail: soumen_sen@cmeri.res.in

S. N. Shome
e-mail: snshome@cmeri.res.in

S. S. Roy
National Institute of Technology, Durgapur, Durgapur 713209, India
e-mail: ssroy99@yahoo.com

© Springer Nature Singapore Pte Ltd. 2019
D N Badodkar and T A Dwarakanath (eds.), *Machines, Mechanism and Robotics*, Lecture Notes in Mechanical Engineering,
https://doi.org/10.1007/978-981-10-8597-0_32

377

design and operation of such systems for energy minimization always have been the most desirable requirement. This article presents an approach for motion planning of underwater redundant manipulator which attempts to keep the energy requirement in overcoming the hydrodynamic and dynamic forces at minimum, under the constraint of the presence of an obstacle, in the same time keeping away from singularity.

Literature is rich with many methods proposed for redundancy resolution. Author in [1] proposed redundancy resolution using Jacobian pseudoinverse; it was subsequently improved by authors in [2]. A scheme to reduce joint torques through inertia-weighted pseudoinverse of Jacobian was proposed in [3], whereas authors in [4] attempted minimization of instantaneous joint torques by jacobian pseudoinverse. Dynamic modelling of underwater manipulator systems is found in [5, 6]. In rigid-body framework for hydrodynamic modelling, three dominant effects are recognized [6, 7], namely, inertial effect, hydrodynamic drag and buoyancy. Standard empirical expressions are available in fluid mechanics literatures to represent the effects. Again for the hydrodynamic drag, only the dominant component, namely, the pressure drag is generally considered (see [7, 8]); other components like skin friction drag do not contribute appreciably in the net hydrodynamic force, given water as the medium. The hydrodynamic drag forces and inertia-related forces due to added mass become function of instantaneous configuration of the manipulator moving underwater. Good amount of work is also found in the literature for motion planning of redundant manipulators in the presence of obstacles [9, 10], including techniques of artificial potential field, even with dynamic obstacles.

This article considers minimization of total energy in overcoming hydrodynamic and dynamic forces in order to do redundancy resolution and motion planning, avoiding obstacle and singularity. The formulation for optimization is based on standard empirical hydrodynamic models (pressure drag, added mass, etc.) used for underwater moving bodies, obtained from literature; for example, [6, 7, 11] can be referred. Validations of the models are beyond the scope of the paper.

2 Dynamics/Hydrodynamics of Underwater Manipulator

When the motion of rigid body is analysed in an underwater environment, a number of additional effects must be considered as a result of various hydrodynamic forces and interactions. One valid modelling approach followed in literature is to formulate the hydrodynamic effects in a rigid-body mechanics framework. Under this framework, net hydrodynamic forces can be divided into forces due to hydrodynamic drag (dominating pressure drag), inertia/added mass force and buoyancy force. The general form of rigid-body equation for underwater manipulator is given by

$$M(\theta)\ddot{q} + C(\theta, \dot{\theta})\dot{\theta} + D(\dot{\theta})\dot{\theta} + G(\theta) = \tau \tag{1}$$

where $\theta \in \Re^n$ is the vector of generalized coordinates of joint variables, $M(\theta) \in \Re^{n \times n}$ is the inertia matrix including rigid body and added mass inertia, $C(\theta, \dot{\theta}) \in$

$\mathfrak{R}^{n \times n}$ is the Coriolis and centrifugal matrix including added mass effect, $D(\dot{\theta})$ is the hydrodynamic damping matrix, $G(\theta)$ is the vector of restoring forces and τ is the vector of input forces and moments G.

2.1 Added Mass

When a manipulator link is accelerated or decelerated underwater, some of water in the neighbourhood also moves along with the link. The force, responsible to accelerate surrounding water, causes a reaction force opposite to the direction of accelerating manipulator link. This force, acting opposite to the direction of acceleration, is named as added mass (inertia) force. The added inertia can be expressed by a 6-by-6 tensor. Manipulator links can be designed to have symmetries in order to have simpler form of the inertia tensor. Having a body-fixed coordinate frame with the axes aligned along the axes of symmetries, added inertia in general form can be expressed in body-fixed frame as [7]

$$M_A = -diag\{X_{\dot{u}}, Y_{\dot{v}}, Z_{\dot{w}}, K_{\dot{p}}, M_{\dot{q}}, N_{\dot{r}}\} \tag{2}$$

Literature provides empirical formulae of added mass for various standard geometries [7, 11]. For right circular cylindrical bodies, added mass is given by (2) with

$$\begin{aligned}
X_{\dot{u}} &= 0; \\
Y_{\dot{v}} &= -\pi \rho d^2 L/4; \\
Z_{\dot{w}} &= -\pi \rho d^2 L/4; \\
K_{\dot{p}} &= 0; \\
M_{\dot{q}} &= -\pi \rho d^2 L^3/12; \\
N_{\dot{r}} &= -\pi \rho d^2 L^3/12.
\end{aligned}$$

$X_{\dot{u}}$ denotes added mass component along acceleration direction of $\dot{u}$; u, v, w, p, q, r are the linear and angular velocities according to SNAME convention [7]. This article considers the link of the manipulators as right circular cylindrical bodies. Added mass in (2) is contained in the inertia term in (1).

2.2 Centrifugal/Coriolis Effect Due to Added Mass

Added mass also contributes to the centrifugal and Coriolis effect. In the body-fixed frame, these effects are expressed through a skew-symmetric matrix (subscript A denoting effect due to added mass) [7]:

$$C_A(v) = \begin{bmatrix} 0 & 0 & 0 & 0 & -a_3 & a_2 \\ 0 & 0 & 0 & a_3 & 0 & -a_1 \\ 0 & 0 & 0 & -a_2 & a_1 & 0 \\ 0 & -a_3 & a_2 & 0 & -b_3 & b_2 \\ a_3 & 0 & -a_1 & b_3 & 0 & -b_1 \\ a_2 & a_1 & 0 & -b_2 & b_1 & 0 \end{bmatrix}$$

where

$a_1 = X_{\dot{u}}u + X_{\dot{v}}v + X_{\dot{w}}w + X_{\dot{p}}p + X_{\dot{q}}q + X_{\dot{r}}r,$

$a_2 = X_{\dot{v}}u + Y_{\dot{v}}v + Y_{\dot{w}}w + Y_{\dot{p}}p + Y_{\dot{q}}q + Y_{\dot{r}}r,$

$a_3 = X_{\dot{w}}u + Y_{\dot{w}}v + Z_{\dot{w}}w + Z_{\dot{p}}p + Z_{\dot{q}}q + Z_{\dot{r}}r,$

$b_1 = X_{\dot{p}}u + Y_{\dot{p}}v + Z_{\dot{p}}w + K_{\dot{p}}p + K_{\dot{q}}q + K_{\dot{r}}r,$

$b_2 = X_{\dot{p}}u + Y_{\dot{p}}v + Z_{\dot{p}}w + K_{\dot{p}}p + K_{\dot{q}}q + K_{\dot{r}}r,$ and

$b_3 = X_{\dot{r}}u + Y_{\dot{r}}v + Z_{\dot{r}}w + K_{\dot{r}}p + M_{\dot{r}}q + N_{\dot{r}}r,$

with notations as described in Sect. 2.1 above.

2.3 Drag Force

Due to high density of water (nearly 1000 times compared to air), underwater manipulators/vehicles experience considerable drag forces, even in slow motions. Among all the components, pressure drag has the dominant contribution to the net drag. The drag force is function of link geometry, joint angles and relative link velocities with respect to fluid and assumes a form $f_d = -0.5 * \rho C_d A \|v^n\| v^n$, where A is the projected area of the body normal to the velocity, ρ is the density of water, v^n is the normal velocity component and C_d is the drag coefficient, whose value for standard geometry and flow conditions can be found in fluid dynamics literature [7, 11]. In the treatment of this article, strip theory is applied, where each cylindrical link is divided into small strips of finite width. Drag forces on each strip are computed using above formula, eventually giving rise to the net drag force on a moving link of the manipulator as a sum of forces on all the strips:

$$f_{di} = -0.5 * \rho \sum_{s=1}^{s=Ns} C_{di} D_{si} \|v_i^n\| v_i^n \delta x \tag{3}$$

where N_s represents the number of strips on the ith link, $\delta x = L_i/N_s$ is the strip width, L_i is the length of ith link, D_{si} is the sth strip diameter, ρ is the density of water and v_i^n is the velocity component normal to the strip area, $\delta x D_{si}$. The hydrodynamic damping force term $D(\dot{q})\dot{q}$ in (1) is determined using (3).

2.4 Buoyancy Force

Buoyancy force on a submerged body is a hydrostatic effect and is simply a function of the volume of displaced water by the body and is directed upward opposite to gravity. The force acts at the centre of buoyancy, which is the centre of mass of the displaced fluid volume. Buoyancy force is given by the following expression:

$$B = \rho V g \tag{4}$$

where V is the volume of the displaced fluid and g is the acceleration due to gravity.

3 Avoiding Obstacle and Singularity

For each obstacle present in the manipulator workspace, the obstacle avoidance procedure runs through several layers. First, during the task performance, the obstacle distance from the manipulator links is calculated at every step. Second, having known the instantaneous distance of obstacle from each link, a secondary criterion is evaluated. Finally, that configuration is selected towards redundancy resolution, which satisfies the secondary criterion (along with finding the joint rates that avoid collision of the links with obstacles). This article does not consider self-collision among the links. Self-collision is avoided by choosing appropriate joint ranges. However, the method can be extended to incorporate self-collision as well.

Singularity avoidance is treated in this article by taking a strategy that joint rates should not reach a very high velocity. Mathematically, the procedure ensures that the manipulator Jacobian at end effector does not become ill-conditioned.

In the procedure, each link is modelled as a line connecting the origins of the link coordinate frames and obstacles are considered as point object. Coordinate frames and axis assignments are done according to Denavit–Hertenberg convention. The unit direction of link i is given by

$$e_i = (X_{i+1} - X_i)/L_i \tag{5}$$

The projection α_i of the line (as shown in Fig. 1) from joint i to centre of obstacle point X_0 on the link i is

$$\alpha_i = e_i^T (X_0 - X_i) \tag{6}$$

A *critical point* is defined by the base of the perpendicular from the obstacle on the link. Hence, Cartesian coordinate of critical point is given as

$$X_{ci} = X_i + \alpha_i X_i \tag{7}$$

Fig. 1 Relation between
obstacle and link

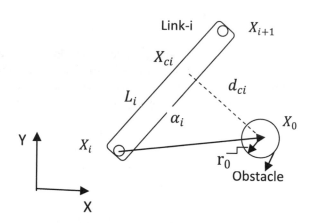

Critical point distance d_{ci} from the obstacle point and its direction u_i are, respectively, expressed as

$$d_{ci} = \|X_{ci} - X_0\|$$ (8)

$$u_i = (X_{ci} - X_0)/d_{ci}$$ (9)

When the critical point lies on link, the distance is computed by (8). Otherwise, the distance is computed between the obstacle and X_i or X_{i+1} depending on which side the intersection point between the extended link and the perpendicular lies.

Thus, for each link i, the secondary criterion is defined by the function

$$z_i = f_i(q, t) = r_0 - d_{ci}$$ (10)

where r_0 is the radius of a safe region, around the obstacle point. The obstacle avoidance secondary criterion ensures that the links steer clear of the safety region. Desired rate of the secondary task is zero on the boundary of the safety region, i.e.

$$\dot{z}_i^d = 0$$ (11)

If x is the point in task space to be reached by the end effector of the manipulator, then the primary task of reachability satisfies

$$x = f(q(t))$$ (12)

and

$$\dot{x} = J_e \dot{q},$$ (13)

along with the secondary task described by $\dot{z}$,

$$\dot{z} = J_c \dot{q}. \tag{14}$$

Denoting desired velocities of main task and additional task by $\dot{x}^d$ and $\dot{z}^d$, respectively, the joint rates $\dot{q}$ are evaluated such that the errors for primary task and secondary tasks are minimized. The singularity avoidance is also taken care of in the formulation by penalizing high joint rates [12], which also include high joint velocities resulted due to ill-conditioning of Jacobian (inverse kinematics). Thus, the above minimization formulation ensures that jacobian stays away from becoming ill-conditioned in the vicinity of configuration singularity. The composite cost function to be minimized is formulated as

$$F = \left(J_e \dot{q} - \dot{x}^d\right)^T W_e \left(J_e \dot{q} - \dot{x}^d\right) + \left(J_c \dot{q} - \dot{z}^d\right)^T W_c \left(J_c \dot{q} - \dot{z}^d\right) + \dot{q}^T W_v \dot{q}, \tag{15}$$

where W_e, W_c, and W_v are positive definite weighting matrix of proper dimension. Following joint rates minimizes the above cost function:

$$\dot{q} = \left(J_e^T W_e J_e + J_c^T W_c J_c + W_v\right)^{-1} \left(J_e^T W_e \dot{x}^d + J_c^T W_c \dot{z}^d\right). \tag{16}$$

4 Optimization for Underwater Motion Planning

The redundancy resolution is obtained by choosing those configurations (among all possible configurations) which minimize energy against overcoming the hydrodynamic drag and other effects under given constraints of reachability, obstacle and singularity avoidance. Using (1) and (16), instantaneous dynamic power can be expressed as

$$P(q, \dot{q}, \ddot{q}, t) = \sum_{i=1}^{n} |\tau_i| |\dot{q}_i| \tag{17}$$

Referring to (12) and (16), a constrained optimization problem is thus formulated with an objective to minimize total energy for following a geometric path in the task space with specified end and intermediate motion specification.

$$\min_{q} \int_{t_0}^{t_f} P(q, \dot{q}, \ddot{q}, t) \, dt$$

Subject to $x = f(q(t))$, $\dot{q}(t) = (J_e^T W_e J_e + J_c^T W_c J_c + W_v)^{-1} J_e^T W_e \dot{x}$,

$$q_{jl} < q_j < q_{ju}, \quad j = 1 \text{ to } n \tag{18}$$

Joint accelerations are computed from inverse kinematics.

This article considers only serial link manipulators. A recursive algorithm is developed for inverse dynamics computations (due to dynamic and hydrodynamic loading) in a Newton–Euler approach, which is used for determination of joint torques (τ) used in (17); however, discussion on the recursive formulation is out of the scope of the present article. Outcome of above optimization (when feasible) gives solution trajectories in joint space while following a path in the task space defined by (12). Since development of an efficient optimization algorithm was not an objective of the paper, a simple and direct grid search algorithm has been employed to find the solution.

5 Simulation: Results and Discussion

The procedure delineated above is applied for a planar three degrees-of-freedom manipulator moving in a vertical plane against gravity and fully submerged underwater. The links of the manipulator are considered to be long hollow cylindrical objects of outer and inner diameters 60 mm and 40 mm, respectively, of aluminium alloy with density 2830 kg/m^3. The lengths of the links are 0.5 m, 0.4 m and 0.3 m, respectively, from base to the distal one. It is intended to make the end effector follow a straight line path, starting at rest from a point in space (0.50, 0.70 m) and reaching a point (–0.40, 0.55 m) with zero velocity and in time 1 s following a cubic polynomial task trajectory. A point obstacle is placed at (0, 0.30 m), and radius of the safe region is taken as 0.05 m for obstacle avoidance.

The simulation results are reported in the following figures. Figure 2 shows the manipulator configuration corresponding to the minimum total energy in overcoming the hydrodynamic and dynamic forces. Corresponding joint rates are shown in Fig. 3.

Fig. 2 Series of manipulator configuration in Cartesian path following the end effector avoiding obstacle with minimum total energy

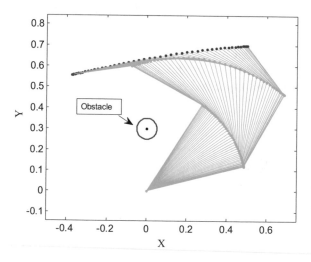

The power requirement in executing the minimum energy path following is given in Fig. 4 (the bold red line).

Figure 5 shows the power requirement in overcoming only the hydrodynamic drag forces in the above Cartesian task following. Clearly, energy required in overcoming hydrodynamic drag is not necessarily the minimum along the minimum total energy trajectory. Unlike conventional industrial manipulators, where gravity loading plays a major part, in underwater scenario, buoyancy reduces the gravity effect considerably. Instead, it is seen in most of the cases that the hydrodynamic drag forces playing dominant role.

Figure 6 shows total energy requirement in each iteration of the optimization solution process. Each iteration corresponds to one feasible solution, where total energy is

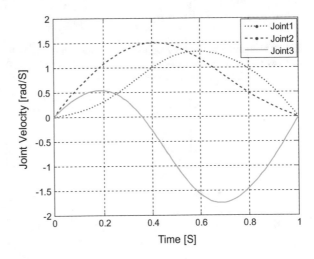

Fig. 3 Joint rates corresponding to the minimum energy trajectory

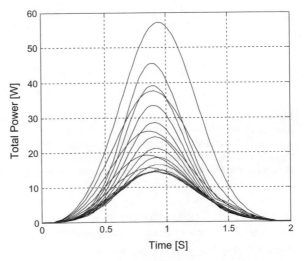

Fig. 4 Instantaneous total power requirement for various non-optimal and the *minimum energy* motions while following the Cartesian path. The solid red line corresponds to the minimum energy trajectory tracking

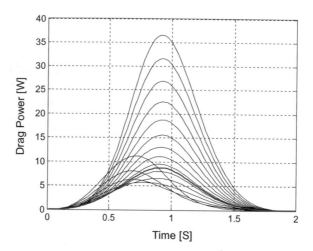

Fig. 5 Instantaneous power required to overcome only the hydrodynamic drag effect for various non-optimal and *minimum energy* motions. The solid red line is the power due to only drag, corresponding to the minimum total energy trajectory

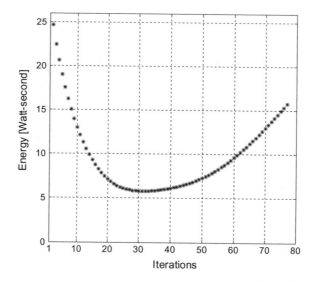

Fig. 6 Total energy requirement at various iterations. At each iteration, configurations (redundancy resolution) and joint trajectories are solved along the entire path for the given desired task requirement of rest-to-rest straight line following by the end effector in Cartesian space avoiding both obstacle and singularity, in the presence of hydrodynamic effects. The optimal solution is obtained at iteration no. 33 with the chosen precision and step size of the iteration process

computed for the entire trajectory (at all instantaneous configurations, velocities and accelerations, obtained from inverse kinematics) in following the rest-to-rest straight line following task by the end effector in the Cartesian space. The evolution clearly shows that there exists a minimum, where the optimal configurations (redundancy resolution) and joint trajectories are obtained for the entire Cartesian path, satisfying obstacle and singularity avoidance. In the grid search method employed here, totally 77 iterations take place for the chosen grid sizes (step sizes for the variables). The optimal (minimum energy) solution is found at iteration number 33 in the reported simulation. Please note that the time to accomplish the task has been kept invariant. It is to be noted that, within the same time of task accomplishment, there exist several feasible sets of configurations and trajectories, among which optimal solution exists.

6 Conclusion

This article presents an approach for optimal motion planning of redundant underwater manipulator in the presence of obstacle based on minimization of total energy in overcoming hydrodynamic and dynamic forces. Validated empirical formulations exist in literature to estimate the hydrodynamic effects, which are applied here in a rigid-body dynamics framework. Strip theoretic approach is taken for estimation of hydrodynamic drag forces on each link and finding the centre of drag. A recursive formulation is developed for inverse dynamics computations involving the hydrodynamic effects for serial link manipulators. The considered manipulator essentially has redundancy in joint space, which is beneficial in manoeuvring and steering clear of obstacle, maintaining reachability and trajectory following with the energy requirement minimized. The procedure developed in this article has the inbuilt ability to avoid singular configurations. The method is applied to a planar vertically moving three degrees-of-freedom manipulator for a line following task by the end effector. Simulation results are reported to show the effectiveness of the proposed formulation as an optimization problem for redundancy resolution and trajectory planning of underwater manipulator in the presence of hydrodynamic effects and avoiding obstacle and singularity. Future work requires experimental validation of the method proposed and obtaining extended formulation for spatial avoidance of multiple and possibly moving obstacles.

Acknowledgements The work has been done under the activities of the Network project ESC-0113 (CSIR, Govt. of India) and the DST (Govt. of India) sponsored project GAP-152812, both being carried out in CSIR-CMERI, Durgapur, India.

References

1. D.E. Whitney, Resolved motion rate control of manipulators and human prostheses. IEEE Transaction on Man-Machine Syst. **MMS-10**(2), 47–53 (1969)
2. A. Liegeois, Automatic supervisory control of the configuration and behavior of multibody mechanisms. IEEE Trans. System, Man Cybern. **SMC-7**(12), 868–871 (1977)

3. O. Khatib, Unified approach for motion and force control of robot manipulators: The operational space formulation. IEEE J. Robot. Autom. **RA-3**(1), 43–53 (1987)
4. J.M. Hollerbach, K.C. Suh, Redundancy resolution of manipulators through torque optimization. IEEE J. Robot. Autom. **RA-3**(4), 308–316 (1987)
5. J. Yuh, Modeling and control of underwater robotic vehicle. IEEE Trans. Syst. Man Cybernet. **20**, 1470–1483 (1990)
6. B. Levesque, M.J. Richard, Dynamic analysis of a manipulator in a fluid environment. Int. J Robot. Res. **13**, 221–231 (1994)
7. T.I. Fossen, *Guidance and Control of Ocean Vehicles* (Wiley), ISBN 0-471-94113-1
8. G. Antonelli, *Underwater Robot* (Springer, Cham, Heidelberg, New York, Dordrecht, London), ISBN 978-3-319-02876-7
9. F. Fahimi, H. Ashrafiuon, C. Nataraj, Obstacle avoidance for spatial hyper-redundant manipulators using harmonic potential functions and the mode shape technique. J. Robot. Syst. **20**(1), 23–33 (2003)
10. A.N. Scott, C.R. Carignan, A Line-based obstacle avoidance technique for dexterous manipulator operations, in *Proceedings of IEEE International Conference on Robotics and Automation*, art.no. 4543722 (2008) pp. 3353–3358
11. J.N. Newman, Marine Hydrodynamics. The MIT Press, Cambridge Massachusetts ISBN: 9780262140263
12. Y. Nakamura, H. Hanafusa, Inverse kinematic solutions with singularity robustness for manipulator control. ASME J. Dyn. Syst. Meas. Control **108**, 163–171 (1986)

Indigenous Mobile Robot for Surveillance and Mapping

K. Y. V. Krishna, A. Wadnerkar, G. M. Patel, G. Baluni, A. K. Pandey and R. M. Suresh Babu

Abstract Remote surveillance of hazardous areas necessitates the deployment of mobile robots for carrying out planned work. These robots are equipped with sensors to enable monitoring and recording of the critical parameters of the remote hazardous areas. The sensed parameters need to be localized to gain better insights of site conditions and take corrective actions. By forming a system that offers combination of human intelligence with mobile robot's reach and onboard machine intelligence, a teleoperated mobile robot provides a flexible and versatile solution for remote safe operation (Mukherjee et al. in National Symposium on Nuclear Instrumentation, Mumbai, Nov 2013) [1]. In addition, the robot's ability to build the map of remote environment and self-localize with reference to map all by itself provides a basis for overlaying of sensed data onto the map for easier visualization and assessment by the user. This paper addresses the design and development of an indigenously developed mobile robot capable of carrying out surveillance and map building in remote environment.

Keywords Mobile robot · Surveillance · 3D vision · SLAM · Map generation Radiation mapping

K. Y. V. Krishna (✉) · A. Wadnerkar · G. M. Patel · G. Baluni · A. K. Pandey
R. M. Suresh Babu
EISD, Bhabha Atomic Research Centre, Mumbai, India
e-mail: vamshi@barc.gov.in

A. Wadnerkar
e-mail: anshuw@barc.gov.in

G. M. Patel
e-mail: gmpatel@barc.gov.in

G. Baluni
e-mail: gbaluni@barc.gov.in

A. K. Pandey
e-mail: amitkp@barc.gov.in

R. M. Suresh Babu
e-mail: subabu@barc.gov.in

© Springer Nature Singapore Pte Ltd. 2019
D N Badodkar and T A Dwarakanath (eds.), *Machines, Mechanism and Robotics*, Lecture Notes in Mechanical Engineering,
https://doi.org/10.1007/978-981-10-8597-0_33

389

1   Introduction

Remote surveillance and manipulation tasks in hazardous areas, such as active plants, require deployment of mobile work agents for surveillance and corrective actions. These work agents are sent for short period of time to carry out the tasks such as sensing the conditions prevailing in remote area. The sensed parameters need to be localized in order to gain better insights of site conditions and take corrective actions. Localization of sensed parameters requires a *topographic map* of the remote area under surveillance. Maps of the remote environment serve two purposes:

- Performing situation assessment and localizing themselves inside buildings;
- Path planning and high-level autonomous behaviors of robot systems.

In most of the cases, these maps are not known beforehand due to various reasons including inaccessible site conditions, dynamically changing environment, and modeling constraints associated with area size and complexity. To address the problem of remote sensing of inaccessible areas while navigating safely, a *teleoperated mobile robot* incorporating machine intelligent modules has been built for map building of an unknown environment while simultaneously keeping track of its own location. In addition, the sensed parameters during the campaign can be interrelated and overlaid with reference to the map coordinate system. This technique finds its uses in factory automation, search/rescue operations, guidance, and transportation tasks.

Section 2 describes the architecture and design aspects considered during the system development. Section 3 describes implementation mechanism used for achieving remote navigation and map building capability. Section 4 describes the results of our experiments on SLAM. Section 5 describes the possible applications of system, and the paper concludes in Sects. 6 and 7 with possible value additions.

2   System Architecture and Design

2.1   System Mechanism

The mobile robot hardware comprises chassis housing mechanical sub-assemblies, power source, actuators, and control electronics (see Fig. 1). Locomotion is achieved using two drive wheels at the rear end and a castor wheel at the front for stability and free pivoting. Robot control is based on *differential steering* principle, whereby the difference between the speeds of left and right wheels regulates the direction of *vehicle steering*. The kinematics of differential drive robot can be found in [2]. Two independent 24 V BLDC motors with gear reduction of 30 have been employed to drive the left and right wheels. The *power bank* of the system is 24 V, 40 AH lead acid batteries mounted inside the robot platform, and power is distributed to electrical/electronic components through voltage converters. A *wireless transceiver* on the mobile robot is used to communicate with the remote host.

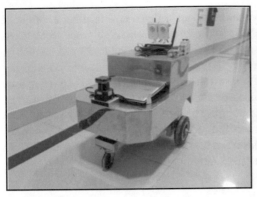

Fig. 1 Mobile robot equipped with 2D laser scanner and stereo camera; (left) side view; (right) front view

2.2 Control System

The mobile robot locomotion is based on the torque differential produced between the left and right wheels located at the rear side of vehicle. The onboard controller is responsible for giving the motion control commands to the actuators and steer the robot in the desired direction. Position sensing of the wheels is obtained using *optical encoders* attached to the wheel shafts. The position signals from the sensors are fed to the onboard controller for *closed-loop control*. The controller operates the actuators in *speed control mode* to achieve the desired trajectory independent of the inclination of terrain. Position control of the robot is achieved through a *position control loop* which sits on top of the speed control loop. The onboard controller periodically polls the state of the vehicle and sends the status data to the host on request. The host-side software integrates instantaneous speed data to calculate the 2D *pose* of the robot. This calculated 2D pose obtained using odometry considerably differs from the actual robot pose and degrades over the course of robot operation. The pose error can be attributed to various reasons including modeling inaccuracies, wheel slippages, wheel misalignments, mismatched wheels, etc. and can be reduced using state estimation techniques using data from exteroceptive sensors.

2.3 Communication

The onboard controller communicates with the host through 2.4 GHz wireless ISM band. The wireless transceiver on the robot acts as an access point and communicates with wireless module at the host end which operates in client mode. To extend the reach of wireless communication in addition to overcoming the signal losses due to barriers, repeaters can be employed at various places to get full site coverage. The onboard controller ensures that the communication with the host is intact throughout the system operation. To achieve this, it implements a *watchdog timer* to check if communication with host is alive. In case the communication breaks and cannot be reestablished even after multiple attempts, the controller halts the vehicle to avoid any untoward damage to itself and the external environment. The signal strength between robot and the host is continuously monitored and in cases where the robot has reached areas with no link with the host, the robot may be directed to move back in the same path until the connection gets reestablished. To incorporate this feature, the robot must have robust directed sensing hardware and software for obstacle avoidance to prevent any damage during the signal searching phase.

3   Mobile Robot Navigation

3.1   Telecontrol Mode

In telecontrol mode, the human operator controls the robot from a remote location through external visual feedback. Based on visual feedback and other sensor data rendered on HMI, the operator uses his judgment to manually steer the robot in the desired path. The images relayed from the onsite location should have minimal delay for good controllability of the robot. The operator end software provides supervisory control and issues control commands to the onboard controller to move the robot in the desired path. The host software periodically acquires the instantaneous wheel positions from onboard controller to estimate the robot pose. The calculated robot pose is rendered onto the user console showing its estimated 2D position and orientation in the remote environment (see Fig. 2). Any error conditions such as communication failure and obstacle confrontation are indicated on console for further action and remediation by the user.

In telecontrol mode, the robot can be operated in two modes: joystick control mode and programmed mode for simple point-to-point traversal.

3.1.1   Joystick Control Mode

In manual mode, the operator uses a joystick to control the speed and direction of robot. A commercial-off-the-shelf joystick has been used for controlling the robot in different operational sub-modes: manual steering, left wheel turn, right wheel turn, and in-place rotation. The horizontal (X) and vertical (Y) axes of the joystick are used to control the steering angle and average speed of the robot. The horizontal axis position of the stick sets the *speed ratio* of the left and right wheels from which the desired heading of the robot is derived. The digital buttons on the joystick are used to switch between different sub-modes within manual operation mode. The throttle wheel is used to set the maximum average speed of operation and depending on the

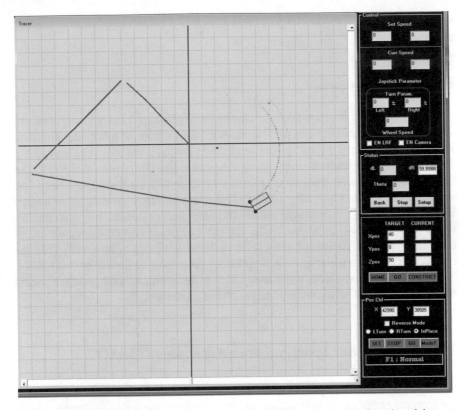

Fig. 2 Operator console. Left pane shows the robot control in programmed modes, right pane contains control panel and status display

position of the handle in Y-direction, the vehicle speed is dynamically increased or decreased.

3.1.2 Programmed Mode

This mode is an extension of manual operating mode and is used to automate execution of simple point-to-point traversals along straight line or curved path. The user specifies the destination point and optionally a set of intermediate points to avoid obstacles in its path (Fig. 2). The guide points are set by the operator based on visual feedback of onsite conditions. The *traversal* between two points is in straight line. Each point-to-point traversal comprises two steps: Automatic orientation of the vehicle in the direction of the subsequent point followed by movement in straight line. The user is also provided with the option of reaching the destination at one stretch by following a circular path. Given a destination point, the software calculates the required speed ratio between left and right wheels and executes on the robot to reach the destination.

3.1.3 Visual Feedback

In telecontrol mode, it is imperative that the operator has some kind of visual feedback for operating the robot from remote location. In cases where the robot operating area is inaccessible for direct viewing, camera-based viewing is the only option available for the operator to guide the robot along free space and perform needed tasks. The robot is equipped with a *wireless camera* of 640 × 480 resolution to stream live video as seen by the robot. Higher resolution and frame rates provide better quality images but at the cost of increased bandwidth. Monocular views can help the operator realize the presence of obstacles, walls, and other objects in the remote environment but cannot help in visualizing their relative distance or depth. In order to aid the operator in getting a better depth perception of the remote environment, the robot is equipped with *calibrated stereo camera pair* and the operator can experience *remote 3D views* using shutter glass-based stereoscopic technique.

3.2 Simultaneous Localization and Mapping (SLAM)

When the operator is remotely controlling the robot, visual feedback provided by the onboard camera is local in nature, i.e., it provides information about the robot's immediate vicinity. To provide the operator with *global perspective* of the work environment, a topological or metric map is required. In cases where the map is not known beforehand or difficult to measure due to dynamically changing conditions, SLAM technique provides the necessary solution to incrementally build the map during robot navigation. In SLAM, the robot has to estimate its own position in addition to building the map of remote environment using its sensor feedback. The complexity of SLAM arises from the fact that for localization a map is needed and to build a consistent map, the robot position has to be known beforehand. Probabilistic approaches to solving the problem are increasingly used as modeling of uncertainty makes these methods very robust. These techniques work in an iterative way using recursive state estimation where noisy system dynamics and sensor measurements are integrated in a way so as to minimize the overall error.

SLAM is a fundamental primitive for many applications of autonomous mobile robots. Once the robot is able to build a map of its surroundings and determine its own location, then it will be able to navigate to desired locations in previously unknown environments for performing its tasks. It is increasingly being employed in self-driving cars, unmanned aerial vehicles (UAV), autonomous underwater vehicles, domestic robots, etc. where it is not feasible to accurately pre-model the environment due to its size constraints or dynamic nature.

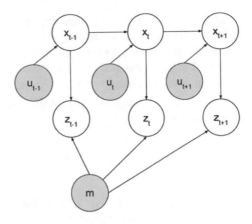

Fig. 3 SLAM problem
representation

3.2.1 SLAM Problem

Figure 3 represents the generalized graphical representation of SLAM problem. Here, x_t is the robot position at time t. Position in case of planar workspace is typically three-dimensional vector with two-dimensional coordinate and robot's orientation angle. u_t represents odometry. It is often derived from robot wheel encoders or control commands. z_t represents measurements of the environment at position x_t at time t. Commonly used measurement sensors are LIDAR, Kinect, sonar sensor, etc. m denotes the map of the environment. Position x_t is related to both previous (x_{t-1}) and the following positions (x_{t+1}).

The SLAM problem is defined as the estimation of m and robot position x_t using measurements "z" and odometry data "u".

Solutions for SLAM problem can be classified into four broad categories [3, 4]. They are Extended Kalman Filter (EKF) SLAM [5], Particle filter-based SLAM [6], Graph-based SLAM [7], and scan matching-based SLAM [8]. In our implementation, we have used Hector SLAM algorithm. It is scan matching-based SLAM algorithm and has been proved to be sufficiently accurate as to not require explicit loop closing techniques in considered scenarios.

3.2.2 Hector SLAM Algorithm

Hector SLAM is an open-source 2D SLAM technique based on robust scan matching of range data. It uses LIDAR sensor for building map of the surroundings. Unlike other SLAM techniques, Hector SLAM does not need odometry data which makes it possible to implement even in aerial robots or ground robots operating in uneven terrains. It estimates the pose of the robot using scan matching algorithms. Very high scan rate and low measurement noise of modern LIDAR systems allow it to obtain fast and accurate pose estimates.

Hector SLAM uses Gauss–Newton minimization technique for scan matching. It maintains a map of its surroundings. On receiving a new scan from LIDAR, it finds the optimum alignment of the scan with the map obtained so far. The endpoints are projected in the actual grid map and the occupancy probabilities are estimated.

Let p_x and p_y represent the position of the robot and ψ the orientation, and let $\xi = (p_x, p_y, \psi)^T$ represent pose of the mobile robot. Then, the algorithm finds ξ that minimizes

$$\xi^* = \operatorname*{argmin}_{\xi} \sum_{i=1}^{n} [1 - M(S_i(\xi))]^2$$

where the function $M(S_i(\xi))$ returns the map value at $S_i(\xi)$ which is the world coordinates of the scan endpoints.

The optimum value of ξ is obtained by applying correction $\Delta\xi$ such that

$$\sum_{i=1}^{n} [1 - M(S_i(\xi + \Delta\xi))]^2 \to 0$$

Applying first-order Taylor expansion to $M(S_i(\xi + \Delta\xi))$ and setting the partial derivative with respect to $\Delta\xi$ to zero yields the Gauss–Newton equation for the minimization problem

$$\Delta\xi = H^{-1} \sum_{i=1}^{n} \left[\nabla M(S_i(\xi)) \frac{\partial S_i(\xi)}{\partial \xi} \right]^T [1 - M(S_i(\xi))]$$

where

$$H = \left[\nabla M(S_i(\xi)) \frac{\partial S_i(\xi)}{\partial \xi} \right]^T \left[\nabla M(S_i(\xi)) \frac{\partial S_i(\xi)}{\partial \xi} \right]$$

Based on the value of ξ, the map is updated with each new scan and the algorithm calculates new optimized robot pose and map. It was proved in [8] that this technique is sufficiently accurate to close loops in small-scale scenarios without use of an approach for explicit loop closure. Hector SLAM is also capable of 6D pose estimation using data obtained from inertial measurement unit. On uneven surfaces, the LIDAR has to be stabilized around roll and pitch axes to keep the laser aligned with the ground plane. 6D pose estimation has not been implemented in our present work.

3.2.3 Implementation

In our system, we have used 2D LIDAR sensor for acquiring depth scan of the surrounding. This sensor has a range of 30 m and worst-case accuracy of ± 50 mm. It provides 2D scan depth data for a beam angle of 270° at 40 scans per second.

For mapping and localization, we have used Hector SLAM technique [8]. Various modules of our software including SLAM integration are based on Robot Operating System (ROS) [9]. ROS is a flexible framework which provides a set of drivers, tools, and libraries in order to help develop robotics applications with hardware abstraction. A ROS system is comprised of a number of independent nodes, each of which communicates with the other nodes using publish/subscribe messaging model. It provides versatile communication infrastructure for nodes/processes and allows easy integration of a wide range of tools including visualization of robot pose, kinematics, sensor data, and perception algorithms. Our software nodes implemented in ROS include robot control/tracking module, joystick interfacing module, laser data acquisition module, and hector SLAM module. All the nodes are independent of each other and communicate among others using ROS topic publish/subscribe messaging system.

4 Results and Discussion

Experiments were conducted with the robot teleoperated inside the rooms and lobby area of our office building. Figure 4a shows the robot in the lobby. Figure 4b shows the generated map, trajectory followed, start position, and current position estimate of the robot. The robot's actual position (X, Y) was recorded and compared to the ground truth data at seven different locations, results of which are shown in Table 1 and observation points are shown in Fig. 5. Maximum error in X and Y coordinates was observed to be 13.3 cm for actual position of 497.9 cm (2.6%). It can also be observed that the error does not go unbounded over the course of operation.

(a)   **(b)**

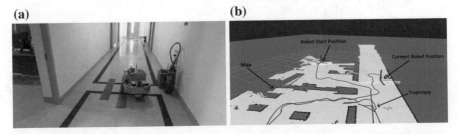

Fig. 4 **a** Image of the mobile robot operating in the lobby area; **b** Mobile robot's start and current position marked in the generated map while also keeping track of the robot's path traced

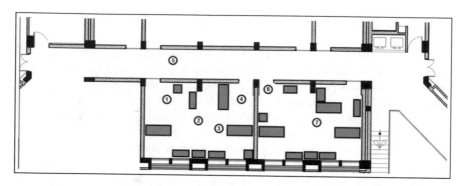

Fig. 5 Actual map of the area to be mapped (Ground truth data). Observation points at various places are numbered 1–7

Figure 5 shows the actual ground truth map, and Fig. 6 shows map generated for our test run. It can be seen that our implementation is able to generate consistent and accurate maps preserving the wall boundaries, obstacles, and overall structure of the lobby area and two rooms under observation. From the above results of test run, it can be concluded that Hector SLAM gives satisfactory results for both localization and map building and can provide accurate and useful results enabling autonomous operation.

One limitation of Hector SLAM observed in our course of experiments was with respect to failure in laser data acquisition in the middle of campaign. The algorithm compares instantaneous laser scan data with most recent map due to which it can lose track of its location if the laser data is not continuously available. This can lead to erroneous map generation after the mapping node starts receiving data after outage period.

Table 1 Comparison of robot actual position with ground truth data

Sr. no.	Robot actual position (X, Y) (mm)	Robot estimated position (X, Y) (mm)	Error (ΔX, ΔY) (mm)
1	(1461, 3859)	(1461, 3947)	(0, −89)
2	(3598, 2447)	(3624, 2397)	(26, −50)
3	(4979, 1785)	(5112, 1819)	(133, 34)
4	(6379, 3889)	(6376, 3918)	(−3, 29)
5	(1836, 6467)	(1806, 6510)	(−30, 43)
6	(8140, 4567)	(8243, 4503)	(103, −64)
7	(11,274, 2530)	(11,297, 2499)	(23, −31)

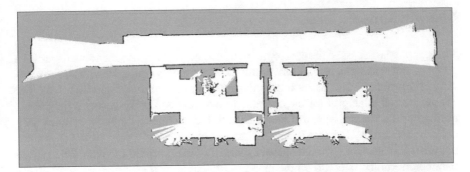

Fig. 6 Final map generated by Hector SLAM

Fig. 7 Sample heat map of
an area

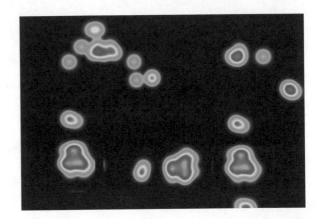

5   Applications

The present system can be used for remote surveillance in hazardous areas like sites
with the presence of toxic gases, biological contamination, and nuclear radiation.
During the campaign, the mobile robot can periodically collect the environmental
parameters while simultaneously performing map building and localization. The
sensed parameters can be overlaid onto the map and displayed in the form of a *heat
map* [10] for easier visualization as shown in Fig. 7. This heat map can then be used
for further assessment by the user.

Possible application scenarios of this system include

- Radiation mapping,
- Signal strength mapping,
- Tracking of objects of interest, and
- Exploration of remote hazardous areas.

6 Conclusions

This paper has discussed the development of a telecontrolled mobile robot capable of carrying out sensing in remote environment. The robot is equipped with stereo camera setup to aid operator in getting depth perception of the remote environment. The 3D perception is helpful for the operator to evaluate and make accurate judgments during navigation in telecontrol mode. During the operation, the robot continuously collects and fuses 2D LIDAR data to incrementally build a map of the surrounding environment while simultaneously localizing itself within the map. The sensed parameters can be overlaid on the map and rendered as a heat map for graphically pinpointing the area of interest for corrective actions.

7 Future Enhancements

In our present work, the robot is teleoperated to generate a map of its surroundings. The work can be extended to facilitate the robot with *autonomous* behavior and operate in remote areas using *in situ based reactive* approaches with minimal user guidance. This requires incorporating diversified sensor hardware and development of *robust algorithms* which implement obstacle avoidance and path planning techniques. We also plan to explore other SLAM algorithms in order to improve accuracy and make the system more robust to problems including kidnapped robot scenario and overcome problems associated with LIDAR in ranging transparent objects.

References

1. J.K. Mukherjee, K.Y.V. Krishna, A.K. Pandey, indigenously developed mobile work agent, in *National Symposium on Nuclear Instrumentation*, Mumbai, Nov 2013
2. R. Siegwart et.al., *Introduction to Autonomous Mobile Robots* (MIT Press, 2011)
3. H. Durrant-Whyte, T. Bailey, Simultaneous localization and mapping: part I. IEEE Robot. Autom. Mag. **13**(2), 99–110 (2006)
4. T. Bailey, H. Durrant-Whyte, Simultaneous localization and mapping (SLAM): Part II. IEEE Robot. Autom. Mag. **13**(3), 108–117 (2006)
5. S. Thrun, J.J. Leonard, *Simultaneous localization and mapping, Springer handbook of robotics* (Springer, Berlin Heidelberg, 2008), pp. 871–889
6. M.W.M.Gamini Dissanayake et al., A solution to the simultaneous localization and map building (SLAM) problem. IEEE Trans. Robot. Autom. **17**(3), 229–241 (2001)
7. M. Montemerlo, et al., FastSLAM: a factored solution to the simultaneous localization and mapping problem (Aaai/iaai, 2002)
8. S. Kohlbrecher, J. Meyer, O. von Stryk, U. Klingauf, A flexible and scalable SLAM system with full 3D motion estimation, in *Proceeding of IEEE International Symposium on Safety, Security and Resue Robotics*, Kyoto, Japan, Nov 2011
9. M. Quigley et al., ROS: an open-source robot operating system, in *ICRA workshop on open source software*, Vol. 3, No. 3.2
10. T. Jilek, Radiation intensity mapping in outdoor environments using a mobile robot with RTK GNSS, in *International Conference on Military Technologies* (2015), Brno

Vision-Based Automated Target Tracking System for Robotic Applications

A. K. Pandey, K. Y. V. Krishna and R. M. Suresh Babu

Abstract Moving object detection and tracking has significant importance in machine vision and robotic applications. The objective of tracking is to ensure that the targeted object always remains in camera view. In this paper, Speeded-Up Robust Features (SURF) technique is used to develop a robust automated target tracking system that relies on local features (corner, edge) rather than global features (intensity and shape) of the object. SURF provides an efficient scale- and rotation-invariant detector that is robust to partial occlusion and noise. System based on SURF presents more accurate and efficient automated target tracking system. This system is developed for the application where user has to locate and orient camera manually to target an object in its workplace.

Keywords Vision system · Object detection and tracking · SURF · SIFT
Feature detection · Feature description · Integral image

1 Introduction

Object detection and tracking is most researched topic in machine vision. It has a wide range of applications including traffic surveillance, vehicle navigation, gesture understanding, security camera systems and so forth. It also has significant importance in robotic applications where user has to locate and orient robot eye (camera) manually to target an object in its workplace. Object detection accuracy completely depends on parameters being used to define the object. Visual features and motion of object are the primary sources of information which have long been used for object

A. K. Pandey (✉) · K. Y. V. Krishna (✉) · R. M. Suresh Babu
EISD, Bhabha Atomic Research Centre, Mumbai, India
e-mail: amitkp@barc.gov.in

K. Y. V. Krishna
e-mail: vamshi@barc.gov.in

R. M. Suresh Babu
e-mail: subabu@barc.gov.in

© Springer Nature Singapore Pte Ltd. 2019
D N Badodkar and T A Dwarakanath (eds.), *Machines, Mechanism and Robotics*, Lecture Notes in Mechanical Engineering,
https://doi.org/10.1007/978-981-10-8597-0_34

detection in computer vision applications. Feature-based detection process examines an image to extract unique features present on the objects. The effectiveness of any feature-based technique depends upon the level of invariance exhibited with respect to photometric and affine transformations primarily scale and rotation and it should also detect when parts of the object are occluded. Local features such as corners and edges are more efficient, resistant to partial occlusion, and are relatively insensitive to changes in viewpoint [1]. Several algorithms have been proposed that use local features. Scale-Invariant Feature Transform (SIFT) is one of the most popular feature detection algorithms introduced by Lowe [2]. The Speeded-Up Robust Features (SURF) is another algorithm based on the same principles and steps, but it utilizes a different scheme and provides faster results [3] with the same level of accuracy. The system presented here uses SURF algorithm for object detection and tracking which is entirely based on the local features of an object.

Local features are described using close neighbourhood around a feature point. Detection and description of these features are influenced by geometric and photometric deformations associated during scene capture. Feature detectors such as SIFT, PCA-SIFT, SURF and GLOH are designed to be robust to these variations by using various techniques. All these detectors possess a different complexity, speed and accuracy for object detection. SURF presents an efficient scale and rotation-invariant detector and descriptor which surpass all other feature detection techniques in terms of repeatability, distinctiveness, robustness and speed using the concept of integral image and Hessian approximation [4, 5]. Automated target tracking system setup based on SURF presented in this paper comprises a wireless IP camera mounted on Pan Tilt Unit (PTU). The software featuring SURF-based module segments target object from its background, estimate its position in the image and automatically adjusts camera orientation to invariably keep the object in camera's field of view.

2 Related Work

2.1 Overview of SURF: Speeded-Up Robust Feature

Feature-based object detection using Speeded-Up Robust Features (SURF) comprises three steps:

- Feature point detection.
- Feature point description.
- Matching.

Feature point detection
Feature point detector detects the feature point unique to objects present in the scene. This detector should be repeatable and robust so that same feature point could be detected under varying viewing conditions. SURF detector examines the image at different scales and extracts feature points as local extrema in its local neighbour-

Fig. 1 Three octaves with three levels. The neighbourhood for the 3 × 3 × 3 non-maximum suppression used to detect features is highlighted [5]

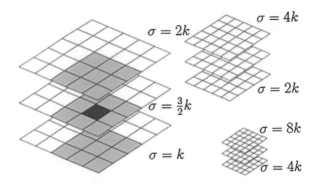

hood for scale invariance. Scale-space generation is done using Gaussian kernel of different σ values to generate a pyramid of response maps constituting of levels and octaves. Doubling the σ value of Gaussian kernel corresponds to an octave which is further divided into uniformly spaced levels. After generation of response maps, non-maximum suppression is done in a 3 × 3 × 3 neighbourhood surrounding the current pixel which is considered as a potential feature point if it is extrema among eight neighbours in the current level and 18 neighbours in level above and below. The relation between levels, octaves and neighbourhood are illustrated in Fig. 1.

Hessian matrix detector:

SURF uses Hessian matrix to detect blob-type feature by convolving it with the image and estimating the determinant to find potential feature points.

$$\mathcal{H}(x,\sigma) = \begin{bmatrix} L_{xx}(x,\sigma) & L_{xy}(x,\sigma) \\ L_{xy}(x,\sigma) & L_{yy}(x,\sigma) \end{bmatrix} \tag{1}$$

Equation 1 shows Hessian matrix. L_{xx} and L_{yy} are the convolutions of the image with the second-order derivative of the Gaussian with respect to x- and y-direction vectors. L_{xy} is the convolution of the image with second-order partial derivative of Gaussian in xy direction. Non-maximal suppression of the determinants of Hessian matrices is done to extract more localized potential feature points. The process of detection is further speeded up by using the concept of integral images [6] and approximated kernels which make it feasible for implementation in real-time applications.

An integral image I(x) is a derived image where each point $x = (x, y)^T$ stores the cumulative sum of all pixels within the rectangular boundary region surrounded by the origin and point (x). Mathematically, it can be represented as shown in Eq. 2.

$$I(x) = \sum_{i=0}^{i \le x} \sum_{j=0}^{j \le y} I(x, y) \tag{2}$$

The use of integral images enables calculating the response in a rectangular area with arbitrary size using only four look-ups as illustrated in Fig. 2. For digital imple-

Fig. 2 Filter response
calculation using integral
image

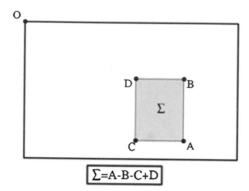

$$\Sigma = A\text{-}B\text{-}C\text{+}D$$

Fig. 3 L_{xx} and L_{xy}
discretization and the
approximations D_{xx} and
D_{xy} [3]

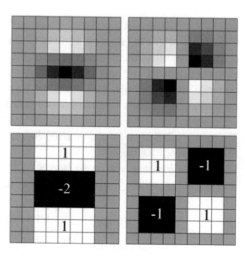

mentation and more speeded-up operation, SURF uses approximate box filters corresponding to Hessian matrix which is illustrated in Fig. 3, where grey, white and black areas correspond to 0, positive and negative values, respectively. This determinant of the box filter response is expressed by Eq. 3. The approximated and discrete kernels are referred to as D_{xx} for L_{xx} and D_{xy} for L_{xy}. The multiplying factor w is used to compensate for errors introduced due to usage of approximated Gaussian kernel and is roughly equal to 0.9.

$$Det\left(\mathcal{H}_{approx}\right) = D_{xx}D_{yy} - \left(wD_{xy}\right)^2 \tag{3}$$

SURF examines several octaves and levels to detect features across scale and calculates the responses with arbitrary larger kernels (of varying box filter size as illustrated in Fig. 4), whereas SIFT scales the image down for each octave and uses progressively larger Gaussian kernels (of varying σ value). For more details, refer to [4, 5].

Fig. 4 Illustration of
varying filter size using box
filter [3]

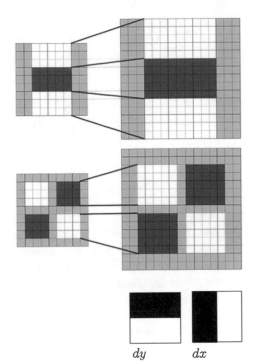

Fig. 5 Haar wavelets filter
response where black and
white areas correspond to a
weight −1 and 1

dy dx

Feature point description

Feature point descriptor provides a unique and robust description of a feature using local neighbourhood. Haar wavelet (Fig. 5) responses in local neighbourhood are used for generating descriptor vector of a feature point. Rotational invariance is achieved by assigning a direction to feature point which is obtained by calculating dominant orientation of the Gaussian weighted Haar wavelet response in sliding window of size $\pi/3$ centred to this feature point. The local neighbourhood area surrounding the feature point is oriented to this direction before calculating the descriptor.

Local neighbourhood spatial distribution illustration is shown in Fig. 6. The descriptor selects 20 s neighbourhood area centred to the feature point which is further subdivided into 4×4 subareas. The wavelet response in x- and y-directions is given by dx and dy, respectively. The interest areas are weighted with a Gaussian centred at the feature point to give some robustness for deformations and translations.

$$v = \left\{ \sum dx, \sum |dx|, \sum dy, \sum |dy| \right\} \tag{4}$$

The vector v (Eq. 4) is calculated for each subarea and the concatenation of the vector for all the 16 subareas defines descriptor of the single feature. This results in a 64-dimensional vector defining each feature point followed by descriptor normalization to achieve contrast invariance. For more details about descriptor generation, refer to [3–5].

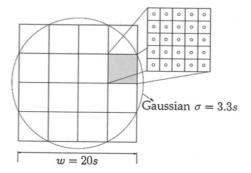

Fig. 6 A 20 s area is divided into 4 × 4 subareas that are sampled 5 × 5 times [5] to get the wavelet response (Fig. 5)

Matching

The feature points matching is based on the distance between the vectors. The best match for each feature point is obtained by finding its nearest neighbour in the extracted feature points from template images. Euclidean distance is used as a similarity measure for finding the nearest neighbour. In scenarios such as target tracking in robotic applications which are governed by real-time constraints, the dimensionality and distinctiveness of the descriptor become very crucial. Smaller dimensions are desirable for fast feature point matching but may give less distinctive descriptor than their high-dimensional counterparts. SURF has been found to be suitable for more accurate real-time implementation of object detection and tracking with most distinct descriptor using lower dimensional vectors.

2.2 Tracking

After the object detection, description and matching, tracking is used to segment the object from its background and localize it within image. This location information is a key parameter in commanding the PTU controller to set pan and tilt axes so as to always keep the object within the camera view.

3 Overview of System

Block diagram of system (Fig. 7) shows basic constitutes of automated target tracking system. The system comprises a vision sensor mounted on PTU. After the user selects a target object, the feature definition of this object is determined, stored in database and passed onto SURF detector/descriptor module. The continuous image streams acquired by the camera are processed through SURF module to segment the object in the image and estimate its actual position. This position information is fed to PTU controller to automatically set the camera view vector in accordance to the

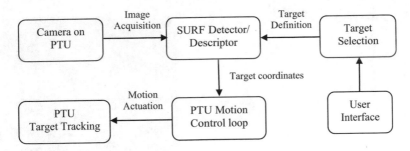

Fig. 7 System block diagram

object's varying position. This process of automatic adjustment of the camera head in accordance to moving target is known as view locking capability.

Software for automated target tracking system is written in C# for PTU control loop operation, and SURF implementation uses openCV library for its realization on PC-based platform.

3.1 Hardware Specification

Figure 8 shows the hardware setup of the current system. A wireless IP camera mounted on PTU is used for tracking the object of interest. Although the setup (shown in the Fig. 8) comprises two cameras (used for stereo setup experiments not in scope of this paper), only the left camera was used for target tracking application. Resolution of camera is 640×480 at 20 frames per second. Higher resolution camera could be used for sharper and better feature point detection at the cost of decreasing processing speed. Higher resolution images provide larger data size for same viewing area, thus providing more feature points and increased chance of tracking. However, the frame processing time increases due to which the maximum speed of moving target for detection decreases compared to low-resolution image. Detected object image coordinate is used actuate PTU in desired direction to track object. The PTU is controlled over serial RS232 interface with position accuracy of $0.052°$ and maximum speed of $300°/s$. In addition to image resolution, tracking efficiency depends on the speed of target object and its distance from camera. Further, objects generate lesser feature points compared to closer ones resulting in poor detection and matching accuracy. Similarly, closer object increases the chance of detection and tracking. The maximum speed of moving target is directly proportional to its relative distance from camera. Object should not move in such a manner that it goes out of view of camera before PTU could respond. In our system, for successful tracking, it was observed that the speed of object located at relative distance of 1 m from camera should not be more than 1 m/s. Objects away by more than 1 m can move relatively faster while closer ones must move at slow speed for successful tracking. Detection would not be possible for extremely fast moving object.

Fig. 8 System setup

3.2   User Interface

Figure 9 shows the User Interface (UI) for automated target tracking system. This utility implements SURF-based feature detection, recognition and tracking. It features PTU control interface for orienting camera towards the target in workspace. Images are acquired over Ethernet and are processed through SURF-based target tracking module.

System operates in two modes of operation:

1. *Manual mode*: This mode facilitates user in searching and locating targeted object in workspace.
2. *Automated target tracking mode*: In this mode, after the user selects the target or region of interest, the camera automatically follows the motion of object using its feature definition.

Details of UI components are as follows:

Camera console: This pane renders the camera view where the user can select the target object of interest.

PTU control pane: This pane is used to interactively adjust the camera orientation and locate the target in manual mode of operation.

Target tracking pane: This pane features SURF-based object tracking and allows switching mode of operation from manual mode to automated target tracking mode.

Targeted object pane: This pane shows objects stored in database that can be tracked.

Message pane: This pane shows the status of system and instructs user about subsequent operation for efficient process flow.

The user can select the area of interest by drawing a rectangle (red colour rectangle in Fig. 9) on the console panel and start target tracking operation. After the object

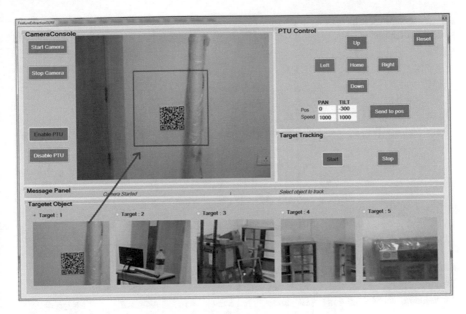

Fig. 9 User interface

selection, selected image area is processed through SURF module, and its feature points and associated descriptor information are stored in database under selected target definition. Once target tracking is enabled, current image stream passes through SURF module for detection and identification. As the object appears in camera view, the tracking module detects the object, segments it from the background and estimates its current location (x, y) in the image coordinate system (Fig. 10). This location (x, y) is used to drive PTU control loop to orient it to keep object always in the centre of camera view with object coordinate in threshold window around coordinate (0, 0). Position control loop for PTU is developed and implemented to provide smooth tracking. Coordinates are fed continuously to the PTU controller via serial communication to automatically orient the axes of PTU and keep the object in camera view. The software allows the user to store multiple areas of interest in the database. When the user changes the target, the PTU starts scanning the entire workspace and locks its view onto the object after detection.

3.3 Results and Discussion

Tests were carried out to evaluate the performance of system. In this regard, various objects at different distances, elevations and orientations were tested. It was found that as distance between the object and camera increases, the size of the object starts to decrease consequently; only bigger object features points are identified and

Fig. 10 Image coordinate system realization

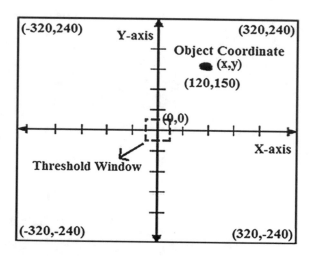

Table 1 Evaluation at various distances, elevations and angles of rotation

Distance effect		Elevation effect		Rotation effect	
Distance in cms	Matching in %	Elevation angle in degree	Matching in %	Angle of rotation in degrees	Matching in %
45	95	0	95	0	95
75	88	15	90	60	91
105	76	30	76	120	89
130	58	45	30	180	85

smaller object features begin to disappear. This results in less efficient detection and matching. Elevation of object also affects the matching. Object recognition and tracking were found to be best when the object elevation is below 45°. Above 45°, object features tend to get deformed compared to reference object and do not generate best results. Rotation of object with respect to reference object has nominal effect on system performance. Table 1 shows test results demonstrating the effect of all the above parameters on system performance in terms of matching percentage for referenced object placed at 45 cm. Matching percentage is given by the ratio of feature points present on detected object in live image to feature points present in referenced object image.

For automated target tracking system, we need to continuously update definition of reference object as the matching percentage goes down to a specific value (55% in present setup). Updating the reference object shall mitigate effects of above-discussed parameters on the system behaviour and assure high system performance and reliability.

4 Conclusion

Automated target tracking system has been developed for applications where the camera viewing vector has to be invariably adjusted by the operator to keep track of moving objects in workspace. The system uses SURF technique which approximates or even outperforms all other feature-based schemes with respect to repeatability, distinctiveness, robustness and speed. The system can serve to upgrade legacy systems which use PTU-based camera heads for focussing on the areas of interest. It eases burden on the operator by allowing him to focus on the job at hand (e.g. visual inspection, object handling, etc.) rather than bothering about object searching and camera head adjustment towards the targeted object.

References

1. Y. Ke, R. Sukthankar, PCA-SIFT: a more distinctive representation for local image descriptors, in *CVPR*, vol. 2 (2004), pp. 506–513
2. D.G. Lowe, Distinctive image features from scale-invariant key-points. Int. J. Comput. Vis. (2004)
3. H. Bay, T. Tuytelaars, L. Van Gool, SURF: speeded up robust features, in *ECCV* (2006)
4. H. Bay, A. Ess, T. Tuytelaars, L. Van Gool, S. U. R. F. (SURF). Elsevier preprint (2008)
5. J.T Pedersen, Study group SURF: Feature detection & description, Q4 (2011)
6. P. Viola, M. Jones, Rapid object detection using a boosted cascade of simple features, In *CVPR*, vol. 1 (2001), pp. 511–518

An Eight-Wire Passively Driven Parallel Manipulator: Development and Analysis

Pratibha Vishnu Shinde, Soumen Sen, Pratik Saha
and Dheeraj Singhal

Abstract The article presents development of an eight-wire passively driven parallel manipulator and discusses its workspace and stiffness behaviour. The uniqueness is in the passively driven design. The device can be used in biomechanics study of human movements and for calibration of manipulator arms, among many others. Manipulator kinematics and the *force closure* workspace (with inextensible wires) are analysed. A procedure is presented to numerically determine the workspace. *Task space stiffness* at end effector is examined through a stiffness tensor for directional stiffness behaviour in the workspace. A *stiffness index* characterizes the degree of isotropy of the stiffness. Experimental validation of forward kinematics and simulation results of force closure workspace and stiffness behaviour of actuated manipulator are reported.

Keywords Wire/cable-driven manipulator · Force closure · Workspace
Stiffness tensor

P. V. Shinde
IIEST, Shibpur,
Shibpur 711103, West Bengal, India
e-mail: shindepratibha31@gmail.com

S. Sen (✉) · P. Saha · D. Singhal
Robotics and Automation Division, CSIR-Central Mechanical Engineering Research Institute,
Durgapur 713209, West Bengal, India
e-mail: soumen_sen@cmeri.res.in

P. Saha
e-mail: pratik_saha@cmeri.res.in

D. Singhal
e-mail: dheerajsinghal101@gmail.com

© Springer Nature Singapore Pte Ltd. 2019   413
D N Badodkar and T A Dwarakanath (eds.), *Machines, Mechanism
and Robotics*, Lecture Notes in Mechanical Engineering,
https://doi.org/10.1007/978-981-10-8597-0_35

1 Introduction

Wire-driven parallel manipulator is a closed mechanism where a platform is moved by a set of wires/cables, which, in turn, are pulled by motors or passive devices on pulleys at the other ends. Generally, the pulling motors or passive load ends are mounted on a framed structure. Manipulation of the platform is achieved by changing the lengths of the wires. Lightweight structure, large workspace, few moving parts, improved inertial properties and high payload-to-weight ratio are making wire-driven parallel manipulator a promising alternative to conventional rigid link ones in many industrial applications as well as rehabilitation and assist devices. However, unilateralist nature of wires, which allows them to only pull, adds complexity in design and requires actuation redundancy in the system. This calls for examining the *force closure* conditions underwire tensions.

Research work on wire/cable-driven parallel manipulators started sometimes in 80s as an alternative to rigid link parallel manipulators to obtain large workspace with lightweight structure. Author in [1] presents a detailed review on wire/cable-driven parallel manipulators and includes a review on kinematics and statics introducing the definition of wrench matrix, followed by dynamics and control on cable-driven parallel system, with their application. However, it excludes discussion on stiffness analysis. Expressing force closure conditions using concepts of convex hull and hyperplanes are popular in literature. Authors in [2] proposed a recursive dimension reducing algorithm for examining force closure conditions using Gauss elimination method. Authors of [3] used null space solution of the transpose of Jacobian matrix for getting the force closure workspace. Authors in [4] gave a systematic method for the analysis of force closure workspace of six degrees-of-freedom manipulators with seven or more cables. The article in [5] discusses about open issues in wire-driven parallel manipulators, including singularity in the wire-driven one, compared to conventional rigid link parallel manipulator. There exist only few literatures on stiffness analysis and in one such paper in [6] authors carried out stiffness analysis to examine system stability.

The present article describes development of an eight-wire passively driven parallel manipulator, presents experimental validation of forward kinematic procedure, considers determination of force closure workspace (with inextensible wires) and gives an account on the task space stiffness behaviour of an *actuated* manipulator with simulation results.

2 Development of an Eight-Wire Passively Driven Parallel Manipulator

An octahedron design of the fixed frame (structure) is a conventional design; however, lack of *form closure* (complete restraint) may pose an issue to achieve all six degrees-of-freedom with only six cables passing through the six vertices of the octahedron.

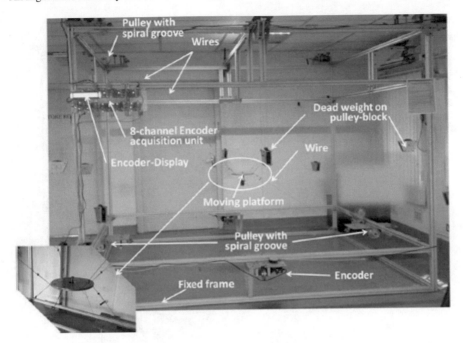

Fig. 1 An eight-wire passively driven parallel manipulator. Moving platform is shown in the inset, showing eight connecting points of the wires

For ease of construction using off-the-shelf extruded bars, a hexahedron design of fixed frame is chosen. Arrangement of eight wires is a natural choice in this design, which meets the form closure requirement (and thereby *force closure*), given the fact that a minimum of seven wires are needed for complete restraint in general (irrespective of the presence of gravity) [7, 8]. Hence, an eight-wire passively driven parallel manipulator is developed, a photograph of which is shown in Fig. 1.

The fixed frame of the developed manipulator is of 2016 mm length, 2016 mm breadth and 2047 mm height. The moving platform is circular in shape of radius 100 mm and on the periphery eight wires are anchored at equidistant points. In analysis, the platform is considered as a regular octagon, each apex being connected by a wire. Four of the wires emanate from four top corners of the fixed frame. Remaining four wires emerge from four points, located at the mid-point of the bottom four sides of the fixed frame. Figure 2 illustrates the routing of wires from one top corner and bottom mid-point of the fixed frame. Each wire is supported by a dead weight hung on pulley block, routed through idle pulleys. On the pulley block side, each wire runs on an intermediate positive drive pulley having spiral groove. Solid model of the assembly of the routing pulleys, positive drive pulley with spiral groove, encoder with timing belt–pulley and the passive weight on pulley block are depicted in Fig. 3. The circular moving platform is made to reach a desired pose within the work volume by winding and unwinding the wires on the spiral grooves, and counterbalanced by

Fig. 2 Illustration on routing of wires: four wires emanate from top four corners of the fixed frame, while the remaining four come from four mid-points of bottom four sides of fixed frame

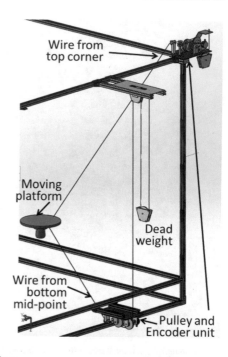

Fig. 3 Solid model of arrangement of the positive drive pulley with spiral groove, encoder with timing pulley-and-belt and the dead weight (passive) on pulley block

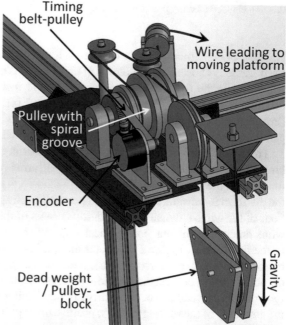

dead weights on pulley blocks, keeping the wires always in tension. Encoders fixed on the intermediate pulley shafts measure the change in lengths of the wires. The manipulator platform stays in equilibrium nearly at the centre under the equal passive dead loads (without external load).

2.1 Kinematics

Computation of the length of the wires is straightforward for a given pose of the manipulator (inverse kinematics). However, the forward kinematics is difficult. The present assembly is only a positioning manipulator due to the presence of regular polygonal platform. So orientation is not considered in the forward kinematics. An iterative procedure is followed for forward kinematics computation.

As shown in Fig. 4, a is a wire attachment point on fixed frame, a to h are attachment points on the moving platform and $\{O\}$ is the reference frame . Body frame $\{e\}$ is attached on the platform at the centre, where an end effector is mounted. Here, $a_i \in \mathbb{R}^3$ is position vector of ith attachment point in $\{O\}$, $b_i \in \mathbb{R}^3$ is position vector of ith attachment point $l_i \in \mathbb{R}^3$ is vector along ith wire and $p \in \mathbb{R}^3$ is position vector of the end effector in $\{O\}$. Clearly,

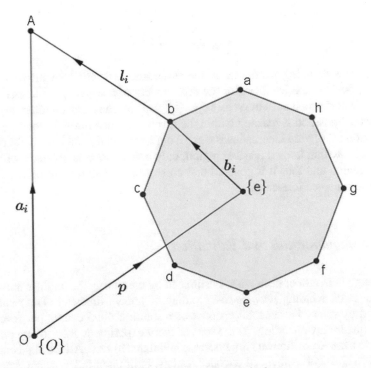

Fig. 4 Kinematics of eight-wire passively driven parallel manipulator

$$\| \, a_i - p \, \|_2 = \| \, l_i + b_i \, \|_2, \tag{1}$$

$i = 1$ to 8. $\| \cdot \|_2$ denotes Euclidean norm. Length of wire being always positive, triangle inequality gives $\| \, l_i + b_i \, \|_2 \leq l_i + \| \, b_i \, \|_2$. Therefore, from Eq. 1:

$$\| \, a_i - p \, \|_2 \leq l_i + \| \, b_i \, \|_2 . \tag{2}$$

Equation 2 represents set of circles with centres at a_i and radii $l_i + \| \, b_i \, \|_2, i = 1$ to 8. Bounds for common region are obtained as

$$p_i^1 = a_i - (l_i + \| \, b_i \, \|_2)[1, 1, 1]^T ; \quad p_i^2 = a_i + (l_i + \| \, b_i \, \|_2)[1, 1, 1]^T. \tag{3}$$

Hence, lower and upper bounds for the feasible region are given by $p^{low} = \max(p_i^1)$ and $p^{high} = \min(p_i^2)$, respectively. Centre of this common region is taken as an initial estimate, and the forward kinematics solution is obtained by iteration through minimizing the *distance norm* of the position error, employing *Levenberg–Marquardt* method [9]. For minimization (least square), positional error function is formed as

$$\phi_i = (\| \, a_i - p - b_i \, \|_2^2 - l_i^2). \tag{4}$$

The signed increment h for the iterative procedure is given by ([9, 10])

$$h = \frac{J_\phi^T \, \phi}{(J_\phi^T \, J_\phi + \mu \, I)} \in \mathbb{R}^3, \tag{5}$$

where μ is a damping parameter in the procedure, $I \in \mathbb{R}^{3 \times 3}$ an identity matrix and $J_\phi \in \mathbb{R}^{8 \times 3}$ is the jacobian for the error function $\phi = [\phi_1, \phi_2, \ldots, \phi_8]^T \in \mathbb{R}^8$. Iteration is performed until the scalar $\phi = \sum_{i=1}^{m} \phi_i^2$ reaches a given tolerance value. The targeted position is reached within the given tolerance through iteration. Since the solution of forward kinematics is carried out numerically and iteratively, starting with a point within known feasible region, only one solution is obtained within the feasible region and thus it is ensured that correct end effector position is achieved within the accepted tolerance.

2.2 Implementation and Validation

The change in length of each wire is estimated by measuring the angular movement of the relevant winding *positive drive* pulley of known diameter. The rotation is measured by rotary incremental encoder of resolution 4096 counts per revolution through quadrature encoding. At the start of every experiment, the moving platform is taken to a home position and the system is initialized to zero. All the eight encoders are read in situ with embedded encoder readers, built upon independent Arduino©

Uno controller boards and data are processed in another controller unit (Arduino©
Mega 2560), which receives data from individual encoder readers over I^2C bus.
Finally, the encoder data are accessed in computer via serial communication at 38.4
kbps. Labview© environment from National Instruments is used for data acquisition,
online computation and visualization. The forward kinematics procedure, described
above, is implemented in Labview programming environment for fast and reliable
development. The procedure is made to run at an update rate of 50 mS for moderately
fast movement of the platform. Presence of friction, backlash and play in the pulleys, wire guides and couplings cause errors in the measurements, however, within
acceptable values.

Two experiments are conducted for repeatability of system measurement and
validation of the forward kinematics procedure. First, a reference frame $\{O\}$ is chosen
(one of the bottom corners of fixed frame) and the home position of the platform
(and system) is identified. Then, location of a chosen point within the workspace
is measured with the end effector several times, in each operation starting from the
home position. The repeatability is found to be $x_r = 2.0$ mm, $y_r = 1.0$ mm (rounded
off) in measuring a point having average values of coordinates ($\bar{x}$, $\bar{y}$) 1416 mm and
719 mm (rounded off), respectively, at a given z (no. of measurements $n = 20$).

To further validate the procedure, a circle is drawn with known diameter (140 mm)
on a horizontal plane located at a given height ($z = 756$ mm). Positional measurements of 10 points on the periphery of the circle are taken with the end effector
manually (keeping the platform horizontal), measured by the encoder readings. The
measured points are fitted on a circle with least square technique and centre and
diameter are estimated from the measurements. Error in diameter measurement is
found to be 2.35%. Figure 5 presents the results of circle measurements.

Fig. 5 Experimental
validation: sample data
points and the circle which
best fits them. Diameter
measurement shows an error
of 2.35%

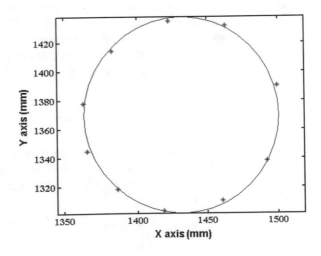

3 Workspace Analysis: Force Closure

The constructed manipulator is having equal length and breadth (sides) of the fixed frame and the moving platform is a regular polygon (octagon). The particular construction imposes restriction on the effective mobility of the platform (see [11]). Rotation about an axis normal to the plane of the moving platform (z-axis) would not be possible from input. It amounts that an external torque about the above normal cannot be supported by pulling forces of the wires. Effective degrees-of-freedom of the platform reduces to five for the present construction of the manipulator.

Being unilateral, all wires must generate positive tension forces and under the passive internal loading, the platform maintains equilibrium. The equilibrium relations for external loads/moments acting on the moving platform are given by

$$\sum_{i=1}^{8} t_i + f = 0, \quad \sum_{i=1}^{8} b_i \times t_i + \tau = 0,$$

where $t_i = t_i \cdot c_i$ is ith tension vector and t_i is magnitude of ith wire force. $c_i \in \mathbb{R}^3$ is unit vector along ith wire, represented in $\{O\}$. External loads/moments are clubbed in a vector $w = \begin{bmatrix} f & \tau \end{bmatrix}^T \in \mathbb{R}^5$ giving rise to:

$$A\, t = w \quad with \quad t \geq 0 , \tag{6}$$

where $A = \begin{bmatrix} c_1 & c_2 & \cdots & c_8 \\ b_1 \times c_1 & b_2 \times c_2 & \cdots & b_8 \times c_8 \end{bmatrix} \in \mathbb{R}^{5 \times 8}$ is wire structure matrix (on removing the row corresponding to torque about z-axis) and $t = [t_1\, t_2\, \dots\, t_8]^T \in \mathbb{R}^8$ is wire tension vector. The structure matrix happens to be equal to transpose of the manipulator Jacobian (J^T), which is described in Eq. 7.

Let l_i denote the length of ith wire, and $l \in \mathbb{R}^8$ the vector of lengths of all the wires. Then, the relation between the time rate of change of wire lengths and the velocities of the moving platform is given by

$$\dot{l} = J \left\{ \begin{matrix} \dot{p} \\ \omega \end{matrix} \right\} , \tag{7}$$

where $\dot{p} \in \mathbb{R}^3$ is the rectilinear velocity vector and $\omega \in \mathbb{R}^2$ the angular velocity vector of the moving platform in $\{O\}$. The Jacobian J can be split into two blocks, namely $J_L \in \mathbb{R}^{8 \times 3}$ and $J_\omega \in \mathbb{R}^{8 \times 2}$ relating the rectilinear velocity and angular velocity, respectively, so that

$$\dot{l} = \begin{bmatrix} J_L \mid J_\omega \end{bmatrix} \left\{ \begin{matrix} \dot{p} \\ \omega \end{matrix} \right\} . \tag{8}$$

The relationship between the linear differential displacements in wire space and the task space is readily expressed as

$$\Delta l = J_L \, \Delta p. \tag{9}$$

Solution for Eq. 6 contains a particular solution and a homogeneous component with the null space defined by

$$A \, t = 0. \tag{10}$$

Force closure is described as a condition under which any arbitrary external load at the end effector can be supported by adjusting the wire tensions (assuming, the motors can provide enough torque, the wires are inextensible and do not fail). The force closure condition can be checked by examining the null space of A having all positive vectors or not, or, equivalently by examining the convex combination of the columns of the structure matrix A to check the convex hull of the set of the columns of A containing the origin or not (see [7]). On satisfying the above condition, it can be ensured that the system is under *force closure* (with wire tensions keeping positive). An algorithm for checking the force closure condition is developed and employed to find the *force closure workspace* of the present wire-driven manipulator (assuming inextensible wires).

For n degrees-of-freedom system with m wires, at first, a set of $n - 1$ linearly independent column vectors are selected from the structure matrix A (for nonsingular configuration) to form a hyperplane, passing through the origin and dividing the whole space into two half-spaces and its normal vector is identified. In the second step, each of the remaining vectors is checked for which half space it belongs to, by taking dot product with the above normal. Similar procedure is applied for all combinations of the column vectors. It is reasoned that if there occurs at least one change in sign (of the dot products), the vectors are ensured to be distributed on both the sides of the hyperplane, thus containing the origin. There will be a total of $^mC_{n-1}$ hyperplanes and their respective normal vectors. Applying the procedures for all vectors, it can be examined whether the origin lies in the interior of convex hull of the column vectors or not. For all positions of the end effector within the fixed frame volume, above condition is checked. The points, where the force closure conditions (*convex hull containing origin*) are satisfied, constitute the *force closure workspace* of end effector of the parallel manipulator. Force closure workspace for the present eight-wire-driven parallel manipulator is computed (at zero orientation of the platform) following the above procedure and the results are shown in Fig. 6. The observed nature of the workspace is influenced by the particular construction, where the top four wires emanate from top four corners and bottom four wires emerge from middle of the four bottom sides of the fixed frame.

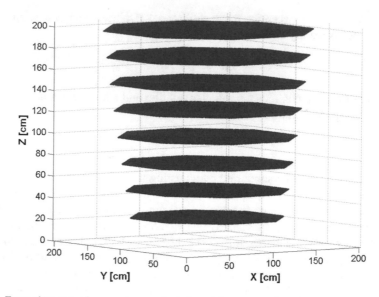

Fig. 6 Force closure workspace at zero orientation of the octagonal platform

Fig. 7 Stiffness ellipsoids at
$z = 102.35\,\text{cm}$

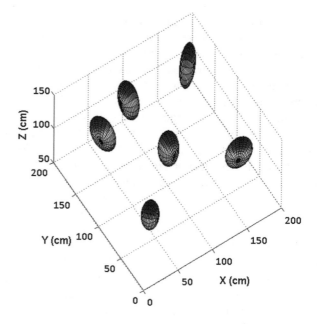

4 Stiffness

The wire-driven parallel manipulator system, under equilibrium of the wire tensions and actuated by motors, manifests directional stiffness about the equilibrium points against external loads. The manipulator stiffness is contributed by the elastic properties of the wires (no more inextensible) and the proportional gain of the motor position controller, when actively controlled.

Denoting an end effector position at an equilibrium as $p \in \mathbb{R}^3$, on application of an external force f, the platform gets deflected by $\Delta p \in \mathbb{R}^3$, resulting in a deflection of wire length by Δl_i. In vector form, for all wires, the relationship between the differential displacements is given by Eq. 9. By force–velocity duality (and referring to Eq. 6)

$$f = J_L{}^T t. \tag{11}$$

A diagonal stiffness tensor (k_l) is formed for all wires (in wire space): $k_l = \begin{bmatrix} k_{li} & 0 & 0 & .. & 0 \\ 0 & k_{l2} & 0 & .. & 0 \\ .. & .. & .. & .. & .. \\ 0 & 0 & 0 & .. & k_{l8} \end{bmatrix}$, where, k_{li} denotes the stiffness of ith wire.

For identical stiffness $k_{li} = k$, $k_l = k I_{8 \times 8}$. Wire tensions and elastic deformations of the wires are related by

$$t = k_l \Delta l. \tag{12}$$

Defining Cartesian stiffness tensor $K \in \mathbb{R}^{3 \times 3}$, by definition of stiffness:

$$f = K \Delta p. \tag{13}$$

Using Eqs. 9–13, the Cartesian stiffness can be derived to be

$$K = J_L{}^T k_l J_L = k J_L{}^T J_L, \tag{14}$$

which is clearly configuration dependent .

The principal values and direction of stiffness are expressed by eigenvalues (λ_i, $i = 1, 2, 3$) and eigenvectors, respectively, of the stiffness tensor. Since only translational stiffness is considered (orientation not happening and not included), the stiffness matrix is dimensionally consistent and so the eigenvalues. The variation of stiffness is illustrated by ellipsoids, where the maximum eigenvalue (λ_{max}) decides the length of semi-major axis aligned along corresponding eigenvector. The other eigenvalues present semi-axes in other orthogonal directions. The shape varies from a sphere to an ellipsoid and on degeneration to an ellipse or a line. A detail delineation through exemplar calculation is out of the scope of this paper. For computational detail, a work of the same authors [12] may be referred, where a general discussion on wire-driven parallel manipulator is presented.

The measure of *stiffness isotropy* can be represented by a *Stiffness index*, $\gamma = \frac{\lambda_{min}}{\lambda_{max}}$. The most isotropic stiffness behaviour occurs when $\gamma = 1$, generating a sphere. Cartesian stiffness for different positions of the end effector is shown in Fig. 7. Result shows that stiffness index is nearer to 1 when equilibrium position is at the centre of the fixed frame.

5 Conclusion

The article presents a brief account of the development of a passive eight-wire-driven parallel manipulator with counterweights. Equal counterweights at equilibrium keep the platform nearly at the centre of the fixed frame. Encoders on positive drive pulley shafts measure the change in length of the wires. The principle for forward kinematics is delineated in brief, supported by experimental results on repeatability and identification of a circle. The paper presents the principle of computing the force closure workspace and reports result on computation of workspace for selected platform configuration. Analysis on the task space stiffness behaviour is done, and results of simulation are presented around various equilibrium points over the workspace. However, experimental validation for force closure workspace and task space stiffness behaviour will require attachment of motors at the wire ends, which is kept as immediate future work.

Acknowledgements The work has been done under the activities of the Network project ESC-0113 (CSIR, Govt. of India) and the DST (Govt. of India) sponsored project GAP-152812, both being carried out in CSIR-CMERI, Durgapur, India.

References

1. C. Gosselin, Cable-driven parallel mechanisms: state of the art and perspectives. Mech. Eng. R. Bull. Jpn. Soc. Mech. Eng. **1**(1) (2014)
2. C. Pham, S. Yeo, S. Mustafa, G. Yang, I. Chen, Force-closure workspace analysis of cable-driven parallel mechanisms. Mech. Mach. Theory 53–69 (2006)
3. M. Gouttefarde, M. Gosselin, Analysis of the wrench-closure workspace of planar parallel cable-driven mechanisms. IEEE Trans. Robot. **22**, 434–445 (2006)
4. X. Diao, O. Ma, Force-closure analysis of 6-dof cable manipulators with seven or more cables. Robotica **27**, 209–215 (2009)
5. J. Merlet, Wire-driven parallel robot: open issues, in *Romansy 19 Robot Design, Dynamics and Control*, ed. by V. Padois, P. Bidaud, O. Khatib. CISM International Centre for Mechanical Sciences, vol. 544 (Springer, 2013)
6. S. Behzadipour, A. Khajepour, Stiffness of cable-based parallel manipulators with application to stability analysis. J. Mech. Des. **128**(6), 303–310 (2006)
7. R. Murray, Z. Li, S. Sastry, *A Mathematical Introduction to Robotic Manipulation* (CRC Press, Boca Raton, FL, 1994)
8. J.P. Merlet, On the redundancy of cable-driven parallel robots, in *5th European Conferences on Mechanism Science (Eucomes)*, Guimares, 16–19 Sept 2014, pp. 31–39

9. K. Madsen, H. Nielsen, O. Tingleff, *Methods for Non-linear Least Squares Problems*, 2nd edn. Technical University of Denmark: Informatics and Mathematical Modelling (2004)
10. A. Pott, An algorithm for real-time forward kinematics of cable-driven parallel robots, in *Advances in Robot Kinematics: motion in man and machine*, (Springer, 2010), pp. 529–538
11. O. Ma, J. Angeles, Architecture singularities of platform manipulators. Int. J. Robot. Autom. **7**(1), 23–29 (1992)
12. P. Shinde, S. Sen, S.N. Shome, Task space stiffness analysis of wire driven parallel manipulator, in *IEEE 1st International Conference on Electronics, Materials Engineering and Nano-Technology, (IEMENTech)*, Kolkata, 28–29 April 2017, https://doi.org/10.1109/IEMENTECH. 2017.8077014

An Open-Section Shell Designed for Customized Bending and Twisting to Ease Sitting and Rising in a Chair

Shamanth Hampali, Pai S. Anoosha and G. K. Ananthasuresh

Abstract This paper is concerned with a compliant-hinge mechanism in an assistive chair that does not use external power in aiding the elderly and arthritics in stand-to-sit and sit-to-stand manoeuvres. The mechanism, attached to the seat of the chair, acts like a nonlinear torsion spring that is effectively pivoted to the frame. A pair of semi-circular open-section shells that are rigidly connected to each other and fastened to the chair frame comprise the spring. A cam profile on a guide plate enables the shells to deform transversely even as they twist to provide customized torque–angle characteristic as per the weight of the occupant. The formulation of the design specification based on biomechanical considerations, kinetics of sitting and rising in a chair, kinetoelastic modelling of open-section shells, a new energy mapping method of designing the guideway for the shells, and simulation of the entire unitized compliant spring mechanism are presented.

Keywords Adjustable stiffness · Assistive chair · Compliant-hinge mechanism
Elastic centre · Geriatrics

1 Introduction

Some elderly people, especially those suffering from arthritis, have difficulty during the act of sitting down and rising from a chair. Many of the available assistive chairs [1–5] use simple springs that merely provide assistive torque for rising and give the 'pushing feeling' even while being fully seated. Many of them are also not

S. Hampali · P. S. Anoosha (✉) · G. K. Ananthasuresh
Indian Institute of Science, Bangalore, India
e-mail: anooshapai@iisc.ac.in; anooshapai@gmail.com

S. Hampali
e-mail: shamanthh@iisc.ac.in

G. K. Ananthasuresh
e-mail: suresh@iisc.ac.in

© Springer Nature Singapore Pte Ltd. 2019
D N Badodkar and T A Dwarakanath (eds.), *Machines, Mechanism and Robotics*, Lecture Notes in Mechanical Engineering,
https://doi.org/10.1007/978-981-10-8597-0_36

427

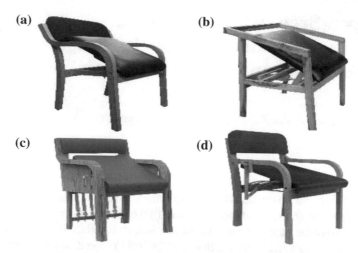

Fig. 1 Assistive chairs with different mechanisms. **a** Torsion spring chair. **b** Gas spring chair. **c** Statically balanced chair. **d** Bistable chair

customizable. With the goal of providing a cost-effective and customizable, fully mechanical solution for an assistive chair, we propose a novel design in this work.

Our interactions with geriatricians and utilization of the concepts of bistability and static balancing [6] led to the design of four assistive chairs shown in Fig. 1. Clinical testing on two of these chairs under the supervision of a geriatrician helped us formulate three objectives: (i) providing resistive support to the elderly while sitting, who tend to slouch into the chair seat because of lack of complete control over their limbs; (ii) offering no resistance while being seated; and (iii) providing gradual assistive support while rising from the chair. In view of these, the seat of the chair was hinged upwardly inclined (Figs. 1 and 2). The work done by the weight of the occupant is stored in specially designed springs that are capable of taking a substantial fraction of the load so as to minimize the effort put by the knee joint. Based on the above observations, after much experimentation and discussions with the subjects and geriatricians, a qualitative torque profile shown in Fig. 2 was decided. Quantitative features of the torque–angle characteristic are explained in the next section.

2 Kinetics of Stand-to-Sit Manoeuver

Stand-to-sit kinetics of a three-segment, three-joint stick model of a human body in the sagittal plane is analysed (Fig. 3). The segment parameters and joint angle profiles are taken from a previous study [7]. Here, t_f is the total time for stand-to-sit transition, and t_s is the time instant when the occupant comes in contact with the seat of the chair. A non-dimensional parameter termed as the Floating Factor (FF)

Fig. 2 Qualitative target
torque profile

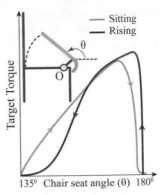

Fig. 3 Three-segment,
three-joint human stick
model

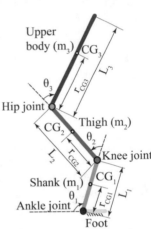

is defined to express any added reactive force F that the occupant feels due to the
spring.

$$FF = \frac{\text{Reaction force of the seat on the occupant}}{\text{Weight of the occupant on the chair seat}} = \frac{F}{W_3 + (W_2/2)} \qquad (1)$$

where W_i is weight of the ith segment. It is desirable to have FF close to zero for
ergonomically comfortable seating.

With the aforementioned model, kinetics of the sitting was analysed for two
different chairs: a normal chair and a chair with inclined seat and a variable stiffness
spring at its hinge. Infinitesimally small sliding is assumed between the thigh segment
at the hip joint and the chair seat when they are in contact. Hence, the reaction force
from the chair-seat is always normal to it. At any given instant $t > t_s$, from the
free-body diagram of each segment (Fig. 4), we have

$$\mathbf{T}_2 = \mathbf{r}_{CG2} \times W_2 + \mathbf{T}_3 + l_2 \times RF_3 + l_2 \times \mathbf{F} = \mathbf{r}_{CG2} \times W_2 + \mathbf{r}_{J2-CG3} \times W_3 + l_2 \times \mathbf{F}$$
$$(2)$$

Fig. 4 Free-body diagrams of links for variable stiffness chair

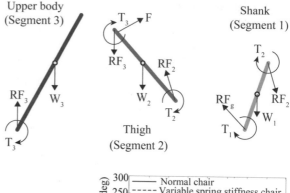

Fig. 5 Knee joint torque variation

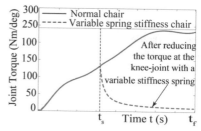

where $\mathbf{T}_i$ and θ_i are the torque and angle at the ith joint, respectively; l_i the length of ith segment; $\mathbf{r}_{CGi}$ the vector along ith segment joining the $(i-1)$th joint and Centre of Mass (CoM) of the ith segment; $\mathbf{r}_{Ji-CGk}$ the vector joining the ith joint and CoM kth link, where $i = 1, 2$ and $k = 2, 3$, where $k > i$ and $\mathbf{F}$ the reaction force due to the spring (Fig. 4) and is normal to the orientation of the chair seat. Since the torque at the knee joint should be always greater than or equal to zero for sitting action, we have

$$\mathbf{T}_2 = \mathbf{r}_{CG2} \times W_2 + \mathbf{T}_3 + l_2 \times \mathbf{F} \geq 0 \tag{3}$$

In Eq. (3), the first two terms in the right-hand side are dependent only on the properties and orientation of the links. The magnitude of $\mathbf{F}$, however, should vary such that it allows the torque at knee joint to be as low as possible. However, it is also appropriate to consider a desired profile for knee joint torque $\mathbf{T}_2$, for $t > t_s$ and in turn compute $\mathbf{F}$ as shown in Fig. 5. This is the spring force that should resist and assist the person while sitting in and rising from the chair, respectively. Now, the total energy of the system can be written as

$$\text{Total Energy} = PE_{\text{mass}} + WD_{\text{joints}} + SE_{\text{torsion spring}} \tag{4}$$

where PE_{mass} is the potential energy due to body mass of the occupant; $SE_{\text{torsion spring}}$ the strain energy stored in the torsion spring and WD_{joints} is the work done by the joints. Due to the addition of a spring, a portion of reduction in PE_{mass} is stored as $SE_{\text{torsion spring}}$, thereby reducing overall WD_{joints} (Fig. 6).

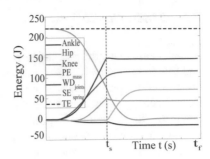

Fig. 6 Energy for a variable stiffness chair

3 Design

We use open-section shells in this work. Open-section shells tend to warp, i.e. they displace axially under torsion. When warping is restrained at any point along the beam, the member undergoes non-uniform torsion; the torque is carried by shear stresses (St. Venant torsion) and axial stresses (warping torsion). The shear stresses are in opposite directions on opposite faces, and hence the torsional stiffness for members with open section is lower than those having closed sections for given size and angle of twist. The concept of the elastic centre has been used in the design and is defined as follows:

The elastic centre (O) of a section is the average location of the shear centre and the torsional centre if the distance between these two centres is sufficiently small to be neglected for practical purposes. The elastic centre, in practice, is calculated as the shear centre [8].

A schematic of a prismatic thin-walled beam and its cross section are shown in Fig. 7. The shell-beam axis is defined by the line of centroids of the cross sections. For an open-section member with cantilever end conditions, torsional stiffness is the lowest when the beam twists about the elastic centre O. If, by any means, the beam is made to twist at a point that is at an offset from the elastic centre, it offers increased stiffness. This can also be achieved by keeping the point of application of the load fixed and bending the beam while twisting it. This feature is utilized in the design to achieve variable stiffness as described later in the paper.

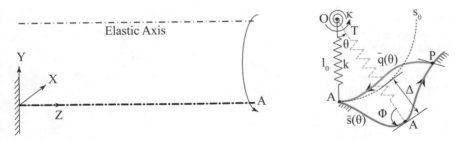

Fig. 7 Representative diagram of thin-walled open-section beam

3.1 Kinetoelastic Model

A shell beam that can bend and twist and its kinetoelastic model are shown in Fig. 8 and Fig. 9, respectively. The translational spring with stiffness $k(s, \theta)$ and the rotational torsion spring at O with a spring constant $\kappa(s, \theta)$ represent the variable nonlinear bending stiffness and torsional stiffness, respectively. Note that l_0 is the free length of the translational spring, i.e., when there is no deformation and s is the absolute magnitude of bending measured along the local y-axis of the member. Furthermore, Δ represents the change in the length of the translational spring at any instant, which is equal to $(s - s_0)$ and θ is the angle of twist. Let F be the axial force applied at A to extend the spring and T be the torque applied at O to rotate the system about O. This system can be actuated in two ways.

Case 1. A two-DoF system: Both F and T are applied incrementally so that point A is traversed along a path. Here, the magnitudes of applied F, T and the total strain energy stored in the system are independent of the order of application of the two external inputs.

Case 2. A one-DoF system: Point A is initially placed in a frictionless guideway $\bar{s}(\theta)$ that commences at s_0. The slot guides the point A along a desired path when only torque T is applied at O. Even though the strain energy stored in the system in this case is equal to that of the energy in Case 1, the magnitude of the applied torque is different. In fact, a torque larger than that in Case 1 is required to actuate the

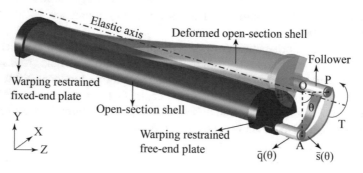

Fig. 8 Open-section shell undergoing coupled bending and twisting

Fig. 9 Kinetoelastic model representing coupled bending and twisting

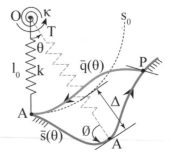

system. The total potential energy of the system is minimized to find the relationship between the applied Torque T and slot $\bar{s}(\theta)$.

$$PE_{\text{total}} = SE_t + SE_r + WP_F + WP_T \tag{5}$$

where SE_t and SE_r are strain energies of the translational and rotating torsional springs, and WP_F and WP_T are the work potentials due to applied force F (zero in this case) and torque T. If s_0 and θ_0 are the initial state variables, we have

$$PE_{total} = \frac{1}{2}k(s, \theta)(s - s_0)^2 + \frac{1}{2}\kappa(s, \theta)(\theta - \theta_0)^2 - F(s - s_0) - T(\theta)(\theta - \theta_0) \tag{6}$$

By taking the Lagrangian along with the constraint $(\bar{s}(\theta))$, minimizing it with respect to s and θ, and using derivatives in polar coordinates, we get

$$T(\theta) = \kappa(s, \theta)(\theta - \theta_0) + \frac{\partial k}{\partial \theta}\frac{(s - s_0)^2}{2} + \frac{\partial \kappa}{\partial s}\frac{(\theta - \theta_0)^2}{2}$$
$$+ \left(k(s, \theta)(s - s_0) + \frac{\partial k}{\partial s}\frac{(s - s_0)^2}{2} + \frac{\partial \kappa}{\partial s}\frac{(\theta - \theta_0)^2}{2} \right) s \cot \phi \tag{7}$$

From Eq. (7), it is evident that the system has a nonlinear torque–angle characteristic. The torque is dependent on the angle made by the transitional spring with the tangent of the slot at the point of contact (ϕ). It may be noted that the SE stored in the system due to the deformation in both the springs for a given s and θ is unique and independent of the path traversed. Thus, for a given energy profile, it is possible to obtain any given nonlinear stiffness variation from this system by guiding the endpoint A through specially designed guideways. Point A (Figs. 8 and 9) can return to its original state along the same slot $\bar{s}(\theta)$ or by a different slot $\bar{q}(\theta)$ starting at the common point P. The slope of the slot $\bar{q}(\theta)$ at P determines the magnitude of torque at O, when point A just starts moving along it. It should be noted that the torque profiles are different. This concept is used here to impart dissimilar torque profiles while sitting and rising (Fig. 1).

3.2 Compliant-Hinge Mechanism

The compliant-hinge mechanism designed in this work is shown in Fig. 10 and its 2D kinetoelastic model is shown in Fig. 11. We have combined two kinematically symmetric building blocks having a common axis of rotation. The arrangement is such that the deformation of one building block is countered by the other building block. This is achieved by connecting the two building blocks by a rigid segment. During pure torsion, the building blocks rotate about the common virtual axis with their free ends tracing a circular arc with centre O. Thus, it functions like a hinge that can allow large rotations beyond $45°$. The mechanism can also exhibit the func-

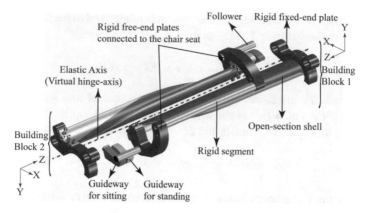

Fig. 10 The variable stiffness complaint mechanism that replaces the hinge of the chair seat

Fig. 11 Kinetoelastic model
of the compliant mechanism

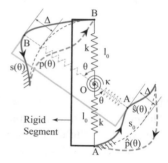

tionality of a variable stiffness torsional spring when guided along a guideway. The guideway is designed using an approach which we call the *energy mapping method*.

3.3 Energy Mapping Method

The work done by the weight of the person is the energy that is stored in the spring. For the given target resistive or assistive torque–angle profiles, the area under the curve gives the magnitude of energy stored in the spring at any instant, which forms the target energy plot for a particular weight of the occupant. Conversely, the slope of the energy curve at any point gives the torque at that point. The compliant-hinge mechanism of fixed dimensions is analysed for various magnitudes of bending and twisting, and the corresponding strain energy data is obtained using commercially available finite element analysis (FEA) software *ABAQUS*. The 2-DoF system explained in Sect. 3.1 is used for this. The characteristic strain energy data are initially parameterized over discrete magnitudes of bending to obtain distinct curves. Thus, one characteristic energy curve represents the strain energy stored in the beam with a

Fig. 12 Characteristic
energy surface

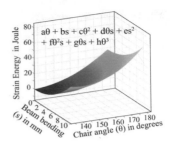

Fig. 13 Energy mapping

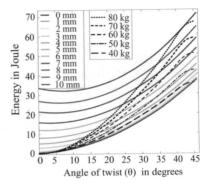

particular magnitude of bending (s) maintained constant throughout the angle of twist (θ).

The data is fit to a multivariate function, that is, second order in s and third order in θ to obtain an energy surface (Fig. 12). Each point on the energy surface corresponds to a unique value of s, θ and SE but the magnitude of torque is determined by the slope of the energy surface at that point in SE-θ plane. In other words, two different energy surfaces, passing through the same point, have a distinct value of torque at that point which is slot-dependent. Subsequently, the target energy curve for a particular weight of the occupant (Sect. 1) is overlaid onto the characteristic strain energy surface to obtain a unique relationship between s and θ (Fig. 13). A cam-like guideway ($s(\theta)$) is designed accordingly (Fig. 14). Both the building blocks in the mechanism are guided by their respective guideways. Therefore, the strain energy stored in the system will vary as per the target requirement.

Finite element simulation was performed to validate a target torque profile when the mechanism deforms along a designed guideway. Results were thus obtained as shown in Fig. 15. The points do not exactly lie on the target torque curve due to numerical artefact of contacts in the quasi-static analysis performed.

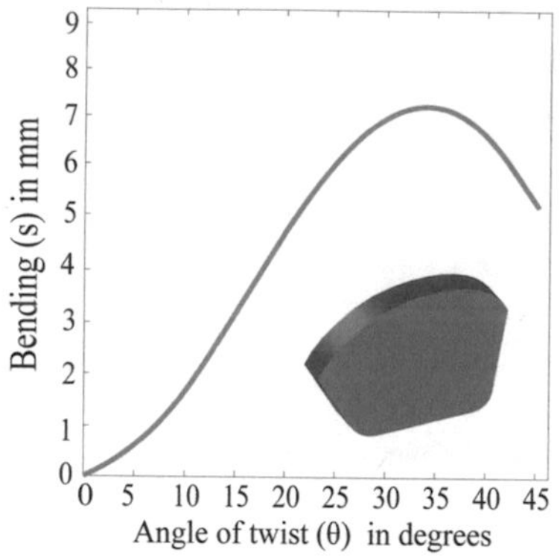

Fig. 14 Figure representing
the design of a guideway slot

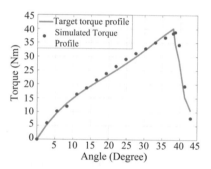

Fig. 15 Plot representing
validation of a torque profile

3.4 Design Specifications for the Assistive Chair

Each building block acts like a spring and the number shells in one stack are chosen
based on the energy requirement. For the assistive chair, each stack consists of three
prismatic shells of 0.8 mm thickness of progressively varying radii. The same cross
section for all beams is chosen to be the variants of circular arcs because this shape
does not need forming and is easy to manufacture by roll bending. The dimensions
of each shell beam are chosen such that (i) all the shells in the stack have the same
elastic axis; and (ii) they lie within the space constraints of the application. Thorough
nonlinear finite element analyses were performed in *ABAQUS*, with spring steel
($E = 210$ *GPa*) as the material. The shell beam undergoes non-uniform torsion [8]
and coupled bending and twisting deformation [9]. The stress distribution in the
deformed configuration was found to be non-uniform, and the peak stresses were as
high as 2000 MPa, which are undesirable. Rigid boundary conditions being crucial
for proper restraint of the mechanism, and in order to make the design feasible in
practice, the following modifications were made:
(i) Two diagonally opposite circular cuts were made on the longitudinal edges of the
shell as shown in Fig. 16. When the shell-beam twists, the cuts allow warping and
axial deformation, consequently reducing the stress. For a given radius and length,
$H_{max} = 1/2$(perimeter of the cross section) and $W_{max} = 1/2$(Length of the open −
section shell). FEA simulations showed that for a given H (or W), increase in W (or

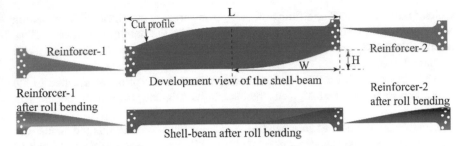

Fig. 16 Shell spring design and modifications

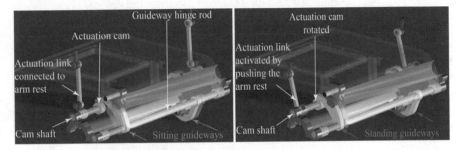

Fig. 17 Actuation mechanism to switch from sitting and standing guideway in the assistive chair

H) gave uniform stress distribution. And the dimensions were chosen suitably to meet these requirements. The cut also induces non-uniform cross section, thereby making the second moment of area vary along the longitudinal axis. As a result of cutting away some material, very high stress (up to 1000 MPa) is concentrated at the fixed edges during bending.

(ii) Two reinforcers (of same geometry to the material removed after the cut) of the same thickness as that of the shell were added on the inside along the longitudinal edges that is devoid of the cut (Fig. 16). Adding these makes the second moment of area of the shell-beam constant along its axis. Thus, reinforcers do not significantly affect the behaviour of the component in torsion but only improve the performance under bending loads.

Both the building blocks have end-plates rigidly that are connected to frame of the chair. The common elastic axis of the building blocks defines the virtual hinge of the chair seat. When a person sits, the mechanism twists and is guided along the *sitting guideway* (Fig. 10) designed using the energy principle to impart the suitable resistive force to the occupant.

An actuation mechanism is used to switch between the guideways during loading (sitting) and unloading (standing) paths. All the guideways are hinged to the rod on one end and are placed on a cam profile on the other end, which in turn is mounted on a camshaft. A three-link mechanism is connected between the shaft and the armrest of the chair as shown in Fig. 17. The follower connected to the end of the open-section shells exerts downward push on the sitting guideway and is always in contact with it. Only when the person decides to rise, a cue must be given by pressing the armrests, which rotates the cam. The sitting guideway is lowered by the virtue of the actuation cam profile, while the follower comes in contact with the standing guideway. Thus, the mechanism deforms along this guideway specially designed as per the target explained in Sect. 1.

This imparts the desired assistive force to the user. A spring is attached to the armrest to retract the actuation mechanism to its original position for consequent use.

Floating factor equal to zero can be effectively achieved with this mechanism so that the user feels like any other normal chair while being seated. Figures 18 and 19 show the assembly of the mechanism on the assistive chair. The full-scale prototype is fabricated, and real-time testing will be done to validate the design.

Fig. 18 3D CAD model of the mechanism on the assistive chair

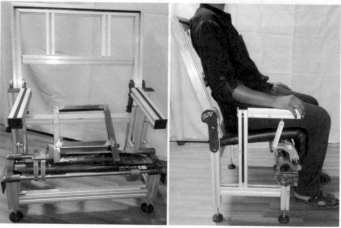

Fig. 19 Full-scale working prototype

4   Closure

A variable-torque compliant mechanism is designed using open-section shells. The shell beams act as nonlinear springs under combined bending and twisting deformations. The magnitude of deformation is regulated by guiding the open-section shells along specially designed guideways. Any torque–angle profile can be achieved for which the energy lies within the range of characteristic energy space of the mechanism. The design space is flexible as the shell-beam dimensions are not critical and number of shells can be varied to suitably accommodate a range of magnitudes of diverse energy variations. This mechanism also functions like an effective hinge exhibiting large rotations beyond 45^0. The mechanism is effectively used in an assistive chair to impart two distinct torque–angle variations for sitting and rising. A user-actuated trigger switches the mechanism from one path of traverse to another. This design is compact, modular and customizable as per user requirement of resistive–assistive force to accommodate occupants of different weights.

References

1. A.W. Peter, W. Bressler, *Lift Chair*, US 7,000,988 B2 (2006)
2. G. Geisler, K. Hausherr, *Stand-Assist Recliner Chair*, US005265935A (1993)
3. D. Newman, *Seat Assist*, US005316370A (1994)
4. R.E. Schiller, Chair *with Occupant Assisting Features*, Patent no. 4,632,455 (1986)
5. H.L. Iversen, *Portable Occupant-Arising Assist Seat With Torsion Springs*, US005116100A (1992)
6. D. Sarojini, T.J. Lassche, J.L. Herder, G.K. Ananthasuresh, Statically balanced compliant two-port bistable mechanism. Mech. Mach. Theor. **102**, 1–13 (2016)
7. K. Wada, T. Matsui, Optimal control model for reproducing human sitting movements on a chair and its effectiveness. J. Biomech. Sci. Eng. **8**(2), 164–179 (2013)
8. O. Stodieck, J.E. Cooper, P.M. Weaver, Interpretation of bending/torsion coupling for swept, nonhomogenous wings. J. Aircr. **53**(4), 892–899 (2016)
9. P.A. Seaburg, C.J. Carter, Torsional analysis of structural steel members. Architect. Eng. **32**(2), 347–358 (1994)

Study of Dynamic Behavior of Active Steering Railway Vehicles

Smitirupa Pradhan, Arun Kumar Samantaray and Chandrajeet Pratap Singh

Abstract In this chapter, we have focused on the link type active steering bogie with an actuator placed in the center of the bogie. The operating principle of actuator is to control the yaw movement of the wheel set according to the location of the vehicle on the track. Active steering vehicle has been co-simulated where the steering vehicle model and control algorithm are modeled in multi-body simulation (MBS) software VI-Rail and MATLAB Simulink environment, respectively. As the railway tracks have different curvatures and cant/superelevations, the estimated steering angle varies from time to time, which affects the dynamics of the vehicle. Hence, the control algorithm is used to control yaw angle of the vehicle. By implementing controlled steering, a significant improvement on ride comfort, derailment speed, creep forces, and creepage have been observed, which helps to reduce the wheel–rail wear and the noise.

Keywords Forced steering bogie · Dynamic behavior · Curving performance
Rail wheel dynamics · Co-simulation

1 Introduction

Generally, due to geographical constraints in the subway lines and in the mountainous regions, railway tracks have many sharp and transition curves with small cant, which are the cause of several problems such as generating large lateral creep force on the rail, severe wear at the flange of the wheel, significant load change at the transition

S. Pradhan (✉) · A. K. Samantaray · C. P. Singh
Systems, Dynamic and Control Laboratory, Mechanical Engineering Department, Indian Institute of Technology Kharagpur, Kharagpur 721302, India
e-mail: smitirupa@gmail.com

A. K. Samantaray
e-mail: samantaray@mech.iitkgp.ernet.in

C. P. Singh
e-mail: chandrajeet29@gmail.com

© Springer Nature Singapore Pte Ltd. 2019
D N Badodkar and T A Dwarakanath (eds.), *Machines, Mechanism and Robotics*, Lecture Notes in Mechanical Engineering,
https://doi.org/10.1007/978-981-10-8597-0_37

441

curves, etc. To solve the abovementioned problems as well as to improve the curving performance, a steering mechanism may be implemented. However, there is a trade-off between the curving performance and stability for the railway vehicles with different wheel profiles. Several mechanical solutions such as cross bracing and primary yaw damping have been recommended to solve this conflict [1]. Still, there is a trade-off between stability and steering/curving of the vehicle. Several researchers have indicated that active control strategy may be a solution to reduce the gap between this trade-off. Different proposed active control strategies are active stability [2], active yaw relaxation [3] and active control of lateral position, and yaw movement of wheel set [4]. Still, a number of practical problems exist, such as measurement of angle of attack and lateral displacement of the wheel set is very difficult and expensive. Another key issue is the lack of information of the contact parameters such as creep coefficients, equivalent conicity of wheel sets and dimensions of the contact patch, etc., which may lead to inaccurate controller design [5].

Hwang et al. [6] have improved steering performance by reducing the longitudinal stiffness of primary axial rubber spring and gave a control algorithm for an actual steering bogie. They have not focused the role of cant/superelevation to estimate steering angle. Recently, a control law for the active steering bogie, which is able to adapt to the cant excess and/or deficiency on a curved track with constant velocity of the vehicle and track design parameters has been proposed.

This article presents the layout of a forced steering bogie where acceleration and braking have been taken into consideration. The procedure relies on the co-simulation between multi-body simulation software VI-Rail and MATLAB/Simulink and the dynamic performance of the vehicle on the curved track has been studied.

The remaining parts of this article are organized as follows: Sect. 2 presents the concept of steering bogies along with estimation of steering angle. Section 3 details the multi-body vehicle and track models. The efficacy of the active steering mechanism in terms of dynamic performance is presented in Sect. 4. Section 5 presents the results and discussions which are followed by conclusions in Sect. 6.

2   Steering Bogies

While a rail vehicle moves on a curved rail track, the wheel set displaces toward the outer rail, hence, the instantaneous diameter of the outer wheel increases and that of the inner wheel decreases. The variation of instantaneous rolling radii in outer and inner wheels leads to self-steering, as shown in Fig. 1. As self-steering is not sufficient to counterbalance the centrifugal force while curving, which may cause derailment, hence, some designers have focused on the passive and active steering to enhance the steering performance. The idea of steering bogie resolves the above-stated problem by steering the wheel sets so that the outer wheelbase is longer than that of inner during curving. Radially steered bogies [7] are classified depending on the control principle used.

Fig. 1 Self-steering
characteristics of the wheel
set

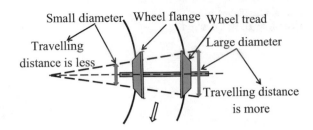

2.1 Active/Assist/Forced Steering

In case of active steering, stability and steering actions are considered separately. The required yaw angle/steering angle is determined from the instantaneous radius of curvature and cant height/superelevation of the track, wheelbase, and the velocity of the vehicle. The steering performance of the vehicle on the curved track depends on both the design parameters of the bogie and the track.

2.2 Steering Angle

The steering angle is mostly dependent on the curvature of track, length of transition curve, and running speed of the vehicle. For a given curve radius at a particular position, the steering angle is defined as the angle by which each axle has to be turned in order to make zero angle of attack of the wheel with the track and align the axle along the radial direction of the track. This steering angle on a track may be calculated as $\alpha = \sin^{-1}(W_b/2R)$, where W_b is the wheelbase, α is the required steering angle, and $1/R = \rho$ is the curvature of the track (see Fig. 2). However, the above formulation does not consider the existing cant in the track. As a result, the vehicle operates in under- or over-steering which leads to yaw oscillations of the wheel set. Also, the vehicle encounters large centrifugal force in high speed and needs more steering angle, whereas, the above formulation is independent of speed. Thus, steering angle in the presence of cant angle in the curved track may be calculated in terms of cant deficiency or cant excess depending on the speed of the train. The instantaneous steering angle/yaw movement at leading and trailing axles, respectively [5], can be modified to

$$\alpha_l = \sin^{-1}\left(\frac{F_c}{2F_{22}}\right) - \sin^{-1}\left(\frac{W_b}{2} \times \frac{1}{R}\right) \approx \frac{F_c}{2F_{22}} - \frac{W_b}{2R}$$

$$\alpha_t = \sin^{-1}\left(\frac{F_c}{2F_{22}}\right) + \sin^{-1}\left(\frac{W_b}{2} \times \frac{1}{R}\right) \approx \frac{F_c}{2F_{22}} + \frac{W_b}{2R} \qquad (1)$$

where $F_c = M(v^2/R - g\sin\phi)$ is the lateral force due to the cant deficiency, v is the velocity, g is the acceleration due to gravity, M is the mass corresponding to static

Fig. 2 Calculation of
steering angle of the wheel
set

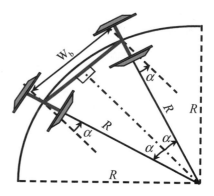

axle load and ϕ is cant angle in radians. The symbol F_{22} is the lateral creep force
which is defined as $F_{22} = E(ab)c_{22}$ [8], where E is the modulus of elasticity of the
wheel material, a and b are semi-axes of the elliptical contact patch between the rail
and the wheels, and c_{22} is the creepage coefficient in lateral direction.

3 Modeling and Simulation

3.1 Multi-body Vehicle Model

A full vehicle model consists of two bogies and car body/coach with steering mechanism. A bogie comprises two wheel sets with axle, primary, and secondary suspension
systems. The primary suspension system of a bogie lies between the wheel set and
bogie frame which consists of four axle boxes, eight flexi-coil springs, and vertical
dampers and four friction dampers. The secondary suspension system in each bogie
contains two air springs, two nonlinear anti-yaw dampers, lateral dampers, and two
nonlinear bump stops as shown in Fig. 3. The important parameters of the bogie components are given in Table 1. The link type steering mechanism consists of steering
beam, lever, and link [9], as indicated in Fig. 3. The model shown in Fig. 3 is used for
dynamic analysis in MBS software VI-Rail. The base bogie design is based on JR
Hokkaido Series 283 DMU express diesel train. An actuator is placed at the center
of the bogie through a revolute joint. The yaw movement of the bogie contributes to
the angle of attack to the wheel set by rotating the steering beam, lever, and link.

The correlation of yaw movement of the steering beam and the axle box is calculated from analysis of steering linkage mechanism in ADAMS (Fig. 4). Reverse
lookup through polynomial fitting is used for inverse kinematics. For a specific set of
chosen link lengths, this correlation can be curve fitted as $\alpha_b = 17\alpha_W^3 - 20\alpha_W^2 + 15\alpha_W$,
where α_b and α_W is the steering beam angle and steering angle at the axle, respectively. The steering linkage applies force directly at the center of the axle box to
which the axle of the wheel set is attached.

Fig. 3 Labeled diagram of the forced steering bogie template developed in ADAMS (VI-Rail)

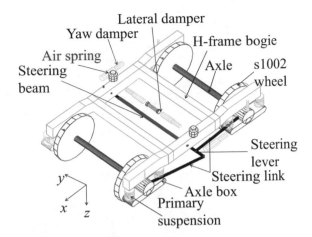

Table 1 Parametric values of important components per bogie

Components of MBS body	Parameter values in SI unit	Quantity
Mass of bogie frame	$M_{frame} = 2615$	1
Mass of wheel set	$M_{wheelset} = 3006$	2
Mass of axle box	$M_{box} = 155$	4
Stiffness of primary suspension	$K_x = 6.8 \times 10^6$ $K_y = 3.92 \times 10^6$ $K_z = 5.756 \times 10^5$ $K_\Theta = K_\alpha = 63.5$	4
Nominal pressure of secondary suspension (air spring)	$P_{static} = 2.0532 \times 10^5$	2
Primary vertical damper (series stiffness)	1.0×10^6	4
Secondary vertical damper (series stiffness)	6.0×10^6	2
Secondary anti-yaw damper (series stiffness)	3.0×10^7	2
Secondary lateral damping (series stiffness)	6.0×10^6	2

Note In the table above, K_x, K_y, and K_z are the stiffness of the primary suspension in x, y, and z directions, respectively; K_θ and K_α are the torsional stiffness in x and y directions, respectively. All the dampers are designed with nonlinear damping and series stiffness (standard data in VI-Rail)

Usually, depending upon the operating speed and track design parameters, a time-varying set point is specified for the axle yaw angle which is converted to a desired steering beam angle. This steering beam angle is controlled by the application of actuator torque through a proportional integral derivative (PID) controller with the measured steering beam angle taken as the feedback to the controller, as shown in Fig. 5. In this study, the control gains in PID controllers are determined by the trial-and-error approach.

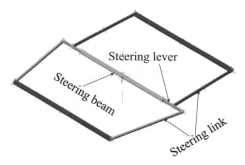

Fig. 4 Analysis of steering linkage in ADAMS

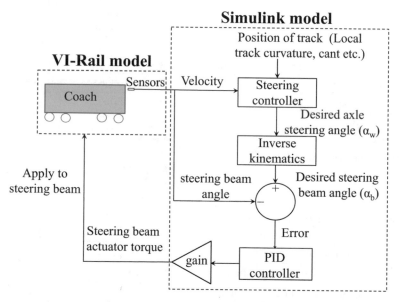

Fig. 5 Block diagram of PID control of steering angle calculation

3.2 Track Parameters

The input parameters for the dynamic analysis are velocity profile, standard wheel–rail profiles (S1002 and UIC 60), design, and flexibility parameters of the track along with track irregularities. For dynamic analysis, we have taken a simple track, which consists of straight (1800 m), transition (320 m) and curved portion (4000 m with curve radius 2500 m), and maximum speed 80 m/s (288 kph). The velocity profile is shown in Fig. 6. The variations of curvature and cant of the designed track are presented in Fig. 7.

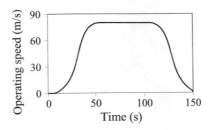

Fig. 6 Velocity profile with acceleration and braking

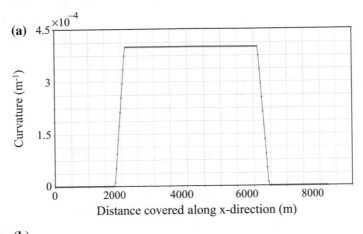

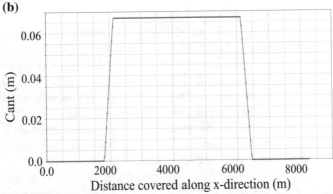

Fig. 7 Variation of **a** curvature and **b** cant in the designed track

4 Dynamic Analysis

The bogie template (Fig. 3) and the car body are assembled to produce the whole coach model in ADAMS VI-Rail as shown in Fig. 8. The design parameters of the tracks may vary according to the applications. To find the derailment and critical

Fig. 8 Assembled coach
model in ADAMS VI-Rail
for dynamic analysis

Fig. 9 Longitudinal creep
for both left and right wheel
of both the axle

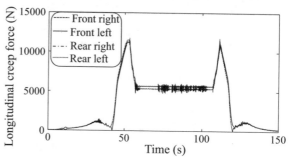

speeds, we have used curved (curve radius 2500 m and cant height 67 mm) and straight tracks with measured and ramp (small perturbation type) irregularities, respectively. The critical speed is the limit above which sustained hunting motion occurs and the derailment speed is the one at which the wheel flange climbs over the rail and the vehicle comes out of the track. From the dynamic analysis, it is found that the critical speed with and without steering are 156 m/s (561.6 kph) and 160 m/s (576 kph), respectively, whereas the derailment speed for the same conditions is 134 m/s (482.4 kph) and 111 m/s (399.6 kph), respectively. Thus, steering bogie increases both the critical speed and derailment speed limit.

The necessary condition required to achieve perfect steering is to ensure equal longitudinal creep force between the wheels of the same axle to minimize excessive wear and damage at the wheel–rail contact surfaces. The longitudinal creep forces for all the wheels of both the axles are shown in Fig. 9 which shows almost equal creep force at all wheels. This leads to reduction in wear and damage to the wheels [8]. There is a significant difference between the developed active steering and conventional bogies in terms of both lateral creep force and normal contact force. It may be noted that contact forces of the passive steering bogie are highly fluctuating with its mean value not differing much from that of the active steering bogie.

There is a significant difference between the developed active steering bogie and conventional bogie in terms of both lateral creep force and normal contact force, which is observed from the simulation (results are not given here). It may be noted that contact forces of the passive steering bogie are highly fluctuating with its mean value not differing much from that of the active steering bogie. The instantaneous contact angle and rolling radius give the information about the location of the contact patch for conventional, passive and active steering bogies. In the case, the vehicle moves on the curved track, the outer wheel of the front axle in the conventional bogie shifts toward the flange of the wheel to increase the steering action, and the average contact angle and rolling radius of bogie are 36° and 0.4656 m, respectively. However, in the presence of active steering, the average contact angle and rolling radius for the same wheel are 1.5 and 0.4599 m, respectively, which means that the contact patch locations remain at the tread of the wheel. This reduces the chance of derailment and also due to less lateral sway movement, the ride comfort felt by the passengers increases.

Due to geometrical configuration of the wheel profile and track (curved portion), the lateral and spin creepage of the conventional bogie are significantly large as compared to the active steering bogie. The average values of lateral creepage for both the conventional and active steering bogies are 0.004 and 0.0011, respectively, and during curving, the spin creepage for both the bogies is 1.2628 m^{-1} and 0.0489 m^{-1}, respectively. From the simulation, it is also seen that the average values of angle of attack of the conventional and the active bogies are 0.182° and 0.07°, respectively, i.e., the angle of attack of the steering bogie is 61.5% lower than that of the conventional bogie.

5 Results and Discussion

5.1 Derailment Quotient

The derailment quotient is defined as the ratio of the lateral force to the vertical force acting at the wheel–rail interface. The derailment quotient of the outer wheel of the front axle of the front bogie for both the conventional and active steering is shown in Fig. 10.

During curving at 80 m/s (288 kph) speed, average derailment quotients of both the bogies are 0.2638 and 0.03266, respectively, where the allowable limit is 0.8 [6]. Derailment quotient indicates how far the wheel is from reaching flange. As speed increases, the quotient increases exponentially. The derailment quotient of the active steering bogie is about 87.62% lower than that of the conventional bogie.

Fig. 10 Derailment quotient

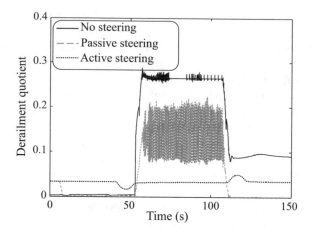

Fig. 11 Wear index

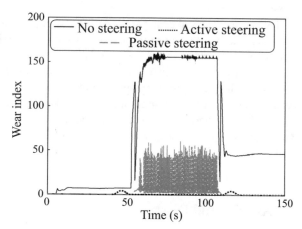

5.2 Wear Index

The wear index indicates how fast the wheel wears out and decides wheel maintenance schedule. It is calculated as wear index $= \sum_{i=1}^{N_{cp}} f_x \upsilon_x + f_y \upsilon_y$, where f_x and f_y are the longitudinal and lateral creep forces; υ_x and υ_y are longitudinal and lateral creepage, respectively; and N_{cp} is the number of contact points. The wear index for the outer wheel of the front axle of the front bogie is shown in Fig. 11, where it is found that the wear index of active steering bogie is 87.65% lower than that of the conventional bogie. The wear index of rear wheel set is similarly lower in steering bogie compared to that of the conventional bogie.

5.3 Ride Comfort

Due to the presence of irregularities on the track, the structural vibration generated at the wheel–rail contact surface is transmitted to bogie through primary suspension and retransmitted to the car body and subsequently to the passenger via the secondary suspension. The degree of comfort felt by the passenger under vibration is termed as ride comfort, which is measured by Sperling ride index (W_z) [10], in this article. We consider the predefined velocity profile (Fig. 6) and the designed track (Fig. 8) with measured/stochastic type of irregularities. For the same operating conditions, W_z in the lateral direction for both the active and passive steering bogie are 2 and 2.3747, respectively, and W_z in the vertical direction is almost same for both the cases. Lower ride index indicates better comfort. Thus, actively steered bogie gives better comfort due to reduced lateral sway on curves. Note that the conventional bogie derails at the same speed and operating condition.

6 Conclusions

The dynamic analysis of a mechatronic railway bogie with forced/active steering mechanism is presented here. The yaw control law adapts to the change in velocity of the vehicle and position on the track. It is shown that the forced/active steering bogie is able to adapt to the cant excess and cant deficiency on curved tracks. The vehicle performances of both active and passive steering bogies are evaluated through dynamic analysis using co-simulation between MBS VI-Rail and MATLAB Simulink. It is found that the dynamic performances related to hunting stability, derailment speed, passenger comfort, wheel wear rate, etc., are improved significantly with an active steering bogie. Nevertheless, the passive steering bogie also gives better performance as compared to the conventional bogie at a lower implementation cost, but higher maintenance cost due to quicker wheel wear.

References

1. R. Illingworth, M.G. Pollard, The use of steering active suspension to reduce wheel and rail wear in curves. Proc. Inst. Mech. Eng. **196**(1), 379–385 (1982)
2. T.X. Mei, R.M. Goodall, Modal controllers for active steering of railway vehicles with solid axle wheel-sets. Vehicle Syst. Dynam. **34**(1), 24–31 (2000)
3. G. Shen, R.M. Goodall, Active yaw relaxation for improve bogie performance. J. Vehicle Syst. Dynam. **28**, 273–282 (1997)
4. J. Perez, J.M. Busturia, R.M. Goodall, Control strategies for active steering of bogie-based railway vehicles. Control Eng. Pract. **10**, 1005–1012 (2002)
5. S. Shen, T.X. Mei, R.M. Goodall, J.T. Pearson, A novel control strategy for active steering of railway bogies. UKACC Control (2004)
6. I. Hwang, H. Hur, T. Park, Analysis of the active control of steering bogies for the dynamic charecteristics on real track conditions. Rail Rapid Transit. 1–12 (2017)

7. R.M. Goodall, T.X. Mei, Active suspensions, in S. Iwnicki (Ed.) *Hand Book of Railway Vehicle Dynamics* (CRC Press, FL, 2006), pp. 327–357
8. W. Zhang, D. Huanyun, S. Zhiyun, J. Zeng, Roller Rigs, in S. Iwnicki (Ed.) *Handbook of Railway Vehicle Dynamics* (CRC Press, FL 2006), pp. 457–506
9. I. Okamoto, How bogies work. Japan Railway Trans. Rev. **18**, 52–61 (1998)
10. V.K. Garg, R.V. Dukkipati, *Dynamics of Railway Vehicle Systems* (Academic Press, Canada, 1984)

Design and Analysis of Spring-Based Rope Climbing Robot

Pinank R. Ratanghayra, Abdullah Aamir Hayat and Subir Kumar Saha

Abstract The robots moving on a rope are an interesting domain with research potential and various applications. This paper reports on the design of a rope climbing robot design and its analysis. The rope climbing robot uses wheels powered by the DC motors for climbing the vertical rope. It can traverse horizontal ropes as well. The springs attached to the wheels are used for passive clinging of the robot to the rope. The stiffness of the spring was calculated on the basis of the payload and the motion capabilities of the robot. The proposed design gives two degrees-of-freedom (DOF) to the robot, i.e., translation and rotation about the rope. The power required for climbing at different inclinations is reported. The design proposed here is of low cost, easy to build, and control. It can be useful for surveillance purposes, for delivering help in disaster situations, inspection of cable suspension bridges, power plant chimneys, and cooling towers.

Keywords Rope climbing robot · Two degrees-of-freedom · Spring-loaded assembly · Self-locking

1 Introduction

A rope climbing robot is a type of a mobile robot that clings to the rope for their locomotion unlike most of the mobile robots that use the plain surface for the motion. One of the main challenges is to design a robot that is stable and can be locked at any desired position on the rope. A wide variety of mechanisms have been developed so

P. R. Ratanghayra
S.V. National Institute of Technology Surat, Surat, India
e-mail: pinank.ratanghayar@outlook.com

A. A. Hayat (✉) · S. K. Saha
Indian Institute of Technology Delhi, New Delhi 110016, India
e-mail: aamir_hayat@rediffmail.com

S. K. Saha
e-mail: saha@mech.iitd.ac.in

© Springer Nature Singapore Pte Ltd. 2019
D N Badodkar and T A Dwarakanath (eds.), *Machines, Mechanism and Robotics*, Lecture Notes in Mechanical Engineering,
https://doi.org/10.1007/978-981-10-8597-0_38

(a) Robot traversing in horizontal rope [2]   (b) A pair of driving mechanism for rope climbing [4]   (c) Pole climbing robot [5]   (d) Pole climbing robot [6]

Fig. 1 Different climbing mechanisms

far for either rope or pole climbing. One of the mechanisms introduced resembled the motion of a sloth bear [1]. This bot had separate grippers. One of them maintained a tight grip on the rope while other moved further. Another design suggested a piston actuated rope climber [2] as shown in Fig. 1a. This robot used a slider and clampers for moving the robot. A robot capable of moving by gripping handrails was presented in [3] where a link mechanism in coordination with belt and pulley system was used. One of the design introduced an autonomous rope climbing robot in [4] as shown in Fig. 1b. Other mechanisms available resemble the motion for pole climbing as in [5, 6] with a wheeled system shown in Fig. 1c, d. A survey of design aspects and technologies for the climbing mechanism is presented in [7]. The design presented here for rope climbing is a wheel-based system since they are highly reliable and easy to build. The robot is actuated by DC motors and stability is provided by a spring-loaded assembly. The robot can be locked at any position on the rope and is controlled wirelessly using Bluetooth communication.

The structure of the paper is as follows. This paper is divided into five sections. Overview of the design and the formulation is presented in Sect. 2. Section 3 presents the experimental evaluation of the prototypes built. The conclusions and discussions are presented in Sect. 4. Finally, the add-ons to the existing device are also proposed in the future work.

2 Methodology

In this section, the mechanical design and assembly are explained. The formulation and the mathematical basis are also described.

2.1 Design

The basic principle used for motion along the rope is rolling. The wheels roll on the surface of the rope which is powered by a DC motor. In presence of sufficient friction between the wheels and the rope, the robot traverses the rope. The design consists of four wheels, spring-loaded system with a chassis explained next.

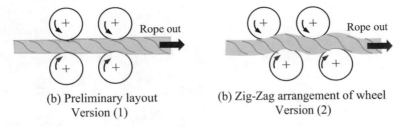

(b) Preliminary layout
Version (1)

(b) Zig-Zag arrangement of wheel
Version (2)

Fig. 2 Arrangement of wheels in the two versions

2.1.1 Wheels Layout

The first design (version 1) consisted of two wheel pairs on either side of the rope as shown in Fig. 2a. However, upon testing this version it was found that wheels did not offer sufficient friction to support the robot in the vertical position but worked well for horizontal traversing. Hence, there was a need to increase the area of contact to increase the friction. This was done by arranging the wheels in a zigzag pattern as shown in Fig. 2b.

2.1.2 Spring-Loaded System

The backbone of the mechanical system is a spring-loaded assembly. It consists of an extension spring which is fixed to a DC motor through a clamp, as shown in Fig. 3c. This DC motor is coupled to a wheel which rolls on the surface of the rope. The assembly is responsible for providing necessary gripping force to the wheels.

2.1.3 Chassis

The chassis holds the entire mechanism in place during its operation. It consists of slots for fixing the motors as depicted in Fig. 3a. Two strong supports are provided

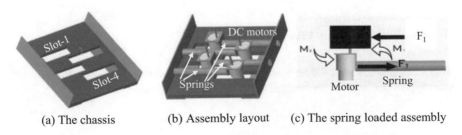

(a) The chassis

(b) Assembly layout

(c) The spring loaded assembly

Fig. 3 The chassis layout and forces on spring-loaded assembly

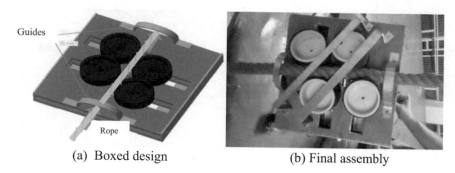

(a) Boxed design   (b) Final assembly

Fig. 4 Assembly

on each side of this base for mounting the springs. This is shown in Fig. 3b. The arrangement allows the motors to slide, and thus, the gap between the wheels can be varied. This allowed the robot to be used for ropes of multiple diameters which are within the range of extension of the spring.

2.2 Assembly of Rope Climbing Robot

The four spring-loaded systems are fixed in their respective slots as shown in Fig. 3b. The springs are mounted such that they are always in tension, and hence, each motor is pulled toward the wall on the opposite side. This provides the necessary force for gripping the rope. In this layout, there is a tendency for the wheels to move away from the rope due to the moment produced by spring force and the force exerted by the rope as shown in Fig. 3c. This moment results in misalignment of the wheels when the rope is inserted and thus cannot provide the required friction to the robot. This is countered by placing an additional plank identical to the base on top of the motors as shown in Fig. 4a resulting in a box-like structure. This arrangement allows the motors to slide only in one direction without any misalignment and the final assembly is shown in Fig. 4b.

3 Mechanical Analysis

This section deals with the selection procedure of the motors and springs. They are selected on the basis of the desired speed and payload capacity.

3.1 Wheels Arrangement

As it can be seen that in version 1, the friction force is concentrated at a particular point and therefore is insufficient to carry the entire load of the robot. Unlike version 1, in version 2, the area of contact is much larger and thus the friction force is uniformly distributed. In the interest of keeping the paper within the page limit, analysis of only version 2 is presented here. Let the radius of the wheel be r, θ is the angle of contact and h is the rope thickness. The surface area S in contact with the wheel is given as

$$S = \frac{2\pi r h \theta}{360} \tag{1}$$

Then, the total surface area in the contact for the four wheels is denoted as $S_{total} = 4S$. If the torque required for the DC motor is T and power consumed is P, then

$$\tau = r \times F_3 \tag{2}$$

$$P = \frac{2\pi N \tau}{60} \tag{3}$$

where N is the rotation per minute (rpm) of the motor, F_3 is the force provided by the motor which is equal to friction. Next the required stiffness of the spring is calculated.

3.1.1 Spring Selection

The stiffness of the spring directly influences the friction force and hence will also determine the payload carrying capacity of the robot. Let the total weight (weight of robot + payload) is W which is supported by friction f, then frictional force acting on each wheel is

$$f = W/4 = \mu N = \mu k x \tag{4}$$

where μ is the coefficient of friction, k is spring stiffness, and x is the extension of spring. For thickness t of the rope the spring will be compressed by half the thickness of the rope, i.e., $x = t/2$. On knowing the modulus of rigidity G of spring material, wire diameter d, and coil diameter D, the number of turns n can be calculated as [8]

$$k = Gd^4/(8D^3 n) \tag{5}$$

Equation 5 was used to select the spring specification. Considering Fig. 5a for version 2, the normal force is F_n. It is this force which presses the rope between the two wheels. The value of F_n can be calculated as

$$F_n = \frac{F_p}{2\cos\left(\frac{\theta}{2}\right)} \tag{6}$$

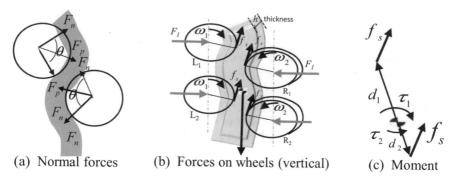

(a) Normal forces   (b) Forces on wheels (vertical)   (c) Moment

Fig. 5 Free body diagram

where F_p is shown in Fig. 5a. Next the friction force, f can be given by

$$f = 2\mu F_n = F_p / \cos\frac{\theta}{2} \tag{7}$$

Now, there are three such junctions and considering equal to 120°, the total frictional force would be from Eqs. (4), (6) and (7) we can write $f_{total} = 3\mu kt$.

3.1.2 Mobility of the Mechanism

The design proposed has two degrees-of-freedom, i.e., one translation and the other one is rotation.

Translation: When all the four wheels rotate at the same speed, the bot moves either upward or downward as shown in Fig. 6a. The linear velocity v with which the robot traverse is given by

$$v = 2\pi R N / 60 \tag{8}$$

where R and N are defined in Sect. 3.1.

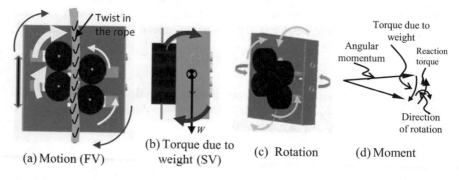

(a) Motion (FV)   (b) Torque due to weight (SV)   (c) Rotation   (d) Moment

Fig. 6 Robot motions and moments

Rotation: The robot can also be made to rotate about the axis of the rope. Consider that the two wheels on the left of the rope rotate at a greater angular velocity than the ones on the right. This will try to rotate the robot toward the right as shown in Figs. 5 and 6a. As the wheels are not symmetric about the center of gravity of the assembly, there exists a net torque on the robot. As the center of gravity of the robot is toward the back due to the presence of motors on one side, the gravitational force also produces a torque about another axis as depicted in Fig. 6b. If I is the moment of inertia about the axis of rotation of the wheels and ω is the angular velocity of the wheels, then the gyroscopic couple is given by

$$C = I\omega\omega_P \tag{9}$$

where ω_p is angular velocity about the rope. The term $\omega\omega_p$ represents the acceleration of the robot about the rotation axis. This gyroscopic torque causes anticlockwise rotation of the robot when viewed from the top about the axis of the rope. The robot could be made to rotate in opposite direction by increasing the speed of the wheels on the right side. The twist in the rope and the nonsymmetric distribution of weight on either side of the robot and grooves on the wheels also affect the rotation about the axis of the rope in a real situation. The gyroscopic couple can be increased by rotating all the four wheels in the same direction, but this might lead to damage of the wheels or even slipping of the robot. This motion is particularly useful for surveillance purposes.

4 Electronic Control

The rope climbing robot was powered by a 12 V DC Lithium polymer recharge-able battery which provides enough power to traverse. This power source is also lightweight. The system architecture is shown in Fig. 7. The microcontroller is the center of all communication. Arduino Uno was chosen because of the ease with which it can be programmed and also is low cost. The motor driver used was Saber-

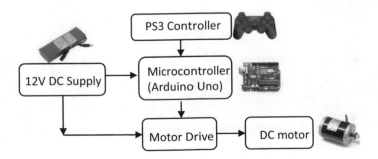

Fig. 7 Electronic control

tooth dual channel driver. The PS3 controller sends the signals to Arduino Uno via a Bluetooth dongle which then sends the corresponding signal to the motor driver and finally controls the rotation speed of the DC motor.

5 Results and Discussions

The clamping force is provided by the springs. This force is proportional to the displacement of the spring which depends on the thickness of the rope. This means that thicker the rope higher will be, the spring force and, consequently, higher will be the friction force. The spring-based system makes the robot self-locking so that it can be stopped passively at any position on the rope. Also, it allows the robot to be used for ropes of multiple diameters and can adjust to irregularities in rope such as knots, etc.

Based on the above considerations, a prototype was developed based on version 2, which is shown in Fig. 6. The motors used had a maximum torque rating of 15 Kg cm at 60 rpm and 12 V. The springs had the stiffness of about 1500 N/m and cotton rope with a thickness of 4 cm. The weight of the robot assembly was approximately 3.6 Kg. The speed for horizontal traversing was around 0.11 m/s while for vertical traversing it was about 0.08 m/s. This assembly was designed to support a maximum payload of 1 Kg. Figure 8 shows the amount of power consumption by the rope climbing robot for the different inclinations of the rope. The power consumption was measured at a speed of about 0.08 m/s and with a payload of 0.7 kg which mainly included the weight of the battery approximately.

Figure 9 shows the energy consumed in two cases, i.e., vertical traversing and the horizontal traversing against the distance moved. The power consumed for the horizontal case is taken from Fig. 8 as 45 W and for the velocity as 0.11 m/s. The energy consumed in traversing will be the product of power and time in traversing the given distance. The time taken to traverse a distance d with velocity for vertical

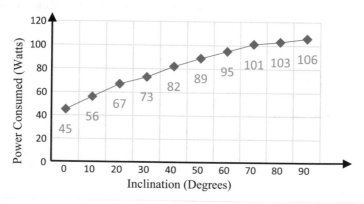

Fig. 8 Power consumed versus inclination of the rope

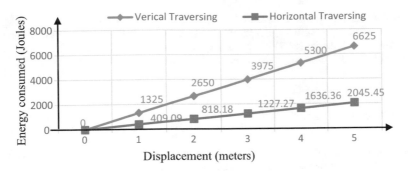

Fig. 9 Power consumed versus inclination of the rope

Table 1 Energy consumed in horizontal and vertical traversing

	Power (P Watt)	v (m/s)	Time $t = d/v$	Energy (Pt)
Horizontal	45	0.11	9.09 d	409.09 d
Vertical	106	0.08	12.5 d	1325 d

and horizontal are listed in Table 1. The energy consumed is directly proportional to distance traveled. For horizontal traversing, traveling a distance of 1 m would require 409.09 J (0.00011 kWh) of energy while for vertical traversing, it would require 1325 J (0.00036 kWh) of energy. In case of irregularities in the rope, power consumption would increase as extra energy would be required to climb the obstacles.

It can be concluded that as the inclination increases the amount of power required to propel the robot against the gravity also increases. The power requirement is maximum for the vertical case, i.e., against the gravity. The videos of the rope climbing robot can be found at the link given in [9].

6 Conclusion and Future Work

A new and effective approach for rope climbing was introduced. The system developed is easy to build and has many applications in real world. As an application, a wiper mechanism can be mounted on this robot which can be used to clean the surface of a chimney. In future, modifications can be made to increase the stability of this design, and a system can be developed in which the robot can rotate about the rope. A PID control can be developed to automatically adjust the speed on nearing the end of the rope or a wifi module can be added to increase the range of its control.

Acknowledgements We are thankful to all the members of robotics club in making the first version of the rope climbing robot at SVNIT. We would like to acknowledge the members of Programme for Autonomous Robotics (PAR) lab (build in collaboration with DRHR/BARC, Mumbai) at IIT Delhi and especially Mr. Anil Patidar for his valuable comments and support.

References

1. S. Urankar, P. Jain, A. Singh, A. Saxena, B. Dasgupta, Robo-sloth: a rope-climbing robot. IIT J. 21 (2003), http://www.nacomm03.ammindia.org
2. Y. Koo, A. Elmi, W.A.F. Wajdi, Piston mechanism based rope climbing robot. Procedia Eng. **41**, 547–553 (2012)
3. K. Vidyasagar, S. Ahmadsaidulu, M. Sumalatha, Rope climbing robot. Int. J. Comput. Appl. **108**(12) (2014)
4. D. Tandon, K. Patil, M. Dasgupta, Designing a modular rope climbing Bot, in *2015 Annual IEEE India Conference (INDICON)* (IEEE, 2015), pp. 1–4
5. A. Baghani, M.N. Ahmadabadi, A. Harati, Kinematics modeling of a wheel-based pole climbing robot (UT-PCR), in *Proceedings of the 2005 IEEE International Conference on Robotics and Automation, 2005. ICRA 2005* (IEEE, 2005), pp. 2099–2104
6. H. Kawasaki, S. Murakami, H. Kachi, S. Ueki, Novel climbing method of pruning robot, in *SICE Annual Conference, 2008* (IEEE, 2008), pp. 160–163
7. D. Schmidt, K. Berns, Climbing robots for maintenance and inspections of vertical structures a survey of design aspects and technologies. Robot. Auton. Syst. **61**(12), 1288–1305 (2013)
8. V. Bhandari, *Design of Machine Elements* (Tata McGraw-Hill Education, 2010)
9. Rope climber videos—Google drive, https://drive.google.com/drive/folders/0B-yf6g2sYvUPSjdqQUs5bHppUE0. Accessed on 28 Aug 2017

Generalized Method for Real-Time Object-Oriented Modeling and Simulation of Systems Applied to a Vehicle Wheel Suspension Mechanism

Rajat Dandekar and Frédéric Etienne Kracht

Abstract It is becoming increasingly important to simulate the dynamic behavior of complex systems in order to make real-time predictions about the performance of the system. The modeling technique has to be computationally efficient and accurate. In this work, a novel object-oriented modeling method is presented, which is characterized by high modularity and computational efficiency. This method is particularly useful for performing real-time simulations and is characterized by a high degree of configurability, scalability and is found to be faster than the established multibody simulation software like ADAMS and DYMOLA. The developed method can be used to predict the dynamic behavior of open-loop as well as closed-loop systems in real time. The method is demonstrated by using it to model a vehicle suspension system for predicting the dynamic response of the mechanism.

Keywords Modeling · Mechanism · Object-oriented · Euler angles · Suspension

1 Introduction

A variety of modeling methods have been developed in the past to simulate and predict the physical behavior of dynamic systems. Due to the increasingly complex simulation tasks today, such as the real-time control in closed-loop applications or the optimization of systems with more and more parameters, modeling methods have to be particularly efficiently designed. On the other hand, the model should be such that adjustments can be quickly and easily made and complex systems can be easily built.

R. Dandekar (✉)
Department of Engineering Design, Indian Institute of Technology Madras, Chennai, India
e-mail: rajatdandekar@gmail.com

F. E. Kracht
Department of Mechatronics, University of Duisburg-Essen, Duisburg, Germany
e-mail: frederic.kracht@uni-due.de

© Springer Nature Singapore Pte Ltd. 2019
D N Badodkar and T A Dwarakanath (eds.), *Machines, Mechanism and Robotics*, Lecture Notes in Mechanical Engineering,
https://doi.org/10.1007/978-981-10-8597-0_39

463

Fundamentally, in every model, the governing equations of motion of the system are set up and solved. As an alternative to classic forward-looking methods on the basis of the state equations, during the last decades object-oriented methods for modeling are being developed. These are characterized among other things by high modularity, interdisciplinarity, configurability, and a simple operation for the end user. Furthermore, you can reuse existing model components. This leads to a significant increase in the efficiency of the development process. Complex mechanical systems are dismantled into individual objects which directly represent the physical components. This can be, for example, a robot, running machines or even suspension of vehicles simply put together and simulated in connection [1]. The disadvantage of this type of modeling is that your application, usually takes up a longer calculation time. This is mainly because of the special description by means of differential-algebraic equations whose solution requires special complex integrators and equation solver. In addition, mechanical systems generally consist of either open or closed kinematic chains. Closed chains are associated with the problem that they usually only can be solved iteratively. For real-time applications, such as the simulation of a kinematically closed vehicle suspension in a driving simulator, this method is therefore not easily usable. The widespread use and the access to object-oriented modeling methods are still not prevalent in the industries. This is on the one hand due to license fees, but also due to the lack of knowledge in this field. There are also large parts of models already in the history which are created and stored in other modeling languages. The link by co-simulations is possible, but it also has disadvantages, such as the use of different equation solver and the resulting synchronization problems of the increment.

In this contribution, the development of a run-time optimized type of object-oriented modeling method that represents the dynamics of a mechanical multibody system will be demonstrated. The widespread simulation environment SIMULINK is used as it integrates well with other models. Complex systems can be easily assembled from individual elements of a model library. The modeling technique can be easily used to represent both open- and closed-loop systems. In the past, thanks to the strong increase in efficiency of the algebraic equation solver, self-algebraic loops are quickly predictable. The already mentioned advantages of the high degree of modularity, free scalability, and increased user-friendliness are retained. In the next section, the modeling technique is described with the help of governing equations of motion. Then, the method of modeling systems with open and closed kinematic chains is demonstrated. The simulation results will then be demonstrated with the help of a vehicle suspension system example. The computational efficiency and accuracy are compared with other established modeling methods. The last section summarizes the article together and gives an outlook for further research approaches.

2 Object-Oriented Modeling

In this section, a general process of object-oriented modeling is discussed. Each physical component is shown as a block that interfaces in both directions connected to other components. The blocks are taken from an object library which contains a description of their physical behavior. This approach leads to a fast method of modeling with reduced time and efforts [1]. The topology of the model is maintained similar to the real system, so that a high level of user-friendliness is ensured [2]. The interfaces in the system represent the potential and the flow variables. In the physical domain of mechanics, the potential variable is the acceleration, and the flow variable is the force. These interfaces represent actual existing connections such as joints. At the nodal points of the individual elements, the potential variables are the same, and the sum of the flow variables is zero.

Figure 1 represents the model of a mechanical object, "ac" represents across variables, and "th" represents through variables. The governing equations describing this object consists of ordinary differential equations f_d on the one hand and implicit algebraic equations f_a on the other hand. These equations consist of x_d, whose time derivates occur in the set of governing equations and x_a whose time derivates do not occur. The combination of the two forms results in a differential-algebraic equation system (DAE), for the solution of which special DAE solvers are necessary [1].

A modified object-oriented method is the kinetostatic transfer elements [3]. The global kinematics are solved by means of the generalized coordinates in connection with the Jacobi matrices. Furthermore, energy-neutral kinetostatic transmission, i.e., identical virtual work of the input and output states, is assumed. Movements are thereby transmitted forward through the element, forces in the opposite direction. For the resolution of kinematic loops, iterative or analytical methods are used depending on the design of the system. For the analytical solution, the kinematic loops are depicted as "kinematic transformers", which contain the explicit equations of the individual components of the closed chain. If no explicit equations can be determined, iterative methods are used.

In this work, each physical body is modeled and stored in a model library. Analogous to the described classical method, variables of type x_d and also of type x_a are obtained. In contrast to MODELICA, however, the underlying equations are already resolved after the desired variable in order to avoid an implicit equation in the element. The existing holonomous constraints are integrated into the object. For this

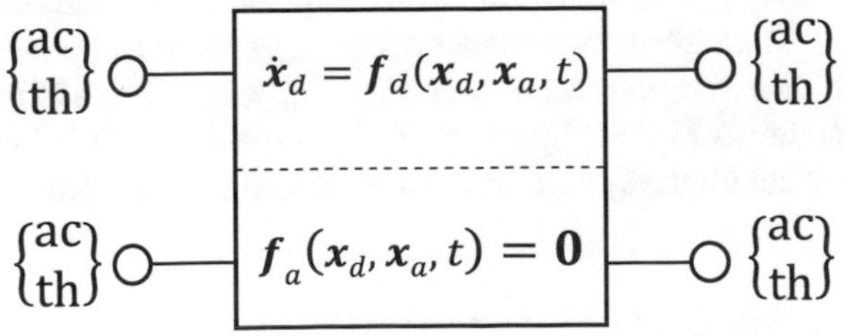

Fig. 1 Schematic representation of object-oriented model [7]

Fig. 2 Rigid body object [7]

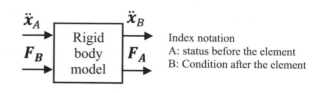

Index notation
A: status before the element
B: Condition after the element

purpose, generalized coordinates are used. Each block, considered separately, thus consists only of explicit equations and has a unique signal flow direction. This results in a block with the inputs and outputs as shown in Fig. 2. The combination of different objects can create a complete system that can be highly complex. The possibly present kinematic chains are reflected by algebraic loops in the system. These are solved internally in MATLAB/SIMULINK numerically before each integration step of the integrator for ordinary differential equations [4]. A detailed modeling method is now shown for a few different elements which are later required for a vehicle suspension.

2.1 Single Rod with Universal Joint

For the simple representation of the basic principle of the modeling methodology, an example of a single rod is demonstrated. The method can be easily extended to complex mechanisms involving more number of joints. The rigid body bar has two end points A and B, and C represents the center of gravity of the body (refer to Fig. 3). An external force F_B acts on the body at point B, and the translational acceleration of the body at point A a_A is known. In the case of a fixed joint, this acceleration would be 0. For an easy explanation of the general procedure, it is assumed that the center of gravity in the exact center of the rigid body lying. Furthermore, the body is assumed to be symmetric about the center of mass and homogeneous. The inertia tensor of the body is known. The main aim is to predict the dynamic behavior of the body; hence, we need to calculate the variation of the Euler angles θ, ϕ (refer to Fig. 3) with time. The following steps must be performed in order to obtain the differential equations in terms of the Euler angles. (a) Determination of the forces and moments acting on the body in the body-fixed coordinate system. (b) Use the Newton–Euler equations to obtain and solve three linear equations in terms of the angular accelerations (α_x, α_y, α_z) setting up the double rate of change of the Euler angles $\ddot{\phi}$, $\ddot{\theta}$ as a function of the angular accelerations α_x, α_y, α_z.

The global coordinate system is represented by $E(x_E, y_E, z_E)$ and the local coordinate system is represented by $i(x_i, y_i, z_i)$ which is located at the center of gravity (refer to Fig. 3). Using the Euler angles θ, ϕ, it is possible to represent the forces acting on the system in the body coordinate system.

Fig. 3 Schematic representation of a rigid body model [7]

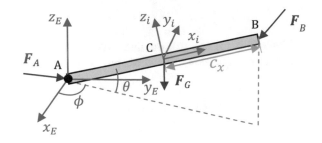

$$
{}^{i}\mathbf{F}_B = \begin{bmatrix} {}^{i}F_{B,x} \\ {}^{i}F_{B,y} \\ {}^{i}F_{B,z} \end{bmatrix} = \begin{bmatrix} \cos(\theta)\cos(\phi) & \cos(\theta)\sin(\phi) & \sin(\theta) \\ -\sin(\phi) & \cos(\phi) & 0 \\ -\sin(\theta)\cos(\phi) & -\sin(\theta)\sin(\phi) & \cos(\theta) \end{bmatrix} \begin{bmatrix} {}^{E}F_{B,x} \\ {}^{E}F_{B,y} \\ {}^{E}F_{B,z} \end{bmatrix}. \quad (1)
$$

The same transformation matrix can be used for the transformation of the moments in the body-fixed frame of reference.

In the next step, the dynamics of the rigid body will be represented. The translation and the rotational dynamics is represented by the Newton–Euler set of equations written in the i frame of reference which is body fixed and located at the center of gravity [5].

$$
{}^{i}\mathbf{F}_A + {}^{i}\mathbf{F}_B + {}^{i}\mathbf{F}_G = m\mathbf{E}_3{}^{i}\mathbf{a}_C, \quad (2)
$$

$$
{}^{i}\boldsymbol{\tau}_C = \mathbf{I}_C{}^{i}\boldsymbol{\alpha} + {}^{i}\boldsymbol{\omega} \times \left(\mathbf{I}_C{}^{i}\boldsymbol{\omega}\right), \quad (3)
$$

where m the mass of the body, ${}^{i}\mathbf{F}_A$, ${}^{i}\mathbf{F}_B$ are the external forces acting on the system at joints A and B, respectively, in the body frame of reference. ${}^{i}\boldsymbol{\tau}_C$ is the torque acting on the body about the center of gravity. $\mathbf{E}_3$ is the unit matrix and $\mathbf{a}_c$ is the acceleration vector of the center of gravity. ${}^{i}\boldsymbol{\omega}$ is the angular velocity and ${}^{i}\boldsymbol{\alpha}$ the angular acceleration of the system in the body frame of reference. $\mathbf{I}_{cm}$ is the moment of inertia of the body about the principal axis passing through the center of gravity.

When the Newton–Euler equations are written about the point A, the following are the resulting equations:

$$
{}^{i}\mathbf{F}_A + {}^{i}\mathbf{F}_B + {}^{i}\mathbf{F}_G = m\mathbf{E}_3{}^{i}\mathbf{a}_A - m\left({}^{i}\mathbf{c} \times {}^{i}\boldsymbol{\alpha}\right) + m\left({}^{i}\boldsymbol{\omega} \times \left({}^{i}\boldsymbol{\omega} \times {}^{i}\mathbf{c}\right)\right), \quad (4)
$$

$$
{}^{i}\boldsymbol{\tau}_A = m\left({}^{i}\mathbf{c} \times {}^{i}\mathbf{a}_A\right) + \mathbf{I}_C{}^{i}\boldsymbol{\alpha} - m\left({}^{i}\mathbf{c} \times \left({}^{i}\mathbf{c} \times {}^{i}\boldsymbol{\alpha}\right)\right) + {}^{i}\boldsymbol{\omega} \times \left(\mathbf{I}_C{}^{i}\boldsymbol{\omega}\right) - m{}^{i}\boldsymbol{\omega} \times \left({}^{i}\mathbf{c} \times \left({}^{i}\mathbf{c} \times {}^{i}\boldsymbol{\omega}\right)\right),
$$
$$
(5)
$$

${}^{i}\mathbf{a}_A$ is the translational acceleration of the body at point A in the body frame of reference. The vector $\mathbf{c}$ is the position vector from A to the center of gravity in the body-fixed coordinate system and is $\mathbf{c} = (c_x, 0, 0)^T$. $\mathbf{I}$ is the inertia tensor of the body.

The torque acting at point A can be written as

$$^{i}\tau_A = {}^{i}r_{AB} \times {}^{i}F_B + {}^{i}r_{AC} \times {}^{i}F_G. \tag{6}$$

From Eqs. (5) and (6), the linear equations of the angular accelerations can be obtained by expansion of the cross products as follows:

$$^{i}\alpha_x I_{xx} = -{}^{i}\omega_y {}^{i}\omega_z (I_{zz} - I_{yy}), \tag{7}$$

$$^{i}\alpha_y \left(m\,c_x^2 + I_{yy}\right) = m\left(c_x {}^{i}a_{A,z}\right) - {}^{i}\omega_x {}^{i}\omega_z (I_{xx} - I_{zz})$$
$$+ m\left({}^{i}\omega_x {}^{i}\omega_z\, c_x^2\right) - mg\,c_x \sin(\theta)\sin(\phi) - 2c_x {}^{i}F_{B,z}, \tag{8}$$

$$^{i}\alpha_z \left(m\,c_x^2 + I_{zz}\right) = m\left(-c_x {}^{i}a_{A,y}\right) - {}^{i}\omega_x {}^{i}\omega_y (I_{yy} - I_{xx}) - m\left({}^{i}\omega_x {}^{i}\omega_y\, c_x^2\right) - mgc_x \cos(\phi) + 2c_x {}^{i}F_{B,y}. \tag{9}$$

The angular velocities are calculated in the body-fixed frame of reference as follows:

$$^{i}\boldsymbol{\omega}_i = \begin{bmatrix} {}^{i}\omega_x \\ {}^{i}\omega_y \\ {}^{i}\omega_z \end{bmatrix} = \begin{bmatrix} \dot{\phi}\,\sin(\theta) \\ -\dot{\theta} \\ \dot{\phi}\,\cos(\theta) \end{bmatrix}. \tag{10}$$

Similarly, angular accelerations can be calculated in the body-fixed frame of refrence as follows:

$$^{i}\boldsymbol{\alpha}_i = \begin{bmatrix} {}^{i}\alpha_x \\ {}^{i}\alpha_y \\ {}^{i}\alpha_z \end{bmatrix} = \begin{bmatrix} \dot{\theta}\dot{\phi}\,\cos(\theta) + \ddot{\phi}\,\sin(\theta) \\ -\ddot{\theta} \\ -\dot{\theta}\dot{\phi}\,\sin(\theta) + \ddot{\phi}\,\cos(\theta) \end{bmatrix}. \tag{11}$$

To determine the double rate of change of the Euler angles $\ddot{\phi}, \ddot{\theta}$ in terms of the angular accelerations, we have the following equations:

$$\ddot{\theta} = -{}^{i}\alpha_y, \tag{12}$$

$$\ddot{\phi} = {}^{i}\alpha_x \sin(\theta) + {}^{i}\alpha_z \cos(\theta). \tag{13}$$

From Eqs. (7)–(13), we can obtain the Euler angles as a function of time. The resulting set of equations can be modeled in MATLAB SIMULINK in the form of a block diagram which is easily configurable and scalable.

3 Connection of Elements

The individual elements of the body can now be assembled into a total system together. This results in the formation of open-loop or closed-loop kinematic chains. Modeling for both these cases is described in this section.

Fig. 4 Double pendulum [7]

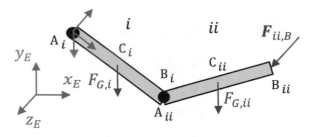

Fig. 5 Modeling of double pendulum [7]

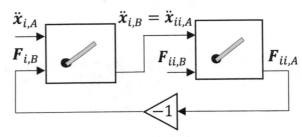

3.1 Open-Loop Kinematic Chain

An example of two rigid body links connected at a joint is considered (double pendulum). Figure 4 shows two links i and ii connected a joint with external forces acting on the system. The method of solution can be extended to any number of links very easily which is an advantage of object-oriented programming.

The force $F_{ii,B}$ acting at point B_{ii} and the acceleration of point A_i are known. The two rigid bodies are connected at the same physical point represented by A_{ii} in link i and B_i in link ii. The following are the properties of the multibody system:

(1) The sum of forces at point B_i is 0.
(2) The acceleration at point A_{ii} and B_i are identical.

Figure 5 shows the object-oriented modeling of the composite system. Thus, due to the unique flow direction of the input and output variables, the mechanical systems consisting of a finite number of open-loop kinematic chains are easy to model.

3.2 Closed-Loop Kinematic Chain

An example of a four-bar mechanism is considered to demonstrate the concept of modeling a closed-loop chain (refer to Fig. 6).

The forces acting at points A_1 and D_1 are not known. If we consider the flow direction from A_1 to D_1 considering F_{D1} as the external force acting on the system, then the system can be modeled as an open-loop system (refer to Fig. 7a) which shows the block diagram of the resulting open-loop system. This problem cannot be solved

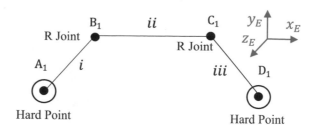

Fig. 6 Four-bar mechanism [7]

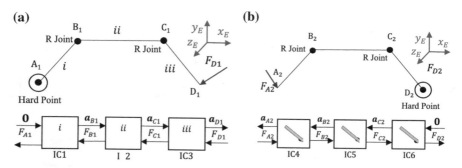

Fig. 7 a Four-bar mechanism—open chain 1. **b** Four-bar mechanism—open chain 2

using a single chain, the solution to this problem uses the application techniques of a recursive Newton–Euler algorithm [6]. If we consider flow direction from D_1 to A_1, then we can model another open-loop system with the external force F_{A2} acting on the system at point A_1. All the elements in this chain will be the vertical mirror images of the first chain (Fig. 7a). Hence, the initial conditions of all the links will change by $180°$. Figure 7b shows the block diagram of the second open-loop mechanism. The overall block diagram consists of the superposition of the two open-loop kinematic chains (refer to Fig. 8).

In the next section, the modeling theory developed in the earlier section will be applied to a practical automotive example of a double wishbone suspension system.

4   Modeling of the Double Wishbone Suspension

Suspensions of vehicles are increasingly using mechatronic functions, whether it is through the use of active spring/damper elements and stabilizers or the measurement of various states of different elements of the suspension and tires by sensors. For the design and optimization of a suspension in relation to the driving comfort and safety, it is, therefore, necessary to first mechanically model the overall suspension system to dynamically predict the suspension behavior in real time. Object-oriented

Fig. 8 Modeling of a
closed-loop four-bar
mechanism [7]

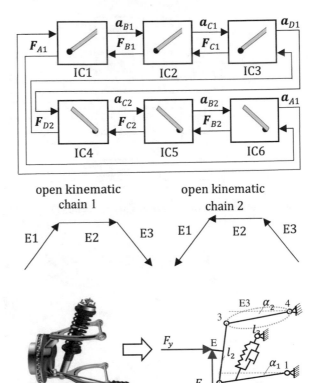

Fig. 9 Double wishbone
suspension

methods of modeling are ideal for a vehicle suspension in the design phase itself. This is because although there exist a number of different suspension topologies, the elements of a suspension such as arms with multiple connection points, springs, and dampers are used in almost every configuration.

4.1 Modeling with Modified Object-Oriented Approach

The modeling of a double wishbone suspension is demonstrated in this section, as it has a wide range of applications. Figure 9 represents the schematic representation of the simplified double wishbone suspension system. By applying the single rod, spring damper elements to the concept of modeling closed-loop kinematic chains, the overall structure of the system is represented in the block diagram format in Fig. 10.

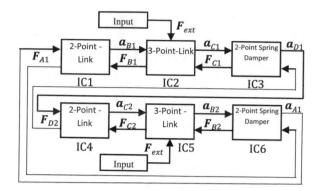

Fig. 10 Double wishbone suspension block diagram [7]

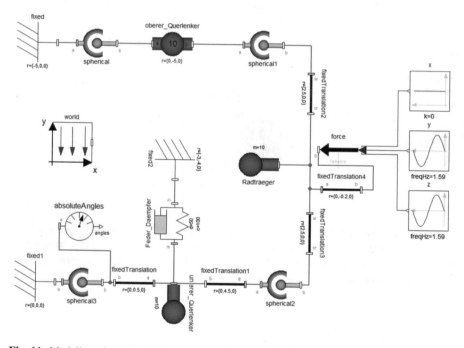

Fig. 11 Modeling of double wishbone suspension system in DYMOLA [7]

4.2 Comparison with Other Modeling Approaches

In this section, the simulation time and the accuracy of the modeling approach are compared with some established modeling software. The first comparison is made with the object-oriented programming language MODELICA. The composition of the model is shown in Fig. 11. In addition to MODELICA, the multibody simulation environment ADAMS/VIEW is used for comparison. All models are parameterized

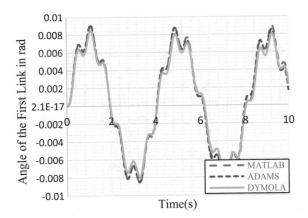

Fig. 12 Euler angles of the first arm (ADAMS, DYMOLA, and MATLAB/SIMULINK)

Table 1 Comparison of the model computational efficiency with ADAMS and DYMOLA for a double wishbone suspension system (Processor: Intel Core i7-6700 K 4.00 GHz 16.0 GB RAM)

Simulation tool	CPU time (s)
MATLAB/SIMULINK (developed model) • Object Orientied (ode 2—Heun)	0.157
DYMOLA • Object Oriented (DASSL—DAE-Solver)	0.269
ADAMS • Multibody system (GSTIFF—I3)	1.641

with the same geometrical properties, e.g., the length, moment of inertia, relative position of the joints, etc. An attempt is made to eliminate all the external processes while calculating the CPU time required to solve the mechanism. An external sinusoidal force $F_{ext} = 10$ N with a frequency of 10 rad/s is applied to the wheel carrier. Euler angle θ of the first link is compared for the abovementioned modeling approached. Before comparing the CPU time, the accuracy of the model is established. Figure 12 shows the comparison of accuracy made with DYMOLA and ADAMS. It can be seen from the figure that the change in Euler angle is identical which establishes the accuracy of the proposed method. The determined calculation times are shown in Table 1. The step size has been set to 0.05 s, and the motion was simulated for 201 time steps for each modeling method. It can be clearly seen that the proposed object-oriented method gives the least calculation time and hence is more efficient compared to DYMOLA and ADAMS. Also, the use in a real-time system, such as the use in the driving simulator at the University of Duisburg-Essen, is feasible

5   Summary

In this work, a signal flow based, object-oriented modeling method for mechanical systems is described. The basis of the method was the application of the Newton–Euler equations applied in the body-fixed frame of reference. Open kinematic chains can be represented easily; also closed-loop chains can be modeled by the superposition of two open-loop chains. Due to the algebraic loop solver in SIMULINK, fast simulation times are obtained. In comparison with the modeling language MODELICA and the multibody simulation environment of ADAMS, the model performed better with respect to the computational efficiency in the case of a vehicle suspension system.

References

1. D. Schramm, *Modeling and Simulation*, vol. 2. University Duisburg Essen: Plain Text Media Workshop GmbH, Essen, in 2017
2. I. S. Drogies, Object-oriented modeling of the dynamic behavior with MODELICA, in *Driving Dynamics Control* (Springer, 2006), pp. 71–91
3. A. Kecskemethy, *Object-Oriented Modeling of the Dynamics of Multibody Systems with the Help of Transmission Elements [Dr]*, *Thesis, University of Duisburg* (VDI Verlag, Germany, 1993)
4. Math Works, *Algebraic Loops* (2016), https://de.mathworks.com/help/simulink/ug/algebraic-loops.html
5. R. Featherstone, *Rigid Body Dynamics Algorithms* (Springer, 2014)
6. G.F. Schanzer, *Optimal Control of a Multi Finger Gripper with Competing Controls Under Consideration of Ph.D. Thesis Elasticities* (Technical University of Munich, 2007)
7. F.E. Kracht, R. Dandekar, T. Bruckmann and D. Schramm, *Real Time Object Oriented Modeling with the Example of a Vehicle Wheel Suspension*, IFToMM DACH, TU Chemnitz (2017)

Kinematic and Dynamic Analyses of Four Bar Clamping Mechanism Operating in Liquid Sodium

Anu Krishnan, Jose Varghese, R. Vijayashree, S. Raghupathy
and P. Puthiyavinayagam

Abstract Future fast breeder reactors envisage the use of Offset Handling Machine for ex-vessel handling. In order to avoid the inadvertent lifting of transfer pot (TP) by in-vessel handling machine, an actuator operated four bar clamping mechanism is being used. Kinematic analysis of the mechanism is very important to ensure the positional accuracy of clamping link. Accurate determination of forces in links are essential for linear actuator sizing, which necessitates the need for dynamic analysis. A code has been developed for the kinematic and dynamic analysis of the mechanism. Position analysis ensures that clamping link moves out thereby enabling the easy removal of TP. Analysis shows that maximum velocity at the tip of clamping link is very small and hence do not influence the positional accuracy. Dynamic analysis with and without considering the effects of friction are carried out and pushing/pulling force requirements of clamping mechanism are established.

Keywords Fast breeder reactor · Offset handling machine · Subassembly transfer flask · Transfer pot · Four bar clamping mechanism · Kinematic analysis Dynamic analysis

A. Krishnan (✉) · J. Varghese · R. Vijayashree · S. Raghupathy · P. Puthiyavinayagam
Reactor Design Group, Indira Gandhi Center for Atomic Research, Kalpakkam,
Tamil Nadu, India
e-mail: anukrishnan@igcar.gov.in

J. Varghese
e-mail: varghese@igcar.gov.in

R. Vijayashree
e-mail: rviji@igcar.gov.in

S. Raghupathy
e-mail: rags@igcar.gov.in

P. Puthiyavinayagam
e-mail: vinayaga@igcar.gov.in

© Springer Nature Singapore Pte Ltd. 2019
D N Badodkar and T A Dwarakanath (eds.), *Machines, Mechanism and Robotics*, Lecture Notes in Mechanical Engineering,
https://doi.org/10.1007/978-981-10-8597-0_40

1 Introduction

Second stage of Indian nuclear power program involves establishing Fast Breeder Reactors (FBRs) for power generation which uses liquid sodium as coolant. Fuel handling system is one of the critical systems of fast reactor having influence on both availability and safety of the plant. The functions of fuel handling system include receipt, inspection, storage and loading of fresh sub-assemblies into the core; removal of spent sub-assemblies from the core, sodium washing, storage and shipping of spent sub-assemblies to reprocessing plant. In FBRs, design of fuel handling machine is challenging considering the fact that in-vessel handling is a blind operation due to the opacity of sodium and most of the fuel handling operations are carried out remotely.

Future FBRs envisage the use of a combination of Offset Handling Machine (OHM) within the main vessel and a simple shielded Subassembly Transfer Flask (STF) located outside the main vessel, for ex-vessel handling of sub-assemblies in sodium filled transfer pot (TP). OHM links the sub assembly transfer between in-vessel handling machine (IVHM) and STF. Spent sub assembly lowered into sodium filled TP by IVHM is transferred to higher elevation by OHM, from where STF takes the TP with sub assembly out of main vessel. Reverse operations are carried out for fresh sub assembly. While the IVHM takes out the fresh sub assembly from TP, there is a chance of lifting of TP along with the sub assembly. In order to avoid the lifting of TP a clamping mechanism is required. The clamping mechanism has to be moved out while the STF takes TP out. This paper details the kinematic and dynamic analysis of four bar mechanism designed for this purpose.

2 Description of Clamping Mechanism

Figure 1 shows the sketch of actuator operated four bar clamping mechanism in closed condition.

A hinged lever (Link-4) at the top of transfer pot prevents the upward movement of pot during transfer, except at the position from where STF takes the TP out. Link-4 needs to be rotated counter clock wise to facilitate the removal of TP by STF. The operation of hinged lever (Link-4) is carried out by an electrically operated linear actuator. The motion of actuator is transmitted to the Link-4 through an actuator rod, hinged bell crank lever (Link-2) and connecting link (Link-3). Link-2 and Link-4 are prismatic links of 20 mm thickness and are hinged to the stationary link (Link-1) of the mechanism through fork shaped brackets. Connecting link (Link-3) is hinged to Link-2 and Link-4 at either ends. For the required link opening, θ_2 is varied from 45° to 53.3°.

A metallic bellow is connected to the actuator rod for sealing cover gas and sodium aerosols. Link lengths as shown in the figure are obtained by solving the Freudenstein equation, optimizing for minimum bellow displacement and ensuring transmission angle greater than 50°. Bracket connecting Link 4 and Link-1 is kept close to TP

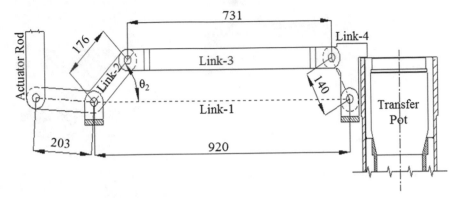

Fig. 1 Four bar clamping mechanism (closed position)

holder so as to reduce the bending moment and stresses when TP hits the Link-4 when IVHM inadvertently lifts the TP up. In order to reduce the effect of self-weight of Link-3, it is kept in horizontal position in closed condition, thereby ensuring a state of stable equilibrium. The angle that left hand portion of Link-2 makes with horizontal is chosen as ~4° in order to reduce the lateral bellow displacement.

2.1 Requirement of Kinematic and Dynamic Analysis

As θ_2 is varied it should be ensured that the Link-4 moves out and easy removal of TP is possible. Positional accuracy requirements of components operating in radioactive environment are stringent, necessitating the need of kinematic analysis of the clamping mechanism for a range of θ_2 values between 45° and 53.3°. Since the clamping mechanism is operating in high temperature, radioactive and inaccessible area, its reliability of operation should be very high. Pushing/pulling force requirements of Link-2 has to be accurately estimated for linear actuator sizing. Hence accurate determination of forces in links is important. Further, the forces act as an input for the wear study of pin joints. Thus dynamic analysis of links for θ_2 values ranging from 45° to 53.3° is required.

3 Code Development

A computer code has been developed for the kinematic and dynamic analysis, which can give the results of position, velocity, acceleration and force (with and without friction) for any value of θ_2 between 45° and 53.3°. Basis of the code developed is discussed in the following section.

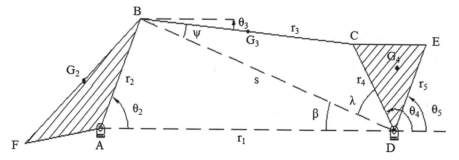

Fig. 2 Simplified four bar clamping mechanism

3.1 Position Analysis

Four bar clamping mechanism is simplified as shown in Fig. 2 for position analysis.

Tip of the clamping link (Link-4) is represented by the point E and is the critical point with reference to kinematic analysis. G_2, G_3 and G_4 denote the center of gravity (CG) of links 2, 3 and 4 respectively.

From trigonometric relations [1]:

$$s = \sqrt{r_1^2 + r_2^2 - 2r_1r_2 \cos \theta_2}, \tag{1}$$

$$\beta = \cos^{-1} \frac{r_1^2 + s^2 - r_2^2}{2r_1s} \tag{2}$$

$$\psi = \cos^{-1} \frac{r_3^2 + s^2 - r_4^2}{2r_3s}, \tag{3}$$

$$\lambda = \cos^{-1} \frac{r_4^2 + s^2 - r_3^2}{2r_4s} \tag{4}$$

$$\theta_3 = \psi - \beta, \tag{5}$$

$$\theta_4 = \pi - \lambda - \beta \tag{6}$$

Thus co-ordinates of points can be written as: $A = (0, 0)$, $B = (r_2 \cos \theta_2, r_2 \sin \theta_2)$, $C = (r_2\cos\theta_2 + r_3\cos\theta_3, r_2\sin\theta_2 + r_3\sin\theta_3)$, $D = (r_1, 0)$, $E = (r_1 + r_5\cos\theta_5, r_5\sin\theta_5)$

Similarly co-ordinates of other points like G_2, G_3 and G_4 can be written for position analysis.

3.2 Velocity Analysis

It is assumed that the push/pull velocity of linear actuator is 15 mm/s. Thus the angular velocity of Link-2, $\omega_2 = 15/AF = 15/203 = 0.074$ rad/s. Since the lateral movement of actuator rod is negligible, ω_2 is considered to be constant throughout. Using loop closure equation for the link system and converting the vector equation into x and y components: [1]

$$\mathbf{DA + AB + BC + CD = 0} \tag{7}$$

$$r_1 \cos 180 + r_2 \cos \theta_2 + r_3 \cos \theta_3 + r_4 \cos(\pi + \theta_4) = 0 \tag{8}$$

$$r_1 \sin 180 + r_2 \sin \theta_2 + r_3 \sin \theta_3 + r_4 \sin(\pi + \theta_4) = 0 \tag{9}$$

Differentiating Eqs. 8 and 9 with respect to time and representing in matrix format

$$\mathbf{A} \times \boldsymbol{\omega} = \mathbf{B} \tag{10}$$

where, $\mathbf{A} = \begin{bmatrix} -r_3 \sin \theta_3 & r_4 \sin \theta_4 \\ r_3 \cos \theta_3 & -r_4 \cos \theta_4 \end{bmatrix}$, $\mathbf{B} = \begin{bmatrix} \omega_2 r_2 \sin \theta_2 \\ -\omega_2 r_2 \cos \theta_2 \end{bmatrix}$, $\boldsymbol{\omega} = \begin{bmatrix} \omega_3 \\ \omega_4 \end{bmatrix}$

where, ω_3 and ω_4 are angular velocities of link 3 and 4 respectively.

From Eq. 10 values of ω_3 and ω_4 can be obtained.

Velocities of points B, C and E are further found out using following equations:

$$V_{B,x} = -r_2\omega_2\sin\theta_2, \tag{11}$$

$$V_{B,y} = r_2\omega_2 \cos \theta_2, \tag{12}$$

$$V_{C,x} = -r_2\omega_2\sin\theta_2 - r_3\omega_3\sin\theta_3, \tag{13}$$

$$V_{C,y} = r_2\omega_2 \cos \theta_2 + r_3\omega_3 \cos \theta_3, \tag{14}$$

$$V_{E,x} = -r_5\omega_4\sin\theta_5, \tag{15}$$

$$V_{E,y} = r_5\omega_4 \cos \theta_5, \tag{16}$$

Velocities of other points can be found similarly.

3.3 Acceleration Analysis

Since linear actuator is pushing/pulling the Link-2 with constant angular velocity, angular acceleration of Link-2 is 0. For determining the angular accelerations of link 3 and 4 Eqs. 8 and 9 are differentiated twice with respect to time and representing in matrix format as:

$$\mathbf{A} \times \boldsymbol{\alpha} = \mathbf{C} \tag{17}$$

where,

$$C = \begin{bmatrix} r_2\omega_2^2 \cos\theta_2 + r_3\omega_3^2 \cos\theta_3 - r_4\omega_4^2 \cos\theta_4 \\ r_2\omega_2^2 \sin\theta_2 + r_3\omega_3^2 \sin\theta_3 - r_4\omega_4^2 \sin\theta_4 \end{bmatrix}, \alpha = \begin{bmatrix} \alpha_3 \\ \alpha_4 \end{bmatrix}$$

where, α_3 and α_4 are angular accelerations of link 3 and 4 respectively. A is same as that in Eq. 10.

Acceleration of point C in Fig. 2 can be written as:

$$A_{C,x} = -r_2\omega_2^2 \cos\theta_2 - r_3\alpha_3 \sin\theta_3 - r_3\omega_3^2 \cos\theta_3 \tag{18}$$

$$A_{C,y} = -r_2\omega_2^2 \sin\theta_2 + r_3\alpha_3 \cos\theta_3 - r_3\omega_3^2 \sin\theta_3 \tag{19}$$

Similarly, accelerations of other required points are written. Acceleration values of CG is a pre-cursor for dynamic analysis and thus acceleration of points G_2, G_3 and G_4 are obtained as mentioned above.

3.4 Dynamic Force Analysis

Free body diagram of links is shown in Fig. 3.

m_i and I_i denote the mass and moment of inertia of 'ith' link respectively and are manually given as an input to the code. Masses of link 2, 3 and 4 are 2.2 kg, 6.8 kg and 2.8 kg respectively and moment of inertia of links 2, 3 and 4 are 29.4 kgm^2, 544 kgm^2 and 12.7 kgm^2 respectively. T_{ij}^f denote the frictional moment at pin joints [2].

$$\left| T_{ij}^f \right| = r\mu\sqrt{\left(F_{ij}^{x2} + F_{ij}^{y2} \right)} \tag{20}$$

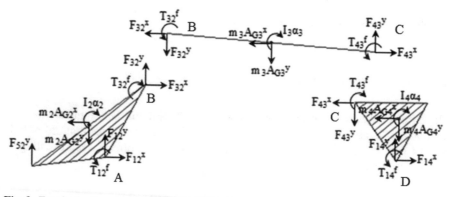

Fig. 3 Free body diagram of links

where, 'r' is the radius of the pin and μ (Coefficient of friction between steel and steel in sodium environment) $=0.7$ [3].

Direction of T_{ij}^f depends on the relative angular velocity of the links connected to pin joint and is dependent on the direction of link movement (clock wise or counter clock wise). This effect is included in the code using 'If-else' command. Weight of the links is acting vertically downwards through CG (Not shown in Fig. 3).

Force and moment equilibrium equations (about C) of Link-4 can be written as:

$$F_{14}^x - F_{43}^x - m_4 A_{G4}^x = 0 \tag{21}$$

$$F_{14}^y - F_{43}^y - m_4(9810 + A_{G4}^y) = 0 \tag{22}$$

$$- cT_{43}^f - m_4(9810 + A_{G4}^y)(x_{G4} - x_C) - m_4 A_{G4}^x(y_C - y_{G4}) + F_{14}^x y_c$$
$$+ F_{14}^y(x_D - x_C) - I_4\alpha_4 + dT_{14}^f = 0 \tag{23}$$

If $(\omega_3 - \omega_4) < 0$, $c = 1$ else $c = -1$. If $\omega_4 < 0$, $d = 1$ else $d = -1$.

Similarly equations of equilibrium are written for other links. Thus there will be 9 such equations and 9 unknowns. Since the equations are nonlinear in nature, iterative solution technique Newton-Raphson method is employed. For initial trial of solutions, results from dynamic analysis without friction is used (Obtained by putting $T_{ij}^f = 0$ in the equations, thereby obtaining 9 linear simultaneous equations).

3.5 Algorithm of Computer Code

Algorithm of the computer code developed is shown in Fig. 4.

4 Results and Discussion

4.1 Position Analysis

Link locations at extreme positions are shown in Fig. 5 (Link-2 shown partially only). It is observed that when θ_2 rotates from 45° to 53.3°, θ_4 rotates from 117.9° to 127.6° thereby enabling the smooth removal of TP.

4.2 Velocity Analysis

Velocity of point E (During link closing) is plotted against Link-2 angle in Fig. 6 and is observed that velocity maintains almost a linear relationship with θ_2. The maximum velocity of point E is observed to be 14.074 mm/s. Since the maximum

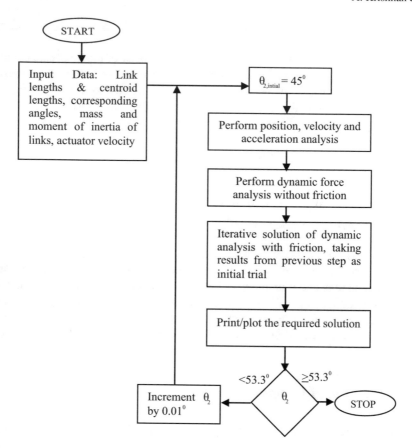

Fig. 4 Algorithm of code

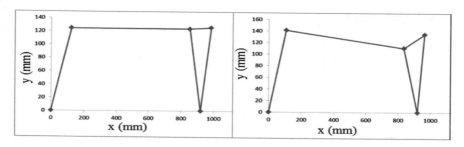

Fig. 5 Link-4 position (locked and un-locked)

velocity is very small, its influence on the positional accuracy of the clamping link is almost negligible.

Fig. 6 Velocity of point E

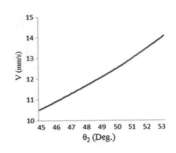

Fig. 7 Force to open/close the mechanism

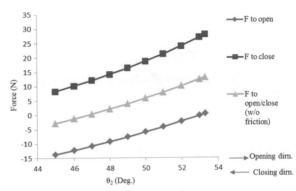

4.3 Dynamic Analysis

It is observed from Fig. 7 that in order to open the mechanism a pushing force of 13.9N is to be given initially. Further, the pushing force decreases with θ_2 (Becomes less negative). This is due to the assistance of self-weight of links in opening (Specifically that of Link-3).Further it is noted that a pulling force of 27.9N is to be given initially to close the mechanism. The effect of self-weight is maximum at extreme position of $\theta_2 = 53.3°$ and decreases as θ_2 decreases. Also, when the effect friction is not being considered, the force to push/pull is same and is independent of whether link is in opening/closing mode.

5 Static Analysis

Maximum pulling force exerted by IVHM is 15 kN. Hence the clamping mechanism should be able to provide a clamping force of 15 kN in static condition. Static force analysis is performed to determine the force rating of actuator (Fig. 8):

$$\sum M_B = 0 \rightarrow F_{34} = \frac{15 \times 65.5}{124.5} = 7.89 \, \text{kN} \tag{24}$$

$$F_{34} = F_{43} = F_{23} = F_{32} = 7.89 \, \text{kNZ} \tag{25}$$

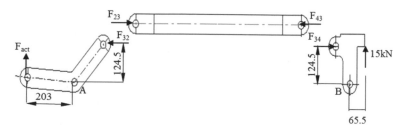

Fig. 8 Free body diagram for static analysis

$$\sum M_A = 0 \rightarrow F_{act} = \frac{7.89 \times 124.5}{203} = 4.84\,\text{kN} \tag{26}$$

Thus a pulling force of 4.84 kN acts on actuator and needs to be sized for the same.

6 Conclusion

Kinematic and dynamic analysis is performed for the four bar clamping mechanism for a range of θ_2 values from 45° to 53.3°. Results of position, velocity, acceleration and dynamic analysis are obtained. Position analysis ensures that clamping link (Link-4) rotates and enables the smooth removal of TP. Maximum velocity at the tip of Link-4 is very small and thus doesn't influence the positional accuracy of the mechanism. Dynamic force analysis with and without friction is performed. It is observed that the force to open/close the mechanism is very small when compared to the static load requirements of the linear actuator.

References

1. J.E Shigley, Theory of machines and mechanism (Oxford university press, 2015)
2. S. Mitsi, I. Tsiafis K.D. Bouzakis, Dynamic analysis of six-bar mechanical press for deep drawing, in *Proceedings ROTRIB-16, IOP Conference Series*, vol. 174, conf. 1 (2017)
3. AFCEN, RCC-MRx Section III Subsection K-Examination, handling or drive mechanisms

Telepresence System with 3D Mouse and Path-Planning Functionality

Abhishek Jaju, Pritam Prakash Shete, P. V. Sarngadharan
and Surojit Kumar Bose

Abstract Telepresence system provides interfaces to remotely teleoperate robot and execute hazardous task. These tasks are generally executed by human operator in master–slave mode. Telepresence interface provides a small haptic device to manipulate robot, stereoscopic view to see the environment and moreover force reflection capability. Bilateral master–slave tele-manipulation depends upon operator's experience and agility to a large extent. In this article, we discuss the concept of 3D mouse and path-planning functionality for an autonomous stereo vision guided telerobotics system. These augmented reality functionalities will assist operator to perform pick and place operations more efficiently.

Keywords Telepresence · Augmented reality · Assistive technique
Remote operation · Haptic feedback · Stereo vision and stereo measurement

1 Introduction

Identical master–slave systems have been in vogue for many years from now. Advancements in computer-assisted master–slave manipulation technology made

A. Jaju (✉)
Division of Remote Handling and Robotics, Bhabha Atomic Reaseach Centre,
Mumbai, Trombay, Mumbai, India
e-mail: ajaju@barc.gov.in

P. V. Sarngadharan
Division of Remote Handling and Robotics, Bhabha Atomic Reaseach Centre,
Mumbai, Mumbai 400085, India
e-mail: sarang@barc.gov.in

P. P. Shete · S. K. Bose
Computer Division, BARC Mumbai, Mumbai, India
e-mail: ppshete@barc.gov.in

S. K. Bose
e-mail: bose@barc.gov.in

© Springer Nature Singapore Pte Ltd. 2019
D N Badodkar and T A Dwarakanath (eds.), *Machines, Mechanism
and Robotics*, Lecture Notes in Mechanical Engineering,
https://doi.org/10.1007/978-981-10-8597-0_41

Fig. 1 Setup of telepresence station

it practical to use a small haptic device as a master, while a standard industrial robot can be slave [1–3]. In teleoperation, the workspace of the slave manipulator is seen through multiple views from monoscopic cameras. Instead, here we use live feeds from two IP-cameras to construct a stereoscopic view (3D) of the slave environment [4]. The remote operator manipulates the slave using a small haptic device as a master. All together, this haptic and visual (3D) immersion of the operator in the remote environment can be thought of as a telepresence interface (Fig. 1). This interface can be made accessible through Ethernet network for doing remote operation jobs. Overcoming the problems arising from this separation of operator and robot is the essence of telepresence research [5]. The remote operator's corrective action is based on the live camera feed from the remote site. Thus, a virtual position loop is established between the operator's action and robot manipulator. However, latency in camera feed results in undesirable correction commands to the slave manipulator. This is due to the fact that the cameras and the network have limited frame rate for relaying and reconstructing the images [6].

Thus, a need for automation in telepresence system arises. Automated systems can and have replaced human operators in structured jobs, but the introduction of automation does not always lead to their complete replacement. Rather, it changes the nature of the work they do. The role of operators in this system tends to switch from worker to supervisor when automation is introduced [7].

We present an augmented reality interface which assists the operator to perform teleoperation task autonomously [8]. For this, we have devised two technique, viz. 3D mouse and path planning. 3D mouse is an AR-based cursor which can be moved using ordinary mouse on the live 3D video stream. This mouse is calibrated with the remote environment; thus, it gives position coordinate of any object in the scene.

Once the coordinates of object are available, we can use path-planning utility to move the robot and pick the object. The trajectory of the robot is defined by selecting intermediate points on the live video stream.

2 System Setup

We will discuss the architecture and setup of our telepresence system (see Fig. 2) in detail in this section. Our system consists of two different geographical sites, namely, manipulator site and remote site.

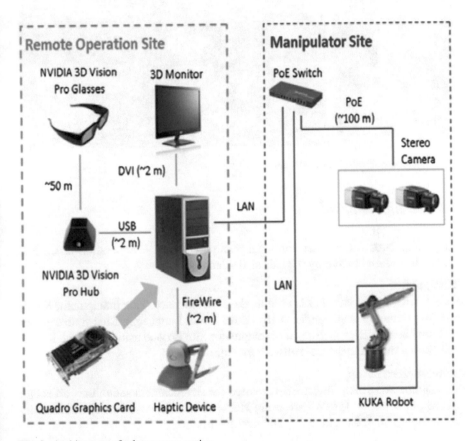

Fig. 2 Architecture of telepresence station

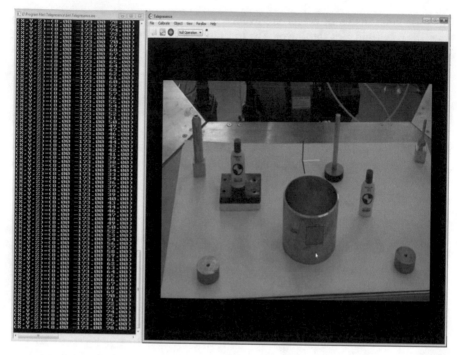

Fig. 3 Augmented reality-based 3D mouse

2.1 Manipulator Site

The manipulator site has the industrial manipulator and teleoperation tasks. It is viewed from Remote Site by the pair of IP-Cameras.

Manipulator

KUKA KR6 industrial robot is used as slave manipulator. This manipulator has its own programming language, i.e. KRL (Kuka Robot Language). Real-time communication between Remote Site and Manipulator Site is done using real-time KUKA RSI (Robot Sensor Interface) software module.

Stereocamera Setup

Two Dinion HD 1080p IP-cameras are used for stereocamera setup; they offer Full HD resolution at 30 fps. We are using H.264 format for real-time streaming with latency ranging, 120 (minimum)–240 ms (maximum).

Force–Torque Sensor

Sense of touch is very important in online tele-manipulation jobs. To get realistic force reflection at remote site, ATI F/T sensor is used. This sensor is mounted on the wrist of the robot, and subsequently, the gripper is mounted on the F/T sensor using an adapter plate. The sensor's data is transmitted at the remote location, and F/T values are then mapped onto the haptic device for force reflection.

2.2   Remote Site

The remote site is separated by 1.5 km from the manipulator site. The operator controls the robot from the remote site using following equipment.

Workstation
Our workstation configuration is Intel Core i7 (3.30 GHz) processor with 8 GB DDR3 RAM. Windows 7 64 bit is the installed operating system.

3D Display
We are using a 22" LCD monitor from Viewsonic (VX2268WM) as 3D display. Its refresh rate is 120 Hz. Normal monitors have refresh rate of 60 Hz. 3D application needs high refresh rate monitor because alternate Left and Right images are shown to the corresponding eyes. Thus, the effective refresh rate is 60 Hz for each eye.

3D Vision Pro and Graphics Card
To view stereoscopic content on 3D display we are using NVIDIA Quadro 4000 graphics card with 3D vision PRO RF Hub and Glasses. The stereoscopic format is Side by Side and viewing method is OpenGL Quad Buffered. The advantage of this method is that one can view 3D content even without full screen. This method can work under both Linux and Windows operating system.

Haptic Device
We have used the Phantom haptic device as a master to manipulate the slave KUKA robot remotely by visual feedback from the live stereoscopic view from IP-cameras. The haptic device has force feedback capability from slave environment. Motion mapping from haptic master to slave robot is achieved by the using constant scaling mapping [9].

3   Implementation

We will discuss the implementation details of our telepresence system with 3D mouse and path-planning functionality, in this section. Real-time robot manipulation is realized using C# programming language and KUKA RSI, whereas the stereoscopic vision system is implemented in C++.

3.1   Camera and Stereo Calibration

We are using 9×6 chequerboard pattern with 32 mm^2 size for both camera and a stereo calibration. The camera and the stereo calibration are performed using specifically designed 48 image sequence for high accuracy. The calibration is performed such that the entire working volume is covered by chequerboard pattern. Calibration images are taken at twelve unique orientations by maintaining symmetry and covering the entire camera (individual) as well as a stereo view region. Forty-eight calibration images ensure abundant set of views and are utilized at each calibration phase for better accuracy.

3.2 Online Stereo-Rectification

After individual camera calibration and stereo calibration, we got camera parameters and relationship between both the cameras. We then carried out stereo-rectification to remap left and right camera images. This is been done for pixel-level alignment of image rows with each other (left and right). Stereo-rectification can accurately align two cameras at image level which is very hard to achieve using manual camera alignment. Image re-mappings are calculated using OpenCV library. These maps are then subsequently applied to each image for a real-time stereo image rectification in OpenGL. This process is done in real time by implementing it on the graphics card. It takes 6.7 ms processing time for each frame of HD resolution [10].

3.3 AR 3D Mouse and Path Planning

Augmented reality technology is utilized to superimpose computer-generated objects on a stereoscopic view of the robot working environment. Here, real-world view is augmented by computer-generated virtual objects such as 3D axis, 3D marker and so on to enhance 3D stereoscopic view for enriched 3D experience. The OpenCV calibration module and the OpenGL graphics library are utilized for inserting virtual objects in a real world. Initially, both left and right camera views are stereo rectified using OpenGL graphics processing. Thereafter, a chequerboard calibration pattern is utilized for extrinsic camera calibration. A rotation matrix and a translation vector computed from extrinsic calibration are utilized to calculate OpenGL projection and OpenGL model view matrices for both left and right camera views. Virtual objects are drawn using these OpenGL matrices on stereo rectified camera views. This is registered to computer's mouse movement. To move in Z (depth), one has to use scroll button, left click to select the object and right click to mark intermediate points for path planning. The operator has the option to define the trajectory as linear or point-to-point.

3.4 3D Coordinate Mapping

Both the stereo cameras and the robot have their own coordinate systems and origins. A 3D coordinate mapping is performed to align their respective coordinate systems and origins. An extrinsic camera calibration is carried out for left camera using the chequerboard pattern in order to transform the 3D coordinate system and the origin to the predefined world coordinate system. As shown in Fig. 4, the common reference coordinate system is mapped onto the chequerboard plane with Z coordinate equal to zero on the plane, whereas X and Y coordinates are given by the chequerboard square size. The chequerboard corners are identified using OpenCV library, which provides one rotation matrix and one translation vector of the chequerboard plane with respect to the camera. Then, these matrices are utilized to calculate a transformation matrix, which transforms the camera coordinate system to the common reference coordinate system. Now, using the three-point method, we transform robot's base coordinate system to reference coordinate system using the same chequerboard pattern.

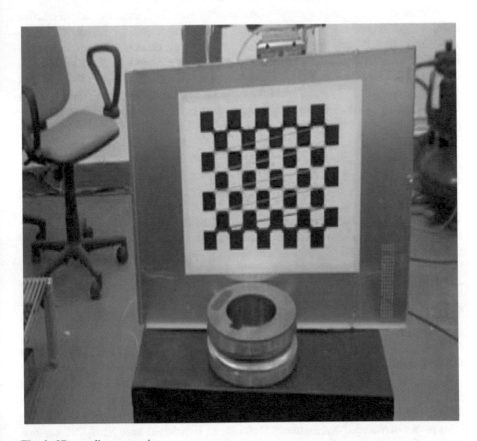

Fig. 4 3D coordinate mapping

Table 1 Accuracy and repeatability of 3D mouse interface

Axis	Max error (mm)	Accuracy (mm)	Repeatability (mm)
X	1.36	4.67	2.76
Y	1.33		
Z	4.86		

3.5 Robot Control

Industrial robots are programmed for repetitive tasks such as welding, painting and palletizing. Its path is preprogrammed and not altered in real time. For non-repetitive tasks such as hot cell manipulation, the user has to change and correct robot's movement from time to time depending upon the task and object. Our job is of non-repetitive nature and requires correction in robots path on the fly. KUKA Ethernet RSI XML software package is used to control the robot in real time. The Cyclical data transmission (IPO Cycle) from the external system to the robot controller and vice-a-versa is 12 ms. We can directly intervene in the path of the robot using the position commands from either haptic device or AR-based 3D mouse.

4 Experiments and Results

After implementing 3D mouse and path-planning functionality successfully in our telepresence system, we wanted to compare and evaluate the efficacy of this interface. So we conducted following experiment sets.

4.1 Accuracy and Repeatability

Our robot is highly accurate to 1 mm with repeatability of 1 mm. We use 3D mouse to find coordinates of the tip of the gripper. We already know the actual coordinate of the tip of the gripper through robot (tool calibration). We then transform both the coordinates with respect to common reference system and calculate the accuracy and repeatability of 3D mouse, using Euclidian distance as a measure (Table 1). We have also calculated the maximum deviation in individual axis X, Y, Z from our data set. We found that X, Y axis has very less deviation compare to Z axis (depth). The accuracy and repeatability are at par with other real-time stereo measurement software [11].

Fig. 5 Peg pick and place teleoperation task in progress

4.2 Comparison with Marker-Based Technique

We now compare our 3D mouse with marker-based technique. For this, we have placed predefined marker on the object (see Fig. 3). The operator moves the 3D mouse at the centre of the marker and gets its coordinates. Similar, we also get coordinates of the marker's centre using marker detection technique [12]. Having both coordinates, we then calculate error in measurement by using marker as ground truth. This test is essential to quantify how accurately operator can place AR cursor on the centre of the marker using stereoscopic 3D view. Mean error is reported as 1.88 mm which is around 20-pixel error. Thus, we are able to position 3D mouse quite accurately (Fig. 5).

4.3 Comparison with Haptic Manipulation

Majority of teleoperation tasks are of pick and place type. So we compare our 3D mouse interface (autonomous) with haptic interface (manual) by performing picking and placing task. The task is to pick the peg and put it on the lead platform.

Table 2 Mean completion time of teleoperation task

Manipulation technique	Mean completion time (s)
Haptic device	39.6
3D mouse and path planning	15.2

The clearance of gripper is 40 mm, and diameter of peg is 25 mm. We compare both by the mean time taken to finish the job (see Table 2). We have taken 10 trials and conducted ANOVA analysis. We found $p = 0$. Since $p < 0.05$, the result is statistically significant.

5 Conclusion

First set of experiment indicates that 3D mouse interface has good accuracy in X-Y plane but in depth its accuracy decreases to −5 mm. Thus, this interface could be used in gross manipulation where high accuracy is not required, such as reaching to the neighbourhood of the object. For finer job operator has to rely on haptic manipulation. This interface can also be used to align gripper parallel to object autonomously. This interface is better than any marker-based technique because it is difficult to put markers on every object. Also, this interface gives freedom to the operator to dynamically select any object in the scene and can be very useful for any unplanned activity.

The second experiment establishes that this interface is equivalent to marker-based method. The operator can easily select the point of interest on the object. The error in positioning the cursor is of the order of few pixels.

In the third experiment, we compare this interface with the manual haptic interface. This interface was significantly faster than haptic. This is due to the fact that in autonomous mode one can utilize full speed of robot whereas in manual mode the speed is hampered by latency in communication, inadequate control and insufficient feedback. Thus, this interface along with path-planning utility enhances telepresence system by providing autonomous functionality to an inherit master–slave system. This AR interface will enable the operator to utilize the full functionality of industrial robot and decrease the operation time significantly.

References

1. F. Conti, O. Khatib, Spanning large workspaces using small haptic devices, in *Proceedings of 1st Joint Eurohaptics Conference and Symposium on Haptic Interfaces for Virtual Environment and Teleoperator Systems* (Pisa, Italy, 2005)
2. J. Park, O. Khatib, A haptic teleoperation approach based on contact force control. Int. J. Robot. Res. **25**, 575–591 (2006)

3. P. Chotiprayanakul, D.K. Liu, Workspace mapping and force control for small haptic device based robot teleoperation, in *Proceedings of IEEE International Conference on Information & Automation* (Macau, China), pp. 1613–1618
4. A. Jaju et al., Development and evaluation of a telepresence interface for teleoperation of a robot manipulator, in *Proceedings of 10th International Conference on Ubiquitous Robots and Ambient Intelligence*, October–November 2013
5. B. Glass, G. Briggs, *Evaluation of Human versus Teleoperated Robotic Performance in Field Geology Tasks at a Mars Analog Site*
6. A. Banerji, A. Jaju, P.K. Pal. Experiments on telemanipulation with 'delayed live video', in *International Conference on Control Automation Robotics and Embedded Systems (CARE)* (2013)
7. R. Parasuraman, V. Riley, Humans and automation: use, misuse, disuse, abuse. Human Fact. **39**(2), 230–253 (1997)
8. P.P. Shete, A. Jaju, S.K. Bose, P. Pal, Stereo vision guided telerobotics system for autonomous pick and place operations, in *Proceedings of the 2015 Conference on Advances in Robotics —AIR '15* (2015)
9. A. Jaju, A.P. Das, P.K. Pal, Evaluation of motion mappings from a haptic device to an industrial robot for effective master-slave manipulation, Int. J. for Robot. Automat. (2013)
10. P.P. Shete et al., A real-time stereo rectification of high definition image stream using GPU, in *Proceedings of IEEE International Conference ICACCI-2014*, September 2014
11. W. Sankowski et al. Estimation of measurement uncertainty in stereo vision system. Image Vis. Comput. **61**(2017), 70–81
12. H. Kato, M. Billinghurst, Marker tracking and HMD calibration for a video-based augmented reality conferencing system, in *Proceedings of 2nd IEEE and ACM International Workshop on Augmented Reality (IWAR'99)*. IEEE (1999)

Defect-Free Analytical Synthesis of Four-Bar Linkage for Four Precision Positions Using Perimeter Algorithm

Hitesh Kumar Prajapat, Ramanpreet Singh and Himanshu Chaudhary

Abstract This paper presents a defect-free analytical synthesis of four-bar linkage for four precision positions using the proposed algorithm. The proposed algorithm poses several constraints such as extremity of transmission angle, Grashof conditions, and the minimum perimeter condition, to obtain a defect-free and compact four-bar linkage. Besides these constraints, one more constraint is applied which keeps the moving pivot of driving link outside the wedge-shaped region, which is consistent with the Filemon's construction. This constraint ensures that mechanism has no circuit defect. In this work, motion generator mechanism is synthesized by considering four precision positions. This work proposes an algorithm named as perimeter algorithm, and a realistic example is considered to demonstrate the effectiveness of the algorithm.

Keywords Filemon's construction · Burmester curve · Transmission angle
Circuit defect · Perimeter

1 Introduction

1.1 Background and Objective

Mechanism designer finds mechanism dimensions through the coordinates of fixed and moving pivots for crank and follower links, respectively. In general, kinematic synthesis is divided into three subcategories: motion generation, path generation, and

H. K. Prajapat · R. Singh (✉) · H. Chaudhary
Department of Mechanical Engineering, Malaviya National Institute of Technology, Jaipur, India
e-mail: ramanpreet.gurdutta@hotmail.com

H. K. Prajapat
e-mail: ermehitesh@gmail.com

H. Chaudhary
e-mail: hchaudhary.mech@mnit.ac.in

© Springer Nature Singapore Pte Ltd. 2019
D N Badodkar and T A Dwarakanath (eds.), *Machines, Mechanism and Robotics*, Lecture Notes in Mechanical Engineering,
https://doi.org/10.1007/978-981-10-8597-0_42

function generation. These syntheses are differentiated by mechanism output parameter, i.e., prescribed precision positions. In case of motion generation, mechanism output parameter is rigid body positions while in path generation, it is path of a point on the body. In function generation relation between, angular displacements of the input and output links are maintained.

The ungrounded mechanism joints or moving pivots of a planar four-bar mechanism and the grounded joints of the mechanism, i.e., fixed pivots can be used for identifying a mechanism from infinities of available mechanism. The locus of moving and fixed pivots are known as Burmester curves which confirm the existence of infinite four-bar solutions for given four precision positions [1]. From these curves, one or more infeasible or defected solutions may be present. Therefore to eliminate the defected solutions Filemon's construction can be used.

The objective of this study is to develop an algorithm which can produce Burmester curve containing infinite number of mechanism solutions and simultaneously removing a segment from this curve which contains defected mechanisms. To remove that segment Filemon's construction is used. From the remaining mechanism solutions, one or more defect-free solution is identified which follows all the constraints like limits of transmission angle, Grashof condition, and mechanism minimum perimeter.

1.2 Literature Review

The four-bar mechanism synthesis is done through graphical method as well as by analytical method [2]. Analytical method contains the work of Martin and Russell [3]. They proposed an algorithm for generating planar four-bar motion generator having some constraints of transmission angle, minimal perimeter, and Grashof condition. Erdman [2] work provides a method of modeling the dyads by complex numbers in several different equation forms for three prescribed positions of either path or motion generation with prescribed timing. Garcia et al. [4] proposed an approach which uses exact differentiation to obtain gradient elements for function generation, path generation, and rigid body guidance in kinematic synthesis of mechanism. Brake et al. [5] gave a complete solution of Alt-Burmester curve synthesis problems for four-bar linkages which is an analytical approach. Lebedev [6] gave a method for synthesis of 2-D mechanism by using vector relationship between centrode and link lengths. In the work of Khare and Dave [7], crank-rocker mechanism is optimized by maximizing, the minimum transmission angle. Whereas Chiang [8] proposed a method of synthesis for four-bar function generators by means of equations of three relative poles, instead of conventional four opposite poles. Thompson [9] presented a graphical synthesis of four-bar mechanisms by three positions, instant center specification. By specifying the location of the instant center, constraints the solution by one free choice per dyad, it reduces the number of free choices available. The work of Sun and Waldron [10] includes graphical iteration method for locating regions of Burmester circle point curve which give full rotatable crank. Sancibrian et al. [11] proposed a method for the optimal synthesis of mechanisms using prescribed instant center positions.

Singh et al. [12] proposed reduced number of constraints to obtaining a defect-free crank-rocker mechanism for n-point synthesis using nature-inspired algorithms.

2 Burmester Curve Generation

The planar four-bar mechanism is divided into two dyads, i.e., a set of two links connected together with a joint. As shown in Fig. 1, a planar four-bar linkage has two dyads: left dyad made of vector **W** and **Z** and right-hand dyad made of vectors **S** and **U**. Vectors **W** and **U** represent lengths of crank and follower, respectively.

The vector $\mathbf{P}_{j1}$ represents the displacement of the coupler point, P, when the crank rotates counterclockwise by an angle β_j w.r.t to the positive x-axis. α_j is the angle turned by the vector **Z**, and it represents the distance between moving pivot and coupler point. Vector **Z** makes an angle Φ to the X−axis. In Fig. 1, the position of both dyads is shown according to which the angle turned by follower is γ_j to reach jth position. By loop closure equation [13, 14]:

For left side dyad:

$$W_1 e^{i\Theta} + Z_1 e^{i\Phi} + P_{j1} e^{i\delta_j} - Z_1 e^{i(\Phi+\alpha_j)} - W_1 e^{i(\Theta+\beta_j)} = 0 \tag{1}$$

For right side dyad:

$$U_1 e^{i\sigma} + S_1 e^{i\psi} + P_{j1} e^{i\delta_j} - S_1 e^{i(\psi+\alpha_j)} - U_1 e^{i(\psi+\gamma_j)} = 0 \tag{2}$$

Fig. 1 Four-bar mechanism with both dyads at its initial and jth position

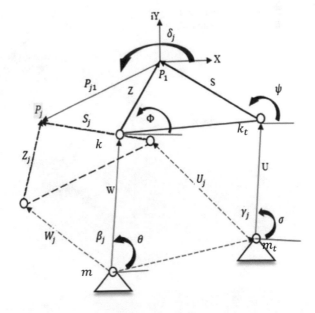

Now for $j = 4$, four prescribed coupler positions, three standard form equations are formed. The displacement from position 1 to 2, 1 to 3, and 1 to 4 can be presented by Eqs. (3)–(5), respectively. These three equations give five unknowns, namely, W, Z, β_2, β_3, β_4.

$$W_1 e^{i\Theta}\left(e^{i\beta_2} - 1\right) + Z_1 e^{i\Phi}\left(e^{i\alpha_2} - 1\right) = P_{21} e^{i\delta_2} \tag{3}$$

$$W_1 e^{i\Theta}\left(e^{i\beta_3} - 1\right) + Z_1 e^{i\Phi}\left(e^{i\alpha_3} - 1\right) = P_{31} e^{i\delta_3} \tag{4}$$

$$W_1 e^{i\Theta}\left(e^{i\beta_4} - 1\right) + Z_1 e^{i\Phi}\left(e^{i\alpha_4} - 1\right) = P_{41} e^{i\delta_4} \tag{5}$$

Equations (3)–(5) can be solved analytically using an algorithm [13] for planar four-bar synthesis. For a range value of β_2, a locus of moving and fixed pivots can be obtained where $k = -z$ (moving pivot) and $m = k - w$ (fixed pivot) as shown in Fig. 2. These curves of moving and fixed pivots known as circle and center point curves, respectively, or Burmester curves. Figure 2 shows a four-bar mechanism for which Burmester curve is produced. Every point on the circle point curve represents a moving point of a mechanism and each point on the center point curve is a fixed point of that same mechanism.

Synthesized mechanism can attain all the prescribed precision positions but it is not necessary that mechanism is free from circuit defect. Therefore, to remove the possibility of defects in the mechanism Filemon's construction [15] is applied to the generated Burmester curve. According to her method, if the crank of a selected mechanism has its moving pivot out of the wedge-shaped region (shown in Fig. 3), then the motion generator will attain all the prescribed precision positions in a circuit.

Fig. 2 Burmester curve for a planar four-bar mechanism

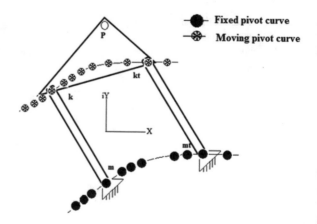

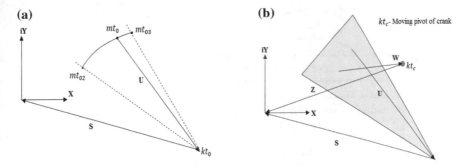

Fig. 3 **a** Wedge-shaped region for a four-bar mechanism. **b** A four-bar mechanism is having crank moving pivot outside the wedge region

3 Perimeter Algorithm

In this section, an algorithm is proposed to obtain a circuit defect-free mechanism. The algorithm begins with the generation of Burmester curves for four precision point synthesis of four-bar mechanism. Then, segments on the Burmester curves which contains defected solution mechanisms are identified and removed. The refined (remaining) segment which contains feasible solution mechanisms are considered and other constraints such as transmission angle constraint, Grashof condition, and minimum perimeter condition are applied. Finally, a mechanism is selected from segment which contains feasible solutions and does not violate any constraint. The schematic diagram of the proposed algorithm is shown in Fig. 4.

4 Case Study

Four-bar mechanism synthesis for knee joint of exoskeleton
From the work of Sancibrian et al. [11] prescribed precision points are taken. From a total of 14 prescribed values for the knee flexion, four points are taken for the four-point precision position synthesis as shown in Table 1. For the initial data Burmester Curve is generated on the range of [120°–240°] angle β_2. Figure 5 shows the set of fixed and moving pivot curves for four-bar knee joint mechanism.

In Fig. 5, the yellow highlighted portion (in web version) is removed and the remaining segment contains mechanism solutions which are free from circuit defects. The obtained mechanism is a double-rocker Grashof type mechanism; therefore, the minimum length link should be the coupler link. The constraints like transmission angle, Grashof condition, and minimum perimeter are applied while synthesizing the mechanism. Thus, 16 defect-free mechanisms are found from 120 possible set of mechanisms. From the remaining defected solutions, coupler curve is generated using one defected solution as shown in Fig. 6, and it is found that mechanism cannot

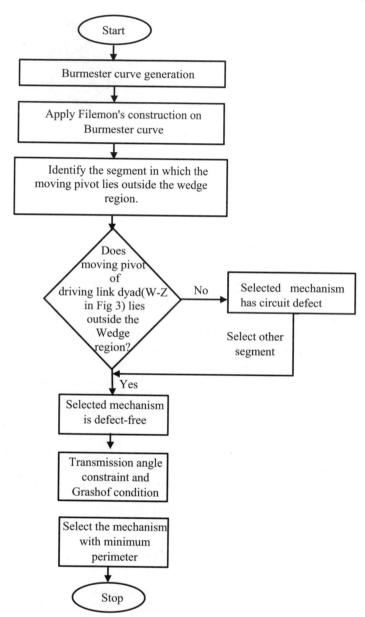

Fig. 4 Flowchart for perimeter algorithm

pass through all the points. Thereafter, the defect-free mechanism (obtained through Filemon's construction) is selected and coupler curve is generated. It is found that mechanism passes through all the prescribed points precisely as shown in Fig. 7. Table 2 shows the parameters of the synthesized mechanism.

Table 1 Knee joint four-bar mechanism prescribed points and dyad displacement angle

Precision position	p_j	α_j {deg.}
1	− 50, 200	0
2	10, 100	14
3	−30, −18	77
4	−40, 0	98

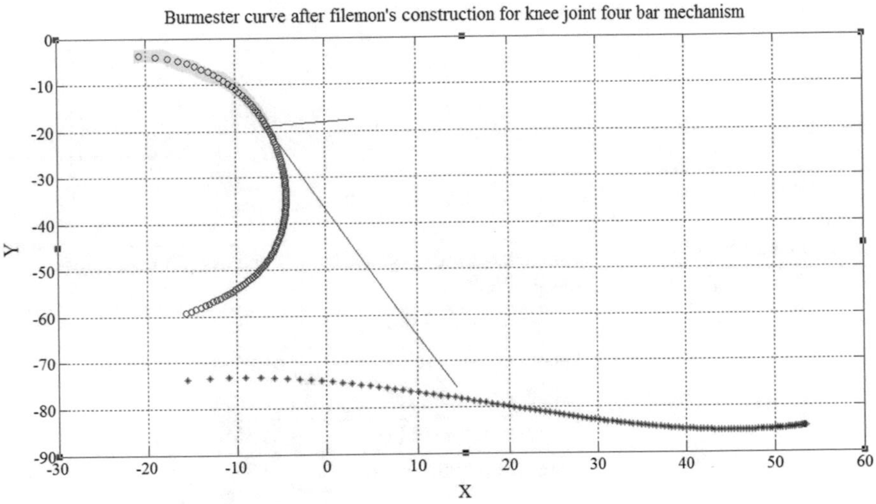

Burmester curve after filemon's construction for knee joint four bar mechanism

Fig. 5 Burmester curve after Filemon's construction for knee joint of exoskeleton

Fig. 6 Coupler curve for a mechanism outside the wedge-shaped region

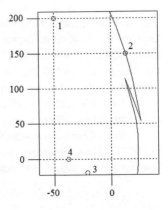

Fig. 7 Coupler curve generated from knee joint four-bar mechanism path generator

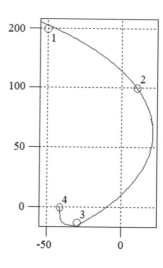

Table 2 Parameters for the synthesized mechanism

Parameters for the synthesized mechanism for knee joint four-bar linkage

Length of ground link (a)	2.8538
Length of crank (b)	61.0588
Length of coupler (c)	2.5265
Length of follower (d)	61.3416
Length of ground link (a)	2.8538

5 Conclusions

To attain the number of predefined coupler points, there are an infinite number of Grashof mechanism solutions present. After applying proposed conditions, out of these solutions a synthesized motion generator can be synthesized in which driving link has generated transmission angles in the feasible range, and this work is done through Burmester curve which is generated numerically by an algorithm. In this work, a double-rocker mechanism is designed to demonstrate the effectiveness of the proposed perimeter algorithm. A designer can change the constraints to obtain other class of four-bar linkages while using this algorithm. The algorithm is coded in MATLAB and an example of knee joint four-bar mechanism is considered, which justifies the algorithm performance.

References

1. K. Russell, Q. Shen, R.S. Sodhi, *Mechanism Design: Visual and Programmable Approaches.* CRC Press (2013)
2. A.G. Erdman, Three and four precision point kinematic synthesis of planar linkages. Mech. Mach. Theor. **16**(3), 227–245 (1981)
3. P.J. Martin, K. Russell, R.S. Sodhi, On mechanism design optimization for motion generation. Mech. Mach. Theor. **42**(10), 1251–1263 (2007)
4. R. Sancibrian, P. García, F. Viadero, A. Fernandez, A general procedure based on exact gradient determination in dimensional synthesis of planar mechanisms. Mech. Mach. Theor. **41**(2), 212–229 (2006)
5. D.A. Brake, J.D. Hauenstein, A.P. Murray, D.H. Myszka, C.W. Wampler, The complete solution of alt–burmester synthesis problems for four-bar linkages. J. Mech. Robot. **8**(4), 041018 (2016)
6. P.A. Lebedev, Vector method for the synthesis of mechanisms. Mech. Mach. Theor. **38**(3), 265–276 (2003)
7. A.K. Khare, R.K. Dave, Optimizing 4-bar crank-rocker mechanism. Mech. Mach. Theor. **14**(5), 319–325 (1979)
8. C.H. Chiang, Synthesis of four-bar function generators by means of equations of three relative poles—1. Finitely separated positions. Mech. Mach. Theor. **10**(1), 81–91 (1975)
9. T.J. Thompson, Graphical synthesis of four-bar mechanisms by three-position, instant-center specification, in *ASME 2012 International Design Engineering Technical Conferences and Computers and Information in Engineering Conference* (American Society of Mechanical Engineers, Aug 2012), pp. 715–724
10. J.W.H. Sun, K.J. Waldron, Graphical transmission angle control in planar linkage synthesis. Mech. Mach. Theor. **16**(4), 385–397 (1981)
11. R. Sancibrian, P. García, F. Viadero, A. Fernandez, A general procedure based on exact gradient determination in dimensional synthesis of planar mechanisms. Mech. Mach. Theor. **41**(2), 212–229 (2006)
12. R. Singh, H. Chaudhary, A.K. Singh, Defect-free optimal synthesis of crank-rocker linkage using nature-inspired optimization algorithms. Mech. Mach. Theory **116**, 105–122 (2017)
13. G.N. Sander, A.G. Erdman, *Advanced Mechanism Design: Analysis and Synthesis volume 2* (Prentice—Hall, Engievsem Cliffs, NJ, 191, 14, 1984)
14. R.L. Norton, *Kinematics and Dynamics of Machinery* (McGraw-Hill Higher Education, 2011)
15. E. Filemon, Useful ranges of centerpoint curves for design of crank-and-rocker linkages. Mech. Mach. Theor. **7**(1), 47–53 (1972)

Tuning Procedure for Correction of Systematic Errors in a Quad Configuration AGV

Vaibhav Dave, Shishir K. Singh, Jagadish Kota, Namita Singh, Rahul Sakrikar, V. K. Shrivastava and P. V. Sarngadharan

Abstract Autonomous Guided Vehicle (AGV) is an ensemble of various parts and subsystems and hence prone to operational errors induced due to manufacturing and assembly tolerances. Moreover, the controls of the various actuators are also prone to inaccuracies due to technical limitation of the control hardware. These mechanical and control limitations along with actuator latencies manifest cumulatively as errors in the motion of the AGV. In presence of these errors, vehicle does not faithfully follow the commands issued by the control algorithm and in turn results in path following and stopping inaccuracies. It is imperative to minimize the effect of these errors to achieve the desired repeatability and precision required for the satisfactory operation of the system. The current paper discusses the methodologies for measurement and compensation of systematic errors like difference in wheels orientation and alignments, offset of laser navigator, uncertainty of wheel diameter, etc. The paper proposes formulation of the tuning procedure for a quad configuration AGV. The

V. Dave (✉) · S. K. Singh (✉) · J. Kota · N. Singh · R. Sakrikar (✉) · V. K. Shrivastava
P. V. Sarngadharan
Division of Remote Handling and Robotics, Bhabha Atomic Research Centre,
Mumbai 400085, India
e-mail: vdave@barc.gov.in

S. K. Singh
e-mail: shishir@barc.gov.in

R. Sakrikar
e-mail: rsakrikar@barc.gov.in

J. Kota
e-mail: jkota@barc.gov.in

N. Singh
e-mail: namita@barc.gov.in

V. K. Shrivastava
e-mail: vk_shri@barc.gov.in

P. V. Sarngadharan
e-mail: sarang@barc.gov.in

© Springer Nature Singapore Pte Ltd. 2019
D N Badodkar and T A Dwarakanath (eds.), *Machines, Mechanism and Robotics*, Lecture Notes in Mechanical Engineering,
https://doi.org/10.1007/978-981-10-8597-0_43

paper also presents the resulting improvements achieved in AGV performance, in path tracking and positional repeatability at material transfer stations.

Keywords AGV · Mobile robots · Systematic errors · Laser navigation Path tracking · Unmanned ground vehicles

1 Introduction

The Autonomous Guided Vehicle (AGV) [1, 2] is an integral part of automated material transfer and storage systems implemented at medium and large size manufacturing units. The work described herein pertains to the development of AGV-based automation for handling of fuel pellets in a nuclear reactor fuel fabrication plant. The AGV's generally can be classified into different categories based on their navigation method and kinematic configuration. The navigation methods include magnetic field track, painted line follower, ultrasonic beacon guided, and laser-based free-ranging types. The traction and steer actuation results in various kinematic configurations ranging from simple differential driven to omnidirectional quad configuration. The application's maneuvering requirements dominate the choice of the wheel configuration. AGV designed for the aforementioned application is a quad configuration, laser free-ranging system; the quad configuration provides good maneuverability and orientation stability and ease of approach at the material transfer stations. The laser navigator [3] based free-ranging technique makes the system easily amenable to the site layout changes and hence offers flexibility in terms of system implementation.

Performance of the AGV is largely effected by the introduction of errors at different levels of the system design and fabrication. These errors can be classified into two categories, namely, systematic and nonsystematic errors [4–6]. The nonsystematic errors are induced by the environment in which AGV is deployed. Estimation and compensation of this category of errors are difficult as their sources are different from one environment to the other. On the contrary, source of the systematic errors are confined to the AGV itself and can be compensated for, to a satisfactory extent.

The work presented herein will discuss the estimation and compensation of systematic errors of the AGV and the process of AGV tuning. The discussion is focused on compensation of systematic errors, introduced due to tolerances in fabrication and assembly of the AGV and limitations of control hardware. The tuning procedure also takes into consideration the possible errors in the mounting of the laser navigator, which is primarily used for the overall system tuning.

This paper covers the conceptual architecture of AGV and its control schematic. The sources of errors and systematic methodology on compensating them are dealt with in detail. The experimental results of the tuning procedure are presented followed by the concluding remarks.

2   AGV Design

The AGV is a battery powered mobile platform facilitating the material transfer on the shop floor at precise locations. The AGV needs to be equipped with appropriate material handling facility, as per the application requirement. The AGV used for the system uses onboard powered roller conveyors for this purpose. The choice of mechanical design and kinematic configuration of the AGV depends heavily on the environment it works in, material transfer interface it uses, navigation space available to name a few. The current system requirements demand high precision on the stopping coordinates and orientation of the AGV to successfully transfer the material at the designated stations. The challenge is to avoid collision with stationary conveyors and at the same time approach the conveyors closely enough to avoid material instability during transfers. The AGV also has to maneuver narrow alleys, sharp turns, and move over curved paths. A laser navigated, quad configuration AGV is selected for the purpose as it fulfills all these requirements.

2.1   Wheel Configuration

As discussed above, a typical manufacturing site requires the AGV to move efficiently along the linear stretches, curves, perform crabbing motion, and turn around its wheel axis center, to negotiate the paths connecting the material transfer points. The quad configuration, having two driven and steered wheels mounted on the AGV's longitudinal axis, satisfies the requisite criteria of motion requirements. The corners of the AGV are provided with passively driven and steered castors for support.

As shown in Fig. 1a–c, quad configuration AGV can perform three different kinds of motions with its wheel configure. The tangential motion makes AGV move on an arc of radius R, while the orientation of AGV remains tangent to the arc. The wheel axis center is the reference point for the motion. In order to achieve satisfactory motion, it is necessary to maintain equal wheels speeds and equal and opposite steer angles, as depicted in Fig. 1a. Equation 1 expresses the relation between the radius of curvature (R), the wheel angles of drive wheels with respect to wheel axis (θ), and the wheel base length (L).

$$R = L/(2\tan\theta) \tag{1}$$

Figure 1b shows the operation of the AGV in crab motion, where the AGV moves sidewise maintaining the same orientation as at the start of the motion. As shown in Fig. 1b, it is necessary to maintain equal wheels speeds and steer angles, as depicted in Fig. 1b. The resultant motion takes the AGV sidewise without changing its own orientation. Velocity vector of AGV will be the same as of the wheels.

The straight motion of the AGV, along the wheel axis, is achieved as a special case in both the tangential and crab mode, by maintaining the wheel angle $\theta = 0$.

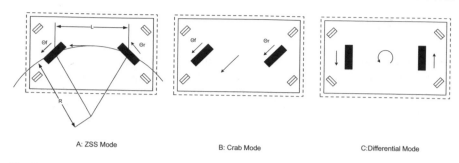

Fig. 1 **a** Tangential mode. **b** Crab mode. **c** Differential mode

Figure 1c shows the AGV operation in the differential mode generating sidewise motions and turn around the wheel axis center (zero turning radius). The wheels in this mode are oriented at right angles to the wheel axis and wheel speed are controlled as per the required motions.

2.2 Control Schematic

The control schematic of the overall system has been shown in Fig. 2. The basic control of the AGV is achieved using PLC. The motion controls of the steer and traction actuators are based on the commands received by the Vehicle Control Program (VCP) being executed by the PLC system. The various sensors on the AGV are interfaced to the PLC which acquires the requisite data and provides the same to the higher level software after due processing. The Plan Executor (PE) module runs on an onboard Industrial computer. PE is responsible for generation of the proper commands to achieve satisfactory path tracking based on adaptive pure-pursuit algorithm [7, 8]. The PE carries out the path tracking based on the amalgamation of the encoder-based odometer data from PLC and laser navigator interfaced to the onboard computer. The path execution and material transfer operations are as per the transfer orders generated by the Supervisory control software, based on the real-time material availability and requirements.

3 Tuning Procedure

It is evident that the satisfactory motion of the AGV relies highly on conformation of front and rear wheel orientation and speed to the commanded parameters. The mechanical mounting and tolerances in the system introduce systematic errors in control of these vital motion parameters. A tuning procedure has been formalized to compensate for these kinds of systematic errors in the system. These errors have

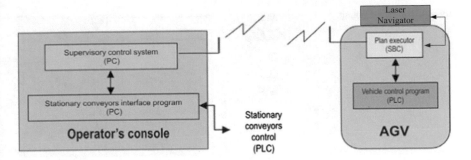

Fig. 2 Control schematic of AGV system

an amalgamated effect on the motion of the AGV, which makes estimation and compensation for them a nontrivial task. The tuning procedure outlines the steps of tuning, in a flow order which compensates for these errors in such a way that the combined effect of these errors is minimally manifested for errors other than the one for which estimation is in progress. The tuning procedure proposed is to be carried out in three ordered steps to achieve the desired results.

3.1 Steering Wheel Home Position Tuning

The wheels of the AGV are equipped with position sensors for homing. The mounting error in this sensor and the inherent hysteresis in the sensor output result in an offset in the home position of the wheels. This error can be estimated using following procedure:

i. As shown in Fig. 3, place a graph chart on a plane surface (probable wall or some holding arrangement) in front of the AGV, approximately 10 m away.

ii. Mount the laser range sensor at AGV's corners, in line with the vehicle centreline. Find distances d1 and d2. Similarly, mount laser range sensor on front wheel, in line with its drive motion. Find the distance d5 and d6.

iii. As shown in Fig. 3, adjust AGV's orientation such that d1 = d2 and B1 = B2, which results in the AGV being positioned perpendicular to the graph chart.

iv. For the wheel to be at home position, the condition d5 = d6 is to be satisfied. The observed deviation from the home position can be corrected using the appropriate changes in the actuation signal from the PLC. The difference Δc between the initial and final actuating signal gives the required signal offset.

v. Same procedure is to be repeated for the other wheel, to obtain the signal offset for that wheel.

Fig. 3 Steer home tuning

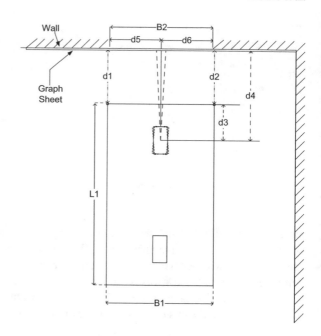

3.2   Estimation of Laser Navigator Offset

AGV uses laser navigator positioning system for precise localization on the floor. It
has to be mounted on the AGV at a known location in vehicles local coordinate system. The current system the mounting is provided at the center of the AGV. However,
the position may not be true due to the manufacturing tolerances. In order to precisely
measure the mounting location and orientation of the sensor, an estimation procedure
has been devised, to estimate navigator position in vehicle's local coordinate system.
Following steps describe the estimation procedure:

i.   **Estimation of angular offset**: As shown in Fig. 4, the AGV is oriented parallel to
the graph paper by making distances d5 and d6 equal, using laser range sensors.
The distances d1 and d2 are measured by another set of laser range sensors
mounted at suitable locations on the navigator mounting platform. The laser
range sensors are rotated together such to a position where the distances d1'
and d2' are minimum. The rotation correction for laser navigator can then be
calculated using Eq. 2.

$$\alpha = arcsin\left(\frac{d1' - d2'}{b}\right) \tag{2}$$

ii. **Estimation of translational offset**: As evident from Fig. 4 following value for
X_{Offset} and Y_{offset} can be estimated using Eqs. 3 and 4, respectively.

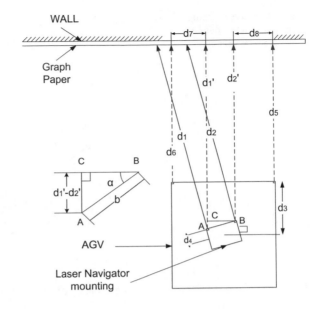

Fig. 4 Laser navigator offset estimation

$$X_{Offset} = (d7 - d8)/2 \tag{3}$$

$$Y_{Offset} = \frac{d'_1 + d'_2}{2} + (d_4 * \cos\alpha) - d6 - d3 \tag{4}$$

3.3 Estimation of Wheel Velocity Difference and Compensation for Unequal Wheel Diameter

Subsequent to the tuning for wheel home position, it is evident that when wheel will be commanded to reach 90°, it will reach there more faithfully. AGV can crab perpendicular to its centerline by orienting both the front and the rear wheel at 90°. But due to the unequal wheel velocities on ground the pure crabbing will not take place instead change in AGV's orientation will be observed. The AGV will move in an arc as in Fig. 5.

We can estimate the compensation for wheel diameter by running the AGV in 90° crabbing mode for sufficient distance so that we can get some prominent value of Ψ. Equation 5 will provide the radius of motion for vehicle's center, R_{CG}, here the arc length is getting calculated by integrating the travel distance S_i which in turn has been calculated by the positions provided by laser navigator. The vehicle's velocity kept to a low value of 50 mm/s so as to keep the value of S_i's low, it will reduce the approximation errors. Equations 6 and 7 provide the actual velocity of the front (V_f) and rear (V_r) wheel, respectively. Value of ω can be calculated by dividing the angle difference Ψ found through laser navigator with the experiment time period.

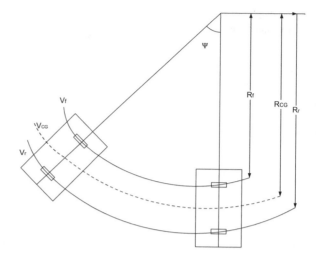

Equations 8 and 9 will provide the estimation of the diameter for both front (D_f) and the rear (D_r) wheels.

$$R_{CG} = \frac{\sum_{i=1}^{n} s_i}{\psi} \qquad (5)$$

$$V_f = \omega * \left(R_{CG} - \frac{L}{2} \right) \qquad (6)$$

$$V_r = \omega * \left(R_{CG} + \frac{L}{2} \right) \qquad (7)$$

$$D_f = \frac{V_f}{\pi * Gear\,Ratio * Motor\,Velocity_{rps}} \qquad (8)$$

$$D_r = \frac{V_r}{\pi * Gear\,Ratio * Motor\,Velocity_{rps}} \qquad (9)$$

4 Results

The tuning procedure as described above was applied on the AGV. The homing errors for both the steering actuators, offsets of laser navigator, and the corrections needed for velocity of both traction actuators were estimated using the described procedure. The corrections required for the steer actuator homing sensor were 0.8 ± 0.05 for front and 1.3 ± 0.05 for rear wheel. Similarly, navigator's offsets were found to be 8 mm, 15 mm, and 1.8° in x, y, and θ, respectively. Furthermore, the errors introduced by unequal wheel velocity of front and rear wheel were largely due to error in estimation of wheel diameters. All these errors introduce inefficiency in performance of the system. After correcting the laser navigator's offset, experiments

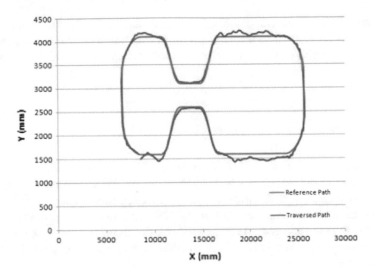

Fig. 6 Test run before tuning of AGV

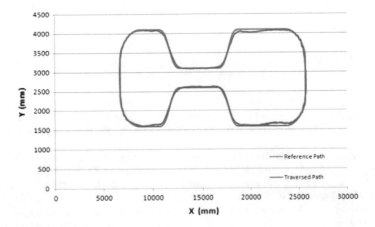

Fig. 7 Test run after tuning of AGV

were conducted to correct the errors in motion and orientation in all operation modes using the navigator. The diameter estimated using the above described experiment was found to be 246.1 mm for front wheel and 248.8 mm for rear wheel instead of 250 mm provided in wheel module's datasheet.

Effectiveness of the tuning procedure gets manifested in the performance improvement of path following algorithm. We are using adaptive pure-pursuit algorithm for path following on a defined path. Results of AGV's test run before and after tuning are shown in Fig. 6 and Fig. 7, respectively.

Average error for the run described in Fig. 6 came out to be 58.05 mm and for Fig. 7, it was 25.13 mm. In the case of Fig. 6, oscillations and offset visible from the path are the consequence of errors in steer wheel homing and laser navigator mounting.

5 Conclusion

A procedure for tuning of AGV which estimated and compensates for various systematic errors of the system has been formalized. An AGV developed for material handling at nuclear fuel fabrication facility has been tuned using this procedure. Compensation for the errors boosted the AGV's performance for path following as well as the stopping accuracy at the material transfer stations. Moreover, proper estimation of wheel diameter in the tuning procedure resulted in an improved odometry of the vehicle.

References

1. P.K. Pal, R. Sakrikar, P.V. Sarngadharan, S. Sharma, V.K. Shrivastava, V. Dave, N. Singh, A.P. Das, Development of an AGV-based intelligent material distribution system, Curr. Sci. J. 101(8) (2011)
2. N. Singh, P.V. Sarngadharan, P.K. Pal, AGV scheduling for automated material distribution—a case study, J. Intelligen. Manufact. 20(4) (2009). https://doi.org/10.1007/s10845-009-0283-9
3. Nav-200 Laser Positioning System for Navigational Support, SICK AG Waldkirch, Germany (2006)
4. J. Borenstein, L. Feng, UMBmark: a bench-mark test for measuring odometry errors in mobile robots, in *SPIE Conference on Mobile Robots* (Philadelphia, Oct 22–26, 1995)
5. J. Borenstein, L. Feng, Measurement and correction of systematic odometry errors in mobile robots. IEEE Trans. Robot. Automat. 12(6) (1996)
6. A. Martinelli, The accuracy on the parameter estimation of an odometry system of a mobile robot, in *Proceedings of IEEE International Conference on Robotics and Automation*, vol. 2, pp. 1378–1383 (2002)
7. R.C. Coulter, *Implementation of the Pure Pursuit Path Tracking Algorithm*. Technical Report CMU- RI-TR-9201, Carnegie Mellon
8. V. Dave, S. Sharma, P.K. Pal, Path tracking of mobile robots with pure pursuit algorithm, in *National Conference on Robotics and Intelligent Manufacturing Process* (Bharat Heavy Electricals Limited, Hyderabad, 2009)

Design of a Linkage-Based Backdrivable Underactuated Gripper

Vinay Kumar, J. P. Khatait and S. Mukherjee

Abstract This paper presents the design of a gripper whose fingers can passively adapt to the shape and size of the object being grasped. Passive shape adaptive behavior of fingers is obtained by implementing underactuation, thus reducing the amount of sensory input required for grasping. The gripper has two identical fingers placed opposite to each other. Each finger has two phalanges and is actuated using a back-drivable electric motor via a linkage mechanism. Thus, the gripper has four degrees of freedom and two degrees of actuation. First, optimization procedure for sizing gripper mechanism and associated variables are explained. Subsequently, learnings from the realization of first two prototypes are presented.

Keywords Underactuation · Gripper · Passive shape adaptability

List of Symbols

α	Angle between palm and link OP
β	Angle between proximal phalanx and link AB
η	Angle between link OA and proximal phalanx
γ	Transmission angle between links OA and AB
λ	Angle between the distal phalanx and the line of action of F_j
ϕ	Angle between the palm and direction of external force u
θ_1	Angle between palm and proximal phalanx
θ_2	Angle between proximal and distal phalanx
θ_{pl}	Preload on torsional spring

V. Kumar (✉) · J. P. Khatait · S. Mukherjee
Mechanical Engineering Department, IIT Delhi, New Delhi, India
e-mail: vinaym815@gmail.com

J. P. Khatait
e-mail: jpkhatait@mech.iitd.ac.in

S. Mukherjee
e-mail: sudipto@mech.iitd.ac.in

© Springer Nature Singapore Pte Ltd. 2019
D N Badodkar and T A Dwarakanath (eds.), *Machines, Mechanism and Robotics*, Lecture Notes in Mechanical Engineering,
https://doi.org/10.1007/978-981-10-8597-0_44

517

φ	Angle between links O_1O_2 and O_1B
a	Length of link OA
ang_1	Angle between positive X-axis and O_1C
ang_2	Angle between positive O_1O_2 axis and O_1C
b	Length of link AB
c	Length of links O_1B, O_1Q and OP
F_j	Force exerted by distal phalanx
F_k	Force exerted by proximal phalanx
F_ϕ	Resultant force exerted by gripper on object
F_{palm}	Force exerted by palm
h	Length of O_1P
j_c	Distance of contact point on distal phalanx from point O_1
k	Stiffness of torsional spring between links O_1B and O_1Q
k_c	Distance of contact point on proximal phalanx from point O
L_0	Half palm length
L_1	Length of proximal phalanx OO_1
L_2	Length of distal phalanx O_1O_2
R	Radius of object being grasped
R_{lo}	Kinematic lower bound of graspable object range
R_{max}	Upper bound of graspable object range
R_{min}	Lower bound of graspable object range
R_{up}	Kinematic upper bound of graspable object range
T	Actuation torque
uv	Frame with origin at $(0, R)$ and at an angle ϕ with X-axis
x, y	Coordinates of object's C.O.M
XY	Frame attached to the center of palm
$F_{lt|1}$	Force because of both mechanical limit being activate
$F_{lt|2}$	Force because of mechanical limit between palm and proximal phalanx being activate
$F_{\phi|max}$	Maximum external force that can be sustained for an object in direction u
$F_{R|max}$	Maximum external force that can be sustained for an object in any arbitrary direction

1 Introduction

Inspired by the ease with which human hands can grasp and manipulate different objects, many dexterous robotic hands have been developed. They usually have twelve or more actuators with a wide array of sensors, which makes them versatile. But this high versatility comes at the cost of complex control and difficult manufacturing. Traditional grippers used with robotic arms are incapable of adapting to different object shapes and sizes, and thus have a small graspable object range. This gripper addresses the gap between dexterous robotic hands and traditional gripper, for activities requiring immobilization of grasped object with respect to the gripper.

Shape adaptation enables grasping of objects having different shapes and sizes while its passive nature reduces the sensory information required for a successful grasp. Passive shape adaptive behavior is obtained by implementing underactuation in finger's structure. An underactuated mechanism has fewer degrees of actuation (DOA) than kinematic DOF. Inverted pendulum is an example of one such system, as it has 2 DOF and 1 DOA. But unlike the inverted pendulum, DOF of underactuated fingers are coupled not by dynamics, but by the use of springs and mechanical motion limits. This coupling is preferable over that from inertial forces due to simplified analysis. Passive shape adaptation coupled with fewer actuators simplifies grasping strategies and hardware required for gripper control.

2 Literature Review

Several underactuated fingers have been proposed in the literature and they are usually one of the two types: tendon actuated or linkage actuated. Tendon-actuated fingers [1, 2] tend to be light and compact but need intricate assembly, and introduce friction and compliance to be accounted for. Therefore, for the purpose of this gripper, only linkage actuated mechanism is considered.

As all the fingers do not establish contacts with object simultaneously, a gripper needs to continue the motion of fingers yet to initiate contact with the object. This has been achieved by actuating all the fingers independently in iHY hand [2], by using a pulley system in SDM hand [1], and by using a differential in SARAH hand [3]. Using a pulley or differential system between fingers further reduces the number of actuators required, but it also allows disturbing forces acting on one finger to influence the behavior of other fingers. To avoid this SARAH hand [3] features non-backdrivable elements, which permit transmission of forces only in one direction, i.e., from actuators toward the fingers. This one-way transmission reduces the actuation forces required to only those necessary for shape adaptation; however, it also allows build-up of large contact forces which may damage the gripper itself. Therefore, the fingers are actuated individually using backdrivable electric motors in this gripper. Independent finger actuation also affords the possibility of predictable fine within hand manipulation of grasped objects.

A holistic approach is adopted for optimizing gripper parameters for increased grasping and holding capabilities, instead of a multistage optimization like that of LARM hand [4]. Performance parameters and disturbance model suggested in [5] are found suitable and incorporated at the design stage itself.

3 Gripper Mechanism

Finger mechanism (Fig. 1) is obtained as a coupling of parallelogram OO_1QP and five-bar mechanism OO_1BA, including a torsional spring and a mechanical stop. Link OP of the parallelogram is fixed to the palm OG, and proximal phalanx OO_1 is shared by both the parallelogram and five-bar chain. A second mechanical stop is introduced between palm and proximal phalanx to avoid hyperflexion of fingers. Link O_1B of five-bar mechanism forms a rigid structure with links O_2B and distal phalanx O_1O_2. The finger mechanism is actuated by applying a torque T on link OA about O. One such finger is attached at both ends of the palm to obtain gripping action.

The mechanical limit and torsional spring between links O_1B and O_1Q make the distal phalanx move perpendicular to palm in the absence of contact along proximal phalanx. This behavior is useful for grasping small objects using distal phalanges [3], and grasps employing it are called *pinch grasps*. In this design, the spring is used to execute pinch grasp and its stiffness requirements are driven by the mass of phalanges. As the spring forces are only a small fraction of actuation forces, spring stiffness was treated as a constant for optimization. This value, i.e., 0.5 N mm/deg with a preload (θ_{pl}) of 37.5°, was computed using simulations involving gravity.

Fig. 1 Schematic half view diagram of gripper

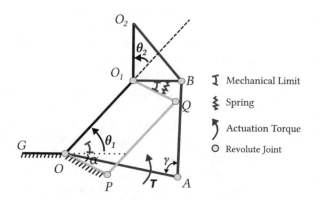

Fig. 2 First version of gripper holding water bottle

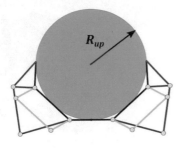
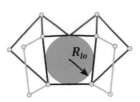

Fig. 3 Gripper configurations for R_{up} and R_{lo}

4   Graspable Object Range

Circular objects have been used to quantify graspable object range, as they are orientation free and their sizes can be described using a single parameter [6]. Friction is assumed to be zero at the contact surfaces, and inertia of fingers is neglected for simplifying force analysis. Further, friction if present will stabilize the object beyond limits derived here. Because of zero friction simplification, enclosing half of the object's periphery becomes a necessary condition for sustaining external forces in any arbitrary direction. Thus, the upper bound of graspable object range becomes radius R_{up} (Fig. 3), for which the gripper just encloses half of objects periphery. The lower bound is equal to object radius R_{lo} (Fig. 3), for which the distal phalanges of fingers come in contact with each other. Radii R_{up} and R_{lo} are geometric bounds of graspable object range and do not take into account the limitation of transmission links to transmit and distribute actuation torque to different phalanges.

To prevent the links from crossing each other or toggling configuration during motion, it is ensured that points A and B do not switch sides with respect to OB and O_1A, respectively, for R_{up}, R_{lo} and pinch grasp configurations. Although the gripper can perform pinch grasps, the analysis is not reported here.

5   Contact Locations and Finger Orientations

Fingers of this gripper can have at most two contact points with a circular object, i.e., one along each phalanx. Depending on the number of contacts between object and fingers, grasps in this paper are further referred as four-point, three-point, and two-point grasps.

For symmetric four-point grasp (Fig. 4), contact locations and finger orientations can be computed using Eqs. 1–4. For asymmetric four-point grasps, same expressions can be used; however, L_0 appearing in them must be changed to $L_0 - x$ for right finger and $L_0 + x$ for the left finger.

Fig. 4 Symmetric four-point grasp

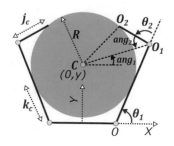

$$\theta_1 = 2\,atan\left(\frac{L_0 + k_c}{y + R}\right) \tag{1}$$

$$\theta_2 = \pi + ang_1 - ang_2 - \theta_1 \tag{2}$$

$$j_c = \begin{cases} R, & \text{if } L_2 < \sqrt{O_1C^2 - R^2} \\ \sqrt{O_1C^2 - R^2}, & \text{if } L_2 \geq \sqrt{O_1C^2 - R^2} \end{cases} \tag{3}$$

$$k_c = L_0^2 + y^2 - R^2 \tag{4}$$

For a finger having lost a contact, computation of its orientation and contact locations cannot be decoupled from force expressions and is established using an iterative algorithm. This iterative algorithm starts with last known value of θ_1 corresponding to a stable grasp and iterates it till the finger mechanism is in static equilibrium. Equations 2 and 3 can be used for three- and two-point grasps as well.

6 Static Analysis

Expressions relating forces exerted by the gripper to contact locations and finger orientations are obtained using static analysis. A dynamic analysis was deemed superfluous as the motion ($\approx$5 s) is quasi-static and the inertia of fingers small.

Forces exerted by distal phalanx, proximal phalanx, and palm on the grasped object are denoted using symbols F_j, F_k, and F_{palm}, respectively. These forces are along the common normal of contacting surfaces because of the zero friction simplification. Static equilibrium expressions for finger mechanism (Fig. 5), assuming contacts along both the phalanges, are written to obtain Eqs. 5–7 for F_j and F_k.

Forces F_{palm}, $F_{lt|1}$, and $F_{lt|2}$ are passive in nature. An active mechanical limit means the corresponding phalanx is being pushed against it. $F_{lt|1}$ has nonzero magnitude if mechanical limits at both the proximal and distal phalanges are activated. Similarly, $F_{lt|2}$ is nonzero if mechanical limit at proximal phalanx is activated, and F_{palm} is nonzero if the object is being pushed against the palm. Nonzero magnitudes of passive forces are such that the grasped object is in static equilibrium under the influence of contact forces applied by gripper and external forces.

Fig. 5 Free-body diagram
of finger mechanism for
static analysis

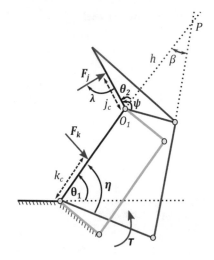

$$F_1 = \frac{T}{a \sin(\eta + \beta)} \tag{5}$$

$$F_j = \frac{F_1 h \sin(\beta) - k(\theta_1 + \theta_2 + \theta_{pl} - \pi/2)}{j_c \sin(\lambda)} + F_{lt|1} \tag{6}$$

$$F_k = \frac{L_1}{k_c} \left[F_1 \sin(\beta) + F_j \sin(\theta_2 - \lambda) \right] + F_{lt|2} \tag{7}$$

If force expressions yield negative values, loss of contact is indicated at the respective phalanx and the grasp transforms to a three-point or two-point grasp.

7 Disturbance Model

Disturbance model suggested in [5] is implemented for computing the maximum external force $F_{\phi|max}$ acting in direction u, that the gripper can sustain for an object of radius R. For finding out $F_{\phi|max}$, grasped object is displaced by small steps in direction u (Fig. 6), while being free to drift in direction perpendicular to it, i.e., v. At every step, the gripper reconfigures to produce a resultant force F_ϕ which together with external forces leads to a static equilibrium of grasped object. Thus, a variation of F_ϕ with u is obtained and the maximum of this variation gives $F_{\phi|max}$ value.

Fig. 6 Disturbance model

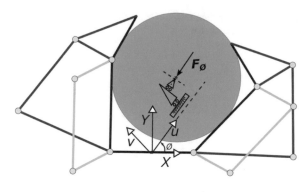

Fig. 7 $F_{R|max}$ versus R for
final gripper parameters
(Table 2)

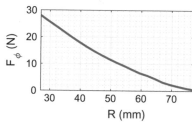

7.1 Gripper Simulations

Figure 8 shows the variation of resultant force F_ϕ with u for parameters listed in
Table 1, obtained using *SimMechanics* simulation and algorithm mentioned above.
The same trajectories in XY plane are shown by dotted lines in Fig. 9. In *MATLAB*
algorithm, everything from contact locations to disturbance model implementation
was hardcoded, while in *SimMechanics* simulation they were computed automatically. The close proximity of two trajectories shows that the developed *MATLAB*
algorithm and force relations are error free. The *MATLAB* code is faster (10x), less
prone to instability, and hence suited for iteration which we do later.

The first peak in Fig. 8 corresponds to transition from four-point grasp to three-
point grasp, while the second peak corresponds to both the mechanical limits of
the right finger being activated. The second peak can also occur in the absence of
mechanical limits being activated, when the iso-force contours of Fig. 9 change in
transition.

It can be observed from Fig. 9 that the gripper has a tendency to move the grasped
object toward a specific equilibrium position. This tendency restores the object back
to its initial stable position once external forces vanish.

Two sets of *SimMechanics* simulations were performed to validate the disturbance model. In the first set, external forces of specific magnitude and direction were
applied on the grasped object, while in the second set, the object was displaced in the
same pattern. The resulting sets of equilibrium position and resultant forces applied
by gripper conform closely show stability under both force and inertia perturbation.

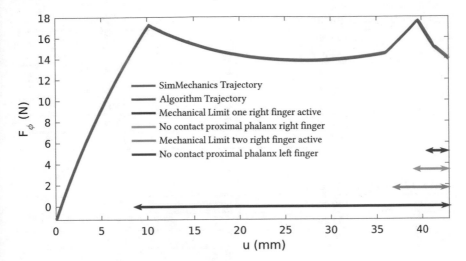

Fig. 8 F_ϕ versus u for parameters listed in Table 1

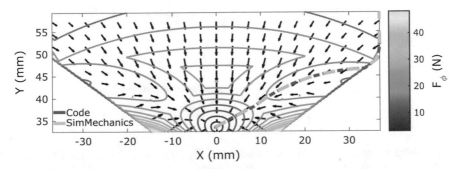

Fig. 9 Vector plot of F_ϕ for parameters listed in Table 1

8 Optimization Setup

Maximum external force $F_{R|max}$ (Eq. 8) which the gripper can sustain for an object of radius R, as defined in [5], is equal to the minimum external force required to move the grasped object out of gripper. Actuation torque T is assumed to be 1 N-m as per the motors. For radii varying from R_{lo} to R_{up}, $F_{R|max}$ is computed and a radius is assumed to be ungraspable if $F_{R|max}$ for it turns out to be less than 4.5 N. Thus, a variation of $F_{R|max}$ versus R is obtained which gives maximum and minimum graspable radii (R_{max} and R_{min}).

Lengths L_0, L_1, L_2, a, b, c, and angle φ were tuned in $MATLAB$ using genetic algorithm to maximize graspable range parameter Q_{grasp} (Eq. 9) suggested in [5].

Table 1 Parameters related to plots of Sect. 7.1

L_0	25 mm	α	30°
L_1	55 mm	θ_{pl}	0°
L_2	30 mm	k	$135 \frac{\text{N mm}}{\text{rad}}$
a	60 mm	R	32.5 mm
b	55 mm	ϕ	30°
c	25 mm	T	1 N m
φ	90°		

Table 2 Final gripper parameters

L_0	30 mm	α	37.5°
L_1	75 mm	θ_{pl}	37.5°
L_2	30 mm	k	$0.5 \frac{\text{N mm}}{\text{deg}}$
a	70 mm	R_{min}	27 mm
b	75 mm	R_{max}	62.5 mm
c	35 mm	T	1 N m
φ	90°	Q_{grasp}	0.5818

$$F_{R|max} = min\left\{[F_{\phi|max}]_{\phi \in \text{disturbance direction}}\right\} \tag{8}$$

$$Q_{grasp} = \frac{\pi}{2}\left(\frac{R_{max} - R_{min}}{L_0 + L_1 + L_2}\right) \tag{9}$$

As the gripper is symmetric, ϕ values 30°, 45°, 60°, and 90° were used for computing $F_{R|max}$ values. Mechanical limit at proximal phalanx is assumed to be at θ_1 corresponding to R_{up} gripper configuration (Fig. 3). Value of α was selected to be 37.5° based on CAD model check for interferences. Table 2 shows the final gripper parameters selected using optimization algorithm, and Fig. 7 shows the $F_{R|max}$ versus R variation for them.

9 Fabrication

Figure 2 shows the first version of gripper holding a water bottle. Its parts are made using 3D printing, and joints using pins and circlips. The design involves a five-bar mechanism sandwiched between two similar parallelogram mechanisms and is over-constrained. These extra constraints require precise alignment of different links

Fig. 10 Second version of gripper assembled without motors

Fig. 11 CAD model of second version

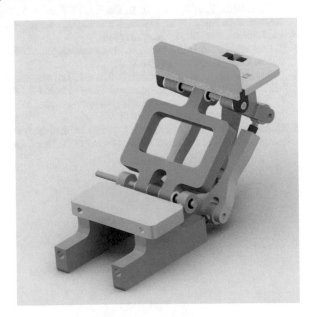

and were therefore relaxed in the second version using spherical joints. The second prototype (Fig. 10) was fabricated using acrylic sheets and laser cutting, and its CAD model is shown in Fig. 11.

10   Conclusion

In this paper, two different versions of underactuated gripper have been presented. Optimized length of the distal phalanx obtained, is outside the search space of optimization procedure suggested in [6]. The average value of transmission angle is about 90° for optimized parameters, which is often used as a design criterion for underactuated gripper. We are currently testing the system for its grasping limits, and the torques required at the motors seem to be on the higher side.

References

1. A. M. Dollar and R. D. Howe, Simple, robust autonomous grasping in unstructured environments, in *Proceedings 2007 IEEE International Conference on Robotics and Automation* (2007), pp. 4693–4700
2. L. U. Odhner, L. P. Jentoft, M. R. Claffee, N. Corson, Y. Tenzer, R. R. Ma, M. Buehler, R. Kohout, R.D. Howe, A.M. Dollar, A compliant, underactuated hand for robust manipulation. Int. J. Robot. Res. **33**(5), 736–752 (2014)
3. T. Laliberté, L. Birglen, C. Gosselin, Underactuation in robotic grasping hands. Mach. Intelligen. Robot. Control **4**(3), 1–11 (2002)
4. S. Yao, M. Ceccarelli, G. Carbone, Q. Zhan, Z. Lu, Analysis and optimal design of an underactuated finger mechanism for larm hand. Front. Mech. Eng. **6**, 332 (2011)
5. G. A. Kragten, J. L. Herder, The ability of underactuated hands to grasp and hold objects. Mech. Mach. Theor. **45**(3), 408–425 (2010)
6. G. A. Kragten, F. C. van der Helm, J. L. Herder, A planar geometric design approach for a large grasp range in underactuated hands. Mech. Mach. Theor. **46**(8), 1121–1136 (2011)

Design of a Teleoperated Mobile Manipulator for Inspection of Cyclotron Vault

Amaren P. Das, S. K. Saha, D N Badodkar and S. Bhasin

Abstract This paper presents the design and control scheme of a mobile manipulator used for radiation survey of Cyclotron vault and cave regions. It discusses the mechanical design of the traction system, the steering gear, and the scissor mechanism. Selection of steering system based on terrain condition and power requirement is also discussed.

Keywords Mobile manipulator · Scissor mechanism · Differential drive · Davis steering mechanism · Cyclotron vault · Radiation mapping

1 Introduction

Cyclotrons are used to accelerate charged particle beam to high energy. These are required for experiments in nuclear physics and nuclear medicine. The particles are accelerated to high energy using a high-frequency alternating voltage which is applied between two hollow "D"-shaped sheet metal electrodes called "Dees" inside a vacuum chamber. The area surrounding the Dee is called the vault, and cave is the area where beamline is available for experimentation. In order to increase the efficiency

A. P. Das (✉) · D N Badodkar
Division of Remote Handling and Robotics, Bhabha Atomic Research Centre,
Trombay, Mumbai, India
e-mail: apdas@barc.gov.in

D N Badodkar
e-mail: badodkar@barc.gov.in

S. K. Saha
Department of Mechanical Engineering, IIT Delhi, Hauz Khas,
New Delhi 110016, Delhi, India
e-mail: saha@mech.iitd.ac.in

S. Bhasin
Department of Electrical Engineering, IIT Delhi, Hauz Khas, New Delhi, India
e-mail: sbhasin@ee.iitd.ernet.in

© Springer Nature Singapore Pte Ltd. 2019
D N Badodkar and T A Dwarakanath (eds.), *Machines, Mechanism and Robotics*, Lecture Notes in Mechanical Engineering,
https://doi.org/10.1007/978-981-10-8597-0_45

529

and estimate the neutron field in the vault and cave areas of the two cyclotrons K-130 and K-500 operational at VECC, Kolkata, in situ radiation measurement was needed.

The interaction between an accelerated beam of charged particles and the target produced by Bremsstrahlung and characteristic X-rays prompts γ-rays, neutrons, and delayed radiation (β and γ). Hence, the vault and cave areas are inaccessible to human during operation. A teleoperated mobile robot was designed and developed at BARC to carry out in situ measurement and mapping of radiation level in these areas.

Most of the mobile robots presented in the literature use differential wheel drive with passive castor, as in [1–3]. The other common methods for locomotion of mobile robots are the omnidirectional wheels [4, 5] and tracked wheel system [6, 7]. According to Nagatani et al. [8], a vehicle with Mecanum wheels is susceptible to slippage and same is the case for tracked vehicle, which are inherently skid steered. The slippage of the wheels prevents the most popular dead-reckoning method, using rotary shaft encoders, from being performed well. In this paper, we present design of mobile manipulator based on Davis steering mechanism. The Davis steering system modifies the heading of the front wheels in a way that, at low speeds, all the wheels are in pure rolling without lateral sliding [9]. The kinematics and control of such systems are discussed in [10] and references therein but no detailed design is presented. This paper discusses the design methodology of mobile manipulators based on environmental requirements. We also highlight the advantage of Davis steering over castor wheels or other steering methods from the perspective of this mobile manipulator. A control framework for teleoperation is also presented.

2 Design Overview

The objective of mobile robot is to navigate inside the cyclotron vault and collect radiation intensity data at all the required points decided by the operator. Data is to be collected not only at different planer locations of the floor but also at varying height from the floor. To cater this operational requirement, a mobile platform with a vertically extendable manipulator arm was developed. Together, they are referred henceforth as mobile manipulator. The 3-D model of the mobile manipulator with its major subsystems is shown in Fig. 1, whereas the actual system is shown in Fig. 2.

The environmental condition required that the vehicle be either autonomous or teleoperated. To keep the complexity low, it was decided to have wireless teleoperated navigation and control. This gives an operator full flexibility to drive and control the system from a remote station using visual feedback provided by the onboard camera. The key parameters of the mobile manipulator are listed in Table 1.

The mobile manipulator has a footprint of 700 mm × 400 mm based on the narrow passage which the system has to negotiate. These passages are formed inside the vault area by the pipelines and structural supports of the cyclotron and its associated equipment. Two DC motors, with speed servo controller, provide the traction to each

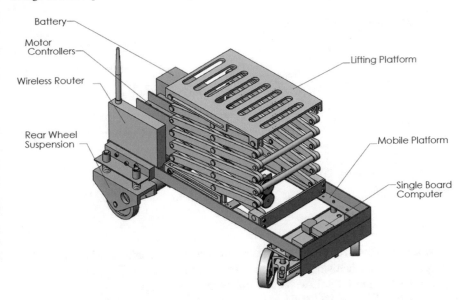

Fig. 1 3-D model of the mobile manipulator

Fig. 2 Photograph of the actual system

Table 1 Key parameters and specifications of the mobile manipulator

Weight	70 kg	Without payload
Payload	10 kg	—
Footprint	700 mm × 400 mm	-
Height	500 mm (Minimum), 1500 mm (Extended)	Along with Z-axis
Steering mechanism	Davis steering	—
Turning radius	415 mm	-
Ground clearance	45 mm	—
Maximum traction speed	2 m/min	On flat terrain
Ramp climb angle	30°	Checkerboard surface

rear wheel. The two front wheels are inter-connected with Davis steering mechanism [11]. A scissor mechanism provides the vertical motion of the detector.

In order to keep the self-weight of the system small, all the structural parts are made of aluminum alloy AL6061, apart from the base frame. Stainless steel (SS304) angle sections are used for the base frame, which give it an excellent strength-to-weight ratio.

2.1 Design of the Traction System

Traction is provided by the two rear wheels. Each wheel is driven by a Maxon DC RE50 200 W Motor through a 26:1 reduction gearbox. The motors are mounted at an offset to the wheel axis for increased ground clearance. See Fig. 3. Spring suspension is provided at each wheel to ensure sufficient contact force on uneven ground. The diameter of the wheel is 100 mm (D_w), which is sufficient to ride over obstacle of height 20 mm (Max). They are made of aluminum alloy-6061 with 5-mm-thick molded polyurethane (PU) liner. The PU liner provides large traction on cement flooring while being resistant to wear.

The load distribution was optimized to generate maximum normal reaction, F_n, at the rear wheels without overturning while moving up the ramp of 30°. Maximizing rear wheel reaction by increasing "b" as per Eq. 1 ensures increased traction, $F_T = \mu F_N$ (μ is the coefficient of friction), but at the same time decreases the stability margin indicated by "X" in Fig. 4:

$$F_{N2} = \frac{b}{a} F_{N1}, \quad F_{N1} + F_{N2} = mg \cos \theta \tag{1}$$

The stability margin X was fixed as 30 mm so as to achieve maximum acceleration of 0.144 g over the ramp of 30° without overturning. This was done based on the dynamic stability, Eq. 2.

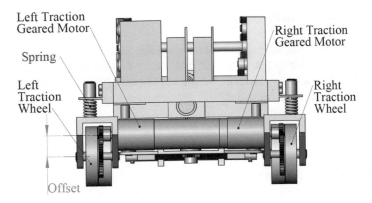

Fig. 3 Rear suspension

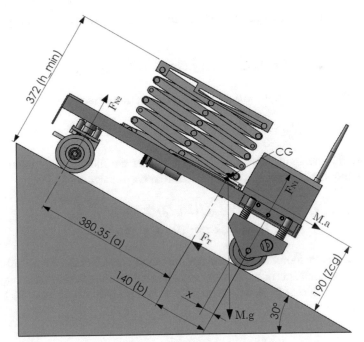

Fig. 4 Mobile manipulator on slope

$$mgb\cos\theta = (mg\sin\theta + ma)z_{cg}, \quad \Rightarrow g(\frac{b}{z_{cg}}\cos\theta - \sin\theta) = a \quad (2)$$

where m: mass of vehicle and g: acceleration due to gravity.

2.1.1 Selection of Motor and Gearbox

The torque requirement for each rear wheel was calculated based on the static moment balance with the assumption that each rear wheel shares equal load and the total suspended weight is 80 kg. From the free-body diagram (Fig. 4), using moment and force balance, we get the following:

$$F_{N1} = \frac{aM\cos\theta}{a+b-\mu Z_{cg}}, \qquad F_T = \mu F_{N1} \tag{3}$$

In order to estimate the traction motor size, we take worst-case scenario $\theta = 0$ and $\mu = 0.3$.

$$F_{N1} = 66\,\text{kg}, \qquad F_T = 0.3 * 66 \approx 20\,\text{kg}$$

Since the traction is provided by the two rear wheels, the torque required per wheel (T_w) is given by

$$T_w = (F_T/2)(D_w/2) = (20/2) * 50 = 500\,\text{kg mm} \simeq 5\,\text{N m} \tag{4}$$

The motor torque T_M, required based on the assumption of factor of safety, $FS = 1.5$ is

$$T_M = (FS) * T_w = 1.5 * 5 = 7.5 \simeq 8\,\text{N m} \tag{5}$$

Assuming the maximum speed, $V_{ramp} = 1$ m/s, of the mobile manipulator over a ramp, the required power, P_M, of the traction motor is calculated as

$$\omega_w = V_{ramp}/(D_w/2) \simeq 200\,\text{rpm}$$
$$P_m = \omega_w T_m = 20 * 8 = 160\,\text{W} \tag{6}$$

The nearest Maxon motor available as per the catalogue [12] is 200 W, RE50-370354 motor. The nominal speed, N_s is 5680 rpm. Therefore, the gearing ratio required is $N_s/\omega_w = 5680/200 \simeq 28.4$. The nearest gear box available is of ratio 26:1, which was chosen.

2.2 Design of Steering System

This mobile manipulator uses Davis steering mechanism, Fig. 5, on the front wheels. Caster was not used as they tend to align with small obstacles and thus get stuck. On the other hand, tracked wheels have excellent rough terrain capabilities, but is power intensive due to skid steering, whereas omnidirectional wheels need complex controller for coordination.

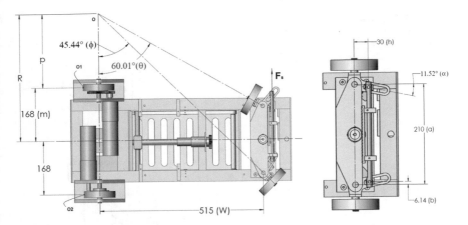

Fig. 5 Davis steering mechanism

Davis mechanism satisfies the steering Eq. 7, which ensures pure rolling of all wheels over the entire steering range. This makes the system suitable for odometry and energy efficient. The mechanism being positively driven by position controlled servo motor does not align with the obstacles and thus are able to cross over it. The dimensions of the links used in the steering mechanism are shown in Fig. 5, and are based on the Ackerman steering law given in Eq. 7

$$\cot \phi - \cot \theta = a/w, \quad \frac{2b}{h} = \frac{a}{w} \qquad (7)$$

Figure 5 shows the extreme values of ϕ and θ, limited by mechanical construction. The minimum turning radius can then be calculated as $a/2 + w \cot \theta = 210/2 + 515 \cot 59.8 = 415$ mm.

2.2.1 Calculation of Steering Torque

The torque required to steer the front wheel is estimated based on a simplified assumption that the wheel deforms under normal load and the contact area thus generated is circular in shape with diameter that of the wheel width, W_w, as shown in Fig. 6. In order to estimate the normal reaction on each wheel, we assume that the total weight of 80 kg is equally shared by the four wheels. Therefore, $N_s = 80/4 = 20$ kg. Next, we apply the uniform pressure formula used to design brakes/clutches, given in Eq. 8, to find the resistance torque T_s, between the ground and the wheel.

$$T_s = \frac{N_s \mu}{3} W_w = 0.4 \, \text{N m} \qquad (8)$$

Fig. 6 Wheel ground interaction

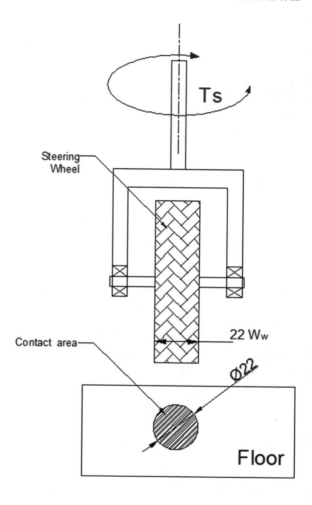

The resistance torques, T_s, of both the wheels are balanced by the force F_s acting on the rack as shown in Fig. 5. The rack is coupled to the steering motor by a pinion of diameter, $D_p = 40$ mm. The motor torque, T_{m_s} in Eq. 9 is calculated with a high factor of safety, $FS = 3$. This is because T_S is estimated based on a simplified model of break design. The power, P_{m_s} of the steering motor based on torque T_{m_s} and the steering speed ω_s of 100 rpm is

$$T_{m_s} = (FS)\frac{2T_s}{h}\frac{D_p}{2} = 1.6\,\text{N m} \quad \text{and} \quad P_{m_s} = T_{m_s} * \omega_s = 17\,\text{W} \qquad (9)$$

Based on the above specifications, a 20 W, RE25 DC motor of Maxon make and a gear box GP32 of ratio 159:1 was chosen for the steering mechanism.

2.3 Design of Scissor Mechanism

The vertical stage was designed to move up to a height of 1.5 m from the floor level. This motion was generated using a scissor mechanism, as shown in Fig. 7. The scissor mechanism has two major advantages over other lifting methods such as telescopic pillar, etc. First, the ratio of height in extended and collapsed condition is very large. In our case, it is 3:1. Second, the self-weight of the mechanism is very low as it is made of rectangular links.

The scissor mechanism, Fig. 7, has six stages, where one "X" denotes one stage. The scissor is connected to the top platform by a pivot joint O_2 and a prismatic joint A_2. This is coupled to the base frame by pivot joint O_1 and a prismatic joint A_1. The linear actuation of joint A_1 is provided by a lead screw of pitch (P) 1.5 mm and mean diameter (d_m) 10 mm. This results in vertical motion of the top platform. From geometry we get

$$y = l \sin \theta, \ x = l \cos \theta, \ \Rightarrow dy = l \cos \theta d\theta, \ dx = -l \sin \theta d\theta$$
$$h = Ny \rightarrow dh = Ndy$$

(10)

where N = 6 is the number of stages. From the principle of virtual work, we get

$$-F_x dx = W dh, \ \Rightarrow F_x = \frac{WN}{\tan \theta}$$

(11)

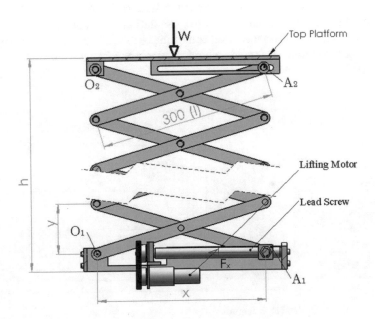

Fig. 7 Scissor Mechanism

where F_x is the axial force on the prismatic joint, A_1 and W is the payload. From Eq. 11, it is clear that as $\theta \rightarrow 0$, the force $F_x \rightarrow \infty$. In the present design, $\theta_{min} = 5°$ and $\theta_{max} = 45°$. Therefore, the extended height $h_{max} = Nl \sin \theta_{max} = 1.3$ m and the collapsed height $h_{min} = 156$ mm. The maximum force $F_x = 342$ kg is required at $\theta_{min} = 5°$, assuming $W = 8$ kg as payload. This was used in formula for screw jack [11], Eq. 12, to calculate the motor torque of the scissor mechanism.

$$T_L = \frac{F_x d_m}{2} \left(\frac{p + \pi \mu d_m \sec \alpha}{\pi d_m - \mu p \sec \alpha} \right) = 7.5 \, \text{N m} \qquad (12)$$

where coefficient of friction, $\mu = 0.1$, ACME thread angle $2\alpha = 60°$ and pitch $p = 1.5$ mm, is used. Based on the above specification, 10 W RE20 DC motor with a gear box of 25:1 ratio is chosen from Maxon motor catalogue [12].

3   Control Architecture and Hardware

The mobile manipulator is planned to be teleoperated over a wireless network. The control block diagram and architecture are shown in Fig. 8. It has a remote control station which is the interface for the operator and a local controller on the mobile manipulator. They communicate over a WiFi network. The remote station sends data packet every 50 ms to the mobile manipulator. The commanded velocity, the steer angle, the z position of the platform, and the state of the detector and headlamps constitute the data packet sent by the remote station. The onboard control of the mobile robot replies with a data packet consisting of the X, Y position and orientation of the robot, the current steer angle, angular velocities of each wheel, the z position of the top platform, and bumper status.

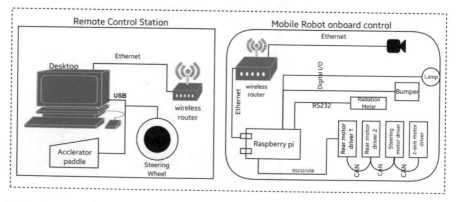

Fig. 8 Control architecture block diagram

3.1 Local Onboard Controller

The onboard computer receives the command from the remote station and controls the robot hardware through robot operating system (ROS). The computer is daisy chained to the four Maxon EPOS2 motor controllers/drivers. The communication between the onboard computer and the first Maxon controllers is over USB/RS232 interface using Maxon's proprietorial protocol [13]. The first controller serves as CAN master for the rest of the controllers. The rear wheel motor drivers are configured in velocity servo loop. The steering and the z-axis motors drivers are configured in position control loop. The camera mounted on the mobile robot and Raspberry Pi is connected over Ethernet via a wireless hub.

3.2 The Remote Control Station

The local station consists of a desktop computer running Windows XP. A steering wheel and two foot switches are connected to the desktop. The steering wheel is used for turning mobile robot. One of the two foot switches acts as an accelerator to set the mean velocity and the other is used to brake the vehicle.

The screen of the desktop displays the video streaming from the mobile robot onboard camera. A graphical user interface (GUI) also displays the robot's parameters such as current steer angle, velocity of each rear wheel, and the position of the z-axis. Buttons on the GUI operate the z-axis, healamps, etc.

4 Conclusion

Design calculation for a mobile manipulator is presented in this paper. Different aspects based on the requirements of radiation inspection around cyclotron were taken into account. Advantage of positively steered wheels over caster wheel was highlighted for mobile robots. A control architecture is proposed for the teleoperation of the mobile manipulator.

In future, the system will be tested for its performance and will be reported separately.

References

1. Y. Yamamoto, X. Yun, Coordinating locomotion and manipulation of a mobile manipulator, in *Proceedings of the 31st IEEE Conference on Decision and Control* (IEEE, 1992), pp. 2643–2648
2. S. Rajendran et.al., Mobile robot for reactor vessel inspection, in *National Conference on Advanced Manufacturing and Robotics* (CMERI, Durgapur, WB, 2004), pp. 2527–2532

3. S.K. Saha, J. Angeles, Kinematics and dynamics of a three-wheeled 2-DOF AGV, in *Proceedings of IEEE International Conference on Robotics and Automation* (IEEE, 1989), pp. 1572–1577
4. F.G. Pin, S.M. Killough, A new family of omnidirectional and holonomic wheeled platforms for mobile robots. IEEE Trans. Robot. Autom. **10**(4), 480–489 (1994)
5. J.E.M. Salih, M. Rizon, S. Yaacob, A.H. Adom, M.R. Mamat, Designing omni-directional mobile robot with mecanum wheel. Am. J. Appl. Sci. **3**(5), 1831–1835 (2006)
6. J. Suthakorn, S.S.H. Shah, S. Jantarajit, W. Onprasert, W. Saensupo, S. Saeung, S. Nakdhamabhorn, V. Sa-Ing, S. Reaungamornrat, On the design and development of a rough terrain robot for rescue missions, in *2008 IEEE International Conference on Robotics and Biomimetics, ROBIO* (IEEE, 2009), pp. 1830–1835
7. M. Guarnieri, R. Debenest, T. Inoh, E. Fukushima, S. Hirose, Development of HELIOS VII: an arm-equipped tracked vehicle for search and rescue operations, in *2004 Proceedings of IEEE/RSJ International Conference on Intelligent Robots and Systems (IROS)* (IEEE, 2004), vol. 1, pp. 39–45
8. K. Nagatani, S. Tachibana, M. Sofne, Y. Tanaka, Improvement of odometry for omnidirectional vehicle using optical flow information, in *2000 Proceedings of IEEE/RSJ International Conference on Intelligent Robots and Systems (IROS)* (IEEE, 2000), vol. 1, pp. 468–473
9. J.Y. Wong, *Theory of Ground Vehicles* (Wiley, 2008)
10. B. d'Andrea Novel, G. Bastin, G. Campion, Dynamic feedback linearization of nonholonomic wheeled mobile robots, in *1992 Proceedings of IEEE International Conference on Robotics and Automation* (IEEE, 1992), pp. 2527–2532
11. T. Bevan, *Theory of Machines*, 3rd edn. (CBS Publishers & Distributors, Delhi, India, 1984)
12. *Motor catalogue 2014*. Switzerland: Maxon Motors, 2017
13. *EPOS Application Note: RS232 to CANopen Getway*. Maxon Motors, 2012

Design and Development of an Efficient Onion Harvester for Indian Farms

Amogh Parab, Chinmay Sonar, Prasannajeet Mane, Janga Sai Kiran, Panna Lal Saini and Vineet Vashista

Abstract In this paper, we focus on the problem of onion harvesting using one possible methodology. The current method of harvesting onions in India involves farmers sitting on the ground and plucking the onion withholding the stem of the crop. We have developed a prototype of manually operated onion harvester which will increase the efficiency of the harvesting and reduce the manual labor. To visualize our idea for mechanism, we made an interactive geometry model in Cinderella software. For validating our results, we did static force analysis and ground penetration testing. The mechanism can be potentially automated which will increase the efficiency even further.

Keywords Onion harvesting · Manual labor · Slider crank · Claw · Automation

1 Introduction

The onion crop is one of the widespread crops in India, and it has been cultivated for a long time. India is one of the major contributors to onion production by producing

A. Parab · C. Sonar · P. Mane · J. S. Kiran
P. L. Saini · V. Vashista (✉)
Indian Institute of Technology Gandhinagar, Ahmedabad, Gujarat, India
e-mail: parab.amogh@iitgn.ac.in

C. Sonar
e-mail: sonar.chinmay@iitgn.ac.in

P. Mane
e-mail: prassanjeet_mane@iitgn.ac.in

J. S. Kiran
e-mail: janga.sai@iitgn.ac.in

P. L. Saini
e-mail: panna.saini@iitgn.ac.in

V. Vashista
e-mail: vineet.vashista@iitgn.ac.in

© Springer Nature Singapore Pte Ltd. 2019
D N Badodkar and T A Dwarakanath (eds.), *Machines, Mechanism and Robotics*, Lecture Notes in Mechanical Engineering,
https://doi.org/10.1007/978-981-10-8597-0_46

19% of the world's total production. There are multiple phases in the production of onion crop. There are many different methods and machines used for onion harvesting. In order to analyze the current situation in this regard, one needs to have a literature survey which shall be found in the later part of the section.

In the case of onion, some portion of the bulb is over the ground. Hence, the exact location, shape, and the area spanned by each onion can be inferred easily unlike other ground vegetables which are completely underground. Vegetables such as carrot are long and deep-rooted. Potatoes grow as a bunch and are spread out underground. These crops require a technique that imparts a larger force and which spans a larger depth into the ground.

1.1 Onion Life Cycle and Current Methods Used in Harvesting

The basic details of onion plantation and harvesting are presented in [1]. It is observed that one onion cycle lasts for around 5 months. In the last stage of the cycle, the harvesting step is assumed to be one of the most important steps. Since the improper harvesting can affect the overall production quality to a large extent, analyzing the current situation, it is found that there are two methods followed by the majority: (i) Handpicking the stems and pulling the onions off or (ii) by removing the complete layers of soil and then separating onions from that.

The first method is very labor intensive and it is largely practiced in India. The method is very slow and requires a large amount of time and human labor. The source [2] explains the procedure of hand removing the onions. The bulbs of onions grow over the ground level to about 4 cm height. Hence, it can be very easily seen where the plants are located, which would assist in plucking the onions. A lot of studies have also gone into analyzing the concentration of different microorganisms and the chemical compositions of air on onion field in the different seasons. Specifically, the paper [3] talks about the ill effect on the cornea, and hence the caused eye diseases for the workers in the onion field. The paper specifically studies Taiwan but also mentions that the environmental conditions resemble India to a large extent. Hence, we assume that reducing manual labor will be useful in onion farms.

The second method of removing the complete layer of soil to remove onion uses a huge machinery. The patent [4] shows an example of early machinery developed in 1980s. Today, there are many modern machines which are available to do this task. The one such example is shown in [5]. This describes the machine and the methodology to use in farms. As shown, generally these machines are very large, and hence they can be used only on large farms due to economical and space constraints.

1.2 Need for New Mechanism

As a summary of above discussion, we can see that the methods available in the market for onion harvesting task are either very labor intensive or include very large machinery. Hence, we assume that the problem of onion harvesting has not been addressed to the extent of its importance for small/medium-sized Indian farms. So, in this paper, we narrowed down our focus to find an economically viable option of a harvesting mechanism with potential to automate it for use in small/medium Indian farms.

2 Methodology

The developed model is a five-bar mechanism which has acquired the form of two slider crank mechanisms. The parts include a claw, central link, supporting side links, and a handle to actuate the mechanism.

Figure 1 shows the interactive geometry model of the mechanism. This was made in order to visualize the mechanism. The model was made in Cinderella software. The dimensions in the geometry model are up to the scale. The CAD model [6] provided us with insights into the finer attributes of the model. The video of CAD model has been appended to better understand the working and trajectory of the claw.

In order to verify the working feasibility of the proposed solution, we developed a rudimentary/primary prototype of the model. Although the link-slider–claw movement patterns were according to our expectations, we did get insights into the shortcomings of the current model, specifically in terms of joint mating and ergonomic, esthetic factors.

Figure 2, the right model, represents the first prototype we developed. The model in the left represents the final developed model. We also tested our model on different types of soil to test the ground penetration. The mechanism could easily penetrate wet/watered soil or clay. Efforts required to penetrate hard soil were greater than that of clay. Videos of the same are added in bibliography [7, 8].

Following factors were specifically considered in the designing aspect of the mechanism (Fig. 3):

1. Modification in the claw size and curvature: Claw radius and curvature are designed in a way to accommodate different sizes of onions in claws. Typically, the sizes of onions harvested in India vary from 5 to 10 cm (2–4 inches). The claw is designed such that, when in open position, maximum diameter is 10 cm and the distance between 2 claws is 3 cm so that the onion does not slip from the claws.
2. Restricting the claws rotation to the required extent: To avoid the potential damage to outer onion surface while plucking.
3. Height of the mechanism to provide comfort to the farmer: The mechanism has height slightly less than one meter which will make the force application point (handles) come close to heap. This will ease the efforts of force application.

Fig. 1 Cinderella model for mechanism

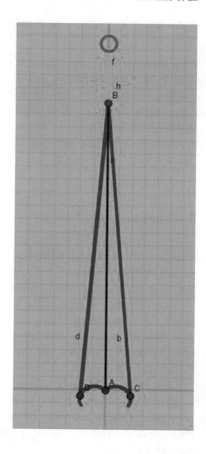

4. Making the joints sturdier in order to being able to sustain large amount of force.
5. Handle like structure at the top of the mechanism to be able to move the mechanism from place to place. Since the onions come out at different places in the ground, it will be necessary to move mechanism from one place to another while harvesting the onions.

3 Analysis

The mechanism developed by us is a five-bar slider crank mechanism which is essentially two slider crank mechanisms actuated by a single slider. The slider is the input link where vertical force will be applied. Output will be taken at the claw through connecting links (refer Fig. 4). Considering the symmetry of the mechanism, one can only consider the right side of the mechanism. Thus, the mechanism is reduced to a simple three-bar slider crank mechanism, which is explained in detail in the next section.

Fig. 2 Developed model

Fig. 3 Claw

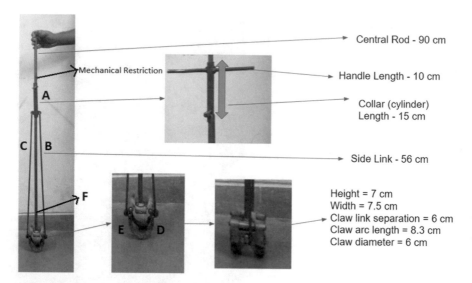

Fig. 4 Dimensions of our mechanism

3.1 Mapping to Simpler Slider Crank Mechanism

Figure 4 shows a picture of the prototype developed. Links A, B, C, D, and E together make five-bar mechanism with A as slider. Link F is central link on which the whole mechanism is built. If we consider links A, B, and D, then this will form a slider crank mechanism. Similarly, links A, C, and E will make another slider crank mechanism. Point to be noted is that both the mechanisms have common actuating slider A. Output crank links are mirror images of each other, also even though links D and E are cranks, they are not used for the full rotation.

3.2 Position Analysis

For position analysis, consider the following two parameters. 1. Claw diameter 2. Slider Position, as they decide how much slider has to move in order to grab the onion. Define the claw diameter at the given position to be the maximum distance between claws. The slider position is measured with reference to the mechanical restriction (shown in Fig. 4). There two critical positions in our mechanism, one at which the claw is completely open and other at which it is closed. Following chart shows claw diameter and slider position at those positions (Table 1).

Average onion diameter is 5 cm, and maximum onion diameter is 7 cm, and thus we can pluck average sized onion fairly easily. To achieve this moment, we need to move the slider by 36 mm.

Table 1 Critical positions

Position	Claw diameter (mm)	Slider position (mm)
Open claw	98	0
Closed claw	68	36

Table 2 Force analysis

Force (N)	Force at each arm (N)	Pressure Generated (K Pa)
40	9.65	60.33
50	12.06	75.42
60	14.48	90.50
70	16.89	105.58

3.3 Force Analysis

For onion farming, one needs clay soil for which penetration pressure is 100 K Pa [9]. We calculated for the given amount of force applied to the handle pressure generated at the claws. Following table shows the static force analysis. Also, keep in mind that an average human being can exert 150 N of force fairly easily (Table 2).

4 Conclusion and Future Work

The developed mechanism requires less physical exertion. Due to rendered consideration of ergonomic factors, a farmer can perform this operation without bending. As per our problem statement, the mechanism has been able to provide the anticipated outcomes. The reduction of manual labor as well as ease in performing the operation (total weight = 2.3 kg) are the highlighting ones.

As the future prospect, further improvement can be made in order to make the mechanism pluck multiple onions at a time. Incorporation of motor in order to automate the operation could be another potential improvement we could embark upon. Sliding moment can be achieved through the motor. The low cost of the model could be another crucial factor. The complete process costs around ₹650–700 which is relatively cheap. Mass production could further reduce the price to a considerable extent.

References

1. Onion farming in india—guide for beginners, http://www.agrifarming.in/onion-farming/
2. Youtube, How to grow onions and garlic, *Better Homes and Gardens*

3. C.-W. Chang, C.-K. Ho, Z.-C. Chen, Y.-H. Hwang, C.-Y. Chang, S.-T. Liu, M.-J. Chen, M.-Y. Chen, Fungi genus and concentration in the air of onion fields and their opportunistic action related to mycotic keratitis. Arch. Env. Health Int. J. **57**(4), 349–354 (2002)
4. Y. Hagiz, Harvesting apparatus for onions, US Patent 4,373,589, 15 Feb 1983
5. Youtube, Harvest of first year onion sets, John Deere + VSS Amac Vru XLM Plantuien Oogst Loonbedrijf SvZ, *Tractorspotter*, https://www.youtube.com/watch?v=7WmO4BDKa0A
6. A. Parab, Autodesk amination, https://www.youtube.com/watch?v=72R64GJCWHM&feature=youtu.be
7. A. Parab, Working of onion plucking mechanism, https://youtu.be/JO3qaTlFFic
8. A. Parab, Working of onion plucking mechanism, https://youtu.be/iFys_4q593E
9. NPTEL, *Design of Shallow Foundations*, http://nptel.ac.in/courses/105101083/download/lec17.pdf

A Simplified Model for Contact Mechanics of Articular Cartilage and Mating Bones Using Bond Graph

Arvind Kumar Pathak and Anand Vaz

Abstract Articular cartilage is a soft tissue between the mating bones of a synovial joint. It prevents direct contact while facilitating load carriage and lubrication with very low friction and wear. Modeling of a synovial joint involves nonuniform geometry of mating bones, available from point cloud data, separated by cartilage. This work proposes a simplified yet efficient model of a ball dropped in a bowl lined with a cartilage layer, to emulate the contact mechanics between mating bones. Multibond graph submodels for the ball and bowl are used to represent their rigid body mechanics. The nature of the intervening cartilage layer is characterized by a nonlinear C-field. Simulation code has been written algorithmically, directly from the bond graph model. Results indicate that the proposed model holds significant promise for applications in biomechanics.

Keywords Contact mechanics · Articular cartilage · Nonlinear stiffness · Bond graph · 3D animation

1 Introduction

Articular cartilage is a soft tissue between two mating bones of a synovial joint. It facilitates high load carriage − 7 to 10 times body weight, lubrication with very low frictional coefficient and wear [1]. It does not permit direct contact between the surfaces of mating bones during dynamic interaction. The modeling of a synovial joint is intricate due to nonuniform geometry of mating bones and intermediate cartilage layer. The bone geometry is available from digital scans in the form of point cloud data. The presence of a soft cartilage layer relaxes the rigid geometrical

A. K. Pathak (✉) · A. Vaz (✉)
Department of Mechanical Engineering, Dr. B. R. Ambedkar National Institute of Technology
Jalandhar, Jalandhar, G.T. Road, Bye Pass, Jalandhar 144011, Punjab, India
e-mail: pathakarvindk@gmail.com

A. Vaz
e-mail: anandvaz@ieee.org

© Springer Nature Singapore Pte Ltd. 2019
D N Badodkar and T A Dwarakanath (eds.), *Machines, Mechanism and Robotics*, Lecture Notes in Mechanical Engineering,
https://doi.org/10.1007/978-981-10-8597-0_47

549

constraints imposed by mating bone surfaces and distributes the contact forces over the contact area. Understanding the distribution of contact forces and their evolution over time is interesting and significant for biomechanical joints [2].

Conventionally, finite element analysis is used to model the soft contact mechanics at synovial joints [3]. The computational complexity required for nearly exact dynamic models is extremely high. It is desirable to obtain a simplified model, with lesser computational complexity, which behaves approximately identically to the exact system. The behavioral effect of the soft cartilage at a synovial joint is modeled using a combination of stiffness and damping elements. This renders the model more realistic, simpler to derive, and easier to numerically simulate. A nonlinear stiffness field has been used previously [4] to constrain the bone movement by surrounding soft cartilage at the synovial joint within a limiting boundary specified by geometry of mating bone surfaces. To capture the dynamic behavior at the contact interface, the forces acting at the contact surface have to be computed. The extent of penetration of the cartilage layer at the contact interface yields the resulting forces and their distribution over the contact area.

To demonstrate the simplified conceptual model and its implementation, a bond graph model of a ball dropped in a bowl with an intermediate virtual cartilage layer is considered here. The surface geometry of each mating body is represented by unstructured point cloud, i.e., sets of point primitives that sample the positions and respective normals of the underlying surfaces. This framework is illustrative of the inflexible bone and delicate articular ligament in real natural joints. The stiffness of the soft material has nonlinear characteristics, and its constitutive relations have been logically and systematically derived. The equations governing the dynamics of the system have been derived from the bond graph model, which also facilitates the coding for simulation [5, 6]. This paper is organized as follows. Section 2 elaborates the complete physics behind the proposed model. Multibond graph model for contact mechanics is developed and discussed in Sect. 3. A discussion of simulation results for the multibond graph model is carried out in Sect. 4. Section 5 represents the concluding remarks and potential for future work.

2 Proposed Model

With the above motivation, this work proposes a simplified yet efficient alternative biomechanical model, to emulate the contact mechanics between mating bones at the human synovial joint. To demonstrate the proposed concept, an example of a ball dropped in a bowl with an intermediate virtual cartilage layer is considered, as shown in Fig. 1a. The surface of both, the ball and bowl, is considered to be rigid. The geometries of the ball and the bowl are available in the form of a point cloud. Multibond graph submodels for the ball and bowl are used to represent their rigid body mechanics. The frame {1} is fixed on the ball at its center. The frame {2} is fixed at the center of the bowl, while the inertial frame {0} is fixed at the bottom center of the bowl as shown.

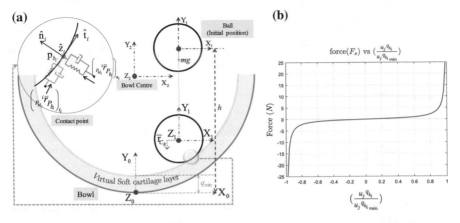

Fig. 1 **a** Basic configuration of ball in bowl with cartilage layer. **b** Behavior of soft cartilage layer

A nonlinear stiffness field is used to characterize the behavior of the intervening virtual soft cartilage layer. This soft layer comes into action when the relative position of peripheral points on the ball and bowl approaches within a predefined limit. Initially, the ball is dropped from a certain center height h under the action of gravity, as shown. Contact mechanics between the ball and bowl with the soft cartilage layer is divided into two parts: (a) contact detection and (b) reaction forces on the ball and the bowl offered by the cartilage layer. Since the geometries are in the form of point cloud, to identify the contact detection, the relative distance $_{bl_j}q_{b_i}$ of peripheral point b_i on the ball with respect to the point bl_j on the bowl is calculated at every instant of time t.

$$_{bl_j}q_{b_i}(t) = \sqrt{\left(x_{b_i}(t) - x_{bl_j}(t)\right)^2 + \left(y_{b_i}(t) - y_{bl_j}(t)\right)^2 + \left(z_{b_i}(t) - z_{bl_j}(t)\right)^2}. \quad (1)$$

When the value of $_{bl_j}q_{b_i} >$ thickness of soft cartilage layer, contact between two bodies will not occur. Consequently, the soft cartilage material will not apply any reaction force F_s.

Contact between two bodies will take place when the value of $_{bl_j}q_{b_i}$ will lie within a predefined limit. In this condition, the soft layer comes into action and starts getting deformed. Accordingly, the ball and bowl experience reaction forces applied by the soft cartilage layer at the contact interface. The stiffness of soft cartilage layer is considered to be nonlinear. Its magnitude increases and tends to infinity as $_{bl_j}q_{b_i} \rightarrow {}_{bl_j}q_{b_{i_{min}}}$, a predefined clearance limit which ensures that the ball does not penetrate the surface of the bowl. Consequently, the reaction force F_s experienced by the mating bodies at the area of contact interaction also tends toward infinite magnitude. A suitable candidate function satisfying the above conditions is proposed as

$$
{}_{blj}F_{s_{b_i}} = \frac{k_{s\,blj}q_{b_i}}{\left({}_{blj}q_{b_{i\,min}}^2 - {}_{blj}q_{b_i}^2\right)}, \quad -{}_{blj}q_{b_{i\,min}} < {}_{blj}q_{b_i} < {}_{blj}q_{b_{i\,min}}, \quad {}_{blj}q_{b_{i\,min}} > 0. \quad (2)
$$

k_s is a constant. Equation (2) can be rearranged as

$$
{}_{blj}F_{s_{b_i}} = \frac{k_{s\,blj}q_{b_i}}{{}_{blj}q_{b_{i\,min}}^2\left[1 - \left(\frac{{}_{blj}q_{b_i}}{{}_{blj}q_{b_{i\,min}}}\right)^2\right]}, \quad -{}_{blj}q_{b_{i\,min}} < {}_{blj}q_{b_i} < {}_{blj}q_{b_{i\,min}}, \quad {}_{blj}q_{b_{i\,min}} > 0.
$$

$$(3)$$

The characteristics of this nonlinear stiffness are illustrated in Fig. 1b. The force F_s developed by the soft cartilage material tends to increase asymptotically toward infinity as the deformation in soft material tends to the permissible limit ${}_{blj}q_{b_{i\,min}}$. Physically, it implies that the ball can never penetrate into the bowl.

3   Multibond Graph Modeling

A bond graph model, based on rigid body dynamics, is developed for the ball and bowl [7], and is shown in Fig. 2. The model is initiated using flow mapping which

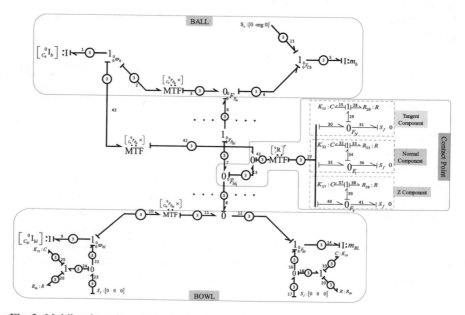

Fig. 2 Multibond graph model for ball and bowl with intermediate virtual cartilage layer

represents the kinematics of the system under consideration. Velocity ${}^{0}_{0}\dot{\bar{r}}_{P_{b_i}}$ of any point P_{b_i} on the periphery of the ball is given as

$$
{}^{0}_{0}\dot{\bar{r}}_{P_{b_i}} = {}^{0}_{0}\dot{\bar{r}}_{C_b} - \left[{}^{0}_{C_b}\bar{r}_{P_{b_i}} \times \right] {}^{0}_{0}\bar{\omega}_b, \tag{4}
$$

where ${}^{0}_{0}\dot{\bar{r}}_{C_b}$ is the velocity of center of mass and ${}^{0}_{0}\bar{\omega}_b$ is the angular velocity of ball, both of which are observed and expressed in inertial frame. $\left[{}^{0}_{C_b}\bar{r}_{P_{b_i}} \times \right]$ is the skew-symmetric matrix obtained from position vector ${}^{0}_{C_b}\bar{r}_{P_{b_i}} = \left\{ {}^{0}_{C_b}x_{P_{b_i}} \quad {}^{0}_{C_b}y_{P_{b_i}} \quad {}^{0}_{C_b}z_{P_{b_i}} \right\}^{T}$. Similarly, for the bowl, velocity ${}^{0}_{0}\dot{\bar{r}}_{P_{bl_j}}$ of any point P_{bl_j} on the periphery of bowl is given as

$$
{}^{0}_{0}\dot{\bar{r}}_{P_{bl_j}} = {}^{0}_{0}\dot{\bar{r}}_{C_{bl}} - \left[{}^{0}_{C_{bl}}\bar{r}_{P_{bl_j}} \times \right] {}^{0}_{0}\bar{\omega}_{bl}, \tag{5}
$$

where ${}^{0}_{0}\dot{\bar{r}}_{C_{bl}}$ is the velocity of the center of mass and ${}^{0}_{0}\bar{\omega}_{bl}$ is the angular velocity of bowl observed and expressed in the inertial frame.

The translational and rotational motion of the bowl is restricted by constraints, which are suitably relaxed to eliminate derivative causality, using a combination of spring and damper elements. Equations (6) and (7) represent the generalized efforts applied at the translational and rotational side of bowl.

$$
\bar{F}_T = e_{16} = e_{19} + e_{20}. \tag{6}
$$

$$
\bar{\tau}_R = e_{22} = e_{25} + e_{26}. \tag{7}
$$

Due to the presence of soft cartilage layer, contact interaction between the ball and bowl is modeled using nonlinear stiffness field. To capture the viscoelastic behavior at the contact interface, stiffness **C** having constitutive relation based on (2), and matching damping **R** element are chosen. The $0_{0 \bar{F}_{P_{b_i}}}^{bl_j}$ junction in the bond graph structure is used to obtain the relative velocity ${}^{0}_{P_{bl_j}}\dot{\bar{r}}_{P_{b_i}}$ of the point P_{b_i} on the ball with respect to the point P_{bl_j} on the bowl, as in (8). It also represents the force transmitted between the points P_{b_i} and P_{bl_j} on either side of the soft cartilage.

$$
{}^{0}_{P_{bl_j}}\dot{\bar{r}}_{P_{b_i}} = {}^{0}_{0}\dot{\bar{r}}_{P_{b_i}} - {}^{0}_{0}\dot{\bar{r}}_{P_{bl_j}}. \tag{8}
$$

When the contact condition, discussed in Sect. 2 is satisfied, the relative velocity vector ${}_{P_{bl_j}}{}^{i}\dot{\bar{r}}_{P_{b_i}}$ is obtained using Eq. (9). This kinematic relation makes use of a modulated transformer element MTF : $\left[{}^{0}_{i}R \right]^{T}$, $\in \mathbb{R}^{3 \times 3}$. $\left[{}^{0}_{i}R \right]$ represents the orientation of the localized frame $\{b_i\}$ fixed on the ball, with respect to the inertial frame $\{0\}$. It may be noted that a localized frame is fixed at each point in the cloud for the ball. Its angular velocity remains the same as that of the ball, even though its orientation may be different from that of the frame fixed on the ball.

$$P_{blj} {}^{i} \ddot{\vec{r}}_{P_{bi}} = [{}^{0}_{i}R]^{T} \left\{ {}^{0}_{P_{blj}} \ddot{\vec{r}}_{P_{bi}} + \left[{}^{0}_{P_{bli}} \ddot{\vec{r}}_{P_{bi}} \times \right] {}^{0}_{0} \bar{\omega}_{b} \right\}. \tag{9}$$

Since the problem is considered to be planar, the orientation of frame $\{b_i\}$ is given by

$$[{}^{0}_{i}R] = \begin{bmatrix} {}^{0}\hat{t}_i & {}^{0}\hat{n}_i & {}^{0}\hat{z}_i \end{bmatrix} \tag{10}$$

${}^{0}\hat{t}_i$, ${}^{0}\hat{n}_i$ and ${}^{0}\hat{z}_i$ are $\in \mathbb{R}^{3 \times 1}$, corresponding to unit vectors along the common tangent, common normal, and a direction perpendicular to them, respectively. For the planar case, ${}^{0}\hat{z}_i = \{0\ 0\ 1\}^{T}$.

Equation (11) represents normal reaction force applied by the combination of nonlinear stiffness $C{:}K_{32}$ and damper $R{:}R_{33}$ at point P_{b_i}.

$$ {}^{i}F_{N_i} = e_{35} = {}^{i}F_{N_K} + {}^{i}F_{N_R}. \tag{11}$$

The combination of $C{:}K_{15}$ and $R{:}R_{28}$ is used to model the frictional force given by (12) along the direction opposite to the relative motion between the two mating bodies, i.e., along the tangent at point P_{b_i}.

$$ {}^{i}F_{t_i} = e_{30} = {}^{i}F_{t_K} + {}^{i}F_{t_R}. \tag{12}$$

The static and dynamic friction are modeled as follows:

$$\begin{aligned} {}^{i}F_{R_i} &= {}^{i}F_{t_i} \leq \mu_S^i F_{N_i}, & P_{blj} {}^{i}\dot{x}_{P_{bi}} = 0, \\ &= \mathrm{sign}({}^{i}_{P_{blj}}\dot{x}_{P_{bi}})\mu_K^i F_{N_i}, & P_{blj} {}^{i}\dot{x}_{P_{bi}} \neq 0, \end{aligned} \tag{13}$$

where μ_S and μ_K are coefficients of static and dynamic friction, respectively. Total force at the contact interface between the ball and bowl expressed in the moving frame $\{b_i\}$ is

$$ {}_{blj}{}^{i}\bar{F}_{b_i} = \left\{ {}^{i}F_{R_i}\ {}^{i}F_{N_i}\ {}^{i}F_{Z_i} \right\}^{T}. \tag{14}$$

The force vector at the contact point P_{b_i}, expressed in the inertial frame, is represented by junction $0_{blj}{}^{0}F_{bi}$ in the bond graph as

$$ {}_{blj}{}^{0}\bar{F}_{b_i} = [{}^{0}_{i}R]\, {}_{blj}{}^{i}\bar{F}_{b_i}. \tag{15}$$

The force ${}_{blj}^{0}\bar{F}_{b_i}$ acting at the contact point P_{b_i} on the ball is equal in magnitude and opposite in direction to the force ${}_{bi}^{0}\bar{F}_{blj}$ acting at the contact point P_{blj} on the bowl,

$$_{bl_j}{}^0\bar{F}_{b_i} = -{}_{b_i}^0\bar{F}_{bl_j}. \tag{16}$$

At every instant of time, if N number of points on the bowl are in the contact interface with the point P_{b_i} on the ball, the total force ${}^0\bar{F}_{b_i}$ at the point P_{b_i} is given as

$$^0\bar{F}_{b_i} = \sum_{j}^{N} {}_{bl_j}{}^0\bar{F}_{b_i}. \tag{17}$$

Since the ball is dropped under the action of gravity an additional force $\left\{0 \ -mg \ 0\right\}^T$ acts on the ball. The resultant of all forces acting on the ball, which causes change of its translational momentum ${}^0\bar{p}_b$, is given as

$$\frac{d}{dt}\{^0\bar{p}_b\} = e_5 = \sum_{i=1}^{N} {}^0\bar{F}_{b_i} + \left\{0 \ -mg \ 0\right\}^T. \tag{18}$$

The resultant moment produced by the contact forces about the center of mass of the ball, expressed in the inertial frame, results in change of angular momentum ${}_{C_b}^0\bar{p}_b$ and is given as

$$\frac{d}{dt}\{_{C_b}\bar{p}_b\} = e_1 = \sum_{i}^{N} \left[{}_{C_b}^0\bar{r}_{P_{b_i}} \times\right]{}^0\bar{F}_{b_i}. \tag{19}$$

Similarly, the resultant force acting on the bowl which causes change in its translational momentum ${}^0\bar{p}_{bl}$ is given as

$$\frac{d}{dt}\{^0\bar{p}_{bl}\} = e_{14} = \sum_{j=1}^{N} {}^0\bar{F}_{bl_j} + \bar{F}_T, {}^0\bar{F}_{bl_j} = \sum_{i}^{N} {}_{b_i}^0\bar{F}_{bl_j}. \tag{20}$$

The resultant moment produced by the contact forces about the center of mass of the bowl, expressed in the inertial frame, causes change in its angular momentum ${}_{C_{bl}}^0\bar{p}_{bl}$ and is given by

$$\frac{d}{dt}\{_{C_{bl}}^0\bar{p}_{bl}\} = e_9 = \sum_{j}^{N} \left[{}_{C_{bl}}^0\bar{r}_{P_{bl_j}} \times\right]{}^0\bar{F}_{bl_j} + \bar{\tau}_R. \tag{21}$$

Equations (18)–(21) are a set of first-order differential equations obtained from the model, which represent its complete dynamics.

4 Simulation Results

The contact mechanics between articular cartilage and mating bones with the help of proposed model has been simulated. Simulation code has been written directly from the bond graph in an algorithmic manner using MATLAB. The ball mass is 0.02 kg. The radius of the ball and bowl is 0.04 m and 0.15 m, respectively. The minimum thickness of the virtual soft cartilage material is 0.015 m. An offset of 0.005 m is provided on the ball along the positive X-direction with respect to the frame fixed on the bowl. The ball is being dropped from an initial height of 0.70 m along the Y-direction under the action of gravitational force on the ball. The coefficients of static and dynamic friction, which provides low friction and low wear to articular cartilage surfaces are 0.01 and 0.003 [8], respectively. Figure 3 shows the position trajectory of the ball center over a time period with respect to inertial frame. The ball initially drops from a height of 0.70 m, and bounce back due to force applied by the virtual cartilage material modeled as nonlinear stiffness field. It rolls in the bowl while oscillating about the center at the bottom of the bowl surface. There is no motion of the ball along the Z-direction, since it moves in the X-Y plane, as expected.

Figure 4 shows the different animation frames for the position of the ball within the bowl cavity and simultaneously, the normal and frictional forces offered by the virtual soft cartilage material. Figure 4a shows the initial position of the ball; at this instant, the ball is not in contact with the virtual cartilage layer. Hence, the surface of the ball and the bowl is not experiencing any normal and tangential force. Figure 4b shows the first striking moment of the ball in the soft cartilage material. At this instant, the ball and the bowl experiences normal and tangential forces applied by nonlinear stiffness of the cartilage layer. A minimum thickness of virtual soft cartilage layer is maintained. Figure 4c shows that the ball rolls over the virtual soft cartilage material due to the angular momentum of the ball developed over a period of time. Figure 4d

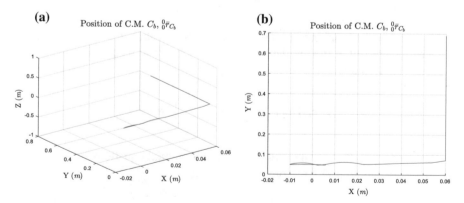

Fig. 3 Position trajectory of the ball center with respect to bowl: **a** 3D coordinate system and **b** 2D coordinate system (X-Y plane)

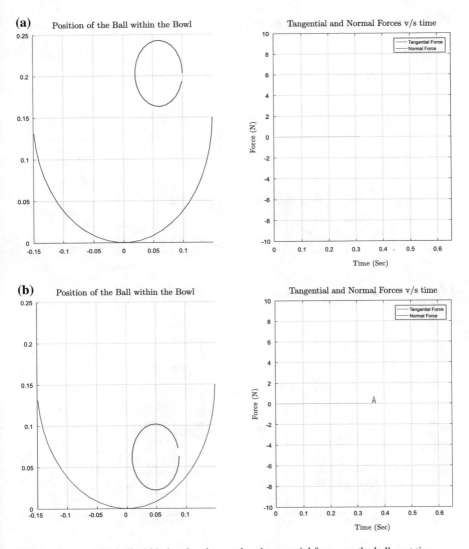

Fig. 4 Motion of the ball within bowl and normal and tangential forces on the ball w.r.t time

shows the final position of the ball when it comes to rest due to frictional force offered by the soft cartilage material at the contact surface of the ball.

(c)

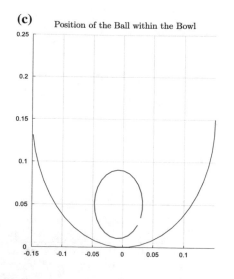

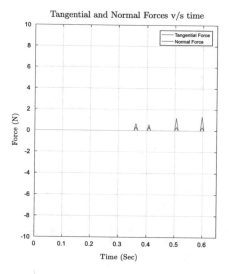

(d)

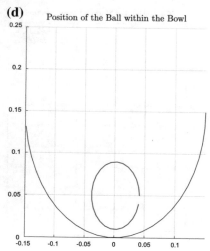

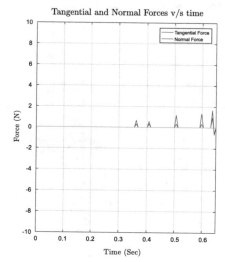

Fig. 4 (continued)

5 Conclusion

The effect of soft cartilage between two mating bones at a synovial joint is emulated using an example of a ball and a bowl. The behavior is analyzed using a nonlinear stiffness between the ball and bowl, modeled using bond graph. The ball moves within the bowl and at every instant of time, a minimum thickness of virtual soft cartilage material is maintained between the mating surfaces. The constitutive relation for the stiffness of the cartilage material is considered such that the force developed by the cartilage material at the area of contact interaction between the ball and bowl increases asymptotically as the ball surface approaches closer to the predefined clearance limit with respect to the bowl. The contact area continuously changes during ball motion and development of forces and moments at the contact interface are determined and analyzed. The present work provides an opportunity to emulate contact mechanics between mating bones, while taking into account their surface geometries in the form of point clouds. The bond graph technique is especially convenient and computationally advantageous for dynamic analysis of such systems.

References

1. C.P. Neu, K. Komvopoulos, A.H. Reddi, The interface of functional biotribology and regenerative medicine in synovial joints. **14**(3), 235–247 (2008)
2. M. Pauly, L.J. Guibas, D.K. Pai, Quasi-rigid objects in contact, in *Proceeding SCA'04 Proceedings of the 2004 ACM SIGGRAPH/Eurographics Symposium on Computer Animation* (2004), pp. 109–119
3. A. Kumar, A. Vaz, K.D. Gupta, Bond graph modeling of dynamics of soft contact interaction of a non-circular rigid body rolling on a soft material. MAMT **86**, 265–280 (2015)
4. A. Vaz, S. Hirai, A simplified model for a biomechanical joint with soft cartilage, in *2004 IEEE International Conference on Systems, Man and Cybernetics* (2004), pp. 756–761
5. A. Mukherjee, R. Karmakar, *Modeling and Simulation of Engineering Systems through Bondgraphs* (Narosa Publishing House, New Delhi, 2000)
6. D.C. Karnopp, D. Margolis, R.C. Rosenberg, *System Dynemics: Modeling and Simulation of Mechatronic Systems* (Wiley-Interscience, New York, 2000)
7. N. Mishra, A. Vaz, *Bond Graph Modeling of a 3-Joint String-Tube Actuated Finger Prosthesis*, vol. 117 (2017), pp. 1–20
8. R. Serway, J. Faughn, *College Physics*, 6th edn. (Brooks/Cole- Thomson Learning, Canada, 2003), p. 101

Modeling and Estimation of Closed-Loop Impact for Multi-arm Space Robot While Capturing a Tumbling Orbiting Object

Deepak Raina, Sunil Gora and Suril Vijaykumar Shah

Abstract In this paper, an attempt has been made to develop a framework for closed-loop impact modeling of a multi-arm robotic system mounted on a servicing satellite while capturing a tumbling orbiting object. When the satellite is in broken state or does not have provision for grapple and tumbling, the interception is very difficult. In such cases, interception using multi-arm robotic system can be appealing as this will certainly increase the probability of grasp in comparison to a single-arm robot. When multiple arms of a robot will capture only one target object from different points of contact, then it is termed as closed-loop impact. In this paper, first, the dynamic models of a multi-arm robot and a tumbling orbiting object are obtained. The target dynamics has been modeled considering it to be a rigid body. Then, the three phases of the capturing operation, namely, approach, impact, and postimpact have been modeled. Efficacy of the framework is shown using a dual-arm robot mounted on a servicing satellite performing capturing operation when both arms of robot capture a single target object. The effects of relative velocity and angle of approach on the impact forces would also be investigated.

Keywords Space robot · Closed-loop impact · Dynamic simulation

1 Introduction

Space robotics have been an active area of research for the last few years [1]. Autonomous on-orbit services (OOS), such as capturing, refueling, and repair and refurbishment of an on-orbit satellite using a robot mounted on service satellite,

D. Raina (✉) · S. Gora · S. V. Shah (✉)
Mechanical Engineering Department, Indian Institute of Technology Jodhpur,
Jodhpur, Rajasthan, India
e-mail: raina.1@iitj.ac.in

S. Gora
e-mail: sunil.1@iitj.ac.in

S. V. Shah
e-mail: surilshah@iitj.ac.in

© Springer Nature Singapore Pte Ltd. 2019
D N Badodkar and T A Dwarakanath (eds.), *Machines, Mechanism and Robotics*, Lecture Notes in Mechanical Engineering,
https://doi.org/10.1007/978-981-10-8597-0_48

561

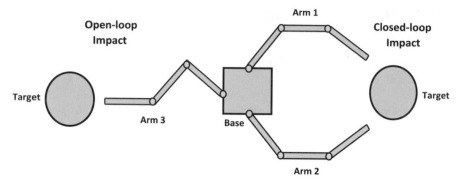

Fig. 1 Open-and closed-loop impact in case of multi-arm floating base robotic system

will be one of the important components of the space missions in future. The main objective of capturing faulty satellites/debris is to avoid their possible collision with a working satellite in the same orbit. Use of space robots boosts the reliability, safety, and ease of execution of operations.

In the case of a multi-arm robotic system, the impact can be classified into two types: open-loop impact and closed-loop impact as shown in Fig. 1. When r—arms of a robot will capture r—target objects, then it is referred to as an open-loop impact. When multiple arms of a robot will capture only one target object from different points of contact, then it is termed as closed-loop impact. Recently, a framework for modeling and estimation of open-loop impact for multi-arm space robot while capturing tumbling orbiting objects was proposed in [2]. In this paper, the work presented in [2] will be extended to model closed-loop impact

1.1 Literature Survey

The space debris capture and handling require passive object handling capabilities. The first step is to securely grasp the passive object. This task is called docking. Studies in this field have provided several theoretical approaches [3] some of which resulted in experimental servicers [4]. On-orbit object handling has similarities to cooperative manipulation of objects on earth [5] with the additional complexities that in space no fixed support exists, thus letting momentum changes to play a key role in body motion. The work presented in [6] provided the detailed derivation of the model of a space robot with multiple arms based on its geometric features and momentum conservative property of the system. The work in [7] proposes a method for berthing a target and reorientating the base using manipulator motion only after the capture. In [8], the manipulator damps out the target's angular and linear momentums as quickly as possible considering the constraint that the magnitude of the exerted force and torque remain below their prespecified values in the post-grasping phase. In [9], a new strategy is used for capturing a free-floating satellite initially having angular momentum, and proposes two control laws for angular momentum management during the postimpact phase. In [10], a mechanism is proposed to close the tether-net around the debris for application in the net-based space debris capture mission.

Impact modeling of multi-arm space robot is exploited but no extensive study is reported on closed-loop impact. Closed-loop impact eases the capture of tumbling orbiting object and also enhances the capture capability of the manipulator. Although the closed chain mechanism induces complexity but it also ensures improved manipulation accuracy as compared to the serial manipulator. So closed-loop impact must be studied for multi-arm space robot. In this paper, closed-loop impact model is developed for 4-link dual-arm space robot while it captures a tumbling orbiting object with both arms.

The capture operation includes three phases, namely, approach, impact, and postimpact. In approach phase the end effector moves with a predefined trajectory to the target object. During the impact phase, end effector makes contact at a distinct point on the target object and impact forces are generated. The postimpact phase is simulated by determining the change in generalized velocities of the end effector and object during impact. Those end effector velocities are used to simulate the closed-loop of the space robot. The change in impulse force with the change in end effector pose and relative velocity is also studied in this paper.

The rest of the paper is organized as follows: Dynamic modeling for free-floating robot and target objects are presented in Sect. 2. Modeling of impact is presented in Sect. 3, while the implementation of the proposed framework on planar dual-arm space robot is presented in Sect. 4. Finally, conclusions are given in Sect. 5.

2 Dynamic Modeling

In this section, the dynamic models of a multi-arm robot and a tumbling orbiting object are obtained. In dynamic modeling of a multi-arm robot, the equations-of-motion (EOM) have been obtained using the DeNOC [11] based formulation and closed-loop constraint equations. The target dynamics have been modeled considering it to be a rigid body.

2.1 Dynamics of Multi-arm Robot

In the preimpact phase, multi-arm space robot will be an open-loop system. Thus, the EOM given in [2] will be used as

$$I\ddot{\theta} + c = \tau + J^T F_e \tag{1}$$

Fig. 2 Constraint forces (λ) in closed dual-arm robot

The multi-arm robot will become a closed-loop system in postimpact phase if two or more arms will capture the same target objects from different contact points. Hence, EOM given in (1) can be written for closed-loop system as

$$I\ddot{\theta} + c = \tau + J^T F_e + J_c^T \lambda \tag{2}$$

where J_c is the constrained Jacobian matrix [12] for the closed-loop system and is defined in a way so that $J_c\dot{\theta} = 0$. Moreover, λ is the vector of Lagrange multipliers representing the constraint forces at the cut opened joints as shown in Fig. 2.

2.2 Target Dynamics

The EOM for target [2] can be written as

$$I_{ti}\dot{t}_{ti} = \tau_{ti} - J_{ti}^T F_e \tag{3}$$

In closed-loop impact modeling, multiple arms of a robot will capture only one target object from different points of contact. Thus, the matrix I_{ti} would be same for each contact point, though matrices $\dot{t}_{ti}$, J_{ti} would change depending on the location of the contact point on the target by the ith arm.

3 Impact Model

To model the impact, let us consider that the target object collides with the end effector of the robot arm mounted on a service satellite at a known single point and as a result of this collision, impact force F_e is induced.

By combining (1) and (3), the impact force F_e can be eliminated to obtain the following equation:

$$J^T J_t^{-T} I_t \dot{t}_t + I \ddot{\theta} = -c + \tau + J^T J_t^{-T} \tau_t \qquad (4)$$

Let the duration of impact be T seconds. Now (4) would be integrated over T time period as

$$J^T J_t^{-T} I_t (t_{tf} - t_{ti}) + I(\dot{\theta}_f - \dot{\theta}_i) = \int_0^T [-c + \tau + J^T J_t^{-T} \tau_t] dt$$

Recalling the assumptions stated in [2], the above equation can be written as

$$J^T J_t^{-T} I_t (t_{tf} - t_{ti}) + I(\dot{\theta}_f - \dot{\theta}_i) = 0 \qquad (5)$$

The above equation represents conservation of generalized momenta and is valid for all collisions. To calculate magnitude of impulse, (1) is then rearranged and integrated over time duration of impact T as

$$\overline{F} = J^{-T} I(\dot{\theta}_f - \dot{\theta}_i) \qquad (6)$$

In this paper, impact is assumed to be inelastic, thus the coefficient of restitution (e) is zero and the velocity of end effector and contact point would be same, i.e.,

$$J \dot{\theta}_f = J_t t_{tf} \qquad (7)$$

The generalized velocities of the target can be written in terms of manipulator velocities to get

$$t_{tf} = J_t^{-1} J \dot{\theta}_f \qquad (8)$$

Substitution of (8) into (5) yields

$$\dot{\theta}_f = G^{-1} H \qquad (9)$$

where

$$G = J^T J_t^{-T} I_t J_t^{-1} J + I$$

$$H = J^T J_t^{-T} I_t t_{ti} + I \dot{\theta}_i \qquad (10)$$

From (9), we can obtain final velocities for space robot, which can be used to calculate the change in target velocities using (8). The final base velocities $\dot{t}_{bf}$ can be obtained using the momentum equation [13] as given by

$$\dot{t}_{bf} = I_b^{-1} \left(\begin{bmatrix} p \\ l - c_o \times p \end{bmatrix} - I_{bm} \dot{\theta}_f \right) \qquad (11)$$

From (9) and (11), we get generalized velocity vector as an initial condition for the postimpact dynamic simulations.

4 Results and Discussions

Numerical experiments have been performed with 4-link dual-arm robot mounted on a service satellite. The solid sphere rotating about its z-axis has been considered as a target object. The link length, mass, and inertia properties of the base and robot, used in [2, 14] for the purpose of simulation, are provided in Table 1. The COM of the satellite is located at (0, 0). The mass, mass moment of inertia (MOI), and location of the target object are given in Table 2.

In the numerical experiments, three phases of impact are modeled, and the behavior of the system undergoing impact is estimated. In the approach phase, the initial and final positions for both end effectors as in Table 3 are given as input. Moreover, the target is assumed to have angular velocity of 0.2 rad/s in the anticlockwise direction. The preimpact simulations were carried out using ReDySim [15] for the time period of 30 s.

The trajectory following proportional and derivative (PD) control law given by (12) was used for carrying out dynamic simulations.

Table 1 Model parameters of dual-arm robot and base

	Base	Robot								
		Arm 1				Arm 2				
Link	0	1	2	3	4	5	6	7	8
Length (m)	1	1	1	1	1	1	1	1	1
Mass (kg)	500	10	10	10	10	10	10	10	10
MOI (kg m^2)	83.61	1.05	1.05	1.05	1.05	1.05	1.05	1.05	1.05

Table 2 Model parameters of target

	Target
Mass (kg)	10
Radius (m)	0.5
MOI (kg m^2)	1
Location (m)	(0, 1.73)

Table 3 Initial and final end effectors' position

	P_{e1x}	P_{e1y}	P_{e2x}	P_{e2y}
Initial	3.03	2.00	−3.03	2.00
Final	0.50	1.73	−0.50	1.73

$$\tau = K_p(\theta_d - \theta) + K_v(\dot{\theta}_d - \dot{\theta}) \tag{12}$$

where K_p and K_d are the diagonal matrices of proportional and derivative gains and $\dot{\theta}_d$ and $\dot{\theta}$ are desired and actual joint velocities, respectively. The preimpact and impact phase simulation results are shown in Figs. 3a, b. The total momentum of the system before impact is shown in Fig. 4.

Table 4 Impulse (N s) estimation

Case	Impulse ($\overline{F}$)	
	Contact point 1	Contact point 2
Case 1	0.1483	0.1373
Case 2	0.0679	0.0676
Case 3	0.1373	0.1483
Case 4	0.1548	0.1697
Case 5	0.0923	0.1803

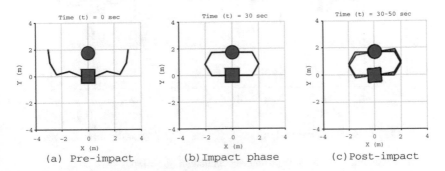

(a) Pre-impact   (b) Impact phase   (c) Post-impact

Fig. 3 Case 1: $\theta_e = 180°$; $\omega_t = 0.2$ rad/s

In the impact phase, (7)–(11) were used to model impact and estimate the change in velocities of the robot and target. The generalized velocity vector so obtained was used as an initial condition for post dynamic simulations. Since we assumed that the target is captured rigidly by the end effector as a perfectly inelastic case, so the robot and target would become one closed-loop system in postimpact phase. The postimpact simulations were also carried out using ReDySim [15] for 20 s. Further, cases of change in relative velocity and approach angle are also simulated. The postimpact dynamic simulations for the abovementioned cases are shown in Figs. 3c, 5 and 6. The magnitude of impulse in these cases is shown in Table 4.

It is evident from Figs. 4 and 7 that total momentum of the system is almost same before and after impact. Thus, the laws of inelastic collision are satisfied.

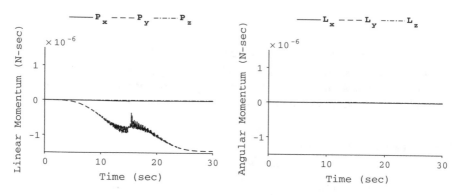

Fig. 4 Total momentum before impact

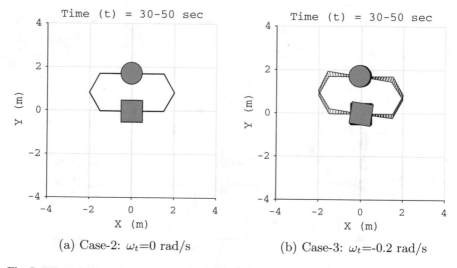

(a) Case-2: $\omega_t=0$ rad/s   (b) Case-3: $\omega_t=-0.2$ rad/s

Fig. 5 Effect of relative velocity on postimpact simulation ($\theta_e = 180°$)

5 Conclusions

In this work, a framework for closed-loop impact modeling and estimation of a multi-arm space robot has been presented for capturing a tumbling orbiting object. The impact of orbiting target with two arms of a space robot has been modeled and postimpact dynamics of a dual-arm space robot and target has been simulated. It may be noted that postimpact uncontrolled dynamics will result in undesirable motion, thus a control scheme will be proposed to achieve postimpact stabilization in future work. Experimental implementation and validation of the proposed method on an earth-based dual-arm robot will also be carried out in future.

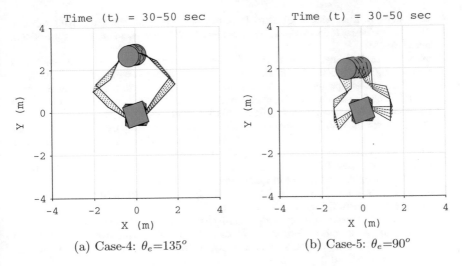

(a) Case-4: $\theta_e = 135^o$　　　　　　(b) Case-5: $\theta_e = 90^o$

Fig. 6 Effect of approach angle on postimpact simulation ($\omega_t = 0.2\,\text{rad/s}$)

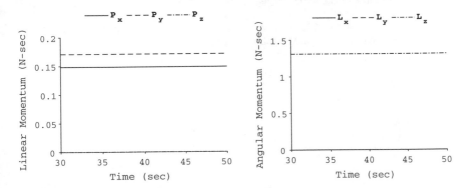

Fig. 7 Total momentum after impact

References

1. J.-C. Liou, An active debris removal parametric study for LEO environment remediation. Adv. Space Res. **47**(11), 1865–1876 (2011)
2. D. Raina, S. Shah, Impact modeling and estimation for multi-arm space robot while capturing tumbling orbiting objects, in *Proceedings of Conference on Advances in Robotics*, (ACM, 2017), pp. 1–6
3. G. Rouleau, I. Rekleitis, R. L'Archeveque, E. Martin, K. Parsa, E. Dupuis, Autonomous capture of a tumbling satellite, in *2006 Proceedings of IEEE International Conference on Robotics and Automation, ICRA*, (IEEE, 2006), pp. 3855–3860
4. K. Yoshida, ETS-VII flight experiments for space robot dynamics and control, in *Experimental Robotics VII* (2001) pp. 209–218
5. O. Khatib, Mobile manipulation: the robotic assistant. Robot. Auton. Syst. **26**(2–3), 175–183 (1999)

6. K. Yoshida, R. Kurazume, Y. Umetani, Dual arm coordination in space free-flying robot, in *1991 Proceedings of IEEE International Conference on Robotics and Automation* (IEEE, 1991), pp. 2516–2521
7. W. Xu, C. Li, B. Liang, Y. Xu, Y. Liu, W. Qiang, Target berthing and base reorientation of free-floating space robotic system after capturing. Acta Astronaut. **64**(2), 109–126 (2009)
8. F. Aghili, Pre-and post-grasping robot motion planning to capture and stabilize a tumbling/drifting free-floater with uncertain dynamics, in *2013 IEEE International Conference on Robotics and Automation (ICRA)* (IEEE, 2013) pp. 5461–5468
9. D.N. Dimitrov, K. Yoshida, Momentum distribution in a space manipulator for facilitating the post-impact control, in *2004 Proceedings of IEEE/RSJ International Conference on Intelligent Robots and Systems, IROS,* vol. 4 (IEEE, 2004), pp. 3345–3350
10. I. Sharf, B. Thomsen, E.M. Botta, A.K. Misra, Experiments and simulation of a net closing mechanism for tether-net capture of space debris. Acta Astronaut. (2017)
11. S. Shah, S. Saha, J. Dutt, Modular framework for dynamic modeling and analyses of legged robots. Mech. Mach. Theory **49**, 234–255 (2012)
12. P.E. Nikravesh, *Computer-Aided Analysis of Mechanical Systems* (Prentice-Hall, Inc., 1988)
13. A. Gattupalli, S. Shah, K.M. Krishna, A. Misra, Control strategies for reactionless capture of an orbiting object using a satellite mounted robot, in *Proceedings of Conference on Advances in Robotics* (ACM, 2013), pp. 1–6
14. F. James, S. Vyas, P. Bandikatla, P. Mithun, S.V. Shah, Design and development of an earth based experimental setup for testing algorithms on space robots," in *Proceedings of the 2015 Conference on Advances in Robotics* (ACM, 2015), p. 38
15. S.V. Shah, P.V. Nandihal, S.K. Saha, Recursive dynamics simulator (ReDySim): a multibody dynamics solver. Theor. Appl. Mech. Lett. **2**(6) (2012)

Non-dimensionalized Feasibility Maps for Designing Compliant Mechanisms

Kishor K. S. Bharadwaj, T. Ramesh and G. K. Ananthasuresh

Abstract A Spring-Lever (SL) model with two degrees of freedom is a lumped model for a single-input-single-output (SISO) compliant mechanism just as a spring is a single degree-of-freedom model for an elastic structure under one load. Three parameters of an SL model help visualize compliant mechanisms in a database juxtaposed with a feasible map constructed using quantitative specifications of a given design problem. In the past work, this approach is shown to be effective in selection and re-design based method of designing compliant mechanisms. This work extends the method to designing compliant mechanisms at multiple length scales through non-dimensionalization of two stiffness parameters in the SL model. Non-linear large-displacement behavior of compliant mechanisms and user-specifications are accurately captured in non-dimensionalized stiffness maps. After describing the procedure for constructing non-dimensionalized stiffness maps, the method of designing compliant mechanisms using the maps is illustrated through examples and case-studies.

Keywords Spring-Lever model · Elastica · Scaling · Dimensional analysis

1 Introduction

There are many methods to design compliant mechanisms. Some of them are developed for much longer time than some that are proposed recently. As the focus of this paper is on combining two new methods, it is pertinent to compare and contrast different methods first.

K. K. S. Bharadwaj · T. Ramesh (✉)
Mechanical Engineering, National Institute of Technology Tiruchirappalli, Tiruchirappalli, India
e-mail: tramesh@nitt.edu

K. K. S. Bharadwaj
e-mail: bharadwaj.kishor@gmail.com

G. K. Ananthasuresh
Mechanical Engineering, Indian Institute of Science, Bengaluru, India
e-mail: suresh@iisc.ac.in

© Springer Nature Singapore Pte Ltd. 2019
D N Badodkar and T A Dwarakanath (eds.), *Machines, Mechanism and Robotics*, Lecture Notes in Mechanical Engineering,
https://doi.org/10.1007/978-981-10-8597-0_49

Pseudo rigid-body (PRB) modeling-based methods effectively utilize rigid-body mechanism synthesis methods by modeling stiffness using a torsion spring [1]. They have all the advantages of loop-closure synthesis methods but also inherit their short-comings. Simplified modeling of large bending of beams of certain boundary conditions is the highlight of this method. Topology optimization methods [2–4] approach the compliant mechanism design problem as a structural optimization problem. This method is ideally suited for the conceptual design stage but becomes involved when strength and nonlinear performance are considered. These two methods have proved to be effective but require considerable expertise from the user. Some new methods address this problem by aiding user-intuition. Selection from a database using feasibility maps [5, 6], building-block based interactive design [7, 8], force-flow method [9, 10], and non-dimensional kinetoelastic maps are some examples of the methods that ease the design process. Much more development is needed to make these and other methods general enough for designing a variety of compliant mechanisms. In this work, we combine the feasibility and non-dimensional maps towards an improved method of designing compliant mechanisms.

1.1 Feasibility Maps Using a Database of Compliant Mechanisms

Much of the past work on compliant mechanism design has led to a number of distinct compliant mechanisms [11] that can be classified based on functionality. There are nearly 100 fully compliant mechanisms that do not have any kinematic joints. There are grippers, direction-changing mechanisms, displacement-amplifying compliant mechanisms, force-amplifying compliant mechanisms, clamping mechanisms, compliant suspension mechanisms, bistable compliant mechanisms, shape-morphing compliant mechanisms, etc. Figure 1 shows a dozen representative compliant mechanisms from a database built over a period of time in our group.

A question then arises as to whether a new design problem can be solved using an existing compliant mechanism in a database. This requires a common model for all types of compliant mechanisms, a way to compare given design specifications with the capabilities of candidate mechanisms, a method of selection, guidance for selecting a material and manufacturing process, and a procedure for re-designing when that becomes necessary. All these were discussed by Hegde and Ananthasuresh in [5, 6]. We review them briefly.

Any compliant mechanism may be represented using a spring-lever (SL) and spring-mass-lever (SML) models for describing static and dynamic responses, respectively. SL and SML models have two degrees of freedom (DoFs) because most compliant mechanisms have input and output DoFs. Figure 2 shows an SL model, which has three parameters: input-side stiffness (k_{ci}), output-side stiffness (k_{co}), and inherent amplification factor (n). These are not specific to a type of compliant mechanism and are hence general enough to describe not only small but also

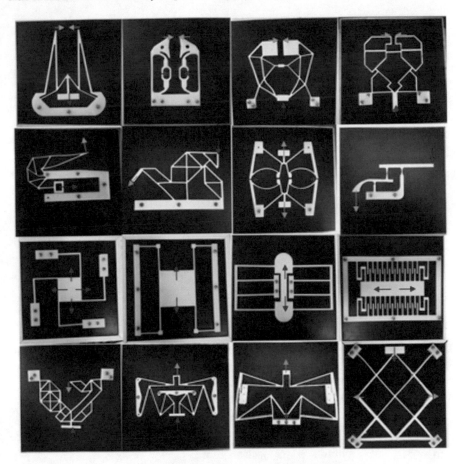

Fig. 1 Extract from the database of different types of compliant mechanisms

large-displacement behavior. When large-displacement behavior is considered, the three SL parameters vary with a motion parameter such as input displacement, output displacement, input force, etc. The three parameters essentially capture the instantaneous input and output stiffness parameters (k_{ii}, k_{io}, k_{oo}) [12] but with useful physical insight. The equivalence between $\{k_{ii}, k_{io}, k_{oo}\}$ and $\{k_{ci}, k_{co}, n\}$ has been reported [6].

$$
\begin{aligned}
k_{ci} &= k_{oo} \\
n &= -k_{io}/k_{oo} \\
k_{co} &= k_{ii} - k_{io}^2/k_{oo}
\end{aligned}
\tag{1}
$$

The SL parameters may be considered as "properties" of compliant mechanisms just as materials have properties such as density, Young's modulus, yield strength, etc.

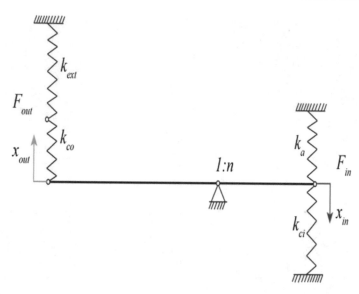

Fig. 2 Spring lever model of a compliant mechanism [5, 6]

This notion enables linking design specifications with the properties of elements in a database as in Ashby's method of material selection [13] for a given design problem. Hegde and Ananthasuresh [5] had followed a similar approach by representing quantitative user-specifications for a compliant mechanism design problem as follows.

$$
\begin{aligned}
F_{in}^{min} \leq F_{in} \leq F_{in}^{max} \quad & u_{in}^{min} \leq u_{in} \leq u_{in}^{max} \\
F_{out}^{min} \leq F_{out} \leq F_{out}^{max} \quad & u_{out}^{min} \leq u_{out} \leq u_{out}^{max} \\
k_{a}^{min} \leq k_{a} \leq k_{a}^{max} \quad & k_{ext}^{min} \leq k_{ext} \leq k_{ext}^{max}
\end{aligned}
\tag{2}
$$

It may be noted that the last two sets of inequalities include information about actuator stiffness (k_a) as well as workpiece stiffness (k_{ext}). Thus, a user can specify up to 12 scalar values (min and max values of six quantities of interests) depending on the design problem on hand. The 12 inequalities and two equilibrium equations of the SL-model can be solved to create feasible triplets of $\{k_{ci}, k_{co}, n\}$. The user needs to specify the required range of force and overall size of the mechanism in terms of F_{ref} and L_{ref} which are used to non dimensionalize the input and output stiffness of the compliant mechanisms. Hence user needs to specify totally 16 scalar values (min and max values of eight quantities of interests).

This leads to a feasible volume in the 3D space of $\{k_{ci}, k_{co}, n\}$. 2D projection in the $k_{ci} - k_{co}$ space of the feasible volume is shown in Fig. 3. This process has been automated and is proved to be a singly jointed set [6].

Every point in the feasible space of $\{k_{ci}, k_{co}, n\}$ satisfies the user-specifications in Eq. (2). Now, it is useful if we also show compliant mechanisms on this feasibility

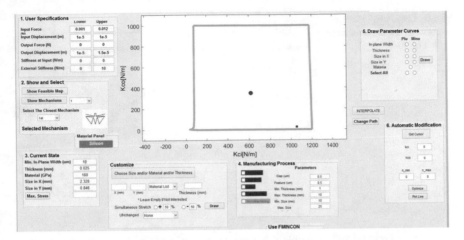

Fig. 3 Feasibility map showing the feasible region for a given specification by user

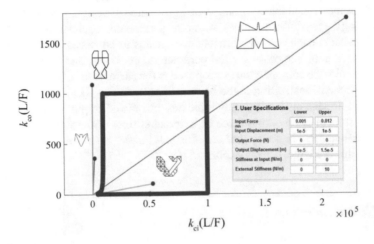

Fig. 4 Feasibility map showing the feasible region and compliant mechanisms for a given specification by user

map using their SL parameters. For this, the 2D map of $k_{ci} - k_{co}$ is more useful than the 3D map of $\{k_{ci}, k_{co}, n\}$. This is shown in Fig. 4. Each compliant mechanism is now a curve with the point indicating the SL parameters in the unloaded configuration.

If the curve lies entirely inside the feasibility map, it would mean that the corresponding compliant mechanism satisfies the user-specifications. If multiple mechanisms lie entirely inside the feasible map, anyone of them can be selected based on other considerations such as size, shape, fixed portions, etc. If none lie inside, [5, 6] showed how they can be re-designed interactively by changing the size, cross-section parameters of the beam segments, etc. Performance parameters such as maximum

Fig. 5 Large displacement
analysis of a cantilever beam
with a tip load

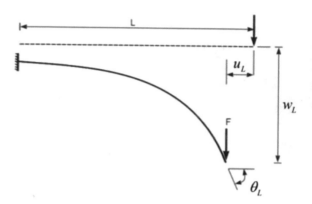

stress and manufacturing considerations such as min/max thickness, min/max values
of cross-section parameters are displayed to the user in real time.

The aforementioned selection and re-design method of designing compliant mechanisms using the feasibility map and SL-model parameters is quite effective. But there
is one drawback: each compliant mechanism needs to be stored in the database in
multiple sizes, multiple cross-section parameters, thickness, and material variants.
This is an avoidable complication as proposed in the current work. This can be solved
using non-dimensionalization of the SL parameters. Among $\{k_{ci}, k_{co}, n\}$, the last is
already non-dimensional as it simply indicates the ratio of output and input displacements when there is no output force or external stiffness. The first two need to be
non-dimensionalized in a way that remains valid under nonlinear conditions when
displacements are large. This is explained next.

1.2 Non-dimensionalization

Topology and shape are the principal contributors to the functionality of a compliant
mechanism. Topology is decided by the number of beam segments and their connectivity. Shape is decided by the shapes of the beam segments. The rest are secondary.
The rest include material, size, and cross-section dimensions of the beam segments.
There is a useful way to capture the large-displacement response of compliant mechanisms of given topology and shape. For this, we assume that the proportions of
lengths and cross-section dimensions of all beam segments do not change. This has
two implications. First, if proportions of the lengths of beam segments are the same,
it means that the shape of the compliant mechanism does not change. Second, if the
proportions of cross-section dimensions of all beam segments remain the same, then it
leads to fixed non-dimensionalized responses such as displacements, stiffness, maximum stress, natural frequency, etc. This remains so even under large-displacement
conditions. This subtle point can be understood by considering the large displacement
solution of a cantilever beam under a single transverse load (Fig. 6).

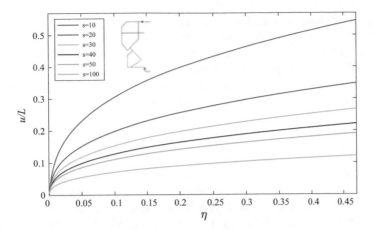

Fig. 6 Non-dimensional input displacement versus η for a compliant gripper

The axial and transverse displacements of the end of a cantilever beam, w_L and u_L, are obtained using elliptic integrals [14, 15]. By referring to Fig. 5, we write

$$\frac{w_L}{L} = \sqrt{\frac{1}{\eta}}\{\mathbf{F}(p,\ \pi/2) - \mathbf{F}(p,\ \phi_L) - 2\mathbf{E}(p,\ \pi/2) + 2\mathbf{E}(p,\ \phi_L)\} \qquad (3a)$$

$$\frac{u_L}{L} = 1 - \sqrt{\frac{2}{\eta}(2p^2 - 1)} \qquad (3b)$$

where $\eta = \frac{FL^2}{EI}$, which is used to solve for p (and hence ϕ_L, which is the slope of the tip of the cantilever) using

$$\int_{\phi_L}^{\pi/2} \frac{d\phi}{\sqrt{1 - p^2 \sin^2 \phi}} = \sqrt{\eta} \qquad (3c)$$

where

$$\phi_L = \sin^{-1}\left(\frac{1}{p\sqrt{2}}\right) \qquad (3d)$$

$F =$ force applied at the tip of the cantilever, $L =$ length, $E =$ Young's modulus, and $I =$ second moment of inertia. Furthermore, $\mathbf{F}$ and $\mathbf{E}$ are elliptic integrals of the first and second kinds, respectively. It is important to notice that non-dimensionalized w_L and u_L nonlinear functions of the non-dimensional number η as a whole rather than individual quantities that describe the cantilever geometry and material as well as applied force. This means that the value of η, which can be understood as the *index of bending*, determines the behaviour of the beam.

The analytical solution for a cantilever given in the preceding equations can be generalized to any planar compliant mechanism by defining η slightly differently and by introducing another non-dimensional number s, called the *slenderness ratio*. For rectangular cross-section with breadth b and depth d, we write [16]:

$$\eta = \frac{Fs^2}{Ebd}; \quad s = \frac{L}{d} \tag{4}$$

It is reported in [16] that any static mechanical response can be non-dimensionalized and expressed as a function of η and s. Figure 5 shows a sample non-dimensionalized kinetoelastic map for the input displacement of a compliant mechanism. It may be noticed that different curves exist for different values of s, whose range is from 10 (as per Euler-Bernoulli beam theory) to an upper threshold until which the compliant mechanisms deforms without any abnormalities such as self-contact, buckling, etc.

Geometric advantage (ratio of output and input displacements), mechanical advantage (ratio of output and input forces), maximum stress, multi-axial stiffness, natural frequency, etc., can all be expressed in this manner. A few finite element analysis simulations performed for different instances of compliant mechanisms are enough to draw such non-dimensional maps.

The highlight of the non-dimensional portrayal described in this section is that the overall size (indicated by representative length L), cross-section size (indicated by representative b or d), material property (E), and applied force(s) (indicated by representative F if they are multiple forces) together decide the non-dimensional response. So, a micron-sized mechanism made of silicon and macro-sized polypropylene with the same value of η and s would have the same non-dimensional response, even under the nonlinear conditions of large-displacement motion. We exploit this feature in the current work by storing the essential characteristics (i.e., SL parameters) in dimensional form in the database. This is explained next.

2 Non-dimensionalization of Stiffness Parameters in the SL Model

In this work, we non-dimensionalize k_{ci} k_{co} and $\hat{\sigma}_{max}$ as follows.

$$\hat{k}_{ci} = k_{ci}\frac{L}{F_{in}} \text{ and } \hat{k}_{co} = k_{co}\frac{L}{F_{in}}, \quad \hat{\sigma}_{max} = \sigma_{max}\left(\frac{1000}{E}\right) \tag{5}$$

Now, we can plot non-dimensionalized input and output-side stiffness parameters of any compliant mechanism for chosen values of s against η. The range of η varies for different compliant mechanism topologies and their shapes. It may again be

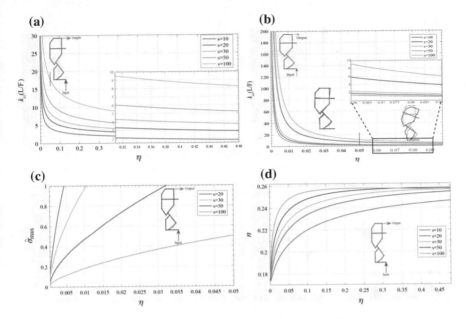

Fig. 7 Non-dimensionalized SL-maps of a compliant gripper. **a** Non-dimensional input stiffness ($\hat{k}_{ci}$) versus bending index (η), close-up view of a particular range of η; **b** non-dimensional output stiffness ($\hat{k}_{co}$) versus bending index (η) showing deformations at different values of η; **c** non-dimensional stress ($\hat{\sigma}_{\max}$) versus bending index (η); **d** intrinsic amplification/attenuation factor (n) versus bending index (η)

noted that only the topology (connectivity) and shape (proportions of different beam segments and their cross-sections) are enough to compute non-dimensionalized $\hat{k}_{ci}$ and $\hat{k}_{co}$.

Thus, irrespective of the size, cross-section size, material, and applied forces, the behavior of all compliant mechanisms can now be conveniently stored in a database. It is also important to note that each compliant mechanism in the database needs to be analyzed once for each value of s (typically not more than five or six times) in a parametric sweep of η from 0 to a value until which no abnormality occurs (as noted earlier, buckling, self-contact, etc.). Figures 7 and 8 show the non-dimensionalized SL parameters for three different compliant mechanisms.

2.1 Using Non-dimensional Kinetoelastic Maps

Non-dimensional kinetoelastic maps can be used for quick analysis as well as design. For analysis, the user needs to compute the non-dimensional parameter η by using representative values of F, L, b, d, E of the compliant mechanism. Choosing the average values of these parameters is one way to do it. Then, by noting the curve

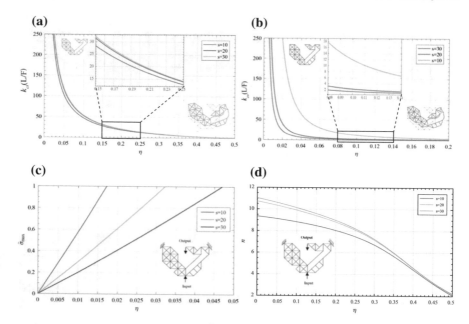

Fig. 8 **a** Non-dimensional Input stiffness ($\hat{k}_{ci}$) versus bending index (η), close-up view of a particular range of η; **b** non-dimensional output stiffness ($\hat{k}_{co}$) versus bending index (η), close-up view of a particular range of η; **c** non-dimensional stress ($\hat{\sigma}_{max}$) versus bending index (η); **d** intrinsic amplification/attenuation factor (n) versus bending index (η)

corresponding to the value of $s = L/d$, the non-dimensional response can be obtained from the kinetoelastic map. For example, by referring to Fig. 7a–d, considering the following values, we get $\eta = 0.05$ and $s = 100$.

$$F = 0.1\,N;\ L = 0.1\,m;\ E = 200\,GPa;\ b = 1 \times 10^{-4}\,m;\ d = 1 \times 10^{-3}m$$

Using Fig. 7a–d, for $\eta = 0.05$ and $s = 100$, we get

$$\hat{k}_{ci} = k_{ci} \Rightarrow \hat{k}_{ci}(F/L) = 18\,\text{N/m}$$

$$\hat{k}_{co} = k_{co} \Rightarrow \hat{k}_{co}(F/L) = 2.5\,\text{N/m}$$

$$\hat{\sigma}_{max} = \sigma_{max} \Rightarrow \hat{\sigma}_{max}\left(\frac{E}{1000}\right) = 100\,\text{MPa}$$

As evident here, we are able to obtain the SL parameters quickly from the non-dimensional SL map, without having to perform finite element analysis. By using the SL parameters, one can assess if a given compliant mechanism meets the requirements of a problem.

For design, we need to first draw the feasibility map using user-specifications of the upper and lower bounds of six parameters noted in Eq. (2). Additionally, the user needs to enter the representative size (i.e., L) and force (i.e., F). By using these, the feasibility map can be drawn using the non-dimensionalized SL parameters. This can be seen in Fig. 4. The same figure can now also show the non-dimensional SL parameters of the compliant mechanisms in the database. Figure 4 shows four mechanisms for clarity rather than showing many. It may be noted that each compliant mechanism is a curve in the feasibility map when we consider large-displacement behavior. However, for the compliant mechanisms considered in Fig. 4, all curves turn out to be straight lines in the non-dimensionalized $k_{ci} - k_{co}$ map. In the next section, we explain how to use this in design.

3 Design Case Studies

Let us consider a compliant mechanism that needs to be designed for the following user specifications. Here the intension is to amplify the applied input displacement. The maximum actuator stiffness is 10 N/m and has an external stiffness (stiffness of the workpiece) of 10 N/m.

$$1.5 \leq F_{in} \leq 3 \quad 0.001 \leq u_{in} \leq 0.002$$
$$0 \leq F_{out} \leq 0 \quad 0.001 \leq u_{out} \leq 0.01$$
$$1 \leq k_a \leq 2 \quad 0 \leq k_{ext} \leq 10$$

Figure 9, shows the non-dimensional feasibility map where an amplifying mechanism shown inside the map satisfies the aforementioned requirements while the other compliant mechanism (a Gripper) does not.

Fig. 9 Feasibility map showing the compliant mechanisms for a given user-specifications

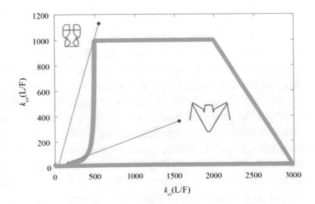

Fig. 10 Compliant
mechanisms for three
different user-specifications

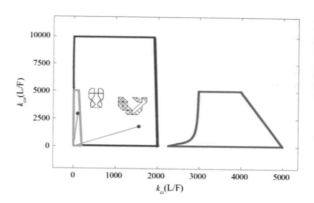

Any compliant mechanism may satisfy many specifications sets. Now we shall compare three different specification sets with the compliant mechanisms compared.

In Fig. 10, specification set-1 corresponds to Feasibility map in green color. Set-2 and set-3 correspond to purple and orange colored maps respectively.

Specification set-1	Specification set-2	Specification set-3
$2 \leq F_{in} \leq 2.5$ $0.005 \leq u_{in} \leq 0.007$	$2 \leq F_{in} \leq 10$ $0.005 \leq u_{in} \leq 0.007$	$1 \leq F_{in} \leq 10$ $0.05 \leq u_{in} \leq 0.07$
$0 \leq F_{out} \leq 0$ $0.01 \leq u_{out} \leq 0.014$	$0 \leq F_{out} \leq 0$ $0.009 \leq u_{out} \leq 0.01$	$0 \leq F_{out} \leq 0$ $0.1 \leq u_{out} \leq 0.14$
$0 \leq k_a \leq 10$ $0 \leq k_{ext} \leq 10$	$0 \leq k_a \leq 10$ $0 \leq k_{ext} \leq 100$	$0 \leq k_a \leq 10$ $0 \leq k_{ext} \leq 10$

Figure 10 shows the compliant mechanisms that satisfy the aforementioned specification sets. The gripper satisfies specification set 1; both the compliant mechanisms satisfy specification set 2, neither satisfies specification set 3.

4   Closure

In this paper, we combined two recent methods of designing compliant mechanisms. The first method is the feasibility map-based selection of compliant mechanisms and the second is using non-dimensional kinetoelastic maps. By extending non-dimensionalization to input and output-side stiffness parameters in the SL-model, we are able to draw the feasibility map using the non-dimensional parameters. As a result, the large-displacement behavior of compliant mechanisms in the database can also be represented in non-dimensional form as curves in the same non-dimensional feasibility map. Therefore, micro/meso/macro or any other sized compliant mechanism can be designed using the new technique presented in this paper. Two case studies are presented to illustrate the method. By having the software implementation of non-dimensional maps and corresponding non-dimensional SL parameters of more than 100 compliant mechanisms in a database, designers can easily design a compliant mechanism of any size, cross-section parameters, force, and material. Thus, the method presented in this paper has much practical utility. The notable point is that the method applies to large-displacement applications where other methods are not easily amenable or require a lot of effort from the designers.

References

1. L.L. Howell, A. Midha, Parametric deflection approximations for end-loaded, large-deflection beams in compliant mechanisms. J. Mech. Des. **117**(1), 156 (1995), https://doi.org/10.1115/1.2826101
2. M.I. Frecker, G.K. Ananthasuresh, S. Nishiwaki, N. Kikuchi, S. Kota, Topological synthesis of compliant mechanisms using multi-criteria optimization. J. Mech. Des. **119**(2), 238–245 (1997)
3. A. Saxena, G.K. Ananthasuresh, On an optimal property of compliant topologies. Struct. Multi. Optim. **19**(1), 36–49 (2000)
4. S.R. Deepak, M. Dinesh, D. Sahu, G.K. Ananthasuresh, A comparative study of the formulations and benchmark problems for the topology optimization of compliant mechanisms. ASME J. Mech. Robot. **1**(1), 20–27 (2008)
5. S. Hegde, G.K. Ananthasuresh, Design of single-input-single-output compliant mechanisms for practical applications using selection maps. J. Mech. Des. **132**(8), 081007 (2010)
6. S. Hegde, G.K. Ananthasuresh, A spring-mass-lever model, stiffness and inertia maps for single-input, single-output compliant mechanisms. Mech. Mach. Theor. **58**, 101–119 (2012)
7. C.J. Kim, Y.M. Moon, S. Kota, A building block approach to the conceptual synthesis of compliant mechanisms utilizing compliance and stiffness ellipsoids. J. Mech. Des. **130**(2) 022308 (2008)
8. G. Krishnan, C.J Kim, S. Kota, An intrinsic geometric framework for the building block synthesis of single point compliant mechanisms, J. Mech. Robot. **3**(1), 011001 (2011)
9. G. Krishnan, C.J. Kim, S. Kota, A kinetostatic formulation for load-flow visualization in compliant mechanisms. J. Mech. Robot. **5**(2), 021007 (2013)
10. G. Krishnan, C.J. Kim, S. Kota, Transmitter constraint sets: part II—a building block method for the synthesis of compliant mechanisms, in *Proceedings of 2010 ASME International Design Engineering Technical Conferences and, Computers and Information in Engineering Conferences*, ASME
11. L.L. Howell, S. Magleby, *Handbook of Compliant Mechanisms* (Wiley, 2013)
12. M.Y. Wang, A kinetoelastic formulation of compliant mechanism optimization. J. Mech. Robot. **1**(2), 021011 (2009)
13. M.F. Ashby, K. Johnson, *Materials and Design: The Art and Science of Material Selection in Product Design* (Butterworth-Heinemann, 2013)
14. R.H. Burns, F.R. Crossley, Kinetostatic synthesis of flexible link mechanisms. in *Mechanical Engineering*, vol. 90 (11. 345 E 47th St, New York, Ny 10017: ASME-AMER Soc Mechanical Eng, 1968)
15. R. Frisch-Fay, *Flexible Bars* (Butterworths, 1962)
16. S.D.B. Bhargav, H.I. Varma, G.K. Ananthasuresh, Non-dimensional kinetoelastostatic maps for compliant mechanisms, in *ASME 2013 International Design Engineering Technical Conferences and Computers and Information in Engineering Conference, Paper No. DETC*, vol. 12178 (2013)

Design Modification for Anti-choking Mechanism in Thresher Machine

Yasir Mahmood, Gowripathi Rao, Prem Singh and Himanshu Chaudhary

Abstract This paper suggests a modified thresher machine design for minimizing the problem of choking in the concave. As surveyed in the district of Dantaramgarh, Rajasthan, the major hitch faced by the farmers in employing multi-crop thresher machine is the choking of straw and chaff in concave clearance as the speed of feed is increased. As the feed is increased, the chaff aggregate increases considerably and is forced down the clearance and chokes it subsequently. To resolve the issue, a design was suggested that entailed a concave frame to hold the concave instead of being an integral part of mainframe of machine. The mechanism introduced to move the concave frame was termed as anti-choking mechanism.

Keywords Anti-choking · Offset slider crank · Multi-crop thresher · Concave frame · Concave

1 Introduction

Rajasthan is an agrarian state, where the majority of the total population resides in the rural area and largely dependent on agriculture as the source of their livelihood. The economy of the state is mostly depended on agriculture. Reducing instability in agricultural production has been a major policy concern over the years since the stability and growth in agriculture are vital for providing food and nutrition security to burgeoning population.

Y. Mahmood (✉) · G. Rao · P. Singh · H. Chaudhary
IET, GLA University, Mathura, India
e-mail: yasir.mahmood1125@gmail.com

G. Rao
e-mail: gowripathiraofmpe@gmail.com

P. Singh
e-mail: premsingh001@gmail.com

H. Chaudhary
e-mail: hchaudhary.mech@mnit.ac.in

© Springer Nature Singapore Pte Ltd. 2019
D N Badodkar and T A Dwarakanath (eds.), *Machines, Mechanism and Robotics*, Lecture Notes in Mechanical Engineering,
https://doi.org/10.1007/978-981-10-8597-0_50

585

Table 1 Availability of thresher power operated with respect to the net cultivated area [2]

Year	Thresher power operated (no./1000 ha)
1972–73	1.4631
1982–83	7.3058
1992–93	18.2630
2002–03	35.8569
2012–13	53.1709
2022–23	70.7360

1.1 Agricultural Mechanization Status in Rajasthan

Farm power availability (Power available per unit area) has increased tremendously from 0.32 kW/hac (1965–66) to 2.02 kW/hac (2013–14). In Rajasthan, there has been consistent development in adopting farm mechanization technologies for agricultural operations and use of improved high-value cash crops, which increases the farm income and productivity. Rajasthan constitutes the major tractor market in India [1].

The data available in literature was used to analyze and project the population of different agricultural machines in India [2]. The use of threshers is being projected to be increased till 2022–23. Table 1 shows availability of threshers with respect to net cultivated area. There has been a considerable increase in the use of threshers for the agricultural operations. This shows the importance of threshers used for agricultural operations among farmers.

1.2 Market Survey

The area of survey was localized to nearby cities of Jaipur such as Chomu, Sikar and Danta Ramgarh, as these regions hold a high number of agriculture equipment workshops. These workshops mainly manufacture thresher and reaper machines of different types. The workshops visited are as follows: Vishwakarma Agro Industries (Jaitpura Industrial Area, Rajasthan), Shri Vishwakarma Udyog (Jaipur Chomu Road, Jaipur, Rajasthan) and Kumawat Machine Workshop (Danta District, Rajasthan). The parameters such as clearance between threshing cylinder and concave were studied and based on which the solutions were proposed [3]. Several farmers in the nearby regions were interviewed. Proper field level working and the major problem in present multi-crop thresher machine was identified.

1.3 Thresher Machine

The agricultural operations vary according to the type of crops, rainfall and the soil condition. These operations consist of tillage process by ploughing, pulverizing and levelling the soil. Then comes the sowing of the seed followed by irrigation, spraying, harvesting and threshing. Then, the crops are prepared for the market and stored simultaneously.

Thresher is a machine which separates the food grains from the crop and provides a clean grain. The grain loss, unthreshed grain and blown grain should be minimum. According to the BIS standards, the total grain loss should not be more than 5%, and the broken grain should be less than 2% among the grain threshed.

Working: The harvested crop is kept on the belt drive which through rollers is fed to the threshing unit. This unit consists of a cylinder which has spiked teeth enclosed in a concave cylinder with a slight clearance ranging from 20 to 30 mm based on requirement and crops. The crop is rubbed in between the clearance and grain is separated without cutting the chaff. The straws separated are vacuumed outside the machine using aspirator fan while seeds fall down through the concave openings. The remains land on sieve which is shaking at high frequency using slider crank mechanism and using filter sheets unwanted materials in remaining grains are separated and the grains are collected (Fig. 1).

1.4 Choking Problem in Concave

In threshing operation, choking of concave portion is generally observed. Basically, the crop quantity is fed into the threshing drum and the separation of grain occurs through the crop beating by cylinder. Grain seeds fall down to the concave and then on to sieve for cleaning purpose. During this time the amount of crop entering the cylinder increases the chaff produced by separating grain which results in the choking of the openings of the concave as shown in Fig. 2. To solve this problem whole machine is to be stopped and through thin rods choking is to be unclogged which takes around 20–30 min. Thus to avoid this problem, farmers generally opt for slow feed rate of the crop in the threshing operation thereby decreasing the grain separation rate.

2 Materials and Methods

Madanlal Kumawat's patented design of multi-crop thresher with conveyor belt for feeding (Patent Number 253863, PG Journal Number 35/2012, Publication date 31 August 2012) was observed thoroughly in the field and dimensions were taken at their workshop. The design modifications proposed are for the same existing machine.

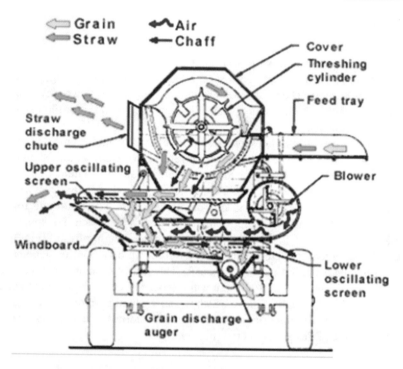

Fig. 1 Basic threshing operation (*Source* Multicrop Thresher, Balaji Engineering)

Fig. 2 Choking in thresher drum's concave

In the present machine, the crop is fed through the conveyor belt and is beaten in the threshing cylinder. As the grain seeds fall through the fixed concave, the chaff is vacuumed out the machine.

A concave frame is designed in contrast to the integrated concave of existing machines. The concave frame has bearing wheels which fitted inside the slots pro-

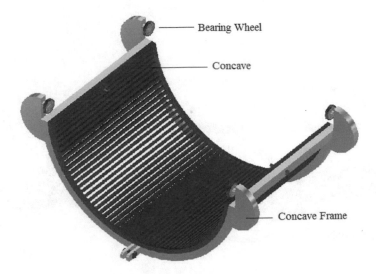

Bearing Wheel

Concave

Concave Frame

Fig. 3 Concave frame and concave

vided in the mainframe of the thresher machine. The concave is fitted inside the frame in contrast to being an integrated part of the mainframe in the existing machines.

The concave frame is free to move in horizontal line of motion along with the fitted concave inside it. The frame is made the slider of an offset slider crank mechanism through a connecting rod to crank. The crank rotated takes input from sieve crankshaft using gears. The gears used are of the same specification as the conveyor belt gearbox so as to keep maintenance still in the ease as before, i.e. easy replacement. The gear ratio is 1:1 so as to get the same angular velocity as the sieve crank hence getting the same shaking frequency as the sieve. However, the unbalanced forces have to be taken into account in further research and optimum crank rotation speed based on experimental results is to be obtained (Figs. 3 and 4).

As the speed of feed is increased from the gearbox of conveyor belt, the gear for engaging anti-choking mechanism is engaged as can be seen in Fig. 5 labelled 'Concave Gear System' thereby giving a shaking movement to the concave frame. Since the concave now shakes continuously, the chaff does not rest and hence is not pushed down the concave openings to clog it and is immediately vacuumed out the machine (Table 2).

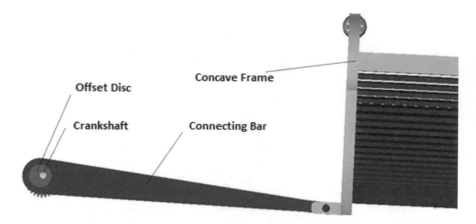

Fig. 4 Offset slider crank mechanism for shaking concave frame

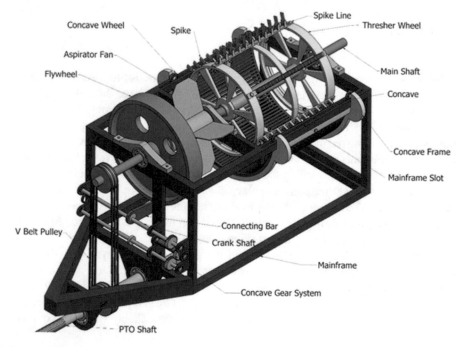

Fig. 5 Complete modified design for thresher machine

3 Analysis and Results

The whole modified thresher machine with anti-choking mechanism is designed using Autodesk Inventor 2016 based on the dimensions taken from Madanlal's workshop. The dimension for the introduced component concave frame is taken according to the existing mainframe while the concave is just added a feature for attaching it to the movable frame.

The offset in the disc is taken to be 15 mm based on the sieve stroke length of the already existing patented Madanlal's thresher; hence, the stroke length becomes 30 mm for the concave frame because the offset acts as the crank length. The shaking frequency for concave frame has been taken according to the shaking frequency of sieve, as the optimization will be experimental-based, which lies in the future scope of the work. The kinematic analysis is performed using Altair Motionview 11. The theoretical results are mapped using MATLAB, and the results are verified. The kinematic analysis includes the position, vector and acceleration analysis of concave frame with respect to time.

3.1 Theoretical Analysis

The vector loop equation for a 4 bar slider crank mechanism as used for shaking the concave frame is written with same dimensioning as our offset slider crank. The equations were given complex number notations and solved using Euler equivalents to derive a relation between crank angle 'θ' and slider position 'd'.

$$d = a cos\theta - b cos\left[sin^{-1}\left(\frac{a sin\theta - c}{b}\right)\right] \tag{1}$$

$$\dot{d} = -a\omega sin\theta + b\left\{\frac{a}{b}\frac{cos\theta}{cos\left[sin^{-1}\left(\frac{a sin\theta - c}{b}\right)\right]}\omega\right\} sin\left[sin^{-1}\left(\frac{a sin\theta - c}{b}\right)\right] \tag{2}$$

$$\ddot{d} = -a\alpha sin\theta - a\omega^2 cos\theta + b\alpha_{cr}sin\theta_{cr} + b\omega_{cr}^2 cos\theta_{cr} \tag{3}$$

a   offset of disc (15 mm)
b   connecting bar length (972 mm)
c   vertical offset of slider (46 mm)
d   horizontal distance of slider from the pivot crankshaft
θ   crank angle
ω   crank angular velocity (800 rpm)

Table 2 Parts introduced in the already existing machine

S. no.	Part name	Quantity	Mass (kg)
1	Concave frame	1	43.24
2	Bearing wheels	4	0.64
3	Bearing	1	21.67
4	Slots in mainframe	2	–

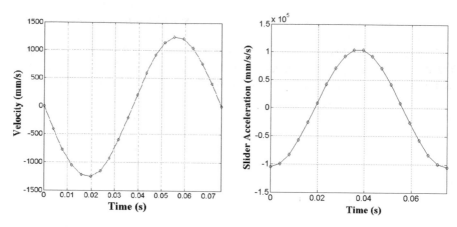

Fig. 6 Velocity and acceleration of concave frame versus time for one complete rotation

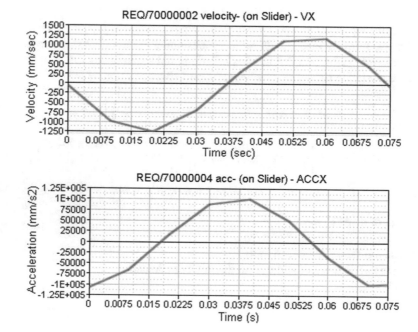

Fig. 7 Motion view results for velocity and acceleration of concave frame versus time

The above equations are coded in MATLAB and are plotted for one complete revolution of crankshaft as shown in Fig. 6.

The modified design created was exported to Altair Hyperworks and is run through Motionview 12.0 to make kinematic analysis. The results obtained were in reasonable agreement with the theoretical analysis [4] (Fig. 7).

The effect of acceleration and velocity on the choking problem will be identified in further research by developing the prototype and finding the results experimentally.

4 Conclusions

In this paper, the choking problem in multi-crop thresher machine was identified. The proposed solution is the anti-choking mechanism which with continuous shaking of concave does not let the chaff rest on the concave opening and is immediately vacuumed out. However, the results have to be verified experimentally through a prototype which is the ongoing work and has not been reflected in the paper. The calculations for optimum frequency of oscillation and life cycle will be analysed further. A kinematic analysis was performed using analytical and software simulations which match approximately.

Acknowledgements The authors are grateful to Mr. Ramanpreet Singh (Ph.D. Scholar MNIT) for his constant guidance.

References

1. S. Singh, R.S. Singh, S.P. Singh, Farm power availability on Indian farms. Agri. Eng. Today **38**(4), 44–52 (2014)
2. K.K. Tyagi, S. Jagbir; K.K. Kher, V.K. Jain, S. Surendra, *A Project Report on 'Study on Status and Projection Estimates of Agricultural Implements and Machinery'*. IASRI New Delhi (2010)
3. C.O. Osueke, Study of the influence of crop, machine and operating parameters on performance of cereal threshers. Int. J. Eng. Res. Develop. **7**(9), 01–09 (2013); H.A. Rothbart, *Cam Design Handbook: Dynamics and Accuracy*, McGraw-Hill Professional (2003)
4. Altair Hyperworks Results

Development of an Automated System for Wire Wrapping and Spot Welding of PFBR Fuel Pin

Anupam Saraswat, Prateek Pareek, Madhusudan Sharma, Farman Ali, Rajashree Dixit, P. S. Somayajulu, Sibasis Chakraborty and Vrinda Devi

Abstract In the upcoming fuel fabrication facility for Indian prototype fast breeder reactor (PFBR), automation of fuel fabrication is required to be done. Fuel pin carries spacer wire wrapped around its surface. This pin contains groove at bottom end plug for bead entanglement. Wire has to be welded on the bottom end plug. Crimping is done to restrain the tension in the wire before weld bead. The scope of this paper is to present development of an automated system required for remote handling of wire wrapping process. A prototype has been designed to simulate various processes of wire wrapping. This is an automated system for handling of pin and wire wrapping processes.

Keywords Automatic wire wrapping system · Spacer wire · PFBR fuel pin

A. Saraswat (✉) · P. Pareek · M. Sharma · F. Ali · R. Dixit · P. S. Somayajulu
S. Chakraborty · V. Devi
Radio Metallurgy Division, Bhabha Atomic Research Centre, Mumbai, India
e-mail: anupams@barc.gov.in

P. Pareek
e-mail: prateekp@barc.gov.in

M. Sharma
e-mail: mssharma@barc.gov.in

F. Ali
e-mail: farman@barc.gov.in

R. Dixit
e-mail: rajashree@barc.gov.in

P. S. Somayajulu
e-mail: somaya@barc.gov.in

S. Chakraborty
e-mail: sibasis@barc.gov.in

V. Devi
e-mail: kvvdevi@barc.gov.in

© Springer Nature Singapore Pte Ltd. 2019
D N Badodkar and T A Dwarakanath (eds.), *Machines, Mechanism and Robotics*, Lecture Notes in Mechanical Engineering,
https://doi.org/10.1007/978-981-10-8597-0_51

1 Introduction

India is pursuing a three-stage nuclear programme. In the second stage, fast breeder reactors are planned to generate electricity. Short cooled, fast reactor reprocessed fuel is expected to have high radiological activity [1]. The high amount of dose rate in the feed material necessitates remote operability and automation in the fuel fabrication facility [2].

Fuel pins for prototype fast breeder reactor (PFBR) are required to be wrapped with spacer wire. There is a provision provided in the bottom end plug of the pin to entangle the spacer wire. This spacer wire is welded to the top end plug. Spacer wire is wound on the pin with a pitch of 200 mm, which is a crucial parameter and needs to be maintained.

The scope of this paper is to present development of an automated system for remote operation of complete wire wrapping process. A prototype has been designed to simulate wire wrapping of 6–8 pins in an hour on true scale. This paper presents the design philosophy and constraints of an automated wire wrapping system.

2 Design Considerations

For a system which is required to perform in a high radiation environment, some important design considerations shall be incorporated into the design. Apart from the mechanical loadings, other design parameters listed below are very important for a foolproof design.

1. Static loads: It includes dead weights of components like moving slide system, fuel pin, structural supports and housing are considered for design load. The system is designed to handle one fuel pin at a time from 8 pins kept in a tray. The pick and place mechanism has to lift one pin at a time and place it on the wire wrapping machine. The pin is of 2580 mm in length and 6.6 mm diameter weighing close to 2 kg. This has to be rotated on the V-groove platform for wire wrapping process. A wire of the same length approximately is to be lifted from a similar tray placed adjacent to it. Automation is required to mechanize this complete process with minimum or negligible human intervention.
2. Dynamic loads: All the forces experienced by the structural elements while the system is in motion, i.e. forces required to rotate the pin or position them on the V-grooves, turning moment experienced by the pin during rotation, force applied during crimping, etc. comes under dynamic loads.
3. System shall be modular in construction. It is important that in the case of failure of any one component operator should be able to remove/repair that component without disturbing the entire system.
4. Material and components selection shall be carried out based on the high radiation background levels. Since this is a prototype, radiation resistant electronics and

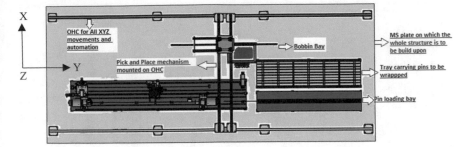

Fig. 1 Overall schematic of the wire wrapping machine

components may not be required at present. But a provision for a replacement at a later date shall be available.

5. System shall be easy to maintain. This requires maximum use of standard and uniform size components like bolts, nuts, etc. in the assembly. All the mechanisms used shall be rugged in construction.

3   System and Component Details

The main system has various subsystems which are designed for carrying out different operations in the wire wrapping of the fuel pin. These subsystems manoeuvre various parts of the pin hence require various degrees of motion. Each direction travel has been provided with an independent drive and control units. The overall dimensions of the system are 7800 mm (along Y-axis), 2870 mm (along X-axis) and 2000 mm (along Z-axis) as shown in Fig. 1. Length of the pin is 2580 mm, and various subsystems are placed around this pin. Dimension along the pin shall be identified as Y-direction for all further references. The wire feed and bend system has to travel along the complete length of the pin. Wire feed system also provides the perpendicular feed of the wire for entanglement of the bead. This dimension shall be identified as X direction for all further references. Crimping and welding system are placed below the pin area. These subsystems move up as and when required, for performing required operation. This dimension shall be identified as Z direction for all further references.

Following are the main components of the system:

3.1   Fuel Pin Tray and Wire Tray

The fuel pin tray has been designed to accommodate 8 number of fuel pins as shown in Fig. 2a. A typical fuel pin is shown in Fig. 2b. Fuel pin tray is made of stainless steel base for support and aluminium profile with V-grooves to hold fuel pins.

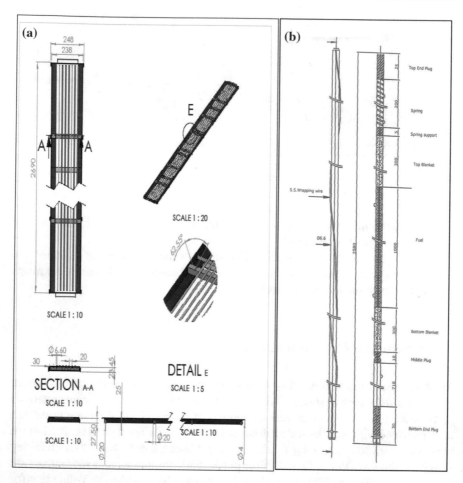

Fig. 2 **a** Fuel pin tray drawing and **b** a typical fuel pin of PFBR

Table 1 Details of the fuel pin

Material	Mild steel (mm)
Outside diameter	6.6 ± 0.02
Length of finished pin tube	2580 ± 0.5

The opening of each V-groove is slightly more than fuel pin diameter such that pin can be supported on more than half of the circumference. Sufficient distance is provided between V-grooves to allow the pins to be handled by a gripper individually. Design of pin tray has been standardized and the operator for various operations can use the same tray interchangeably. Each pin tray is provided with hooks to enable easy locking with pick and place mechanism. The pin details are provided in Table 1.

The wire tray is also similar to the pin tray in design. It is designed to hold wires required in wire wrapping process. Wire details are provided in Table 2.

Table 2 Details of wire to be wrapped around the pin

Material	Titanium modified stainless steel (mm)
Outside diameter	1.65 ± 0.02
Pitch on the pin	200 ± 1

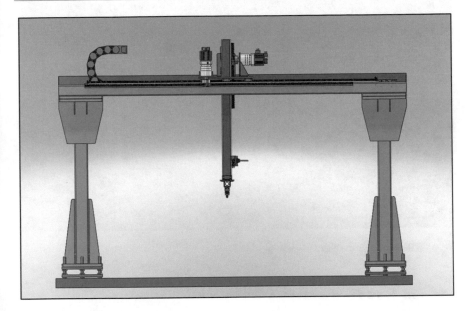

Fig. 3 Pin handling mechanism

3.2 Pin Handling System

Once pin trolley is in home position for loading of the pin on wire wrapping fixtures, the pin handling system will pick the pin from the tray and place it on V-shaped wrapping fixtures. Pin handling mechanism is shown in Fig. 3. Pick and a place mechanism have a specially designed groove to hold the pin as well as the wire from the adjacent tray. Pin handling mechanism shall move from its home position to loading position with the help of X and Z slide gantry. Then, gripper shall grip the pin in rhombus-shaped Teflon coated cavity so as to prevent scratch or dent onto the surface of the pin. Pin shall now be kept on the fixtures provided for wire wrapping process. Then, this system shall move back to home position for handling of wire. Wire comes in a tray which is placed near the pin tray and it has to be fed to the wire tensioning subsystem.

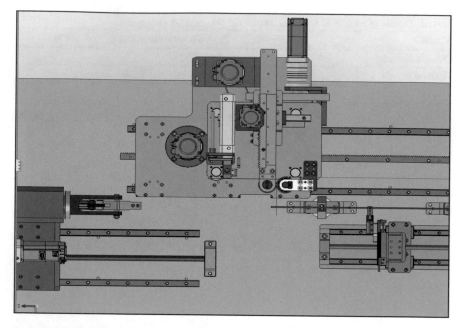

Fig. 4 Wire feed system schematic drawing

3.3 Pin Wire Feed System

Tension of the wire is an important parameter to be controlled in the wire wrapping process. Moreover, it has to be ensured that the wire is straight and does not have any permanent deformation which may lead to gap between the wire and the pin surface after the wire wrapping process. To ensure the same a wire feed subsystem has been provided to provide adequate tension and feed the wire during wire wrapping process.

Grooved wheels also help in removing any localized deformation. Wire coming out from the feed subsystem gets wound around the pin. Starting point of the wire consists of a bead which has to entangle in a groove on the pin.

Wire feed system aims at proper orientation of the wire so as to make sure the entanglement of bead in the groove. This complete system is mounted over LM Guide and ball screws and moves through the complete length of the pin. This system feeds the wire as it gets wrapped around the pin. Details of the system are given in Fig. 4.

3.4 Pin Positioning and Rotation

Once the pin is placed in the groove on the table, its start and end position needs to be detected for proper positioning of other subsystems and calculation of the pitch. Two sensors are provided, one on each end to detect the start and end position of the

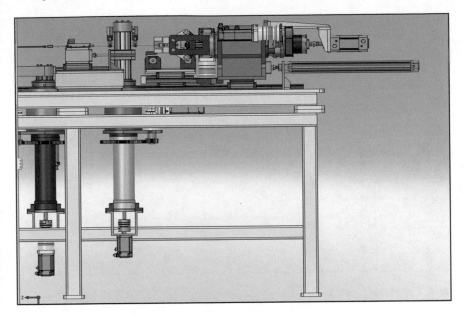

Fig. 5 Right-hand slide (RHS) pin rotation and positioning

pin. These sensors are mounted on the left-hand slide system and right-hand slide system, respectively, as shown in Fig. 5.

Left-hand slide and right-hand slide both have independent motors and gearbox. These are synchronized with a motion controller. Pin is gripped on left-hand side and rotated so as to find the degree of rotation required to bring the crimping position on the end side while rotating from the pin groove from the front side.

This helps in determining the degree of rotation required to achieve the pin crimping position while starting from bead position on the front end. The sensors attached to the two slides help in calculation of exact length of the pin. Pitch of the wire is maintained by synchronous rotation of the pin and movement of the wire feed system.

3.5 Pin Crimping System

Once the wire reaches the bottom end plug it has to be welded. Weldment requires some time to cool and gain strength. If tension is applied on the weld pool, it may lose its strength. The tension of the wire is restrained little before the welding point by crimping the wire into the pin so the wire is relaxed beyond this point.

Crimping is done by putting the wire in a cavity and applying sufficient load to cause permanent deformation of the cavity so that it holds the wire firmly and limits the tension in the wire. Wire is without tension and relaxed beyond this point.

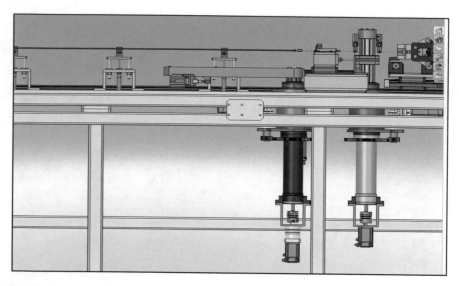

Fig. 6 Pin crimping system

Crimping force is calculated by considering tube with a mandrel. It's also taken care that it is sufficient to cause permanent deformation of the tube but at the same time does not cause any damage to the pellets inside the pin. To avoid crowding on the wire wrapping area crimping system has been placed under the wire wrapping table as shown in Fig. 6. It's provided with a lift gearbox and crimping mechanism.

After the wire is wrapped, it is actuated and lifts up. Arm of the crimping system rotates precisely as per the position of the pin provided by the sensors and reached the crimping position on the fuel pin. Hydraulic mechanism is used to make sure that force does not exceed the maximum limiting force. This is crucial in preventing damage to the pellets inside the pin.

3.6   Wire Cutting and Disposal System

Wire that comes in the wire tray has length little more than the required. After welding, some length of the wire is extra and needs to be cut before wire wrapping process is complete. This extra wire poses a problem during handling of pin in other processes.

Hence, a wire cutting system is also placed below the table and has a gear and motor attached to it for precise movement of the system when required. After the crimping process, the wire cutting system gets actuated and rises above the table. It has a scissor-like arrangement to cut the extra wire coming out of the pin. Wire cutting and disposal system is shown in Fig. 7.

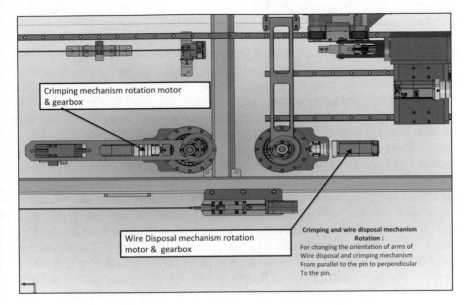

Fig. 7 Wire cutting and disposal system

3.7 Wire Welding System

Welding of the wire is done on the top end plug. This is required to hold the wire in place. Crimping is just to provide support for proper welding by eliminating tension from the wire. The aim of holding the wire on bottom plug is achieved by Welding.

Welding subsystem is placed adjacent to wire wrapping system. Pick and place mechanism lifts the pin and places it on the welding station. Since welding is a hot process as it is being achieved by spot welding so care has been taken to isolate the welding process from other processes. Welding system welds the wire onto the pin by spot welding. Here, the chuck in which the pin is held places the pin in proper orientation and recedes back to uncover the top end plug. The electrode of the spot weld has circular cross section area with diameter little more than that of wire so as to provide sufficient weld area for strong welding.

4 Operational Details

Wire wrapping system is fully automatic in operation involving multiple drives operating in a synchronized manner to perform various interlinked operations. This requires very precise manipulation and coordination between various subsystems. To achieve this motion, controller is used instead of PLC. Process is completely automated and is controlled through motion controller. System automated various processes of wire wrapping along with retrieval of pin tray and wire tray.

Once pin trolley is in home position, pin handling system moves to its position and pick and place mechanism lifts one pin from the tray and places it on the V-grooves provided on the wire wrapping machine. These V-grooves are in form of floating supports and are subdued when the wire feed system reaches close to them so as to avoid any hindrance in the wire wrapping. Once the pin is placed on these supports its exact position is sensed by the sensor provided on the positioning and rotation system. These systems are provided on either side of the pin rest area. The sensors on mounted on it provide the exact location of the pin and the length of the pin. Once the pin length is known pin is rotated to get the angular difference between the groove on bottom end plug and crimping spot on the top end plug. These two values are important for controller to maintain the required pitch of the wire to 200 mm. Pick and place mechanism meanwhile places the wire on to the wire feed mechanism, which provides the adequate tension in the wire which is 5–7 kg. This system first helps in entanglement of bead of the wire in grove on lower end plug and then it moves along the complete length of the pin. Pin is rotated in controlled manner with the help of servo motor so as to get the required pitch of 200 mm. As the wire feed system reaches the end of pin the wire is held on top of the slot provided on the top end plug. The crimping mechanism applies force on the crimping spot so as to make plastic deformation and hold the wire tightly. A cutting and dispose mechanism cuts the wire leaving behind a sufficient for welding. The cut out part is dropped into a bin attached to the system. Wire beyond the crimp spot does not have any tension. This is important to make sure proper welding and cooling of the weld bead. Welding is done by principle of spot welding on to the welding area adjacent to wire wrapping area in Y-direction. A welding arm comes up and the wire is spot welded onto the top end plug of the pin. After the welding this wire wrapping process is complete. Pick and place mechanism lifts the pin and places in another tray which takes it out for further process.

5 Control and Operator Interface

Automated operation of individual components and coordination of various components have to be done by the Motion controller. Necessary interlocks were provided to ensure safe and reliable operation of the system. All necessary operating parameters were made available at the control station. It was possible to set the necessary parameters from the control station. The controller was programmed to prompt the operator for necessary actions, whenever operator intervention is necessary. The controller has features for fault detection and diagnosis. Database of tension in the wire, pitch crimping force, etc. is to be available to the control station.

6 Conclusion

A system for automatic wire wrapping of PFBR fuel pin has been developed. This system shall be able to retrieve pin from a tray and do the complete wire wrapping process without any manual intervention. The system has all the essential features required for handling radioactive materials like modular design, parts interchangeability, etc.

References

1. G. Pandikumar, V. Gopalakrishnan, P. Moahanakrishnan, Multiple recycling of fuel in prototype fast breeder reactor. Pramana-J. Phys. **72**(5), 819–832 (2009)
2. S. Chakraborty, A. Saraswat, K. Danny, P. Somayajulu, A. Kumar, Design of MOX fuel fabrication plant for Indian PFBR, in *Proceedings of the Second International Conference on Advances in Nuclear Materials* (Mumbai, 2011)

Experiences in Process Automation of Injection Casting Equipment Inside Glove Box

M. Bala Parandhama Raju, Abhishek Kumar Yadav, R. Lava Kumar, G. Yathish Kumar, G. Nantha Kumar, N. Kathiravan, T. V. Prabhu and S. Anthonysamy

Abstract Fabrication of metallic (U-6%Zr) slugs involves melting of binary alloy under vacuum and injection casting into quartz moulds at high pressure. Injection casting system contains high vacuum, high pressure, motion control, crucible handling and glove box pressure control systems in addition to melting, preheating and cooling systems inside a glove box. Injection casting process is the primary and important operation of the metal fuel fabrication process and is in the critical path linked to productivity. It is pertinent to implement high level of automation to improve batch mode productivity, accuracy and reduce risk hazards associated with radioactivity. The technology development and process automation on fabrication of U-6%Zr binary alloy and qualification experiences are outlined in this paper. This paper deals with the experience gained in process automation of injection casting equipment, crucible lifting mechanism and its integration inside glove box which is maintained at high purity inert atmosphere.

Keywords Injection casting · Crucible lifting mechanism · Automation · Glove box · High-temperature furnace · Manufacturing · Nuclear fuels

1 Introduction

Injection casting is a well-established technique for producing fuel slugs (U-Zr) for fabrication of metallic fuel pins. Injection casting method was started in the early 1950s, and this technique was applied to fuel slug fabrication for the Experimental Breeder Reactor-II (EBR-II) driver and the Fast Flux Test Facility (FFTF) fuel pins in large numbers [1].

M. Bala Parandhama Raju · A. K. Yadav · R. Lava Kumar · G. Yathish Kumar
G. Nantha Kumar · N. Kathiravan · T. V. Prabhu (✉) · S. Anthonysamy
MC&MFCG, Indira Gandhi Centre for Atomic Research, Kalpakkam, India
e-mail: prabs@igcar.gov.in

M. Bala Parandhama Raju
e-mail: mbpraju@igcar.gov.in

© Springer Nature Singapore Pte Ltd. 2019
D N Badodkar and T A Dwarakanath (eds.), *Machines, Mechanism and Robotics*, Lecture Notes in Mechanical Engineering,
https://doi.org/10.1007/978-981-10-8597-0_52

In the metallic fuel fabrication line, fuel slugs are produced by injection casting method. Injection casting was chosen, as this method is suitable for remote operation and is capable of mass production with minimum radioactive waste generation in the glove box.

2 Injection Casting Equipment

The injection casting equipment consists of stainless steel high-temperature furnace/process chamber, dome closing mechanism, mould and chamber loading mechanism, transmission drives from servo motor, lead screw-nut mechanisms, swing mechanism, etc. Operation of C-clamps for bottom chamber and top chamber are driven by servo drives. The motors for lifting mechanism are mounted below the glove box through double rotary seals. The chamber lifting mechanism travels at a speed of 3 mm/s and the overall accuracy is ±0.5 mm. This accuracy helps in precisely dipping the quartz mould during casting.

PLC and SCADA based instrumentation controls are implemented for operation of high vacuum, high-pressure system, motion control, melting and preheating systems based on commands from user and field parameters. PLC is integrated with SCADA system on PC thereby realizing real-time interface depicting status of pumps, valves and heaters as well as values of all the field parameters mentioned above. All field parameter data are stored and trended on the PC for analysis and quality control. Batch reports collect history for points and events that occurred during the casting process production run. A SCADA MMI is used as an interface between the process operator and the injection casting system and its automation hardware.

2.1 Design and Fabrication of Casting Equipment

An engineering scale injection casting equipment of 10 kg (U-6Zr) capacity was designed and fabricated for glove box operation. The injection casting equipment is housed inside an inert atmosphere glove box in the laboratory in IGCAR. The casting process involves preparation of charge, melting of metal alloy and casting of metal alloy rod (slug). Melting of metal alloy with temperature rise up to 1500 °C is a heat-intensive process. Heating of metal takes place through induction heating process. An appearance of the injection casting apparatus is shown in Fig. 1.

A medium frequency induction heater (7 kHz, maximum power: 50 kW) was designed to meet the bulk heating requirement. The heating system heats both components of graphite crucible and charge effectively. The maximum design temperature of crucible was set to 1600 °C. Instead of directly sensing the temperature of molten alloy, the sheathed thermocouple sensor of type-B (Pt-30%Rh and Pt-6%Rh) measures temperature (up to 1700 °C) is provided at the bottom of the graphite crucible.

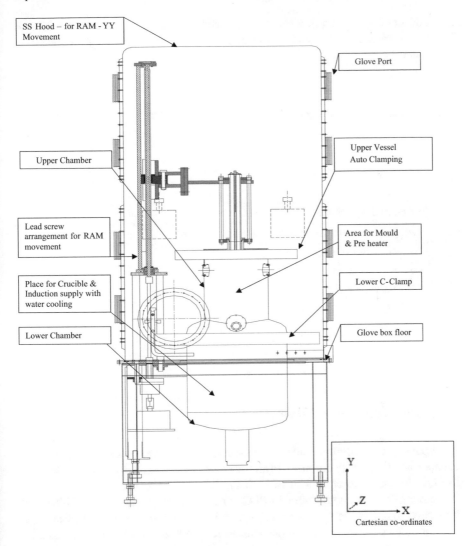

Fig. 1 Fabrication of injection casting equipment

A two-colour pyrometer is provided to measure the temperature of the molten metal through the viewport. The casting equipment is facilitated by automated chamber lifting and automated swing mechanisms which is operated by PLC panel. The vessel has double-shell structure for cooling by water to keep surface temperature below 60 °C. All components including power supply, 'Ar' gas accumulation tank, vacuum system and control panel are installed in the operating area. A PLC-based mimic control panel with SCADA system provides power, temperature control and data collection of casting process. In each batch operation, the molten fuel alloy is injected into a bundle of moulds. After de-moulding, the cut fuel slugs are taken for encapsulation.

2.2 Design Parameters for the Injection Casting Equipment

a	Susceptor crucible	Graphite 155 mm ID, 195 mm OD, 150 mm deep, and 180 mm high
b	Vacuum during melting	1×10^{-5} mbar
c	Inert gas pressure during injection casting	2 kg/cm^2
d	Design pressure of process chamber	3 kg/cm^2
e	Density of the metal alloy	18.6 g/cc
f	Temperature of molten metal alloy	1450 °C
g	Total weight	500 kg
h	Total load on glove box floor	200 kg

2.3 Automation and Control

Field parameters including vacuum, pressure, temperature, coolant flow, status of clamps (open/close), position of lifting arm, coolant flow, etc. are communicated to PLC. Temperature of coolant of each system, chambers, crucible and preheater is measured and communicated to PLC. Local operating panel is provided with indication to reflect the status of pumps, proximity sensors, position of lifting arm, coolant flow and sufficient argon pressure in accumulator tank to ease the operation of entire system [2].

PLC is integrated with SCADA system on PC thereby realizing real-time interface depicting status of pumps, valves and heaters as well as values of all the field parameters mentioned above. Interlocks are programmed in PLC by ladder logic to ensure the safe operation of the entire system. In addition, interlocks are also established to make sure that process requirements and steps are correctly executed and also minimize the erroneous operations. Safety interlocks include the following:

- Tripping heater power supplies and raising an alarm in case of coolant flow ceases or increase in coolant/chamber skin temperature or over temperature of crucible/moulds.
- Interlocks to avoid top chamber/top flange colliding with structural materials [3].

- Shutting argon supply to argon accumulator tank in case when it reaches the maximum safe value due to operator negligence and raising an alarm.
- Isolation between vacuum and high-pressure system ensured by more than one valve (isolation valve, high vacuum valve and roughing valve). This interlock prevents opening of argon inlet valve when the chamber is not isolated from vacuum system.
- Preventing connecting the chamber to vacuum line/high-pressure line when any of the clamps is not closed.
- Preventing opening of clamps when the chamber is in pressurized/evacuated condition. Realizing the argon from chamber if pressure increases beyond permissible limit.
- Preventing opening of argon inlet valve in case chamber argon pressure lesser than that of accumulator tank.

2.4 C-clamp and Its Drive Mechanism

C-clamps are used to get uniform compression of O-ring and to maintain required level of leak tightness inside the process chamber. The clamping mechanism should maintain integrity when the chamber is in vacuum or positive pressure. Bottom C-clamp is used to connect bottom and top chambers, and the top C-clamp is used to connect top chamber and cover flange. The ends of C-clamp are connected with lead screw driven by motor to facilitate closing and opening. The first half of lead screw is left-hand square thread (dia. 40 mm, 4 TPI) and the second half is right-hand square thread (dia. 40 mm, 4 TPI) of material EN-46. Groove is provided on bottom flange of connecting members to house O-ring (10 mm diameter and Viton material). The planarity of C-clamps is maintained to meet the functional tolerance.

A brushless DC geared motor drives the lead screw to clamp and de-clamp the C-clamps on to the chamber flanges. Compactness of equipment was maintained. The opening/closing speed is about 100 mm/min. The output shaft of gearhead and lead screw has timer pulley coupled by timer belt. A manual override is provided for lifting and opening/closing lead screws in case of power failure. The operating voltage of motors is chosen to operate in argon atmosphere without approaching the breakdown voltage.

3 Charge Preparation

Uranium ingots were received of diameter 12.0 and 10 mm length. Zirconium was in the form of sponge. For charge preparation, amount of zirconium was adjusted against the weight of the uranium (Figs. 2 and 3).

Fig. 2 Uranium ingots

Fig. 3 Charge in the crucible

4   Melting and Injection

For alloying of uranium with zirconium, crucible temperature was elevated to the alloying temperature around 1500 °C corresponding to the superheat by over 50–100 °C above liquidus temperature of U-6Zr alloy. After alloying operation, the vacuum system is turned 'ON' and casting was carried out automatically. The equipment was designed to operate automatically from the steps of mould descent and preheat, mould dipping into melt and injection by pressurization, holding in melt, to mould raise. The time sequences were optimized. During injection casting, a bundle of moulds descended into molten alloy and 'Ar' gas was introduced into vessel from accumulation tank by opening a solenoid valve. The pressurizing rate was measured to be 1.7 bar/s. After casting, moulds were held in the same position for few seconds (Figs. 4 and 5).

Fig. 4 Injection casting
chamber

Fig. 5 SCADA MIMIC
screen

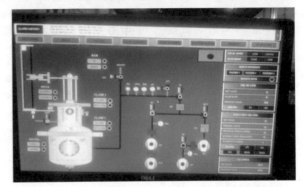

5 Crucible Lifting Mechanism

Automated crucible lifting mechanism assists in place/pick of the crucible with
charge into/from the casting chamber. It is fixed automation scheme where the
pick/place equipment executes a fixed sequence of processing or assembly operations. Each of the operations in the sequence is plain linear, rotational motion and
combination of two. It is designed with compact bases to conserve floor space and
programmed to move within strict work envelope limits. It cannot accommodate
changes in product shape and dimension. It is chain sprocket mechanism assisted
by counterweight and driven by servomotors. It is designed for an angular motion
of 130° with good accuracy and repeatability to place the crucible concentrically in
the induction coil. The end effector is suitably designed for adaptability for handling
fragile graphite crucible and the cylindrical shields. The design incorporates a taper
lock arrangement for attaining concentricity. The 'Y' motion is achieved by a tele-
scopically extendable arm with an end effector. It was demonstrated for a payload

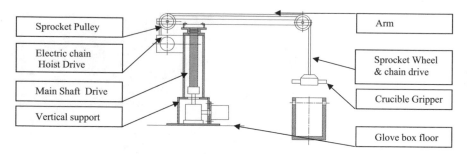

Fig. 6 Automated crucible lifting mechanism

capacity (50 kg), reach (600 mm) and repeatability of ±0.5 mm. An electrically operated parallel jaw gripper mounted with reed switches acts as end effector (Fig. 6).
Vision guided by operator assistance was tried with pan-tilt cameras mounted at different locations inside the glove box. The operator initiates the system by through
user interface to facilitate the operator to choose the target object by selecting the
object image (crucible) from database. In the object detection phase, the snapshot
of a scene is taken in real time, and then matching the objects in the current scene
image was tried. The development work towards vision guided pick-place is yet to
be standardized and is in preliminary stage.

From the various experiments, it is concluded that the approach proved effective
in terms of robustness, ability to handle and grasp the crucible firmly. The effective performance of the complete pick-place system along with the accuracy was
demonstrated.

5.1 Design Calculations for Basic Mechanisms

(a) Lifting mechanism

In the lifting mechanism, lead screw provides transfer of rotary motion to linear
motion. Standard lead screws which are precision rolled from 304 stainless steel with
a lead accuracy of 0.01 (mm/mm), positional repeatability to within 0.05 mm was
used. The design calculations were made by using standard formulas in data book.
The maximum safe column load, torque required to raise and lower, rotary to linear
driving efficiency, critical shaft speed, etc. was carried out.

The torque to move a load up the thread: $T_u = \frac{F \cdot D_p}{2}\left[\frac{L + \pi \cdot f \cdot D_p}{\pi D_p - f \cdot L}\right]$	Where F—Force to be moved D_p—Pitch diameter L—Lead of the screw f—Coefficient of friction
To check for elastic instability, Euler formula was used: $\frac{F}{A} = \frac{C \cdot \pi^2 \cdot E}{\left(\frac{b}{r}\right)^2}$	F—Total load A—Area of section E—Modulus of elasticity b/r—Slenderness ratio C—Coefficient of constraint

Fig. 7 Free body diagram of the clamp mechanism

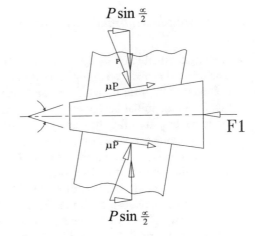

$P\sin\frac{\infty}{2}$

F1

$P\sin\frac{\infty}{2}$

(b) **Clamping mechanism**

The integrity of the chamber seal depends on the external clamping to maintain compression on the O-ring. The force per linear cm of seal circumference as a function of shore hardness and percentage squeeze was calculated. Clamping is achieved by wedge action in the form 'C' shaped clamps. The action of wedge is based on friction relations.

One side of the wedge bears against the flange and the other side is supported by a surface in the fixture.

To calculate F1, the forces P are resolved into their components with respect to the axis of the wedge as shown in Fig. 7. To withdraw a wedge that holds the flange with a pressure P requires a force F2, which was calculated as

$$F2 = -2P\ \sin\frac{\infty}{2} + 2\mu P\ \cos\frac{\infty}{2}$$
$$= 2P(-\ \sin\frac{\infty}{2} + 2\mu\ \cos\frac{\infty}{2})$$

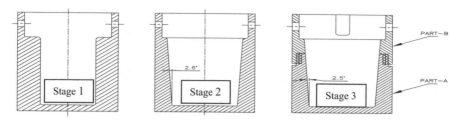

Fig. 8 Crucible developments

5.2   Crucible Modifications and Stages

- A straight crucible of 10 kg capacity of charge with 70% free space at top was machined. It is made up of high density (~1.85 g/cc) graphite where inner surface is coated with yttria to avoid carbon contamination into the charge (Stage-1 in Fig. 8). In the initial design of the crucible, the residual U-Zr ingot which is left out in the crucible after the casting was difficult to be removed.
- As the graphite was very brittle, load could not be applied to remove residual ingot from the crucible. Hence, the design of the crucible has been changed to taper of 5° from the top to bottom (Stage-2 in Fig. 8).
- This facilitated easy removal of residual U-Zr Ingot after casting. The next stage of development in design of crucible was split type crucible, which can be easily split into two parts by use thread, which is provided at the centre of the vertical surface of the crucible (Stage-3 in Fig. 8). Split of crucible is done for the ease of vacuum plasma coating on the inner surface of the crucible.

6   Trail Castings

The primary purpose of trial casting was to explore and understand various injection casting variables, e.g. casting temperature and pressure, pressurizing rate, mould preheating temperature and its coating method.

Two trial runs with U-6 wt%Zr alloy were carried out. In each trial run, 15 slugs were cast and a total of 30 slugs were cast (Fig. 9).

7   Discussion

During testing of automation system with pick up and place operation, few errors were noticed and troubleshooting was done. The occurrence of the error is because of the deviation is assembly tolerances and poor rigidity of mechanism structures. Maximum error was noticed in the rotating angle 130°. By controlling the thickness of

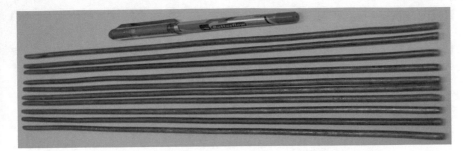

Fig. 9 Copper casted slugs

structural members, resulting stiffness (static/dynamic) was maintained. Components of the arm were designed on the basis of stiffness and stability. Thus, deflection and deformation of all components along the line of action of forces were kept minimum.

The system was fully tested in terms of hardware, software and comparing the mathematical calculation practically. After trial runs, the functional tolerances were met by operating in harsh glove box environment.

Good quality castings were produced free of internal and external defects consistently with the automation scheme.

8 Conclusions

The mechanical components, assembly, hardware, PLC/SCADA of the automation system and pick-place system was successfully designed and tested. The results of the mechanical testing of the complete system were obtained for ten cycles. Evaluation of the reach/work envelope, repeatability, manipulability and accuracy was carried out. The automation scheme was demonstrated successfully by producing qualified fuel slugs.

- Injection casting of fuel slug from metal alloy ingots has demonstrated in automated line successfully.
- The automation of graphite crucible lifting mechanism is also demonstrated and the system helped for injecting casting process. The design modification adopted in crucible has improved the process efficiency and life of crucible.

Acknowledgements The authors would like to thank Dr. M. Joseph, Director, MC&MFCG, IGCAR, Dr. S. Anthonysamy, AD, MFRG and Shri P. Muralidaran, Head, MFFD for their valuable guidance throughout the project and also would thank the whole MFFD team of IGCAR for cooperating to prepare this paper.

References

1. IGCAR Internal report no—IGCAR/ROMG/DFMF/IC/02
2. G. Yathish Kumar, J. Jagadeesh Chandran, PLC and SCADA based automation of injection casting process for casting of uranium-zirconium blanket fuel slugs for metallic fuel fabrication
3. J. Singh, M. Tiwari, M. Shrivastava, Industrial automation—a review. Int. J. Eng. Trends Technol. (IJETT) 4(8) (2013)

Degenerated Degree of Freedom Sensing Without Loss of Accuracy While Estimating the Rigid Body Parameters for the Calibration of a Two-Axis Robotic Arm for Prototype Fast Breeder Reactor, Steam Generator Inspection System

S. Joseph Winston, Joel Jose, D. Jagadishan, S. Sakthivel, P. Visweswaran, S. Murugan, G. Amarendra and P. V. Manivannan

Abstract The Prototype Fast Breeder Reactor (PFBR) has eight Steam Generators (SG), each with 547 tubes connecting top and bottom headers. The integrity of these tubes is ascertained using periodic In-Service Inspection (ISI) procedures. Two-Axis Tube Locator Module (TLM) is a robotic manipulator designed to be used to precisely locate all 547 tubes. The difference in the device work plane and the tube sheet plane is mainly due to error from tolerances in fabrication and error due

S. Joseph Winston · J. Jose (✉) · D. Jagadishan · S. Sakthivel · P. Visweswaran · S. Murugan
G. Amarendra
Indira Gandhi Centre for Atomic Research, Kalpakkam 603102, India
e-mail: joel@igcar.gov.in; joeljosej@gmail.com

S. Joseph Winston
e-mail: winston@igcar.gov.in

D. Jagadishan
e-mail: jagan@igcar.gov.in

S. Sakthivel
e-mail: ssvel@igcar.gov.in

P. Visweswaran
e-mail: visweswaran@igcar.gov.in

S. Murugan
e-mail: murugn@igcar.gov.in; murugan@igcar.gov.in

G. Amarendra
e-mail: amar@igcar.gov.in

P. V. Manivannan
Indian Institute of Technology Madras, Chennai, India
e-mail: pvm@iitm.ac.in

© Springer Nature Singapore Pte Ltd. 2019
D N Badodkar and T A Dwarakanath (eds.), *Machines, Mechanism and Robotics*, Lecture Notes in Mechanical Engineering,
https://doi.org/10.1007/978-981-10-8597-0_53

to mounting the device. These errors hinder the accurate positioning of inspection device over the tubes for inspection. In this work, a novel approach to calibrate the TLM is attempted by using motor encoder as sensors, to calibrate the TLM without using any external calibration devices. In this work, a three-point calibration is used to compute transformation matrix using two-axis motor encoder as sensors, for measuring the displaced position of calibration point tubes and using SVD on the correlation matrix formed from the original and transformed points. Even though three independent measurements (x, y, z axis) are required to spatially ascertain the positioning error of the probe with respect to calibration point tube, it proved that planar 2D measurement using readily available servo motor encoder sensors itself is adequate for the calibration of TLM without much loss of accuracies. The degenerated sensing reduces the cost, effort, and time for calibrating the TLM for use in inspection.

Keywords Steam generators · Tube locator module · SVD · Degenerated sensing · Robot calibration · Error estimation

1 Introduction

In the Steam Generator (SG) used in Prototype Fast Breeder Reactor (PFBR), the integrity of water/steam tubes that connect top and bottom headers of SG is to be ascertained periodically, as per In-Service Inspection (ISI) procedures; since sodium flows in the shell side and water/steam in the tube side. It is mandatory to perform the Pre-Service Inspection (PSI) to qualify the SG for operation. A Remote Field Eddy Current (RFEC) type sensor is generally used for the inspection of the tubes, as the SG tubes are made of ferromagnetic material. Figure 1 shows the typical PFBR SG. The inspection device for PFBR SG has a Tube Locator Module (TLM), with two-axis robotic arm to precisely locate all 547 tubes for pushing the RFEC probe through 23 m length of the SG tube through the expansion bends up to the bottom raised spigot weld for inspection. Damped Least Squares (DLS) Inverse Kinematics (IK) algorithm has been developed and implemented in the motion controller for the two-axis manipulator [1]. When the device is placed on the manhole of SG and deployed into the header, the two-axis manipulator is deployed to work just above the tube sheet for a planar reach orienting to the tubes distinctly. Figure 2 shows the difference in the device work plane and the tube sheet plane which is due to error from tolerances in fabrication, deviant orientation of the device while mounting on the SG manhole. The precise reach of tubes is often limited due to these errors introduced during device deployment and fabrication. This has bearing on the accurate positioning of the inspection probe to be pushed on the desired tube. Manually reorienting the device is time consuming and may result in introducing further errors.

This paper details the use of a novel technique using the joint axis motor encoders as sensors for the estimation of the errors between tube sheet plane and the robotic

Fig. 1 Steam generator

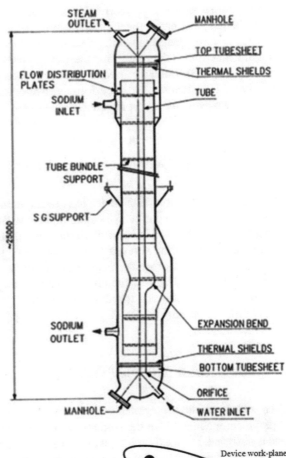

Fig. 2 Device plane and tube sheet reference path

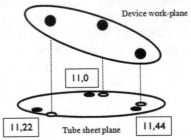

arm workspace plane (2D). Generally, the z axis movement (i.e., tube sheet to manipulator arm distance) is sensed by a range sensor and is used along with motor encoder data for spatial sensing of errors between the tube sheet and manipulator. However, in this work, it is proved that neglecting the z measurement does not affect the calibration which is estimating the rigid body parameters. This leads to only insignificant reduction in accuracy, even in the absence of the third dimension data which comes from the range sensor. Error correction method has been simulated using python coding language in detail for the degenerated degree of sensing and a calibration test setup is developed and used to prove that degenerated degree of sensing induces insignificant errors in the system and these errors are well within the tolerable limits. The proposed methodology is used in the manipulator calibration for the eight steam generators in PFBR and found to perform with reasonably very good accuracies. The degeneracy reduces the cost, effort and time of tube inspections.

2 PFBR Steam Generator Inspection System (PSGIS)

The comprehensive inspection device has several modules performing various tasks such as device deployment, tube locating and cable pushing, etc. For the successful inspection, it is mandated to identify all the tubes uniquely and point to point move from tube to tube in the shortest path. Tubes have to be designated with unique numbering scheme to store the inspection results against each tube and used for comparing the RFEC signatures in the subsequent inspection campaigns. The Tube Locator Module (TLM) is a two-axis robotic manipulator which orients to all 547 tubes of SG for pushing the RFEC probe or visual probe for inspection.

3 Tube Locator Module (TLM)

Tube locator module integrates the cable pusher module and is fitted inside the deployment module. Since the workspace is planar in nature a selective complaint arm is designed. It is used for uniquely identifying the tube to be inspected by means of kinematic movement of its axes with the help of inverse kinematic algorithm developed and implemented in this research work. Figure 3 shows the actual TLM, and Fig. 4 shows the TLM reach configuration simulated respectively. Tubes in the SG are arranged in a hexagonal pattern increasing in row from 0 to 14 as shown in Fig. 4. Each tube is uniquely addressed by (n, h) numbering scheme where n represents the row and h represents the position of the tube in that row. Each row has 6 * n possible location for the tubes to be placed. Polar and Cartesian coordinates of tubes are obtained using Eqs. 1 and 2. Tube pitch (i.e., "a" in Eq. 1) is 32.2 mm for PFBR tube sheet.

$$(r, \theta) = \left(a\sqrt{n^2 + h^2 - nh}, \ \cos^{-1}\left(\frac{a(2n - h)}{2r} \right) \right) \tag{1}$$

$$\begin{bmatrix} x \\ y \end{bmatrix} = \begin{pmatrix} r \cos \theta \\ r \sin \theta \end{pmatrix} \tag{2}$$

Fig. 3 Tube locator module (TLM)

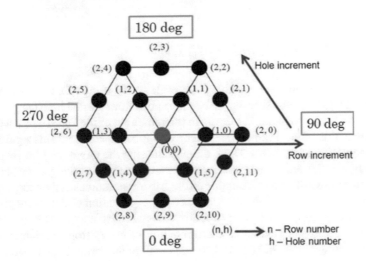

Fig. 4 SG tube ordering scheme

The geometrical shape of TLM is designed to have the manipulator arm fit inside the deployment module which is placed into the manhole at the top header of the SG from where the system is deployed into the header.

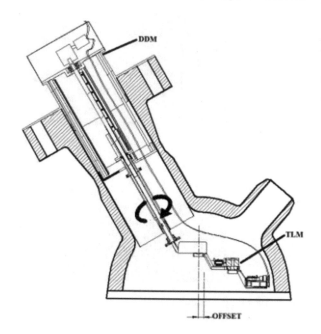

3.1 Three-Point Calibration of TLM

TLM is inserted through the manhole at an angle of 60° using a Device Deployment Module (DDM). The tube sheet has to be referenced from the manhole flange surface where the DDM is mounted. The errors in the mounting of the DDM cause a change in the orientation of the TLM with respect to the tube sheet plane. This significantly affects the performance of the TLM, thereby missing the target tube for inspection which is by rotation and translation errors as shown in Fig. 5 and Fig. 6, respectively. These errors as such are not measurable through external sources as the access into the manhole is limited to the device only. Hence the exploitation of the motor encoders which are generally present in any robotic two-axis systems to easily accomplish without any additional devices. The culmination of errors from the fabrication as well as mounting of the DDM and TLM can result in the form of combined rotation as well as translation errors which are nonlinear.

3.2 Methodology for Calibration of TLM

The two axes of TLM by virtue of interconnected rigid bodies will trace all the coordinates in its workspace which is a plane. Hence, tube sheet coordinate points always will get transformed respecting the rigid body transformation. Converse to the transformation of a set of tube sheet points to device workspace points by trans-

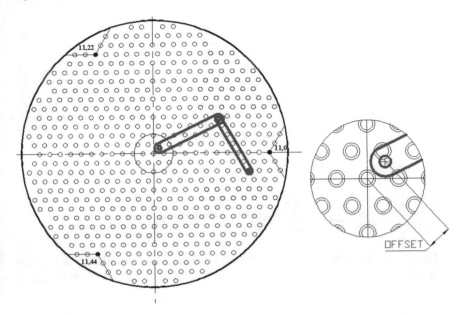

Fig. 6 Translational error

formation matrix; one has to deduce the transformation matrix from the actual tube sheet points to the device workspace points considering the rigid body transformation. Three calibration points which are easily identifiable from the tube sheet through vision sensors have been used to compute the actual transformation that exists between the coordinate center of tube sheet and device work plane in terms of base offsets in X and Y direction as well as three rotations that exist between tube sheet plane and device work plane. The error vectors on the three calibration points are measured by jogging the motors on forward kinematic moves to orient the RFEC probe on the manipulator arm to align the calibration point tubes. The difference in the angle generated from IK solution after jogging gives the differential angle which represents the error vectors. These error vectors are computed through finding the new end effector point through the forward kinematics using the differential angles obtained after manual jogging and correcting the errors to orient the tube.

Let us assume the set of coordinate points from the tube sheet selected for the calibration be {mi}. The transformed set of {mi} points is denoted as {di} which is after the error measurement. **R** and **T** are the rotation and translation matrices that transformed {mi} points to {di}. Solving the optimal transformation that maps the set {mi} onto {di} requires minimizing a least squares error criterion [2] provides the final transformation matrix (M) and will be used to transform all 547 tube center in the tube sheet before running the inverse kinematic algorithm to reach tube centers.

$$\sum{}^2 = \sum_{i=1}^{N} \|di - Rmi - T\|^2 \qquad (3)$$

$$\bar{d} = \frac{1}{N} \sum_{i=1}^{N} di \tag{4}$$

$$d_{ci} = di - \bar{d} \tag{5}$$

$$\bar{m} = \frac{1}{N} \sum_{i=1}^{N} mi \tag{6}$$

$$m_{ci} = mi - \bar{m} \tag{7}$$

Equation 3 can be rewritten as

$$\sum{}^2 = \sum_{i=1}^{N} (d_{ci}^T d_{ci} + m_{ci}^T m_{ci} - 2d_{ci}^T R m_{ci}) \tag{8}$$

This equation is minimized when the term $2d_{ci}^T R m_{ci}$ is maximized which is equivalent to maximizing trace (RH), where H is a correlation matrix which is defined by;

$$H = \sum_{i=1}^{N} m_{ci} d_{ci}^T \tag{9}$$

If the singular value decomposition of H is given by $H = U \sum V^T$, then the optimal rotation matrix, **R** that maximizes the desired trace [3] is;

$$R = VU^T \tag{10}$$

In order to correct the rotation matrix on some case which represents reflection rather than rotation as suggested by Umeyama [2] and Kanatani [4], the rotation may be computed as

$$R = U \begin{pmatrix} 1 & 0 & 0 \\ 0 & 1 & 0 \\ 0 & 0 & \det(UV^T) \end{pmatrix} V^T \tag{11}$$

The optimal translation can be now deduced as follows:

$$T = \bar{d} - R\bar{m} \tag{12}$$

$$M = TR \tag{13}$$

The transformation matrix (M) as in Eq. 13 corrects the error for the entire tube sheet for precise reach [5]. The dimension of M matrix is 4×4.

4   Three-Point Calibration with Degenerated Sensing

The spatial estimation of the transformed points due to errors in the device requires a range sensor to supplement the encoder data for a spatial three degree of freedom sensing of the transformed location in three coordinate axes. However, a considerable advantage will be derived if the third axis sensing is removed and the sensing is degenerated to only two axes. The SG tube ID is 12.6 mm and tube pitch is 32.2 mm. Any error more than 16.1 mm in magnitude will result in wrong tube orientation by the device. Maximum fabrication tolerance for the manhole is $\pm 1°$. For the conservative side, simulation has been carried out up to $5°$, and error is considered to be insignificant if its magnitude is less than 3 mm absolute for any tubes. The deformed points [x', y', z'] are given by multiplying M with original points [x, y, z] in the workspace.

$$
\begin{bmatrix} x' \\ y' \\ z' \\ 1 \end{bmatrix} = [M] * \begin{bmatrix} x \\ y \\ z \\ 1 \end{bmatrix}
\tag{14}
$$

M_{act} represents the transformation matrix with sensing all three axes, and M_{deg} represents the transformation matrix with degenerated sensing (without measuring the height using range sensor, in z axis). In both cases, x and y axes deviations in the plane are measured using axes encoder as sensors. In this, the error induced in the x and y axis is only taken as the net error as device is kept at a conservative height to avoid any inference of the probe with tube sheet which is due to variation of z axes and probe is inserted in an orthogonal manner after calibration.

Actual transformation is given by multiplying each point with M_{act} and is given by

$$
\begin{bmatrix} x' \\ y' \\ z' \\ 1 \end{bmatrix} = [M_{act}] * \begin{bmatrix} x \\ y \\ z \\ 1 \end{bmatrix}
\tag{15}
$$

Transformation of tube using the degenerated sensing is given by multiplying each point with M_{deg} and is given by

$$
\begin{bmatrix} x'' \\ y'' \\ z'' \\ 1 \end{bmatrix} = [M_{deg}] * \begin{bmatrix} x \\ y \\ z \\ 1 \end{bmatrix}
\tag{16}
$$

The error induced due to degeneration is given by

$$\begin{bmatrix} e_x \\ e_y \\ e_z \end{bmatrix} = \begin{bmatrix} x' - x'' \\ y' - y'' \\ z' - z'' \end{bmatrix} \tag{17}$$

Error magnitude as a result of degeneration is given by

$$e_{mag} = \sqrt{e_x^2 + e_y^2} \tag{18}$$

The Z axis is not required for orientation to a point on a 2D plane. However, the Z data only gives the tube sheet plane to device work plane gap.

4.1 Error Magnitude with Tilt in X and Y Axis

Max error limit is set to 3 mm for a tube of 12.6 mm ID and cut off limit for missing the tube is 16.1 mm. In simulation M_{deg} is calculated for each degree of tilt using python code and highest error magnitude among 547 tubes is calculated in each iteration of tilt angle and is plotted. It is observed that in the range of 0°–5° error induced by degenerative method is within the tolerance limits (<3 mm). Tilt in X and Y tilt is calculated by considering the uniform tilt in each axis as shown in Fig. 7 and Fig. 8, respectively. Figure 9 shows the error induced due to uniform tilt in X and Y.

Fig. 7 Error versus X tilt

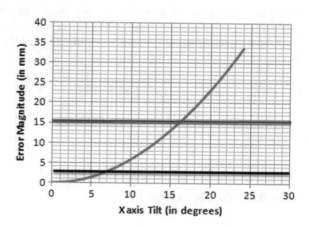

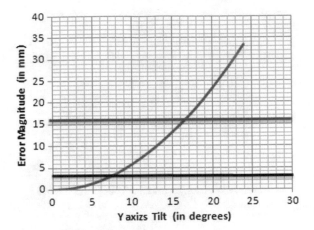

Fig. 8 Error versus Y tilt

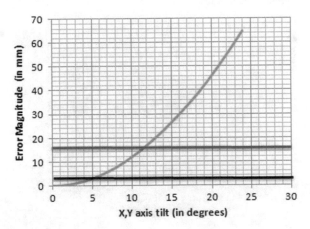

Fig. 9 Error versus X, Y tilt

4.2 *Error Distribution for Degenerated Sensing*

Surface plots are generated for X, Y, and Z axis considering the max tilt of 5°. In the combined X, Y tilt uniform tilt in X and Y is considered.

4.2.1 Error Due to Tilt of X Axis and Y Axis

It is observed in Fig. 10 that error is increasing in a linear fashion in the Y axis and minimum along the X axis for a tilt about X axis for 5° and max error magnitude is 1.5 mm which is well within the tolerance limits. Figure 11 shows that error is increasing in a linear fashion in the X axis and minimum along the Y axis for a tilt

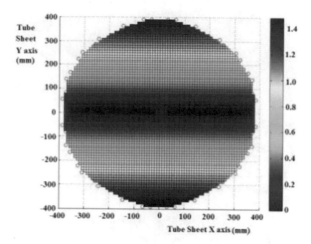

Fig. 10 Error distribution due to X tilt

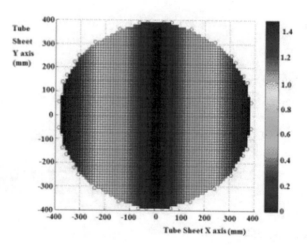

Fig. 11 Error distribution due to Y tilt

about Y axis for 5° and max error magnitude is 1.5 mm which is well within the tolerance limits.

4.2.2 Error Due to Tilt of XY Axis and Rotation of Z Axis

In XY case, error is minimum in the axis which passes through origin at 45° and error is increasing in a linear fashion along the perpendicular axis and max error magnitude is 3.0 mm as shown in Fig. 12. No error is induced due to Z rotation (on XY plane) as shown in Fig. 13 as there is no loss of accuracy due to Z axis rotation.

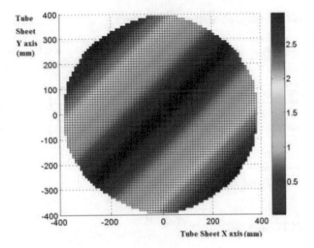

Fig. 12 Error distribution due to XY tilt

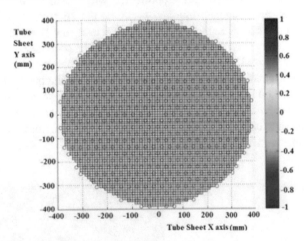

Fig. 13 Errror distribution due to Z axis rotation

Table 1 shows clearly that error details in the calibration tube points in the 11th row. The maximum error induced due to X and Y axis tilt of 5° is 0.4329 mm which is very insignificant for a tube ID of 12.6 mm. The error percentage corresponding to radial vector of each point and a maximum value of 0.1222% is obtained. These numbers clearly indicate that the error induced due to degenerated sensing is insignificant and will not affect the accuracy in tube inspection.

Table 1 Error induced in the calibration tube points due to X an Y tilt 5° each due to degenerated sensing

Row no.	Hole no.	Error x (Δx)	Error y (Δy)	Resultant error (e_r)	Error percentage (% e_r)
11	0	−0.2125	0.2123	0.3004	0.0848
11	11	0.0778	−0.1087	0.1337	0.0377
11	22	0.2903	−0.3212	0.4329	0.1222
11	33	0.2125	−0.2127	0.3007	0.0849
11	44	−0.0778	0.1083	0.1333	0.0376
11	55	−0.2903	0.3208	0.4327	0.1221

5 Implementation

A Raspberry pi system with python is connected wireless to the motion controller to acquire the real-time encoder data and populate the {di} set of points after the jogging of the motors correcting the errors manually using a vision system. Figure 14 and Fig. 15 shows the TLM calibration and test setup respectively.

This degenerated sensing scheme has been applied on the procedure of calibration of the manipulator on all the steam generators of PFBR during preservice inspection campaign and verified that error induced due to degenerated sensing is insignificant and successfully completed the campaign by means of inspecting all 547 tubes of SG without loss of accuracy. Figures 16 and 17 show the transformation matrix and deviation of tubes derived for all SGs.

Fig. 14 TLM calibration

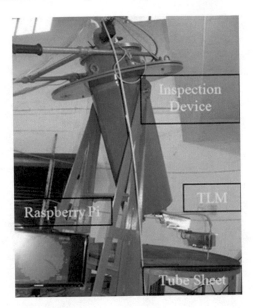

Fig. 15 Test setup

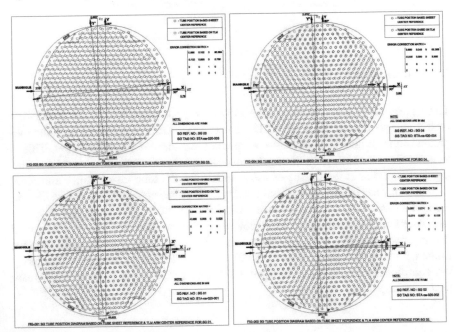

Fig. 16 SG01 to SG04 net deviation

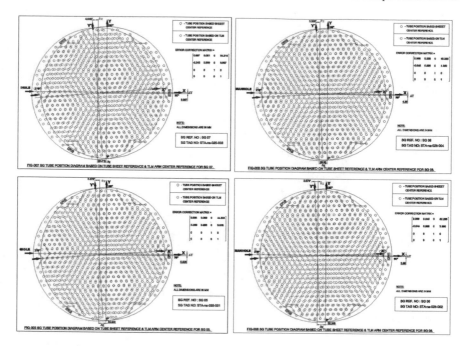

Fig. 17 SG05 to SG08 net deviation

6 Conclusion

Three point calibration scheme using SVD decomposition [6–8] of the correlation matrix was proposed in this paper. The correlation matrix is obtained from the theoretical tube centers to the measured deviated position of the tube center. This is used for the error correction during the inspection. These errors are unavoidable during the mounting of the device on the manhole for SG tube inspection. Calibration methodology has been enhanced with degenerative sensing by avoiding the measurement in the third axis. This is achieved using readily available servo motor encoders (shoulder and elbow actuators) in the device itself. It has been simulated and verified that error induced due to degenerative sensing is linear and is within the tolerance limits with very little effect on the overall accuracy. This degenerative methodology has significantly reduced the cost, time and effort during the inspection of steam generator inspection campaign.

References

1. S.R. Ross, Introduction to inverse kinematics with jacobian transpose, pseudoinverse and damped least squares method (Department of Mathematics, University of California, San Diego, 7 Oct 2009)
2. S. Umeyama, Least squares estimation of transformation parameters between two point patterns. IEEE Trans. Pattern Anal. Mach. Intell. **13**, 376–380 (1991)
3. J.H. Challis, A procedure for determining rigid body transformation parameters. Biomechanics **28**, 733–737
4. K. Kanatani, Analysis of 3-D rotation fitting. IEEE Trans. Pattern Anal. Mach. Intell. **16**, 543–549 (1994)
5. S. Joseph Winston, J. Jose, A. Subramaniyan, S. Murugan, A.K. Bhaduri, Rigid body transformations for calibration of prototype fast breeder reactor, steam generator inspection device, in *Advancement is Automation, Robotics and Sensing, Springer, Communications in Computer and Information Science Book Series* (CCIS, vol. 627), pp. 23–40
6. D. Kalman, A singular value decomposition: the SVD of a matrix (The American University, Washington DC 20016, 13 February 2002)
7. S. Wei, Z, Lin, Accelerating iterations involving eigenvalue or singular value decomposition by block Lanczos with warm start. Microsoft Technical Report#MS-TR_2010-162
8. G.H. Goloub, C.F. Van Loan, *Matrix Computations* (The John Hopkins University Press, Baltimore, London, 1996), pp. 448–460

Quintic Interpolation Joint Trajectory for the Path Planning of a Serial Two-Axis Robotic Arm for PFBR Steam Generator Inspection

G. Perumalsamy, P. Visweswaran, Joel Jose, S. Joseph Winston
and S. Murugan

Abstract Prototype Fast Breeder Reactor (PFBR) has eight Steam Generators (SGs). Inspection of SGs requires a remote tooling to reach the probe pusher module to each of the 547 tubes present. Since the tube sheet reach has a planar workspace, a two-axis Selective Compliant Assembly Robotic Arm (SCARA) type of manipulator suits well. However, the geometry and size of the manipulator are based on the workspace and space constraints which are very well represented in the kinematic studies through the DH parameters. However, the position or velocity inverse kinematics solution for the tube to tube movement results in discrete position or velocity points. So for precision movements with good control on speed and position, we prefer position and velocity-based moves through the motion controller. In order to maintain continuity on accelerations and jerks while controlling velocity points require a choice of higher order polynomial. This paper presents the quintic interpolation method (quintic polynomial trajectory) for planning a joint trajectory of two-axis robotic arm. The quintic interpolation and the case study of PFBR steam generator inspection are presented. The quintic interpolation ensures the continuity of displacement, velocity and acceleration for the planned motion of joint trajectory of two-axis robotic arm.

Keywords Joint trajectory planning · Quintic polynomial · Steam generator inspection · Trajectory generation · Jerk

G. Perumalsamy (✉) · P. Visweswaran · J. Jose · S. Joseph Winston · S. Murugan
Indira Gandhi Centre for Atomic Research, Kalpakkam 603102, India
e-mail: psamy@igcar.gov.in; perumalsamy2012mdes@gmail.com

P. Visweswaran
e-mail: visweswaran@igcar.gov.in

J. Jose
e-mail: joel@igcar.gov.in

S. Joseph Winston
e-mail: winston@igcar.gov.in

S. Murugan
e-mail: murugan@igcar.gov.in; murugn@igcar.gov.in

© Springer Nature Singapore Pte Ltd. 2019
D N Badodkar and T A Dwarakanath (eds.), *Machines, Mechanism and Robotics*, Lecture Notes in Mechanical Engineering,
https://doi.org/10.1007/978-981-10-8597-0_54

637

1 Introduction

The PFBR Steam Generator Inspection System (PSGIS) has been designed and developed at IGCAR to carry out the pre-service and in-service inspection of the eight installed PFBR steam generators. PFBR Steam generator has 547 tubes connecting the top and the bottom headers. Liquid Sodium is flowing outside the tube, whereas high-pressure de-mineralized water is flowing inside the tube. For maximum reachable workspace condition, 2R (Revolute) Planar robotic arm is used. In the PSGIS device, the tube locator module uses a two-axis serial robotic arm for the precise movement of the end effector and distinctly orients to 547 Steam generator tubes for pushing the Remote Field Eddy Current (RFEC) probe into the tubes for inspection. Inverse kinematic algorithm linearizes the non-linear Cartesian space move to the joint space through the Jacobian matrix. Thus, any computational step in two consecutive estimates of the joint space parameter results in a discontinuity which needs to be resolved by means of interpolation. As the two-axis serial robotic arm requires a end effector Cartesian space linear velocity should be constant at 20 mm/s, the joint space needs to be controlled as a two closed-loop control system with velocity in the inner loop and position in the outer loop.

2 Description of the Two-Axis Manipulator and Kinematics

Tube Locator Module (TLM) is a two-axis robotic arm used for precisely locating SG tubes in the steam generator. TLM is an R-R type manipulator and uses IK algorithm for precisely reaching the end effector to the selected tube. The shoulder and elbow axes of TLM have to move in a synchronous manner to reach the selected tube in the shortest distance (Fig. 1).

2.1 Forward Kinematics

The position and orientation of robotic end effector knowing the arm length and joint angle can be determined by forward kinematics.

The relationship between end effector position (X, Y) of the two-axis robotic arm (Fig. 2) of link length $(L_1$ and $L_2)$ and angular position $(\theta_1$ and $\theta_2)$ is given by [1]

$$X = L_1 \cos(\theta_1) + L_2 \cos(\theta_1 + \theta_2) \tag{1}$$

$$Y = L_1 \sin(\theta_1) + L_2 \sin(\theta_1 + \theta_2) \tag{2}$$

Fig. 1 Two-axis robotic arm
tube locator module

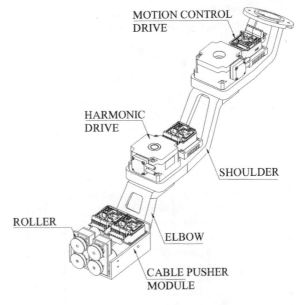

Fig. 2 Schematic
representation of 2R axis
robotic arm of steam
generator inspection

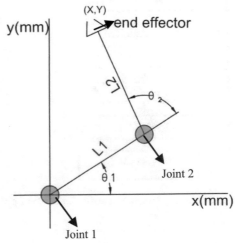

2.2 Inverse Kinematics

The joint angle of robotic arm knowing the robotic end effector position and orientation can be determined by Eq. (3)

$$\Delta\theta = J^{-1}\Delta e \tag{3}$$

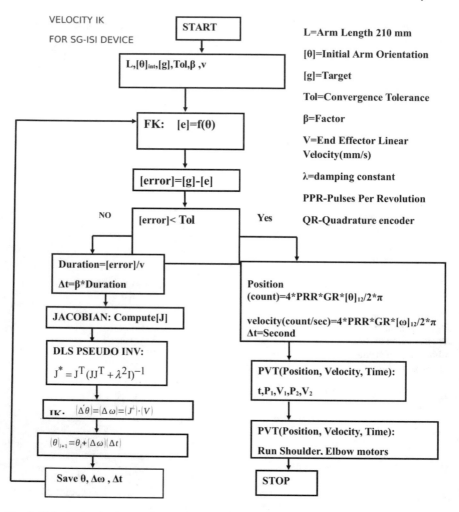

Fig. 3 Velocity inverse kinematics for SG-ISI DEVICE

The end effector position is mapped to joint coordinates by Jacobian matrix (J) [2] as given by Eq. (4)

$$J = \begin{bmatrix} -L_1 \sin(\theta_1) - L_2 \sin(\theta_1 + \theta_2) & -L_2 \sin(\theta_1 + \theta_2) \\ L_1 \cos(\theta_1) + L_2 \cos(\theta_1 + \theta_2) & L_2 \cos(\theta_1 + \theta_2) \end{bmatrix} \tag{4}$$

$$\begin{bmatrix} \Delta\theta_1 \\ \Delta\theta_2 \end{bmatrix} = \begin{bmatrix} -L_1 \sin(\theta_1) - L_2 \sin(\theta_1 + \theta_2) & -L_2 \sin(\theta_1 + \theta_2) \\ L_1 \cos(\theta_1) + L_2 \cos(\theta_1 + \theta_2) & L_2 \cos(\theta_1 + \theta_2) \end{bmatrix}^{-1} \begin{bmatrix} \Delta x \\ \Delta y \end{bmatrix} \tag{5}$$

The inverse kinematics algorithm is shown in Fig. 3.

Table 1 Boundary conditions for different splines

Boundary conditions	First derivative	Second derivative	Third derivative
Natural spline	–	$\theta''(t = t_s) = 0$ $\theta''(t = t_f) = 0$	–
Clamped spline	$\theta'(t = t_s) = \theta'_s$ $\theta'(t = t_f) = \theta'_f$	–	–
Not-a-knot spline		–	$\theta'''_i(t = t_i) = \theta'''_{i+1}(t = 0)$

IK solution is at discrete time steps and hence while running the motion controller requires a proper trajectory planning or else undesirable effects as that of motor trips would happen due to discontinuities in accelerations and jerks. This also induces a lot of dynamic forces on the arm and lead to oscillations or deviations from the desired path.

3 Trajectory Planning

The trajectory planning is normally carried out in the joint space of the robot, after a kinematic inversion of the given geometric path. The joint trajectories are then obtained by means of interpolating functions which meet the imposed kinematic and dynamic constraints.

Planning a trajectory in the joint space rather than in the operating space has an advantage that the control system acts on the robot's joints rather than on the end effector, so it would be easier to adjust the trajectory according to the design requirements if working in the joint space. Trajectory generation in the joint space would allow to avoid the problems arising with kinematic singularities.

The trajectory generation must fulfil the constraint set on the maximum values of the generalized joint torques and must be such that no mechanical resonance mode is excited. This can be achieved by smooth trajectories (continuity in position, velocity and acceleration). The joint variables as that of position, velocity, acceleration, etc. must be a continuous function of time and also smooth.

Piecewise cubic polynomial (third order) will provide continuous position and velocity and zero velocity at the start and end [3]. The acceleration is not zero at the start and end point, this will produce jerk at the starting and ending [2, 4]. The discontinuous acceleration in cubic polynomial can be avoided by fifth-order polynomial.

Depending upon the start and end point boundary conditions, cubic spline (piecewise cubic polynomial) are classified into natural, clamped and not-a-knot spline. The boundary conditions are shown in Table 1.

3.1 Joint Space Trajectory Interpolation

The smoothness of trajectories in joint space, which directly affects the stability of the output torque of actuators, is vital in trajectory planning. Quintic interpolation profile is characterized by good smoothness.

The quintic polynomial in Eq. (6) used for planning joint axis trajectory movement for two-axis robotic arm [5]. It is the lowest degree polynomial for which velocity and acceleration profile is continuous and smooth. The disadvantage of quintic interpolation is more deviation from the actual profile between the interpolated points. This can be rectified by increasing the number of sampling points. The two-axis serial robotic arm joint position, velocity, acceleration and jerk for one segment in a time interval t are given by Eq. (6)

$$\theta(t) = a_0 + a_1 t + a_2 t^2 + a_3 t^3 + a_4 t^4 + a_5 t^5$$

$$\dot{\theta}(t) = a_1 + 2a_2 t + 3a_3 t^2 + 4a_4 t^3 + 5a_5 t^4$$

$$\ddot{\theta}(t) = 2a_2 + 6a_3 t + 12a_4 t^2 + 20a_3 t^3$$

$$\dddot{\theta}(t) = 6a_3 + 24a_4 t + 60a_3 t^2 \qquad (6)$$

where $a_0, a_1, a_2, a_3, a_4, a_5$ are polynomial coefficients, and t is the time of motion.

4 Simulation Result

Two-axis serial robotic arm end effector straight line path from tube location $(11, 0)$ to $(11, 8)$ in Fig. 4 can be achieved by intermediate points $P_1, P_2, P_3, P_4, P_5, P_6, P_7$ [6, 7]. These start $(11, 0)$ and end $(11, 8)$ and intermediate points can be mapped to joint angles by inverse kinematics. The intermediate points are selected in such a way that tracking error is less. More the number of intermediate points, lesser the deviation (Fig. 5).

The discrete joint angles for the joint 1 (θ_1) and joint 2 (θ_2) of a two-link serial robotic arm are given in Table 2.

The piecewise polynomial is being used to interpolate two points. To interpolate 9 points 8 segments are used. Piecewise polynomial is joined by continuity condition.

θ_{1cd} represents polynomial for joint 1 with initial interval point c and final point d.

The eight segment polynomial for joint 1 and joint 2 is given by Eq. (7)

Fig. 4 Two-link robotic arm end effector movement from (11, 0) to (11, 8)

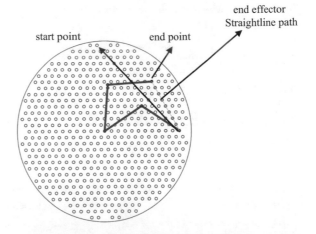

start point   end point   end effector Straightline path

Fig. 5 Experimental setup of two-link robotic arm

Table 2 Joint angles of two-link robotic arm for a straight line path (11, 0) to (11, 8)

Tube no.	(11, 0)	P1	P2	P3	P4	P5	P6	P7	(11, 8)
x	354.36	338.26	322.17	306.07	289.98	273.9	257.8	241.7	225.6
y	0	27.81	55.69	83.58	111.46	139.3	167.22	195.1	222.9
Theta 1 (θ_1)	32.48	40.81	48.71	56.24	63.35	69.97	75.99	81.26	85.66
Theta 2 (θ_2)	−64.97	−72.21	−77.8	−81.92	−84.63	−85.99	−86.00	−84.65	−81.95

$$\theta_{1(11,0)P1}(t) = a_0 + a_1 t + a_2 t^2 + a_3 t^3 + a_4 t^4 + a_5 t^5$$
$$t_1 \leq t \leq t_2[(11,0) \to (P1)]$$

$$\theta_{2(11,0)P1}(t) = b_0 + b_1 t + b_2 t^2 + b_3 t^3 + b_4 t^4 + b_5 t^5$$
$$t_1 \leq t \leq t_2[(11,0) \to (P1)]$$

$$\theta_{1(P1P2)}(t) = a_6 + a_7 t + a_8 t^2 + a_9 t^3 + a_{10} t^4 + a_{11} t^5$$
$$t_2 < t \leq t_3[(P1) \to (P2)]$$

$$\theta_{2(P1P2)}(t) = b_6 + b_7 t + b_8 t^2 + b_9 t^3 + b_{10} t^4 + b_{11} t^5$$
$$t_2 < t \leq t_3[(P1) \to (P2)]$$

$$\theta_{1(P2P3)}(t) = a_{12} + a_{13} t + a_{14} t^2 + a_{15} t^3 + a_{16} t^4 + a_{17} t^5$$
$$t_3 < t \leq t_4[(P2) \to (P3)]$$

$$\theta_{2(P2P3)}(t) = b_{12} + b_{13} t + b_{14} t^2 + b_{15} t^3 + b_{16} t^4 + b_{17} t^5$$
$$t_3 < t \leq t_4[(P2) \to (P3)]$$

$$\theta_{1(P3P4)}(t) = a_{18} + a_{19} t + a_{20} t^2 + a_{21} t^3 + a_{22} t^4 + a_{23} t^5$$
$$t_4 < t \leq t_5[(P3) \to (P4)]$$

$$\theta_{2(P3P4)}(t) = b_{18} + b_{19} t + b_{20} t^2 + b_{21} t^3 + b_{22} t^4 + b_{23} t^5$$
$$t_4 < t \leq t_5[(P3) \to (P4)]$$

$$\theta_{1(P4P5)}(t) = a_{24} + a_{25} t + a_{26} t^2 + a_{27} t^3 + a_{28} t^4 + a_{29} t^5$$
$$t_5 < t \leq t_6[(P4) \to (P5)]$$

$$\theta_{2(P4P5)}(t) = b_{24} + b_{25} t + b_{26} t^2 + b_{27} t^3 + b_{28} t^4 + b_{29} t^5$$
$$t_5 < t \leq t_6[(P4) \to (P5)]$$

$$\theta_{1(P5P6)}(t) = a_{30} + a_{31} t + a_{32} t^2 + a_{33} t^3 + a_{34} t^4 + a_{35} t^5$$
$$t_6 < t \leq t_7[(P5) \to (P6)]$$

$$\theta_{2(P5P6)}(t) = b_{30} + b_{31} t + b_{32} t^2 + b_{33} t^3 + b_{34} t^4 + b_{35} t^5$$
$$t_6 < t \leq t_7[(P5) \to (P6)]$$

$$\theta_{1(P6P7)}(t) = a_{36} + a_{37} t + a_{38} t^2 + a_{39} t^3 + a_{40} t^4 + a_{41} t^5$$
$$t_7 < t \leq t_8[(P6) \to (P7)]$$

$$\theta_{2(P6P7)}(t) = b_{36} + b_{37} t + b_{38} t^2 + b_{39} t^3 + b_{40} t^4 + b_{41} t^5$$
$$t_7 < t \leq t_8[(P6) \to (P7)]$$

$$\theta_{1(P7(11,8))}(t) = a_{42} + a_{43} t + a_{44} t^2 + a_{45} t^3 + a_{46} t^4 + a_{47} t^5$$
$$t_8 < t \leq t_9[(P7) \to (11,8)]$$

$$\theta_{2(P7(11,8))}(t) = b_{42} + b_{43} t + b_{44} t^2 + b_{45} t^3 + b_{46} t^4 + b_{47} t^5$$
$$t_8 < t \leq t_9[(P7) \to (11,8)]$$

$$(7)$$

The eight-segment quintic interpolation polynomial has 48 unknown coefficients ($8 \times 6 = 48$), which are calculated from the initial and final boundary conditions as well as intermediate point position continuity, velocity continuity, acceleration continuity, jerk continuity and derivative of jerk continuity. The initial and final joint rates and acceleration must be zero for starting and stopping at rest. After applying the initial and boundary condition, simultaneous equations are obtained and solved to get the unknowns. The 48 conditions are given in Eq. (8).

The comparison of cubic and quintic interpolation for joint 1 and joint 2 is shown in Figs. 6 and 7. The corresponding end effector path is shown in Fig. 8.

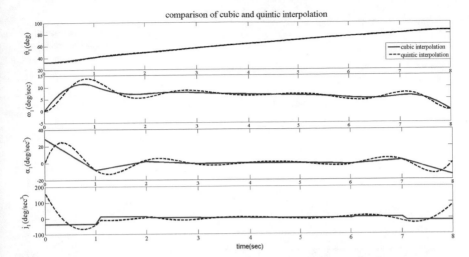

Fig. 6 Comparison of joint 1 positions, velocity, acceleration, jerk for cubic and quintic interpolation

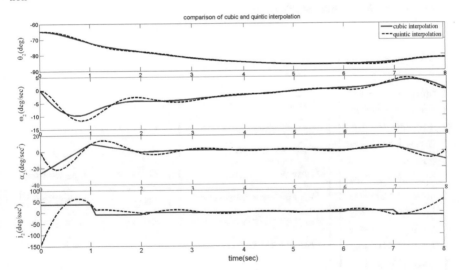

Fig. 7 Comparison of joint 2 position, velocity, acceleration, jerk for cubic and quintic interpolation

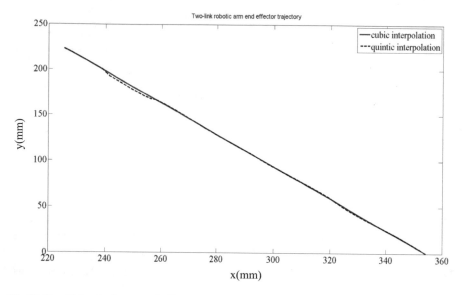

Fig. 8 Two-link robotic arm end effector path

$$\left\{ \begin{array}{l} \theta_{1(11,0)P1}(t=t_2) = \theta_{1P1} \\ \theta_{1(P1P2)}(t=0) = \theta_{1P1} \\ \theta_{1(P1P2)}(t=t_3) = \theta_{1P2} \\ \theta_{1(P2P3)}(t=0) = \theta_{1P2} \\ \theta_{1(P2P3)}(t=t_4) = \theta_{1P3} \\ \theta_{1(P3P4)}(t=0) = \theta_{1P3} \\ \theta_{1(P3P4)}(t=t_5) = \theta_{1P4} \\ \theta_{1(P4P5)}(t=0) = \theta_{1P4} \\ \theta_{1(P4P5)}(t=t_6) = \theta_{1P5} \\ \theta_{1(P5P6)}(t=0) = \theta_{1P5} \\ \theta_{1(P5P6)}(t=t_7) = \theta_{1P6} \\ \theta_{1(P6P7)}(t=0) = \theta_{1P6} \\ \theta_{1(P6P7)}(t=t_8) = \theta_{1P7} \\ \theta_{1(P7(11,8))}(t=0) = \theta_{1P7} \end{array} \right\}$$

$$\left\{ \begin{array}{l} \dot\theta_{1(11,0)P1}(t=t_2) = \dot\theta_{1P1P2}(t=0) \\ \dot\theta_{1(P1P2)}(t=t_3) = \dot\theta_{1(P2P3)}(t=0) \\ \dot\theta_{1(P2P3)}(t=t_4) = \dot\theta_{1(P3P4)}(t=0) \\ \dot\theta_{1(P3P4)}(t=t_5) = \dot\theta_{1(P4P5)}(t=0) \\ \dot\theta_{1(P4P5)}(t=t_6) = \dot\theta_{1(P5P6)}(t=0) \\ \dot\theta_{1(P5P6)}(t=t_7) = \dot\theta_{1(P6P7)}(t=0) \\ \dot\theta_{1(P6P7)}(t=t_8) = \dot\theta_{1(P7,(11,8))}(t=0) \end{array} \right\}$$

$$\left\{ \begin{array}{l} \ddot\theta_{1(11,0)P1}(t=t_2) = \ddot\theta_{1P1P2}(t=0) \\ \ddot\theta_{1(P1P2)}(t=t_3) = \ddot\theta_{1(P2P3)}(t=0) \\ \ddot\theta_{1(P2P3)}(t=t_4) = \ddot\theta_{1(P3P4)}(t=0) \\ \ddot\theta_{1(P3P4)}(t=t_5) = \ddot\theta_{1(P4P5)}(t=0) \\ \ddot\theta_{1(P4P5)}(t=t_6) = \ddot\theta_{1(P5P6)}(t=0) \\ \ddot\theta_{1(P5P6)}(t=t_7) = \ddot\theta_{1(P6P7)}(t=0) \\ \ddot\theta_{1(P6P7)}(t=t_8) = \ddot\theta_{1(P7,(11,8))}(t=0) \end{array} \right\}$$

Position continuity   Velocity continuity   Acceleration continuity

$$\left.\begin{cases} \dddot{\theta}_{1(11,0)P1}(t = t_2) = \dddot{\theta}_{1(P1P2)}(t = 0) \\ \dddot{\theta}_{1(P1P2)}(t = t_3) = \dddot{\theta}_{1(P2P3)}(t = 0) \\ \dddot{\theta}_{1(P2P3)}(t = t_4) = \dddot{\theta}_{1(P3P4)}(t = 0) \\ \dddot{\theta}_{1(P3P4)}(t = t_5) = \dddot{\theta}_{1(P4P5)}(t = 0) \\ \dddot{\theta}_{1(P4P5)}(t = t_6) = \dddot{\theta}_{1(P5P6)}(t = 0) \\ \dddot{\theta}_{1(P5P6)}(t = t_7) = \dddot{\theta}_{1(P6P7)}(t = 0) \\ \dddot{\theta}_{1(P6P7)}(t = t_8) = \dddot{\theta}_{1(P7,(11,8))}(t = 0) \end{cases}\right\} \quad \left.\begin{cases} \ddddot{\theta}_{1(11,0)P1}(t = t_2) = \ddddot{\theta}_{1(P1P2)}(t = 0) \\ \ddddot{\theta}_{1(P1P2)}(t = t_3) = \ddddot{\theta}_{1(P2P3)}(t = 0) \\ \ddddot{\theta}_{1(P2P3)}(t = t_4) = \ddddot{\theta}_{1(P3P4)}(t = 0) \\ \ddddot{\theta}_{1(P3P4)}(t = t_5) = \ddddot{\theta}_{1(P4P5)}(t = 0) \\ \ddddot{\theta}_{1(P4P5)}(t = t_6) = \ddddot{\theta}_{1(P5P6)}(t = 0) \\ \ddddot{\theta}_{1(P5P6)}(t = t_7) = \ddddot{\theta}_{1(P6P7)}(t = 0) \\ \ddddot{\theta}_{1(P6P7)}(t = t_8) = \ddddot{\theta}_{1(P7(11,8))}(t = 0) \end{cases}\right\}$$

Jerk continuity   Snap continuity

$$(8)$$

The 48 conditions for joint 1 are given in Eq. (8). Similarly 48 conditions can be formulated for joint 2.

In cubic interpolation initial point at $(t = 0)$ and final point $(t = 8)$ has some finite acceleration. This will create jerky motion and lead to wear on the robotic arm. This can be avoided by fifth-order polynomial (quintic interpolation).

4.1 Implementation of Elmo Motion Controller

The cubic interpolation for joint 1 and joint 2 has been tested in Elmo motion controller. The joint 1 cubic interpolation is shown in Fig. 9 similarly for joint 2, respectively. The Elmo's Gold Maestro motion controller is used for experimental validation. The harmonic drive FHA-C mini series (gear ratio = 50) servo actuators with incremental line driver encoder (2000 ppr) are used. Encoder is used in 4x counting mode, thereby deriving (2000 * 4 * gear ratio) counts/rev which is 400,000 counts/rev.

5 Conclusion

PFBR, steam generator inspection device uses a two-axis manipulator for orienting to all the 547 tubes distinctly. Movement from one tube to another tube though is a straight line path; the inverse kinematic solution at discrete steps has discrete joint space position points. Precision operation requires a velocity inner loop control with position control on the outer closed-loop control. Cubic order interpolation on the position points is adequate if velocity control is not demanded. In the trajectory planning, it is desired to have both velocity and position paths to reach any tube destination. It is quite obvious that when velocity also needs to be controlled, a cubic

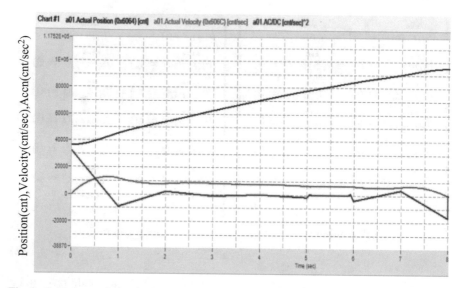

Fig. 9 Cubic interpolation for joint 1 in Elmo motion controller

order interpolation will cause severe discontinuities in accelerations and jerks. Hence, this paper deals with the implementation of the quintic interpolation to overcome this problem. Also by careful control on more solution points, a smooth trajectory is generated for the tube to tube motion. The quintic interpolation is programmed and checked through the motion controller and proved to have no discontinuities on accelerations as well as on jerks proving to be a good choice for position and velocity closed loops for the SG inspections.

References

1. R.N. Jazar, *Theory of Applied Robotics* (Springer, 2010)
2. J. Craig, *Introduction to Robotics—Mechanics and Control* (Pearson Prentice Hall, 2005)
3. C.S. Lin, P.R. Chang, J.Y.S. Luh, Formulation and optimization of cubic polynomial joint trajectories for industrial robots. IEEE Trans. Autom. Cont. **AC-28**, 1066–1074 (1983)
4. J. Angeles, Fundamentals of robotic mechanical systems: theory, methods, and algorithms (Springer, 2003)
5. R.L. Williams II, Simplified robotics joint-space trajectory generation with a via point using a single polynomial. J. Robot. 2013:735958 (2012)
6. C.S Lin, P.R. Chang, Joint trajectories of mechanical manipulators for Cartesian path approximation. IEEE Trans. Syst. Man Cybern. **SMC-13**, 1094–1102 (1983)
7. J.Y.S. Luh, C.S. Lin, Approximate joint trajectories for control of industrial robots along Cartesian paths. IEEE Trans. Syst. Man. Cybern. **SMC-14**(3), 444–450 (1984)

On the Dynamic Response of Rigid Rotor Supported by Rolling-Element Bearing

Chintamani Mishra, Abhishek Kumar Kashyap
and Arun Kumar Samantaray

Abstract A prototype of a system is a numerical model. It is used to generate large amount of data and can be a successful replacement to experiment,which is often difficult to conduct and moreover is expensive. This article deals with the development of two models of rotor supported by deep groove rolling-element bearings to study the dynamic response. The bearing models are 5-DOFs and multi-body dynamics is developed using Matlab–Simulink and the bond graph environment. The systems of equations generated by modeling rolling-element bearing using these two approaches are theoretically simulated. The effects of speed variations in the dynamic response using these two models are investigated. The three regions namely, periodic, quasi-periodic, and chaotic are seen on the 5-DOFs rotor supported by rolling-element bearing model with increasing speed, whereas bearing model based on multi-body dynamics approach gives only chaotic response for each speed. Thus, using these two modeling approaches, a comparative study of the magnitude and characteristics of rotor motion can be done, and can be used to infer the vibratory nature of rotor in rolling-element bearing.

Keywords Rolling-element bearing · Dynamic response · Bond graph
Poincare map · Multi-body dynamics

1 Introduction

The vibration generated by rolling-element bearing is unavoidable in many types of rotating machines. Under the effects of radial load, a parametric vibration as a function of ball diameter, number of balls, and pitch diameter appears. This vibration

C. Mishra (✉) · A. K. Kashyap
School of Mechanical Engineering, KIIT University, Bhubaneswar, India
e-mail: chintamani.mishrafme@kiit.ac.in

A. K. Samantaray
Department of Mechanical Engineering, Indian Institute of Technology Kharagpur,
Kharagpur 721302, India
e-mail: samantaray@mech.iitkgp.ernet.in

© Springer Nature Singapore Pte Ltd. 2019
D N Badodkar and T A Dwarakanath (eds.), *Machines, Mechanism
and Robotics*, Lecture Notes in Mechanical Engineering,
https://doi.org/10.1007/978-981-10-8597-0_55

is generally called as VC vibration as it is due to the varying compliance of the bearing [1]. A balanced/unbalanced rotor supported by rolling-element bearing constitutes a nonlinear system. Generally, the effects of unbalance force in the rotor-bearing system cannot be avoided. The nonlinearity characteristic is because of radial internal clearance, Hertzian contact between different elements, and so on [2]. Tiwari et al. [2] studied the dynamic response of balanced rotor supported by a deep groove ball bearing. The same authors studied the dynamic response for unbalanced rotor supported by bearing [3]. In both the work, they studied the response to analyze the stability with the help of Floquets method and higher order Poincare map. The rotor-bearing system taken for that analysis was a 2-DOFs, where it was assumed that outer race of the bearing is fixed to rigid support and the inner race is fixed rigidly to shaft.

Harsha and Kankar [4] studied the dynamic response of rotor-bearing system, where the effects of number of balls and surface waviness are taken into consideration. Harsha [5] similarly studied the dynamic response of rolling-element bearing due to cage run out and number of balls. In both the analysis, the frequency map and Poincare map were used to analyze the response of rotor supported by bearing.

Modeling of rolling-element bearing can be of quasi-static or dynamic. Quasi-static modeling approach considers the force and moment balance equations, whereas the dynamic modeling approach considers the differential equations of motion of rolling-element bearing [6]. Many computer codes and multi-body dynamics simulation software are commercially available, which can be used for modeling rolling-element bearing. A dynamic model of rolling-element bearing, developed using Matlab–Simulink approach is reported in [7]. The ball dynamics and cage dynamics are not taken into consideration while developing the model. A model of rolling-element bearing which considers planar multi-body dynamics formulation which considers the effects due to preload, unbalance, traction, and cage dynamics are reported in [7, 8].

In the present analysis, two models of rolling-element bearings are taken into consideration to infer the dynamic response of rotor supported by rolling-element bearing. The first model is a kinematics-based model that considers planer motion of rolling-element bearing and it does not consider the cage, contact, and traction between different elements, and is developed in Matlab–Simulink environment, whereas the second model is a multi-body dynamics model of rolling-element bearing developed using multi-energy domain-based bond graph simulation tool SYMBOLS where the cage, contact, and traction dynamics are taken into consideration for modeling.

The response of the rotor is analyzed for rotor supported by rolling-element bearing using both the modeling approach with the help of higher order Poincare and frequency maps.

The Matlab–Simulink model and bond graph model of rolling-element bearing are explained in Sect. 2 and Sect. 3, respectively. The simulation results are discussed in Sect. 4. The conclusion and scopes are discussed in the final section.

2   Matlab–Simulink Model of Rolling-Element Bearing

A simple bearing model using MATLAB–Simulink tool is developed here using the method proposed in [6]. The effects due to inertia of inner and outer races and contact force are taken into consideration, whereas the cage and balls inertia are neglected while developing the model. Most of the planer models of rolling-element bearing generally consider balls at equal angular spacing and constant angular speed of cage. A spring damper system representing structural parameter is used to connect the outer race to pedestal. A high-frequency resonance response of the bearing is generated by including an extra sprung mass. Thus, the model is a five degrees of freedom model which includes two degrees of freedom of inner and outer races and one degree of freedom due to sprung mass to represent high-frequency structural response.

A simplified bearing model is shown in Fig. 1 where the rotor shaft is driven at a constant speed $\dot{\theta}_i = \omega_i$, the outer race is supported by flexible support, and the inner race is anchored to inertial frame through flexible supports (representing rotor shaft flexibility). In Fig. 1, K_P and R_P are stiffness and damping between the outer race and pedestal support, respectively, K_S and R_S are similarly the stiffness and damping of rotor shaft, respectively, and K_R, R_R and m_R are the stiffness, damping, and mass of sprung mass system and the load-deflection factor of rolling element is represented by K_b. The development of model is based on assumptions taken in [9].

The angular position of jth ball at time elapsed t, θ_j, as a function of cage angular frequency, number of balls N_b, and initial reference position θ_0 can be expressed as:

$$\theta_j = \frac{2\pi(j-1)}{N_b} + \omega_c\, t + \theta_0 \quad \text{for} \quad j = 1, \ldots, N_b. \tag{1}$$

Fig. 1 5-DOF model of rolling-element bearing

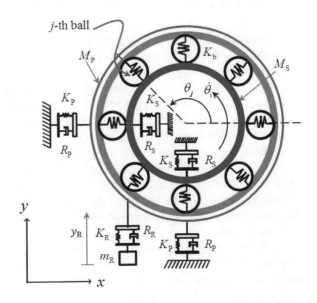

From simple kinematics cage angular velocity can be expressed as:

$$\omega_c = \frac{\omega_i}{2}\left(1 - \frac{d}{D}\right) \tag{2}$$

Assuming surface contact, Hertzian contact force in horizontal (F_x) and vertical (F_y) directions are calculated as proposed in [6]. It is to be noted that traction or frictional forces are not modeled in the 5-DOF model.

The outer race with pedestal is modeled as a two degrees of freedom system which can have translational motion in x- and y-directions. The inner race is a two degrees of freedom system, which is fixed rigidly to the rotor shaft and it rotates with a constant angular speed. The sprung mass is attached in y-direction of the pedestal to generate structural response. The equations of motion of inner race, pedestal with outer race, and sprung mass are given in Eqs. 3, 4, and 5, respectively.

$$
\begin{aligned}
M_S\ddot{x}_i + R_S\dot{x}_i + K_S x_i + F_x &= 0, \\
M_S\ddot{y}_i + R_S\dot{y}_i + K_S y_i + M_S g + F_y &= 0,
\end{aligned}
\tag{3}
$$

$$
\begin{aligned}
M_P\ddot{x}_o &= F_x - R_P\dot{x}_o - K_P x_o, \\
M_P\ddot{y}_o &= F_y - M_P g - (R_P + R_R)\dot{y}_o - (K_P + K_R)y_o + K_R y_R + R_R\dot{y}_R,
\end{aligned}
\tag{4}
$$

$$m_R\ddot{y}_R = K_R(y_o - y_R) + R_R(\dot{y}_o - \dot{y}_R) - m_R g. \tag{5}$$

3 Model of Bearing: A Bond Graph Approach

A more advanced model is developed in the present article using bond graph [10, 11] multi-body dynamics approach as presented in [6–8]. This model considers slip, traction, motor torque, preload, unbalance, and cage dynamics. Similar to the planer model, this model considers constant angular spacing of rolling element.

In developing the model, major parts of bearings such as the outer and inner races, rolling elements, and the cage are considered as different rigid bodies. This model considers flexible rotor shaft and structural flexibility of pedestal. The free body diagrams of major parts are shown in Fig. 2.

The model considers planer motion of rolling element, inner race with rotor and cage. Thus, all these elements have linear translation along two axis and rotation around the third axis, a three degrees of freedom system for each. The outer race is fixed to a pedestal and it does not allow rotation and hence it is a two-degrees-of-freedom system.

All the rolling elements are constrained to move inside the cage. The dynamics of the system determines the locations of centers of cage, inner race and outer races. The computation of these centers are used to find out the contact points of rolling element

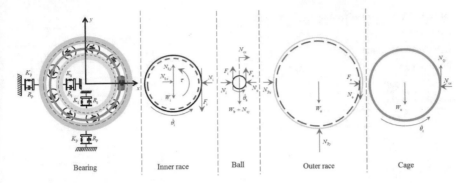

Fig. 2 FBD of rolling-element bearing

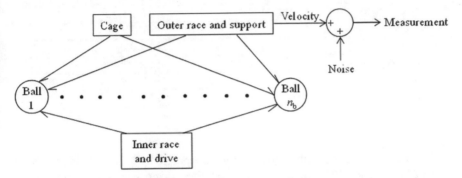

Fig. 3 Integrated model of bearing using bond graph

with races. This model considers surface contact for mating surfaces. Figure 2 shows the rolling-element bearing as a spring-mass-damper system and free body diagram (FBD) of its different parts.

The model developed in this article is in a modular manner as proposed in [6, 7]. Different sub-models of inner and outer races, cage, and rolling elements are modeled using the method proposed in [6, 7]. All the sub-models are developed as capsules using SYMBOLS software. The sub-models are assembled to generate the complete models of rolling-element bearing (Fig. 3).

4 Results and Discussion

In the present analysis, a deep groove ball bearing (MB-ER-16K) supported by a rigid rotor is taken into consideration. The parameters taken by Mishra et al. [6] are the main parameters for this study. Table 1 shows the different parameters of rolling-element bearing using Matlab–Simulink and bond graph modeling approach.

Table 1 Parameters of rolling-element bearing

Parameter	MS model	BG model
Ball diameter (mm)	4.76	4.76
Pitch diameter (mm)	23.5	23.5
Number of balls	9	9
Rotor mass (kg)	0.6	0.6
Rotor stiffness	–	–
Rotor damping (Ns/m)	200	200
Pedestal mass	–	3 kg
Pedestal stiffness	–	4×10^7 N/m
Pedestal damping	–	1000 Ns/m
Ball mass	–	0.002 kg
Ball stiffness (N/m)	7.055×10^9	7.055×10^9
Ball damping	–	1000 Ns/m
Cage mass	–	0.002 kg
Cage stiffness	–	1×10^8 N/m
Cage damping	–	1 Ns/m
Preload (μm)	20	20

The FFT map of a horizontal balanced rotor supported by rolling-element bearing for speed 2100 and 9700 rpm in X- and Y-directions using Matlab–Simulink model are shown in Figs. 4 and 5, respectively. The corresponding Poincare maps are shown in Figs. 6 and 7, respectively. Chaotic solution at 2100 rpm is shown in Fig. 4 where the frequency spectrum has VC and its multiples. With increasing speed to 5300 rpm, periodic doubling with chaos can be observed by Poincare map (not shown). The chaotic solution extends upto 6300 rpm where fourth sub-harmonic appears and the solution is quasi-periodic and after which chaos appears. As the speed increases to 6800 rpm, torus solution appears and the stability returns (Fig. 7). The corresponding FFT map is shown in Fig. 5, where VC and its harmonics with sidebands at interval of shaft frequency appears. With the increase in speed to 9700 rpm, the chaotic solution and 12th sub-harmonic appears (not shown).

Using the bond graph model, the FFT map of rotor supported by rolling-element bearing at rotor speed of 4500 and 9900 rpm in X and Y are shown in Figs. 8 and 9. The corresponding Poincare maps are shown in Figs. 10 and 11. Ninth sub-harmonics and its multiples which leads to chaos can be seen in 4500 rpm (Fig. 10) and corresponding Poincare map is shown in Fig. 11. With increasing speed to 5800 rpm, periodic doubling with numbers of sub-harmonics appears in the spectrum (not shown), which eventually leads to chaotic solution. The chaotic solution continues when the speed increases upto 7100 rpm. Torus-like solution can be found when the speed increases to 9900, and which can be evident from the Poincare map (Fig. 11) but at this speed number of sub-harmonics appears in this speed (Fig. 9), the response is chaotic.

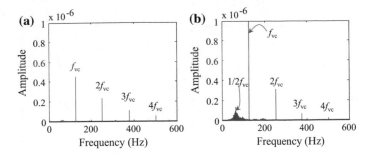

Fig. 4 FFT at 2100 rpm (MS)

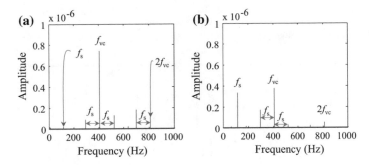

Fig. 5 FFT at 6800 rpm (MS)

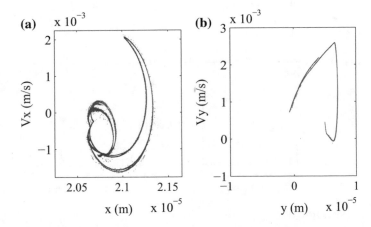

Fig. 6 Poincare map at 2100 rpm

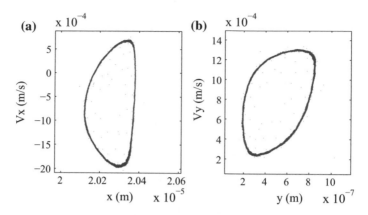

Fig. 7 Poincare map at 6800 rpm

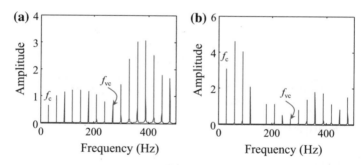

Fig. 8 FFT at 4500 rpm (BG)

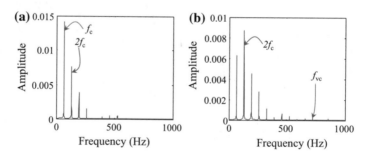

Fig. 9 FFT at 9900 rpm (BG)

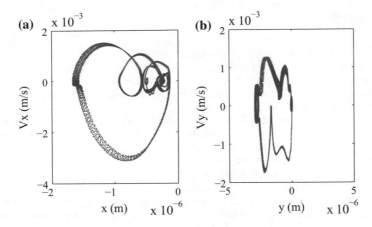

Fig. 10 Poincare map at 4500 rpm

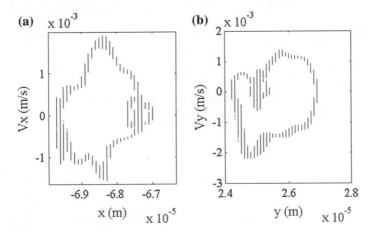

Fig. 11 Poincare map at 9900 rpm

5 Conclusion

In the present analysis, two models of rotor supported by rolling-element bearing with increasing complexity are presented to study the dynamic response. In the first rolling-element bearing model, the stability of system comes as the speed increases, similarly to the conclusion drawn in [3]. The second model, where the traction and cage dynamics are taken into consideration the response of the rigid rotor supported by bearing is always chaotic for each speed. A model should be accurate enough to represent a real system. As the second model considers the traction as well as cage dynamics of rolling-element bearing, it can be inferred that the rotor response is always chaotic irrespective of speed of the rotor.

References

1. B. Mevel, J.L. Guyader, Routes to chaos in ball bearing. J. Sound Vib. **162**(3), 471–487 (1993)
2. M. Tiwari, K. Gupta, O. Prakash, Effect of radial clearance of a ball bearing on the dynamics of a balanced horizontal rotor. J. Sound Vib. **238**, 723–756 (2000)
3. M. Tiwari, K. Gupta, O. Prakash, Dynamic response of an unbalanced rotor supported on ball bearing. J. Sound Vib. **238**, 757–779 (2000)
4. S.P. Harsha, P.K. Kankar, Stability analysis of a rotor bearing system due to surface waviness and number of balls. Int. J. Mech. Sci. **46**, 1057–1081 (2004)
5. S.P. Harsha, Nonlinear dynamic analysis of rolling element bearings due to cage run-out and number of balls. J. Sound Vib. **289**, 360–381 (2006)
6. C. Mishra, A.K. Samantaray, G. Chakraborty, Ball bearing defect models: a study of simulated and experimental fault signatures. J. Sound Vib. **400**, 86–112 (2017)
7. C. Mishra, A.K. Samantaray, G. Chakraborty, Bond graph modelling and experimental verification of a novel scheme for fault diagnosis of rolling element bearings in special operating conditions. J. Sound Vib. **377**, 302–330 (2016)
8. C. Mishra, G. Chakraborty, A.K. Samantaray, Rolling element bearing fault modelling to develop a diagnosis scheme for oscillating and non-uniform shaft rotation. Proc. INACOMM **2013**, 86–94 (2013)
9. N. Sawalhi, R.B. Randall, Simulating gear and bearing interactions in the presence of faults part i. The combined gear bearing dynamic model and the simulation of localised bearing faults. Mech. Syst. Signal Process. **22**, 1924–1951 (2008)
10. A. Mukherjee, R. Karmakar, A. Samantaray, *Bond Graph in Modelling* (CRC Press, Simulation and Fault Identification, 2006)
11. R. Merzouki, A. Samantaray, P. Pathak, B.O. Bouamama, *Intelligent Mechatronic Systems: Modeling* (Springer, Control and Diagnosis, 2012)

On High-Precision Large-Range Resonant-Amplified Scanning with Limited Range Actuation

Nilesh Bansod, Abhijit Tanksale and Prasanna Gandhi

Abstract Compliant mechanisms have found applications in high-precision micro-measurement, microfabrication, micro-manipulation, and other areas. These mechanisms have inherent advantage of being highly precise, backlash-free, low energy consuming, and frictionless and hence durable. However, typical range of motion and speeds with these mechanisms are limited because of large deformation nonlinearities and complex dynamics. Furthermore, achieving higher range of motion with much lower stroke non-collocated actuator is another challenge. Displacement amplifying compliant mechanisms, found in the literature, provides solution for higher range with lower stroke actuation. However parasitic errors are high, complex structure with several moving masses makes their usage in dynamic applications (higher speeds) difficult. We propose, in this paper, alternate method using resonant displacement amplification using simple double parallelogram compliant mechanism (DPCM) toward higher but fixed speed applications. With limited stroke of actuation, we develop control algorithms to maintain a stable limit cycle. Parametric study using lumped mass model offers pathways for design decisions and unfolds interesting results. Experimental results validate the proposed method but point to limitations of the lumped mass model.

Keywords Pulsed-input · Compliant mechanism · Scanning · Parasitic error

N. Bansod (✉) · A. Tanksale · P. Gandhi (✉)
Suman Mashruwala Advanced Microengineering Laboratory,
Indian Institute of Technology Bombay, Powai, Mumbai 400076, India
e-mail: gandhi@iitb.ac.in

N. Bansod
e-mail: nileshbansod@iitb.ac.in; nileshsbansod@gmail.com

A. Tanksale
e-mail: 144100009@iitb.ac.in

© Springer Nature Singapore Pte Ltd. 2019
D N Badodkar and T A Dwarakanath (eds.), *Machines, Mechanism and Robotics*, Lecture Notes in Mechanical Engineering,
https://doi.org/10.1007/978-981-10-8597-0_56

1 Introduction

Traditionally, motion stages have used rails or guides which have frictional losses and backlash. In recent years, compliant mechanisms such as double parallelogram beam structures have been used for motion stages. Compliant mechanisms have the advantage of being highly precise, backlash-free, low energy consuming, and frictionless [1, 2]. These characteristics have proved very useful in microscale high precision, high-speed motion applications such as microstereolithography [3], nanopositioning platforms [4], comb drives in micro-electro-mechanical-systems (MEMS) [5], and so on.

Double parallelogram compliant mechanism involves beams undergoing intermediate to large deformation. Due to large deformation, accurate modeling of such systems requires considering the nonlinearities involved. Beam constrained model (BCM) is a method proposed by Awtar and Sen [6] to capture the geometric nonlinearities. We deploy chained constrained beam model (CBCM) by Ma and Chen [7]. In this method, each beam is divided into few elements and each element is modeled using BCM. It requires fewer elements compared to discretization methods like FEM. It is also able to capture elasto-kinematic effects because BCM captures those.

The range of such motion stages has been limited by the range of noncontact actuators such as the magnetic voice-coil actuator. Our work attempts to achieve high precision and high displacement using collocated system with a novel pulsed-input resonant control strategy. We seek to tackle this problem even without using displacement amplification by proposing to use collocated actuator giving input only over a part of resonant motion. The objective is to achieve a stable limit cycle at fixed but higher speed while minimizing parasitic error.

2 Modeling

The system under consideration is a double parallelogram compliant mechanism. We call the mass connected to the ground as Mass 1 (m_1) and the other mass as Mass 2 (m_2). The four outer beams are connected between with the ground and Mass 1 and the four inner beams connect Mass 1 and Mass 2. We will actuate the system at Mass 2 and the encoder for position and velocity feedback is also located at Mass 2. We define the parasitic error in the system as the absolute displacement in axial direction of Mass 2 with respect to its steady state position (as shown in Fig. 1) The initial study was undertaken on MATLAB–Simulink, where the double parallelogram mechanism was modeled as a two mass-spring-damper system. In the lumped mass model, Mass 1 is connected to the ground with a spring constant k_1 equivalent to the bending stiffness of the four outer beams. The springs between Mass 1 and Mass 2 have stiffness k_2 corresponding to the bending stiffness of the four inner beams. The damping constants c_1 and c_2 try to model the mass damping in

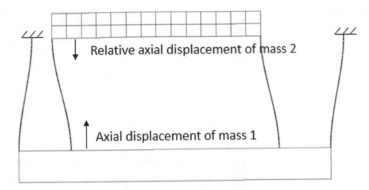

Fig. 1 Schematic for parasitic error

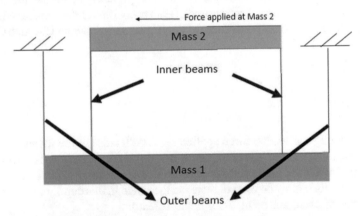

Fig. 2 Schematic of the double parallelogram compliant mechanism

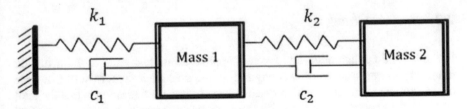

Fig. 3 Lumped mass model for DPCM

the beams. Figure 2 shows the schematic for the setup and Fig. 3 shows the lumped mass model for the same setup.

The main idea is for the actuation pulse to provide energy equal to the energy lost in the non-actuated region. Using simplifications, this energy was calculated and used to simulate the system in open loop. For the initial study, a square-wave pulse is applied such that the force is constant in the actuation range and the direction of force matches the direction of the motion. A stable limit cycle was established by giving

Table 1 Lumped mass model properties

k_1	1041.7 N/m
k_2	1027.9 N/m
m_1	1.325 kg
m_2	2.172 kg

the same force in each cycle, thus establishing a stable open-loop limit cycle. After successfully establishing stable limit cycle in open loop, a semi-closed loop was implemented where the force applied in the actuation range was the variable input. A proportional control was applied on this value of force by calculating the error between the desired amplitude and amplitude achieved in the last cycle. Accordingly, the value of force will be increased if the desired amplitude is more than the achieved amplitude and the vice versa. The mass and beam properties of the considered DPCM are given in Table 1 below. The stiffness of flexible beams is obtained through CBCM-based model.

2.1 Center-Actuated

In the first configuration, the force applied is on both sides of the mean position of Mass 2. One advantage of this configuration is that the system is self-starting since the system at rest is within the actuation zone. The disadvantage here is that a voice-coil-type actuator cannot be used to increase the range in this configuration. But this problem can be overcome using other linear actuators.

2.2 End-Actuated

In the second configuration, the force is applied at the two ends of the actuation range. By its construction, this configuration requires the system to start from one of the extreme positions. Another disadvantage of this configuration is that the total range of the motion gets fixed once the actuator are located. It cannot be altered significantly without moving the actuators.

Since the energy to be transferred in both the cases is same and the range of actuation is also same, the power requirement in the end-actuated configuration would be smaller because the time spent by mass in actuation range is greater in this configuration as the speed of the mass is lower.

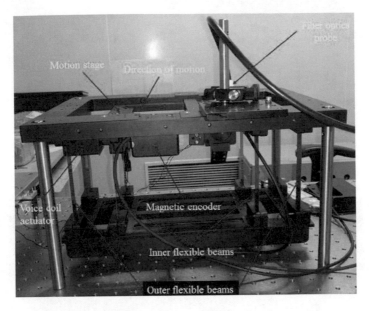

Fig. 4 Photo of the experimental setup used

3 Experimental Results and Discussion

A DPCM setup with beam dimensions shown in Table 2 has been used to perform experiments. A Simulink model developed, was run in real-time controller dSPACE DS1103. An optical encoder mounted at Mass 2 gives position and velocity feedback for Mass 2. A voice-coil actuator is used to actuate Mass 2. Figure 4 shows the location of actuator and encoder.

3.1 Limit Cycle Behavior

A stable limit cycle obtained for 12 mm range using 3 mm actuation (25% actuation) has been shown in Fig. 5. This establishes the feasibility of the proposed control strategy. For very small actuation range, some irregularities are seen in the experimental

Table 2 DPCM beam dimensions

Beam length	109 mm
Outer beam thickness	0.5 mm
Inner beam thickness	0.52 mm
Outer beam width	16.1 mm
Inner beam width	28 mm

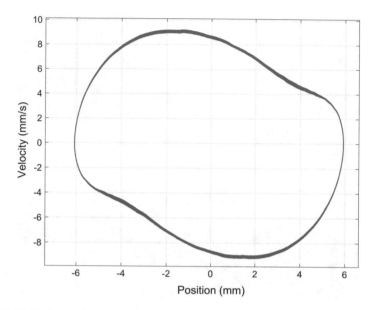

Fig. 5 Stable limit cycle in experimental center-actuation over 25%

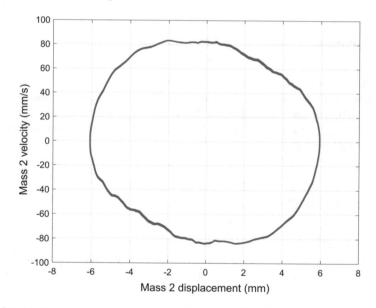

Fig. 6 Irregularities in limit cycle for very small actuation (8.33%)

results. Figure 6 shows the limit cycle for 8.33% actuation range. Although the limit cycle is still repeated, the jagged velocity profile may not be suitable for scanning applications. The model fails to predict this behavior.

3.2 Parasitic Error

We are interested in the parasitic error produced due to this actuation. For simulation, the CBCM-based model is used to predict the axial displacement as a function of transverse displacement for each mass. This function is used to calculate the axial displacement of each mass at any given time, and the difference between the two gives the parasitic error at any given time. The resulting parasitic error is shown compared with the experimentally observed parasitic error in Fig. 7 the positive direction of parasitic error is downward, or in the direction of gravity. For experimental measurement of parasitic error, we use a fiber-optic probe to measure the parasitic error at Mass 2. The error for 25% actuated system is plotted with the parasitic error simulated in the model in Fig. 7.

As seen from Fig. 7, the experimental parasitic error does not match the simulated parasitic error. One of the possible reasons can be that in the dynamic case, the axial displacement versus transverse displacement function of the beams may be different from the static case. In order to test the hypotheses and ascertain, the cause of disparity a magnetic encoder was placed at Mass 1. The parasitic error in Mass 1 was measured in a quasi-static actuation and our resonant control strategy. The variation of parasitic error with position was plotted together, and it was found to have a very good match (Fig. 8). This suggests that even in dynamic case, the relation between the axial displacement and transverse displacement remains the same.

The other reason could be that model does not accurately represent the system, most likely because of insufficient modeling of the damping components. The springs

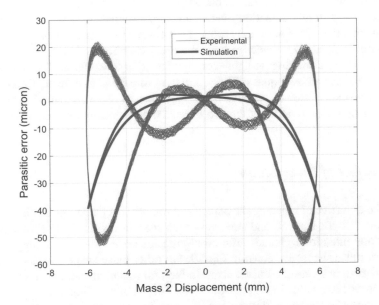

Fig. 7 Experimental parasitic error 25% resonant actuation versus simulated parasitic error

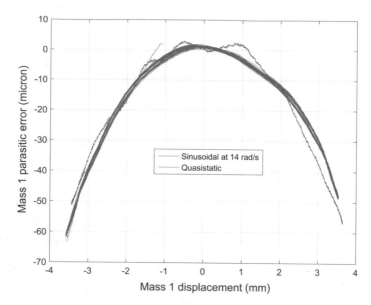

Fig. 8 Comparison of Mass 1 parasitic error for quasistatic and resonant actuation

are accurately modeled and as proved by the match between the results of quasi-static actuation in simulation and experimentation. A plot between total displacement of Mass 2 versus displacement of mass 1 shows the difference in simulation and experiment (Fig. 9). The model is able to predict fairly accurate force required for actuation for different actuation ranges and pulse shapes as seen in Fig. 10. This suggests that the model accurately models the energy loss per cycle due to damping effects but is not able to correctly model the exact variation of damping force within a cycle. Figure 9 also brings to light another interesting observation. The beams were designed to have almost equal stiffness, and therefore equal transverse displacement resulting in cancelation of parasitic error. However, in resonant actuation, the ratio of the maximum amplitudes of the two masses is significantly different from 1.

3.3 Effect of Pulse Shape

With the objective of reducing the parasitic error, other actuation pulse shapes were explored viz. cos-squared and sine waves, as seen in Fig. 11. The 25% actuation case is presented for each and variation of parasitic error versus actuation range for different pulse shapes is shown in Fig. 12. No other pulse shape shows significant improvement in terms of parasitic error. In fact, for higher actuation percentage, the square wave has notably lower parasitic error. The simulation is also able to correctly predict the order and trend for the effect of pulse shape and actuation range, although the absolute magnitude is off due to inadequate dynamics modeling as discussed in

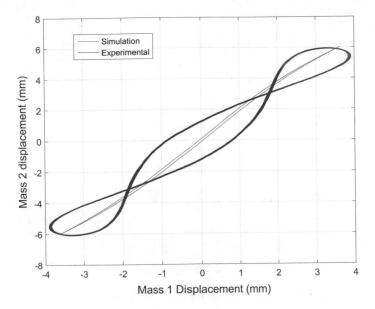

Fig. 9 Simulated versus experimental dynamics of two masses with 25% actuation

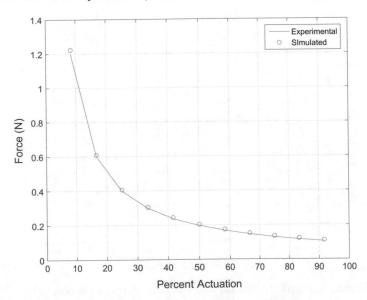

Fig. 10 Force required versus percent actuation for center-actuated square-wave pulse

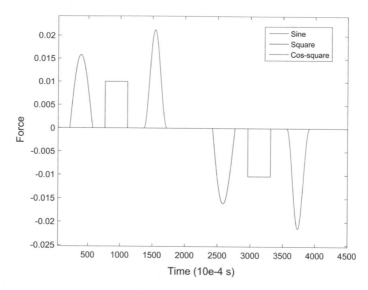

Fig. 11 Comparison of maximum force required in different pulse shapes

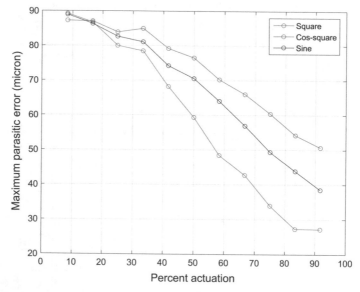

Fig. 12 Experimental maximum parasitic error comparison between pulse shapes

the previous section. The peak force required in case of square-wave pulse is the least (Fig. 13) and therefore, it is the preferred pulse shape out of the options considered.

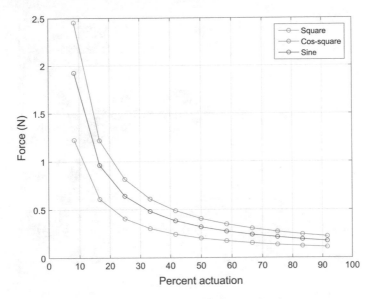

Fig. 13 Comparison of maximum force required in different pulse shapes

3.4 Center-Actuated Versus End-Actuated

Although the end-actuated strategy was discarded, for the academic purposes, the experimental parasitic error for end-actuated was compared to the center-actuated configuration. For the same range of actuation, the max parasitic error was much larger in end-actuated, thus confirming the superiority of center-actuated configuration. Figure 14 compares parasitic error for 75% actuation in both configurations.

4 Conclusion and Future Scope

In the present work, a novel control strategy for resonant actuation of double parallelogram compliant mechanism has been presented. A stable limit cycle has been established, thus confirming the feasibility of such a control for scanning purposes. CBCM-based model predicts the behavior of system at low speeds. However, the model does not allow us to predict behavior at high speeds. The lumped mass model developed to add on to CBCM has shown good promise in predicting the dynamic behavior and trends in the parasitic error as a function of various system parameters. The estimation of force required also shows a good match with the experimental results. But accurate prediction of the dynamic behavior has not been possible and is a topic for further work.

The present work also explores multiple pulse shapes for resonant amplification and the square wave is shown to incur minimum parasitic error among cos-squared

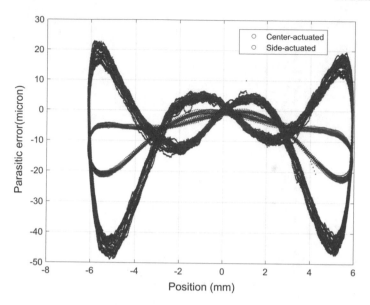

Fig. 14 Experimental parasitic error for end-actuated and center-actuated

pulse, sine pulse, and square-wave pulse. The work also discusses the advantages of center-actuated configuration over end-actuated configuration. The work sets up a platform for further work on linear actuators for limited range actuation. This can lead to substantial increase in the range of double parallelogram compliant motion stages.

References

1. L.L. Howell, *Compliant Mechanisms* (Wiley, 2001)
2. S. Kota, Compliant systems using monolithic mechanisms. Smart Mat. Bull. **2001**(3), 7–10 (2001)
3. S. Deshmukh, P. Gandhi, Optomechanical scanning systems for microstereolithography (msl): analysis and experimental verification. J. Mat. Process. Technol. **209**(3), 1275–1285 (2009)
4. S.S. Aphale, B. Bhikkaji, S.R. Moheimani, Minimizing scanning errors in piezoelectric stack-actuated nanopositioning platforms. IEEE Trans. Nanotechnol. **7**(1), 79–90 (2008)
5. J. Clark, Modeling a monolithic comb drive for large-deflection multi-dof microtransduction, in *University/Government/Industry Micro/Nano Symposium, 2008. UGIM 2008. 17th Biennial* (IEEE, 2008), pp. 203–207
6. S. Awtar, S. Sen, A generalized constraint model for two-dimensional beam flexures: nonlinear load-displacement formulation. J. Mech. Des. **132**(8), 081008 (2010)
7. F. Ma, G. Chen, Modeling large planar deflections of flexible beams in compliant mechanisms using chained beam-constraint-model. J. Mech. Robot. **8**(2), 021018 (2016)

Dynamic Analysis and Design Optimization of Automobile Chassis Frame Using FEM

Shrinidhi Rao and Ajay Bhattu

Abstract In this paper, dynamic analysis of a ladder chassis frame has been done using Ansys. First, modal analysis of the chassis was done using structural steel material. The first six nonzero natural frequencies and their corresponding mode shapes were extracted. It was observed that the second natural frequency of the chassis was close to the engine excitation frequency at idling condition, and the fifth natural frequency was close to the engine excitation frequency at high-speed cruising condition. Thus, the chassis may experience structural resonance at these conditions. The chassis design was optimized so as to obtain the natural frequencies in the desired range, and avoid the possibility of resonance. A harmonic response analysis was done on the original and optimized chassis to check the response under a harmonic force.

Keywords Vibration · Resonance · Chassis · Dynamic analysis · FEM
Optimization · Taguchi method

1 Introduction

Vibration problem occurs where there are rotating or moving parts in machinery. The effects of vibration are excessive stresses, undesirable noise, looseness of parts, and partial or complete failure of parts [1]. The chassis frame is the basic framework of the automobile. All the automobile systems like transmission, steering, suspension, braking system, etc., are attached to and supported by the chassis frame. The frame provides strength as well as flexibility to the automobile. When the vehicle travels along the road, the chassis is subjected to excitations from the engine and transmission system as well as due to the road profile. Due to these excitations, the chassis begins

S. Rao (✉) · A. Bhattu (✉)
Mechanical Engineering Department, College of Engineering Pune, Pune, India
e-mail: mail2shrinidhi@gmail.com

A. Bhattu
e-mail: bhattuajay@gmail.com; apb.mech@coep.ac.in

© Springer Nature Singapore Pte Ltd. 2019
D N Badodkar and T A Dwarakanath (eds.), *Machines, Mechanism and Robotics*, Lecture Notes in Mechanical Engineering,
https://doi.org/10.1007/978-981-10-8597-0_57

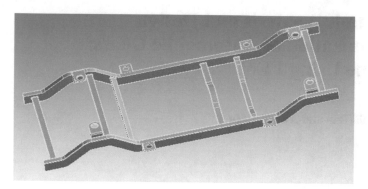

Fig. 1 3D model of chassis frame

to vibrate [2]. If the natural frequency of vibration coincides with the frequency of external excitation, resonance occurs, which leads to excessive deflections and failure [3].

In the current paper, dynamic analysis of a ladder chassis frame has been done using Ansys software. Structural steel material properties were used in modal analysis of the chassis. The chassis design was modified and optimized such that natural frequency lies beyond the resonance range. Harmonic analysis was done on the original and optimized chassis to check the response under a harmonic force.

2 Dynamic Analysis and Design Optimization of Ladder Chassis Frame

2.1 Modal Analysis of Chassis Frame

A ladder chassis frame has been chosen for analysis. The chassis frame consists of long members and cross members as shown in Fig. 1. The long members are of hollow rectangular box section with 5 mm thickness. The overall length of chassis is 3825 mm. The FE model of the chassis frame is shown in Fig. 2. Modal analysis of the chassis frame has been carried out in Ansys in free-free condition. Material considered for the chassis frame is structural steel ($\rho = 7850$ kg/m^3, E = 200 GPa, $\nu = 0.3$). Since free-free condition has been used, the first six natural frequencies are either zero or very close to zero. They correspond to rigid body motion and have been neglected. The first six nonzero natural frequencies and their corresponding mode shapes have been extracted (Table 1).

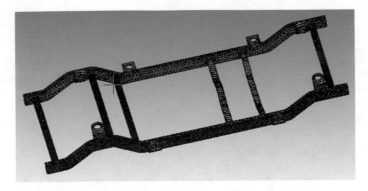

Fig. 2 FE model of chassis frame

Table 1 Natural frequencies and deformations for structural steel chassis

Mode	Frequency (Hz)	Max. deformation (mm)
1	14.211	3.9435
2	25.595	2.4555
3	36.627	4.2618
4	37.933	4.3112
5	48.59	4.7416
6	62.499	6.561

2.2 Design Optimization

As can be seen from the previous discussion, the first six natural frequencies for the structural steel chassis lie in the range from 14 to 63 Hz. In practice, the road excitation has typical values varying from 0 to 100 Hz. At high-speed cruising, the excitation is about 3000 rpm or 50 Hz [2, 4, 5]. Diesel engine is known to have operating speed varying from 8 to 33 rps [6]. In low-speed idling condition, the speed range is about 8–10 rps. This translates into excitation frequencies varying from 24 to 30 Hz [2]. From modal analysis results of structural steel chassis, we can see that the second natural frequency (F2) lies in the 24–30 Hz range, while the fifth frequency (F5) is close to 50 Hz. Thus, the chassis may experience structural resonance at idling and high-speed cruising condition. We have tried to avoid the occurrence of resonance by incorporating minimum changes to the original design, by way of optimization of the design. No extra components have been added to the original design. Only the position and cross-section of two cross members have been optimized to get the frequency values in the desired range.

Parameters for chassis optimization: Four parameters (x1, y1, a, and b) have been chosen for optimization. Out of these four, two are related to the position of the cross members (x1, y1) and the other two are related to the cross-sectional area of the cross members (a, b). The two cross members (CM3 and CM4) undergoing a change

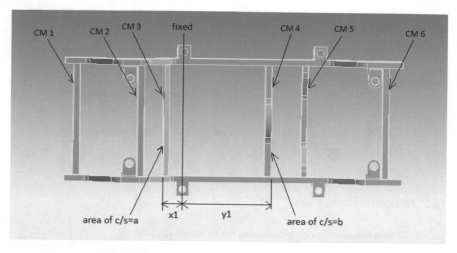

Fig. 3 Parameters for chassis optimization

in position and cross-sectional area are highlighted in Fig. 3, along with the four parameters to be varied.

As seen in Fig. 3,

$$x1 = \text{distance of CM3 from fixed,}$$
$$y1 = \text{distance of CM4 from fixed,}$$
$$a = \text{c/s area of CM3,}$$
$$b = \text{c/s area of CM4.}$$

For original chassis, $x1 = -238.3$ mm, $y1 = 1005$ mm, $a = 624$ mm^2, and $b = 2400$ mm^2.

Methodology of optimization: The cross members indicated by CM1, CM2, CM5, and CM6 are fixed as per their original configuration. The position and area of cross-section of cross members CM3 and CM4 will be varied to find optimum configuration. Next, using Taguchi method, the optimum configuration would be obtained.

Taguchi method makes use of orthogonal arrays (OAs) to conduct a set of experiments. Selection of proper control factors is essential to obtain the optimum results of the process. Taguchi recommends the use of the loss function to measure the performance characteristics that are deviating from the desired target value. The value of this loss function is further transformed into signal-to-noise (S/N) ratio. Usually, there are three categories of the performance characteristics to analyze the S/N ratio. They are: nominal-the-best, larger-the-better, and smaller-the-better [7].

In our case, since we want to reduce the fifth natural frequency (F5), we have chosen smaller-the-better type. We have chosen x1 and y1 as our control factors.

Optimization results: In Table 2, the highlighted rows indicate the configuration selected for the subsequent steps. The basis for selection is minimum value of frequency F5. However, in steps 3 and 4, it is observed that the value of F5 goes on decreasing continuously with increase in cross-sectional area of members. So, in these two steps, we have not selected the configuration giving minimum F5, but an intermediate configuration.

The final selected configuration is the one highlighted in step 4 of Table 2. Now, we keep the selected values of a and b fixed and chose x1 and y1 as our control factors. By adding and subtracting half the step size (i.e., $135/2 = 67.5$ mm) to the selected values of x1 and y1, we get three values (levels) each for x1 and y1. The control factors and their levels are shown in Table 3. By taking different combinations of these values, we get Table 4.

Out of the nine iterations shown in Table 4, the configuration in iteration 3 gives the lowest value of frequency F5. Hence, the iteration 3 seems to be the most optimum configuration under the given considerations. We will further check this by finding out the S/N ratios for the iterations.

The S/N ratios for all the iterations are tabulated as shown in Table 5. The average S/N ratio for each control factor is shown in Table 6.

The factor levels corresponding to the highest S/N ratio were chosen to optimize the condition. Thus, the optimum values of the control factors and their levels are as given in Table 7.

It can be seen from Table 8 that the second and fifth frequencies have moved away from the resonance zone. The optimized chassis configuration is shown in Fig. 4.

Thus, for the optimum chassis configuration, x1 = 742.5 mm, y1 = 607.5 mm, a = 1568 mm^2, and b = 3344 mm^2.

2.3 Harmonic Response Analysis of Original and Optimized Chassis

A harmonic force having a magnitude equal to engine weight (1000 N) is applied to one of the cross member (Fig. 5), and the average response of the entire chassis to this harmonic force at different frequencies is recorded.

From the frequency response curves (Figs. 6 and 7), we can see that the maximum amplitude of vibration under the given force is 6.5799 mm at 93 Hz for the original chassis, and 6.138 mm at 90 Hz for the optimized chassis. Thus, the maximum vibration amplitude for the optimized chassis is slightly lower than that for the original chassis.

Table 2 Parameters for optimization

Step no.	Iteration no.	x1 (mm)	y1 (mm)	a (mm^2)	b (mm^2)	F5 (Hz)
1	1	−275.06	1005	624	2400	48.645
	2	−311.82	1005	624	2400	48.685
	3	−348.59	1005	624	2400	48.738
	4	−385.19	1005	624	2400	48.792
	5	0	1005	624	2400	48.356
	6	135	1005	624	2400	48.284
	7	270	1005	624	2400	48.224
	8	405	1005	624	2400	48.169
	9	540	1005	624	2400	48.124
	10	675	1005	624	2400	48.099
	11	**810**	**1005**	**624**	**2400**	**48.09**
	12	1160	1005	624	2400	48.253
2	1	810	135	624	2400	48.55
	2	810	270	624	2400	48.219
	3	810	405	624	2400	47.946
	4	**810**	**540**	**624**	**2400**	**47.759**
	5	810	675	624	2400	47.697
	6	810	945	624	2400	47.953
	7	810	1080	624	2400	48.279
	8	810	1215	624	2400	48.658
3	1	810	540	848	2400	47.679
	2	810	540	1080	2400	47.597
	3	810	540	1320	2400	47.513
	4	**810**	**540**	**1568**	**2400**	**47.428**
	5	810	540	1824	2400	47.327
	6	810	540	2088	2400	47.24
	7	810	540	2360	2400	47.152
4	1	810	540	1568	2624	47.349
	2	810	540	1568	2856	47.263
	3	810	540	1568	3096	47.175
	4	**810**	**540**	**1568**	**3344**	**47.076**
	5	810	540	1568	3600	46.993
	6	810	540	1568	3864	46.894
	7	810	540	1568	4136	46.798

Table 3 Control factors and their levels

Factors	Levels		
	1	2	3
x1 (mm)	742.5	810	877.5
y1 (mm)	472.5	540	607.5

Table 4 Parameters for optimization

Iteration no.	x1 (mm)	y1 (mm)	a (mm^2)	b (mm^2)	F5 (Hz)
1	742.5	472.5	1568	3344	47.128
2	742.5	540	1568	3344	47.011
3	**742.5**	**607.5**	**1568**	**3344**	**46.932**
4	810	472.5	1568	3344	47.192
5	810	540	1568	3344	47.082
6	810	607.5	1568	3344	46.988
7	877.5	472.5	1568	3344	47.256
8	877.5	540	1568	3344	47.158
9	877.5	607.5	1568	3344	47.079

Table 5 Tabulated S/N ratios

Iteration	S/N (dB)
1	−33.46558
2	−33.44399
3	−33.42938
4	−33.47737
5	−33.4571
6	−33.43974
7	−33.48914
8	−33.47111
9	−33.45654

Table 6 Average S/N ratio for each factor

Level	x1	y1
1	−33.45	−33.48
2	−33.46	−33.46
3	−33.47	−33.44
Delta	0.03	0.04
Rank	2	1

Table 7 Optimum values of control factors and their levels

Factors	Optimum value	Level
x1	742.5	1
y1	607.5	3

Table 8 Comparison of natural frequencies for original and optimized chassis

Mode	Frequency (original) (Hz)	Frequency (optimized) (Hz)
1	14.211	14.926
2	25.595	30.17
3	36.627	32.31
4	37.933	35.115
5	48.59	46.932
6	62.499	62.874

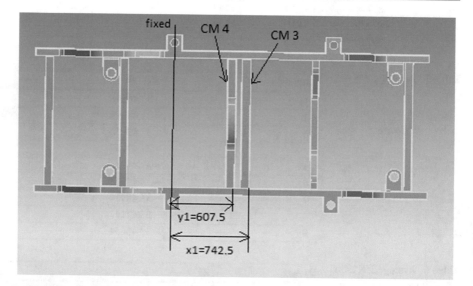

Fig. 4 Optimum chassis configuration

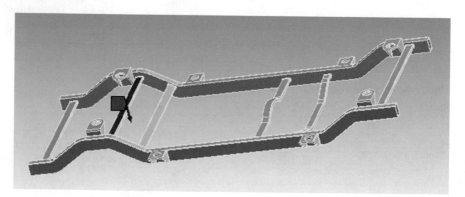

Fig. 5 Harmonic force applied to chassis

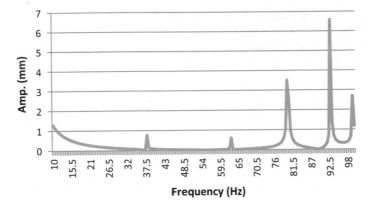

Fig. 6 Frequency response curve—original chassis

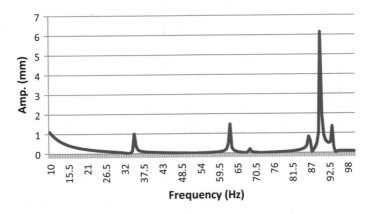

Fig. 7 Frequency response curve—optimized chassis

3 Conclusion

In this paper, dynamic analysis of a ladder chassis frame was carried out and based on the results, the chassis was optimized so as to get the natural frequencies in the desired range with minimum changes in the original design. The following conclusions can be drawn from this work:

- The first six significant natural frequencies for the structural steel chassis are in 14–63 Hz range. These frequencies lie in the range of excitation frequencies due to engine vibrations and road profile excitations.
- From Table 2, it is clear that by increasing the cross-sectional area of members CM3 and CM4, the fifth natural frequency F5 of the chassis decreases and moves away from the 50 Hz mark. The greater the cross-sectional area, the more the value of F5 moves away from 50 Hz. The extent to which the area is to be increased will depend on the operational considerations.

- For the optimized chassis, the second and fifth natural frequencies have moved away from the resonance zone.
- Harmonic analysis showed that for the given inputs, the maximum amplitude of vibration for the optimized chassis is marginally lower than that for the original chassis.

References

1. G.K. Grover, *Mechanical Vibrations*, 8th edn. (Nem Chand & Bros, 2009)
2. T.H. Fui, R.A. Rahaman, Static and Dynamic structural analysis of a 4.5 ton truck chassis. J. Mekanikal (24), 56–67 (2007)
3. S.S. Rao, *Mechanical Vibrations*, 3rd edn. (Wesley, 1995)
4. K. Mekonnen, Static and dynamic analysis of a commercial vehicle with van body. M.Sc. Thesis (School of Graduate Studies, Addis Ababa University, 2008)
5. M. Hadipour, F. Alambeigi, R. Hosseini, R. Masoudinejad, A study on the vibrational effects of adding an auxiliary chassis to a 6-ton truck. J. Amer. Sci. 7(6), 1219–1226 (2011). ISSN: 1545-1003
6. I. Johansson, S. Edlund, Optimization of vehicle dynamics in trucks by use of full vehicle FE-models (Göteborg, Sweden, Department of Vehicle Dynamics & Chassis Technology, Volvo Truck Corporation)
7. S. Athreya, Y.D. Venkatesh, Application of taguchi method for optimization of process parameters in improving the surface roughness of lathe facing operation. Int. Ref. J. Eng. Sci. (IRJES) 1(3),13–19 (2012). ISSN (Online) 2319-183X, (Print) 2319-1821

Active Vibration Absorber for a Nonlinear System with Time-Delay Acceleration Feedback for Superharmonic and Subharmonic Resonance Conditions

S. Mohanty and S. K. Dwivedy

Abstract In the present work, dynamic analysis of a spring, mass, and damper-based nonlinear active vibration absorber, and a nonlinear primary system are carried out by time-delay acceleration feedback. The primary system is subjected to multi-harmonic hard excitation and parametric excitation. It is proposed to reduce vibration of both the primary system and the absorber by attaching a lead zirconate titanate (PZT) stack actuator connected in series with which it acts as an active vibration absorber. Due to the external excitation, strain is developed in the PZT sensor, which produces voltage and this voltage is converted into a counteracting force by the PZT actuator to suppress the vibration of the primary system. Second-order method of multiple scales (MMS) is used to obtain the approximate solution of the system. Frequency responses and time responses for the different parameter of the system are studied for simultaneous superharmonic and subharmonic resonance conditions.

Keywords Dynamic vibration absorber · MMS · PZT actuator

1 Introduction

Dynamic vibration absorber (DVA) consists of spring, mass, and damper system, which is used to attenuate the vibration of the primary system by shifting the resonant natural frequency of the primary system [1]. However, DVAs have only suppressed the vibration at the resonating frequency of operation and also increases the struc-

S. Mohanty (✉) · S. K. Dwivedy
Department of Mechanical Engineering, Indian Institute
of Technology Guwahati, Guwahati 781039, Assam, India
e-mail: siba.mech@gmail.com

© Springer Nature Singapore Pte Ltd. 2019
D N Badodkar and T A Dwarakanath (eds.), *Machines, Mechanism
and Robotics*, Lecture Notes in Mechanical Engineering,
https://doi.org/10.1007/978-981-10-8597-0_58

tural weight of the system [2]. But the use of various optimization techniques, smart materials and model design, and the vibration of the system are reduced for larger band frequency of operation [3] with minimal weight. The absorber used for attenuating the vibration of primary mass vibrates itself at a higher amplitude, which arises to the nonlinearity behavior in the frequency response of the absorber. Also, many dynamical systems are inherently nonlinear because of the prolonged use and various applications [4] so the nonlinear vibration absorber is more practical in nature.

In the present work, a new design for the absorber is proposed in which a PZT stack actuator is connected in series with a spring in the absorber configuration. Also, the mass ratio of 0.01 between the absorber and primary system is considered. The analysis is carried out by considering time-delay acceleration feedback, which is not explored more in the previous literature. The primary system in the proposed model is subjected to multi-harmonic hard excitation and parametric excitation, and the analysis is carried out for the simultaneous sub- and superharmonic resonance conditions.

2 Active Nonlinear Vibration Absorber

In the proposed model, m_i, c_i and k_i denotes mass, damping, and stiffness of the primary system and the absorber, respectively, for $i = 1, 2$ as shown in Fig. 1. k_3 denote spring stiffness which is connected in series with PZT actuator having stiffness k_P^E. The controlling force produced by the combination of spring stiffness k_3 and actuator is denoted as F_c. The terms k_{12}, k_{13}, k_{21}, and k_{23} denotes quadratic and cubic nonlinear stiffness in the primary system and the absorber, respectively. Two harmonic excitation force of $F_{11} \cos(\Omega_{11} t)$, $F_{21} \cos(\Omega_{21} t)$ and a parametric excitation force of $x_1 F_{31} \cos(\Omega_{31} t)$ are acting on the primary system [5]. The mathematical model of the system is described by two ordinary coupled differential equations of motion as:

$$m_1 \ddot{x}_1 + k_1 x_1 + k_{12} x_1^2 + k_{13} x_1^3 + k_2 (x_1 - x_2) + k_{21} (x_1 - x_2)^2 + k_{23} (x_1 - x_2)^3 + c_1 \dot{x}_1$$
$$+ c_2 (\dot{x}_1 - \dot{x}_2) = F_{11} \cos(\Omega_{11} t) + F_{21} \cos(\Omega_{21} t) + x_1 F_{31} \cos(\Omega_{31} t) - F_c \quad (1)$$
$$m_2 \ddot{x}_2 + k_2 (x_2 - x_1) + k_{21} (x_2 - x_1)^2 + k_{23} (x_2 - x_1)^3 + c_2 (\dot{x}_2 - \dot{x}_1) = F_c \quad (2)$$

Fig. 1 Nonlinear active vibration absorber

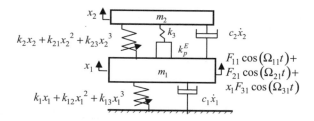

$$F_c = k_r(x_1 - x_2 + nd_{33}k_c\ddot{x}_1(t - \tau_d)) \tag{3}$$

where $k_r = (k_3 k_p^E)/(k_3 + k_p^E)$, $n =$ number of wafers, $d_{33} =$ dielectric charge constant, $k_c =$ controller gain, and $\tau_d =$ time delay in the feedback. Assuming $\omega_1^2 = (k_1 + k_2 + k_r)/m_1$ and non-dimensional time $\tau = \omega_1 t$, the Eqs. (1) and (2) are non-dimensionalized by considering a small bookkeeping parameter ε as given below.

Variable	ξ_1, ξ_2, F_3	$\mu^{-1}, \alpha_{12}, \alpha_{13}, \alpha_{21}, \alpha_{23}, F_{c1}$
Scaling	ε	ε^2

The final equation of motion after ordering can be written as:

$$\frac{d^2x_1}{d\tau^2} + \omega_{n1}^2 x_1 + \left(2\varepsilon\xi_1 + \varepsilon^3\frac{\omega_r}{\mu}2\xi_2\right)\frac{dx_1}{d\tau} = \varepsilon^2\left(\frac{\omega_r^2}{\mu}\right)x_2 + \varepsilon^3 2\xi_2\frac{\omega_r}{\mu}\frac{dx_2}{d\tau} - \varepsilon^2\alpha_{12}x_1^2$$
$$- \varepsilon^2\alpha_{13}x_1^3 - \varepsilon^2\alpha_{21}(x_1 - x_2)^2 - \varepsilon^2\alpha_{23}(x_1 - x_2)^3 + F_1\cos(\Omega_1\tau) \tag{4}$$
$$+ F_2\cos(\Omega_2\tau) + \varepsilon x_1 F_3\cos(\Omega_3\tau) - \varepsilon^2 F_{c1}\left(\frac{d^2x_1(\tau-\tau_d)}{d\tau^2}\right)$$

$$\frac{d^2x_2}{d\tau^2} - \omega_r^2 x_1 + \omega_r^2 x_2 + \varepsilon^2\mu\alpha_{21}(x_2 - x_1)^2 + \varepsilon^2\mu\alpha_{23}(x_2 - x_1)^3 + \varepsilon 2\xi_2\omega_r\left(\frac{dx_2}{d\tau} - \frac{dx_1}{d\tau}\right)$$
$$= \mu F_{c1}\left(\frac{d^2x_1(\tau - \tau_d)}{d\tau^2}\right) \tag{5}$$

where

$$\omega_{n1} = 1, 2\xi_1 = \frac{c_1}{m_1\omega_1}, \omega_r = \left(\frac{\omega_2}{\omega_1}\right), \omega_2 = \sqrt{\frac{k_2+k_r}{m_2}}, \mu = \frac{m_1}{m_2}, \omega_1 = \sqrt{\frac{k_1+k_2+k_r}{m_1}},$$
$$2\xi_2 = \frac{c_2}{m_2\omega_2}, \alpha_{12} = \frac{k_{12}}{m_1\omega_1^2}, \alpha_{13} = \frac{k_{13}}{m_1\omega_1^2}, \alpha_{21} = \frac{k_{21}}{m_1\omega_1^2}, \alpha_{23} = \frac{k_{23}}{m_1\omega_1^2}, F_1 = \frac{F_1}{m_1\omega_1^2},$$
$$F_2 = \frac{F_2}{m_1\omega_1^2}, F_3 = \frac{F_3}{m_1\omega_1^2}, F_{c1} = \frac{k_r k_c nd_{33}}{m_1}, \Omega_1 = \frac{\Omega_{11}}{\omega_1}, \Omega_2 = \frac{\Omega_{21}}{\omega_1}, \Omega_3 = \frac{\Omega_{31}}{\omega_1}$$

In the following section, second-order method of multiple scales is used to obtain the approximate solutions of the Eqs. (4) and (5).

2.1 Approximate Frequency Analysis Using MMS

The method of multiple sales is employed for an approximate solution the system. The perturbed solutions and time derivatives in the new time scale are expanded as:

$$x_1 = x_{10}(\tau_0, \tau_1) + \varepsilon x_{11}(\tau_0, \tau_1) + \varepsilon^2 x_{12}(\tau_0, \tau_1) \tag{6}$$
$$x_1(\tau - \tau_d) = x_{10}(\tau_0 - \tau_d, \tau_1 - \varepsilon\tau_d) + \varepsilon x_{11}(\tau_0 - \tau_d, \tau_1 - \varepsilon\tau_d) + \varepsilon^2 x_{12}(\tau_0 - \tau_d, \tau_1 - \varepsilon\tau_d) \tag{7}$$
$$x_2 = x_{20}(\tau_0, \tau_1) + \varepsilon x_{21}(\tau_0, \tau_1) + \varepsilon^2 x_{22}(\tau_0, \tau_1) \tag{8}$$

The time derivatives along different time scales lead to the differential opera-
tors $\frac{d}{d\tau} = D_0 + \varepsilon D_1 + \varepsilon^2 D_2$ and $\frac{d^2}{d\tau^2} = D_0^2 + 2\varepsilon D_0 D_1 + \varepsilon^2 (D_1^2 + 2D_0 D_2)$ where
$D_n = \partial/\partial T_n$. Substituting the above equations into Eqs. (4) and (5), collecting the
coefficients of ε^n and equating them to zero, one obtains for

$$\varepsilon^0 : D_0^2 x_{10} + \omega_{n1}^2 x_{10} = F_1 \cos(\Omega_1 \tau) + F_2 \cos(\Omega_2 \tau) \tag{9a}$$

$$\varepsilon^0 : D_0^2 x_{20} + \omega_r^2 x_{20} = \omega_r^2 x_{10} + \mu F_{c1} D_0^2 x_{10}(\tau_0 - \tau_d) \tag{9b}$$

$$\varepsilon^1 : D_0^2 x_{11} + \omega_{n1}^2 x_{11} = -2D_0 D_1 x_{10} - 2\xi_1 D_0 x_{10} + x_{10} F_3 \cos(\Omega_3 \tau) \tag{9c}$$

$$\varepsilon^1 : D_0^2 x_{21} + \omega_r^2 x_{21} = 2\omega_r \xi_2 D_0 x_{10} - 2\omega_r \xi_2 D_0 x_{20} + \omega_r^2 x_{11}$$
$$- 2D_0 D_1 x_{20} + \mu F_{c1} D_0^2 x_{11}(\tau - \tau_d) + 2\mu F_{c1} D_0 D_1 x_{10}(\tau - \tau_d) \tag{9d}$$

$$\varepsilon^2 : D_0^2 x_{12} + \omega_{n1}^2 x_{12} = -D_1^2 x_{10} - 2D_0 D_2 x_{10} - D_0^2 F_{c1} x_{10}(\tau_0 - \tau_d)$$
$$- 2D_0 D_1 x_{11} + \frac{\omega_r^2 x_{20}}{\mu} - \alpha_{12} x_{10}^2 - \alpha_{13} x_{10}^3 - \alpha_{21} x_{10}^2 + 2\alpha_{21} x_{10} x_{20} - \alpha_{21} x_{20}^2$$
$$- \alpha_{23} x_{10}^3 + 3\alpha_{23} x_{10}^2 x_{20} - 3\alpha_{23} x_{10} x_{20}^2 + \alpha_{23} x_{20}^3 - 2\xi_1 D_1 x_{10} - 2\xi_1 D_0 x_{11} + x_{11} F_3 \cos \Omega_3 \tau \tag{9e}$$

$$\varepsilon^2 : D_0^2 x_{22} + \omega_r^2 x_{22} = -\omega_r^2 x_{12} - D_1^2 x_{20} - 2D_0 D_2 x_{20} - 2D_0 D_1 x_{21} - \omega_r^2 x_{10}^2 \alpha_{21}$$
$$+ 2\omega_r^2 x_{10} x_{20} \alpha_{21} - \omega_r^2 x_{20}^2 \alpha_{21} + \omega_r^2 x_{10}^3 \alpha_{23} - 3\omega_r^2 x_{10}^2 x_{20} \alpha_{23} + 3\omega_r^2 x_{10} x_{20}^2 \alpha_{23} - \omega_r^2 x_{20}^3 \alpha_{23}$$
$$+ 2\omega_r \xi_2 D_1 x_{10} + 2\omega_r \xi_2 D_0 x_{11} - 2\omega_r \xi_2 D_1 x_{20} - 2\omega_r \xi_2 D_0 x_{21} + \mu F_{c1} D_1^2 x_{10}(\tau - \tau_d)$$
$$+ 2\mu F_{c1} D_0 D_2 x_{10}(\tau - \tau_d) + \mu F_{c1} D_0^2 x_{12}(\tau - \tau_d) + 2\mu F_{c1} D_0 D_1 x_{11}(\tau - \tau_d) \tag{9f}$$

The solution of the Eq. (9a) can be written as:

$$x_{10} = A_1 \exp(i\omega_{n1}\tau_0) + \frac{F_1 \exp(i\Omega_1 \tau_0)}{2(\omega_{n1}^2 - \Omega_1^2)} + \frac{F_2 \exp(i\Omega_2 \tau_0)}{2(\omega_{n1}^2 - \Omega_2^2)} + cc \tag{10}$$

where "cc" stands for complex conjugate of preceding terms. A_1 is an unknown
complex function of non-dimensional time τ_1. Substituting Eq. (10) into Eq. (9b)
and considering 1:1 internal resonance condition, i.e., when $\omega_{n1} = \omega_r + \varepsilon\sigma$, the
secular term and the solution of the Eq. (9b) are expressed in the Eqs. (11) and (12),
respectively.

$$A_1 = \mu F_{c1} \omega_{n1}^2 A_{1d} \exp(-i\omega_{n1}\tau_d) \tag{11}$$

$$x_{20} = B_1 \exp(i\omega_r \tau_0) + \frac{F_1 \exp(i\Omega_1 \tau_0)(\omega_r^2 - \mu F_{c1}\Omega_1^2 \exp(-i\Omega_1 \tau_d))}{2(\omega_r^2 - \Omega_1^2)(\omega_{n1}^2 - \Omega_1^2)}$$
$$+ \frac{F_2 \exp(i\Omega_2 \tau_0)(\omega_r^2 - \mu F_{c1}\Omega_2^2 \exp(-i\Omega_2 \tau_d))}{2(\omega_r^2 - \Omega_2^2)(\omega_{n1}^2 - \Omega_2^2)} + cc \tag{12}$$

Substituting x_{10} and x_{20} in the Eqs. (9c) and (9d) and considering for simultaneous
superharmonic ($\Omega_1 = \frac{\omega_{n1}}{3} + \varepsilon\sigma_1$), subharmonic ($\Omega_2 = 3\omega_{n1} + \varepsilon\sigma_2$), principal parametric ($\Omega_3 = 2\omega_{n1} + \varepsilon\sigma_3$), and 1:1 internal resonance condition, the secular terms
($2i\omega_{n1} D_1 A_1$ and $2i\omega_{n1} D_1 B_1$) are obtained. After eliminating the secular terms from
Eqs. (9c) and (9d), the solutions x_{11} and x_{21} are obtained. Similarly, the secular terms

$2i\omega_{n1}D_2A_1$, $2i\omega_{n1}D_2B_1$ and solutions (x_{12} and x_{21}) for ε^2 order Eqs. (9e) and (9f) are obtained by considering the terms D_1A_1, $D_1^2A_1$, D_1B_1, and $D_1^2B_1$ present in the equation is equal to zero [6]. Now, the modulation of the complex amplitude to the second nonlinear order with respect to the original timescale τ is obtained as:

$$2i\omega_{n1}\frac{dA_1}{dt} = \varepsilon 2i\omega_{n1}D_1A_1 + \varepsilon^2 2i\omega_{n1}D_2A_1 \tag{13}$$

$$2i\omega_{n1}\frac{dB_1}{dt} = \varepsilon 2i\omega_{n1}D_1B_1 + \varepsilon^2 2i\omega_{n1}D_2B_1 \tag{14}$$

The amplitude functions A_1 and B_1 may be expressed in polar form as $A_1 = \frac{1}{2}a_1e^{i\beta_1}$ and $B_1 = \frac{1}{2}a_2e^{i\beta_2}$. Separating real and imaginary part from the Eqs. (13) and (14), the final steady-state autonomous equation is expressed as:

$$a_1'\omega_{n1} = \frac{\varepsilon a_1(F_3\sin 2\gamma_1 - 2\omega_{n1}\xi_1)}{8} + \varepsilon^2(P_1\sin(\gamma_1 - \gamma_2) + P_2\sin 3\gamma_1 + P_4\sin(\gamma_1 + 2\gamma_2))$$

$$+\varepsilon^2\left(P_3\sin\gamma_1 + P_5\sin 2(\gamma_1 - \gamma_2) + P_6 - F_{c1}\omega_{n1}^2 a_1\sin(\omega_{n1}\tau_d)/2 - \xi_1\Omega_2 F_2 F_3\cos\gamma_1/(r_3 r_4)\right) \tag{15a}$$

$$a_1\gamma_1'\omega_{n1} = a_1\omega_{n1}\sigma_1 + \varepsilon a_1 F_3\cos(2\gamma_1)/4 + \varepsilon^2(P_1\cos(\gamma_1 - \gamma_2) + P_2\cos 3\gamma_1)$$

$$+\varepsilon^2\left(\begin{array}{c} P_3\cos\gamma_1 + P_4\cos(\gamma_1 + 2\gamma_2) + P_5\cos(2(\gamma_1 - \gamma_2))/8 \\ +F_{c1}\omega_{n1}^2 a_1\cos(-\omega_{n1}\tau_d)/2 + \xi_1\Omega_2 F_2 F_3\sin\gamma_1/(r_3 r_4) + P_7 + P_8 \end{array}\right) \tag{15b}$$

$$b_1'\omega_r = \varepsilon\left(\begin{array}{c} \omega_r\omega_{n1}\xi_2 a_1\cos(\gamma_2 - \gamma_1) - b_1\omega_r^2\xi_2 - \xi_1 a_1\mu F_{c1}\omega_{n1}\cos(\gamma_2 - \gamma_1 - \omega_{n1}\tau_d) \\ +a_1 F_3\mu F_{c1}\omega_{n1}\sin(\gamma_2 + \gamma_1 - \omega_{n1}\tau_d)/4\omega_{n1} + \varepsilon Q_1\sin(\gamma_2 - \gamma_1) \end{array}\right)$$

$$+\varepsilon^2\left(\begin{array}{c} Q_2\sin(2\gamma_1 + \gamma_2) + Q_3\sin\gamma_2 + Q_4\sin 3\gamma_2 + Q_5\sin(-\omega_{n1}\tau_d) \\ +Q_6\sin(2(\gamma_2 - \gamma_1))/8 + Q_7\sin(\gamma_2 - \gamma_1 - \omega_{n1}\tau_d) + Q_8\sin(2\gamma_1 + \gamma_2 - \omega_{n1}\tau_d) \\ +Q_9\sin(\gamma_2 - \omega_{n1}\tau_d) - \mu F_{c1}\xi_1\Omega_2 F_2 F_3\cos(\gamma_2 - \omega_{n1}\tau_d)/(r_3 r_4) + Q_{10} \end{array}\right) \tag{15c}$$

$$b_1\omega_r\gamma_2' = b_1\omega_r(\sigma_1 + \sigma) + \varepsilon\left(\begin{array}{c} \xi_1 a_1\mu F_{c1}\omega_{n1}\sin(\gamma_2 - \gamma_1 - \omega_{n1}\tau_d) - \omega_r\omega_{n1}\xi_2 a_1\sin(\gamma_2 - \gamma_1) \\ -a_1 F_3\mu F_{c1}\cos(\gamma_2 + \gamma_1 - \omega_{n1}\tau_d)/4 + \varepsilon Q_1\cos(\gamma_2 - \gamma_1) \end{array}\right)$$

$$+\varepsilon^2\left(\begin{array}{c} Q_2\cos(2\gamma_1 + \gamma_2) + Q_3\cos(\gamma_2) + Q_4\cos(3\gamma_2) + Q_5\cos(-\omega_{n1}\tau_d) + \\ Q_6\cos(2(\gamma_2 - \gamma_1))/8 + Q_7\cos(\gamma_2 - \gamma_1 - \omega_{n1}\tau_d) + Q_9\cos(\gamma_2 - \omega_{n1}\tau_d) + \\ Q_8\cos(2\gamma_1 + \gamma_2 - \omega_{n1}\tau_d) + \mu F_{c1}\xi_1\Omega_2 F_2 F_3\sin(\gamma_2 - \omega_{n1}\tau_d)/(r_3 r_4) + Q_{11} + Q_{12} \end{array}\right) \tag{15d}$$

where
$$\gamma_1 = \sigma_1\tau_1 - \beta_1, \quad \gamma_2 = (\sigma_1 + \sigma)\tau_1 - \beta_2 \text{ and } \sigma_1 = \sigma_2/3 = \sigma_3/2.$$

The steady-state equations of the system are obtained by equating $a_1' = \gamma_1' = a_2' = \gamma_2' = 0$. Further, the stability of the obtained steady-state solution is obtained by finding eigenvalue of the Jacobian matrix. In the following section, taking physical system parameters, the numerical results and discussion have been varied out.

3 Results and Discussion

In this section, non-dimensional frequency responses and time responses of the primary system and the absorber are studied from the steady-state Eqs. (15a–15d) using Newton-Raphson method and fourth-order Runge–Kutta method, respectively. Considering mass ratio between the absorber and the primary system as $\mu = 0.01$ and $\varepsilon = 0.1$, the numerical analyzes have been carried in this work. The time response

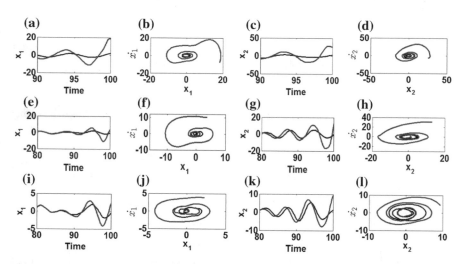

Fig. 2 Time response and phase portrait of the primary system and the absorber with time delay for $F_{c1} = 0.4$ (black) and $F_{c1} = 1.4$ (red) **a–d** σ_1 and σ equal to 1, **e–h** σ_1 and σ equal to 0 and **i–l** σ_1 and σ equal to 0.6 and 2, respectively

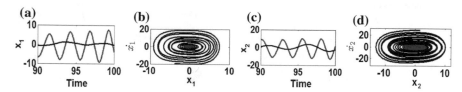

Fig. 3 Time response and phase portrait of the primary system and the absorber without controlling force and time delay for both σ, σ_1 equal to 1 (red) and σ, σ_1 equal to 0 (black)

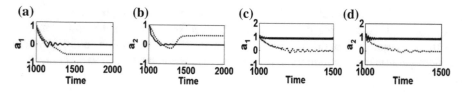

Fig. 4 Time response of the primary system and the absorber obtained from the steady-state equation of second-order MMS with $F_{c1} = 0.4$ and time delay of 1 for **a, b** $\sigma_1 = 0$ (dotted), $\sigma_1 = 1$ (continuous) **c, d** $\sigma_1 = 2$ (dotted), $\sigma_1 = 3$ (continuous)

plot of the primary system and the absorber are shown in Fig. 2 for which non-dimensional parameters are assumed as follows. The damping parameters ξ_1 and ξ_2 of the system are considered as 0.04 and 0.08, respectively. The cubic nonlinearity stiffness is considered to be 0.4% and 0.6% of the linear stiffness for the primary system and the absorber, respectively. The external excitation forces are considered to be $F_1 = 0.6$, $F_2 = 0.6$, and $F_3 = 0.05$, respectively. The time response and the phase portrait of the primary system and the absorber are studied using 'dde23' MATLAB command from the Eqs. (4) and (5) for various values of detuning parameters of σ_1 and σ in Fig. 2 for a time delay of 1 with F_{c1} equal to 0.4 (black color) and 1.4 (red color). In Fig. 2a–d, σ_1 and σ are both considered equal to 1. It can be observed from the Fig. 2a, c that for F_{c1} equal to 0.4, the steady-state response of the primary system and the absorber are periodic with maximum amplitude of 1.6 and 1.4, respectively, but for F_{c1} equal to 1.4, the settling time is more and amplitude responses are increasing with maximum values of 18.7 and 27.8, respectively, for the primary system and the absorber. In Fig. 2e–h σ_1 and σ, both are considered equal to zero. The same trend of curves is observed in Fig. 2e, g in which the primary system and the absorber show periodic responses with maximum amplitude of 2.2 and 5, respectively, for F_{c1} equal to 0.4, and correspondingly for F_{c1} equal to 1.4 the response amplitude is increasing. In Fig. 2i–l σ_1 and σ, parameters are considered

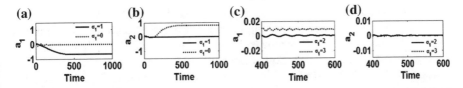

Fig. 5 Time response obtained from the steady-state equation of second-order MMS without controlling force and time delay

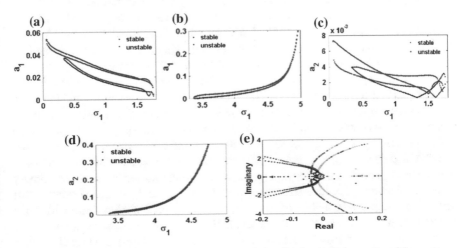

Fig. 6 Frequency response of the primary system and the absorber and eigenvalue of the system

as 0.6 and 2, respectively. From the Fig, 2i, k, the maximum amplitude responses of the primary system and the absorber are 2.2 and 5.6, respectively, for F_{c1} equal to 0.4. When F_{c1} is equal to 1.4, the responses of the primary system and the absorber are increased to 2.9 and 9.8, respectively. The phase portrait of the primary system and the absorber are shown in Fig. 2b, d, f, h, j, and l. From the figures, it is observed that the system is unstable for F_{c1} equal to 1.4 but for F_{c1} equal to 0.4, the system is stable as shown in Fig. 2j, l. It can be observed from the Fig. 2 that with increasing value of F_{c1}, the system shows more vibration and the settling time is also increased. For detuning parameter σ_1 equal to 0.6, both the primary system and the absorber responses are less. Vibration suppression of the system is observed to be better for σ equal to 0 and σ_1 in the range of 0.5–1, and also negative values of σ_1 shows less vibration in the system. In the Fig. 3, times responses and phase portraits for the primary system and the absorber are studied without controlling force using fourth-order Runge–Kutta method from Eqs. (4) and (5). In Fig. 3a, c, the responses of the primary system and the absorber are found to be 1.1 and 3.75, respectively, for σ_1 and σ equal to 0, which is comparatively less than the responses shown in Fig. 3e, g. For σ_1 and σ equal to 1, the responses of the primary system and the absorber are periodic with amplitude 7.3 and 10, respectively. The phase portrait of the primary system and the absorber are shown in Fig. 3b, d, respectively. The system shows a better vibration suppression without the application of F_{c1} when σ_1 is equal to 0 but when σ_1 is not equal to 0 than the response amplitude of both primary system and the absorber keeps increasing same as when F_{c1} equal to 1.4. So, it can be inferred that for a particular value of controlling force F_{c1}, the system shows better vibration suppression when the detuning value σ_1 is away from zero. In Fig. 4, time responses of the primary system and the absorber are obtained from Eq. (15a–15d) with a time delay of 1 using 'dde23' MATLAB command. It is observed from Fig. 4a–d that for F_{c1} equal to 0.4 and 1.4, the amplitude of the primary system is 0.42 and 0.02 and for absorber, it is 0.48 and 0.08 for σ_1 equal to 0 and 1, respectively. Similarly, the amplitude of the primary system is 0.92 and 0.01 and for absorber, it is 0.98 and 0.01 for σ_1 equal to 2 and 3, respectively. In Fig. 5, time response of the primary system and the absorber are obtained without controlling force F_{c1} using 'ode45' MATLAB command. The amplitude of the primary system is 0.62 and 0.001 and for the absorber, it is 0.008 and 0.8 for σ_1 equal to 1 and 0, respectively. Similarly, the amplitude of the primary system is 0.92 and 0.01 and for absorber, it is 0.98 and 0.01 for σ_1 equal to 2 and 3, respectively. The response obtained in the Fig. 3 and Fig. 5 are closely matched with each other when there is no controlling force and time delay in the system for σ_1 equal to 0 and 1. But for the other cases, the amplitude responses are different as in Fig. 5. The frequency response of the primary system and the absorber are obtained by solving Eqs. (15a–15d) using Newton's method which are shown in Fig. 6 for F_{c1} equal to 0.4. In the Fig. 6a, b, the frequency response of the primary system is shown for the different values of σ_1. From Fig. 6a, b, it can be observed that for σ_1 in the region of 0.4–1.6 and 3.4–4.2, the system has a stable solution. Multiple unstable solutions also exist in this region. In Fig. 6c, d, the frequency response of the absorber is shown. In Fig. 6c, the absorber shows stable and unstable branches when σ_1 is in the region of 0.4–1.6. From Fig. 6d, one can observe Hopf bifurcation where the stable solution becomes unstable for σ_1 equal to 4.4. The primary system and the absorber shows better vibration suppression for σ_1 in the range of 1.6–3.4. The amplitude obtained in the frequency plots are closely matched with results obtained in the Fig. 4. In Fig. 6e shows the variation of real and imaginary part of eigenvalues corresponding to responses shown in Fig. 6a–d. Figure 6e clearly shows both static and dynamic bifurcation of the system as the eigenvalues crossing the imaginary axis either through zero or nonzero values, respectively.

4 Conclusions

In the present paper, an active nonlinear vibration absorber by time-delay acceleration feedback is investigated. From the analysis, the non-dimensional amplitude of the primary system is found to be maximum value of 2 for the simultaneous principal parametric, 1:1 internal resonance, sub- and superharmonic resonance conditions with an applied controlling force equal to 0.4. Without the applied control force, the primary system amplitude reduces to 0.02 but only at the resonating operating frequency outside this frequency region the system amplitude increases and becomes unstable. Also increasing the controlling force to 1.4 produces more vibration in the system. From the analysis, it is inferred that the effect of controlling force in reducing the amplitude of the primary system and the absorber for the simultaneous primary resonance, principal parametric, and 1:1 internal resonance condition is better when the frequency of operation varied for σ_1 in the range of 1.6–3.4 or at the resonant frequency of operation. The stability of the system is studied for different values of detuning parameter showing the stable and unstable region of the frequency of operation. The time response plots and the frequency response plots obtained by MMS-II are closely matched at the steady-state conditions. In the proposed model, a spring is connected in series with the PZT actuator. So that the counteracting force developed by the actuator can be controlled more easily without much dependent upon on voltage supply. This can be done using a higher order stiffness spring in series with the actuator by producing more blocking force to the PZT actuator. Since the PZT actuator requires more blocking force and in the proposed model, the mass ratio is considered to be 0.01 so the spring in series with the actuator will provide the more blocking force.

References

1. J.P.Den Hartog, *Mechanical Vibrations* (Dover publications, 1985)
2. T. Asami, Optimal design of double-mass dynamic vibration absorbers arranged in series or in parallel. J. Vib. Acoust. **139**(1), 011015 (2017)
3. J.Q. Sun, M.R. Jolly, M.A. Norris, Passive, adaptive and active tuned vibration absorbers—a survey. J. Mech. Des. **117.B**, 234–242 (1995)

4. M. Sayed, Y.S. Hamed, Stability and response of a nonlinear coupled pitch-roll ship model under parametric and harmonic excitations. Nonlinear Dyn. **64**(3), 207–220 (2011)
5. M. Rabelo, L. Silva, R. Borges, R. Goncalves, M. Henrique, Computational and numerical analysis of a nonlinear mechanical system with bounded delay. Int. J. Non-Linear Mech. **91**, 36–57 (2017)
6. S.K. Dwivedy, R.C. Kar, Nonlinear response of a parametrically excited system using higher-order method of multiple scales. Nonlinear Dyn. **20**(2), 115–130 (1999)

Optimal Damping Factor for the Least Squares Inverse Kinematics for the Steam Generator Inspection System

S. Joseph Winston and P. V. Manivannan

Abstract The Steam Generators used in the Prototype Fast Breeder Reactor have sodium on shell side and water/steam on the tube side. Tube inspection and qualification of all 547 tubes, enhances the safety and reduces the operation cost by increasing plant availability. In this work, a two-axis planar reach robotic arm called as Tube Locator Module (TLM) is used for reaching and orienting the Remote Field Eddy Current (RFEC) testing probe at the exact location of individual Steam Generator tube, and the probe is pushed through the entire tube length for inspection and qualification of the same. A conventional method of inverting the Jacobian and using a pseudo inverse will help in running the actuators in joint space to reach the desired position of the end effector. However, as pseudo inverse suffers numerical stability close to singularities of the manipulator, hence it is proposed to use the damped least squares pseudo inverse method by introducing a damping factor to improve the stability. Higher damping factor increases the stability of manipulator, even when the manipulator moves closer to its singular configurations. However, higher damping factors lead to more tracking error in the end-effector trajectory. Hence, in this work, based on the tracking errors and the geometrical constraints, an optimal damping factor is arrived at for the smooth motion of the TLM. This paper also deals with the manipulability study of the TLM to understand the singular configurations, and apply the damping factor to stabilize the joint angular velocities without causing much error in the end-effector trajectory.

Keywords PFBR · SG · Inspection · Manipulator · Inverse kinematics
DH parameter · Forward kinematics · Yoshikawa manipulability · Tracking error

S. Joseph Winston (✉)
Steam Generator Inspection Devices Section, Indira Gandhi Centre
for Atomic Research, Kalpakkam, India
e-mail: winston@igcar.gov.in

P. V. Manivannan
Department of Mechanical Engineering, Indian Institute
of Technology Madras, Chennai 600036, India
e-mail: pvm@iitm.ac.in

© Springer Nature Singapore Pte Ltd. 2019
D N Badodkar and T A Dwarakanath (eds.), *Machines, Mechanism and Robotics*, Lecture Notes in Mechanical Engineering,
https://doi.org/10.1007/978-981-10-8597-0_59

691

1 Introduction

In Prototype Fast Breeder Reactor (PFBR), there are eight Steam Generators (SGs), each having 547 tubes in bundle carrying water/steam inside and sodium surrounds the tube in the shell side. As sodium–water reaction is exothermic, it is highly undesirable to have a breach in the SG tubes. This mandates a stringent qualification of the SG tubes, by checking for any flaws (or) wall thinning prior to commissioning and also during maintenance operation. Ferritic steel is used to make the SG tubes, due its inherent ability to withstand Stress Corrosion Cracking (SCC), in addition to its high thermal conductivity. However, since ferritic steels are ferromagnetic in nature, only the Remote Field Eddy Current (RFEC) probe can be used for inspecting the tubes. Lot of effort has been put all over the world towards the development of remote inspection systems [1] for SG tube qualifications using RFEC probe, along with the necessary data acquisition system. International experiences reveal that the plant availability for power generation depends highly on the SG availability. Hence, the efforts are to increase the plant availability with due importance to the plant safety through proper tube inspections and qualifications. A two-axis precision robotic manipulator is designed to orient the end effector to all the 547 tubes uniquely for locating the steam tubes and to push the probe into the tubes for inspection. The kinematic algorithm developed is programmed and simulated using the Python language. The position kinematics and velocity kinematics have been implemented for a point-to-point (tube to tube) movement of the device. The singular configurations are understood for the TLM and a strategy of increasing the stability of the numerical solution has been adapted through the implementation of the Damped Least Squares pseudo inverse method. A detailed study has been performed to compare the tracking error of the TLM end effector due to the damping factor. An optimal damping factor has been arrived, so that the device has least tracking error with highest stability close-in region of the singularity configurations of the TLM. After the simulating the system using Python scripting language, the same methodology has been implemented on the commercially available ELMO motion controller, which facilitates the coding through Structured Text (ST) complying with the IEC 61131-3 OpenPLC coding format to run and check in the actual system.

2 Tube Locator Module (TLM)

Since the tube sheet is planar, a typical Selective Compliant Assembly Robotic Arm (SCARA) type device called as Tube Locator Module (TLM) is designed (Fig. 1). The DH parameters of the TLM is given in Table 1.

The geometry of TLM is designed such that it can be assembled into the inclined manhole of SG. The TLM unfolds into the header during the deployment, to reach all the row tubes covering a radial distance of 420 mm. It becomes a prime importance to do the kinematic analysis of the manipulator, to estimate the singular configura-

Fig. 1 Tube locator module

Table 1 DH parameters for TLM

Joint no. (i)	θ_i	α_i	χ_i	d_i
0	$\theta_{shoulder}$	0	210.0	115.0
1	θ_{elbow}	0	210.0	115.0

tion for mitigating the sudden accelerations/jerks. The arm motion becomes highly unstable, when it is close to the singular pose. This is due to large change in the joint space angles for small change in the end-effector Cartesian space moves, which causes undesirable arm motor tripping due to overcurrents. The best way to estimate the closeness to the singular configuration is to properly analyze the manipulator Jacobian. It is also evident that this singular configuration is independent of the first joint (shoulder) angle.

3 Inverse Kinematics for TLM

In order to avoid singularity, a Damped Least Squares (DLS) [2] inverse kinematics methodology has been followed. Formulating the inverse of Jacobian through a pseudo inverse using the DLS method provides good system stability close to its singular configuration. However, as the damping factor increases, the tracking error of the manipulator also increases. Hence, to find the optimal damping factor that results in minimum tracking error, a kinematic algorithm is coded in python scripting language. Simulation were carried out for finding the reachability of end effector in the given task space. To study the behavior of the arm close to its singular configurations, the arm is made to move from the coordinate [420.0, 0.0] to [−420.0, 0.0] (both are singular configuration points of the SG tube sheet). This point-to-point movement makes the manipulator to start close from its first singular configuration and move through the vicinity of center tube with [0.0, 0.0] coordinate (which is also a singular configuration point) and reach the destination. The best way to estimate the closeness to a singular configuration is to estimate the manipulability of the manipulator. The Yoshikawa manipulability [3, 4] is computed to define the condition of the Jacobian

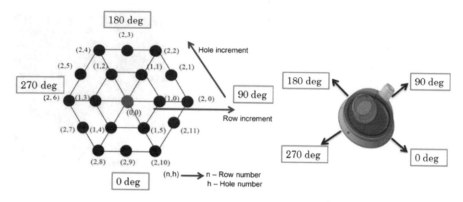

Fig. 2 SG tube ordering scheme (hexagonal array pattern)

at every kinematic step. Since, the tubes are in a hexagonal array form, a numbering scheme has been evolved to obtain the coordinate values, if the user selects the row number and tube number in the array. Figure 2 shows the numbering scheme adapted for the SG tube sheet. Equations 1 and 2 show the tube center coordinates in Polar and Cartesian coordinate system, respectively.

$$(r, \theta) = \left(a\sqrt{n^2 + h^2 - nh}, \cos^{-1}\left(\frac{a(2n - h)}{2r}\right)\right) \tag{1}$$

$$\begin{bmatrix} x \\ y \end{bmatrix} = \begin{pmatrix} r\cos\theta \\ r\sin\theta \end{pmatrix} \tag{2}$$

where "r" and θ are polar coordinates of the tube centers, "a" is tube pitch, "n" is row number, "h" is tube number in the row. The joint space variables are related to the end-effector position (in Cartesian space coordinates) through the Jacobian matrix. Generally, when the Jacobian matrix is a non-square matrix, a pseudo inverse is carried out to obtain the inversion of Jacobian. The forward kinematics shows the end-effector position is a function of joint space variables, which is expressed by the Eq. 3. Its inverse kinematics expression is given by Eq. 4.

$$[e] = J[\theta] \tag{3}$$

$$[\theta] = J^{-1}[e] \tag{4}$$

The Jacobian matrix (J) in the above equation is an $m \times n$-matrix, where "m" represents the DOF of the manipulator and "n" represents independent joints in the manipulator. When "m" is not equal to "n", a pseudo-inverse technique is implemented to find the inverse of Jacobian. In all practical cases, to mitigate the stability issue, when the manipulator end effector is close to the singular position, the Damped Least squares (DLS) Jacobian Inverse ($J^{\dagger}$) [2] is used and is mathematically represented by Eq. 5.

$$J^{\dagger} = J^T(JJ^T + \lambda^2 I)^{-1} \tag{5}$$

where "λ" is a damping factor [5, 6]. When the value of $\lambda = 0$, the inverse of Eq. 5 will typically work as a pseudo-inverse. Further, this "λ" strengthens the diagonal elements of Jacobian near manipulator's singular positions, by reducing the tendency of matrix to have determinant value equalizing zero. Implementing DLS induces the deviation in tracked path from shortest path; but simultaneously improving stability at singular positions.

The velocity kinematics [7] can be implemented as follows:

$$[\dot{\theta}] = J^{\dagger}[\dot{e}] \tag{6a}$$

$$[\Delta\theta] = [\dot{\theta}][\Delta t] \tag{6b}$$

$$[\theta_{i+1}] = [\theta_i] + [\Delta\theta] \tag{6c}$$

where θ is joint angle vector and "e" is change in end-effector position in the given time interval. In order to have a good linearization, the discrete time step is chosen with smaller interval, so that the joint angles and end-effector position changes with smaller steps. This is implemented to reduce large change in joint velocities when higher times are used, that will mask the velocity changes due to manipulability near the singular configurations.

4 Manipulability Study for TLM

Manipulability is a measure of the ability of the manipulator to move in specific directions. This study is important, as the manipulator close to its singular configurations will have very less ability to move in specific directions and requires very large torque for motion. This results in motors drawing more current. In addition, the velocities have a sudden spike causing a lot of accelerations in the manipulator arms, producing undesirable dynamic forces in the system.

Considering, a set of joint velocities with constant unit norm, i.e., a unit sphere in the joint velocity space given in Eq. 7

$$\dot{q}^T\dot{q} = 1 \tag{7}$$

If v_e is the end-effector velocity in Cartesian space, the joint velocity is given by the following expression:

$$\dot{q} = J(\theta)^{\dagger}v_e \tag{8}$$

Now, the Eq. 7 now becomes:

$$\left[J(\theta)^{\dagger}v_e\right]^T\left[J(\theta)^{\dagger}v_e\right] = 1 \tag{9}$$

where, pseudo inverse is as follows:

$$J(\theta)^{\dagger} = J(\theta)^{T}[J(\theta)J(\theta)]^{-1} \tag{10}$$

Simplifying the Eq. 9, we get,

$$v_e^T \left[J(\theta)J(\theta)^T \right]^{-1} v_e = 1 \tag{11}$$

The expression above defines the points on the surface of an ellipsoid in the end-effector velocity space. The shape and size of the ellipsoid is given by the eigen-decomposition of the matrix $J(q)J(q)^T$. For a 2R manipulator, the ellipsoid becomes an ellipse. The directions of the principal axes of the ellipse is given by the direction of the eigenvectors of $J(q)J(q)^T$ and the lengths of the axes of the ellipse by the square root of the eigenvalues. In the case of a planar manipulator, as in the case of TLM, the $J(q)J(q)^T$ has two orthogonal eigenvectors with corresponding its eigenvalues.

Figure 3 shows the manipulability ellipse of the TLM. The direction of major and minor axes is given by corresponding eigenvectors, while their magnitude is given by eigenvalues. Figure 4 shows the manipulators velocity manipulability of TLM in its task space. It also shows three configurations A, B and C, which are close to singular poses. A large diagonal scalar value (i.e., eigenvalue) indicates high manipulability in the corresponding direction. The condition number in Eq. 12, k—is defined as the ratio of the smallest and largest eigenvalue of $J(q)J(q)^T$ matrix. If the value of the condition number (k) is close to unity, we have an isotropic ellipse (which is a circle). On the other hand, if the value of "k" is either very small (or) high, it indicates that the manipulator is close to its singular point. Having an isotropic ellipse is preferable, as it indicates good manipulability in all directions. The condition number k is given as:

$$k = \sqrt{\frac{\lambda_2}{\lambda_1}} \tag{12}$$

where λ_1 and λ_2 are major and minor axis of ellipse. The area of the ellipse gives the manipulability index. The Manipulability index, μ is given as:

$$\mu = \sqrt{\left| J(\theta)J(\theta)^T \right|} \tag{13}$$

For a 2R planar manipulator, as in the present case of TLM, the manipulability is independent of the first joint angle (i.e., the shoulder angle) [8]. This is indicated through Eq. 16. The end-effector function for a 2R planar can easily be written as follows:

$$e = \begin{bmatrix} e_x \\ e_y \end{bmatrix} = \begin{bmatrix} l_1 \cos \theta_1 + l_2 \cos(\theta_1 + \theta_2) \\ l_1 \sin \theta_1 + l_2 \sin(\theta_1 + \theta_2) \end{bmatrix} \tag{14}$$

Fig. 3 Manipulability
ellipse

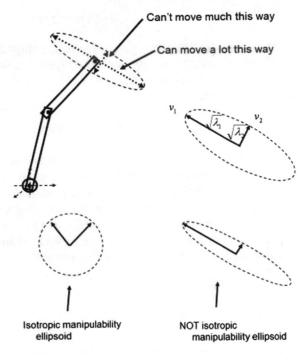

Fig. 4 Manipulability on the
task space

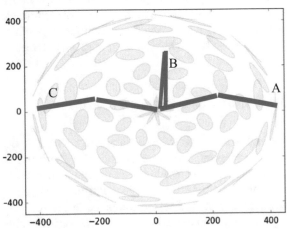

The Jacobian matrix is calculated as:

$$J(\theta) = \begin{pmatrix} -l_1 \sin \theta_1 & -l_2 \sin(\theta_1 + \theta_2) \\ l_1 \cos \theta_1 & l_2 \cos(\theta_1 + \theta_2) \end{pmatrix} \qquad (15)$$

The manipulator will be in a singular configuration, when the determinant of Jacobian becomes zero;

$$\therefore \ |J(\theta)| = l_1 l_2 \sin \theta_2 \tag{16}$$

It is obvious from the Fig. 4, the manipulability ellipse tends to a straight line, when the elbow arm aligns with the shoulder arm. Hence, the manipulator suffers from velocity manipulability in that particular direction. This configuration of manipulator can be generalized as:

$$\theta_2 = \{n\pi \ : \ n\varepsilon N\} \tag{17}$$

In the TLM workspace, the central and peripheral tubes locations gives rise to manipulability. However, a considerable effort has been put to handle this manipulability, when the manipulator pose is close to A, B, (or) C, as shown in Fig. 4. The same figure gives us the understanding for choosing any two points diametrically opposite to study the manipulability; which will be a worst-case scenario. Further, due to circular symmetry, the manipulability will be same for all angles in the polar space of the TLM in diametrical direction motions.

5 Effect of Damping Factor

In order to study the manipulability and the tracking error, inverse kinematics algorithm has been developed in the computer scripting language—Python. Python has been chosen, as it has many library routines to graphically represent the results easily through plots. It also has the linear algebra routines as a built-in library.

5.1 Simulation Through Python

The algorithm uses the DH parameters as input data. Using forward kinematics method, the position of the end effector is calculated. The Inverse kinematic algorithm computes the joint space values for the movement of end effector from present position of the end effector to goal position. The joint space parameters (joint angular positions and velocities) are computed in discrete steps. After each step movement, the code recomputes the Jacobian matrix for further inversions in an iterative scheme.

Once the IK code is functional, the velocity manipulability is computed in every discrete step to analyze the manipulators configuration for further motion towards the target goal point [9]. In our case study, it has been chosen to start the end-effector position from close to [420.0, 0.0] and move to position [−420.0, 0.0] by passing through the center singular point [0.0, 0.0].

Table 2 shows the manipulability, manipulability index and the eigenvalues at the point closer to [420.0, 0.0]. The manipulability "μ" and the manipulability index as discussed earlier are computed for various damping factors "λ". It can be noticed that the increase in damping factor results in increased area of the ellipse, i.e., shown

Table 2 Manipulability close to the first singular point A [420.0, 0.0]

λ	μ	$k = \sqrt{\frac{\lambda_1}{\lambda_2}}$	λ_1	λ_2
0	1539.1	20513.9	220435.5	10.7
20	9524.0	537.6	220835.5	410.7
40	18911.4	137.8	222035.5	1610.7
60	28441.8	62.0	224035.5	3610.7
100	48029.5	23.0	230435.5	10010.7
200	102079.5	6.5	260435.5	40010.7

Table 3 Manipulability close to the second singular point B [0.0, 0.0]

λ	μ	$k = \sqrt{\frac{\lambda_1}{\lambda_2}}$	λ_1	λ_2
0	769.7	3283.1	44100.0	13.4
20	4289.3	107.6	44500.0	413.4
40	8586.8	28.3	45700.0	1613.4
60	13128.6	13.2	47700.0	3613.4
100	23275.0	5.4	54100.0	10013.4
200	58009.7	2.1	84100.0	40013.4

as "μ". The Manipulability index close to unit indicates a configuration, where the manipulator will have isotropic manipulability. A higher or lower value shows least manipulability in the particular directions. It is also obvious from the Eq. 17 that the manipulator position with elbow angle θ_2 is equal to 0 and π, the manipulator is close to the singularity condition.

Table 3 shows the manipulability for various damping factor at $\theta_2 = \pi$, i.e., the end effector is at position [0.0, 0.0]. Similarly, Table 4 shows the manipulability variation close to the singular configuration "C", i.e., when the end effector reaches the position [−420.0, 0.0]. The angular velocities shoot up close to the singular configuration and at times show discontinuities which causes the joint motors to trip due to severe accelerations and jerks. The Fig. 5 shows the joint angular velocities. The linear speed of the end effector in Cartesian space is limited to uniform 20 mm/s from the safety concerns of device. Figure 5 clearly indicates the high change in motor speeds at configurations A, B and C. The figure also indicates the smoothening of the velocity curves at higher damping factors. At zero damping factor, the system will become highly unstable, when manipulator reaches close to singular configuration. This is evident from Fig. 5, as the angular velocities of the joints reaches close to 5 radians/s, which is very high and it may cause the motor tripping.

Table 4 Manipulability close to the second singular point C [−420.0, 0.0]

λ	μ	$k = \sqrt{\frac{\lambda_1}{\lambda_2}}$	λ_1	λ_2
0	384.8	328277.2	220496.0	0.7
20	9407.8	551.3	220896.0	400.7
40	18854.8	138.8	222096.0	1600.7
60	28405.9	62.2	224096.0	3600.7
100	48011.6	23.0	230496.0	10000.7
200	102078.5	6.5	260496.0	40000.7

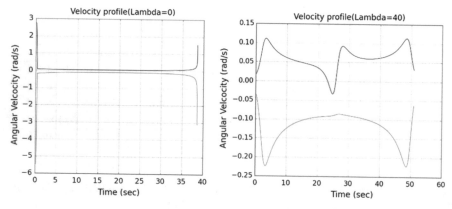

Fig. 5 Joint space velocity variations

5.2 Manipulability

Once, the IK code is functional, the velocity manipulability is computed in every discrete step to analyze the manipulators configuration for further motion towards the target goal point. Similar to the previous case study, it has been chosen to start the end-effector position from close to [420.0, 0.0] and move to position [−420.0, 0.0] by passing through the center singular point [0.0, 0.0].

5.3 Tracking Error

The tracking error is a measure of deviation of actual end-effector path compared to the desired path of the TLM. From the IK solution, the joint angles at various time steps are used to construct the end-effector path by running the forward kinematic routine. The best way to express tracking error is by finding the area enveloped by the end effector from the shortest straight line path.

This algorithm is also coded in Python. First, it computes the vector angle subscribed between the start to end point line and the x-axis. The end-effector tracking

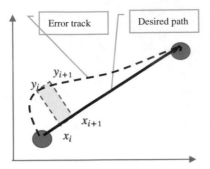

Fig. 6 Error quantification

points is rotated to reference x-axis, so that area integration is easy. This is done by a transformation matrix with rotation angle equal to the computed vector angle. The peak error indicates the peak value of the deviated track of the end effector and the area indicates, how much deviant was the tracking as compared to the original shortest path between point-to-point movements of the manipulator as shown in Fig. 6. The Eq. 18 shows the area integration of the deviated path from the desired path.

$$Tracking\ Error = \sum_{i=1}^{n} (x_{i+1} - x_i)\left(\frac{y_{i+1} + y_i}{2}\right) \tag{18}$$

where "x" is the displacement along the shortest path between the initial and the goal point, while "y" is the perpendicular deviation from the desired trajectory (shortest path). Figure 7 shows the tracking error plot for damping factors 40 and 200. The Fig. 8 shows that the peak error and tracking error measured as area and trend of the curves almost matches. This indicates that the tracking is smooth without sudden spikes. It is quite obvious that for very high damping factors, the tracking error values are very high. This shows that increasing the damping factor beyond the optimal value will give rise to undesirable tracking errors.

5.4 Optimal Damping

It is obvious from the foregoing analysis that the increase in damping factor increases the manipulator's stability. Further, the increase in damping factor reduces the peak angular velocities of the motor in proximity to the singular configuration of the manipulator. However, with high damping factor, the tracking error also increases. Especially, in the SG inspection, if some tubes are plugged (i.e., defecting tubes of the steam generator are normally closed using plugs), the plug head will project up from the tube sheet. Hence, due to excess tracking error, the inspection probe at the manipulator end effector may deviate from planned path and come in contact with

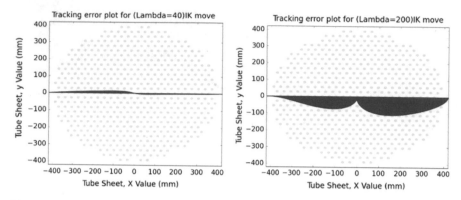

Fig. 7 Tracking error for various damping factors

Fig. 8 Tracking error due to damping factor, λ

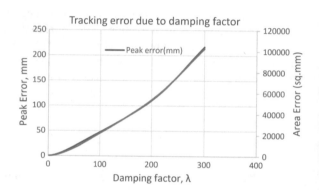

plugs and cause undesirable collisions which will damage the probe. Therefore, to optimize the damping factor for the manipulator, TLM, the peak angular velocities estimated close to the singular points at A and C (in Fig. 4) for various damping factors are compared against the tracking error of the manipulator as shown in Fig. 9. The crossover of these two curves (namely, tracing error and angular vs. damping factor) happen close to the damping factor 35. However, for a damping factor (λ) of 40, though the tracking error is slightly higher (which is acceptable because of large tube—tube pitch), the peak angular velocity is lower; thereby improving the stability. Hence, damping factor of 40 has been chosen as the optimal value for the Damped Least squares (DLS) pseudo-inverse algorithm for the TLM manipulator.

6 Implementation on Motion Controller

The DLS IK algorithm is programmed on the commercially available motion controller, Elmo. The coding is done through the open standard, IEC 61131-3 OpenPLC coding syntax, ST code and Functional Block Diagrams (FBD). The manipulator

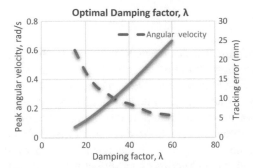

Fig. 9 Optimal damping factor, λ

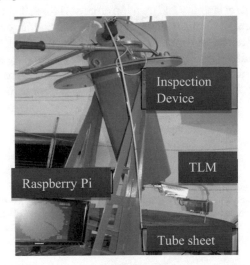

Fig. 10 Experimental setup

is fixed on a test stand as shown in Fig. 10. The system has been under various conditions and found to be highly stable even close to the singular configurations. Also, the tracking error is found to be well within the allowable limits. Hence, the optimal damping factor chosen as 40 is a good choice. It is also ensured through the implementation of the DLS methodology, the convergence to the IK solution and tracking error are within in the allowable limits. This protects the system from any abnormal motor trips and also maintains a highest stability even close to its singular configurations. Subsequently, the device has performed well during the actual inspection campaign on eight PFBR SGs without any single motor trips.

7 Conclusion

Steam Generator of Fast Breeder reactors needs the qualifications of the tubes, in order to reduce operational costs by attaining highest plant availability. A versatile remote Tube Inspection Manipulator (TLM) has been designed. We have also developed required forward and inverse kinematics algorithms, in addition to routines necessary calculating the optimal damping factor. From the simulation studies, it has been found that higher damping factor leads to better manipulator stability; however, it leads to undesirable tracking error. It has been found that a damping factor (λ) value of: 40 results in smooth motion of end-effector motion, with minimal tracking error. This methodology has been implemented on a commercial motion controller ELMO and checked for stability and tracking error deviation. The experimental study indicates that system performs well, even close to its singular configurations. Subsequently, the device has performed well during the actual inspection campaign on eight PFBR SGs without any single motor tripping. This not only gives assurance but also gives utmost safety as the tube-to-tube motion is simulated prior to the actual motion on the robotic arm through manipulability and error estimations through the motion controller.

References

1. L. Obrutsky, J. Renaud, R. Lakhan, Steam generator inspections: faster, cheaper and better, are we there yet?, IV Conferencia Panamericana de END, Buenos Aires, Octubre 2007
2. S.R. Ross, Introduction to inverse kinematics with Jacobian transpose, pseudoinverse and damped least squares method (Department of Mathematics, University of California, San Diego, 7 Oct 2009)
3. T. Yoshikawa, *Foundation of Robotics-Analysis and Control* (Corona Publication Pvt. Ltd., Japan), pp. 127–153
4. T. Yoshikawa, Manipulability of robotic mechanisms. Int. J. Robot. Res. **4** (1985)
5. S. Chiaverini, B. Siciliano, O. Egeland, Review of the damped least-squares inverse kinematics with experiments on an industrial robot manipulator. IEEE Trans. Control Syst. Technol. **2**, 123–134 (1994)
6. L.M. Phuoc, P. Martinet, S. Lee, H. Kim, Damped least square based genetic algorithm with gaussian distribution of damping factor for singularity-robust inverse kinematics. J. Mech. Sci. Technol. **22**, 1330–1338 (2008)
7. C. Peter, Robotics vision and control, in *Fundamental Algorithms in MATLAB* (Springer)
8. B. Tondu, A theorem of manipulability of redundant serial kinematic chains. Eng. Lett. **15**(2), EL_15_2_27, Advance online publication: 17 Nov 2007
9. R. Ishibashi, S. Zou, K. Kawaguchi, N. Takesue, A. Kojima, A proposal of manipulability based model predictive control for the parallelogram linkage, in *10th IFAC Symposium on Robot Control International Federation of Automatic Control* (Dubrovnik, Croatia, 5–7 Sept 2012)

A Partial Compliant Mechanism for Precise Remote-Center Motion

Tanveer ul Islam and Prasanna S. Gandhi

Abstract Remote-center motion (RCM) mechanisms employing compliant links provide friction-less and backlash-free motion of a part of mechanism about a remote-center of desired radius. Such precision mechanisms find use in many medical and engineering applications. A partial RCM mechanism employing an L-shaped cantilever beam is proposed, for the first time, to enable a mounted rigid-link to rotate precisely about one of its edges. The mechanism is conceived with multiple arrangements of the L-shaped cantilever beams to hold the rigid-link against another fixed link such that the "remote-center" of the mechanism coincides with one of the edges of the mounted rigid-link. The link and L-shaped cantilever are connected by means of a higher pair joint, thus a partially compliant mechanism. Remote-center coordinates are located by carrying out nonlinear "finite element analysis" of the cantilever beam. Further, the mechanism is fabricated and experiments are carried out to verify its working at high precision.

Keywords Compliant mechanism · Remote-center · Angular lifting · FEA

1 Introduction

Motion along a circular path about a fixed center without a direct mechanical link connected to the center is defined as remoter-center motion [1]. Motion manipulation about a remote point specifies the application of RCM mechanisms involving an action over/about far-off locations. Use of RCM mechanisms have shown remarkable advancement in "minimal invasive surgeries" (MIS) [2–4], which involves performing an operation deep inside a living body but controlled externally [5, 6].

T. ul Islam (✉) · P. S. Gandhi
Suman Mashruwala Advanced Microengineering Laboratory, Department of Mechanical Engineering, Indian Institute of Technology Bombay, Powai, Mumbai 400076, India
e-mail: tanveerkamgar@gmail.com

P. S. Gandhi
e-mail: gandhi.iitb@gmail.com

Real RCM mechanisms have linkage configurations that allow rotation only about a fixed remote-center (RC). A number of such configurations include Single-revolute-joint [7], Circular-prismatic-joint [8], Parallelogram-based [9, 10], Synchronous-transmission-based [9], and Instantaneous [11] RCM mechanism. Motion manipulation about a remote-center can also be achieved via real-time position correction, employing computer control, called virtual RCM mechanisms [12–15]. Virtual mechanisms could at different times be operated at different remote-center locations but run the risk of being sensitive to external noise or software malfunctioning. A real mechanism, on the other hand, is immune to the noise due to mechanically constrained motions but lacks in accuracy because of friction and backlash existing between the mechanism links. Real RCM mechanisms based on compliant links provides a backlash-free and friction-less motion, thus an ideal mechanism for high-precision motion manipulation. For small deflection of compliant links, such mechanisms have been shown to enable precise control over the end-effector [16].

We propose a partial compliant RCM mechanism to maintain the accuracy of remote-center for large displacement of a rigid-link on one side, whereas the other end/edge remains true to the remote-center. The mechanism proposed uses an L-shaped cantilever beams to precisely rotate a rigid-link about one of its edges. The rigid-link in this mechanism could be contemplated as a flat rectangular plate held by the compliant cantilever links against a ground link or another rectangular plate. The mechanism thus developed allows precise angular rotation of one flat-plate initially held against another flat rectangular plate. Such mechanisms, especially find application in screen-printings [17], controlled debonding of surfaces adhered due to an adhesive or fluid [18], peel-testing, and shaping of fluid sandwiched between two plates into desired patterns [19].

The paper is divided into the following sections: Sect. 1 presents the RCM mechanism and explains its assembly, Sect. 2 discusses the FEA analysis carried out to find remote-center coordinates, Sect. 3 demonstrates the precision working of actual setup fabricated, and finally, Sect. 4 concludes the findings.

2 RCM Mechanism

The mechanism consists of three mechanical links viz. (i) Link-1 is an L-shaped compliant link (cantilever beam) (ii) Link-2 is a rigid-link (flat-plate), mounted onto multiple compliant links, and (iii) Link-3 is a fixed rigid-link (another flat-plate). All the three links are separately shown in Fig. 1a–c. Choice of rigid-links as flat-plates in the RCM mechanism is suited for its testing in RC accuracy.

Link-1 is a cantilever beam fixed at one, and freely hanging at the other end as shown in Fig. 1a. Free end is sharply bent at 90° giving an L-shape (side view) to the cantilever beam. Vertically downward force applied at the link tip would deflect the cantilever as shown in Fig. 1d. Path traced by the cantilever tip is a curve with radius r whose remote-center lies at a horizontal distance of X_{rc} and vertical distance of Y_{rc} from the cantilever base (fixed end). Remote-center, as would be shown later,

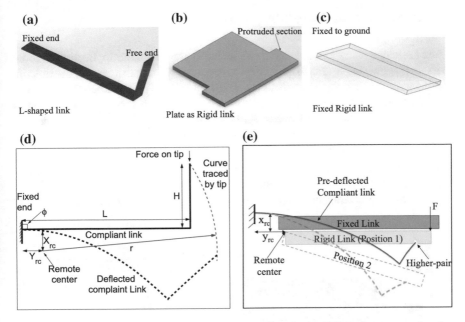

Fig. 1 Figure shows **a** solid model of compliant cantilever beam (link-1), **b** a rectangular plate with protruding sides to act as a rigid-link of the mechanism (link-2), **c** a rectangular plate as fixed rigid-link (link-3), **d** compliant link of length (L) and height (H) and path are traced by tip when a force is applied on its tip along with the RC coordinates, and **e** side view of an assembled mechanism in one of its configuration

always has a negative Y_{rc} coordinate. Its negative nature determines the shape of the rigid-link and overall assembly of the mechanism.

Two compliant links hold the rigid-link (link-2) and form its two sides in a way that one of its edges coincides with the remote-center of the link. Tip of compliant link is located into a notch in the rigid-link, forming a higher pair joint between the two links. Out of the many possible configurations (different ϕ values) to assemble the two links, we chose to test the mechanism at a very large deflection of the compliant link thus selecting $\phi = 90°$, Fig. 1d. The angle ϕ is maintained by means of the "fixed rigid-link" (link-3) of the mechanism.

The fixed link is a flat rectangular plate shown in Fig. 1c, and is a part of the ground whose position remains locked at all times. The fixed link initially holds link-2 parallel to itself and at a position such that its inner edge coincides with the remote-center of the compliant link. An assembled configuration of mechanism in Fig. 1e shows the relative position of the links in two extreme positions of mechanism. Force applied on far end of the rigid-link is transferred to the compliant-link tips, which further deflects while tracing an arc whose center coincides with the inner edge of the rigid-link. The link-2, thus rotates about the inner edge, in touch with the fixed link, for a large deflection of the outer edge/compliant link.

3 FE Analysis and Results

A free L-shaped compliant link and its deflected shape due to the application of force on its tip is shown in Fig. 2a. To find the remote-center of the path traced by the link tip, nonlinear finite element (FE) analysis is carried out in ANSYS Workbench. Nonlinear analysis is needed as the compliant link which undergoes a very large deflection as compared to its width and thickness. Although the link can be installed to undergo less deflection by having a smaller ϕ value in Fig. 1d, the FE analysis is carried out for large deflection to obtain the precise value of remote-center coordinates.

Parameters for FE analysis are chosen by considering Beryllium-Copper as compliant link material with Young's modulus of $131E9$ and a Poisson's ratio of 0.285. A parabolic solid tetrahedral element defined by four corner nodes, six mid-side

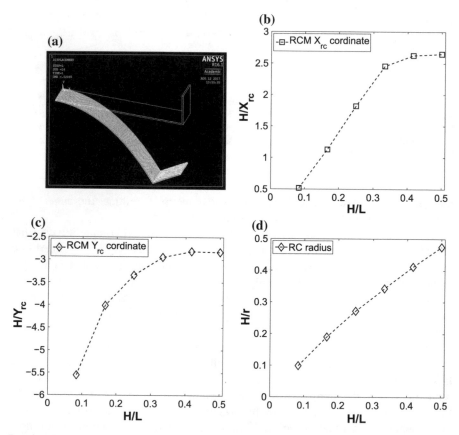

Fig. 2 **a** Free and deflected image from ANSYS. **b** Normalized x-axis coordinate H/X_{rc} of the remote-center obtained through nonlinear FE analysis of the compliant link is plotted against the link height to length ratio H/L. **c** Normalized y-axis coordinate H/X_{rc} is plotted against the H/L ratio. **d** Normalized radius of the remote-center plotted here shows almost a linear variation with the ratio H/L

nodes, and six edges and a smart element size of 200 μm is used. Force applied on the link tip is increased in steps and the position of tip is recorded every time. The recorded data is later used to plot the path traced by the tip. To ensure that the selected mesh size of 200 μm is a stable mesh size, deflection of the link was also analyzed at 10 μm mesh size. Insignificant difference in remote-center coordinates, from two different mesh sizes, justifies the use of higher mesh size for the analysis.

The analysis was carried out for different link length (L) to height (H) ratio's. Tip position, with respect to the cantilever base (0, 0 coordinate), was plotted for different step loads and a curve was fitted. Tip-position coordinates at zero load, intermediate load and at maximum load were initially considered to find the radius and center (remote-center) of a circle passing through these three points. For the tip to trace a perfect circular arc, position coordinates of the tip at other loads should, therefore, fall on the arc calculated from these three points. Cross-referencing of all other points with the arc position verified the perfect circular nature of the curve traced by the cantilever tip. Similar strategy was adopted to verify the circular nature of the curve for all the H/L ratios analyzed.

Normalized horizontal-coordinate H/X_{rc} (along x-axis) of the RC is plotted against H/L ratio in Fig. 2b. Figure shows that as the link height (H) increases the coordinate initially shifts closer and closer to the link fixed end, and then saturates as the H approaches half the link length. Vertical-coordinate (Y_{rc}) on the other hand, shifts farther and farther from the origin before it reaches saturation, Fig. 2c. Convergence towards a saturation happens gradually for Y_{rc} as compared to the X_{rc} coordinate. Given a link H/L ratio, the remote-center coordinates can be found from Fig. 2b, c. Third parameter required to completely define the mechanism is the radius of the remote-center. Figure 2d shows almost a linear decrease in radius with increasing H/L ratio. Thus, for a given link, length L increase in H/L ratio incurvates the arc traced by the cantilever tip.

4   Fabricated Mechanism and Experimental Results

Assembly of the mechanism is always done in a way that the inner edge of link-2 lies in-line/coincides with the remote-center location. Negative sign of Y_{rc}-coordinate, obtained from FE analysis, affirms the positioning of link-2 or a part of it below the cantilever base (link-1). The positioning of link-2 about the RC location could be achieved in many different ways forming different configurations of the mechanism. One such configuration is the designing of link-2 with protruding sections (Fig. 1b) on its two sides to pair with the cantilever tip. Placement of link-2 in concur with the remote-center is achieved by appropriate respective positioning of link-3. It is preferred to have a deflected compliant-link holding link-2 in its initial position as that would ensure a forced-joint between link-1 tip and the notch in link-2. Figure 3a is a solid-model representation of an assembled setup and Fig. 3b is an actual setup fabricated to work as the RCM mechanism.

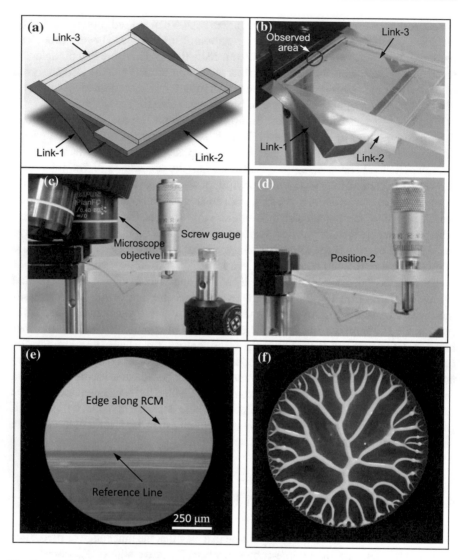

Fig. 3 **a** Soild model of RCM mechanism. **b** Assembled fabricated mechanism. **c** Mechanism in position-1 and microscope position. **d** Mechanism in position-2. **e** Microscopic view of the edge along RC and reference line. **f** Fluid shaped into a branched network by squeezing and debonding two plates held by the RCM mechanism

The fabricated mechanism has a compliant link with $L = 30$ mm, $H = 12$ mm, width $= 5$ mm, and thickness $= 0.3$ mm. FE analysis revealed that the RC coordinates $X_{rc} = 4.478$ mm and $Y_{rc} = -4.288$ mm. Link-2 and link-3 were made from a plexiglass to allow the visualization of the edge lying along the remote-center. To verify the mechanism accuracy, the outer edge of link-2 was deflected by a large vertical distance of 8 mm while the inner edge position was observed under microscope. A manually operated screw gauge was used to deflect the link as shown in Fig. 3c–d. Image of the inner edge and reference line viewed under microscope is shown in Fig. 3e.

The link-2 was deflected with a step size of 1 mm and the edge position with respect to the reference line was measured. For first 3 mm of deflection, no change in edge position was observed, however, for a maximum deflection of 8 mm, a total shift of 14 μm from the reference line was observed. Typical application of the mechanism to test fluid debonding/shaping between the two plates (link-2 and link-3), however, demands a maximum deflection of 2 mm of the outer edge.

5 Conclusion

A partial RCM mechanism was developed to work at high precision for large deflection cases. FE analysis revealed that the RC coordinates always lie below the cantilever base. Out of many configurations possible, flat rectangular links were chosen for their direct use as fluid shaping device and convenient in observing the RC accuracy within small resolution limits under a high-magnification microscope. The mechanism has a wide range in assembling it at different compliant-link angles and geometry of link-2 to pair with link-1. The version of the precision mechanism developed and discussed in this paper, can directly be used to study highly noise sensitive fluid flow process like Saffman-Taylor instability, interface evolution in two-phase flow, adhesive debonding under eccentric loading, etc.

References

1. G. Zong, X. Pei, J. Yu, S. Bi, Classification and type synthesis of 1-dof remote center of motion mechanisms. Mech. Mach. Theory **43**(12), 1585–1595 (2008)
2. M. Vierra, Minimally invasive surgery. Ann. Rev. Med. **46**(1), 147–158 (1995)
3. C.-H. Kuo, J.S. Dai, P. Dasgupta, Kinematic design considerations for minimally invasive surgical robots: an overview. Int. J. Med. Robot. Comput. Assist. Surg. **8**(2), 127–145 (2012)
4. R.H. Taylor, A. Menciassi, G. Fichtinger, P. Fiorini, P. Dario, Medical robotics and computer-integrated surgery, in *Springer Handbook of Robotics* (Springer, 2016), pp. 1657–1684
5. G.S. Guthart, J.K. Salisbury, The intuitive/sup tm/telesurgery system: overview and application, in *IEEE International Conference on Robotics and Automation, 2000. Proceedings. ICRA '00*, vol. 1 (IEEE, 2000), pp. 618–621
6. S.J. Blumenkranz, D.J. Rosa, Manipulator positioning linkage for robotic surgery, 12 June 2001. US Patent 6,246,200
7. M.J.H. Lum, *Kinematic Optimization of a 2-DOF Spherical Mechanism for a Minimally Invasive Surgical Robot*. Ph.D. thesis (University of Washington, 2004)
8. A. Guerrouad, P. Vidal, SMOS: stereotaxical microtelemanipulator for ocular surgery, in *Proceedings of the Annual International Conference of the IEEE Engineering in Engineering in Medicine and Biology Society, 1989. Images of the Twenty-First Century* (IEEE, 1989), pp. 879–880

9. R.H. Taylor, J. Funda, B. Eldridge, S. Gomory, K. Gruben, D. LaRose, M. Talamini, L. Kavoussi, J. Anderson, A telerobotic assistant for laparoscopic surgery. IEEE Eng. Med. Biol. Mag. **14**(3), 279–288 (1995)

10. R. Taylor, P. Jensen, L. Whitcomb, A. Barnes, R. Kumar, D. Stoianovici, P. Gupta, Z. Wang, E. Dejuan, L. Kavoussi, A steady-hand robotic system for microsurgical augmentation. Int. J. Robot. Res. **18**(12), 1201–1210 (1999)

11. D. Kim, E. Kobayashi, T. Dohi, I. Sakuma, A new, compact mr-compatible surgical manipulator for minimally invasive liver surgery, in *Medical Image Computing and Computer-Assisted Intervention MICCAI 2002*, pp. 99–106 (2002)

12. T. Ortmaier, G. Hirzinger, Cartesian control issues for minimally invasive robot surgery, in *Proceedings 2000 IEEE/RSJ International Conference on Intelligent Robots and Systems, 2000 (IROS 2000)* (IEEE, 2000), vol. 1, pp. 565–571

13. M. Michelin, P. Poignet, E. Dombre, Dynamic task/posture decoupling for minimally invasive surgery motions: simulation results, in *Proceedings 2004 IEEE/RSJ International Conference on Intelligent Robots and Systems, 2004 (IROS 2004)* (IEEE, 2004), vol. 4, pp. 3625–3630

14. R.C. Locke, R.V. Patel, Optimal remote center-of-motion location for robotics-assisted minimally-invasive surgery, in *2007 IEEE International Conference on Robotics and Automation* (IEEE, 2007), pp. 1900–1905

15. A. Krupa, G. Morel, M. De Mathelin, Achieving high-precision laparoscopic manipulation through adaptive force control. Advanced Robotics **18**(9), 905–926 (2004)

16. P.S. Gandhi, R.S. Bobade, C. Chen, On the novel compliant remote center mechanism

17. M.S.C. De Sa, Radial screen printing machine, 14 Sept 2005. US Patent App. 11/662,763

18. T. ul Islam, P.S. Gandhi, Spontaneous fabrication of three-dimensional multiscale fractal structures using hele-shaw cell. J. Manuf. Sci. Eng. **139**(3), 031007 (2017)

19. T. ul Islam, P.S. Gandhi, Fabrication of multiscale fractal-like structures by controlling fluid interface instability. Sci. Rep. (2016)

Prototype Fast Breeder Reactor Steam Generator Inspection System for Tube Inspections

S. Joseph Winston, S. Sakthivel, Joel Jose, D. Jagadishan, P. Visweswaran, S. Murugan, G. Amarendra and A. K. Bhaduri

Abstract Prototype Fast Breeder Reactor (PFBR) has eight Steam Generators (SGs), four in each secondary loop for exchanging the heat from the secondary sodium to water/steam. Sodium is present in the shell side and water/steam in the tube side. Internationally, it is seen that SGs are the key factors for the plant availability and hence, SG tube integrity is of prime importance. Significant progress has been made around the world both on the Remote Field Eddy Current (RFEC) testing and the remote automation of the tube inspection. An indigenously designed and built device called PFBR SG Inspection System (PSGIS), which is first of its kind

S. Joseph Winston (✉) · S. Sakthivel · J. Jose · D. Jagadishan · P. Visweswaran · S. Murugan
G. Amarendra · A. K. Bhaduri
Steam Generator Inspection Devices Section/Robotics, Irradiation Experiments and Remote Handling Division, Metallurgy and Materials Group, Indira Gandhi Centre for Atomic Research, Kalpakkam 603102, India
e-mail: winston@igcar.gov.in

S. Sakthivel
e-mail: ssvel@igcar.gov.in

J. Jose
e-mail: joeljosej@gmail.com; joel@igcar.gov.in

D. Jagadishan
e-mail: jagan@igcar.gov.in

P. Visweswaran
e-mail: visweswaran@igcar.gov.in

S. Murugan
e-mail: murugan@igcar.gov.in

G. Amarendra
e-mail: amar@igcar.gov.in

© Springer Nature Singapore Pte Ltd. 2019
D N Badodkar and T A Dwarakanath (eds.), *Machines, Mechanism and Robotics*, Lecture Notes in Mechanical Engineering,
https://doi.org/10.1007/978-981-10-8597-0_61

in the world for FBR SGs is designed and tested on different mock-up test setups and qualified for the use in actual PFBR SG. The device has been used to inspect all the SG installed at PFBR site. This paper brings out the details of the remote tooling designed and used for the inspection of PFBR SG tube.

Keywords PFBR · Steam generator · Tube inspection · RFEC · Remote tooling Kinematics

1 Introduction

Prototype Fast Breeder reactor (PFBR) has eight Steam Generators (SGs) in two secondary loops. The steam generator is a once-through type vertical shell and tube heat exchanger with sodium on the shell side and water/steam on the tube side. Each SG has 547 tubes running through about 23 m from top header to the bottom header. Figure 1 shows the sketch of PFBR SG. The tubes have expansion bends at 5 m from the bottom tube sheet to accommodate the thermal expansion. Internationally [1], it is seen that SGs are the key factors for the plant availabilities and hence, tube integrity is of prime importance as the tube thickness only is the barrier for the sodium coming in contact with water causing a violent exothermic reaction. Since ferritic steels are used for the tubes of SG to counter the Stress Corrosion Cracking (SCC), it becomes important to choose the RFEC method due to the ferromagnetic nature of ferritic steels. According to the Preservice Inspection (PSI) and In-Service Inspection (ISI) requirements of the PFBR SG [1], inspection of the tubes of all the SG using the volumetric RFEC technique with remotely operated ISI equipment is required. Thus, the PSGIS device has been designed and developed for inspection of SG tubes using REFC testing probes through the full length of the tube. Prior to service, tube inspection of the SGs is important to qualify the SGs for safe operation.

2 Steam Generator Technical Data

SGs are the most critical components of Nuclear Power Plants (NPPs), Fig. 1 shows the sketch of PFBR Steam Generator. The main function of SG is to transfer heat from nonradioactive secondary sodium to feed water to generate superheated steam, to make steam in the secondary side with the purpose of driving the turbines for electrical power production. The details of the PFBR Steam Generator are as follows. Table 1 shows the PFBR SG parameters. A variety of degradation modes challenge the integrity of the SG tubing and therefore, the stations' reliability, capacity factor, and cost-effectiveness. Some of these modes generate volumetric material loss due to fretting wear, pitting corrosion, wastage, or flaw-accelerated corrosion (FAC); other modes have directional properties due to intergranular attack (IGA), axial or circum-

Fig. 1 PFBR steam
generator

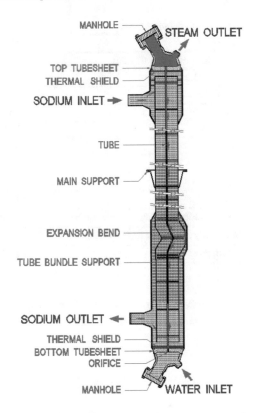

ferential outside diameter (OD), and stress corrosion cracking (SCC). One of the
key life management components for ensuring tube integrity, and thus protecting the
safety of the public and the environment while maintaining cost-effective operation
of NPP is inspection and monitoring aimed at timely detection and characterization
of the degradation [1].

3 Need for Automated Remote Tooling

Manhole flange to tube sheet center hole is 1348 mm. A direct access to the tube
sheet is not possible to push the RFEC probe into the tubes There is a need to deploy
the inspection device inside the manhole to reach SG tubes. There is also a need
to uniquely identify SG tubes during inspection, and also reference the same tubes
at a later time for any repairs. This mandates the need for numerical controlled
inspection system to reference the tubes by unique numbering scheme, and a reach
automated remote tooling of two-axis robotic arm for tube locating operation. It is
also required module for pushing and retrieving RFEC probe to 23 m to reach bottom
tube sheet with accurate localization of the probe. Overall, system control through

Table 1 SG details

Parameter	Value
Tube sheet diameter (inside)	~910 mm
Manhole ID	380 mm
Pitch of the tube array	32.2 mm
Total number of tubes	547 Nos.
Tube size	17.2 OD × 2.3 thick
Tube material	Modified 9Cr1Mo
Tube length	23000 mm, vertical with thermal expansion
SG overall height	25000 mm
Thermal power	158 MW (per SG)
Primary side sodium temp, inlet/outlet	525/355 °C
Secondary side water temp, inlet/outlet	235/493 °C
Steam pressure	17.2 Mpa

sophisticated touch screen needs a comprehensive control system module with a versatile Human–Machine Interface (HMI).

4 International Scenario on SG Inspection System

Manipulator such as Zetec SM23 [2] are typically dedicated to perform only the eddy current testing inspections. Westinghouse ROSA III [3] and AREVA for non-exclusion zone ROGER. More recent robot models are Westinghouse PEGASYS [4], used for European inspections and also optimal for inspection of SGs, and the Zetec ZR-1 designed specifically for PHWR CANDU applications. INETEC Croatia has forerunner [5], which is a light mobile manipulator designed to perform PWR SG inspections. It is adjustable for different tube sheet configurations and inner tube diameters. It has integrated machine vision, fully automated optimal movement, reaching 197 tubes without repositioning-inspection (Figs. 2 and 3).

Table 2 shows various SG tube inspection systems which is used all over the world. Another manipulator developed by INETEC Croatia has Castor; CASTOR is a remote-controlled manipulator, designed for the inspection of VVER SG tubes with eddy current probes, ultrasound examination of collector welds and for tube plugging. Device has the following feature modular design with modules for tube ET inspection, weld UT/ET inspection and tube plugging, easy modules exchange, installation without personnel having to enter the steam generator, real-time 3D visualization and inspection simulation, log file generation via EddyOne Control, machine vision, integrated electronics within the manipulator. Inspection will be by means of a miniature TV camera having a diameter of 17 mm and a length of 250 mm, with a 45° mirror in front of the objective for radial viewing. The optical system's focal dis-

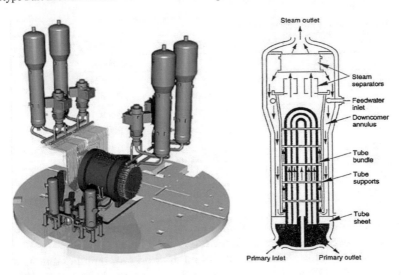

Fig. 2 PHWR and steam generators

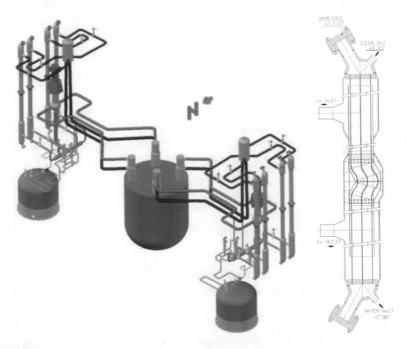

Fig. 3 PFBR and steam generators

tance will allow examination of objects between 10 and 100 mm from the camera. In SUPERPHENIX-1, When the inspected SG has been emptied of sodium, cooled down and filled with nitrogen, its upper manway will be opened. An operator in a

Table 2 Available SG inspection devices

Device name	Manufacturer and country	Reactor type
Zetec SM23	Zetec and USA	PHWR
Zetec ZR1	Zetec and USA	PHWR
ROSA III	Westinghouse and USA	PWR
PEGASYS		PWR
ROGER RANGER	AREVA and USA	PHWR
Forerunner	INETEC and Croatia	PHWR
Tecnatom [6]	Tecnatom, Spain	PWR

special suit with self-contained breathing apparatus will then enter the SG, and move the camera between the layers, from the top of the tube bundle.

A considerable effort has been put around the world for building remote tooling for the Pressurized Water Reactor (PWR), SGs. An indigenously designed and built device called PFBR, SG Inspection System (PSGIS) which is first of its kind in the world for FBR SGs is discussed in this paper.

5 PFBR SG Inspection System (PSGIS)

The PFBR SG inspection device has seven modules for performing various functions. The device is designed in a modular way for easy assembly, dismantling, and can be performance tested as discrete modules. The following are the seven modules:

1. Device deployment module (DDM)
2. Tube locator module (TLM)
3. Cable pusher module (CPM)
4. Cable dispenser module (CDM)
5. Comprehensive control system module (CCM)
6. Inspection system module (ISM)

   (a) Eddy current probe and analysis system (EPAS)
   (b) Vision probe and analysis system (VPAS).

7. Cable Take-Up Module (CTM).

Figure 4 shows the SG manhole with dummy closure, which will be opened to mount the device on the manhole during inspection. The figure shows the deployment operation which deploys the two-axis robotic arm into the top header. The PSGIS device mounted on the SG manhole flange fills the manhole completely. The deployment module, DDM is used to deploy the robotic arm above tube sheet and retract back the device after inspection, and it gives a rigid base reference and support. Total stroke is about 450 mm. TLM is a precision automatic robotic arm which works on the

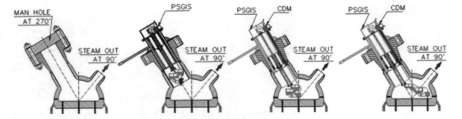

Fig. 4 Design of PFBR SG inspection manipulator based on various operations

Fig. 5 CAD model of
PSGIS

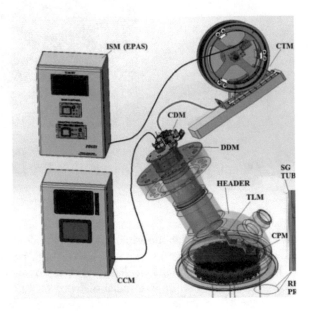

synchronous kinematic motion to reach all the 547 tubes of the SG. The CPM and CDM helps to push the cable from the top header to the bottom making inspection probe travel 23 m down. Synchronous servo motion is applied on four PMDC motors to achieve this insertion and retrieval.

The Cable Take-up Module (CTM) does the cable storage and management. ISM containing RFEC testing data acquiring and analysis system is used to acquire the tube inspection data from all the tubes and vision probe and analysis system is used to view SG tube internals. Figure 5 shows the CAD model of the complete PSGIS device showing all the modules integrated.

TLM is the precision robotic arm designed to uniquely orient to all the tubes for pushing the probe and cable for inspection.

Fig. 6 Precision robotic arm

5.1 Two-Axis Robotic Manipulator Tube Locator Module (TLM)

Tube location operation is an important one in the overall inspection. The TLM module has two-axis robotic arm operated by shoulder and elbow actuator which are AC servo motors. Figure 6 shows the two-axis high-precision robotic arm. The shape is thus arrived to fit into the manhole before deployment and only deployed over the tube sheet must reach up to a radial distance of 420 mm to cover all the tubes in the bundle. The outer most tube radial distance is only 396 mm. The joint actuators are AC servo actuators with central hole to route the cables. The servo drives are accommodated within the arm with the implementation of the Distributed Control system (DCS) to reduce the number of cables running through the arm to the control panel. Comprehensive control system layout is shown in Fig. 7, which is CANopen protocol distributed control system. Open standard DS-402, DS-301 and DS-405 used in motion control. HMI interface with MODBUS over TCP/IP in used to add enhanced touch interface to control the device. Calibration system is interfaced with the motion controller through a TCP/IP socket program.

5.2 Kinematics Analysis of Tube Locator Module

Conventionally, a Jacobian inverse is used to solve the inverse kinematics problem. In order to have a good stability close to the singular configuration, a damped least squares pseudo-inverse technique is used. Equation 1 shows the forward kinematics

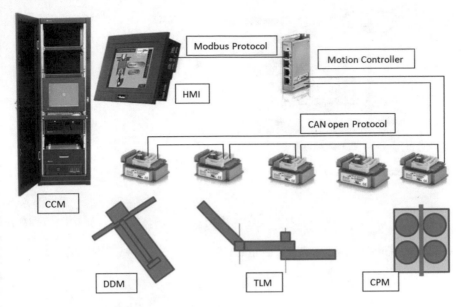

Fig. 7 Distributed control system for the PSGIS

Fig. 8 Joint variables, & end effecter coordinates

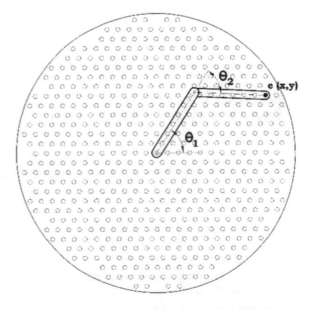

where end-effector Cartesian coordinate frame is expressed in terms of joint space variable. Jacobian matrix is expressed in Eq. 3. The damped least squares pseudo-inverse method [7, 8] is shown in Eq. 4. Figure 8 shows the end effector and joint space coordinate frames.

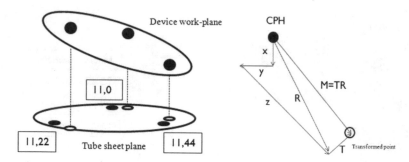

Fig. 9 Resultant error vector

$$[e] = J[\theta] \tag{1}$$

Inverse Kinematics equation is as in Eq. 2;

$$[\theta] = J^{-1}[e] \tag{2}$$

$$J = \frac{\partial f}{\partial \theta} = \left[\frac{\partial f}{\partial \theta_1} \cdots \frac{\partial f}{\partial \theta_n} \right] = \begin{pmatrix} \frac{\partial f_1}{\partial \theta_1} & \cdots & \frac{\partial f_1}{\partial \theta_n} \\ \vdots & \ddots & \vdots \\ \frac{\partial f_m}{\partial \theta_1} & & \frac{\partial f_m}{\partial \theta_n} \end{pmatrix} \tag{3}$$

$$J^\dagger = J^T (J J^T + \lambda^2 I)^{-1} \tag{4}$$

The damping factor increase increases stability close to the singular configuration, whereas a damping factor zero will make the Eq. 4 work like a typical pseudo inverse.

5.3 Device Error Correction Through Calibration

Due to the fabrication tolerances, fabrication errors and mounting of device errors can lead to a large difference in the referencing of the task space tube sheet plane with respect to the actual manipulator workspace. This can go as high as even up to 60 mm if unskilled personnel are mounting the device on SG manhole. Such a large error will lead to wrong orientation of the tubes as the tubes pitch is only 32.2 mm. A novel scheme [9] to calibrate the manipulator using the motor encoders as the error measurement sensors and the corrections applied on the inverse kinematic routines on the fly so that the device works with very high precision even on improper mounting with errors. The rigid body rotation and translation parameters are estimated based on an SVD of the correlation matrix [10–14]. Three calibration points which can be prominently identified from the 11th row tubes are used for the calibration. Figure 9 shows the summation of errors due to rotations and translations.

Fig. 10 TLM IK mock test

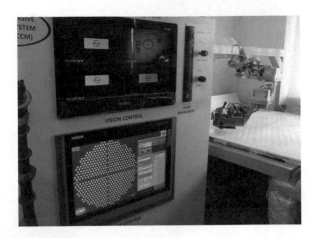

6 Qualification of the SG Inspection Device

In order to maintain the highest order of safety, the developed device was qualified on the following mock-up tests:

Mock-up test-I: kinematic test of the two axis manipulator to reach all 547 tube positions uniquely

Mock Test-II: RFEC system integration and qualification on 4 m test rig with known tube defects

Mock Test-III: 1:1mock-up test qualification of the entire device for full functionality before SG tube inspection.

6.1 Mock Test-I

The robotic manipulator is to reach to the unique position of all the 547 tube locations. The DH parameters are estimated and the link lengths are so chosen to reach even the outer most tube in the tube sheet. The arm actuators are chosen as AC servo actuators and the servo drives to have a good communication bus which is Controller Area Network (CAN) with the CAN open standards DS301, DA 302, and DS 402 for motion control commands. Figure 10 shows the test bench, where the inverse kinematic algorithm developed and ported on the motion controller is tested to reach all 547 tubes. A dummy template representing all 547 SG tubes is used to check the device reachability, repeatability, and accuracies.

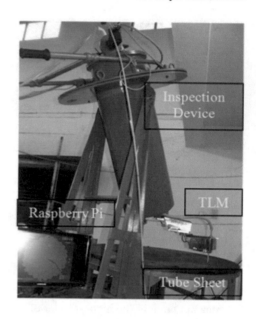

6.2 Mock Test-II

In order to qualify the integrated RFEC system, the TLM is integrated with the other
modules DDM, CDM, and the ISM. Figure 11 shows the specially made test setup to
simulate the 60 SG manhole and tube sheet with some tubes incorporated with known
characterized defects. The complete RFEC system has been qualified by detecting
the known errors in the tubes and system found to perform very well without any
inference from the device side to the RFEC data acquisition. Though the tubes are
incorporated with bends simulating the actual SG tubes, however, the total length of
the tubes were only 4.5 m as against 23 m in the actual case. This has warranted for
another 1:1 full-scale mock-up to check the probe insertability by the device up to
23 m and acquire data.

6.3 Mock Test-III

Figure 12 shows the device PSGIS on 1:1 mock-up setup with top header, tube sheet,
and manhole. The tubes representing various locations as the center of tube sheet,
middle inner zone, and the outer row tubes are simulated with an actual length of
23 m to check the complete insertability of the probe into the full length of the SG
tubes. Also, in this 1:1 mock test setup, it was checked for the device handling and
mounting of the device in the manhole, device calibration, inverse kinematic reach
of the device arm to orient to the tubes, and the pushing and pulling of the probe
with cable to the full length of the SG tube. This qualified the device for the use

Fig. 12 1:1 Mock-up

in the actual SG systems. Also various failure scenarios have been simulated in the 1:1 mock-up test stand to qualify the device for safe operation and safe unmounting. After the mock tests, the device is fully qualified for use in the actual SG system.

7 Preservice Inspection of PFBR SG Tubes

The versatile PSGIS device has been used to carryout the tube inspection and qualification of SG tubes as a part of preservice inspection. The RFEC data is collected for all the SGs and analyzed by the RFEC qualified personnel to qualify the SG tubes. Once the device is coupled with the SG manhole rigidly, then a marking is made aligning the device and the SG manhole. Now, the calibration procedure is followed to estimate the rigid body transformation parameters for the orientation. Once, the device is taken out and reintroduced into the SG manhole as long as we align to the markings, we can bypass the calibration procedure using past calibration data. This was tried and found to be successful and the transformation parameters for all the eight SGs have been recorded for future repeat of the inspections during In-Service inspection (ISI) on the respective SGs. Figure 13 shows the PSGIS mounted on SG manhole, and it also shows the marking for future alignments to avoid recalibration of the device. This saves a lot of cost, time, and effort (Figs. 14 and 15).

8 Conclusion

PFBR Steam Generator Inspection device has been indigenously developed. A stable kinematic algorithm has been developed and ported on the motion controller to uniquely reach all the 547 tubes for inspection. The efficient design of cable pusher and cable dispenser modules with synchronous motion make the seamless travel of the probe even negotiating the thermal expansion bends to reach up to the bottom

S. Joseph Winston et al.

Fig. 13 PSGIS on SG manhole

Fig. 14 PSGIS control panel

Fig. 15 SG internal view
during inspection

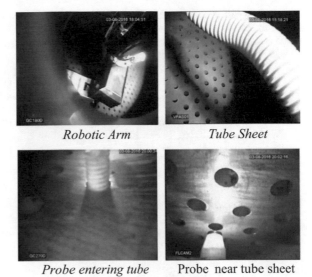

Robotic Arm   *Tube Sheet*

Probe entering tube   Probe near tube sheet

raised spigot weld of the tube to the tube sheet for qualification. The novel method adapted to use the motor encoder as error measurement sensors, which helped to reduce cost and also addition of sensors in the system. The error correction algorithm proved to have a good correction, and a good performance is achieved by the device.

Acknowledgements The help rendered by Mr. K. Purushothaman is duly acknowledged for preparing all the design drawings of the device and also his significant contribution during the tube inspections.

References

1. L. Obrutsky, J. Renaud, R. Lakhan, *Steam Generator Inspections: Faster, Cheaper and Better, are We There Yet?* IV Conferencia Panamericana de END, Buenos Aires—Octubre 2007
2. http://www.zetec.com/products/mechanical-systems/probe-delivery/zr-100
3. https://inis.iaea.org/search/search.aspx?orig_q=RN:23027931
4. http://www.westinghousenuclear.com/Portals/0/operating%20plant%20services/outage%20services/steam%20generator%20services/NS-FS-0025%20Pegasys.pdf
5. http://www.inetec.hr/en/products/robotics/steam-generator/tube-sheet-runner
6. http://tecnatom-ndt.com/products/eddy-current/steam-generator-inspection-system/
7. S.R. Ross, *Introduction to Inverse Kinematics with Jacobian Transpose, Pseudoinverse and Damped Least Squares method*, Department of Mathematics (University of California, San Diego, 2009)
8. T. Yoshikawa, *Foundation of Robotics-Analysis and Control* (Corona Publication Pvt. Ltd, Japan), p. 127
9. S.J. Winston, J. Jose, A. Subramaniyan, S. Murugan, A.K. Bhaduri, Rigid body transformations for calibration of prototype fast breeder reactor, steam generator inspection device, in *Advancements in Automation, Robotics and Sensing* (Springer, 2016), pp. 23–40

10. D.W. Eggert, A. Lorusso, R.B. Fisher, Estimating 3-D rigid body transformation: a comparisonn of four major algorithms. Mach. Vis. Appl. **9**(5), 272–290 (1997)

11. J.H. Challis, A Procedure for determining rigid body transformation parameters. Biomechanics **28**, 733–737 (1995)

12. S. Umeyama, Least squares estimation of transformation parameters between two point patterns. IEEE Trans. Pattern Anal. Mach. Intell. **13**, 376–380 (1991)

13. K. Kanatani, Analysis of 3-D rotation fitting. IEEE Trans. Pattern Anal. Mach. Intell. **16**, 543–549 (1994)

14. D. Kalman, *A Singular Value Decomposition: The SVD of a Matrix* (The American University, Washington DC 2016), 13 Feb 2002

Design and Fabrication of a Partially Statically Balanced Scissor Linkage Made of Bamboo Pieces

Sunil K. Singh and Sangamesh R. Deepak

Abstract This paper investigates the prospects of making linkages made of bamboo pieces for realistic use by taking popular scissor lift as a test case. The paper through prototyping shows that because of weakness in revolute joints formed on bamboo pieces, the popularly used parallel-plane scissor linkage leads to excessive lateral sway. The paper further shows that the lateral sway can be significantly reduced be merely changing the linkage design to triangular-prism-shaped scissor linkage. The paper also formulates an optimization problem where the objective is minimization of actuation effort of scissor lift and optimization parameters are the free-lengths of the springs that are used to partially statically balance the gravity potential energy of the scissor lift. We chose to use normal nonzero-free-length springs instead of well-studied zero-free-length springs since it is less cumbersome and easy to assemble. We could practically demonstrate a 60% reduction in actuation effort. While simple, (1) recognition of advantages of triangular-prism-shaped scissor linkage in the context of making linkages with bamboo and (2) the spring parametrization and manual optimization in the context of static balancing are novel.

Keywords Scissor linkage · Static balancing · Parallel-plane scissor linkage
Triangular-prism-shaped scissor linkage

1 Introduction

Scissor linkage is a well-known mechanism. It is popularly used in scissor lifts or vertical lifts [1]. Some of the other uses of the scissor linkage are in transitional shelters [2], convertible roofs [3, 4], foldable stair [5], and a planar gate [6].

S. K. Singh · S. R. Deepak (✉)
Mechanical Engineering, Indian Institute of Technology Guwahati,
Guwahati 781039, Assam, India
e-mail: sangu@iitg.ernet.in; sangu.09@gmail.com

S. K. Singh
e-mail: sunil.2013@iitg.ernet.in

© Springer Nature Singapore Pte Ltd. 2019
D N Badodkar and T A Dwarakanath (eds.), *Machines, Mechanism and Robotics*, Lecture Notes in Mechanical Engineering,
https://doi.org/10.1007/978-981-10-8597-0_62

Static balancing of a loaded linkage is addition of extra potential energy elements like springs or weights so that the linkage can be moved effortlessly. Static balancing would reduce the actuator force or torque to actuate the linkage. Thus, with small capacity motor or actuator, one can do actuation. If the load on the scissor linkage is constant, it is prudent to completely or partially statically balance the loaded linkage.

Bamboos are abundantly and cheaply available in certain areas. They have been used from a long time to make structures such as bridges, homes, etc. However, they have not been used to make linkages. We wanted to explore the prospects of bamboos for making linkages, especially for scissor lifts. However, when we made the popular parallel-plane scissor lift out of bamboo pieces, we noticed serious presence of lateral sway. We successfully overcame this challenge by replacing parallel-plane scissor linkage with triangular-prism-shaped scissor linkage. Thus, the first contribution of this paper is to highlight smaller lateral sway of triangular-prism-shaped scissor linkage in comparison to parallel-plane scissor linkage when bamboo pieces are used to make links.

Perfect static balancing of any linkage under a gravity load is achieved either by counterweight or by adding zero-free-length springs [7, 8]. Spring-based balancing is preferred since overall weight of the linkage is not significantly increased. However, realizing a zero-free-length spring is cumbersome and can be costly. Hence, we decided to explore the prospect of normal springs for partial static balance of the linkage if not for the perfect balance.

1.1 Organization of the Paper

In Sect. 2, we show the scissor lift based on parallel-plane scissor linkage and its problem of lateral sway. Later, we describe the triangular-prism-shaped scissor lift. Section 3 describes a formulation of optimization problem for static balancing using normal springs. The manual optimization using an applet in SAGE software is also described. We also present experimental evaluation of the solution for static balancing. We conclude the paper in Sect. 5.

2 Design of Linkage

The Fig. 1a shows a scissor lift. Point A shown in the figure is fixed to the ground and point B is constrained to move in a horizontal line passing through A. In the scissor linkages used in industries, point B is guided along the horizontal straight line using a slider joint. However, realizing a slider using bamboo sticks was found to be cumbersome. Hence, we replaced the slider by Chebyshev mechanism that has a point which approximately follows a straight line. Similarly, points at the top of the scissor linkage, C and D, not only undergo vertical motion but their relative horizontal

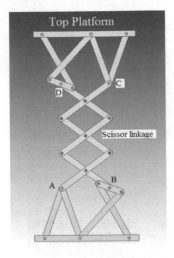

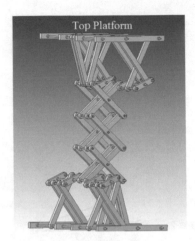

(a) Scissor linkage based vertical lift

(b) A view showing links in parallel planes

Fig. 1 CAD model of parallel-plane scissor mechanism

distance also changes. The top platform which is mounted on these two points C and D has to accommodate the relative change in horizontal distance between these two points. This is again accomplished by incorporating a Chebyshev linkage on the top platform as shown in Fig. 1b.

In the popular design for scissor lift, the links of linkage are placed in parallel planes as shown in Fig. 1b. We did fabricate the parallel-plane scissor linkage using bamboo sticks as shown in Fig. 2a. However, the fabricated linkage showed a significant lateral sway as shown in Fig. 2b. The lateral sway in Fig. 2b is due to the sway in the scissor linkage and also that of Chebyshev linkage at the base.

We attribute the lateral sway observed in parallel-plane scissor linkage to imperfect revolute joint that are formed on bamboo pieces. We find that the imperfection is due to insufficient rigidity in the bearing holes formed on the bamboo pieces. Based on a few insights and physical prototyping, we came to know that triangular-prism-shaped scissor linkage shown in Fig. 4 has much smaller lateral sway in comparison with parallel-plane scissor linkage shown in Fig. 3.

We now describe the steps to construct a single unit of triangular-prism-shaped scissor linkage. A single scissor-cross made of two links is first placed in a vertical plane as shown in Fig. 5a. Further, two replicas of the scissor-cross are made and placed in two different vertical planes such that the three planes form the faces of an equilateral triangle as shown in Fig. 5b. The three scissor-crosses are secured to each other through connectors as shown in Fig. 5c. Because of the connectors, the angle of the three scissor-crosses are synchronized to be equal to each other. The detailed geometry of the connectors is shown in Fig. 5d. The main feature of the connector is that it provides two bearing surfaces whose axes are inclined at an angle

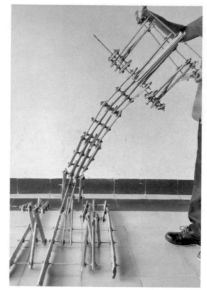

(a) Parallel-plane scissor mechanism made by bamboo pieces

(b) Lateral sway in parallel-plane scissor mechanism

Fig. 2 Fabricated parallel-plane scissor mechanism and observed lateral sway

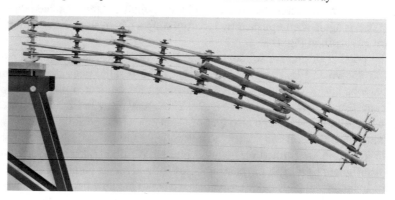

Fig. 3 Parallel-plane scissor mechanism showing lateral swaying

of 120° to each other. The triangular-prism-shaped scissor linkage so formed is an over-constrained linkage and it has ideally single degree of freedom. The degree of freedom corresponds to the change in the angle of the crosses. Several units of triangular-prism-shaped scissor linkage can be stacked one over the other to form multi-unit scissor linkage as seen in Fig. 4.

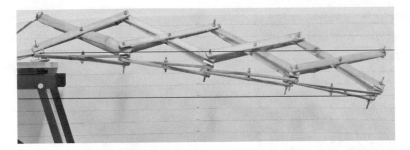

Fig. 4 Triangular-prism-shaped scissor mechanism showing lateral swaying

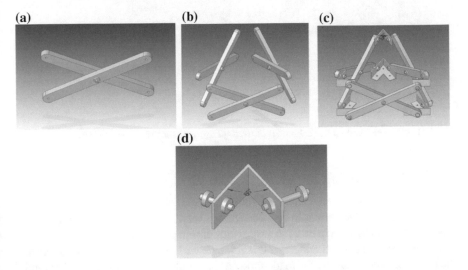

Fig. 5 Construction of a single unit of triangular-prism-shaped scissor mechanism

After confirming the smaller lateral sway property of triangular-prism-shaped scissor mechanism, we redesigned the base of the scissor linkage as well as the top platform of the scissor linkage as shown in Fig. 6a. The base linkage consisting of Chebyshev linkage was strengthened against lateral sway by increasing the effective bearing length. Furthermore, the Chebyshev linkage in the top platform was replaced by Roberts mechanism as shown in Fig. 6a. Based on the design, the prototype was fabricated as shown in Fig. 6b. The prototype demonstrated significant resistance against lateral sway even in the presence of load as is evident in Fig. 6b. We believe that our observation of smaller lateral sway in triangular-prism-shaped scissor linkage can have significant practical utility.

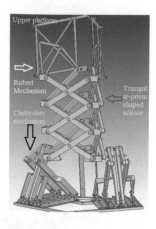

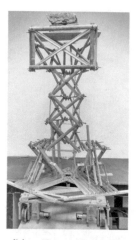

(a) CAD model of triangular-prism-shaped scissor mechanism with upper platform and Chebyshev mechanism in the base.

(b) Triangular-prism-shaped scissor mechanism fabricated with bamboo sticks

Fig. 6 CAD model and fabricated model of triangular-prism-shaped scissor linkage

3 Static Balancing of Scissor Linkage

In the scissor linkage shown in Fig. 6b, when a load is applied on the top platform, the linkage comes down in order to assume minimum potential energy configuration. For spring-based static balancing of this linkage, we have to add extra springs so that the potential energy lost by the load while coming down is transferred to the potential energy of the spring. Similarly, while going up, springs will give back the potential energy to the load. For this transfer of energy to happen, the potential energy of the spring should complement the potential energy of the load so that the sum of the two potential energy functions is a constant.

In theory, it is possible to complement the potential energy of the springs with the potential energy of gravity loads when all the springs have zero-free-lengths. However, when springs have finite free-lengths, it is possible to only approximately complement the gravity load potential energy function. In this work, we decided to use finite free-length springs along the horizontal and vertical lines formed by the revolute joints as shown in Figs. 7 and 8. In Fig. 7 shows one face of a unit of the triangular-prism-shaped scissor linkage having the arrangement of horizontal and vertical springs.

The springs that are accessible to us was in the form of long strip as shown in Fig. 9. The required springs had to be cut from this long strip. Thus, the property of this spring gets decided by the length of the spring that is cut from the strip. In particular, the spring constant of the spring is inversely proportional to length of the spring that

Fig. 7 Face of the triangular-prism-shaped scissor mechanism with the attached horizontal and vertical springs

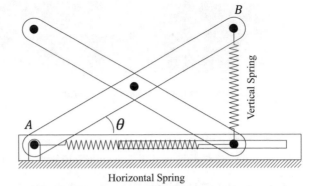

Fig. 8 Balancing springs added on triangular-prism-shaped scissor linkage in horizontal and vertical lines joining the revolute joints

is cut. Furthermore, since the spring strip does not have pretension, the length of the spring is also the free-length of the spring. Thus, for a spring that is cut,

$$k = \frac{\alpha}{f} \tag{1}$$

where k is the spring constant of cut spring and f is the free-length of the cut spring. The proportionality constant α depends only on the spring strip. Since we had only one kind of strip accessible to us, f parameterizes both free-length and spring constant. In our experimental setup, the value of α was found to be 14.9 N.

We have the freedom to choose multiple number of horizontal springs represented by N_h and multiple number vertical springs represented by N_v. For simplicity, all

Fig. 9 Availability of spring in the form of long strip

the horizontal springs are chosen to have the same free-length represented by f_h. Similarly, all the vertical springs are chosen to have the same free-length represented by f_v.

From the Fig. 7 horizontal force F_H and vertical force F_V exerted by the spring are:

$$F_H = \frac{\alpha}{f_h}(l\cos\theta - f_h) \quad \text{and,} \quad F_V = \frac{\alpha}{f_v}(l\sin\theta - f_v) \tag{2}$$

where θ is the angle subtended by the link from the ground and l is the length of the links of the scissor linkage which is equal to length AB as shown in Fig. 7.

Hence, the total horizontal F_h and vertical spring force F_v are:

$$F_h = \frac{\alpha}{f_h}(l\cos\theta - f_h)N_h \quad \text{and,} \quad F_v = \frac{\alpha}{f_v}(l\sin\theta - f_v)N_v \tag{3}$$

So, total spring torque and gravity torque is given as:

$$\tau_{spring} = (\frac{1}{f_h}(\alpha l^2 \cos\theta\sin\theta) - \alpha l\sin\theta)N_h + (\frac{1}{f_v}(-\alpha l^2\cos\theta\sin\theta) + \alpha l\cos\theta)N_v \tag{4}$$

$$\tau_{gravity} = Wl\cos\theta \tag{5}$$

Figure 10a shows the plot of gravity torque denoted by $\tau_{gravity}$, spring torque denoted by τ_{spring} and total torque which is $\tau_{gravity} + \tau_{spring}$. For illustration we take $l = 0.3$ m, and $W = 10$ Kg. With this, we have the task of finding optimal values of N_h, N_v, f_h, and f_v. In order to find the optimal values, we created an applet in SAGE mathematical software. The applet has the facility to vary N_h, N_v, f_h, and f_v in the form of sliders. By manually varying the optimization parameters N_h, N_v, f_h, and f_v we obtained the optimal values has $N_h = 10$, $N_v = 6$, $f_h = 7.8$ cm, and $f_v = 7.8$ cm. The optimal plot corresponding to these values is shown in Fig. 10a. In the plot, the actuation torque before static balancing got reduced by 90%.

3.1 Practical Test of Static Balancing

In order to practically test the performance of the optimal solution, we added springs and weights on the prototype as per the optimal solution. We then measured the

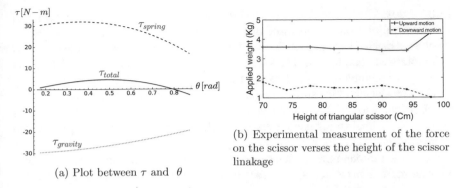

(a) Plot between τ and θ

(b) Experimental measurement of the force on the scissor verses the height of the scissor linakage

Fig. 10 Theoretical and experimental net-torque required for actuation under the load as a function of θ

force required in two cases: (1) to lift the mechanism from its bottom position to its top position and (2) to bring down the mechanism from its top position to bottom position. Both sets of forces are plotted in Fig. 10b. We see that for the same height of the scissor linkage, multiple forces are possible because of friction in joints. From the graph, it is clear that to handle 10 Kg of load, we need to apply at most 4 Kg-wt. Thus, by partial static balance, we have reduced the torque or force required from the actuator by about 60%.

4 Discussion

We now discuss the situations where the prototyping using materials such as bamboos could be advantageous or disadvantageous. Bamboos being organic composites and light in weight are a lot more easy and safe to handle than metals or plastics such as polypropylene or nylon. They are easily amenable to processing such as drilling and cutting through hand tools. Thus, it is possible to obtain a frugal prototype. However, small-scale swaying is always present and this could present difficulties in devising control laws for precisely controlling motion of the top platform which is the end-effector. Furthermore, there is also a limitation on the load carrying capacity. Nevertheless, for frugal proof of concept, bamboo-based prototyping is an attractive option.

5 Conclusion

This paper through prototyping demonstrated that triangular-prism-shaped scissor linkage has much smaller lateral sway in comparison with parallel-plane scissor linkage when revolute joints are imperfect as is typically the case with joints formed on bamboos. The paper also described the complete design, including base and top platform, of a scissor lift made of bamboo pieces. Use of straight line motion generating mechanisms like Chebyshev linkage and Roberts linkage in the place of slider joints was highlighted. The later part of the paper focused on static balancing the designed prototype using normal springs. The balancing solution was obtained by varying free-length of the springs that are cut from a strip. An applet was created in SAGE software to facilitate manual variation of free-lengths and the number springs to arrive at optimal spring parameters where the net torque due to both gravity and springs is minimized through visual judgement. A 90% reduction in torque was accomplished through the minimization. In practice, the reduction was only about 60% due to frictional effects. Overall, a workable scissor lift was made using bamboos as the primary material for links, and it was partially statically balanced with normal springs to obtain about 60% reduction in actuation effort even in the presence of friction.

References

1. C.S. Pan, S.S. Chiou, T.-Y. Kau, B.M. Wimer, X. Ning, P. Keane, Evaluation of postural sway and impact forces during ingress and egress of scissor lifts at elevations. Appl. Ergon. **65**, 152–162 (2017)
2. L.A. Mira, A.P. Thrall, N.D. Temmerman, Deployable scissor arch for transitional shelters. Autom. Constr. **43**, 123–131 (2014)
3. Y. Akgn, C.J. Gantes, W. Sobek, K. Korkmaz, K. Kalochairetis, A novel adaptive spatial scissor-hinge structural mechanism for convertible roofs. Eng. Struct. **33**(4), 1365–1376 (2011)
4. Y. Akgn, C.J. Gantes, K.E. Kalochairetis, G. Kiper, A novel concept of convertible roofs with high transformability consisting of planar scissor-hinge structures. Eng. Struct. **32**(9), 2873–2883 (2010)
5. Modelling, simulation and control of a foldable stair mechanism with a linear actuation technique. Procedia Eng. **97**, 1312–1321 (2014)
6. J.-S. Zhao, F. Chu, Z.-J. Feng, The mechanism theory and application of deployable structures based on SLE. Mech. Mach. Theory **44**(2), 324–335 (2009)
7. S. Deepak, Static balancing of rigid-body linkages and compliant mechanisms, Ph.D. thesis, Department of Mechanical Engineering Indian Institute of Science Bangalore, 2012
8. J.L. Herder, Energy-free system. Theory, conception and design of statically balanced spring mechanism, Ph.D. thesis, Delft University of Technology Delft, The Netherlands, November 2001

Dynamic Analysis of Underwater Vehicle-Manipulator Systems

Anil Kumar Sharma, Vishal Abhishek, Subir Kumar Saha,
N. Srinivasa Reddy and Soumen Sen

Abstract Dynamic model of an underwater robot is nonlinear in hydrodynamic parameters such as added mass, damping, etc. The hydrodynamic coefficients vary with time and configuration of the robot. This paper presents a modeling technique for the Underwater Vehicle-Manipulator System (UVMS) using the DeNOC matrices. Furthermore, as a starting point, some simple hydrodynamic experiments were performed which are used to validate the hydrodynamic simulation in MATLAB environment. For these simulations, the hydrodynamic coefficients were considered to be constant throughout the simulation of the manipulators. Two experiments were performed. In the first experiment, free fall of one-link arm was considered, and in the second, free fall of a two-link manipulator was considered. The simulation results obtained were found in good agreement with the experimental results, even with the constant hydrodynamic coefficients, because of the simple structure of the experiments.

Keywords Underwater manipulator · DeNOC matrices · Hydrodynamics coefficients · Forward dynamics · Matlab simulation · Experimental validation

A. K. Sharma (✉) · V. Abhishek (✉) · S. K. Saha (✉)
Department of Mechanical Engineering, Indian Institute of Technology Delhi,
New Delhi 110016, India
e-mail: agroupofindia@gmail.com

V. Abhishek
e-mail: vishalabhishek1691@gmail.com

S. K. Saha
e-mail: saha@mech.iitd.ac.in

N. Srinivasa Reddy · S. Sen
CSIR-Central Mechanical Engineering Research Institute,
Durgapur 713209, West Bengal, India
e-mail: nsreddy@cmeri.res.in

S. Sen
e-mail: soumen_sen@cmeri.res.in

© Springer Nature Singapore Pte Ltd. 2019
D N Badodkar and T A Dwarakanath (eds.), *Machines, Mechanism and Robotics*, Lecture Notes in Mechanical Engineering,
https://doi.org/10.1007/978-981-10-8597-0_63

1 Introduction

The undersea environment is a vast storehouse of natural resources like minerals (oils, natural gas, chemicals, and metals, etc.), energy (tides and water currents), and food (fish, prawn, lobsters, etc.). The unstructured and hazardous undersea environment poses harsh condition to human divers. Therefore, robotic research has come into place in order to prevent human intervention in the deep sea. The underwater Vehicle-Manipulator System (UVMS) has gained popularity in the robotic research as it offers more flexibility and wider range of applications for underwater robots.

The dynamic modeling of the underwater robots is different from the dynamics of land-based robots and space robots because of the presence of hydrodynamic effects. The hydrodynamic forces significantly impact the dynamics of an underwater manipulator system. The accurate modeling of the underwater robotic system is still a challenging task. However, the modeling of hydrodynamic forces generated during these types of motion is still a big area of research. Furthermore, the presence of hydrodynamic forces also increase the computation cost in comparison to the land-based or space manipulators. An efficient dynamic simulation algorithm of $O(n)$ for an Unmanned Underwater Vehicle (UUV) was developed in [7]. The effect of added mass, viscous drag, fluid acceleration, and buoyancy forces with constant hydrodynamic coefficients was considered. The computation of buoyancy force in local coordinates and drag force using the numerical integration of the local drag force for partially submerged and fully submerged manipulator was presented in [4]. It was demonstrated that the resulting effect of hydrodynamic forces increased the computation time by two to three times the computation time required for the standard dynamics. A more accurate hydrodynamic model for one-link cylindrical underwater manipulator was developed and validated experimentally in [6], where hydrodynamic coefficients were the function of (s/D), and Reynold's number, being s is the displacement of the cylinder and D is its diameter. In [2], the hydrodynamic terms such as added mass, drag, and buoyancy in dynamics of underwater manipulator were obtained by iterative learning control and time-scale transformation. Effectiveness of the method was demonstrated experimentally with one-link and three-link manipulators. The theory and implementation issues which are faced by manipulator designers were discussed in [8]. The kinematics and dynamics modeling of underwater manipulators using Lagrange's approach was developed in [3], and validated with commercial software ADAMS. A detailed dynamic model of UVMS was developed in [10] to investigate the coupling effect between the vehicle and manipulator. A novel design of underwater manipulator with a lightweight multilink structure was proposed in [16], which reduces the coupling effect between the vehicle and manipulator and allow to accomplish free-floating autonomous operations quickly. A survey on the design and control of autonomous underwater robots was provided in [18], which discussed the state-of-art technologies in the key areas of Underwater Vehicle and Underwater Vehicle-Manipulator System (UVMS).

A recursive, computationally efficien,t and numerically stable dynamic analysis method, namely, the DeNOC approach, was proposed in [9], which has been used

Fig. 1 An underwater
vehicle-manipulator system

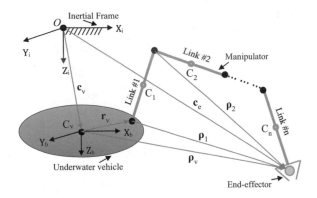

for the dynamics of serial-chain manipulators, closed-loop systems, tree-type robotic systems, parallel manipulators, space robotics, and for flexible multibody systems [11–15]. The DeNOC approach is advantageous for the dynamic analysis of large degree-of-freedom (dof) systems and real-time applications [14]. The dynamics of Kirchhoff's equations describing a submerged body, whose center-of-mass coincides with the center-of-buoyancy, was presented in [1].

As a UVMS has more than six-dof, the DeNOC approach is used for the mathematical modeling of the UVMS. The six-dof underwater vehicle in UVMS was represented with the help of six one-dof joints (3-prismatic for translational motion and 3-revolute for rotational motion, respectively). However, the developed mathematical model was used to simulate the one-link cylindrical arm and two-link manipulator in Matlab environment with constant hydrodynamic coefficients. Experiments were performed to validate the simulation results.

2 Dynamic Modeling

An Underwater Vehicle-Manipulator System (UVMS) is shown in Fig. 1. The manipulator has a moving base and n moving rigid bodies, numbered #1, #2, …, #n, connected by n one-degree-of-freedom kinematic joints, namely, a revolute or a prismatic joint, numbered as 1, 2, …, n. The free body diagram of the ith rigid body is shown in Fig. 2. The mass and mass moment-of-inertia of the body are m_i and $\mathbf{I}_i$, respectively. The body is moving with an angular velocity of $\boldsymbol{\omega}_i$ and linear velocity of $\mathbf{v}_i$. The corresponding hydrodynamic mass matrix and inertia tensor, because of acceleration of the body, are $\mathbf{M}_{a_i}$ and $\mathbf{I}_{a_i}$, respectively. The buoyancy force $\mathbf{f}_{b_i}$ and drag force $\mathbf{f}_{d_i}$ are acting at the center-of-buoyancy $\mathbf{r}_{b_i}$ and drag center, respectively, which are denoted by vector $\mathbf{r}_{b_i}$ and $\mathbf{r}_{d_i}$ from the center-of-mass. The externally applied moment about and force at the center-of-mass are denoted as $\mathbf{n}_{h_i}$ and $\mathbf{f}_{hi}$, respectively.

Using the free-body diagram of Fig. 2, for i th link, the Newton-Euler form of the Kirchhoff's equations of motion (1869) [14], can be written as:

Fig. 2 Free body diagram of
the ith rigid body in water

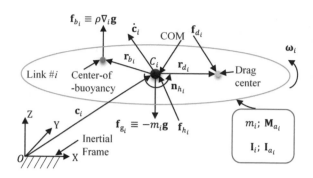

$$\mathbf{I}_{RA_i}\dot{\boldsymbol{\omega}}_i + \boldsymbol{\omega}_i \times \mathbf{I}_{RA_i}\boldsymbol{\omega}_i + \dot{\mathbf{c}}_i \times \mathbf{M}_{a_i}\dot{\mathbf{c}}_i + \mathbf{r}_{b_i} \times \mathbf{f}_{b_i} + \mathbf{r}_{d_i} \times \mathbf{f}_{d_i} = \mathbf{n}_{h_i} \qquad (1)$$

$$\mathbf{M}_{RA_i}\ddot{\mathbf{c}}_i + \mathbf{M}_{a_i}(\dot{\mathbf{c}}_i \times \boldsymbol{\omega}_i) + \boldsymbol{\omega}_i \times \mathbf{M}_{a_i}\dot{\mathbf{c}}_i + \mathbf{f}_{g_i} + \mathbf{f}_{b_i} + \mathbf{f}_{d_i} = \mathbf{f}_{h_i} \qquad (2)$$

The above equations of motion can be written in a matrix-vector form as given
below:

$$\begin{bmatrix} \mathbf{I}_{RA_i} & \mathbf{O} \\ \mathbf{O} & \mathbf{M}_{RA_i} \end{bmatrix} \begin{bmatrix} \dot{\boldsymbol{\omega}}_i \\ \ddot{\mathbf{c}}_i \end{bmatrix} + \begin{bmatrix} -(\mathbf{I}_{RA_i}\,\boldsymbol{\omega}_i) \times \mathbf{1} & -(\mathbf{M}_{RA_i}\dot{\mathbf{c}}_i) \times \mathbf{1} \\ -(\mathbf{M}_{RA_i}\,\dot{\mathbf{c}}_i) \times \mathbf{1} & -\mathbf{M}_{RA_i}(\boldsymbol{\omega}_i \times \mathbf{1}) \end{bmatrix} \begin{bmatrix} \boldsymbol{\omega}_i \\ \dot{\mathbf{c}}_i \end{bmatrix}$$

$$+ \begin{bmatrix} \mathbf{r}_{b_i} \times \mathbf{f}_{b_i} \\ \mathbf{f}_{g_i} + \mathbf{f}_{b_i} \end{bmatrix} + \begin{bmatrix} \mathbf{r}_{d_i} \times \mathbf{f}_{d_i} \\ \mathbf{f}_{d_i} \end{bmatrix} = \begin{bmatrix} \mathbf{n}_{h_i} \\ \mathbf{f}_{h_i} \end{bmatrix} \qquad (3)$$

where $\mathbf{M}_{RA_i} \equiv (m_i \mathbf{1} + \mathbf{M}_{a_i})$, and $\mathbf{I}_{RA_i} \equiv (\mathbf{I}_i + \mathbf{I}_{a_i})$, and $\mathbf{O}$ and $\mathbf{1}$ are the 3×3 null
and identity matrices, respectively. For the ith link, the above equations of motion
can be rewritten in a compact form as:

$$\mathbf{M}_{h_i}\,\dot{\mathbf{t}}_i + \mathbf{W}_{h_i}\,\mathbf{t}_i + \mathbf{g}_{h_i} + \mathbf{d}_{h_i} = \mathbf{w}_{h_i} \qquad (4)$$

where $\mathbf{M}_{h_i}$ is the hydrodynamic mass matrix, $\mathbf{W}_{h_i}$ is the hydrodynamic matrix of
Coriolis, $\mathbf{g}_{h_i}$ is the gravity and buoyancy force vector, $\mathbf{d}_{h_i}$ is the hydrodynamic drag
force vector, $\mathbf{w}_{h_i}$ is the hydrodynamic wrench vector, and $\mathbf{t}_i$ is the twist vector for
the ith link [9]. The Eq. (4) is now written for all n links, i.e., for $i = 1, 2, \ldots, n$, as:

$$\mathbf{M}_h\,\dot{\mathbf{t}} + \mathbf{W}_h\,\mathbf{t} + \mathbf{g}_h + \mathbf{d}_h = \mathbf{w}_h \qquad (5)$$

where $\mathbf{M}_h$ and $\mathbf{W}_h$ are the $6n \times 6n$ generalized hydrodynamic mass matrix, and the
generalized hydrodynamic matrix of Coriolis, respectively. They are given by:

$$\mathbf{M}_h \equiv \mathrm{diag} \cdot [\mathbf{M}_{h_1}, \ldots, \mathbf{M}_{h_n}], \quad \text{and} \quad \mathbf{W}_h \equiv \mathrm{diag} \cdot [\mathbf{W}_{h_1}, \ldots, \mathbf{W}_{h_n}] \qquad (6)$$

Fig. 3 Drag force distribution for ith link

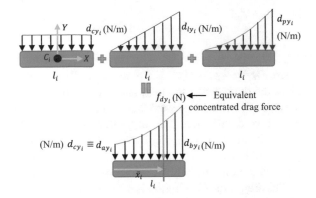

Also, the $6n$-dimensional vectors of generalized twist, gravity and buoyancy, drag, and wrench are defined as

$$\mathbf{t} \equiv \left[\mathbf{t}_1^T, \ldots, \mathbf{t}_n^T\right]^T; \quad \mathbf{g}_h \equiv \left[\mathbf{g}_{h_1}^T, \ldots, \mathbf{g}_{h_n}^T\right]^T \tag{7}$$

$$\mathbf{d}_h \equiv \left[\mathbf{d}_{h_1}^T, \ldots, \mathbf{d}_{h_n}^T\right]^T; \quad \text{and } \mathbf{w}_h \equiv \left[\mathbf{w}_{h_1}^T, \ldots, \mathbf{w}_{h_n}^T\right]^T \tag{8}$$

2.1 Hydrodynamic Effects

When a body moves underwater, the dynamics of the body include several other hydrodynamic effects, which can be characterized in two major categories, namely, hydrostatic forces such as buoyancy, and hydrodynamic forces such as drag, lift, added mass, etc. The mathematical modeling of these hydrodynamic effects is still a big domain of research. Here, the hydrodynamic drag modeling is discussed in detail.

Damping Forces: The damping effect of an underwater manipulator at high speed is highly coupled and nonlinear. Nevertheless, one can approximate the non-coupled motion of a cylindrical link which has three plane of symmetry, and the terms higher than second order are negligible. The drag force corresponds to the velocity component, perpendicular to the longitudinal axis of the link is considered. The velocity and drag force distribution for the first link of the manipulator with revolute joint are linear and parabolic, respectively [17], as shown in Fig. 3. The drag force and drag center location from the origin of the ith link in integral form can be written as:

$$F_i = \frac{1}{2}\rho C_{d_i} D_i \int_0^{a_i} V_{yi}|V_{yi}|dx_i = Dr_i \int_0^{a_i} V_{yi}|V_{yi}|dx_i \tag{9}$$

$$\bar{x}_i = \int\limits_0^{a_i} V_{yi} |V_{yi}| x_i dx_i \Bigg/ \int\limits_0^{a_i} V_{yi} |V_{yi}| dx_i \tag{10}$$

where $Dr_i = \frac{1}{2}\rho C_{d_i} D_i$, ρ is the density of fluid medium, C_{d_i} is the drag coefficient, D_i is the diameter of the link, and V_{yi} is the velocity component perpendicular to the axis of the link. Here, the drag force is calculated in terms of the intensity of the drag force distribution. The drag force intensity at the fixed end of the first link is $d_{ay_1} = 0$ N/m and at other end is d_{by_1} N/m. The equivalent concentrated drag force f_{dy_1} would act at the drag center which is $\frac{3l_1}{4}$ from the origin of the link. The drag force distribution for any ith link of the manipulator is shown in Fig. 3.

The drag force distribution is the combination of constant (d_{cy_i}), linear (d_{ly_i}), and parabolic (d_{py_i}) drag force intensity. The equivalent drag force would act at the drag center $\bar{x}_i$. The expressions for the drag force intensity, equivalent concentrated drag force, and drag center are given below:

$$d_{ay_i} = Dr_i V_{yc_i} |V_{yc_i}|; \ d_{by_i} = Dr_i V_{yv_i} |V_{yv_i}|; \ d_{aby_i} = Dr_i V_{yc_i} V_{yv_i} \tag{11}$$

$$f_{dy_i} = \left[3d_{ay_i} + 3d_{aby_i} + d_{by_i}\right]\frac{l_i}{3} \tag{12}$$

$$\bar{x}_i = \left[\frac{6d_{ay_i} + 8d_{aby_i} + 3d_{by_i}}{3d_{ay_i} + 3d_{aby_i} + d_{by_i}}\right]\frac{l_i}{4} \tag{13}$$

where V_{yc_i} is the constant part of velocity, V_{yv_i} is the varying part of the velocity, and d_{aby_i} is the coupled drag force intensity. Similar expressions can be derived for another perpendicular direction of the link for spatial motion of the manipulator, say, along Z-axis of the link fixed-frame. The key aspect of this drag modeling is that it can capture the drag coefficient variation with respect to the configuration of the UVMS. Further, the calculation of drag center makes its more realistic than merely assuming that the drag force is acting at the center-of-mass. The proposed drag modeling cannot capture the variation in drag coefficient along the link length.

The equations of motion given by Eq. (5) are transformed into the reduced-order equations of motion using the Decoupled Natural Orthogonal Complement (DeNOC) matrices [9], and are expressed below:

$$\mathbf{I}_h(\boldsymbol{\theta})\ddot{\boldsymbol{\theta}} + \mathbf{h}_h(\boldsymbol{\theta}, \dot{\boldsymbol{\theta}}) + \bar{\mathbf{d}}_h(\boldsymbol{\theta}, \dot{\boldsymbol{\theta}}) + \boldsymbol{\gamma}_h(\boldsymbol{\theta}) = \boldsymbol{\tau}_h \tag{14}$$

where $\mathbf{I}_h$ is the hydrodynamic generalized inertia matrix, $\mathbf{h}_h$ is the hydrodynamic vector of convective inertia, $\bar{\mathbf{d}}_h$ is the vector of hydrodynamic damping force, $\boldsymbol{\gamma}_h$ is the vector of gravity and buoyancy forces, $\boldsymbol{\tau}_h$ is the generalized force vector, and $\boldsymbol{\theta}$ is the vector of generalized coordinates.

Fig. 4 Experimental set-up
for one-link cylindrical arm

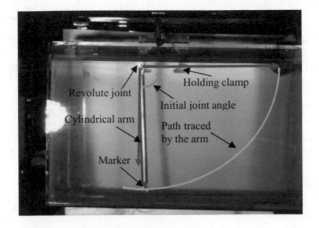

3 Experimental Validations

To investigate the hydrodynamic simulation of an underwater manipulator, three experiments were performed. A transparent water tank of rectangular cross-section, 0.7 m by 0.5 and 0.7 m deep was used to perform these experiments. The density of the water was taken as 1000 kg/m^3 and the drag coefficients were taken from [17].

3.1 Free Fall of One-Link Cylindrical Arm

The experimental set-up is shown in Fig. 4. A one-link cylindrical arm of mass 0.3 kg, length 0.4 m, and diameter 0.02 m fall freely from its initial configuration. The initial joint angle and rate are [$\pi/2$ rad; 0 rad/s]. The drag coefficient for the arm was taken as 0.91. The time taken by the arm to reach equilibrium point was 2 s. The result for joint angle of one-link arm is shown in Fig. 5.

3.2 Free Fall of a Two-Link Manipulator

The experimental set-up is shown in Fig. 6. The physical parameters for the manipulator are summarized in Table 1. The initial configuration is shown in Fig. 7. Initial joint angles and their rates for the manipulator are [-0.07556 rad; 0.0680 rad; 0 rad/s; 0 rad/s]. The time taken by the manipulator to reach at equilibrium point was 1.32 s. The results for the joint angles of the two-link manipulator are shown in Fig. 8a, b.

Fig. 5 Joint angle variation

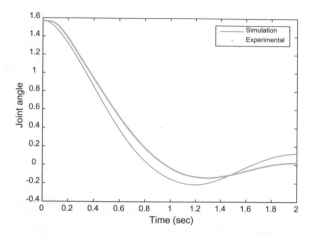

Fig. 6 Experimental set-up
for two-link manipulator

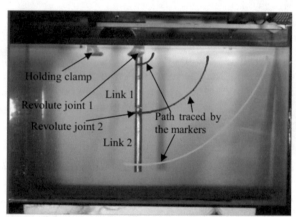

Table 1 Physical parameters
of manipulator

Parameters	Link 1	Link 2
Mass (Kg)	0.136	0.127
Length (m)	0.183	0.17
Diameter (m)	0.02	0.02
Drag coefficient	0.85	0.8

4 Conclusions

The mathematical model of the UVMS has been developed using the DeNOC
approach. However, the developed model was used to simulate one-link cylindrical arm and two-link manipulator. The MATLAB environment is used to simulate
the forward dynamics of underwater manipulator. The experiments were performed
to validate the forward dynamics simulations, and are found closer to the experimen-

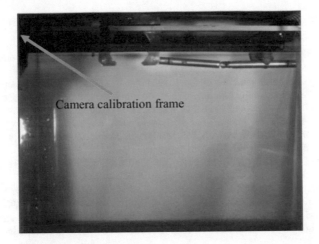

Fig. 7 Initial configuration of the manipulator

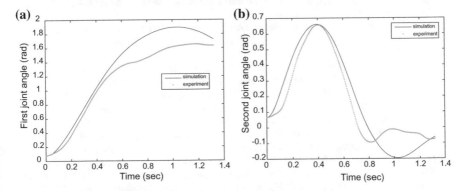

Fig. 8 a Variation in first joint angle, **b** variation in second joint angle

tal results. The equivalent concentrated drag force approach is good over the strip theory of drag modeling [5]. The proposed drag modeling considers the variation in drag center as well as can capture the drag coefficient variation with respect to the configuration of the UVMS if used along with some identification scheme. The use of constant hydrodynamic coefficients for the MATLAB simulation is found in good agreement for simple experimental structure. Future research will concentrate on more accurate drag modeling and estimation of the hydrodynamic coefficients.

Acknowledgements This research was supported by project grant RP02947, from Robotics and Automation Division, CSIR-CMERI, Durgapur, West Bengal, India. I would also like to thank Ms Aparna Pandharkar, for her kind support towards the modeling of UVMS.

References

1. P. Holmes, J. Jenkins, N.E. Leonard, Dynamics of the Kirchhoff equations I: coincident centers of gravity and buoyancy. Elsevier Sci. B. **118**(1998), 311–342 (1998)
2. S. Kawamura, N. Sakagami, Analysis on dynamics of underwater robot manipulator basing on iterative learning control and time-scale transformation, in *Proceedings of the 2002 IEEE International Conference on Robotics & Automation* (Washington, DC, May 2002)
3. R. Li, A.P. Anvar, A.M. Anvar, T.F. Lu, Dynamic modeling of underwater manipulator and its simulation. Int. J. Mech. Aerosp. Ind. Mechatron. Manuf. Eng. **6**(12), 2611–2620 (2012). http://scholar.waset.org/1999.8/11836
4. B. Levesque, M.J. Richard, Dynamic analysis of a manipulator in a fluid environment. Int. J. Robot. Res. **13**(3), 221–231 (1994)
5. K.N. Leabourne, S.M. Rock, Model development of an underwater manipulator for coordinated arm-vehicle control, in *OCEANS'98 Conference Proceedings*, vol. 2 (IEEE, 1998), pp. 941–946
6. T. McLain, S.M. Rock, Development and experimental validation of an underwater manipulator hydrodynamic model. Int. J. Robot. Res. **17**(7), 748–759. http://scholarsarchive.byu.edu/facpub/1521
7. S. McMillan, D. Orin, R. McGhee, Efficient dynamic simulation of an unmanned underwater vehicle with a manipulator, in *Proceedings IEEE International Conference Robotics & Automation* (1994), pp. 1133–1140
8. I.A. Rahman, S.M. Suboh, M.R. Arshad, Theory and design issues of underwater manipulator, in *International Conference on Control, Instrumentation and Mechatronics Engineering*, Johor Bahru, Johor, Malaysia, 28–29 May 2007
9. S.K. Saha, Analytical expression for the inverted inertia matrix of serial robots. Int. J. Robot. Res. **18**(1), 116–124 (1999). https://doi.org/10.1177/027836499901800108
10. M. Santhakumar, Investigation into the dynamics and control of an underwater vehicle-manipulator system. Research Article. https://doi.org/10.1155/2013/839046
11. A.K. Sharma, S.K. Saha, Dynamics of space manipulator: relative vs natural coordinates, in *The 8th Asian Conference on Multibody Dynamics*, Kanazawa, Japan, 07–10 Aug 2016
12. S.K. Saha, S.K. Goel, Dynamic modelling of serial-link mechanisms, in Proceedings of the National Conference on Machines and Mechanisms, IIT Kanpur, India, 12–13 Dec 1997
13. S.K. Saha, Modeling and simulation of space robots, in *Proceedings of the 1993 IEEE/RSJ International Conference on Intelligent Robots and Systems*, Yokohama, Japan, 26–30 July 1993
14. S.K. Saha, S.V. Shah, P.V. Nandihal, Evolution of the DeNOC-based dynamic modelling for multibody systems. Mech. Sci. **4**, 1–20 (2013). https://doi.org/10.5194/ms-4-1-2013
15. S.V. Shah, P.V. Nandihal, S.K. Saha, Recursive dynamics simulator (ReDySim): a multibody dynamics solver. Theor. Appl. Mech. Lett. **2**, 063011 (2012)
16. Y. Wang, S. Wang, Q. Wei, M. Tan, C. Zhou, J. Yu, Development of an underwater manipulator and its free-floating autonomous operation. IEEE/ASME Trans. Mech. **21**(2), 815–824 (2016). https://doi.org/10.1109/tmech.2015.2494068
17. F.M. White, *Fluid Mechanics* (McGraw-Hill, New York, 2011)
18. J. Yuh, Design and control of autonomous underwater robots: a survey. Auton. Robots. **8**, 7–24 (2000)

Briquette Compacting Machine: A Design for Rural Applications

C. Amarnath and Anirban Guha

Abstract This paper enumerates the design and synthesis of a mechanism for a fuel briquette compacting machine. The briquettes are made of a mixture of husk (rice or wheat or any other) and animal waste in appropriate proportions and compacted in the machine. Several experiments were initially conducted to arrive at the right proportions of water, husk, and dung, and to determine the force to compact the biomass. The pellets were dried in the sun and burnt in a stove. The final specifications of the machine were arrived based on these simple trials. There were several challenges in the machine development. The biomass mixture tends to cake and harden if the machine is left idle for long. It is not desirable for a briquette to crumble both in a wet as well as a dry state. The mechanism has to handle these requirements and as the machine, is to be manually operated frictional effects and any tendency to jam ought to be minimized. The engineering drawings of the machine are being freely distributed to rural mechanics who are desirous of replicating the machine, after observing the machine in action at CTARA at IIT Bombay. Several machines have thus been built and are operational in many villages. The paper covers such aspects and how a compact machine was arrived at through synthesis of an appropriate mechanism that is inherently not easily prone to "jamming". The synthesis is based on techniques derived from symmetric coupler curve generation.

Keywords Rural · Briquette · Kinematic synthesis · Coupler curve

C. Amarnath (✉) · A. Guha
Department of Mechanical Engineering, Indian Institute of Technology Bombay,
Mumbai 400076, India
e-mail: c.amarnath@gmail.com

A. Guha
e-mail: anirbanguha@iitb.ac.in

© Springer Nature Singapore Pte Ltd. 2019
D N Badodkar and T A Dwarakanath (eds.), *Machines, Mechanism and Robotics*, Lecture Notes in Mechanical Engineering,
https://doi.org/10.1007/978-981-10-8597-0_64

1 Introduction

Biomass (rice or wheat husk, coconut shells, and other agricultural waste) is used in rural areas as a fuel for burning and also as raw material for composting. Abundant availability of biomass calls for storage and handling of vast quantities of loose biomass. When loose biomass is burnt, there is an adverse environmental impact due to fine particulate matter [1–3]. Compaction (densification) of biomass is often resorted to both for ease of handling the biomass and for reducing if not eliminating environmental pollution. Densification is attractive to large units in view of several advantages, though capital is required for achieving the same. Some amount of densification would help rural households maintain a reasonably safe indoor atmosphere.

Numerous trials were required to understand the nuances of the process of briquetting biomass. We attempted to conduct these trials on simple devices that could be easily replicated rurally. A rudimentary apparatus (Fig. 1) consisting of a tube of about 25 mm in diameter and a piston was built. The cylinder was filled with a mixture of husk and dung, and weights were placed on the piston to compress the biomass. Loose biomass has a typical density of 0.05–0.2 gms per cubic centimeter, and is compacted to about 1.1–1.4 gms per cubic centimeter [4] to obtain a briquette with an adequate level of densification. Trials showed us that a long cylinder with a piston executing a long stroke would be required. The mechanism for the piston press has to be designed accordingly.

2 Auxillary Requirements

Having established the primary requirement of a long stroke, we shall now examine auxiliary requirements. Several possibilities were explored for loading (and unloading) the cylinder with the biomass. The possibilities included top loading, side load-

Fig. 1 Cylinder and piston with dead weight

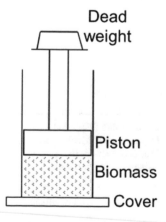

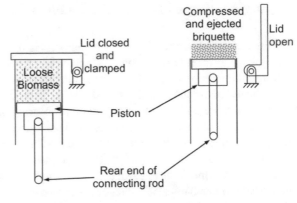

Fig. 2 Lid closed and piston compacting as well as ejecting

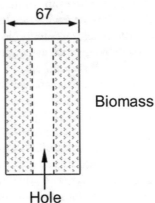

Fig. 3 Cylindrical briquette with central hole (0.5 lt)

ing, and so on. An ejector working in tandem with the motion of the piston could be used for unloading the briquette. Alternately, the piston that compresses the biomass could itself be called upon to eject the briquette too thereby reducing the number of moving parts in the machine. A lid, when closed and locked on the open side of the cylinder, permits compaction (Fig. 2). The size (length) of the briquette (Figs. 2 and 3) depends upon the force applied and the amount of biomass charged into the cylinder. Once compaction is completed by the moving piston, the lid could be opened and as the piston continues to move upward, it could push the briquette out of the cylinder. A long slender rod fitted to the top of the piston and a corresponding axial hole in the cap (both not shown) results in a briquette with an axial hole (Fig. 3) that serves to permit free circulation of air. These are not shown in Fig. 2 but are shown in Fig. 6.

The machine operator banks on his experience and familiarity with the raw material to determine the charge of the biomass to arrive at a reasonable briquette size and density. Once the operator feels the briquette is adequately compressed, the lid is opened and further motion of the input lever causes the briquette to be ejected.

Such a design of the machine with as few moving parts as possible, is easy to service, and maintain, aspects that acquire importance in a rural setting.

3　Engineering a Machine for Usage in Rural Areas

It is preferable to incorporate mostly lower pairs in machinery for rural applications. The links and revolute pairs could be easily fabricated at village level with simple tooling and low expenditure. For a piston press, a prismatic pair has to be necessarily incorporated between the cylinder and piston. Though prismatic pairs are relatively stiffer, it is more difficult to protect the load bearing surfaces from dust. Revolute pairs, by their very nature contain enclosed surfaces and are easy to protect against dust. Side thrust is inherent in engine mechanisms and so also in devices containing higher pairs like a rack and pinion. Devices based on rack and pinion mechanisms provide uniform mechanical advantage throughout the stroke, while one would prefer an increase in mechanical advantage (for example, slider-crank mechanisms) as the piston moves towards the lid at end of the cylinder for compressing the biomass. Also rack and pinion devices are beyond the manufacturing capability of rural mechanics and need enclosures for protection against dust. It would thus be ideal to use revolute pairs to the greatest extent possible in rural designs more so if machine building is to be by self-help groups.

Several mechanisms with lower pairs were examined—beginning with the slider-crank (the engine mechanism). It is well known that in the engine mechanism as the crank pin moves along its circular path, the connecting rod tilts giving rise to side thrust between the piston and cylinder. Also since in this case, the cylinder is a long one, there is a possibility of the connecting rod striking the side of the cylinder. One could use a cross-head as in steam engines, but an alternative, ideal for rural settings, is to use a linkage to guide the rear end of the connecting rod on an approximate straight line along the axis of the cylinder (Fig. 2). This results in the connecting rod having negligible inclination (with respect to the cylinder's axis) throughout the motion of the piston.

There is thus low side thrust between piston and cylinder and consequently friction between the two is theoretically negligible. Minimization of side thrust is important since the mixture of husk and dung has a tendency to cake and offer resistance to motion more so when side thrust is present.

A four-bar linkage with a coupler point tracing an approximate straight line could be used to guide the rear end of the connecting rod. A long straight line motion of the rear end is desired to handle the long travel of the piston.

4　Straight Line Mechanism

There are several techniques to determine a linkage with coupler points generating approximate straight lines. To get reasonably long approximate straight lines [5], one has to resort to use of optimization techniques.

Yet another simple way is to use symmetric coupler curve generators as shown in Fig. 4. The symmetric coupler curve generator is a four-bar linkage obtained by

Fig. 4 Symmetric coupler curve generator

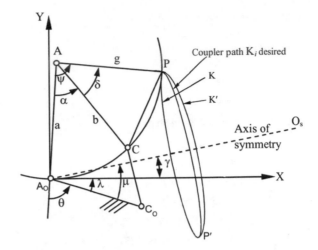

having points Ao, C, and coupler point P lying on a circle centered at the pivot A, i.e., $a = b = g$. Additionally, one must have the angles as $(\gamma + \lambda) = (\psi - \alpha)/2 = \text{constant}$. Os is the axis of symmetry and in this figure, the coupler point P is tracing a flattened ellipse [5].

Let us now consider the dyad OaAP in Fig. 4 which is part of a symmetric coupler curve generator, and let the equation of the straight line desired to be traced by the point P be given as $Y = f(X)$.

For this case as we desire symmetry, we set $a = g$ and the coordinates of the point P are obtained through simple vectorial addition available in several texts [5, 6] as:

$$X = a\,\cos(\theta + \lambda - \psi) - a\cos(\theta + \lambda) \tag{1}$$

$$Y = a\sin(\theta + \lambda) - a\sin(\theta + \lambda - \psi) \tag{2}$$

The first and second derivatives of Eqs. 1 and 2 w.r.t θ are given in Table 1 where Eqs. 1 and 2 are recast for compactness as Eqs. 3 and 4. First and second derivatives of desired path function are also given in the same table. For the present case, the desired path is a straight line. In Table 1, substituting Eqs. 3–6 into Eqs. 7 and 8 leads to the elimination of derivatives of X and Y and expressions are obtained for the derivatives of ψ w.r.t θ. The set of Eqs. 3–6 are essentially those one uses for ISP synthesis of linkages [6].

Using the equations that coordinate ψ and θ one has converted the problem of path generation into one of function generation, namely coordinated motion of links AC and AoCo with AAo being temporarily acting as the fixed link in Fig. 4. We could use the well-known techniques of synthesis of function generators [5–7] for completing the determination of the unknown link lengths (AoCo and CCo) of the four-bar linkage AAoCoC.

Table 1 Position equations and derivatives

Let

$M_C = a \cos(\theta + \lambda)$

$M_S = a \sin(\theta + \lambda)$

$N_C = a \cos(\theta + \lambda - \psi)$

$N_S = a \sin(\theta + \lambda - \psi)$

Primes indicate derivatives with respect to θ

$$X = -M_c + N_c \qquad (3)$$
$$Y = M_S - N_S \qquad (4)$$
$$X' = M_S - N_S(1 - \psi') \qquad (5)$$
$$Y' = M_C - N_C(1 - \psi') \qquad (6)$$
$$X'' = M_c + N_cY'' - N_c(1 - \psi')^2 \qquad (7)$$
$$Y'' = -M_S + N_cY'' - N_S(1 - \psi')^2 \qquad (8)$$

For the path function $y=f(x)$ derivative with respect to θ gives

$$Y' = f_1(X') \qquad (9)$$
$$Y'' = f_1(X'') + f_1(X')^2 \qquad (10)$$

By substituting Eqs. 5–8 in Eqs. 9 and 10, one can obtain expressions for ψ' and ψ'', the first and second derivatives of ψ with respect to θ

5 An Approximate and Long Straight Line

The use of a symmetric coupler curve generator would permit us to obtain a coupler curve that is symmetric, the axis of symmetry Ao Os being as shown [5]. If we were to obtain a linkage by positioning the precision points on one side of the line of symmetry then one could expect a symmetric straight line image (on the other side of the line of symmetry Ao Os) and should the lines on both sides merge we obtain a long approximate straight line as the desired coupler curve. We shall now demonstrate the procedure for synthesis using the relationships in Table 1.

One has to first choose a fixed pivot Ao and the dyad AoAP with AoA = AP as shown in Fig. 5. An axis of symmetry Ao Os is now conveniently chosen. By dropping a perpendicular from P to the axis of symmetry, P' is determined as the reflection of P on the axis of symmetry. PP' is the desired straight line to be generated by the coupler point. We thus know the function Y = f(X) which is the equation of the desired straight line (PP'). We could now determine the derivatives Y' and Y'' using the relations (7) and (8) in Table 1. These quantities are then used to determine Psi prime and Psi double prime using Eqs. 3–6.

The derivatives of ψ w.r.t θ, namely ψ' and ψ'', may now be used to determine the four-bar linkage. Figure 5 shows one such linkage obtained using this procedure. In Fig. 5, the coupler point moves from P to P' along K and the return is along K'.

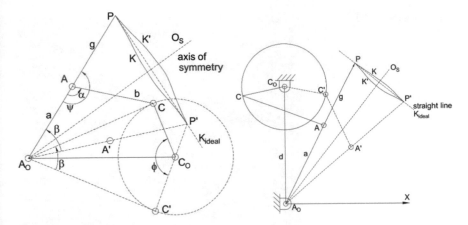

Fig. 5 Mechanisms synthesized

Fig. 6 Scaled drawing of machine

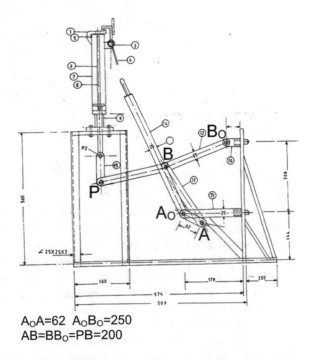

$A_OA=62 \quad A_OB_O=250$
$AB=BB_O=PB=200$

The exact and ideal line is shown as Ki. Note that at least one of K or K′ is close to the ideal straight line Ki.

In the results obtained by us elsewhere [8], the computed error between the ideal and generated paths is around 0.1% of the length of the line.

Fig. 7 Machine in IIT
Bombay

6 Discussions and Conclusions

The machine was constructed using the dimensions of a bar linkage mechanism
obtained from this effort. Figures 6 and 7 are of the first machine that was built
at IIT Bombay. The material and tools, as well as, the skills are readily available
in rural areas of the country. Based on experiments at CTARA, IIT Bombay [9]
adequate guidelines for compaction of various types of biomass material, and their
combustion properties have been reported and this constitutes valuable data on the
entire process of usage of biomass as a fuel.

The main aim here has been to empower the rural artisans in the construction
of these machines—self-reliance being the motto. Consequently, drawings of the
machine have been placed in the open domain, and are available at CTARA (Centre
for Technology Alternatives for Rural Areas) IIT Bombay. The machines have been
replicated by rural teams who have manufactured and used these in many rural areas
through self-help programs. Artisans realize that it would be relatively easy to sustain
and replicate what they have built because the rural ethos has been factored into the
design—unlike modern versions of bullock carts [4] that are yet to be accepted by
the rural users despite several subsidies.

References

1. N. Shekhar, Popularization of biomass briquettes—a means for sustainable rural development. Asian J. Manag. Res. **2**(1) (2011)
2. S.K. Mishra, P.V.R. Iyer, P.D. Grover, Biomass briquetting, in *Proceedings of the National Bio-Energy Convention* (IIT Delhi, 1995)
3. B.S.K Naidu, Biomass briquetting—an Indian perspective, in *ICREGA '14: Renewable Energy Generation and Applications*, ed. by M.O. Hamdan, et al. Springer
4. Down to earth bullock cart in its new avatar. Soc. Environ. Commun. **35**(2) (2010), New Delhi, India
5. R.S. Hartenberg, J. Denevit, *Kinematic Synthesis of Linkages* (McGraw Hill, 1964)
6. G.N. Sandor, A.G. Erdman, *Advanced Mechanisms Design—Analysis and Synthesis* (Prentice Hall of India Pvt Ltd., New Delhi, 1984)
7. F. Freudenstein, Approximate synthesis of four-bar linkages. ASME Trans. **77**(8), 853–861
8. M.S. Joshi, C. Amarnath, Synthesis of six link mechanisms for specified dwell periods. Paper No. DS-3, NaCoMM 81
9. K.V Kadav, Study and characterization of biomass generated fuel for stoves. M.Tech Dissertation, CTARA, IIT Bombay, June 2009

Trajectory Tracking and Control of Car-Like Robots

Suhan Shetty and Ashitava Ghosal

Abstract This paper deals with trajectory tracking control of a car-like robot. By exploiting the differential flatness property of the system based on the dynamics, a trajectory tracking controller using flatness-based control techniques is designed. A singularity in the system for the chosen control inputs, which does not allow direct application of feedback linearization control, is identified and this singularity is overcome by applying the dynamics-extension algorithm to obtain a dynamic feedback linearized controller. This controller results in asymptotic tracking convergence of the system's trajectory to the reference trajectory. Through numerical simulations, the control system is shown to track prescribed trajectories satisfactorily even in the presence of parametric uncertainties.

Keywords Differential flatness · System dynamics · Car-like robot

1 Introduction

Dynamics of a wheeled mobile robot (WMR) is inherently nonlinear, and it is subjected to non-holonomic constraints due to the no-slip condition at the wheel-ground contact. The developments in the control of non-holonomic systems have been a continuing topic of research and are explained in [1]. Most of the literature on trajectory tracking of car-like robots considers only the kinematics aspects of the system, and a detailed presentation of kinematic models of non-holonomic car-like WMR can be found in [2]. However, system dynamics plays a major role in high-speed applications. The trajectory tracking of car-like robots based on system dynamics is a very challenging task due to multiple non-holonomic constraints which complicates the resulting equation of motion. In reference [3], researchers have attempted to use

S. Shetty · A. Ghosal (✉)
Indian Institute of Science, Bengaluru, India
e-mail: asitava@iisc.ac.in; asitava@mecheng.iisc.ernet.in

S. Shetty
e-mail: suhan.n.shetty@gmail.com

© Springer Nature Singapore Pte Ltd. 2019
D N Badodkar and T A Dwarakanath (eds.), *Machines, Mechanism and Robotics*, Lecture Notes in Mechanical Engineering,
https://doi.org/10.1007/978-981-10-8597-0_65

759

dynamics in the trajectory tracking control problem of a differential drive WMR. In reference [4], authors present trajectory tracking of car-like robots based on the dynamics of the system and they use Lyapunov stability theorem to derive control laws. However, reference [4] uses torque on the steering wheel as one of the control inputs and this is not very realistic.

In this work, we derive the dynamic equations of motion of a WMR using a version of the Lagrangian formulation applied to non-holonomic systems known as Maggi's method [5]. We choose the driving force and rate of steering angle as control inputs. Then, we exploit the differential flatness property of the resulting system to design a flatness-based trajectory tracking controller [6, 7]. However, we identify that a direct application of flatness-based controller is not possible due to a singularity in the obtained equation of motion of the robot. We circumvent this by using the dynamic extension [8] of the system and then use flatness-based controller.

The paper is organized as follows: Sect. 2 deals with the modeling of the wheeled mobile robot. In Sect. 3, we identify the differential flatness of the system and design a flat controller. Section 4 presents the verification of the performance of the controller using numerical simulation and in Sect. 5, we present the main conclusions.

2 System Modeling

We assume that the car-like robot uses Ackerman steering and is moving on a plane. We also assume that the car is driven using rear wheels and steered using front wheels. We model the car-like robot as a bicycle moving on a plane. The planar bicycle model is a widely used model for car-like robots as it captures essential kinematic and dynamic characteristics of the system under consideration.

The Fig. 1 represents the planar model of a car-like robot with its corresponding bicycle model. The bicycle model of the car is shown in thicker lines in the same figure. In the figure, $P(x, y)$ represents the mid-point of the rear wheel axle, ϕ represents equivalent steering angle, l represents length of the car, E represents the distance of the center of mass of the car from P, IC represents the instantaneous center of the car, and θ represents the orientation of the longitudinal axis of the car. All the angles are taken positive counterclockwise.

2.1 Kinematic Model

We assume that the wheels are subjected to no-slip condition. This will result in the following two independent non-holonomic constraint equations and are given by:

$$\dot{x}\sin(\theta) - \dot{y}\cos(\theta) = 0 \tag{1}$$

$$\dot{x}\sin(\theta + \phi) - \dot{y}\cos(\theta + \phi) - l\dot{\theta}\cos(\phi) = 0 \tag{2}$$

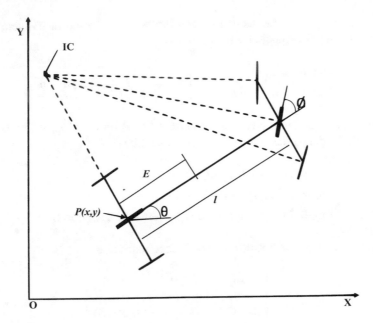

Fig. 1 Schematic of a car-like robot and its equivalent bicycle model

From the Eq. (1), we can write the velocity v of the point P as:

$$v = \dot{x}\cos(\theta) + \dot{y}\sin(\theta) \tag{3}$$

2.2 Dynamic Model

We use the Lagrangian approach to obtain the equation of motion of the wheeled mobile robot. The wheels are subjected to non-holonomic constraints and the traditional Lagrangian approach will involve Lagrangian multipliers. Since we are not interested in the solutions of Lagrange multipliers, we eliminate the Lagrange multipliers and then solve for the equations of motion this is known as Maggi's method [5].

For a mechanical system described using n generalized coordinates (q), m non-holonomic constraints, we define n independent quasi-velocities $(v_i, i = 1\text{--}n)$, among which m of them are made equal to the m non-holonomic constraints. The other $(n - m)$ quasi-velocities are chosen appropriately. Let θ represent the corresponding n quasi-coordinates. We can show that [5] virtual displacements of the quasi-coordinates and the true coordinates are related by:

$$\delta q_i = \sum_{j=1}^{n-m} \Phi_{ij}(q, t)\delta\theta_j, \qquad i = 1, \ldots, n$$

Let $Q_i (i = i, \ldots, n)$ be the generalized forces and L be the Lagrangian of the system. The Maggi's equation is then given as:

$$\sum_{i=1}^{n} \left[\frac{d}{dt} \left(\frac{\partial L}{\partial \dot{q}_i} \right) - \frac{\partial L}{\partial q_i} - Q_i \right] \Phi_{ij} = 0 \quad j = 1, \ldots, n - m \quad (4)$$

Denoting the generalized coordinates of the WMR by (x, y, θ), we have $n = 3$ and $m = 2$. We define the quasi-velocities v_i as follows:

$$v_1 = \dot{x} \cos(\theta) + \dot{y} \sin(\theta) = v$$
$$v_2 = \dot{x} \sin(\theta) - \dot{y} \cos(\theta) = 0$$
$$v_3 = \dot{x} \sin(\theta + \phi) - \dot{y} \cos(\theta + \phi) - l\dot{\theta} \cos(\phi) = 0$$

The above results in the following coefficient matrix:

$$\Phi = \begin{bmatrix} \cos(\theta) & \sin(\theta) & 0 \\ \sin(\theta) & -\cos(\theta) & 0 \\ \tan(\phi)/l & 1/l & -1/l \cos(\phi) \end{bmatrix}$$

Let u denote the force generated by the drive wheel. The generalized forces can be written in terms of u as:

$$Q_x = u \cos(\theta), \quad (5)$$
$$Q_y = u \sin(\theta), \quad (6)$$
$$Q_\theta = 0 \quad (7)$$

We assume that the WMR moves in a plane and hence the Lagrangian, L, is same as the total kinetic energy. The kinetic energy denoted by T is given by:

$$L = T = \frac{1}{2} m (\dot{x}^2 + \dot{y}^2) + \frac{1}{2} I_p \dot{\theta}^2 + m \left(-E\dot{x}\dot{\theta} \sin(\theta) + E\dot{y}\dot{\theta} \cos(\theta) \right) \quad (8)$$

where m is total mass of the WMR, I_p is mass moment of inertia of the WMR about vertical axis through the reference point P and E is the distance of the center of mass of the WMR from P.

Using Eq. (4) we have

$$\left[\frac{d}{dt} \left(\frac{\partial L}{\partial \dot{x}} \right) - \frac{\partial L}{\partial x} - Q_x \right] \Phi_{11} + \left[\frac{d}{dt} \left(\frac{\partial L}{\partial \dot{y}} \right) - \frac{\partial L}{\partial y} - Q_y \right] \Phi_{21}$$
$$+ \left[\frac{d}{dt} \left(\frac{\partial L}{\partial \dot{\theta}} \right) - \frac{\partial L}{\partial \theta} - Q_\theta \right] \Phi_{31} = 0 \quad (9)$$

Using the first column of Φ and substituting Eqs. (8) and (5) into Eq. (9), we get one of the differential equations of motion. The other two equations of motion can be determined by differentiating the constraint equations Eqs. (1) and (2). The equations of motion for the WMR are given as:

$$\ddot{\theta} = \frac{1}{l}[\ddot{x}(\sin(\theta) + \cos(\theta)\tan(\phi)) + \ddot{y}(-\cos(\theta)$$

$$+ \sin(\theta)\tan(\phi)) + \dot{\theta}v + v\frac{d}{dt}(\tan(\phi))] \tag{10}$$

$$\begin{pmatrix} \ddot{x} \\ \ddot{y} \end{pmatrix} = (\dot{\theta}v)\begin{pmatrix} -\sin(\theta) \\ \cos(\theta) \end{pmatrix} + (C_1 u - C_2\dot{\theta}\frac{d(\tan(\phi))}{dt})\begin{pmatrix} \cos(\theta) \\ \sin(\theta) \end{pmatrix} \tag{11}$$

where, $C_1(\phi) = \frac{l^2}{I_\phi}$, $C_2(\phi) = \frac{lI_p}{I_\phi}$ and $I_\phi = ml^2 + I_p\tan^2(\phi)$.

3 Controller Design

We choose the control inputs (u_1, u_2) to be the external force u which is generated by the drive wheel and the rate of steering angle $\frac{d}{dt}(\tan(\phi))$, respectively. Using Eqs. (1)–(3) and Eq. (11), it can be shown that (x, y) is a flat output, i.e., the states of the system $(x, y, \theta, \dot{x}, \dot{y}, \dot{\theta})$, and the control inputs (u_1, u_2) can be expressed in terms of (x, y) and its derivatives [6]. The Eq. (11) can be written in the affine form as:

$$\begin{pmatrix} \ddot{x} \\ \ddot{y} \end{pmatrix} = (\dot{\theta}v)\begin{pmatrix} -\sin(\theta) \\ \cos(\theta) \end{pmatrix} + \begin{bmatrix} C_1\cos(\theta) & -C_2\dot{\theta}\cos(\theta) \\ C_1\sin(\theta) & -C_2\dot{\theta}\sin(\theta) \end{bmatrix}\begin{pmatrix} u_1 \\ u_2 \end{pmatrix} \tag{12}$$

It can be observed that the characteristic matrix is singular in the above equation. To overcome this difficulty, we apply the technique of dynamic extension to the above dynamical system and choose a new variable w_1 as:

$$w_1 = C_1 u_1 - C_2\dot{\theta}u_2 \tag{13}$$

Using w_1, Eq. (11) can be rewritten as:

$$\begin{pmatrix} \ddot{x} \\ \ddot{y} \end{pmatrix} = (\dot{\theta}v)\begin{pmatrix} -\sin(\theta) \\ \cos(\theta) \end{pmatrix} + w_1\begin{pmatrix} \cos(\theta) \\ \sin(\theta) \end{pmatrix} \tag{14}$$

Differentiating the above equation with respect to time we can extend the above system to the following form:

$$\ddot{X} = F + G.W \tag{15}$$

where

$$W = \begin{pmatrix} W_1 \\ W_2 \end{pmatrix} = \begin{pmatrix} \dot{w}_1 \\ u_2 \end{pmatrix}$$

$$\beta = -C_2\dot{\theta}^2 + \frac{v^2}{l}$$

$$X = \begin{pmatrix} x \\ y \end{pmatrix}$$

$$F = (-\dot{\theta}^2 v)\begin{pmatrix} \cos(\theta) \\ \sin(\theta) \end{pmatrix} + (2\dot{v}\dot{\theta} + C_1\dot{\theta}u_1)\begin{pmatrix} -\sin(\theta) \\ \cos(\theta) \end{pmatrix}$$

and

$$G = \begin{bmatrix} \cos(\theta) & -\sin(\theta) \\ \sin(\theta) & \cos(\theta) \end{bmatrix} \begin{bmatrix} 1 & 0 \\ 0 & \beta \end{bmatrix}$$

In Eq. (15), G is non-singular except at $\beta = 0$, i.e., at $v = 0$. Now, we transform the control input by choosing a new control input as:

$$V = F + G.W \tag{16}$$

Substituting the above in Eq. (15) we have

$$\ddot{X} = V \tag{17}$$

This transformed system is in the linear form, and we can use the linear control techniques for designing a trajectory tracking control law for V to track a desired trajectory ($X_d(t)$). Using pole-placement technique we design V as:

$$V = \dddot{X}_d + K_2(\ddot{X}_d - \ddot{X}) + K_1(\dot{X}_d - \dot{X}) + K_0(X_d - X) \tag{18}$$

where K_2, K_1 and K_0 are control gain matrices.

Once we have V, we can get the corresponding W from Eq. (16) as:

$$W = G^{-1}(V - F) \tag{19}$$

and once W is obtained, we can get the original control inputs (u_1, u_2) as follows:

$$u_2 = W_2, \quad w_1 = \int_0^t \dot{w}_1 dt = \int_0^t W_1 dt$$

and from Eq. (13), we have

$$u_1 = \frac{w_1 + C_2 \dot{\theta} u_2}{C_1}$$

To address the problem of singularity of matrix G, that occurs when $v = 0$, we judiciously select inverse as follows:

If $v \neq 0$, then G is invertible, we use

$$G^{-1} = \begin{bmatrix} 1 & 0 \\ 0 & \dfrac{1}{\beta} \end{bmatrix} \begin{bmatrix} \cos(\theta) & \sin(\theta) \\ -\sin(\theta) & \cos(\theta) \end{bmatrix}$$

else if $v = 0$, we choose G^{-1} as:

$$G^{-1} = \begin{bmatrix} 1 & 0 \\ 0 & 0 \end{bmatrix} \begin{bmatrix} \cos(\theta) & \sin(\theta) \\ -\sin(\theta) & \cos(\theta) \end{bmatrix}$$

and keep u_2 unchanged.

The reasoning behind the above choice of the inverse is that when $v = 0$, it can be observed from Eq. (15) that control input $W_2 = u_2$ has no influence on the system dynamics.

4 Numerical Simulation

The controller is validated for commonly used trajectories with car-like robots using MATLAB. For numerical simulations, the nominal system parameters are taken from a typical car as $l = 2$ m, $m = 200$ kg, and $I_p = 100$ kgm^2. An initial offset is added to the desired trajectory so as to test disturbance handling. To make the simulation more realistic and test the controller in the presence of uncertainties in the system parameter values, in the simulation, we use the system parameters as $l = 2.1$ m, $m = 210$ kg, and $I_p = 110$ kgm^2.

The controller gain matrices are chosen as follows for all the simulations:

$$K_2 = \begin{bmatrix} 1.5 & 0 \\ 0 & 1.5 \end{bmatrix}, \quad K_1 = \begin{bmatrix} 0.75 & 0 \\ 0 & 0.75 \end{bmatrix}$$

$$K_0 = \begin{bmatrix} 0.125 & 0 \\ 0 & 0.125 \end{bmatrix}$$

The trajectory tracking performance for two chosen representative trajectories, a semicircle of radius 10 m and lane-change curve, are shown in Figs. 2 and 3. We observe that the error in trajectory tracking converges to zero, and the rate of convergence can be increased by increasing the controller gains. Simulations are performed

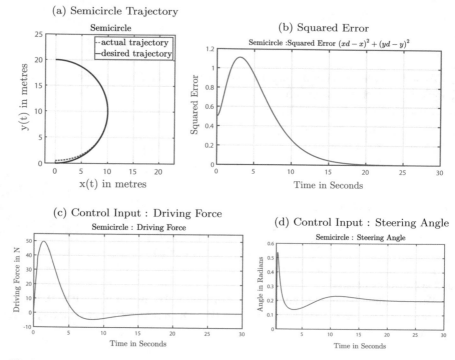

Fig. 2 Semicircle trajectory tracking performance

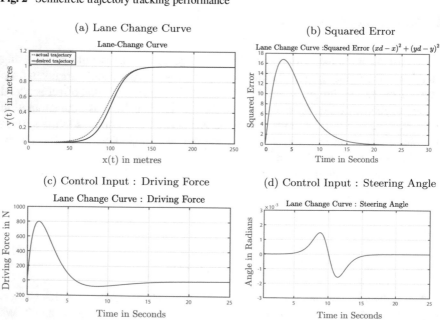

Fig. 3 Lane-change curve tracking performance

for different parametric uncertainties and disturbances in the form of initial offsets of the desired trajectory. The controller is observed to be robust against these uncertainties.

5 Conclusion

In this work, we have proposed a novel trajectory control technique for car-like robots based on the system dynamics. The differential flatness property of the system is exploited to obtain a simple and robust controller. The singularity in the dynamics is identified, and we have used dynamic-extension technique to overcome the singularity issues. The designed controller results in asymptotic convergence of the robot trajectory to a desired trajectory. The controller is validated using numerical simulations for commonly used trajectories.

References

1. I. Kolmanovsky, N.H. McClamroch, Developments in nonholonomic control systems. IEEE Control Syst. Mag. **15**(6), 2036 (1995)
2. A. De Luca, G. Oriolo, C. Samson, Feedback control of a nonholonomic car-like robot. Lect. Notes Control Inf. Sci. Springer **229**, 171–253 (2005)
3. K. Shojaei, A.M. Shahri, A. Tarakemeh, Adaptive feedback linearizing control of nonholonomic wheeled mobile robots in presence of parametric and nonparametric uncertainties. Robot. Comput. Integr. Manuf. **27** (2011)
4. H.H. Lee, A new trajectory control of a car-like wheeled robots, in *Proceedings of the ASME 2012 International Mechanical Engineering Congress and Expositions* (2012)
5. D.T. Greenwood, *Advanced Dynamics*. Cambridge University Press (2006)
6. G.G. Rigatos, *Nonlinear Control and Filtering Using Differential Flatness Approaches: Applications to Electromechanical Systems*. Springer (2011)
7. J. Levine, *Analysis and Control of Nonlinear Systems: A Flatness-based Approach* (Springer, Berlin Heidelberg, 2009)
8. J.-J.E. Slotine, W. Li, *Applied Nonlinear Control* (Pearson, 1991)

Kinematic Analysis of a Suspended Manipulator

Saurabh Gupta, D. C. Kar and K. Jayarajan

Abstract Master–slave manipulators are commonly used for remote handling in nuclear environments. They are generally mechanical, electrical (servo), or power manipulators. They need rigid support or rigid moving platform in the remote area for installation, they cannot be deployed in places, where such preinstalled rigid supports are not available. In such cases, the slave arm of the manipulator could be suspended on an EOT crane and taken to the site for remote operation. BARC has developed one such suspended manipulator and deployed it for remote operation in a radioactive cell. The crane, being flexible, poses challenges in position control of the end effector. Unlike manipulators with rigid base, the position and orientation of the end effector of a suspended manipulator depend on its inertial parameters, in addition to its kinematic parameters. We have developed an algorithm for solving the kinematics of a six degrees of freedom suspended manipulator. The algorithm is validated experimentally on a three degrees of freedom prototype arm.

Keywords Master–Slave manipulator · Suspended manipulator
Kinematic analysis

1 Introduction

Mechanical and electrical manipulators are commonly used in nuclear industry. In both the cases, the facility must be predesigned to accommodate the manipulator. One way to overcome this problem is to suspend the manipulator and transport it to the remote site using an available EOT crane.

S. Gupta (✉) · D. C. Kar (✉)
Division of Remote Handling & Robotics, Bhabha Atomic Research Centre,
Trombay, Mumbai 400085, India
e-mail: saurabhg@barc.gov.in

K. Jayarajan (✉)
BARC Safety Council, Bhabha Atomic Research Centre,
Trombay, Mumbai 400085, India

© Springer Nature Singapore Pte Ltd. 2019
D N Badodkar and T A Dwarakanath (eds.), *Machines, Mechanism and Robotics*, Lecture Notes in Mechanical Engineering,
https://doi.org/10.1007/978-981-10-8597-0_66

Fig. 1 Suspended
manipulator developed at
BARC

Crane Hook

A few literatures are available for suspended manipulators. In most of these works, the manipulators are suspended through multiple wire ropes, which are connected to different points of the transporter. These works focus on how to avoid the movement of the base, when manipulator changes its configuration, when it carries some load, or when it is transported from one place to other [1–3]. In most of the cases, some special arrangement is required in the transporter for multiple wire ropes. Also, some literature suggests controlling the length and position of the attachment (on transporter) of these wire ropes [4, 5], which complicates the system. In [4], the manipulator is suspended by a single wire rope. However, the arm has only two degrees of freedom and the motion is restricted to a 2D plane, which restricts its practical applications.

There are not many literatures available for implementation of suspended manipulators. BARC has developed one such suspendable manipulator [6] and deployed it for remote operation in a radioactive cell (Fig. 1).

When a manipulator is suspended though a EOT crane, the position control and position determination through kinematics become challenging. The first challenge comes from the passive joint at the hook. The orientation of this passive joint depends on the configuration of the active joints. The second challenge comes from transportation. The suspended manipulator swings during transpiration. A skilled operator will be required to operate the EOT crane to reduce oscillations. Here, we address the first issue, i.e., challenges from the passive joint at the hook. To deal with the presence of the passive joint, mathematical model has been developed and simulation has been done. The results of the model have been verified on a prototype RRP manipulator. The effects of various kinematic parameters and inertial parameters on the end-effector position of suspended manipulator are also studied (Fig. 2).

Fig. 2 Prototype RRP
manipulator used for
validation

Crane Hook

2 Basic Parameters of the Manipulator

In this paper, we have simulated a six-degree freedom manipulator with five revolute
joints (joint variables θ_1, θ_2, θ_4, θ_5, and θ_6) and one prismatic joint (joint variable
d_3). The manipulator is suspended by wire ropes from an EOT crane. Coordinate
frames assigned to various joints of the manipulator are shown in Fig. 3. Coordinate
frame-0 is fixed, frames 1–6 are assigned to six joints, and frame-7 is attached to
the end effector. Frame-H is assigned to the point of attachment with the wire rope.
This frame is universal frame. The universal frame is chosen in such a way that the
manipulator maintains its basic pose (Fig. 3), when it is suspended. The description
of universal frame {H} in frame {0} is

$$
{}^0_H T = \begin{bmatrix} 1 & 0 & 0 & -0.225 \\ 0 & 1 & 0 & G(2,1) \\ 0 & 0 & 1 & G(3,1) \\ 0 & 0 & 0 & 1 \end{bmatrix}
$$

where, G is center of gravity of the manipulator in its home in the frame {0}. Frame
on the gripper (no. 7) can be transformed to frame-6 as in the following.

$$
{}^6_7 T = \begin{bmatrix} 1 & 0 & 0 & 0 \\ 0 & 1 & 0 & 0 \\ 0 & 0 & 1 & 0.15 \\ 0 & 0 & 0 & 1 \end{bmatrix}
$$

Fig. 3 Frame fixing of the manipulator

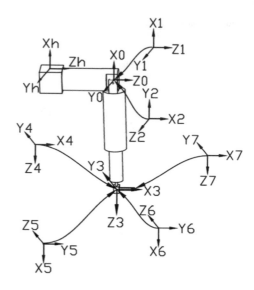

Fig. 4 Schematic diagram of fixed and suspended manipulator

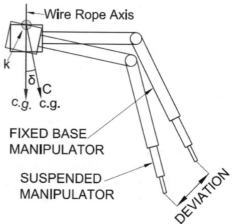

The Denavit–Hartenberg (DH) [7] parameters of the manipulator are shown in Table 1 (a_{i-1} and d_i are in meters and θ_i and α_{i-1} are in degrees). They will be used to calculate the transformation matrix between two adjacent frames, $(i - 1)$ and i as:

$$
{}^{i-1}_{i}T = \begin{bmatrix}
\cos\theta_i & -\sin\theta_i & 0 & a_{i-1} \\
\sin\theta_i \cos\alpha_{i-1} & \cos\theta_i \cos\alpha_{i-1} & -\sin\alpha_{i-1} & -\sin\alpha_{i-1}d_i \\
\sin\theta_i \sin\alpha_{i-1} & \cos\theta_i \sin\alpha_{i-1} & \cos\alpha_{i-1} & \cos\alpha_{i-1}d_i \\
0 & 0 & 0 & 1
\end{bmatrix}
$$

Thus, ${}^{0}_{1}T$ to ${}^{5}_{6}T$ can be found out using the corresponding DH parameters from Table 1.

Table 1 DH parameters of the manipulator

i	α_{i-1}	a_{i-1}	d_i	θ_i
1	0	0	0	$\theta1$
2	−90	0	0	$\theta2$
3	90	0	d3	0
4	0	0	0	$\theta4$
5	−90	0	0	$\theta5$
6	90	0	0	$\theta6$

Table 2 Link mass (m) and cg location (x, y, and z) in link frame

Link	0	1	2	3	4	5	6
x (m)	0	0	0	0	0	0	0
y (m)	0	0	−0.6	0	0	0	0
z (m)	−0.5	−0.175	0	−0.6	−1.25	0	0.06
m (kg)	400	5	20	20	0.150	0.4	1

Fig. 5 DH parameters [7]

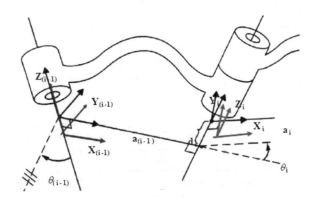

It should be noted that till now frame {H} is not known, as the center of gravity (G) has not been calculated. For determining G, the mass of different links should be known, along with the center of gravities of individual links. These details are provided in Table 2 (link masses are in kg and cg location (x, y, and z) are in meter) (Fig. 5).

3 Mathematical Modeling

In this section, the methodology for the kinematic analysis has been discussed.

3.1 Forward Kinematics Methodology

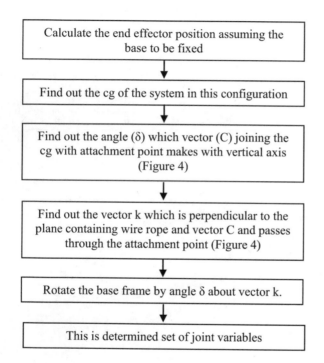

3.2 *Inverse Kinematics Methodology*

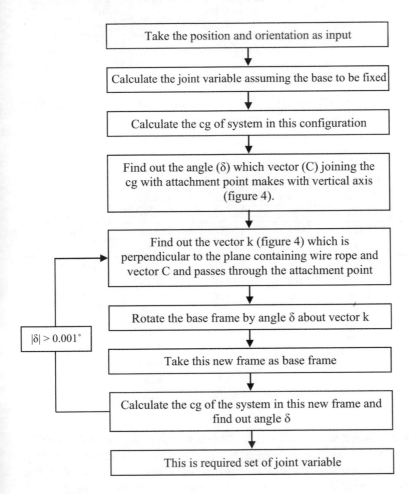

4 Results and Discussion

The forward kinematic code (based on algorithm discussed in previous section) for suspended manipulator was given the following set of joint variables as input (θi is in degree and d_3 is in meter) and we got 4×4 transformation matrix as output.

Input to forward kinematics					
θ_1	θ_2	d_3	θ_4	θ_5	θ_6
40	−70	3	30	30	30

Output of forward kinematics			
0.114	−0.585	−0.803	−3.073
0.967	0.252	−0.045	−1.127
0.228	−0.771	0.595	1.173
0	0	0	1

The above output matrix was given as input to inverse kinematic program, which is iterative. During iteration, the joint variables converge are as follows:

Output of inverse kinematics					
θ_1	θ_2	d_3	θ_4	θ_5	θ_6
22.327	−77.871	3.016	31.925	29.808	33.484
32.428	−73.114	3.003	31.123	29.907	31.477
36.819	−71.258	3.001	30.524	29.959	30.615
38.676	−70.514	3.000	30.227	29.983	30.255
39.451	−70.212	3.000	30.096	29.993	30.105
39.773	−70.087	3.000	30.040	29.997	30.044
39.906	−70.036	3.000	30.017	29.999	30.018
39.961	−70.015	3.000	30.007	29.999	30.007
39.984	−70.006	3.000	30.003	30.000	30.003
39.993	−70.003	3.000	30.001	30.000	30.001
39.997	−70.001	3.000	30.000	30.000	30.001
39.999	−70.000	3.000	30.000	30.000	30.000
40.000	−70.000	3.000	30.000	30.000	30.000

The code developed was used to study the effect of different parameters on the deviation, which is the distance between the end-effector positions, when manipulator is fixed and when it is suspended (Fig. 4). Also, the variations of the error (δ) against iteration steps are studied. These results are discussed in the following heads.

4.1 Variation of Deviation with Joint Variables

The developed code was run for different joint variables and the result was plotted for analysis. From the analysis, we observed that as θ_1 increases, deviation also increases and as θ_2 increases, the deviation decreases. The deviation is always zero in case of d_3, because the variation in d_3 changes the cg only in the vertical direction when manipulator is in its home configuration. In other configurations, the deviation will increase with d_3. Also, the variations of deviation with θ_4, θ_5, and θ_6 have been observed. These deviations are close to zero. Changes in deviation with θ_1 is shown in Fig. 6.

Fig. 6 Deviation with θ_1

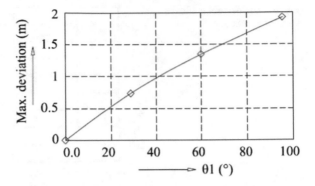

Fig. 7 Maximum deviation with cg of base frame

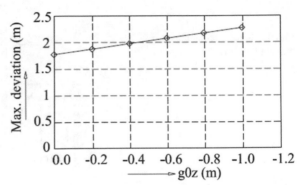

4.2 Variation of Maximum Deviation with CG Location of Links

In this section, the effect of cg on maximum deviation has been studied. The cg of links has been varied in axial direction only. Figure 7 shows the variation of maximum deviation with cg location of base frame g0z (0 stands for link 0 and z is direction in local frame as per Fig. 7). From the figure, it is clear that as cg of link-0 goes away from the end effector, the maximum deviation increases. Similar variations were observed for other joints also.

Figure 8 shows the variation of maximum deviation with the point of attachment of the wire ropes to the manipulator. Point of attachment is made to vary in vertical direction. The variation of maximum deviation is found to be nonlinear, unlike in the previous cases. Here, the cg of the system, as well as the location of end effector in the hook frame, varies with the point of attachment. These two effects are unidirectional in this case. This indicates that the point of attachment should be away from the manipulator base frame in the vertical direction. It is also obvious that point of attachment should never be below the cg of the system, which would decrease stability in the system (Fig. 9).

Fig. 8 Max deviation with
point of attachment

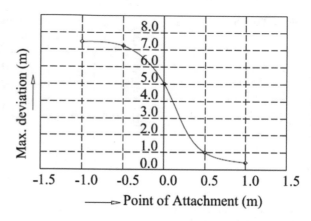

Fig. 9 Max deviation with
mass of link zero

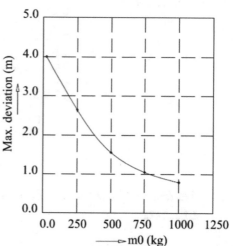

4.3 Variation of Maximum Deviation with Mass of Links

The maximum deviation in end-effector position depends on the masses of links also.
Figure 8 represents the variation of the maximum deviation with mass of link-0 ($m0$).
It is clear that the maximum deviation in end-effector position reduces with increase
in the mass of link-0. In this case, two factors work. First, when the mass of link-0
increases, the position of hook point moves away from the end effector and second
change in the location of cg when the arm is completely stretched is reduced. The
second factor dominates the first one. So, there is reduction in maximum deviation
with mass of link-0. Similar results are observed for other joints also.

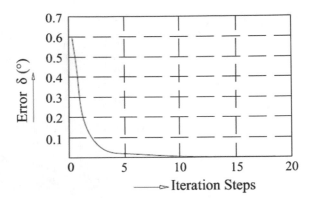

Fig. 10 Variation of error δ with iteration steps

4.4 Variation of Error (δ) with Iteration Steps

The error δ (as shown in Fig. 4) was plotted for different joint variables. It was observed that it has diminishing nature. One such plot is shown in Fig. 10.

Our observations, based on the above analysis are as follows:

(a) To minimize the maximum deviation, the job should be manipulated with the help of last three joints. Use of first three joints should be avoided, wherever possible. Note that the first three joints are generally used for positioning only. Therefore, the crane should be used to place the end effector close to point of interest.

(b) Presence of heavy mass far below the point of attachment reduces the maximum deviation.

(c) The hinge point should be located such that its distance from the end effector is minimum for least maximum deviation.

Out of these three, the first one (a) should be considered during operation and the rest two (b and c) should be considered in the design stage itself.

5 Validation of the Model

In order to validate the model, a prototype manipulator with RRP-type manipulator has been made. The manipulator is suspended by hook of an overhead crane (Fig. 2). As the manipulator does not have any actuator, the joint angles are changed manually. In the experiment, the end-effector positions were observed for different set of joint variables. The experimental results (Xe, Ye, and Ze) against the simulation results (Xm, Ym, and Zm) are plotted in Figs. 11, 12, and 13. In Fig. 14, the individual error ΔX, ΔY, and ΔZ and the absolute error (abs) are plotted. The units of position and errors (in Figs. 11, 12, 13, and 14) are mm. The absolute error is the shortest distance between the end-effector positions in simulation and that in experiment. It

Fig. 11 Experimental
versus model result for X

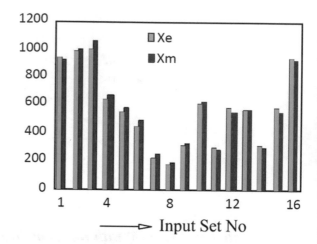

Fig. 12 Experimental
versus model result for Y

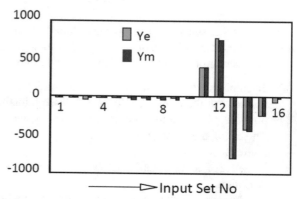

is observed that absolute error varies between 14 and 56 mm, the mean of which is 35 mm. These errors appear to be significant. However, considering the application in master–slave mode, where the operator is always in the control loop, these figures would not pose any practical problem. Of course, such deviations are not permissible in robotic mode. Fine-tuning of various model parameters (kinematic and inertial) using precise measurements can reduce the error.

6 Conclusion

In this paper, a methodology for doing kinematics of a suspended manipulator has been discussed. As algebraic solution of such manipulator is not available, numerical technique has been used. The inverse kinematics algorithm is iterative, where the error was found to be monotonically diminishing. The effects of different variables on the

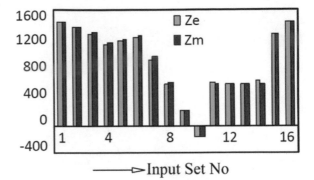

Fig. 13 Experimental versus model result for Z

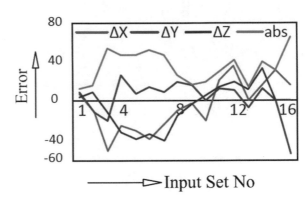

Fig. 14 Error in X, Y, Z and absolute error (mm)

end-effector position were also studied. The methodology for the model was verified with help of RRP-type manipulator.

References

1. H. Osumi, Y. Utsugi, M. Koshikawa, Development of a manipulator suspended by parallel wire structure, in *Proceedings of IEEE/RSJ International Conference on Intelligent Robots and Systems (IROS 2000)*, vol. 1 (2000) pp. 498–503
2. J. Albus, R. Bostelman, N. Dagalakis, The NIST robocrane. J. Rob. Syst. **10**(5), 709–724 (1993)
3. J. Hamedi, H. Zohoor, Kinematic modeling and workspace analysis of a spatial cable suspended robot as incompletely restrained positioning mechanism. Int. J. Aerosp. Mech. Eng. **1**(1), 109–118 (2008)
4. T. Arai, S. Matsumura, Y. Yoshimura, H. Osumi, A proposal for a wire suspended manipulator: a kinematic analysis. Robotica **17**(1), 3–10 (1999)
5. K. Jayarajan, Advances in remote handling technology in nuclear industry. Ann. Indian Nat. Acad. Eng. **IX** (2012)
6. B. Sony, P.V. Sarngadharan, K. Jayarajan, D.N. Bododkar, Suspendable Servo-Manipulator for Hot Cell Applications, BARC Newsletter, Founder's Day Special Issue, Oct 2016, pp. 61–64 (2016)
7. J.J Craig, *Introduction to Robotics, Mechanics and Control*, 3rd edn (Addison-Wesley, 2004)

Development of Tool Delivery System for In-Service Inspection of Pressure Tubes of 220 MWe PHWRs

Kundan Kumar, Sanjay Panwar, D. K. Nathani and K. Madhusoodanan

Abstract Coolant channels of PHWRs have various life-limiting issues due to the existence of a number of degradation mechanisms. In order to ensure safe operation of the coolant channels, various types of tools and techniques like BARCIS, INGRES, Scraping Tool, ID measurement tool, Sag measurement tool, etc., have been developed for monitoring the integrity of the components as an In-Service Inspection activity. Additional tools are being developed as future phase of inspection requirements, such as tools for replication of surface flaw, in situ mechanical properties measurement, and visual examination, etc., for creation of reference data by baseline inspection and to monitor its health to ensure the integrity during operation. This will also provide database for assessing residual operating life of coolant channels, necessary for decision-making. In order to fulfill the regulatory requirement of carrying out large number of inspections for deterministic assessment of the healthiness of the coolant channels of 220 MWe PHWRs, a Tool Delivery System (TDS) has been developed and is under endurance test at BARC. This system would facilitate better and efficient inspection of the coolant channels, thereby reducing the inspection time and man-rem consumption. It facilitates the use of a combination of three or four individual tools; having multiple features to reduce the inspection time. TDS is envisaged to be used for the operation of almost all inspection/examination tools heads. All these inspection heads are connected to control system through a common umbilical cable. The umbilical cable consists of a number of electrical power and signal wires, hydraulic, and pneumatic hoses, etc., required for various types of tools. The tool head is connected to the umbilical cable manually using quick connection

K. Kumar (✉) · S. Panwar · D. K. Nathani · K. Madhusoodanan
Reactor Engineering Division, Reactor Design & Development Group,
Bhabha Atomic Research Centre, Trombay, Mumbai 400085, India
e-mail: kundan@barc.gov.in

S. Panwar
e-mail: spanwar@barc.gov.in

D. K. Nathani
e-mail: dnathani@barc.gov.in

K. Madhusoodanan
e-mail: kmadhu@barc.gov.in

© Springer Nature Singapore Pte Ltd. 2019
D N Badodkar and T A Dwarakanath (eds.), *Machines, Mechanism and Robotics*, Lecture Notes in Mechanical Engineering,
https://doi.org/10.1007/978-981-10-8597-0_67

type connectors. The paper describes various sub-system and components of TDS, their functions, testing, and future plans.

Keywords Coolant channel · Pressure tube · Life management · Inspection tools · Alignment · X-Y-Z precision table · Turret module · Seal plug · Snout

1 Introduction

Coolant channels of Indian Pressurized Heavy Water Reactors (PHWRs) are subjected to several life-limiting degradation mechanisms during their operation. Therefore, In-Service Inspection (ISI) is done for ensuring safety during their operation and to upkeep their operational capabilities. Presently, the parameters, which are being monitored during the ISI program, are axial elongation of coolant channel assembly, inside diameter and wall thickness of pressure tube, garter spring locations, and pressure tube volumetric inspection for flaw [1–5]. However, in future, frequent ISI program may be warranted as additional data may be required for assessment of fitness-for-service of the pressure tube [6–9]. This is more relevant, particularly for Zr-2.5%Nb pressure tubes for which design service life is 30 years. Alternatively, for higher operating years, there may be requirement for more numbers of channels to be inspected for ensuring safety and 100% volume inspection, which would enhance the safety aspect to a great extent. Further, there may be new inspection requirements based on the new researches and findings.

Envisaging these future inspection requirements of the pressure tubes, a remotely operable system namely, Tool Delivery System (TDS) was developed, which would facilitate ISI of pressure tubes by handling all types of inspection tools. TDS will enhance the efficiency of inspection activities as there would be no requirement of handling of multiple and individualistic tool handling systems. This system would also cater to the additional requirements of rehabilitation works. This may result in reduction of the load on the fuelling machines, which is being currently used for many of the inspection requirement [10, 11]. The system has provision to accommodate a combined set of three tools, having a total length of 1500 mm, to carry out inspections of many parameters in one go. This paper describes in brief, design goals, salient features, various modules, and functionality of TDS.

2 Design Goals

Following were design goals for development of the TDS:

- Unique handling system for various inspection tools
- Simple and independent delivery system
- Minimum time for preparatory works in reactor vaults

- Reduction of the inspection load on fuelling machine
- Reduction in total inspection time per channel including preparatory time
- Adaptability for new inspection requirements or inspection tools
- Performance as per all existing and anticipated ISI requirements.

3 Salient Features of TDS

The TDS consists of various modules to fulfill various requirements, such as alignment with any of the coolant channels, clamping on the coolant channel, removal of seal plug, loading and maneuvering of inspection tools, unloading tools, and installing the seal plug into the coolant channel. For site operation, TDS has to be mounted on the Fuelling Machine (FM) bridge. The system is remotely operable from control room. The TDS has the following salient features:

- Capability to handle more than one tool
- In situ calibration feature at tool parking location
- Alignment and sealing with coolant channel
- Two-position tool turret: One for Inspection tool and the other for operating plugs
- Electro-hydraulic umbilical cable and its connector to meet electrical and hydraulic requirement of the tool
- Feedback of all the positions from encoder along with collection of data from the inspection tool
- Radiation resistant sensors
- Telescopic drive to feed the inspection tools in the channel
- Electrical drive of ram
- Safety and functional interlocks for drives
- Multi-camera system for overall viewing and safety.

4 Modules of TDS

The TDS, as shown in Fig. 1, consists of various mechanical, hydraulic, electrical, and control modules in order to fulfill various functions as required to be done for carrying out wet channel (water-filled pressure tube) inspection of pressure tubes. Various functions; like, aligning the TDS with targeted channel with required accuracy; establishing water-tight sealing with the E-face of the channel; creating access to the bore of channel for inserting the inspection tool by way of removing machine plug and seal plug from channel; insertion of inspection tool and maneuvering it for carrying out ISI for the various parameters; retrieval of inspection tool; and bringing the channel to initial condition have to be performed in sequential manner. Suitable interlocks have also been provided in the system, which would prevent any skipping or bypassing of step. Each module of the TDS has been provided with independent

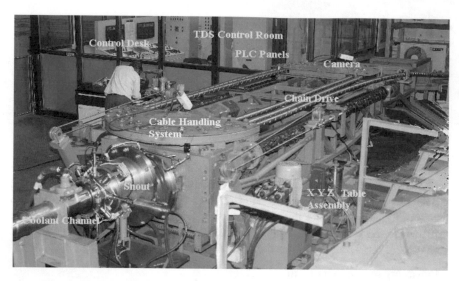

Fig. 1 General arrangement of tool delivery system

motors and feedback system for performing their intended functions safely. These modules are described briefly in the following paragraphs:

4.1 Precision X-Y-Z Table Assembly

The Precision X-Y-Z table is used to move the TDS in all the three directions in order to align the TDS with the target channel. This table comes into action when the TDS is aligned with the target in X-Y plane within ±20 mm. The direction of movement is chosen by the in-built program based on signals from the aligning module. The travel in X and Y directions is ±20 mm and in Z direction is 300 mm.

4.2 Snout Assembly

The front portion of the TDS consists of Snout assembly. Its main function is to form water-tight connection with coolant channel E-face. The snout assembly houses alignment module (Coarse and fine), sealing and clamping module, and a TDS plug. Snout assembly with its other sub-modules is shown in Fig. 2. The sub-modules are described below:

Alignment Module: As the name indicates, this module aligns the TDS with coolant channel within ±0.25 mm. This is achieved in two steps: first, with coarse alignment

Fig. 2 Snout assembly with its sub-modules

Fig. 3 Coarse alignment module

up to ±3 mm and then with fine alignment. The coarse alignment module, as shown in Fig. 3, consists of front plate with four LVDTs. Depending on which LVDT is pressed, the corrective action to align the TDS is taken. The fine alignment consists of four radially loaded balls connected to LVDT with each pair at 90° placed diametrically opposite. Depending of amount by which each LVDT is pressed, corrective action is taken to achieve fine alignment up to 0.25 mm.

Sealing and Clamping Module: TDS consists of self-alignment sealing face mounted on a bellow spring with double convolution to take care of skew angle.

Fig. 4 Main turret housing

Once the sealing is ensured through the feedback of Z traverse of TDS, clamping module is activated to apply load on the sealing face to make a leak tight joint between coolant channel and TDS.

The clamping module consists of four jaws located radialy around the front end of the end fitting. The jaws get clamped on the end fitting by operation of movement of clamping barrel which is moved forward with the help of rotating nut operated hydraulic with the help of a rack.

4.3 Main Turret Assembly

Main turret assembly, as shown in Fig. 4, consists of turret magazine for housing machine plug, seal plug (with spare), duide sleeve, and one for passage of inspection tool. Depending on the operation being performed, respective magazine is aligned with the snout.

4.4 Tool Turret Assembly

Tool turret has a two location position at 120° with third location occupied by dummy for balancing. It either aligns inspection tool or Plug Handling Module (PHM) with TDS depending on operation being performed. The PHM is used to operate machine plug, seal plug, and guide sleeve while the inspection tool location is used when inspection tool has to travel from one end of coolant channel to the other for inspection. The inspection tool is parked in coolant channel mock-up of 2 m with features used for calibration of inspection tool.

Fig. 5 Plug handling module assembly

4.5 PHM Head

PHM head is a modular mechanism used to lock, hold, and unlock shield plug, snout plug, and guide sleeve. As depicted in Fig. 5, it is a three-stage mechanism comprising of O-PHM, M-PHM, and I-PHM. The O-PHM is used to position the PHM head, the M-PHM is used to latch the PHM head onto any of the plugs, and the I-PHM is used to actuate the plug. With help of these operations snout plug, seal plug, and guide sleeve could be operated.

4.6 Calibration Set-Up

Calibration set-up is used for parking and calibration of inspection tools before sending them in the pressure tube, at the start of inspection of each coolant channel assembly. It consists of spool pieces of pressure tube and calandria tubes, two garter springs, and appropriate end connection with sealing arrangement. Features like notches, diameter, and thick variation are provided in the pressure tube for in situ calibration of the inspection tool.

4.7 Tool Feeding Module

Inspection tool needs to move axially inside pressure tube as well should have the rotary movement to inspect the pressure tube at any angle in any specified location. After completing the operations, the inspection tool needs to be taken out of the coolant channel assembly. All these functions are done by tool feeding module. Tool axial and rotary feed drives do the axial/rotary positioning of the inspection tool within the coolant channel assembly.

Fig. 6 Push–pull chain

Tool axial feed comprises of a multi-stage telescopic tube assembly, with an overall stroke of 10 m. The telescopic assembly is driven by push–pull chain, as shown in Fig. 6. The telescopic tube is connected to the inspection tool with the connector assembly. The cables required for carrying signals, data, etc., are bunched together and attached to the inspection tool through the connector assembly. The cable passes through the center of the chain and moves along with the inspection tool.

Tool rotary drive is used to take circumferential scanning of the coolant channel. The tool rotary drive is operable at any axial position of the tool. For this operation, the axial feed telescopic tube is rotated so that the tool, attached to the same, also attains the desired orientation.

4.8 Connector Assembly

As shown in Fig. 7, the connector assembly is composed of a male connector, a female connector for both hydraulic and electrical connections, O ring is used for sealing, and clamping nut is used to keep the both male and female connectors in place.

4.9 Cable Handling System

Cable handling system, as shown in Fig. 8, comprises of a Movable Casing Mechanism (MCM). MCM is having a movable casing and a fixed casing. The movable casing is attached to a set of LM rails and LM shoes. The movable casing is driven by a screw and a nut assembly. The cable is housed through these spiral casing and maximum distance between casings is based on the length of the cable to be inserted

Fig. 7 Connector configuration

Fig. 8 Cable handling system

inside the end fitting. Mechanism needs to be operated when the tool turret is operational. This will work in synchronization with tool axial feed actuator drive to attain some desired tension in the chain.

4.10 Control and Instrumentation

Tool Delivery System controls has been designed based on motion controller-based system, to safely deliver, maneuver, and retrieve inspection tool head in coolant channel. Motion controllers system, with in-built motor drives and limited input/output channels, and programmability with all standard PLC (Programmable logic controllers) languages have been utilized to control all TDS drives. Additional input–output modules have been connected to meet all field input–output requirements.

Three motion controllers have been provided for three main sub-modules of the system; e.g., first, for XYZ drives controlling three axis drive motions, second, for three RAM motions, and the third, for controlling turret motions, axial, and radial motion of inspection tool head. All motion drives are controlled through in-built encoders, in addition to additional encoders, directly installed near load point, for additional safety. All three motion controllers communicate through high-speed

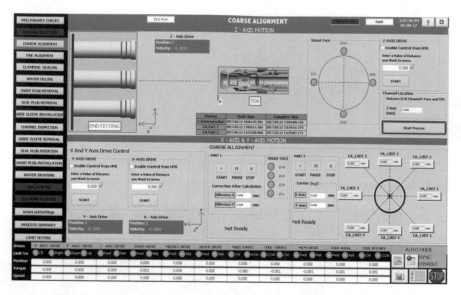

Fig. 9 TDS typical SCADA screen

profinet bus. All motor drives are backed up with motor auto braking system to handle any emergency eventuality. Algorithms have been developed and implemented for remote alignment of TDS with channel E-face; operating of PHM system for handling of seal plug, guide sleeve through electrical drives; and delivery of the inspection tool head in coolant channel for inspection in axial and radial directions. A separate SCADA (Supervisory Control and Aata Acquisition System) based software has been used to animate and control all motion drives through different interactive screens, Fig. 9. A separate manual control panel, as shown in Fig. 10, with software limits and hardwiring with all motion safety limits has been designed to operate the system on unavailability of computerized control system and during commissioning/maintenance work.

Two process control system has been designed to control process parameter of TDS system before connecting to inspection channel and mock-up channel during commissioning stage. Pressure, flow, and temperature are controlled in allowable limits to simulate reactor shut down condition. In addition, CCTV cameras have been mounted to monitor all critical operation from TDS control room. Leak detection system has been provided to monitor any leak at all critical points, and this system is connected to main motion controller system, to initiate suitable corrective action(s).

Fig. 10 TDS control panels

5 Conclusion

TDS has been developed with a view to carry out inspection of large number of coolant channels in minimum time with minimum human intervention. TDS, which has been developed for 220 MWe PHWRs, has the capability to meet this objective. Considering the fact that coolant channels in many of the Indian PHWR have seen more than 12 years of operation, there is an increasing demand for carrying out ISI of more number of coolant channels. A universal delivery system like TDS would be useful in meeting this demand with shorter shut down time and reduced man-rem expenditure. The present form of TDS has to undergo further refinement and qualification trials to make it suitable for reactor deployment.

Acknowledgements The authors are thankful to ex-colleagues Dr. R. K. Sinha, ex-Chairman, DAE, Shri B. B. Runai, Shri J. N. Kayal Shri BSVG Sharma, Shri D. Saha, Dr. P. K. Vijayan, and Shri A. Rama Rao for their guidance and support during development of the system. Authors are also thankful to present and ex-colleagues from NPCIL; Shri S. A. Bhardwaj, Shri S. Vijayakumar, Shri. M. Bharathkumar, Shri S. F. Vora, Shri N. Ramamohan, Shri Joe Peter, Shri D. N. Sanyal, and Shri V. K. Gupta; for their help, guidance and support during various stages of development and functional trials of the system. We are also thankful to M/s L&T Ltd for detailed design, manufacturing, installation and commissioning the system initially at R&D Centre, Tarapur and later at BARC, Mumbai. We are also thankful to Shri Jydeb Sil, R&D Centre Tarapur for providing space and technical support for initial commissioning of the system at Tarapur. We are thankful to all our colleagues at Reactor Engineering Division for their help during commissioning of the system at Hall-7, BARC.

References

1. K. Kumar, S. Panwar, N. Das, T.V. Shyam, B.S.V.G. Sharma, J.N. Kayal, B.B. Rupani, Development of non-conventional NDT techniques for life assessment of components of nuclear power plant. J. NDT Eval. **5**(4) (2007)
2. K. Kumar, N. Das, B.B. Rupani, Evolution of scraping tools for coolant channels of 220 Mwe Indian PHWRs. Report No. BARC/2004/I/009
3. K. Kumar, J.N. Kayal, B.B. Rupani, Development of tool for circumferential scraping of pressure tubes of Indian PHWRs. Report No. BARC/2008/I/008
4. K. Kumar, J.N. Kayal, B.B. Rupani, Development of multi-head scraping technique for pressure tubes of Indian PHWRs. Report No. BARC/2010/I/014
5. K. Kumar, J.N. Kayal, Development of Tools for Life Management of Various Reactor Components, Founders Day Special Issue of BARC News letter, Oct 2012
6. K. Madhusoodanan, T.V. Shyam, K. Kumar, S.K. Sinha, B.B. Rupani, Hydrogen equivalent assessment tool for in-situ measurement of hydrogen in PHWR pressure tubes, in *BRNS Theme Meeting on Assessment of Hydrogen Damage in PHWR Pressure Tubes*, BARC, Mumbai, 28–29 June 2007
7. K. Kumar, S.K. Sinha, Development of flaw replicating technique for pressure tubes of 220MWe Indian PHWRs. BARC Report No. BARC/2013/I/013
8. S. Chatterjee, S. Panwar, K. Madhusoodanan, A. Rama Rao, Estimation of fracture toughness of Zr 2.5% Nb pressure tube of pressurised heavy water reactor using cyclic ball indentation technique. Nucl. Eng. Des. **305**, 9–17 (2016)
9. S. Panwar, S. Chatterjee, N. Das, K. Madhusoodanan, B.S.V.G. Sharma, B.B. Rupani, Development of in-situ property measurement system: signal analysis aspect. J. Non-Destr. Test. Eval. **5**(2) (2006)
10. M.G. Gray, R. Brown, Design of the Bruce and Darlington Universal delivery machine heads, in *Sixth CNS International conference on CANDU maintenance*, Toronto, Ontario, Canada, 16–18 Nov 2003
11. R. Gunn, G. Van Drunen, W.R. Mayo, D. Kalenchuk, Fuel channel inspection with AFCIS Atomic Energy of Canada Ltd, in *7th Technical Committee Meeting on Exchange of Operational Safety Experiences of Pressurized Heavy Water Reactors* (IAEA J8-TC-2000.14, Haiyan, China)

Two-Point Grasp Response

K. Rama Krishna, J. S. Vipin and Dibakar Sen

Abstract This paper for the first time in literature studies the quasi-static behavior of a smooth object when it is being grasped with two rigid point fingers without friction and in the absence of external forces. A simple model of slip for the point finger over the object is proposed and the evolution of the traces of the point of contact of the fingers are computationally determined. The kinematic response of the object as viewed from one finger is assessed with the evolution of the slip. The convergence of the two slip-loci to two distinct points or a single point imply a successful or failed grasp endeavor, respectively. It is argued that the slip-loci are geodesics on the smooth object which gets temporally parametrized, as slip evolves.

Keywords Grasping · Slip · Manipulation · Contact

1 Introduction

Grasping of objects is one of the most common human actions. It is understood from the literature [1] that slipping while grasping is a common experience for humans during interaction with the object. Furthermore, it is observed that often after an initial slip between the object and the hand, the object could be stably held. Hence, the fate of an effort to grasp cannot be adjudged based purely on the concept of stability [2, 3] or quality of a grasp at the initial contacting points alone.

K. Rama Krishna · D. Sen (✉)
Department of Mechanical Engineering, Indian Institute of Science,
Bengaluru 560012, India
e-mail: sendibakar1@gmail.com

K. Rama Krishna
e-mail: ram.itbhu@gmail.com

J. S. Vipin
imk automotive GmbH, Amselgrund 30, 09128 Chemnitz, Germany
e-mail: vipin.jayansylaja@imk-automotive.de

© Springer Nature Singapore Pte Ltd. 2019
D N Badodkar and T A Dwarakanath (eds.), *Machines, Mechanism and Robotics*, Lecture Notes in Mechanical Engineering,
https://doi.org/10.1007/978-981-10-8597-0_68

795

Most of the robotics researchers in grasping primarily focused on determining plausible locations for the grasp of an object and stability of a grasp, rather than the *evolution of the grasp*, except in [4–6], where achievement of stable grasp through slip has been discussed. In [4], two-point stable friction grasp after initial slipping is studied for planar polygonal wedges. This is further extended to spatial polyhedral objects in [6]. However, although it is claimed that the stable grasp is achieved afterslip, no mathematical model of the slip was presented. Literature shows that there are two notions of stable grasp. While one deals with achieving a grasp of an object without slip [4, 6], the other deals with the stability of a grasped object [2, 3] under a perturbation. In this paper, we follow the first notion of a stable grasp wherein a grasp is defined as stable if there is no slip at any of the fingers. Researchers in [7], presented an algorithm for two-point grasp planning on smooth objects represented using b-spline and spherical product surfaces. The flow of this optimization algorithm is numerical in character without any physical relevance to slip in a grasp endeavor.

The present work for the first time in literature studies the response of a smooth object in a grasp endeavor using two-point fingers. For an unstable grasp, a mathematical model of instantaneous slip is presented in Sect. 2. Section 3 deals with evolution of the paths of the points of contact during this endeavor. Kinematic response of the object is studied in Sect. 4. It is assumed that the point fingers are frictionless and there are no other forces acting on the object.

2 Model of Slip

It is obvious that only a contact between the two fingers and object does not ensure a successful grasp. The hand has to exert force to capture the object by establishing a stable grasp. The unbalanced interface forces lead to slippage at the points of contact when the fingers move while maintaining contact with the object until it reaches a stable location or it slips off. Hence, modeling of slip is an important aspect in simulating grasp response.

To explore the kinematics of slipping while grasping, we propose a simple model of slip for the point of contact over the surface of the object. In Fig. 1a, at point P on the surface, the force applied by a point finger is F and its tangential and normal components are F_t and F_n, respectively, which are obtained as:

$$F_n = F \cdot n \tag{1}$$

$$F_t = F - (F \cdot n)\, n \tag{2}$$

where n is the unit normal vector to the surface at the point P. The angle between F and n is called the *grasp-angle* (labeled α in Fig. 1a). Then, we have $\|F_n\| = \|F\| \cos\alpha$ and $\|F_t\| = \|F\| \sin\alpha$. *Equation* (2) *implies that* F_t *lies in the plane defined by* F *and* n. Here, we assume that the slip-vector is proportional to F_t. That is

Fig. 1 Model of slip. **a** Geometry for slip model, **b** two-point grasp

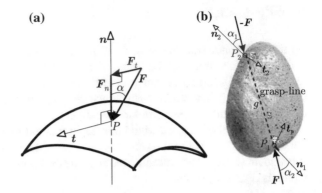

(a) direction of slip is same as the direction of F_t and

(b) speed of slip is proportional to the magnitude of F_t.

Let r be the position vector of the point P. The amount of *infinitesimal slip* of the point finger on the surface is proportional to $\sin \alpha$. That is

$$ds = \|dr\| = \beta \sin \alpha \tag{3}$$

where dr is the line element, ds is the differential arc-length which signifies the infinitesimal distance of the slippage of the point finger on the surface, and β is a positive constant. Let f and t be unit vectors in the directions of F and F_t, respectively. Then, it can be written as:

$$t = \{(n \times f) \times n\}/\{\|(n \times f)\|\} \tag{4}$$

Now, consider a two-point grasp scenario as shown in Fig. 1b where the two points of contact P_1 and P_2 would generally slip instantaneously on the surface of an object. The forces applied by the two fingers at P_1 and P_2 act along the line $P_1 P_2$, which are obviously oppositely oriented and equal in magnitude. The line $P_1 P_2$ is referred to as the grasp-line here and is labeled as g in Fig. 1b. In general, the grasp-angles at the two points of contact, α_1 and α_2, would be different. Let g be the unit vector along the grasp-line g directed from P_1 towards P_2. Using Eq. (4), the unit vectors along the slip directions at P_1 and P_2, labeled t_1 and t_2 (Fig. 1b) respectively, are obtained as:

$$t_1 = \{(n_1 \times g) \times n_1\}/\{\|(n_1 \times g)\|\} \tag{5}$$
$$t_2 = \{(n_2 \times -g) \times n_2\}/\{\|(n_2 \times -g)\|\} \tag{6}$$

It is easy to see that t_1 and t_2 do not have any special geometric relation. The initial slip directions, thus depend upon the local shape of the smooth surface for a given grasp attempt.

3 Slip-Locus

As the grasp endeavor proceeds, the object continuously slips over the two fingers and they produce traces of slip over of the object. Such a trace is named as *slip-locus* in this paper. As slip-locus evolves, the directions of the normals and the direction of the grasp-line change continuously. Since the grasp-line requires the location of both the contact points, *the two slip-loci coevolve as a pair of conjugate curves*. Using the above model of slip, we would develop a method to computationally determine the conjugate slip-loci of the points of contact of the fingers simultaneously, in the subsequent section. The procedure requires the differential geometry of the slip-locus which is discussed below.

3.1 Differential Geometry of Slip-Locus

Slip-vector is related to grasp-angle as given in Eq. (3) which is an intrinsic description. Let us consider that the object being grasped is represented in the parametric form. Equation 3 gives the infinitesimal length of the slip-locus from the instantaneous grasp parameters. We now discuss the relationship between the infinitesimal slip and the rate of change of the parameter/s of representation of the object.

Planar Objects

Let the parametric representation of the boundary of a planar object be given of the form $r(u)$ where u is the independent parameter. Then, we have

$$dr = r_u du \tag{7}$$

where $r_u = \frac{\partial r}{\partial u}$. The infinitesimal distance traveled by a point finger on the object is equal to the length of the arc-length element ds traced on the object which is given by the Eq. (3). From Eqs. (3) and (7), we get

$$|du| = \beta \sin \alpha / \|r_u\| \tag{8}$$

The direction of t is along dr. Hence, from Eq. (7) we have that du is positive if r_u and t are in the same direction; it is negative otherwise. So, we can write the expression for du as:

$$du = \left(\beta \sin \alpha \, r_u \cdot t\right) \big/ \left(\|r_u\|^2\right) \tag{9}$$

Spatial Objects

Let the parametric form of a surface be $r(u, v)$. The differential of the function $r(u, v)$ is written as:

$$dr = r_u du + r_v dv \tag{10}$$

where $r_u = \frac{\partial r}{\partial u}$ and $r_v = \frac{\partial r}{\partial v}$. The unit normal vector at a point is given by:

$$n = (r_u \times r_v)/\|r_u \times r_v\| \tag{11}$$

The square of the differential arc-length of a curve on a surface is given by [8]:

$$ds^2 = \|dr\|^2 = Edu^2 + 2Fdudv + Gdv^2 \tag{12}$$

where $E = r_u \cdot r_u$, $F = r_u \cdot r_v$, and $G = r_v \cdot r_v$. Using Eqs. (3) and (12), we have

$$\beta^2 \sin^2 \alpha = Edu^2 + 2Fdudv + Gdv^2 \tag{13}$$

The direction of slip, i. e., t, is same as that of dr. This implies that $dr \times t = 0$. So, taking cross product of Eq. (10) with t and further dot product with n gives:

$$(r_u \times t) \cdot n \; du + (r_v \times t) \cdot n \; dv = 0 \tag{14}$$

Solving Eqs. (13) and (14) for du, we get

$$|du| = \beta \sin \alpha \left/ \sqrt{E - 2F\left\{\frac{(r_u \times t) \cdot n}{(r_v \times t) \cdot n}\right\} + G\left\{\frac{(r_u \times t) \cdot n}{(r_v \times t) \cdot n}\right\}^2} \right. \tag{15}$$

It can be shown that the algebraic sign of du is opposite to that of $(r_v \times t) \cdot n$. Hence, the expressions for du and dv are written as:

$$du = -|du| \operatorname{sgn}\big((r_v \times t) \cdot n\big) \quad \text{and} \quad dv = -du \frac{(r_u \times t) \cdot n}{(r_v \times t) \cdot n} \tag{16}$$

3.2 Computation of Slip-Locus

As a grasp endeavor progresses with an evolving slip-locus, the two grasp-angles and the grasp-line change continuously which in turn change the instantaneous slip at the two contacts. To emulate the evolution of the slip-locus, the following iterative steps are given below.

Planar Case

Step 1: Choose arbitrary but distinct initial values of u_1 and u_2 for locations of points P_1 and P_2 given by $r_1(u_1)$ and $r_2(u_2)$, respectively.

Step 2: Check if P_1 and P_2 are very close; terminate the procedure if true, else go to Step 3.

Step 3: Compute the unit vector g along the instantaneous grasp-line, normals to the curve at the two points n_1, n_2. Use Eqs. (5) and (6) to determine the slip directions t_1, t_2, respectively.

Step 4: Compute r_u at u_1 and u_2. Taking small value of β (say 0.001), use Eq. (9) to determine du_1 and du_2.

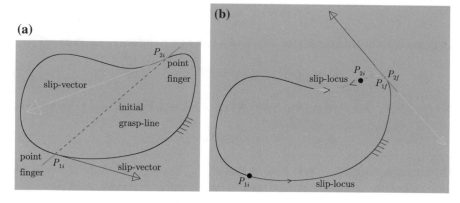

Fig. 2 Grasp endeavor of planar object. **a** Initial configuration, **b** final configuration

Step 5: Compute the new locations of the points P_1 and P_2 given by $r_1(u_1 + du_1)$ and $r_2(u_2 + du_2)$, respectively. Go to Step 2.

Spatial Case

Step 1: Choose arbitrary but distinct initial values of (u_1, v_1) and (u_2, v_2) for locations of points P_1 and P_2 given by $r_1(u_1, v_1)$ and $r_2(u_2, v_2)$, respectively.

Step 2: Check if P_1 and P_2 are very close; terminate the procedure if true, else go to Step 3.

Step 3: Compute the unit vector g along the instantaneous grasp-line, r_u and r_v at $r_1(u_1, v_1)$ and $r_2(u_2, v_2)$. Determine the normal vectors n_1, n_2 using Eq. (11). Use Eqs. (5) and (6) to compute the slip directions t_1 and t_2, respectively.

Step 4: Taking small value of β (say 0.001), use Eq. (16) to compute (du_1, dv_1) and (du_2, dv_2).

Step 5: Find the new locations of the points P_1 and P_2 given by $r_1(u_1 + du_1, v_1 + dv_1)$ and $r_2(u_2 + du_2, v_2 + dv_2)$, respectively. Go to Step 2.

3.3 Examples of Slip-Locus

The above-mentioned method was used to compute the two slip-loci for smooth planar and spatial shapes which are represented using NURBS (Nonuniform Rational B-Splines) curves. Figure 2a shows the initial grasp configuration (grasp-line $P_{1i} P_{2i}$) of a planar object. The *slip-vector* shown at a contact indicates the instantaneous direction of slip of the finger with respect to the object. The length of the slip-vector is proportional to the magnitude of instantaneous slip (i.e., $\beta \sin \alpha$). As slip continues, the two-point fingers trace the slip-locus along the boundary before both converging

(a)   **(b)**

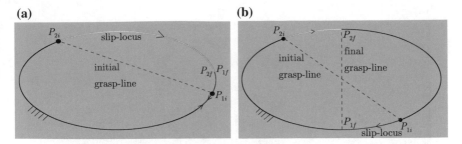

Fig. 3 Slip-locus characterization. **a** Convergence to one point is failure, **b** convergence to distinct points is success

at the same point (P_{1f} and P_{2f} in Fig. 2b). Similar exercise with different initial points of grasping also converged to a common point of "slipping off". Hence, this object is non graspable in absence of friction and other external forces. Figure 3a shows a similar scenario, but, for an elliptic object where the two slip-loci converge at a point. However, in Fig. 3b, for the same elliptic object, when the initial grasp-line is a diameter of the ellipse, it is observed that the two-point fingers converge to the two co-vertices of the ellipse. This is a stable configuration and the slip is arrested for the two grasp-angles being zero. At the stabilized locations of the points of contact, the two normal lines to the ellipse are coincident. Pairs of points on a curve or a surface where the normal lines are coincident has been referred to as *antipodal points* in [7]. We shall be using the same terminology subsequently. Figure 4 shows the computed slip-loci on a smooth surface taking $\beta = 0.001$. The two coevolving slip-loci converge to a common point on the surface. Notice that the two slip-vectors are anti-parallel at the point of convergence (Fig. 4). This means that *the two slip-loci are atleast C^1 continuous at the point of convergence.*

The above procedure works even for polyhedral and tessellated objects [9]. For dihedral grasps where the two normals and the grasp-line are co-planar, the slip-locus is a straight line (Fig. 5a). Dihedral grasp on nonparallel planes generates a pair of conjugate slip-loci which always converge at a point on the intersection of the two planes (Fig. 5b). For a tessellated object (Fig. 5c), the normal changes direction abruptly at an edge common to two adjacent faces which is an additional consideration in such cases.

3.4 Inferences

From the above observations, the following inferences can be made:

(a) *Slipping at the start of a grasp endeavor is not an indication of grap failure.* In a grasp endeavor, there can be two consequences. Either the object moves towards a *stable grasp configuration after the initial slip* or slips off from the fingers.

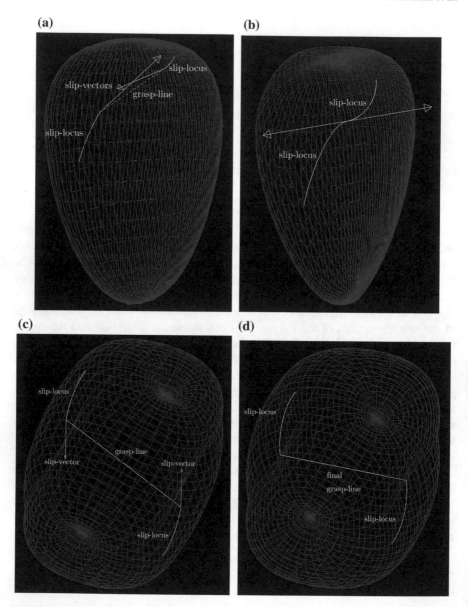

Fig. 4 Computed slip-loci during a grasp endeavor. Failed grasp: **a** evolution, **b** convergence to one point. Successful: **c** evolution, **d** convergence to distinct points

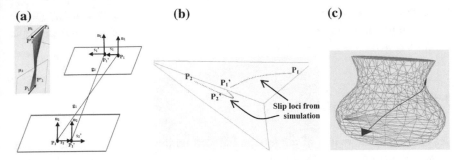

(a)   **(b)**   **(c)**

Fig. 5 Slip-locus during grasping of: **a** parallel faces, **b** dihedral planes, **c** tessellated object

(b) The convergence of slip-loci to a point means that in a physical scenario the point fingers meet at a point; this implies that the object has slipped off from the fingers and stable grasp is not achieved. Hence, *convergence of two slip-loci to a common point indicates a grasp failure.*

(c) When the two slip-loci converge to two distinct points on the surface where the surface normal lines of the object are coincident, these two points are the *locations for frictionless two-point stable grasping of the object.*

4   Slip-Response

Until now, the object was kept fixed and the traces of the point contacts relative to the object are studied. In a physical scenario, the two-point fingers are manipulating the object. We now determine the kinematic response of the object as a result of slip for a squeezing action at the two points of contact. Without loss of generality, one of the fingers is considered fixed and the other is squeezed towards the first finger along a spatially fixed straight line which is nothing but the grasp-line.

4.1   DOF Analysis

The two-point contacts restrict the relative motion between the object and the fingers to the tangent planes at the points of contact. This counts for two constraints on the twist space of the object. Additionally, at a point of contact, not every direction in the tangent plane is available for slip; only the direction prescribed by the model of slip is available. So, we have two additional constraints due to the directions of slip. Finally, the magnitudes of the infinitesimal slips are also given by the model of slip. The ratio of instantaneous slips at the two contacts is a function of the grasp-angles; this provides another constraint. All the afore-mentioned five constraints do not put any restriction on the spin of the object about the grasp-line. Thus, a smooth frictionless object under two-fingered grasping has only 1 degrees of freedom (DOF). As one of the finger is squeezed towards the other one, *the motion of the object is completely determined, except for the spin about the grasp-line.*

4.2 Kinematic Response

Let us analyze the nature of the motion induced on the object during the slipping phase. Let the line $P_{1i}P_{2i}$ be the initial grasp-line and line P_1P_2 be any subsequent grasp-line in the object's frame of reference. A rigid-body transformation which consists of, a translation for moving the point P_1 to P_{1i} and then a rotation about an axis orthogonal to the lines $P_{1i}P_{2i}$ and $P_{1i}P_2$ at P_{1i}, is applied on the spatial object. We used this transformation to visualize the motion of the object. However, rotation about the grasp-line (the free motion) is not visualized. Considering $P_{1i}P_{2i}$ and P_1P_2 to be infinitesimally separated, we can infer that the *instantaneous motion* characteristics of the object *is nothing but a screw motion whose axis is orthogonal to P_1P_2.* Hence, the motion of the object can be decomposed into a screw motion of zero pitch about the grasp-line and a screw motion of finite pitch whose axis is orthogonal to the grasp-line.

5 Discussion

Geodesic slip-locus: The differential geometric properties of the two coevolving of slip-loci have interesting geometric properties. The normal to the locus at a point coincides with the normal to the surface (Sect. 2), which implies that the curve locally lies in the normal plane; this property is also shared by a geodesic curve. Also, there is a unique geodesic curve at a point on a surface in a given direction. Hence, *we believe that the two slip-loci traced are geodesic curves on the surface.* In case of a failed grasp, since the slip directions are same at the point of convergence and there is only one geodesic at the point of convergence in any direction, the two slip-loci must have been part of the same geodesic between the two initial points of grasp. For a successful grasp no comment similar to this can be made based on the studies till now.

Basin of stable grasp: In the case of grasping of an elliptic object (Sect. 3.3), it is seen that for a successful grasp the initial contact points are a pair of ∞^1 available diametrical points and not just a finite number. In a general planar successful grasp, if the two slip-loci converge to antipodal points from the initial contact points, then for starting points in a neighborhood around the previous initial points too, the convergence to the same antipodal points can be expected. In the spatial case, the ∞^1 geodesics converging at the antipodal points are the different paths available for a slip-locus to arrive at. So, for the initial contact points anywhere in the reasonably finite regions in the neighborhood of the antipodal points, consistent convergence phenomena of the slip-loci, implying a successful grasp, can be observed. From a practical point of view, this implies that, we need not be very precise about two antipodal points for a grasp endeavor. Somewhere near the exact locations is likely to lead to a successful grasp after slipping. The computational and analytical assessment of the above mentioned expected grasp responses are under investigation.

6 Conclusions

Slipping of objects in a grasp endeavor is not an indication of grasp failure. A model of slip is proposed for a frictionless point contact over smooth object. Slip-locus is computed for the first time in literature for assessing the grasp potential and behavior of the object. Nature of geodesic at a point provides insight into grasp response. Quasi-static kinematic response of an object with two-point fingers shows that motion of the object with respect to the fingers is deterministic except for the rotation about the line of grasp.

References

1. R.S. Johansson, G. Westling, Signals in tactile afferments from the fingers eliciting adaptive motor responses during precision grip. Exp. Brain Res. **66**(1), 141–154 (1987)
2. D.J. Montana, Contact stability for two fingered grasps. IEEE Trans. Robot. Autom. **8**(4), 421–430 (1992)
3. W.S. Howard, V. Kumar, On the stability of grasped objects. IEEE Trans. Robot. Autom. **12**(6), 904–917 (1993)
4. R.S. Fearing, Simplified grasping and manipulation with dextrous robot hands. IEEE Trans. Robot. Autom. **2**(4), 32–38 (1986)
5. R.S. Fearing, Implementing a force strategy for object reorientation, in *Proceedings of IEEE International Conference on Robotics and Automation* (San Francisco, CA, 1986), pp. 96–102
6. S. Gopalaswamy, R.S. Fearing, Grasping polyhedral objects with slip. IEEE Trans. Robot. Autom. **16**(8), 445–460 (1989)
7. I.M. Chen, J.W. Burdick, Finding antipodal point grasps on irregularly shaped objects. IEEE Trans. Robot. Autom. **9**(4), 507–512 (1993)
8. M.P. Do Carmo, *Differential Geometry of Curves and Surfaces* (Prentice-Hall, Inc., Englewood Cliffs, New Jersey, 1976)
9. J.S. Vipin, *Natural hand based interaction simulation using a digital hand*, Ph.D. thesis, Indian Institute of Science, 2013

New Dynamic Model and Simulation of the Ballbot Using Reaction Wheels

Narendra Raja Sekhar, Mallikarjuna Korrapati, Roshan Hota
and Cheruvu Siva Kumar

Abstract In this paper, a modified approach to stabilize the ballbot is presented using reaction wheels. Unlike recent ballbots, reaction wheels are added to the system. A mathematical model is formulated with the help of Lagrangian mechanics to the modified ballbot. The controllers PID and LQR are considered for position balancing. The effect of reaction wheels to the ballbot is studied and compared to the performance of ballbot without reaction wheels case.

Keywords Ballbot · Inverted pedulum · Reaction wheel · LQR · PID

1 Introduction

Ballbot can be considered as an inverted pendulum balancing on a ball. It has agile motion because of the rolling action of the ball and possess natural instability due to inverted pendulum. Effective control is required as it requires dynamic stability. Lauwers et al. [1] introduced dynamically stable robot with one wheel. Concept of ballbot was introduced with the robot balancing on a ball. Ballbot which is equivalent to size of human and stabilized dynamically was first developed in 2005 by Lauwers et al. [1, 2] with the intention of providing superior capabilities to the robot. Unlike statically stable robots, dynamically stable robots can decelerate and accelerate quickly and have high centre of gravity [3]. Most of the ballbot platforms use control system which approximates the system as linear, enabling to use linear con-

N. Raja Sekhar (✉) · M. Korrapati · R. Hota · C. Siva Kumar
Indian Institute of Technology Kharagpur, Kharagpur, India
e-mail: nraazsekhar@gmail.com

M. Korrapati
e-mail: mallikarjuna.korrapati@iitkgp.ac.in

R. Hota
e-mail: yoursroshanhota@gmail.com

C. Siva Kumar
e-mail: kumar@mech.iitkgp.ernet.in

© Springer Nature Singapore Pte Ltd. 2019
D N Badodkar and T A Dwarakanath (eds.), *Machines, Mechanism and Robotics*, Lecture Notes in Mechanical Engineering,
https://doi.org/10.1007/978-981-10-8597-0_69

807

troller. Sliding mode controller is one of the nonlinear controller that is implemented for ballbot in simulation by Liao et al. [4].

Reaction wheels mechanism was used to stabilize inverted pendulum by Jepson et al. [5]. These reaction wheels were primarily used in spacecraft for attitude control. Dual-axis reaction wheel inverted pendulum was developed by Rouleau [6]. Though different ballbots and different control strategies were developed. There were some limitations like limited torques by motors and limited tilt angles. To outcome the problems, the reaction wheels are added to ballbot so that these reaction wheels can give the additional momentum to the ballbot which can attain to stabilize the system in lesser time. This approach was used to improvise the settling time of the ballbot. The new dynamic model was designed such that two reaction wheels whose axes are orthogonal to each other were mounted at the centre of gravity and perpendicular to the axis of the body. This paper presents the mathematical model of the new ballbot and the simulations results to compare the settling times of both the ballbots with and without reaction wheels case.

2 System Dynamics

This section discusses briefly about the system model. It consists of four bodies as shown in Fig. 1:

1. Spherical ball.
2. Body.
3. Omni wheels.
4. Reaction wheels.

Ballbot makes contact at arbitrary point on the ground. Spherical ball cannot rotate with vertical axis of the ground but can rotate any axis that is parallel to the ground. Spherical ball is actuated with the help of three omni wheels which makes contact at three different points of the spherical ball. A holonomic linkage is made between spherical ball and omni wheels. Tangential forces are applied on the spherical ball by the omni wheels. The reaction wheels are mounted to the body over a motor in such a way that the axes of reaction wheels are perpendicular to the vertical axis of the body. By Newton's third law, the reaction wheels generates a momentum rotates in one direction and the body rotates in opposite direction [7].

The inputs to the system are five torques T_1, T_2, T_3, T_4, T_5 which are generated by the motors.

The following assumptions are to be taken to obtain the system equations:

1. Rolling and Kinetic frictions are negligible.
2. No slip between ball and omni wheels and between ball and ground to manoeuvre the ball.
3. Rigid bodies.
4. Floor is strictly horizontal.
5. No time delay.

Fig. 1 3D model in
solidworks

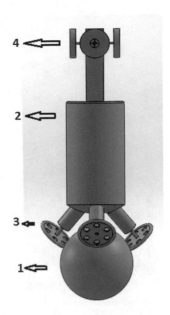

2.1 Coordinate System

Consider I as a inertial frame of reference. A, L are the two reference frames given to the body of the ballbot and the spherical ball, respectively. Inertial frame of reference is rotated about z-axis e_z^I with an angle ϑ_z transforms to L reference frame. By rotating L reference frame about y-axis e_y^L with an angle ϑ_y transforms to A' reference frame. Then, by rotating A' reference frame about x-axis $e_x^{A'}$ with an angle ϑ_x changes to A reference frame. Here, A' reference frame is attached to body of the ballbot and L is attached to the spherical ball as shown in Fig. 2. Coordinates are represented in Euler form because of easiness in calculations. Sensor output convention is matched with Tait-Bryan angle transformation.

$$I \xrightarrow{\vartheta_z} L \xrightarrow{\vartheta_y} A' \xrightarrow{\vartheta_x} A$$

The vectorial representation of angular velocity of the ballbot:

1. **Angular velocity of the ball**

$$_L\vec{\Omega}_B = \begin{bmatrix} \dot{\varphi}_x \\ \dot{\varphi}_y \\ 0 \end{bmatrix} \tag{1}$$

2. **Angular speed of omni wheel**

$$_A\omega_{W1} = \dot{\psi}_1 \quad _A\omega_{W2} = \dot{\psi}_2 \quad _A\omega_{W3} = \dot{\psi}_3 \tag{2}$$

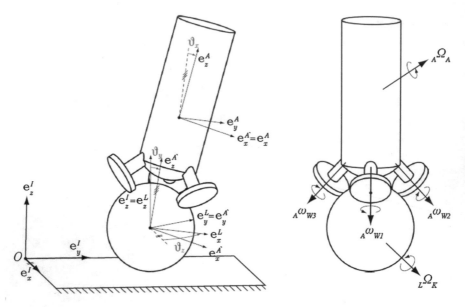

Fig. 2 Representation of reference frames and its angular velocities [7]

3. **Angular velocity of reaction wheels**

$$_A\vec{\Omega}_{RW_1} = \begin{bmatrix} \dot{\gamma}_1 \\ 0 \\ 0 \end{bmatrix} \quad _A\vec{\Omega}_{RW_2} = \begin{bmatrix} 0 \\ \dot{\gamma}_2 \\ 0 \end{bmatrix} \tag{3}$$

4. **Angular velocity of the body**

$$_A\vec{\Omega}_A = \underline{J} \cdot \dot{\vec{\vartheta}} = \begin{bmatrix} \dot{\vartheta}_x - sin\vartheta_y \cdot \dot{\vartheta}_z \\ cos\vartheta_x \cdot \dot{\vartheta}_y + cos\vartheta_y \cdot sin\vartheta_x \cdot \dot{\vartheta}_z \\ -sin\vartheta_x \cdot \dot{\vartheta}_y + cos\vartheta_x \cdot cos\vartheta_y \cdot \dot{\vartheta}_z \end{bmatrix} \tag{4}$$

The vectorial representation of translational speed of the ball is given as:

$$_I\dot{\vec{r}}_P =_I \Omega_B \times_I \vec{BP} \tag{5}$$

2.2 *Parameters*

See Table 1

Table 1 Parameters described as per the generated model [7]

Part description	Symbol	Value
Spherical ball mass	m_B	0.623 kg
Body mass with omni wheels	m_A	18.3 kg
Mass of the reaction wheel	m_{RW}	2 kg
Ball radius	r_B	0.125 m
Omni wheels radius	r_W	0.06 m
Height of the cg of body	l	0.7 m
Ball inertia	Θ_B	0.0064 kg m^2
Body inertia in yz plane	$\Theta_{A,yz}$	2.026 kg m^2
Body inertia in xy plane	$\Theta_{A,xy}$	0.092 kg m^2
Gravitational acceleration	g	9.81 m/s^2
Inertia of motor with wheel	Θ_W	0.00315 kg m^2
Angle of omni wheel	α	45
Angles of the omni wheel directions	$\beta_1, \beta_2, \beta_3$	0, 120, 240

2.3 Dynamics

This section discusses about developing the equations for modified system. Lagrangian approach was used to develop the system equations. The following minimal coordinates $\vec{q}$ is used:

$$\vec{q} = \begin{bmatrix} \vartheta_x & \vartheta_y & \vartheta_z & \varphi_x & \varphi_y & \dot{\gamma}_1 & \dot{\gamma}_2 \end{bmatrix}^T \tag{6}$$

Since γ_1 and γ_2 doesn't effect the behaviour of the system which are not considered in deriving the equations.

Considering the kinetic energies (T) and potential energies (K) of each bodies.

Ball

$$T_B = \underbrace{\frac{1}{2} \cdot m_B \cdot {}_I\dot{\vec{r}}_P^T \cdot {}_I\dot{\vec{r}}_P}_{\text{Translation}} + \underbrace{\frac{1}{2} \cdot {}_L\vec{\Omega}_B^T \cdot {}_L\underline{\Theta}_B \cdot {}_L\vec{\Omega}_B}_{\text{Rotation}} \tag{7}$$

Body

$$T_A = \underbrace{\frac{1}{2} \cdot m_A \cdot {}_I\dot{\vec{r}}_P^T \cdot {}_I\dot{\vec{r}}_P}_{\text{Translation}} + \underbrace{m_A \cdot \left(\underline{R}_{AI} \cdot {}_I\dot{\vec{r}}_P \right) \cdot \left({}_A\vec{\Omega}_A \times_A \vec{r}_{PSA} \right)}_{\text{Coupling}} + \underbrace{\frac{1}{2} \cdot {}_A\vec{\Omega}_A^T \cdot {}_A\underline{\Theta}_A \cdot {}_A\vec{\Omega}_A}_{\text{Rotation}} \tag{8}$$

$$V_A = -m_A \cdot \vec{G} \cdot \underline{R}_{IA} \cdot {}_A \vec{r}_{PSA} \quad \text{with} \quad \vec{G} = \begin{bmatrix} 0 \\ 0 \\ -g \end{bmatrix} \tag{9}$$

Omni wheels

$$T_{Wi} = \frac{1}{2} \cdot {}_A \Theta_{Wi} \cdot {}_A \Omega^2_{Wi} \quad for \quad i = 1, 2, 3 \tag{10}$$

Reaction wheels

$$T_{RW_i} = \underbrace{\frac{1}{2} \cdot m_{RW} \cdot {}_I \dot{\vec{r}}^T_P \cdot {}_I \dot{\vec{r}}_P}_{\text{Translation}} + \underbrace{\frac{1}{2} \cdot ({}_A \vec{\Omega}_A + {}_A \vec{\Omega}_{RW})^T \cdot {}_A \underline{\Theta}_{RW} \cdot ({}_A \vec{\Omega}_A + {}_A \vec{\Omega}_{RW})}_{\text{Rotation}} \tag{11}$$

The dynamic equations of motion were derived by solving the Lagrange equation

$$\frac{d}{dt} \left(\frac{\partial T}{\partial \dot{\vec{q}}} \right)^T - \left(\frac{\partial T}{\partial \vec{q}} \right)^T + \left(\frac{\partial V}{\partial \vec{q}} \right)^T - \vec{f}_{NP} = 0 \tag{12}$$

with

$$T = T_B + T_A + T_{W1} + T_{W2} + T_{W3} + T_{RW1} + T_{RW2}$$

$$V = V_A + V_{RW1} + V_{RW2}$$

Calculations were done using a software Matlab by making smaller, multiple computations and simplified.

The derived nonlinear equations were linearised at initial states and represented in state space form as below.

$$\dot{\vec{x}} = A \cdot \vec{x} + B \cdot \vec{u} \quad \vec{y} = C \cdot x + D \cdot u \tag{13}$$

$$\vec{x} = \left[\vartheta_x, \dot{\vartheta}_x, \vartheta_y, \dot{\vartheta}_y, \vartheta_z, \dot{\vartheta}_z, \varphi_x, \dot{\varphi}_x, \varphi_y, \dot{\varphi}_y, \dot{\gamma}_1, \dot{\gamma}_2 \right]^T \tag{14}$$

$$\vec{u} = \begin{bmatrix} u_1 \\ u_2 \\ u_3 \\ u_4 \\ u_5 \end{bmatrix} = \begin{bmatrix} T_1 \\ T_2 \\ T_3 \\ T_4 \\ T_5 \end{bmatrix} \tag{15}$$

$$\vec{y} = \vec{x} \tag{16}$$

System is linearized at initial states, i.e., $\vec{x} = 0$ and $\vec{u} = 0$.

$$A = \begin{bmatrix} 0 & 1 & 0 & 000000000 \\ -45.9918 & 0 & 0 & 000000000 \\ 0 & 0 & 0 & 100000000 \\ 0 & 0 & -45.9918 & 000000000 \\ 0 & 0 & 0 & 001000000 \\ 0 & 0 & 0 & 000000000 \\ 0 & 0 & 0 & 000010000 \\ 194.567 & 0 & 0 & 000000000 \\ 0 & 0 & 0 & 000000100 \\ 0 & 0 & 194.567 & 000000000 \\ 45.9918 & 0 & 0 & 000000000 \\ 0 & 0 & 45.9918 & 000000000 \end{bmatrix}_{12 \times 12} \tag{17}$$

and

$$B = \begin{bmatrix} 0 & 0 & 0 & 0 & 0 \\ -2.1018 & 1.3695 & 1.3695 & 0.3003 & 0 \\ 0 & 0 & 0 & 0 & 0 \\ 0 & -2.0041 & 2.0041 & 0 & 0.3003 \\ 0 & 0 & 0 & 0 & 0 \\ -5.3929 & -5.3929 & -5.3929 & 0 & 0 \\ 0 & 0 & 0 & 0 & 0 \\ 4.9624 & -3.8288 & -3.8288 & -1.2706 & 0 \\ 0 & 0 & 0 & 0 & 0 \\ 0 & 5.0756 & -5.0756 & 0 & -1.2706 \\ 2.1018 & -1.3695 & -1.3695 & 177.4774 & 0 \\ 0 & 2.0041 & -2.0041 & 0 & 177.4774 \end{bmatrix}_{12 \times 5} \tag{18}$$

and C is 12×12 identity matrix and D is 12×5 zero matrix.

3 Controller Design

In this section, LQR and PID controllers are implemented for linearized system. For 3D model, the linear quadratic state feedback is designed. Control block diagram for the 3D system is shown in Fig. 3.

$$J(u) = \int_0^\infty \left(x^T(t) Q\, x(t) + u^T(t)\, Ru(t) \right) dt \tag{19}$$

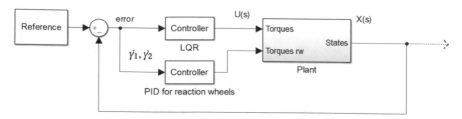

Fig. 3 Block diagram for generated model

Necessary feedback gains are to be calculated with respective to error obtained. LQR control theory is implemented to obtain the required torques for the omni wheel motors. Based on the linearized system with all operating points at zero, the parameters Q and R are chosen as in [7]:

$$Q = diag\,(\,120\ \ 60\ \ 120\ \ 60\ \ 50\ \ 25\ \ 30\ \ 15\ \ 30\ \ 15\ \ 50\ \ 50\,)$$
$$R = diag\,(\,150\ \ 150\ \ 150\ \ 150\ \ 150\,)$$

The weighted matrices Q and R are experimentally tuned. For given Q, R the controller gains can be derived using Matlab *lqr* command.

$$K = \begin{bmatrix} -5.5 & -3.03 & 0 & 0 & -0.37 & -0.34 & -0.36 & -0.49 & 0 & 0 & 0.012 & 0 \\ 3.38 & 1.68 & -5.15 & -2.73 & -0.36 & -0.33 & 0.19 & 0.25 & -0.32 & -0.43 & -0.0076 & 0.01 \\ 3.38 & 1.68 & 5.15 & 2.73 & -0.36 & -0.33 & 0.19 & 0.25 & 0.32 & 0.43 & -0.0076 & -0.01 \end{bmatrix}$$

PID control theory is used to obtain the required angular acceleration for the reaction wheels. These reaction wheels acts as a momentum wheel and conservation of angular momentum is considered, i.e., $\dot{\gamma} = \frac{-I_\theta}{I_{RW}} \cdot \dot{\theta}$. Desired $\dot{\gamma}$ is the reference value for PID controller. Tuning of PID controller in Simulink is done to obtain the gain values, i.e., $K_p = 5.52$, $K_i = 224.91$ and $K_d = 0$.

4 Simulation Results

Considering the same parameters for both the modified model and the existing model as given in Table 1, i.e., $m_{RW} = 2$ kg, radius $r_{RW} = 0.075$ m and CG height $l = 0.7$ m. Initially, the system was in upright position, i.e., in stable condition. Sudden force is given to the system using the pulse generator which makes the system unstable. Generated feedback gain values in Sect. 3 were given to the LQR controller as shown in Fig. 4 which calculates the appropriate torques to the motors that drives the system.

In the Fig. 5, the first graph which shows the settling time for the ballbot with reaction wheels is better than the second graph which shows the settling time for the ballbot without reaction wheels case.

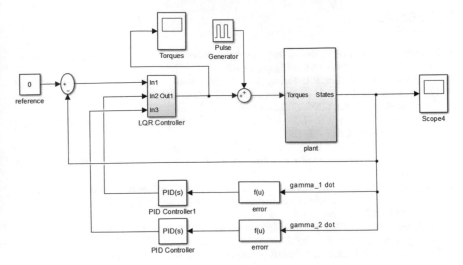

Fig. 4 Simulink model

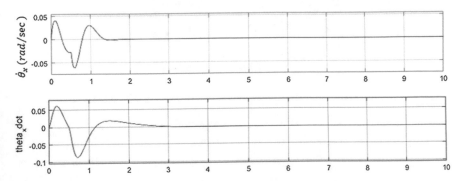

Fig. 5 Angular velocity term $\dot{\theta}_x$ versus time for new ballbot and the existing ballbot

5 Conclusion

This paper presented the design of new dynamic ballbot with the addition of reaction wheels. The LQR controller calculates the appropriate omni wheel motor torques and PID controller calculates the appropriate reaction wheel motor torques based on the measured tilt angle, required to keep the ballbot dynamically stable. Finally, results confirmed that reaction wheels can be used to improvise the behaviour of the ballbot.

References

1. T. Lauwers, G. Kantor, R. Hollis, One is enough!, in *12th International Symposium of Robotics Research* (San Francisco, Oct 2005), pp. 12–15
2. T. Lauwers, G.A. Kantor, R.L. Hollis, A dynamically stable single-wheeled mobile robot with inverse mouse-ball drive, in *Proceedings 2006 IEEE International Conference on Robotics and Automation, 2006. ICRA 2006* (IEEE, 2006), pp. 2884–2889
3. U. Nagarajan, G. Kantor, R. Hollis, The ballbot: an omnidirectional balancing mobile robot. Int. J. Robot. Res. **33**(6), 917–930 (2014)
4. C.W. Liao, C.C. Tsai, Y.Y. Li, C.K. Chan, Dynamic modeling and sliding-mode control of a ball robot with inverse mouse-ball drive, in *SICE Annual Conference, 2008* (IEEE, 2008), pp. 2951–2955
5. F. Jepsen, A. Soborg, A.R. Pedersen, Z. Yang, Development and control of an inverted pendulum driven by a reaction wheel, in *International Conference on Mechatronics and Automation, 2009. ICMA 2009* (IEEE, 2009), pp. 2829–2834
6. M. Rouleau, Self Balancing Stick—Dual axis reaction wheel inverted pendulum, https://redd.it/3n0g8p. Accessed 30 Sept 2015
7. S. Leutenegger, P. Fankhauser, Modeling and control of a ballbot, Bachelor Thesis, ETH Zurich, 2010

Master–Slave Teleoperation of Multi-DOF Cyton Robot with Input from PHANTOM Omni Using Visual Feedback

Mallikarjuna Korrapati, Sahil Raj, Aditya Kameswara Rao Nandula and Cheruvu Siva Kumar

Abstract This paper presents the teleoperation of multi-DOF cyton robot using visual feedback which carries depth information. Teleoperation system consists of PHANTOM Omni device which was set as master and cyton robot as a slave robot. The motion of the slave robot was controlled through direct angle mapping of joints with master. Teleoperation system also uses visual feedback for enabling effective remote manipulability. Visual feedback contains side-by-side frames of left and right IR cameras attached to the Raspberry Pi compute module. Two cameras attached to compute module will capture simultaneous side by side frames and transmitted through network. 3D view of the remote location will be perceived by the user using 3D video transmission in side by side format. Live stream was enabled in smartphone and attached to the VR headset.

Keywords Teleoperation · Master–Slave robot · PHANTOM Omni · Visual feedback

1 Introduction

Robotic technologies are expanding to different fields of application ranging from space robotics to medical rooms. Robots were made autonomous to handle complex environments. In highly complex environments, robotic systems were enabled with

M. Korrapati (✉) · S. Raj · A. K. Rao Nandula · C. S. Kumar
Mechanical Engineering Department, Indian Institute of Technology Kharagpur,
Kharagpur, India
e-mail: mallikarjuna.korrapati@iitkgp.ac.in

S. Raj
e-mail: rajsahildumaribhui@gmail.com

A. K. Rao Nandula
e-mail: akraonandula@gmail.com

C. S. Kumar
e-mail: kumar@mech.iitkgp.ernet.in

© Springer Nature Singapore Pte Ltd. 2019
D N Badodkar and T A Dwarakanath (eds.), *Machines, Mechanism and Robotics*, Lecture Notes in Mechanical Engineering,
https://doi.org/10.1007/978-981-10-8597-0_70

817

human operator or human in loop. This leads to the teleoperation of a robot where a robot is controlled over a distance. At the initial stages, joysticks and keyboard inputs were used in telerobotic systems. With the advancement of robotic technologies, haptic input devices were used for robotic teleoperation. Haptic devices enables kinesthetic sense feedback or force feedback to the operator. These devices can give resistance if the slave robot is obstructed at the remote location.

Robotic teleoperation is performed by using master and slave robot model of communication. Master robot generates a command signal for the slave robot. In other words, motion of the master robot determines the motion of the slave robot. Communication is unilateral in case of master–slave configuration. Many robotic applications are active using robotic teleoperation. One such active field of application was assistive robotic technologies. Teleoperation was also used in assisting disabled with the daily activities. Veras et al. [1] developed a teleoperated system for assisting disabled persons with daily activities. They teleoperated PUMA560 as a slave with PHANTOM Omni as a master robot. Robotic teleoperated systems have also been implemented in a hazardous environment such as nuclear reactors for handling reactive material which ensures the safety of the operator [2].

Teleoperation of wheeled or mobile robot using PHANTOM Omni was implemented using position-position and position-speed command strategy by Farkhatdinov and Ryu [3]. With same position control strategy, a humanoid Baxter robotic arm was teleoperated using Sensable haptic device by mapping the workspaces of the master and slave robot. The effectiveness of such teleoperation was evaluated using free space moving method [4]. A micro hand was teleoperated consisting of two rotational fingers and a master control unit are designed for suitable teleoperation of the slave by Inoue et al. [5]. In the same way, a cost-effective master control unit was designed and used for teleoperation of an anthropomorphic robotic arm by Gupta et al. [6]. In case of surgical robotics, an endoscopic surgical parallel manipulator was teleoperated using PHANTOM Omni by mapping the position of the master robot on to the workspace of the slave robot [7]. A similar configuration of master and slave are chosen and proposed for minimally invasive brain telesurgery by Seung et al. [8].

A robotic system can be effectively teleoperated by including visual and kinesthetic information of the remote location; this enables the user to make an effective decision through sensory information. Many efforts were made to provide sensory information to the operator. The effectiveness of teleoperation with a provision of both visual and force feedback are studied by Alex [9]. Hong et al. [10] proposed a method of providing visual and kinesthetic information of the remote location to operate unmanned vehicles. A highly accurate stereoscopic system was implemented for telerobotics which includes tasks such as autonomous pick and place operation [11].

In this paper, teleoperation of multi-DOF humanoid cyton robotic arm was performed by taking input from a PHANTOM Omni device, and visual feedback was given to the user which enables to perceive 3D view of the remote location.

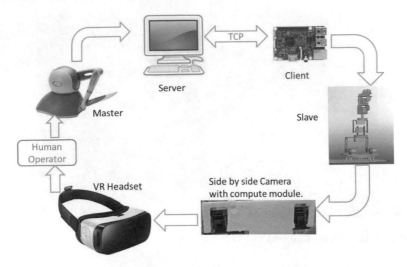

Fig. 1 System description with human in loop

2 System Description

The system developed consists of two modules. One focuses on the robotic teleoperation and the second module consists of a camera module. PHANTOM Omni has been chosen as master manipulator due to its ease of use and low inertia. A cyton robot which has 7-DOF and replicates the motion of humanoid arm was selected as the slave robot. Slave robot was connected to the Raspberry Pi which sends required PWM to the motors to set a position of the robot. A vision system was developed using compute module and placed at the slave robot remote location. A human-in-loop control is implemented in the system. Figure 1 indicates the structure of the teleoperation system.

2.1 Teleoperation

2.1.1 Master Unit

PHANTOM Omni haptic device is mostly used in research for teleoperation which involves haptic feedback. Its usage in many teleoperation systems can be credited due to its low inertia of the device and ease of use. PHANTOM Omni usually consists of six rotational joints as shown in Fig. 2. Translational movements of the end effector are due to the 1–3 rotational joints, and orientation of the end effector is defined by the 1–3 gimbal rotational angles. The kinematic chain was shown in Fig. 3. The kinematics and dynamics were already defined in Openhaptics API software.

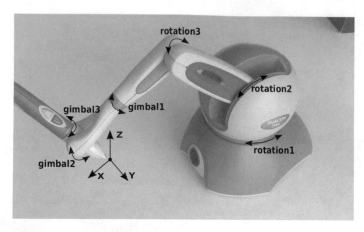

Fig. 2 Rotational joints of the PHANTOM Omni device

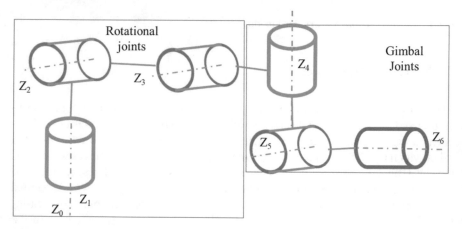

Fig. 3 Kinematic chain of PHANTOM Omni

Kinematics analysis of the device was also stated in San Martin and Trivino [12], Silva et al. [13].

2.1.2 Slave Unit

Cyton robot is a humanoid robot arm which has 7-DOF as shown in Fig. 4. Having configuration of human arm will enable high dexterity for task completion. It can reach through gaps and around obstacles, which makes it possible to place an object or grasp a tool in an unlimited number of ways. It is a redundant manipulator. Kinematic chain of the cyton robot is shown in Fig. 5.

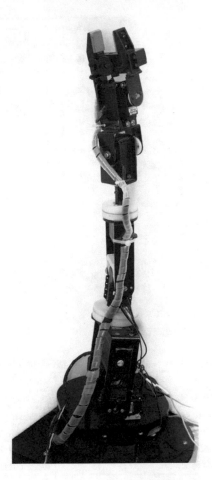

Fig. 4 7-DOF cyton robot

2.1.3 Control Strategy

Command to the slave robot can be given using position-position control strategy. In Ahn et al. [14] investigated the position control strategy with input saturation. In this paper, joint space position-position control is used to control the position of the robot because of its ease of implementation without complexity and speed of operation.

Joint space position-position control
One of the approach to implement position-position control strategy is to map the joint angles of the PHANTOM Omni to the cyton robot directly. Since cyton was a 7-DOF redundant manipulator while omni device has 6-DOF. One of the joint in the cyton robot should be restricted. By taking the geometric structure of the slave

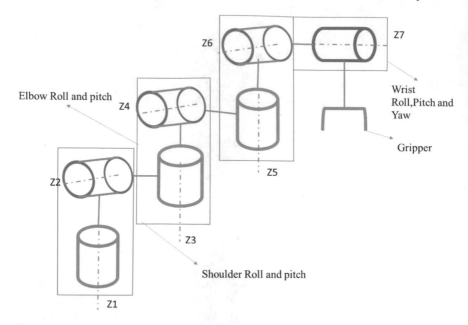

Fig. 5 Kinematic chain of the 7-DOF cyton robot

Table 1 Direct angle mapping between joints of master and slave robots

Master robot joint	Range	Mapped to	Slave robot joint	Range
Rotational joint Z_1	−60 to 60	$\implies$	Shoulder roll Z_1	−100 to 100
Rotational joint Z_2	0 to 105	$\implies$	Shoulder pitch Z_2	0 to 105
Rotational joint Z_3	−30 to 70	$\implies$	Elbow pitch Z_3	0 to 100
Gimbal joint Z_4	−145 to 145	$\implies$	Wrist roll Z_4	−100 to 100
Gimbal joint Z_5	−70 to 70	$\implies$	Wrist pitch Z_5	0 to 110
Gimbal joint Z_6	−145 to 145	$\implies$	Wrist yaw Z_7	−100 to 100

and master robot into consideration, slave robot elbow roll angle was set to zero. All other joints angles are directly mapped to the master device (Table 1).

2.1.4 Communication

Client–server model is a popular model for communicating through the network. The method for communication between a server system and client system uses socket mechanism which establishes server-client model. This mechanism was most popular in the system software such as Linux, Windows, Unix, etc. [15]. The transmission of data uses TCP protocol. Master-side system was considered as a server and slave side system as a client. PHANTOM Omni joint angles are continually transmitted to the Raspberry Pi system to give control signal to the cyton robot.

2.2 Vision System

Robotic teleoperation requires both visual and haptic information to understand the environment. Visual feedback plays a major role in a critical task such as telesurgery. One of the important information required by the visual feedback was depth perception. Depth perception enables to determine distances between the object and understand near and far objects. Lack of depth perception makes the task manipulation difficult. Depth perception can be enabled by a binocular vision, which was achieved by placing two cameras on the same plane, and the same horizontal line to have an overlapping field of view. In this paper, we designed a vision system for the teleoperation.

To achieve such binocular vision, we used Raspberry Pi compute module with camera module v2. A camera mount was designed as shown in Fig. 6, and 3D printed using FDM machine for attaching components together as shown in Fig. 7. The distance between the cameras was selected to approximate the distance between the human eyes. This arrangement was fixed at the remote location site. Raspberry Pi compute module was used to transmit side by side format videos because of its ability to capture frames simultaneously from both left and right camera and transmit through a network.

One can estimate the depth from the left and right images of the two cameras using different matching algorithms such as semi-global matching algorithms. To implement such algorithms, one has to calibrate the camera and map the frames to the calibrated frames. The above process takes a lot of computation for continuous frames and gives precise depth of the location. In this paper, we have implemented

Fig. 6 CAD model of the camera mount

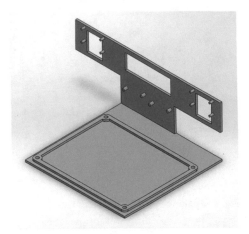

824 M. Korrapati et al.

Fig. 7 Camera module attached to the 3D printed camera mount

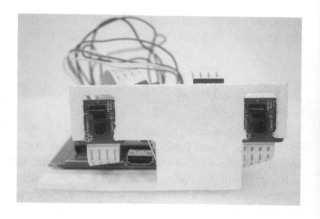

by projecting the left and right frames of the images to the respective eyes using VR headset. This method does not give precise depth of the objects in the locations, however, the user can understand the depth of the remote location intuitively. We generated a network stream of side-by side frames of the left and right cameras, and viewed over a smartphone using a app which was computer networking utility.

3 Results

Joint angle variation of PHANTOM Omni and mapped motion of nyron robot joint angles in degrees are plotted on y-axis, and time series on x-axis for picking up was shown in the following Figs. 8, 9, 10, 11 and 12.

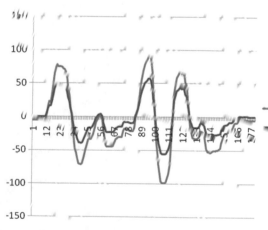

Fig. 8 Motion of joint Z_1 in master and slave

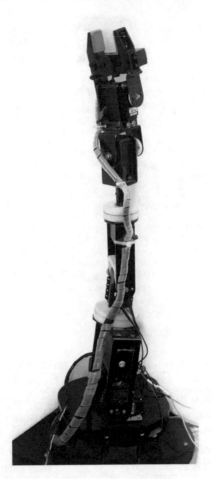

Fig. 4 7-DOF cyton robot

2.1.3 Control Strategy

Command to the slave robot can be given using position-position control strategy. In Ahn et al. [14] investigated the position control strategy with input saturation. In this paper, joint space position-position control is used to control the position of the robot because of its ease of implementation without complexity and speed of operation.

Joint space position-position control
One of the approach to implement position-position control strategy is to map the joint angles of the PHANTOM Omni to the cyton robot directly. Since cyton was a 7-DOF redundant manipulator while omni device has 6-DOF. One of the joint in the cyton robot should be restricted. By taking the geometric structure of the slave

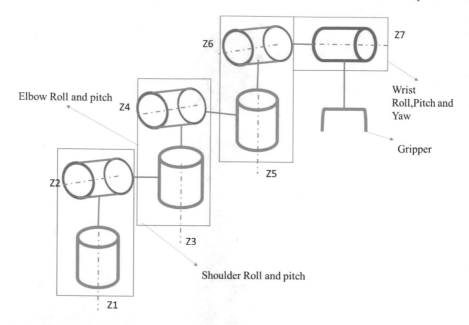

Fig. 5 Kinematic chain of the 7-DOF cyton robot

Table 1 Direct angle mapping between joints of master and slave robots

Master robot joint	Range	Mapped to	Slave robot joint	Range
Rotational joint Z_1	−60 to 60	$\Longrightarrow$	Shoulder roll Z_1	−100 to 100
Rotational joint Z_2	0 to 105	$\Longrightarrow$	Shoulder pitchZ_2	0 to 105
Rotational joint Z_3	−30 to 70	$\Longrightarrow$	Elbow pitchZ_3	0 to 100
Gimbal joint Z_4	−145 to 145	$\Longrightarrow$	Wrist roll Z_4	−100 to 100
Gimbal joint Z_5	−70 to 70	$\Longrightarrow$	Wrist pitch Z_5	0 to 110
Gimbal joint Z_6	−145 to 145	$\Longrightarrow$	Wrist yaw Z_7	−100 to 100

and master robot into consideration, slave robot elbow roll angle was set to zero. All other joints angles are directly mapped to the master device (Table 1).

2.1.4 Communication

Client–server model is a popular model for communicating through the network. The method for communication between a server system and client system uses socket mechanism which establishes server-client model. This mechanism was most popular in the system software such as Linux, Windows, Unix, etc. [15]. The transmission of data uses TCP protocol. Master-side system was considered as a server and slave side system as a client. PHANTOM Omni joint angles are continually transmitted to the Raspberry Pi system to give control signal to the cyton robot.

2.2 Vision System

Robotic teleoperation requires both visual and haptic information to understand the environment. Visual feedback plays a major role in a critical task such as telesurgery. One of the important information required by the visual feedback was depth perception. Depth perception enables to determine distances between the object and understand near and far objects. Lack of depth perception makes the task manipulation difficult. Depth perception can be enabled by a binocular vision, which was achieved by placing two cameras on the same plane, and the same horizontal line to have an overlapping field of view. In this paper, we designed a vision system for the teleoperation.

To achieve such binocular vision, we used Raspberry Pi compute module with camera module v2. A camera mount was designed as shown in Fig. 6, and 3D printed using FDM machine for attaching components together as shown in Fig. 7. The distance between the cameras was selected to approximate the distance between the human eyes. This arrangement was fixed at the remote location site. Raspberry Pi compute module was used to transmit side by side format videos because of its ability to capture frames simultaneously from both left and right camera and transmit through a network.

One can estimate the depth from the left and right images of the two cameras using different matching algorithms such as semi-global matching algorithms. To implement such algorithms, one has to calibrate the camera and map the frames to the calibrated frames. The above process takes a lot of computation for continuous frames and gives precise depth of the location. In this paper, we have implemented

Fig. 6 CAD model of the camera mount

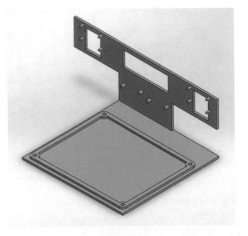

Fig. 7 Camera module
attached to the 3D printed
camera mount

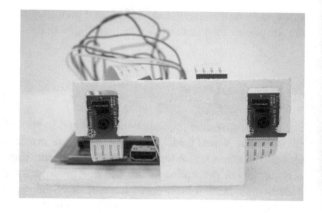

by projecting the left and right frames of the images to the respective eyes using VR headset. This method does not give precise depth of the objects in the locations, however, the user can understand the depth of the remote location intuitively. We generated a network stream of side-by-side frames of the left and right cameras, and viewed over a smartphone using Netcat which was computer networking utility.

3 Results

Joint angle variation of PHANTOM Omni and mapped motion of cyton robot joint angles in degrees are plotted on y-axis, and time series on x-axis for picking an object was shown in the following Figs. 8, 9, 10, 11 and 12.

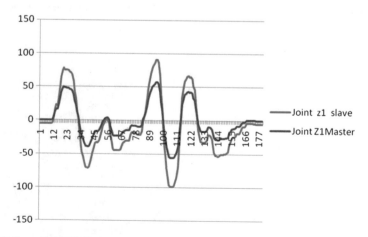

Fig. 8 Motion of joint Z_1 in master and slave

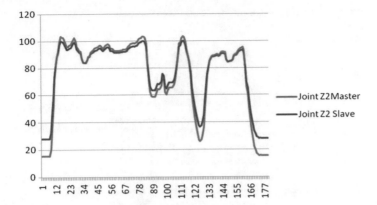

Fig. 9 Motion of joint Z_2 in master and Z_2 in slave

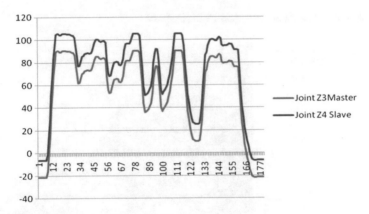

Fig. 10 Motion of joint Z_3 in master and Z_4 in slave

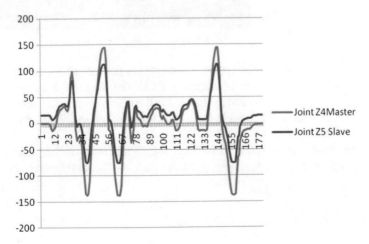

Fig. 11 Motion of joint Z_4 in master and Z_5 in slave

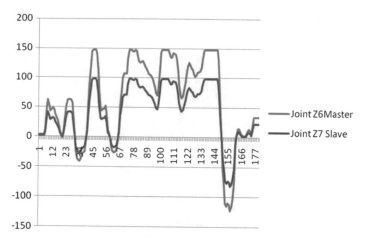

Fig. 12 Motion of joint Z_6 in master and Z_7 in slave

Fig. 13 Side-by-side frame
from the camera module in
the IITkgp lab environment

From the above results, joint angles varies within the range of joint motion and slave robot follows the pattern of master joint angles within the range that was mapped. It was also noticeable that the latency in the teleoperation was not noticeable since amount of data transmitted is less. A side-by-side frame from the compute module was shown in Fig. 13.

An experiment was designed to indicate the significance of the understanding depth at a remote location. A simple slot assembly will indicate the significance of

designed vision system. Ease of operation with live stream of side-by-side frames using visual feedback is greater than with simple one camera feedback because of the depth information in side-by-side frames.

4 Discussion

This paper presents a method of teleoperation of multi-DOF cyton robot using PHANTOM Omni. A joint space position-position control strategy was implemented for teleoperation. A vision system was developed to understand the depth of the remote location. A live stream of side-by-side frames was transmitted through the network to the smartphone. This current framework enables the operator to perform operations such as pick and place with precision by understanding the depth of the remote location. One primary limitation of the adapted framework was network latency in video transmission. One can transmit using a direct wired connection to computer system which can reduce the network delays to 100 ms, but wireless data transfer will give 4 seconds of time delay approximately. Latency is not noticeable in teleoperation since the amount of data transmitted is less.

References

1. E. Veras, K. Khokar, R. Alqasemi, R. Dubey, Scaled telerobotic control of a manipulator in real time with laser assistance for adl tasks. J. Franklin Inst. **349**(7), 2268–2280 (2012)
2. S. Lichiardopol, *A Survey on Teleoperation* (Technische Universitat Eindhoven, DCT report, 2007)
3. I. Farkhatdinov, J.-H. Ryu, Hybrid position-position and position-speed command strategy for the bilateral teleoperation of a mobile robot, in *International Conference on Control, Automation and Systems, 2007. ICCAS'07* (IEEE, 2007), pp. 442–2447
4. Z. Ju, C. Yang, Z. Li, L. Cheng, H. Ma, Teleoperation of humanoid baxter robot using haptic feedback, in *2014 International Conference on Ultisensor Fusion and Information Integration for Intelligent Systems (MFI)* (IEEE, 2014), pp. 1–6
5. K. Inoue, T. Tanikawa, T. Arai, Micro hand with two rotational fingers and manipulation of small objects by teleoperation, in *International Symposium on Micro-NanoMechatronics and Human Science, MHS 2008* (IEEE, 2008), pp. 97–102
6. G.S. Gupta, S.C. Mukhopadhyay, C.H. Messom, S.N. Demidenko, Master-slave control of a teleoperated anthropomorphic robotic arm with gripping force sensing. IEEE Trans. Instrum. Meas. **55**(6), 2136–2145 (2006)
7. A. Khalifa, A. Ramadan, K. Ibrahim, M. Fanni, S. Assal, A. Abo-Ismail, Workspace mapping and control of a teleoperated endoscopic surgical robot, in *2014 19th International Conference on Methods and Models in Automation and Robotics (MMAR)* (IEEE, 2014), pp. 675–680
8. S. Seung, B. Kang, H. Je, J. Park, K. Kim, S. Park, Tele-operation master-slave system for minimal invasive brain surgery, in *2009 IEEE International Conference on Robotics and Biomimetics (ROBIO)* (IEEE, 2009), pp. 177–182
9. M.M. Alex, *Evaluating the Effects of Haptic and Visual Feedback on the Teleoperation of Remote Robots*

10. A. Hong, H.H. Bülthoff, H.I. Son, A visual and force feedback for multi-robot teleoperation in outdoor environments: a preliminary result, in *2013 IEEE International Conference on Robotics and Automation (ICRA)* (IEEE, 2013), pp. 1471–1478

11. P.P. Shete, A. Jaju, S.K. Bose, P. Pal, Stereo vision guided telerobotics system for autonomous pick and place operations, in *Proceedings of the 2015 Conference on Advances in Robotics* (ACM, 2015), p. 41

12. J. San Martin, G. Trivino, *A Study of the Manipulability of the Phantomtm Omnitm Haptic Interface*

13. A.J. Silva, O.A.D. Ramirez, V.P. Vega, J.P.O. Oliver, Phantom omni haptic device: kinematic and manipulability, in *Electronics, Robotics and Automotive Mechanics Conference, CERMA'09* (IEEE, 2009), pp. 193–198

14. S.H. Ahn, B.S. Park, J.S. Yoon, A teleoperation position control for 2-DOF manipulators with control input saturation, in *Proceedings of IEEE International Symposium on Industrial Electronics, ISIE 2001*, vol. 3 (IEEE, 2001), pp. 1520–1525

15. M. Xue, C. Zhu, The socket programming and software design for communication based on client/server, in *Pacific-Asia Conference on Circuits, Communications and Systems, PACCS'09* (IEEE, 2009), pp. 775–777

Liquid Handling Robot for DNA Extraction

Gurpartap Singh, K. D. Lagoo, A. V. S. S. Narayan Rao and D N Badodkar

Abstract Liquid Handling Robots serve to automate the small volume liquid transactions for handling solutions in the research laboratories associated in the field of chemistry, biology, pharmacology, and more. They are used either to eliminate the tedious manual work required in carrying out a large number of pipetting operations or for handling potentially harmful solutions. Liquid Handling Robot is developed for executing simultaneous liquid transaction reactions on a large number of samples to extract DNA molecules from the living cells. This DNA separation reaction is performed by magnetic bead separation method. Multichannel electronic liquid dispensing head is developed to handle biological solutions in microscopic quantities. A robotic positioning system is designed and developed for maneuvering this liquid dispensing head as per the application requirement. A magnet module consisting of an array of permanent magnets operated by a rotary solenoid is developed for DNA extraction. The robotic positioning system and dispensing head is commanded by a customized software interface which provides high throughput. The system is designed for carrying liquids ranging from 30 to 300 µl with repeatability of <5%. The paper discusses the general overview of Liquid Handling Robots, magnetic bead method of DNA extraction, design of a multichannel micropipette, and other major components of the system.

Keywords Liquid handling robot · DNA extraction · Magnetic bead method

G. Singh (✉) · K. D. Lagoo · D N Badodkar
Division of Remote Handling and Robotics, Bhabha Atomic Research Centre,
Trombay, Mumbai 400085, India
e-mail: gpartap@barc.gov.in

A. V. S. S. Narayan Rao (✉)
Molecular Biology Division, Bhabha Atomic Research Centre, Trombay, Mumbai, India
e-mail: narayana@barc.gov.in

© Springer Nature Singapore Pte Ltd. 2019
D N Badodkar and T A Dwarakanath (eds.), *Machines, Mechanism
and Robotics*, Lecture Notes in Mechanical Engineering,
https://doi.org/10.1007/978-981-10-8597-0_71

829

1   Introduction

The Liquid Handling Robot (LHR) is a robotic system that offers an efficient way of handling small volume liquid solutions and performing large-scale liquid handling reactions automatically. The robotic system serves to automate the small volume liquid transactions for handling solutions in the research laboratories associated in the field of chemistry, biology, pharmacology, and more. A multichannel pipetting head carries out the job of liquid collection or dispensing the required volumes of liquid solutions. The dispensing head maneuvered by a robotic positioning system and controlled from a customized software GUI provides an advanced approach in handling increasing numbers of samples, and minimize the possibility of errors during sample handling and preparation, with limited resources. Liquid Handling Robots can be very useful in handling of potentially hazardous solutions [1, 2].

Traditional DNA isolation methods include precipitation and centrifugation steps or use column-based techniques. These processes are time consuming or inefficient in downscaling to small volume samples, hence very difficult to automate. This can be overcome by using the magnetic bead technology which offers fast sample preparation as well as high adaptability for automation [1]. The Liquid Handling Robot system was developed to implement *Magnetic Bead separation method* for extracting DNA from various types of living cells. Sub-micron-sized magnetic particles called magnetic beads, are processed to attain a property of attaching only a selective type of molecules—DNA in this case. During the stages of extraction of DNA protocols such as lysis, elusion, etc., the magnetic beads are required to be collected and resuspended within the liquid solution. This was achieved by incorporating a special developed magnet array module. The magnetic bead separation method provides high yield, high-throughput DNA extraction feasible through automation.

1.1   *Magnetic Bead DNA Separation Method*

The DNA molecules can be extracted from the cells by breaking the cells open. This process is called *Lysis*. When lysis solution is added to the cell solution, it results in a mixture of broken cell membrane, DNA molecules, proteins, and other material from the cell, Fig. 1. Now, the job is to separate the DNA molecules from this heterogenous mixture. For this purpose, the magnetic beads are added to this mixture.

The magnetic beads consist of one or multiple magnetic cores—either of maghemite (gamma Fe_2O_3) or magnetite (Fe_3O_4) with ferromagnetic or superparamagnetic properties; with a coating matrix of hydroxylapatite, silica, and polymers with functionalized terminal groups [1, 3, 4]. The coating matrix of these magnetic beads can be selectively treated so that it attaches to a desired kind of molecule only. In our case, the magnetic beads will attach only DNA molecules. The other molecules will remain in the solution as shown in Fig. 2. Now, if a magnet is brought near the solution tube wall from outside, the magnetic beads—along with the DNA

Fig. 1 Solution tube
containing mixture of broken
cell walls, nucleus walls,
DNA molecules, and other
material from the cell

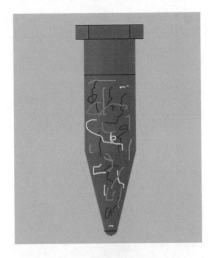

Fig. 2 DNA (red strings)
molecules gets attached to
beads (blue dots)

molecules, will be attracted by the magnet and will stick to the tube wall as shown
in Fig. 3. The remaining solution can be discarded using pipette.

Subsequently, these beads—attached with DNA, are released into the *Wash* buffer
to remove the residual unwanted components. The next step is to separate the DNA
molecules from the magnetic beads. This process is called *Elution*. For this purpose,
elution buffer is added to the solution. The process of elution separates the magnetic
beads from the DNA molecules. After elution, again the magnet is brought near the
tube wall so that only magnetic beads—without DNA molecules, stick to the wall
and the solution containing the DNA molecules can be aspirated out.

The process implemented on the Liquid Handling Robot is a modified version
of the standard protocols mentioned in a commercial magnetic bead-based DNA
extraction kit.

Fig. 3 Magnet attracts
beads containing DNA

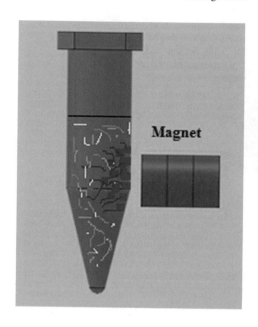

2 Liquid Handling Robot

A Liquid Handling Robot was designed and developed to implement the process of magnetic bead-based genomic DNA separation from bacterial cells. A motorized multichannel micropipette head is the heart of the robotic system. Figure 4 shows major components of the robot which are discussed in the following parts.

2.1 Multichannel Micropipette Head

A 12-channel liquid dispensing head for variable volume pipetting is developed. It can carry 12 different samples ensuring minimal/zero cross contamination. It carries detachable tips arranged in a linear array with a pitch of 9 mm. It works on the principle of air displacement by the movement of a piston [5]. The head consists of a piston-cylinder system in which the piston inside the pipette is isolated from the sample being aspirated into a plastic tip by an air cushion. With an upward movement of the piston, a partial vacuum is created in the tip causing the liquid to be filled into the tip. Figure 5 shows the liquid aspirated into the tips after the piston movement of the actual liquid handling robot.

LHR incorporates a motorized piston mechanism which is driven by a stepper motor coupled to ball screw linear actuator, as shown in Fig. 6. The stepper motor is driven in microstepping mode to obtain fine control over the air being displaced and hence, the dispensed volumes. This maintains the high precision and repeatability is

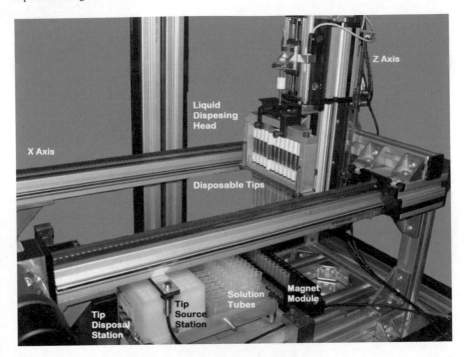

Fig. 4 The major components of the liquid handling robot

required in handling small liquid volumes. The head is capable of pipetting liquid volumes in the range of 30–300 μl, in steps of 1 μl. The pipetting speed can be defined by user from 10 to 300 μl/s, depending upon the density of the desired liquid [6–8]. For viscous liquids, slow aspiration is required along with delay before lifting the pipette out of solution tube to allow the liquid to rise inside the tip. Before transporting this head to dispensing station, the liquid is lifted marginally up from the tip face to provide an air cushion; to avoid residues of liquid solution being filled on the outer surface of the tip and form a droplet.

A spring-loaded push–pull arrangement was developed for automatic removal to tips from the plunger heads into the discarding station, as shown in Fig. 6.

Since, the pipetting head has a variable volume dispensing capability, the accuracy of dispensed volumes is best expressed with *Coefficient of Variation* (CV). It is the ratio of the standard deviation to the mean [9]—Eq. (1). Higher value of Coefficient of Variation indicates larger dispersion about the mean value, hence lesser accuracy.

$$\text{Coefficient of Variation (CV)} = \frac{\text{Standard Deviation } (\sigma)}{\text{Mean Value } (\mu)} \times 100 \qquad (1)$$

A large number of liquid transaction trials were carried to identify the optimum volume and the dispensing accuracy for the LHR micropipette head. An accuracy of the order of <5% CV for volumes from 80 to 300 μl was obtained. For volumes

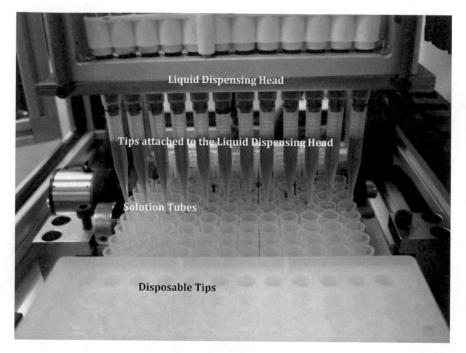

Fig. 5 Detailed view of pipetting

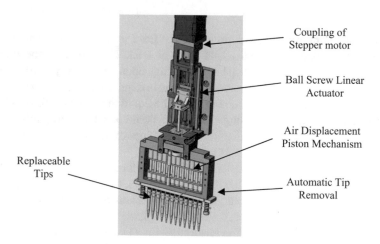

Fig. 6 Multichannel micropipette head

in the range of 30–80 μl s, an accuracy of the order of <10% CV was observed. The CV was measured by making at least five measurements each at 30, 80, 150, 200, and 300 μl, respectively, using distilled water and measuring the mass with a microbalance.

2.2 Holding Tray

The holding tray carries the necessary labware for the required experiments. The robot has four configurable target stations—1 tip rack that can hold 96 tips, 1 reagent rack holding 8 different types of solutions, 1 station for holding reaction wells, and a station for collecting used tips. These racks have 12×8 array configuration with a pitch of 9 mm. Each solution tube is having capacity of 1 ml. They can be used for carrying inventory solutions and samples required for liquid experiments.

2.3 Robotic Positioning System

Two-axes robotic positioning system is designed and developed for maneuvering the multichannel micropipette head as per the application requirement. The robotic system provides movement of the pipetting head to different stations of holding tray including sample holder, TipRack, and tip discarding station. The horizontal axis (X-axis) uses timer belt-based actuators and vertical axis (Z-axis) uses a ball screw-based actuator both driven by hybrid stepper motor. The stepper motors are operated in microstepping mode to achieve the positioning accuracy within ± 0.1 mm for both the axes of the robotic system.

2.4 Magnetic Module

Magnet module is another important component of the magnetic bead DNA separation method. It consists of a single column of 12 solution tubes, called "Test-Tube"—similar to well tray, and an array of permanent magnets arranged at a pitch of 9 mm over a rotary metal block that is operated by a rotary solenoid. The solenoid is operated by the software as per the user command. Normally, the magnets face 120° away from the test tube with minimal impact on the solution in the test tube. They align towards the test tube touching its wall when the rotary solenoid is switched on after the user command so as to provide magnetic field required to clamp the magnetic beads. The field strength was chosen so that it can attract the beads from all the solution in the tube. The arrangement is as shown in Figs. 7 and 8.

2.5 GUI and Software

A user-friendly and intuitive software interface is provided for operators to define a liquid handling method—called protocols, using the standard defined steps like: tip attach, tip dispose, magnet operation, aspirate, dispense, mixing, etc. The robot

Fig. 7 Magnet module with magnets facing 120° away from solution tubes

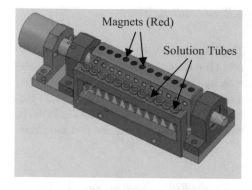

Fig. 8 Magnet module with magnets aligned at side wall of solution tubes

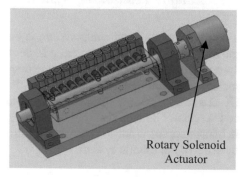

protocols can be easily defined and saved for later use. The LHR application software is designed to execute user-defined liquid handling experiments independent of an operator. To avoid or minimize the cross contamination of samples, the software is implemented with special algorithms to limit the liquid splashing/sputtering during the dispensing head is being transported. It runs over any Windows-based PC/Laptop and uses USB connection for communicating with the robot. The basic outlook of the GUI is shown in Fig. 9.

The LHR can be programmed by users to implement most frequently used dispensing techniques such as diluting, dispensing, sequential dispensing, forward pipetting, and reverse pipetting. Prewetting the tip two or three times is a common practice to improve the accuracy and precision of the pipetting results.

3 DNA Extraction Experiment Results

The Liquid Handling Robot was used to extract genomic DNA from six bacterial samples loaded in alternate wells of the 12-channel head. The yield from all the samples was found comparable to one another.

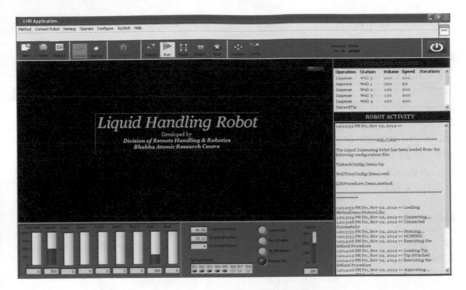

Fig. 9 Software graphical user interface for liquid handling robot

Fig. 10 Agarose gel picture of genomic DNA extracted using the LHR from six replicates of a sample

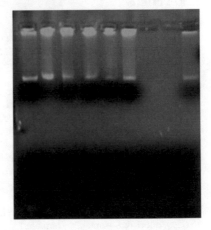

Figure 10 above shows agarose gel electrophoresis of genomic DNA, which is extracted using the LHR from six replicates of a sample—placed in alternate solution tubes in well tray. In the figure above, the lane—counting from left, 1–6 shows results from six replicates of used sample, and lane 9 shows result from a reference genomic DNA sample of known concentration. Thus, the yield is estimated by comparing unknown with a reference genomic DNA sample of known concentration. The DNA yield was estimated by comparing the total DNA obtained to the theoretically estimated DNA yield from 10^8 cells.

4 Conclusion

The Liquid Handling Robot was designed and demonstrated to perform DNA extraction from bacterial cells by magnetic bead separation method. Using 12 channels motorized dispensing head and maneuvering it across various buffers with the help of the user interface, the DNA extraction method was automated. Both inter-experiment and intra-experiment repeatability of the results was assessed and ~80% of the theoretical yields were achieved consistently. With a few modifications, the system can be adapted for any other liquid handling applications viz.—isolation/purification of tagged protein molecules, row-wise and column-wise serial dilution, separation of cell types, etc.

Acknowledgements The authors are thankful to the organization Bhabha Atomic Research Centre for providing conducive environment, efficient work culture and abundant resources to work effortlessly and efficiently to bring up the such systems which, in a way, contribute in the welfare of the society.

References

1. J. Oster, Polyvinyl-alcohol-based magnetic beads for rapid and efficient separation of specific or unspecific nucleic acid sequences. J. Magn. Magn. Mater. (2001)
2. G. Singh, K.D. Lagoo, *Liquid Handling Robot: Brief Communication*. BARC Newsletter, www.barc.gov.in
3. S. Witt, J. Neumann, H. Zierdt, G. Ge'bel, C. Roscheisen, Establishing a novel automated magnetic bead-based method for the extraction of DNA from a variety of forensic samples. Elsevier's J. Forensic Sci. Int. Genet. **6**, 539–547 (2012)
4. T. Gale, *DNA Isolation Methods—World of Forensic Science*, www.encyclopedia.com
5. K. Ewald, *Fundamentals of Dispensing* (Eppendorf AG, Hamburg, Germany)
6. K. Ewald, *Impact of Pipetting Techniques on Precision and Accuracy* (Eppendorf AG, Hamburg, Germany)
7. K. Ewald, *Calibration and Adjustment of Dispensing Systems in the Laboratory* (Eppendorf AG, Hamburg, Germany)
8. K. Ewald, *Influence of Physical Parameters on the Dispensed Volume of Air-Cushion Pipette* (Eppendorf AG, Hamburg, Germany)
9. https://www.insee.fr/en/metadonnees/definition/c1366

Dynamic Modeling of Cooperative Planar Bionic Manipulator

Tsegay Mulu Girmay, Inderjeet Singh, Pushparaj Mani Pathak,
A. K. Samantaray, Rochdi Merzouki
and Belkacem Ould Bouamama

Abstract Bionic robots, imply the robots which are inspired by biological life forms. The manipulator robots inspired from elephant trunk are good example of bionic robots. These are continuous robots with bending backbones and high degrees of freedom. Ideally, the compliant nature of such manipulator delivers infinite degrees of freedom, which makes it difficult to control them at the space task. However, all these degrees of freedoms cannot be actuated, thus these robots are always underactuated, i.e., they provide vast configurations with few inputs. In this paper, a multi-section bionic manipulator, namely the compact bionic handling assistant (CBHA), is dynamically modeled using bond graph. Assuming planar robot that contains a single concentrated mass per section, dynamic equations for each bellow are derived by means of bond graph modeling. Simulation results using lumped model are shown to validate the model.

Keywords Bionic robots · Multi-section bionic manipulator

T. Mulu Girmay · P. M. Pathak (✉)
Mechanical and Industrial Engineering Department, Indian Institute of Technology Roorkee,
Roorkee, India
e-mail: pushpfme@iitr.ac.in; pushp_pathak@yahoo.com

T. Mulu Girmay
e-mail: mulug.dme2015@iitr.ac.in

I. Singh · R. Merzouki · B. O. Bouamama
CRIStAL UMR CNRS 9189, University of Lille,
Polytech Lille, Avenue Paul Langevin, 59655 Villeneuve d'Ascq, France
e-mail: Inderjeet.singh@ed.univ-lille1.fr

R. Merzouki
e-mail: rochdi.merzouki@polytech-lille.fr

B. O. Bouamama
e-mail: belkacem.ouldbouamama@polytech-lille.fr

A. K. Samantaray
Department of Mechanical Engineering, Indian Institute of Technology Kharagpur,
Kharagpur 721302, India
e-mail: samantaray@mech.iitkgp.ernet.in

© Springer Nature Singapore Pte Ltd. 2019
D N Badodkar and T A Dwarakanath (eds.), *Machines, Mechanism and Robotics*, Lecture Notes in Mechanical Engineering,
https://doi.org/10.1007/978-981-10-8597-0_72

1   Introduction

The bionic science involves in imitating working principles of some natural behaviors by based on the current robotics technology. A state-of-the-art of soft robots is established in [1].

The core subject in the fields of continuum robots is finding the greatest improved technology reproducing natural behavior. Ideally, the compliant nature of such robot delivers infinite degrees of freedom. Though, there is a constraint due to the practical incapability to include infinite actuators.

Therefore, most of these robots are underactuated. That is to say, they can attain vast configurations with comparatively few control inputs [2]. Chirikjian and Burdick familiarize a technique for modeling continuum manipulator kinematics by demonstrating the curve-shaping function by means of modal functions [3]. Modeling of hyper degrees of freedom structure kinematics using Serret-Frenet was developed by Mochiyama et al. [4].

For continuum robots, more universal direct kinematics was modeled by integrating the transformations of manipulator sections and stating those in terms of parameters of continuum robot [5]. Overall work of [3–5], is the development of an overall set of procedures for kinematics of continuum manipulator.

Therefore, prototypes of continuum manipulator kinematics have been established and based on these basic control strategies are developed. Recently, the establishment of analytical methods to model dynamics of continuum manipulator is being developed by numerous researchers. Chirikjian developed a model using an infinite degree of freedom model [6]. In [7], recursive algorithms based on the Newton–Euler equations were used to develop the 3D-serial underwater eel-like robot model. Similarly using Cosserat theory of flexible rods, incorporating the effect of material nonlinearity, distributed and payload weight, and geometrically the exact model was established in [8]. By means of virtual work principles, modeling of planar motion of snake-like robot body is presented in [9].

The cooperative behavior of bionic manipulators with mobile base is interesting as it can be used to transport materials from one place to another.

This paper presents the dynamic modeling of the cooperative bionic manipulator Robotino XT [10] for the planar motion. The dynamic model has been prepared using bond graph modeling method [11]. Simulation results are shown to validate the model.

2   Physical System Description

Figure 1 shows the experimental setup for cooperative planar bionic manipulator. The bionic manipulator used here is Robotino XT [12].

Robotino XT consists of a omnidirectional mobile robot called Robotino and bionic handling assistant (BHA) attached to it. The bionic manipulator has seven

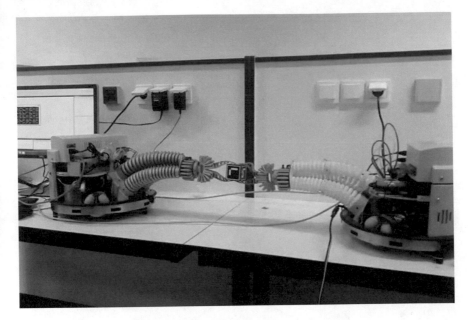

Fig. 1 Experimental setup for cooperative planar bionic manipulator

independent coordinate system consisting of three tubes having two flexible sections and one rotational component. A compliant end-effector is also provided. Each of bending segment is consisting of three bending backbone tubes, manipulated by three electro-pneumatic actuators. The rotational component is manipulated by two bending backbone tubes in the shape of arc.

This bionic manipulator is controlled by means of nine pneumatic actuators (three for each flexible section, two for rotational component, and one for the gripper) and seven sensors (six potentiometers measure the instantaneous tubes lengths using cables and the last one measures the angle of the rotational component).

To model the cooperative bionic manipulator, first, a single bionic manipulator has been modeled. Next section presents the modeling of bionic manipulator.

3   Bond Graph Model

Figure 2 represents the schematic planar model of left bionic manipulator shown in Fig. 1. In this Figure {A} is the inertial frame, {C} is the frame attached at the center of mass of mobile base, {B} is the frame at the base of the manipulator, {1} is the frame at the end of first section, {2} is the frame at the end of second section. ϕ is the angle of inclination of the line joining frame {C} and frame {B} with reference to frame {A}, l_1 is length of backbone of first section, l_2 is

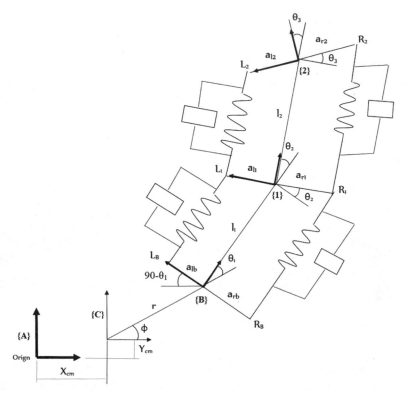

Fig. 2 Schematic diagram of one planar bionic manipulator

length of backbone of second section, θ_1 is the angle of inclination of l_1 with reference to frame {B}, θ_2 is the angle of inclination of l_2 with reference to frame {1},
θ_3 is the angle of inclination of end-effector with reference to frame {2}, L_B and R_B
are left- and right- extreme points at the base of first section, respectively, L_1 and R_1
are left-and right-extreme points at the end of first section, respectively, L_2 and R_2
are left- and right-extreme points at the end of second section, respectively. a_{rb} is
the base radius of right tube of first section, a_{lb} is the base radius of left tube of first
section, a_{r1} is the tip radius of right tube of first section, a_{l1} is the tip radius of left
tube of first section, a_{r2} is the tip radius of right tube of second section, a_{l2} is the tip
radius of left tube of second section, X_{cm} is X-position of frame {C} with reference
to {A}, and Y_{cm} is Y-position of frame {C} with reference to {A}.

The three backbone points, i.e., origin of frames {B}, {1}, and {2} are (X_B, Y_B), (X_1, Y_1), and (X_2, Y_2), respectively. Let the coordinates of points L_B, L_1, L_2, R_B, R_1, and R_2 are (X_{LB}, Y_{LB}), (X_{L1}, Y_{L1}), (X_{L2}, Y_{L2}), (X_{RB}, Y_{RB}), (X_{R1}, Y_{R1}), and (X_{R2}, Y_{R2}), respectively. Then these coordinates can be given as :

$$X_{LB} = X_b - a_{lb} \sin(\phi + \theta_1). \tag{1}$$

$$Y_{LB} = Y_b + a_{lb} \cos(\phi + \theta_1). \tag{2}$$

$$X_{L1} = X_1 - a_{l1} \sin(\phi + \theta_1 + \theta_2). \tag{3}$$

$$Y_{L1} = Y_1 + a_{l1} \cos(\phi + \theta_1 + \theta_2). \tag{4}$$

$$X_{L2} = X_2 - a_{l2} \sin(\phi + \theta_1 + \theta_2 + \theta_3). \tag{5}$$

$$Y_{L2} = Y_2 + a_{l2} \cos(\phi + \theta_1 + \theta_2 + \theta_3). \tag{6}$$

$$X_{RB} = X_b + a_{rb} \sin(\phi + \theta_1). \tag{7}$$

$$Y_{RB} = Y_b - a_{rb} \cos(\phi + \theta_1). \tag{8}$$

$$X_{R1} = X_1 + a_{r1} \sin(\phi + \theta_1 + \theta_2). \tag{9}$$

$$Y_{R1} = Y_1 - a_{r1} \cos(\phi + \theta_1 + \theta_2). \tag{10}$$

$$X_{R2} = X_2 + a_{r2} \sin(\phi + \theta_1 + \theta_2 + \theta_3). \tag{11}$$

$$Y_{R2} = Y_2 - a_{r2} \cos(\phi + \theta_1 + \theta_2 + \theta_3). \tag{12}$$

The time derivative of these coordinates can be given by:

$$\dot{X}_{LB} = \dot{X}_b; \qquad\qquad \dot{Y}_{LB} = \dot{Y}_b. \tag{13}$$

$$\dot{X}_{L1} = \dot{X}_1 - a_{l1} \cos(\phi + \theta_1 + \theta_2)\dot{\theta}_2. \tag{14}$$

$$\dot{Y}_{L1} = \dot{Y}_1 - a_{l1} \sin(\phi + \theta_1 + \theta_2)\dot{\theta}_2. \tag{15}$$

$$\dot{X}_{L2} = \dot{X}_2 - a_{l2} \cos(\phi + \theta_1 + \theta_2 + \theta_3)(\dot{\theta}_2 + \dot{\theta}_3). \tag{16}$$

$$\dot{Y}_{L2} = \dot{Y}_2 - a_{l2} \sin(\phi + \theta_1 + \theta_2 + \theta_3)(\dot{\theta}_2 + \dot{\theta}_3). \tag{17}$$

$$\dot{X}_{RB} = \dot{X}_b; \qquad\qquad \dot{Y}_{RB} = \dot{Y}_b. \tag{18}$$

$$\dot{X}_{R1} = \dot{X}_1 + a_{r1} \cos(\phi + \theta_1 + \theta_2)\dot{\theta}_2. \tag{19}$$

$$\dot{Y}_{R1} = \dot{Y}_1 + a_{r1} \sin(\phi + \theta_1 + \theta_2)\dot{\theta}_2. \tag{20}$$

$$\dot{X}_{R2} = \dot{X}_2 + a_{r2} \cos(\phi + \theta_1 + \theta_2 + \theta_3)(\dot{\theta}_2 + \dot{\theta}_3). \tag{21}$$

$$\dot{Y}_{R2} = \dot{Y}_2 + a_{r2} \sin(\phi + \theta_1 + \theta_2 + \theta_3)(\dot{\theta}_2 + \dot{\theta}_3). \tag{22}$$

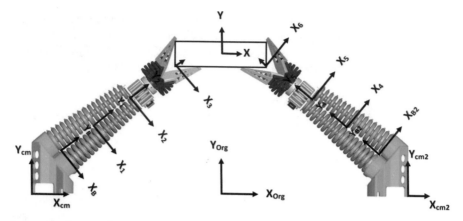

Fig. 3 Schematic diagram of cooperative planar bionic manipulator

Fig. 4 Schematic of object
handled by cooperative
bionic manipulator

Then, change in length of left- and right segments for the robot are given by:

$$\dot{L}_1 = \left(\frac{X_{L1} - X_{LB}}{L_1}\right)(\dot{X}_{L1} - \dot{X}_{LB}) + \left(\frac{Y_{L1} - Y_{LB}}{L_1}\right)(\dot{Y}_{L1} - \dot{Y}_{LB}). \qquad (23)$$

$$\dot{R}_1 = \left(\frac{X_{R1} - X_{RB}}{R_1}\right)(\dot{X}_{R1} - \dot{X}_{RB}) + \left(\frac{Y_{R1} - Y_{RB}}{R_1}\right)(\dot{Y}_{R1} - \dot{Y}_{RB}). \qquad (24)$$

$$\dot{L}_2 = \left(\frac{X_{L2} - X_{L1}}{L_2}\right)(\dot{X}_{L2} - \dot{X}_{L1}) + \left(\frac{Y_{L2} - Y_{L1}}{L_2}\right)(\dot{Y}_{L2} - \dot{Y}_{L1}). \qquad (25)$$

$$\dot{R}_2 = \left(\frac{X_{R2} - X_{R1}}{R_2}\right)(\dot{X}_{R2} - \dot{X}_{R1}) + \left(\frac{Y_{R2} - Y_{R1}}{R_2}\right)(\dot{Y}_{R2} - \dot{Y}_{R1}). \qquad (26)$$

Now consider the two such bionic robots handling a common object as shown in
Fig. 3. The equations for the robot 2 can be derived similarly. Considering the common handled object as shown in Fig. 4. X and Y coordinates of points p_1 and p_2 on
body are given by:

$$Xp_1 = -l/2; \qquad Yp_1 = 0; Xp_2 = l/2; \qquad Yp_1 = 0 \qquad (27)$$

After sometime, let the position of these points be given by $p_1{}'$ and $p_2{}'$. Then, X and Y coordinates of these gripping points after θ rotation of the floating object about the axis can be given by:

$$\begin{bmatrix} Xp_1{}' \\ Yp_1{}' \\ 1 \end{bmatrix} = \begin{bmatrix} \cos\theta & -\sin\theta & 0 \\ \sin\theta & \cos\theta & 0 \\ 0 & 0 & 1 \end{bmatrix} \begin{bmatrix} \frac{-l}{2} \\ 0 \\ 1 \end{bmatrix} = \begin{bmatrix} \frac{-l}{2}\cos\theta \\ \frac{-l}{2}\sin\theta \\ 1 \end{bmatrix} \tag{28}$$

$$\begin{bmatrix} Xp_2{}' \\ Yp_2{}' \\ 1 \end{bmatrix} = \begin{bmatrix} \cos\theta & -\sin\theta & 0 \\ \sin\theta & \cos\theta & 0 \\ 0 & 0 & 1 \end{bmatrix} \begin{bmatrix} \frac{l}{2} \\ 0 \\ 1 \end{bmatrix} = \begin{bmatrix} \frac{l}{2}\cos\theta \\ \frac{l}{2}\sin\theta \\ 1 \end{bmatrix} \tag{29}$$

Displacement of gripping points in X and y directions can be given as:

$$X_1 = \Delta Xp_1 = Xp_1{}' - Xp_1 = \frac{-l}{2}\cos\theta - \left(\frac{-l}{2}\right) = \frac{l}{2}(1 - \cos\theta) \tag{30}$$

$$Y_1 = \Delta Yp_1 = Yp_1{}' - Yp_1 = \frac{-l}{2}\sin\theta - 0 = \frac{-l}{2}\sin\theta \tag{31}$$

$$X_2 = \Delta Xp_2 = Xp_2{}' - Xp_2 = \frac{l}{2}\cos\theta - \frac{l}{2} = \frac{1}{2}(\cos\theta - 1) \tag{32}$$

$$Y_2 = \Delta Yp_2 = Yp_2{}' - Yp_2 = \frac{l}{2}\sin\theta - 0 = \frac{l}{2}\sin\theta \tag{33}$$

Thus gripping point velocities can be evaluated as:

$$\dot{X}_1 = \frac{l}{2}\sin\theta\,\dot{\theta}; \quad \dot{Y}_1 = \frac{-l}{2}\cos\theta\,\dot{\theta}; \quad \dot{X}_2 = \frac{-l}{2}\sin\theta\,\dot{\theta}; \quad \dot{Y}_2 = \frac{l}{2}\cos\theta\,\dot{\theta} \tag{34}$$

Based on the above equations, the bond graph model is developed as shown in Fig. 4. In this bond graph, stiffness in Y-direction and torsional stiffness of different section has been modeled using C elements.

4 Simulation Results

The system equations are generated using bond graph model shown in Fig. 5, and are solved numerically using Runge–Kutta method. Table 1 shows parameters used in simulation. Figure 6 shows initial conditions used in simulation.

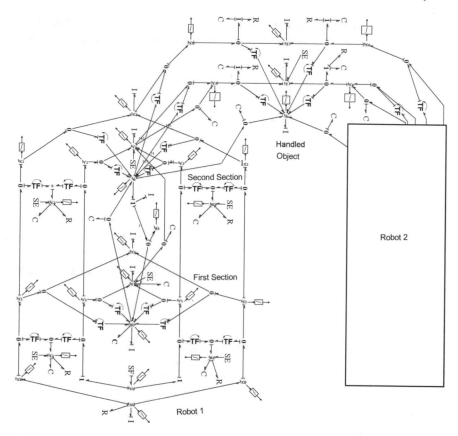

Fig. 5 Bond graph model of planar bionic manipulator

Table 2 summarizes simulation result for different values of actuator forces, which has been obtained by multiplying the pressures values with assumed average value of uniform cross-section area. Y-position of the Object for instants 1, 2, 3, 4, and 5 is 0.238, 0.262, 0.258, 0.304, and 0.319, respectively, (unit of measurement for forces and Positions are Newton (N) and Meter (m), respectively).

Figure 7a–d shows the result for $F_{1L} = 300$ N, $F_{2L} = 300$ N, $F_{1R} = 0$, $F_{2R} = 0$, $F_{4L} = 300$ N, $F_{5L} = 300$ N, $F_{4R} = 0$, and $F_{5R} = 0$. Simulation result is as per anticipated.

Table 1 Simulation parameter of bionic manipulator

Parameter	Value
Angle of inclination of base ϕ	50°
Dead length of first section	2.3 cm
Base diameter of first and second tube	5.37 cm
Tip diameter of first and second tube	4.64 cm
Base diameter of fourth and fifth tube	4.64 cm
Tip diameter of fourth and fifth tube	3.91 cm
First section length at atmospheric pressure	10.14 cm
Second section length at atmospheric pressure	10.46 cm
Dead length above the second section	0.28 cm
Thickness of rotational part	3.5 cm
Gap between second section and rotational part	0.2 cm
Gap between rotational part and end-effector	0.2 cm
Length of end-effector base	2.67 cm

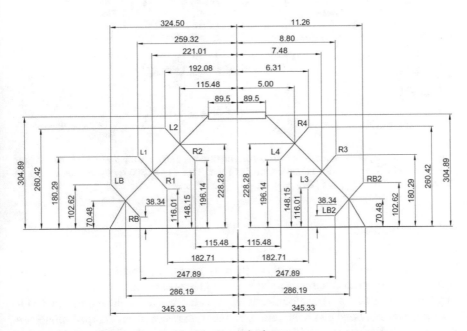

Fig. 6 Initial conditions of cooperative bionic manipulator

T. Mulu Girmay et al.

Table 2 Summarizes simulation result for different values of actuator pressures

	Robot 1					Robot 2				
	F_{1L}	F_{2L}	F_{1R}	F_{2R}	Y_3	F_{4L}	F_{5L}	F_{4R}	F_{5R}	Y_6
1	0	0	0	0	0.239	0	0	300	300	0.247
2	0	0	0	0	0.265	300	300	0	0	0.268
3	300	300	0	0	0.264	0	0	0	0	0.260
4	300	300	0	0	0.308	0	0	300	300	0.309
5	300	300	0	0	0.317	300	300	0	0	0.318

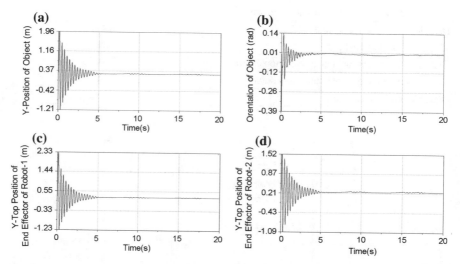

Fig. 7 **a** Y-position of the object (m), **b** object orientation (radians), **c** Y top position of end-effector of robot 1 and **d** Y top position of end-effector of robot 2 for $F_{1L} = 300$ N, $F_{2L} = 300$ N, $F_{4L} = 300$ N, $F_{5L} = 300$ N, $F_{1R} = 0$, $F_{2R} = 0$, $F_{4R} = 0$, and $F_{5R} = 0$

5 Conclusions

In this paper, dynamic modeling of cooperative planar bionic manipulator is developed using bond graph method. Considering a planar manipulator that consists of a single concentrated mass per module, dynamic equations for each module are developed by means of bond graph modeling. Simulation results using lumped model are shown to validate the model. The body displacements and tip displacements are as expected. In future, the experimental results will be compared with the simulated one.

References

1. D. Trivedi, C.D. Rahn, W.M. Kier, I.D. Walker, Soft robotics: biological inspiration, state of the art, and future research. Appl. Bionics Biomech. **5**(3), 99–117 (2008)
2. N. Giri, I.D. Walker, Three module lumped element model of a continuum arm section, in *2011 IEEE/RSJ International Conference on Intelligent Robots and Systems (IROS)* (IEEE, 2011), pp. 4060–4065
3. G.S. Chirikjian, J.W. Burdick, A modal approach to hyper-redundant manipulator kinematics. IEEE Trans. Robot. Autom. **10**(3), 343–354 (1994)
4. H. Mochiyama, E. Shimemura, H. Kobayashi, Direct kinematics of manipulators with hyper degrees of freedom and frenet-serret formula, in *Proceedings of the 1998 IEEE International Conference on Robotics and Automation*, vol. 2 (IEEE, 1998), pp. 1653–1658
5. B.A. Jones, I.D. Walker, Kinematics for multisection continuum robots. IEEE Trans. Robot. **22**(1), 43–55 (2006)
6. G.S. Chirikjian, Hyper-redundant manipulator dynamics: a continuum approximation. Adv. Robot. **9**(3), 217–243 (1994)
7. W. Khalil, G. Gallot, O. Ibrahim, F. Boyer, Dynamic modeling of a 3-d serial eel-like robot, in *Proceedings of the 2005 IEEE International Conference on Robotics and Automation, ICRA 2005* (IEEE, 2005), pp. 1270–1275
8. D. Trivedi, A. Lotfi, C.D. Rahn, Geometrically exact dynamic models for soft robotic manipulators, in *2007 IEEE/RSJ International Conference on Intelligent Robots and Systems, IROS 2007* (IEEE, 2007), pp. 1497–1502
9. N. Li, T. Zhao, Y. Zhao, The dynamic modeling of snake-like robot by using nominal mechanism method, in *Intelligent Robotics and Applications* (2008), pp. 1185–1194
10. C. Escande, T. Chettibi, R. Merzouki, V. Coelen, P.M. Pathak, Kinematic calibration of a multisection bionic manipulator. IEEE/ASME Trans. Mechatron. **20**(2), 663–674 (2015)
11. R. Merzouki, A.K. Samantaray, P.M. Pathak, B. Ould Bouamama, *Intelligent Mechatronic Systems: Modeling, Control and Diagnosis* (Springer Science & Business Media, 2012)
12. http://www.festo.com/cms/en_corp/9655.htm

Author Index

© Springer Nature Singapore Pte Ltd. 2019
D N Badodkar and T A Dwarakanath (eds.), *Machines, Mechanism and Robotics*, Lecture Notes in Mechanical Engineering,
https://doi.org/10.1007/978-981-10-8597-0

Printed in the United States
By Bookmasters